Operating Grants
for Nonprofit Organizations
2004

ORYX PRESS

2004

© **2004 by The Oryx Press**

An imprint of Greenwood Publishing Group, Inc.

Westport, Connecticut 06881

www.greenwood.com

Published simultaneously in Canada

Printed and Bound in the United States of America

∞ The paper used in this publication meets the minimum requirements of American National Standard for Information Science—Permanence of Paper for Printed Library Materials, ANSI Z39.48, 1984.

ISBN 1-57356-603-9

Contents

Introduction

For more than three decades, the GRANTS Database has provided those seeking funding with up-to-date information. One of the most difficult types of grants to find is operating grants, those that fund the day-to-day expenses of running a nonprofit organization. Costs may include overhead, salary support, administration, utilities, and other ongoing expenses of an organization that may not be related to a specific project. Because operating grants do not fund a specific goal, the struggle to find and fund these grants is fierce. *Operating Grants for Nonprofit Organizations* is a tool to help with this difficult task.

SCOPE OF THIS DIRECTORY

This fifth edition of *Operating Grants for Nonprofit Organizations* contains more than 1,300 current funding programs that offer support for some or all general operating expenses of nonprofits and other institutions. Funders come from the private, public, nonprofit, and for-profit sectors and include private, family, and corporate grantmaking foundations; federal and state organizations; corporations; and other nonprofit grantmaking organizations.

Inclusion in the book indicates that the funder gives some form of operating support, has an active funding program that accepts unsolicited inquiries, and gives monetary awards. Funders' interests cover a wide range of areas, including the arts, child development, social services, youth programs, economic development, education, environmental programs, health care, religious programs, community development, and more.

Information for each program listed in this guide has been taken from a sponsor's update of a program statement, from a questionnaire returned by a sponsor, from materials published by the sponsor and furnished to the editors, or from the funder's official Web site. The program information in this guide is current as of March 10, 2004.

Main Entries

The main section of this guide, the Grant Programs section, is sorted alphabetically by state. Grant programs by funders based in that state are listed under each state in alphabetical order. For sponsoring organizations located outside the grant seeker's state but that may give awards in the grant seeker's state or geographic region, the Geographic Index should also be consulted. Both the main listings and the Geographic Index should be used to pinpoint funders that give in the grant seeker's locale. Federal funders who give nationwide are listed under "District of Columbia" and under "Maryland," where their offices are located.

Each entry is composed of the sponsor name and address, contact information, the sponsor's areas of interest, and the following when available: fax numbers, e-mail addresses, Web page addresses, eligibility requirements and contact procedures, restrictions, and samples of previously awarded grants.

Indexes

The most effective way to locate funding is to use the three indexes provided in this directory. The Subject Index contains all program titles—with accession numbers—under their applicable subject terms. The subject terms all come from a controlled vocabulary of terms listed in the *GRANTS Subject Authority Guide* (Oryx Press, 1991). These subject terms are also listed in each grant entry in the Grant Programs section under "Areas of Interest." The Subject Index has been enhanced with cross-references to make searching by subject area more efficient. The Sponsoring Organizations Index lists program sponsors. The Geographic Index lists funders that fund in specific states or regions. The Geographic Index is included to pinpoint funders who are based in one state but that may give grants in other states or over an entire region.

Users are advised to consult the Geographic Index in addition to looking under their state in the main section to find all grants awarded to their state or region. See "How to Use This Guide" on page vii for sample index entries.

The GRANTS Database—A Current Source of Information

By using this guide, grant seekers can match the needs of their particular organizations with those sponsors offering funding in their areas of interest. The current information listed is meant to eliminate the cost incurred by both grant seekers and grant makers when inappropriate proposals are submitted to a funder. However, because the GRANTS Database is updated on a daily basis, with programs continually added, deleted, and revised, grant seekers using this guide may also search the GRANTS Database on the Web through *GrantSelect* grantselect.com. The database is also updated monthly online through both the Dialog Corporation and Knowledge Express Data Systems (KEDS), and on CD-ROM, through Dialog, with bimonthly updates. Online and CD-ROM users may wish to use the *GRANTS Subject Authority Guide,* which lists the descriptors used to index all programs in the database.

The GRANTS family of print and electronic products includes seven specialized publications that serve distinct portions of the research, performance, and service-based community.

Program officers, scholars, researchers, artists and performers, citizen groups, local and regional governments, and public agencies are served by the *Directory of Research Grants*, the *Directory of Biomedical and Health Care Grants*, the *Directory of Grants in the Humanities, Operating Grants for Nonprofit Organizations, Funding Sources for Community and Economic Development, Funding Sources for K–12 Education,* and *Funding Sources for Children and Youth Programs.*

The following people have devoted a great deal of patience, hard work, and thought to keep this project and the database an informative service for the user. It is especially important to mention Millie Hannum and Emily Fassett for their diligent research, editorial work, and development and assignment of index terms; and Sandi Bourelle for production, as well as all others at the Greenwood Publishing Group (GPG) who have contributed to the GRANTS effort.

While the editors have made every effort to verify that all information is both accurate and current within the confines of format and scope, the publisher does not assume and hereby disclaims any liability to any party for loss or damage caused by errors or omissions in this directory, whether such errors or omissions result from accident, negligence, or any other cause. Anyone having any questions regarding the content, format, or any other aspect of *Operating Grants for Nonprofit Organizations* or the GRANTS Database should contact the The Editors, GRANTS, Greenwood Publishing Group (GPG), Millie.Hannum@greenwood.com.

How to Use This Guide

Operating Grants for Nonprofit Organizations is designed to allow the user quick and easy access to information regarding funding programs in the user's area of interest. This guide is composed of a main section listing grant programs alphabetically by state. Three indexes follow the main section: the Subject Index, the Sponsoring Organizations Index, and the Geographic Index.

GRANT PROGRAMS

Each listing in this section consists of some or all of the following elements: sponsor information and contacts, Web page, applicant requirements explaining eligibility, restrictions explaining exclusions, the sponsor's areas of funding interest, and samples of previously awarded grants.

GRANT TITLE ——————— **Avon Products Foundation Grants**   821 ——————— **ACCESSION NUMBER**

Avon Products Foundation

SPONSOR INFORMATION

1345 Avenue of the Americas
New York, NY 10105-0196

Contact Kathleen Walas, President, (212) 282-5518; ——————— **CONTACT INFORMATION**
fax: (212) 282-6049

Internet http://www.avoncompany.com/women/
avonfoundation ——————— **WEB PAGE**

REQUIREMENTS ——————— **Requirements** Applying organizations must be tax-exempt; national and municipal organizations are eligible. Request the guidelines brochure prior to submitting a formal proposal.

RESTRICTIONS ——————— **Restrictions** Grants do not support individuals; memberships; lobbying organizations; political activities and organizations; religious, veteran, or fraternal organizations; fundraising events; and journal advertisements.

Areas of Interest Breast Cancer; Cancer Detection; ——————— **AREAS OF INTEREST**
Children and Youth; Cultural Outreach; Elderly; Humanities; Minorities; Performing Arts; Women; Women's Education; Women's Employment; Women's Health

Sample Awards George Washington U Medical Faculty ——————— **SAMPLE AWARD(S)**
Assoc (Washington, DC)—for salary support for a bilingual health educator and a social worker for the Mobile Mammography Program, $100,000 (2003). National Domestic Violence Hotline (Austin, TX)—to produce Spanish-language outreach materials for a public-awareness campaign about domestic violence, $25,000 (2003). State U of New York at Albany (NY)—for scholarships that enable nontraditional female students to transfer from community colleges, $72,000 over two years (2003). Women's Housing and Economic Development Corp (New York, NY)—to provide financial-education and financial-counseling services to 100 low-income mothers, through the Self Sufficiency Project, $25,000 (2003).

SUBJECT INDEX

The most effective way to access specific funding programs is through the Subject Index. Subject terms, assigned to all entries in the directory, are used to create the Subject Index. Terms have been assigned, using the *GRANTS Subject Authority Guide* (Oryx Press), to target the specific areas of interest of each sponsor. Subject Index terms are arranged alphabetically, and grant program titles—and their accession numbers—are listed alphabetically under each term.

Following are general guidelines that will make your search of the Subject Index more suc-cessful. First, check under the specific topic of interest rather than under a more general term. For instance, if your organization hosts after-school programs for at-risk youth, look first under At-Risk Youth or After-School Programs rather than Youth Programs or Children and Youth.

If you can't find a specific topic, or when you want grants covering broader areas, use more general terms. For example, many grants list funding for arts and humanities, educational programs, or youth programs. To find these grants, use such general descriptors as Arts, General; Humanities; Education; or Youth Programs.

SUBJECT TERM ───────────── **Children and Youth**
Aspen Valley Community Foundation Grants, 204
Atkinson Foundation Community Grants, 46
Bass and Edythe and Sol G. Atlas Fund Grants, 819
PROGRAM TITLE ───────── Avon Products Foundation Grants, 821 ───── **ACCESSION NUMBER**
Clayton Baker Trust Grants, 526
Baltimore Community Foundation Grants, 527

SPONSORING ORGANIZATIONS INDEX

This index lists all program sponsors alphabetically, each followed by the accession numbers of their funding programs.

Atran Foundation, 820

Marilyn Augur Family Foundation, 1149

SPONSORING ORGANIZATION ───────────────── Avon Products Foundation, 821 ───────── **ACCESSION NUMBER**

Azadoutioun Foundation, 555

Mary Reynolds Babcock Foundation, 969

GEOGRAPHIC INDEX

This index lists grants by funders who may fund in one or more states or throughout an entire region. Applicants must be residents of or located in the specific state or region listed to qualify for grants. The Geographic Index is arranged by state and lists grant programs titles and their accession numbers.

STATE ——————————————— **Arkansas**

Albertson's Charitable Giving
   Grants, 370
ARCO Foundation Education
   Grants, 45
Bridgestone/Firestone Grants,
   1132

PROGRAM TITLE ——————— Clorox Company Foundation   **ACCESSION**
   Grants, 67 ——————— **NUMBER**
GenCorp Foundation Grants,
   97

Grant Programs

Alabama

Alabama Power Foundation Grants   1
Alabama Power Foundation
600 N 18th St
Birmingham, AL 35291-0011
Contact William Johnson, President, (205) 257-2508;
fax: (205) 257-1860
Requirements Applications are accepted from Alabama
nonprofit organizations whose programs fall within
foundation guidelines.
Restrictions Grants are not made to individuals, for sectarian religious purposes, or for political activities.
Areas of Interest Arts, General; Civic Affairs; Cultural
Activities/Programs; Economic Development; Elementary Education; Health Care; Higher Education; Preschool Education; Secondary Education; Social Services
Sample Awards Stillman College (Tuscaloosa, AL)—
to construct the Cordell Wynn Humanities, Communications, and Fine Arts Ctr, $65,000.

Alabama State Council on the Arts   2
 Operating Support
Alabama State Council on the Arts
201 Monroe St
Montgomery, AL 36130-4076
Contact Albert Head, Executive Director, (334)
242-4076 ext 245; fax: (334) 240-3269; e-mail: staff@
arts.state.al.us
Internet http://www.arts.state.al.us/grants/
index-grants.html
Requirements Alabama nonprofit 501(c)3 organiza-
tions are eligible to apply.
Areas of Interest Art Education; Arts Administration;
Community Service Programs; Cultural Outreach; Or-
chestras
Sample Awards Central Baldwin Middle School
(Robertsdale, AL)—for the Arts in Education program,
$9924. Red Mountain Chamber Orchestra (Birmingham,
AL)—project grant, $1500.

J.L. Bedsole Foundation Grants   3
J.L. Bedsole Foundation
PO Box 1137
Mobile, AL 36633
Contact Mabel Ward, Executive Director; fax: (344)
432-1134
Requirements Alabama nonprofits may submit applica-
tions.
Areas of Interest Arts Administration; Civic Affairs;
Community Development; Economic Development;
Economics Education; Elementary Education; Health
Care; Higher Education; Hospitals; Libraries; Secondary
Education; Social Services

Sample Awards Alabama Council on Economic Education (AL)—operating support, $2000 (2000). Mobile
Arts Council (AL)—operating support, $37,500 (2000).

Community Foundation of Greater   4
 Birmingham Grants
Community Foundation of Greater Birmingham
2100 First Ave N, Ste 700
Birmingham, AL 35203
Contact Sandy Killion, Vice President Grants and
Initiatives, (205) 328-8641; fax: (205) 328-6576;
email: sandy@foundationbirmingham.org or info@
foundationbirmingham.org
Internet http://www.foundationbirmingham.org
Requirements IRS 501(c)3 organizations that provide
services in the greater Birmingham metropolitan area are
eligible.
Restrictions Grants are not made to or for individuals,
operating expenses of organizations, religious organizations for religious purposes, national fund-raising drives,
conference or seminar expenses, tickets for benefits, political organizations or candidates for public office, organizations with IRS 501(h) status, budget deficits, replacement of government funding cuts, or scholarships
or endowment funds.
Areas of Interest Arts, General; Cultural Activities/Pro-
grams; Education; Environmental Programs; Health
Care; Higher Education; Housing; Japanese Language/
Literature; Social Services
Sample Awards Habitat for Humanity (AL)—to hire a
part-time executive director. Space One Eleven (AL)—
to continue the City Ctr Art program and to raise funds
for the City Ctr Art and Brick Works, $60,000. Birming-
ham Area Consortium for Higher Education (AL)—to
add a Japanese-language component to its Asian studies
program, $20,000.

Community Foundation of South Alabama   5
 Grants
Community Foundation of South Alabama
PO Box 990
Mobile, AL 36601-0990
Contact Grants Manager, (334) 438-5591; fax: (334)
438-5592; e-mail: info@communityendowment.com
Internet http://communityendowment.com/grants/
grants.htm
Requirements Nonprofit, tax-exempt organizations
providing services to the southern Alabama area are eligible.
Restrictions Grants generally are not provided for or to
individuals, recurring requests for the same purpose for
which foundation grant funds have already been
awarded, research that is noncommunity-related or that
does not have short-range results, films, conferences and

workshops, lobbying activities, and tickets to fund-raising events.

Areas of Interest Arts, General; Civic Affairs; Education; Health Care; Recreation and Leisure; Social Services

Vulcan Materials Company Foundation Grants   6

Vulcan Materials Company Foundation
PO Box 385014
Birmingham, AL 35238-5014
Contact Mary Russom, (205) 298-3229; e-mail: giving@vmcmail.com
Internet http://www.vulcanmaterials.com/social.asp?content=guidelines
Requirements Nonprofits in Alabama, Arizona, Arkansas, California, Florida, Georgia, Illinois, Indiana, Iowa, Kansas, Kentucky, Louisiana, Maryland, Mississippi, Missouri, New Mexico, North Carolina, Pennsylvania, South Carolina, Tennessee, Texas, Virginia, and Wisconsin are eligible.
Areas of Interest Arts, General; Children and Youth; Community Development; Criminal Justice; Economic Development; Education; Environmental Programs; Family; Health Care; Higher Education; Humanities; Law; Literacy; Minorities; Scholarship Programs, General; Social Services; Women; Youth Programs
Sample Awards Auburn U Foundation (Auburn U, AL)—for scholarships and fellowships, $45,000. Family and Child Services (Birmingham, AL)—for youth programs, $20,000. Metropolitan Arts Council (Birmingham, AL)—for general support, $79,233.

Susan Mott Webb Charitable Trust Grants   7

Susan Mott Webb Charitable Trust
PO Box 11426
Birmingham, AL 35202
Contact Carla Gale, Trustee, c/o AmSouth Bank, (205) 326-5382; fax: (205) 581-7433; e-mail: cgale@amsouth.com
Requirements Alabama 501(c)3 tax-exempt organizations, colleges and universities, religious organizations, school districts, schools, and state and local government agencies are eligible.
Restrictions Grants do not support advertising, individuals, international organizations, or political organizations.
Areas of Interest Arts, General; Civic Affairs; Community Development; Cultural Activities/Programs; Elementary Education; Environmental Programs; Health Care; Higher Education; Public Affairs; Religion; Secondary Education; Social Services; Technology; Women

Alaska

ACF General Support Grants   8

Alaska Conservation Foundation
441 W Fifth Ave, Ste 402
Anchorage, AK 99501-2340
Contact Program Officer, (907) 276-1917; fax: (907) 274-4145; e-mail: acfinfo@akcf.org
Internet http://www.akcf.org/grants/grant_os.htm

Requirements Applicant organizations must be engaged in environmental advocacy, incorporated as a nonprofit corporation in Alaska, a 501(c)3 or (c)4 organization for at least three years from application date, and have a dues-paying membership of more than 300. Applicants must first send a letter of inquiry to the program officer.
Restrictions Proposals received via fax or e-mail will not be accepted.
Areas of Interest Ecology; Environmental Programs; Nature Centers; Sustainable Development; Water Resources; Wildlife
Sample Awards Chickaloon Village Traditional Council (AK)—for the tribal school's wind/solar project, $25,000 (2002). Alaska Youth for Environmental Action (AK)—for a summer youth gathering, $1000 (2002). Alaska Natural Resources and Outdoor Education Assoc (AK)—to introduce environmental education activity guides to rural K-12 educators, $2000 (2002).

Alaska State Council on the Arts Operating Support Grants   9

Alaska State Council on the Arts
411 W Fourth Ave, Ste 1E
Anchorage, AK 99501-2343
Contact Program Contact, (907) 269-6610 or (888) 278-7424 (toll free, within Alaska only); fax: (907) 269-6601; TTY: (800) 770-8973; e-mail: aksca_info@eed.state.ak.us
Internet http://www.eed.state.ak.us/aksca/grants2.htm#OSLA
Requirements The council awards funds only to Alaskan nonprofit organizations, schools, or government agencies. Eligible organizations must: be involved in producing, presenting, or undertaking a series of events or ongoing arts programs; provide proof of 501(c)3 status; be at least three years from the date of incorporation; and have a cash budget of at least $50,000. A maximum award amount is not set; however, applicants must provide matching funds, and grants will not exceed 50 percent of the total cash expenses.
Areas of Interest Arts Administration; Cultural Heritage Preservation; Dance; Dramatic/Theater Arts; Folk/Ethnic Arts; Literature; Media Arts; Music; Native Americans; Visual Arts

James and Elsie Nolan Charitable Trust Grants   10

James and Elsie Nolan Charitable Trust
PO Box 927
Wrangell, AK 99929
Contact Judith Baker, c/o National Bank of Alaska, Trust Department, (907) 874-2323
Requirements Alaska nonprofit organizations are eligible.
Restrictions Individuals are ineligible.
Areas of Interest Community Outreach Programs; Education; Health Care; Hospitals; Museums; Public Administration
Sample Awards Catholic Community Services of Juneau (AK)—for wheelchair-accessible vehicles, $17,000. Junior Achievement in Anchorage (AK)—for computer equipment. Wrangell Medical Ctr (AK)—for mammogram machine and endoscopes, $105,000. Irene

Ingle Public Library (Wrangell, AK)—for library book purchases and a learning project, $4164.

Skaggs Foundation Grants 11
Skaggs Foundation
PO Box 20510
Juneau, AK 99802
Contact Samuel Skaggs Jr., President, (907) 463-4843
Requirements Nonprofit organizations are eligible. Preference is given to requests from Alaska.
Restrictions Individuals are ineligible.
Areas of Interest Civic Affairs; Conservation, Natural Resources; Cultural Activities/Programs; Disabled; Environmental Programs; Land Management; Museums; Natural History; Water Resources; Youth Programs
Sample Awards Homer Society of Natural History (AK)—general support to Pratt Museum, $10,000. Kachemak Heritage Land Trust (Homer, AK)—for protection of the Riparian corridors in the Kanai, $2500. Trust for Public Land (Seattle, WA)—for general support, $3000. Earth Island Institute (San Francisco, CA)—to support the Alaska Clean H20 Project, $4000.

Arizona

America West Airlines Foundation Grants 12
America West Airlines Foundation
4000 E Sky Harbor Blvd
Phoenix, AZ 85034
Contact C.A. Howlett, President, (480) 693-5733; fax: (480) 693-5546
Internet http://www.americawest.com/aboutawa/community/aa_communityfoundation.htm
Requirements 501(c)3 nonprofits located in one of the following cities are eligible: Anchorage, AK; Phoenix and Tucson, AZ; Burbank, Long Beach, Los Angeles, Oakland, Ontario, Orange County, Sacramento, San Diego, and San Francisco, CA; Colorado Springs and Denver, CO; Washington, DC; Atlanta, GA; Chicago, IL; Indianapolis, IN; Kansas City and Wichita, KS; Boston, MA; Baltimore, Minneapolis/Saint Paul, MN; Saint Louis, MO; Las Vegas and Reno, NV; Newark, NJ; Albuquerque, NM; New York, NY; Columbus, OH; Portland, OR; Philadelphia, PA; Austin, Dallas/Fort Worth, El Paso, Houston, and San Antonio, TX; Salt Lake City, UT; Seattle, WA; or Milwaukee, WI.
Restrictions Program exclusions include salaries, stipends, or grants for personal expenses; political campaigns; discriminatory organizations; churches; endowment funds or grantmaking foundations; purchase of tickets or tables for dinners and/or benefits; purchase of program advertisements; air transportation donations; travel expenses; community emergency requests that do not have proper tax-exempt status; debt retirement or operational deficits; or scholarships to individuals other than for dependent children of the airline's employees.
Areas of Interest Arts, General; Aviation; Business Education; Children and Youth; Civic Affairs; Cultural Activities/Programs; Disabled; Education; Entrepreneurship; Health Care; Higher Education; Leadership; Parent Involvement; Scholarship Programs, General; Science; Social Services; Voter Educational Programs; Youth Programs

Sample Awards Kids Voting USA (Phoenix, AZ)—to educate youths about the importance of voting and of an informed electorate, $50,000 in-kind services. Wilson Elementary School District (Phoenix, AZ)—to support Parents and Teachers: Together We Can Make a Difference, $4000. Arts Genesis (Tucson, AZ)—to support Old Pascua Youth Artists, $2000.

American Foundation Grants 13
American Foundation
4518 N 32nd St
Phoenix, AZ 85018
Contact Grants Administrator, (602) 522-8800 or (602) 955-4770; e-mail: grantinfo@americanfoundation.org
Internet http://www.americanfoundation.org
Requirements 501(c)3, 509(a)1, and 509(a)2 public charities are eligible.
Restrictions Funding will not be considered for the following requests: organizations without tax-exempt 501(c)3, 509(a)1 or 509(a)2 public charity status; general endowment funds; direct aid to individuals; or governmental or quasi-governmental entities or activities other than colleges or universities.
Areas of Interest Philanthropy

APS Foundation Grants 14
Arizona Public Service Foundation
PO Box 53999, MS 8510
Phoenix, AZ 85072-3999
Contact Sandie Jones, Corporate Contributions, (602) 250-2257; fax: (602) 250-2113; e-mail: sandie.jones@aps.com
Internet http://www.aps.com/general_info/aboutaps_14.html
Requirements Arizona 501(c)3 nonprofits are eligible.
Restrictions The foundation does not fund individuals or individual scholarships; religious, political, fraternal, legislative, or lobbying efforts; or travel or hotel expenses.
Areas of Interest Arts, General; Children and Youth; Community Development; Cultural Activities/Programs; Education; Environmental Programs; Health Care; Hospices; Independent Living Programs; Performing Arts; Social Services
Sample Awards Hospice of the Valley (Phoenix, AZ)—for operating support, $10,000. Arizona Bridge to Independent Living (Phoenix, AZ)—for program support, $3000. Arizona Wolf Trap—to sponsor a series of field trips for children to visit performing arts centers.

Arizona Commission on the Arts Local Aid 15
Arizona Commission on the Arts
417 W Roosevelt St
Phoenix, AZ 85003-1326
Contact Patrick Demers, Schools and Locals Director, (602) 229-8221; fax: (602) 256-0282; e-mail: pdemers@ArizonaArts.org; Mollie Lakin-Hayes, Assistant Director, (602) 229-8220; fax: (602)256-0282; e-mail: mlakinhayes@ArizonaArts.org
Internet http://www.arizonaarts.org/guide/gos_local_arts.htm
Requirements The applicant must be an Arizona 501(c)3 nonprofit or a division of an Arizona city gov-

ernment for a minimum of five years and must be the officially designated (city or county) local arts agency; have a full-time paid professional management and evidence of sound management practices; show evidence of long-range planning for the effective use of resources and development of the goals for the organization; and submit an education plan approved by its board that designates financial resources to support the plan.

Restrictions Funding excludes public art in private development, Percent for Art project costs, and public funds other than city or county (federal or state).

Areas of Interest Arts; Arts Administration; Cultural Activities/Programs; Multidisciplinary Arts

Arizona Commission on the Arts Organization Development Program I Grants   16

Arizona Commission on the Arts
417 W Roosevelt St
Phoenix, AZ 85003
Contact Program Contact, (602) 255-5882; fax: (602) 256-0282; general@ArizonaArts.org
Internet http://www.arizonaarts.org/guide/gos_level_I.htm
Requirements Arizona 501(c)3 tax-exempt organizations, schools, or units of government may apply. An unincorporated Arizona organization may apply through a 501(c)3 fiscal agent or a government organization. Applicants must have at least a one-year track record of ongoing arts programming.
Areas of Interest Arts Administration; Arts and Culture; Community Development; Cultural Activities/Programs

Arizona Commission on the Arts Organization Development Program II Grants   17

Arizona Commission on the Arts
417 W Roosevelt St
Phoenix, AZ 85003
Contact Jo Kobert, (602) 255-5882; fax: (602) 256-0282; voice: (800) 842-4681; TTY: (800) 367-8939; e-mail: jkobert@ArizonaArts.org
Internet http://www.arizonaarts.org
Requirements Arizona 501(c)3 nonprofits, schools, or units of government may apply. The organization must commit to provide full financial support of a permanent full-time managerial position. A minimum of two years of fiscal and administrative stability must be demonstrated.
Areas of Interest Arts Administration

Arizona Commission on the Arts Tribal Museum Assessment Program Grants   18

Arizona Commission on the Arts
417 W Roosevelt St
Phoenix, AZ 85003
Contact General Information, (602) 255-5882; fax: (602) 256-0282; e-mail: general@ArizonaArts.org
Internet http://www.arizonaarts.org/guide/gos_tribal.htm
Requirements Arizona 501(c)3 tax-exempt organizations, schools, and units of government may apply.
Areas of Interest Museums; Native Americans

Arizona Community Foundation Grants   19

Arizona Community Foundation
2122 E Highland Ave, Ste 400
Phoenix, AZ 85016
Contact Sandy Doubleday, Vice President, Marketing and Communications, (602) 381-1400; fax: (602) 381-1575; e-mail: rmayberry@azfoundation.com
Internet http://www.azfoundation.org/rfp/index.xpl
Requirements Arizona 501(c)3 organizations are eligible as well as public schools, Native American tribes and their component agencies, and selected public programs.
Restrictions Grants will not be made to individuals; for deficit financing; endowment funds; employee matching gifts; basic research; conferences and seminars; religious organizations for religious purposes; direct lobbying or influencing of elections; tax-supported governmental functions or programs; fund-raising campaigns and expenses; telephone and/or mail solicitation, capital campaigns; or support of veteran, fraternal, and labor organizations.
Areas of Interest Children and Youth; Civil/Human Rights; Disabled; Economic Development; Education; Elderly; Environmental Programs; Family; Food Banks; Health Care; Hearing Impairments; Housing; Mental Health; Neighborhoods; Performing Arts; Poverty and the Poor; Prisoners; Science Education; Youth Programs
Sample Awards Southwest Food Bank (Phoenix, AZ)—for operating support. Habitat for Humanity (Phoenix, AZ)—for a low-income housing community project, $45,000. Arizona Cactus Pine Girl Scout Council (Phoenix, AZ)—for the Scouts Behind Bars project, $25,000.

Arizona Foundation for Legal Services and Education Grants   20

Arizona Foundation for Legal Services and Education
111 W Monroe, Ste 1800
Phoenix, AZ 85003-1742
Contact Kelly Carmody, Legal Services Director, (602) 340-7356; fax: (602) 271-4930; e-mail: kelly.carmody@azflse.org
Internet http://www.azflse.org/AZFLSE/legalservices/ioltagrants.cfm
Requirements Arizona nonprofits are eligible.
Areas of Interest Legal Services; Poverty and the Poor; Refugees
Sample Awards Community Legal Services (Phoenix, AZ)—to maintain pro bono legal services, $150,000 operating support. Florence Immigrants and Refugee Rights Project (Florence, AZ)—to help persons seeking political asylum.

Arizona Republic Foundation Grants   21

Arizona Republic Foundation
200 E Van Buren
Phoenix, AZ 85004
Contact Gene D'Adamo, Vice President, Community Relations, (602) 444-8202
Internet http://www.azcentral.com/relations
Requirements Arizona nonprofits may apply.
Areas of Interest Arts, General; Child Abuse; Children and Youth; Civic Affairs; Cultural Activities/Programs; Education; Elderly; Family; Homelessness; Hunger; Literacy; Neighborhoods; Sexual Abuse; Shelters

Sample Awards Aunt Rita's Foundation (Phoenix, AZ)—AIDS assistance program. East Valley Child Crisis Center (Phoenix, AZ). Valley Citizen's League (Phoenix, AZ). Kids Voting Arizona (Phoenix, AZ). Foundation for Senior Living Programs (Phoenix, AZ).

**Arizona Republic Newspaper Corporate   22
  Contributions Grants**
Arizona Republic Newspaper
200 E Van Buren
Phoenix, AZ 85004
Contact Gene D'Adamo, Vice President, Community Relations, (602) 444-8202; fax: (602) 444-8242
Internet http://www.azcentral.com/relations/initiatives.html
Requirements Arizona nonprofits may apply.
Restrictions Funding is not provided for: programs that address behavioral and mental health issues; physical and mental disabilities; diseases or other specific health issues; recreational programs; capital requests; and grant requests for less than $2,500.
Areas of Interest After-School Programs; Arts and Culture; Assisted-Living Programs; Child Abuse; Childcare; Children and Youth; Civic Affairs; Counseling/Guidance; Cultural Activities/Programs; Domestic Abuse; Domestic Abuse; Democracy; Economic Development; Education; Elder Abuse; Elderly; Food Distribution; Higher Education; Job Training Programs; Literacy; Neighborhoods; Preschool Education; Poverty and the Poor; Reading Education; Recreation; Shelters
Sample Awards Downtown Neighborhood Learning Ctr (Phoenix, AZ)—for general support, $15,000. Area Agency on Aging (Phoenix, AZ)—to support an elderly abuse prevention program, $20,000.

Bank One Corporate Contributions   23
Bank One Corporation
201 N Central Ave, AZ1-1018
Phoenix, AZ 85004
Contact Lydia Lee, (602) 221-2230; fax: (602) 221-1535
Internet http://www.bankone.com/answers/BolAnswersTable.aspx?top=all&segment=ABO&topic=CorporateContributions
Requirements 501(c)3 organizations serving Bank One communities are eligible.
Restrictions Contributions will not be considered for grants to individuals, religious or sectarian activities, private grantmaking or operating foundations, endowments, fraternal or veterans organizations and professional associations, national health organizations, United Way member agencies, individual scholarships or fellowships, sponsorships, service club activities, or political organizations/candidates.
Areas of Interest Arts, General; Business Development; College-Preparatory Education; Cultural Activities/Programs; Disadvantaged (Economically); Economic Development; Early Childhood Education; Education; Elderly; Health Care; Housing; Industry; Job Training Programs; Literacy; Microenterprises; Minorities; Museums; Social Services; Women
Sample Awards Heard Museum (AZ)—for program support, $45,000. Ronald McDonald House of Phoenix (AZ)—for operating support, $25,000.

**Community Foundation for Southern   24
  Arizona Grants**
Community Foundation for Southern Arizona
2250 E Broadway Blvd
Tucson, AZ 85719
Contact Grants Administrator, (520) 770-0800; fax: (520) 770-1500; e-mail: philanthropy@cfsoaz.org
Internet http://www.cfsoaz.org/Pages/GrantSeekers.html
Requirements Nonprofit and grassroots organizations in southern Arizona communities are eligible. Southern Arizona communities include all of Cochise, Santa Cruz, and Pima Counties; and the areas of Yuma, Mariposa, Pinal, Graham, and Greenlee Counties that lie south of the Gila River.
Restrictions Funds are generally not available for ongoing operating or capital campaigns, debt retirement, endowments, individuals, individual schools, sectarian activities, or underwriting of fund-raising events.
Areas of Interest AIDS; Alcohol/Alcoholism; Arts, General; Children and Youth; Counseling/Guidance; Drugs/Drug Abuse; Education; Environmental Programs; HIV; Health Care; Humanities; Mental Disorders; Parent Education; Recreation and Leisure; Rehabilitation/Therapy; Sexual Abuse; Social Services
Sample Awards A Mountain Betterment Assoc (Tucson, AZ)—for grandparenting education and support classes, $3500 (2000). Southern Arizona AIDS Foundation (AZ)—to support a recreational therapy program for clients diagnosed with substance abuse issues and mental illness, as well as HIV/AIDS, $1800 (2000). Southern Arizona Ctr Against Sexual Assault (AZ)—to provide culturally appropriate and bilingual counseling at El Pueblo Neighborhood Ctr, $8100 (2000). Tucson Museum of Art (AZ)—to support children's art projects in the community, $7500 (2000).

Dorrance Family Foundation Grants   25
Dorrance Family Foundation
7600 E Doubletree Ranch Rd, Ste 300
Scottsdale, AZ 85258
Contact Carolyn O'Malley, Executive Director, (480) 367-7233
Restrictions Grants are not made to individuals.
Areas of Interest AIDS; Arthritis; Arts Administration; Arts, General; Botanical Gardens; Civic Affairs; Cultural Activities/Programs; Dramatic/Theater Arts; Education; HIV; Health Care; Higher Education; Hospices; Hospitals; Kidney Diseases and Disorders; Museums; Music; Orchestras; Private and Parochial Education; Religion; Science; Social Services; Special Education; Technology; Zoos
Sample Awards Arizona Museum of Science and Technology (Phoenix, AZ)—for the capital campaign, $591,278. Phoenix Symphony Orchestra (Phoenix, AZ)—as part of a five-year pledge to support the capital campaign, $50,000.

Flinn Foundation Grants Programs   26
Flinn Foundation
1802 N Central Ave
Phoenix, AZ 85004-1506
Contact Program Contact, (602) 744-6800; fax: (602) 744-6815; e-mail: info@flinn.org

Internet http://www.flinn.org/what/request/index.html
Requirements Arizona-based institutions or organizations whose programs are operated for the benefit of Arizona institutions and individuals are eligible to apply. Applications are accepted at any time. There is no application form, but a preliminary letter of inquiry or phone call is requested to determine the appropriateness of a full submission.
Restrictions The foundation rarely provides grants to individuals, building projects (capital campaigns), purchase of equipment, endowment projects, annual fund-raising campaigns, ongoing operating expenses, or deficit needs. Requests to support conferences and workshops, publications, or the production of films and video are considered only when these activities are an integral component of a larger foundation initiative.
Areas of Interest Adolescent Health; Biological Sciences; Biomedical Research; Child/Maternal Health; Dance; Disadvantaged (Economically); Health Care; Health Care Access; Health Services Delivery; Medical Education; Performing Arts; Scholarship Programs, General; Social Services; Teacher Education, Inservice; Undergraduate Education; Visual Arts
Sample Awards Northern Arizona U (Flagstaff, AZ)—to expand teacher-preparation programs in the biological sciences, $517,100 over three years. Homeward Bound (Phoenix, AZ)—to coordinate access to health care services for disadvantaged children, $10,000. Ballet Arizona (Phoenix, AZ)—for 15 months of support, $200,000.

J.W. Kieckhefer Foundation Grants   27
J.W. Kieckhefer Foundation
PO Box 1151, 116 E Gurley St
Prescott, AZ 86302
Contact John Kieckhefer or Eugene Polk, Trustees, (928) 445-4010
Restrictions Grants are not awarded to individuals or for seed money, deficit financing, scholarships, or demonstration projects.
Areas of Interest Biomedical Research; Child Welfare; Community Development; Conservation, Natural Resources; Cultural Activities/Programs; Disabled; Education; Family Planning; Health Care; Higher Education; Hospices; Medical Education; Public Planning/Policy; Social Services; Youth Programs

Armstrong McDonald Foundation Grants   28
Armstrong McDonald Foundation
PO Box 900
Cortaro, AZ 85652-0900
Contact Laurie Bouchard, Vice President, (520) 878-9627; fax: (520) 797-3866; e-mail: armmcdfdn@aol.com
Requirements 510(c)3 nonprofit organizations, colleges and universities, schools, and school districts are eligible.
Restrictions Grants do not support advocacy organizations, individuals, international organizations, political organizations, or state and local government agencies.
Areas of Interest Animal Care; Arts, General; Biomedical Research; Civic Affairs; Community Development; Computer Grants; Cultural Activities/Programs; Disabled; Elementary Education; Environmental Programs;

Health Care; Higher Education; Housing; Humanities; Minorities; Public Affairs; Recreation and Leisure; Religion; Science; Secondary Education; Social Services; Visual Impairments; Women; Youth Programs
Sample Awards Big Brothers Big Sisters of the Midlands (Omaha, NE)—to support an after-school program for at-risk children of single parents, $2500. Cook College and Theological School (Tempe, AZ)—for a literacy program for older Native American students to qualify for college, $30,000. National Jewish Ctr (Denver, CO)—to support nutrition services for chronically ill children who attend Kungsberg onsite school and for support of a pediatric asthma center, $98,000. Zoo Atlanta (GA)—for the cost of diagnostic equipment for endangered species, $25,000.

Margaret T. Morris Foundation Grants   29
Margaret T. Morris Foundation
PO Box 592
Prescott, AZ 86302
Contact Eugene Polk, Trustee, (520) 445-4010
Areas of Interest Animal Care; Arts, General; Biomedical Research; Children and Youth; Cultural Activities/Programs; Environmental Programs; Family; Higher Education; Hospices; Marine Sciences; Mental Health; Music; Social Services

Phelps Dodge Corporation Grants   30
Phelps Dodge Corporation
1 N Central Ave
Phoenix, AZ 85004
Contact Community Affairs Information Line, (800) 528-1182 ext 8050 or (602) 366-8050; e-mail: communityaffairs@phelpsdodge.com
Internet http://www.phelpsdodge.com/index-community.html
Requirements Nonprofit organizations in corporate and subsidiary operating locations are eligible, including Henderson, KY; Atlanta, GA; Norwich, CT; El Paso, TX; Coral Gables, FL; Fort Wayne, IN; Tyrone, NM; and Morenci, AZ.
Restrictions Grants will not be awarded to individuals or for seed money, emergency funds, deficit financing, research, special projects, or conferences.
Areas of Interest Arts, General; Civic Affairs; Cultural Activities/Programs; Elementary Education; Health Care; Higher Education; Secondary Education; Social Services

Phoenix Suns Charities Grants   31
Phoenix Suns
201 E Jefferson
Phoenix, AZ 85004
Contact Program Contact, (602) 379-7900; fax: (602) 530-2251
Internet http://www.nba.com/suns/news/charities_index.html
Requirements Arizona 501(c)3 organizations, primarily in Maricopa County, may submit grant requests.
Areas of Interest Arts, General; Business; Children and Youth; Children's Museums; Cultural Activities/Programs; Drugs/Drug Abuse; Elementary Education; Family; Health and Safety Education; Preschool Education;

Recreation and Leisure; Rehabilitation/Therapy; Science; Secondary Education; Social Services
Sample Awards Junior Achievement of Central Arizona (Phoenix, AZ)—for youth and business partnership, $5000. Teen Challenge (Phoenix, AZ)—for drug prevention/rehabilitation program, $5000. East Valley Boys and Girls Club (Mesa, AZ)—for recreation programs, $10,000.

Virginia G. Piper Charitable Trust Grants   32
Virginia G. Piper Charitable Trust
6720 N Scottsdale Rd, Ste 350
Scottsdale, AZ 85253
Contact Karin Bishop, Grants Manager, (480) 948-5853; fax: (408) 348-1316; e-mail: info@ pipertrust.org
Internet http://www.pipertrust.org
Requirements Arizona nonprofit organizations, primarily in Maricopa County, are eligible.
Restrictions Individuals are not eligible.
Areas of Interest Biomedical Research; Children and Youth; Elderly; Arts, General; Cultural Activities/Programs; Health Care; Education; Preschool Education; Religion
Sample Awards Mesa Arts and Entertainment Alliance (Mesa, AZ)—for the capital campaign for a new Mesa Arts Center, a complex for performing arts, galleries, and outdoor spaces, $500,000 (2003). Stardust Non-Profit Building Supplies (Mesa, AZ)—to provide home repair and safety enhancements for elderly homeowners, $50,000 (2003). Volunteer Ctr (Phoenix, AZ)—to strengthen volunteer management at local nonprofit organizations, $135,333 over three years (2003). Phoenix Indian Ctr (AZ)—for a mentoring program for American Indian youths, $60,000 (2003).

Salt River Project Grants   33
Salt River Project
PO Box 52025
Phoenix, AZ 85072-2025
Contact Program Contact, (602) 236-2573; e-mail: contrib@srpnet.com
Internet http://www.srpnet.com/community/ contributions
Requirements Arizona nonprofits in SRP service communities may apply.
Restrictions SRP does not donate services, including water or electricity, or equipment for which a fee is normally charged.
Areas of Interest Arts Administration; Arts, General; Civic Affairs; Cultural Activities/Programs; Economic Self-Sufficiency; Education; Electric Power; Elementary Education; Engineering Education; Environmental Programs; Food Distribution; Health Care; Housing; Leadership; Mathematics Education; Minorities; Minority Education; Music; Public Planning/Policy; Recreation and Leisure; Science; Science Education; Shelters; Social Services Delivery; Vocational/Technical Education; Volunteers; Water Resources; Women's Education; Youth Programs
Sample Awards Globe-Miami Community Concert Assoc (Globe-Miami, AZ)—for program support. City of Peoria Parks and Recreation Festival of Lights (Peoria, AZ)—for program support. Queen Creek Elementary School (Queen Creek, AZ)—for operating support.

Women's Foundation of Southern Arizona   34
Grants
Women's Foundation of Southern Arizona
6418 E Tanque Verde, Ste 110
Tucson, AZ 87515
Contact Bernadette Wilkinson, Program Officer, (520) 795-5088; fax: (520) 795-5499; e-mail: BernadetteW@ WomenGiving.org
Internet http://www.womengiving.org/grantmaking
Requirements Nonprofit organizations with 501(c)3 status, or emerging grassroots organizations or informal groups who have come together for a program that is consistent with the fund's mission may apply. Groups without tax-exempt status must consist of more than five women and have some type of governing body.
Restrictions The fund does not provide funds for individuals, capital fund drives, endowments, campaigns to elect candidates to public office, programs that promote religious activities, programs outside the southern Arizona area, programs that are inconsistent with nondiscrimination ordinances regarding equal employment opportunity, and agencies that have been funded by SAWF for the last three consecutive years.
Areas of Interest Disabled; Domestic Violence; Education; Homelessness; Homosexuals, Female; Housing; Immigrants; Scholarship Programs, General; Sexual Abuse; Single-Parent Families; Social Change; Women; Women's Education; Youth Programs
Sample Awards Boys and Girls Club of Tucson (AZ)—for the SMART Girls program, a health, fitness, prevention/education, and self-esteem enhancement program for girls ages 10 to 15, $3000 (2003). Planned Parenthood (AZ)—for TAG, an active group of young women providing peer-to-peer outreach, education, and traning and support to young women in southern Arizona as it relates to holistic sexuality and prevention, $4000 (2003).

Arkansas

Charles A. Frueauff Foundation Grants   35
Charles A. Frueauff Foundation
900 S Shackleford, Ste 300
Little Rock, AR 72211
Contact Grants Administrator, (501) 219-1410; fax: (501) 219-1416
Internet http://www.frueau5ffoundation.com/ application/default.asp
Requirements Applicants must be private nonprofit corporations with 501(c)3 status. Giving is limited to the US with emphasis on areas east of the Rockies, the South, and Northeast.
Restrictions The foundation funds nationwide except the Pacific states, Michigan, and Texas. K-12 schools are ineligible. Grants are not awarded to individuals, provide emergency funds, fund research, or for loans.
Areas of Interest Health Care; Higher Education, Private; Natural Sciences; Social Services
Sample Awards Melmark Home (Berwyn, PA)—for classroom and office renovation, $50,000. Stetson U

(Deland, FL)—to provide scholarships to students majoring in the natural sciences, $100,000.

Willard and Pat Walker Charitable Foundation Grants   36
Willard and Pat Walker Charitable Foundation
PO Box 5000
Springdale, AR 72765-5000
Contact Tommy Karr, (501) 756-7031
Requirements Arkansas nonprofit organizations are eligible.
Restrictions Individuals are not eligible.
Areas of Interest Arts, General; Health Care; Higher Education; Hospitals; Social Services
Sample Awards U of Arkansas (Fayetteville, AR)—to construct a building as part of the College of Business, $8 million (2003).

Walton Family Foundation Grants   37
Walton Family Foundation
PO Box 2030
Bentonville, AR 72712
Contact Buddy Philpot, Executive Director, (479) 464-1570; fax: (479) 464-1580
Internet http://www.wffhome.com/application.html
Requirements 501(c)3 nonprofit organizations and public entities are eligible.
Restrictions The foundation generally does not approve applications for grants to individuals, endowment, scholarships that are not part of the foundation's current program, local church-related construction projects, travel expenses for groups to compete or perform, unestablished medical research programs, business-related activities such as start-up costs, or expenses related to groups or individuals participating in noncurricular enhancement programs.
Areas of Interest Adult and Continuing Education; Cultural Activities/Programs; Economic Development; Education; Elementary Education; Higher Education; Radio; Scholarship Programs, General; Secondary Education; Youth Programs
Sample Awards Foundation for the Mid South (Jackson, MS)—to develop community-building methods designed to improve education and foster economic development in specific areas of the Delta, $150,000 (2003). College of Wooster (OH)—for an endowed scholarship fund and for unrestricted use as part of its capital campaign, $9 million (2003). U of Texas (Austin, TX)—for the U of Texas Elementary Charter School, $150,000 (2003). Walton Arts Ctr Council (Fayetteville, AR)—to enhance the center's programs and to attract high-profile artists and events to northwestern Arkansas, $2.8 million over three years (2003).

California

Abelard Foundation West Grants Program   38
Abelard Foundation West
1221 Preservation Pkwy, Ste 101
Oakland, CA 94612
Contact Program Contact, c/o Common Counsel Foundation, (510) 834-2995; fax: (510) 834-2998; e-mail: ccounsel@igc.apc.org
Internet http://www.commoncounsel.org/pages/foundation.html#abelhard
Requirements 501(c)3 organizations located in the Northern Rockies, the Great Basin, the Northwest, the Southwest, and California are eligible.
Restrictions The foundation does not support social service programs offering ongoing or direct delivery of service; medical, educational, or cultural institutions; capital expenditure, construction, or renovation programs; programs undertaken at government initiative; or scholarship funds or other aid to individuals.
Areas of Interest Agriculture; Civil/Human Rights; Community Development; Criminal Justice; Domestic Violence; Environmental Programs; Grassroots Leadership; Hispanics; Minorities; Poverty and the Poor; Social Change; Urban Areas; Violent Behavior
Sample Awards C-Beyond (Concord, CA)— renewal grant for this youth organizing project in working class suburbs which seeks to address both the pervasive racism in the area and local issues such as access to job and recreational opportunities for youth, $12,000. Ctr for Third World Organizing (Oakland, CA)—for a national project to address violence in and against low-income urban communities of color, $8000. Northern Plains Resource Council (Billings, MT)—to address the growing antagonism between environmental organizations and conventional agriculture within the council's Montana Waters project, $9000. Prison and Jail Project (Americus, GA)—to support grassroots coalition building to address systemic discrimination and abuse in rural Georgia's criminal justice system, $7000. Hermanas Unidas/Ayuda (Washington, DC)—to organize Latina survivors of domestic violence to develop leadership skills to act on issues concerning their lives and communities, $6500.

Thomas C. Ackerman Foundation Grants   39
Thomas C. Ackerman Foundation
600 W Broadway, Ste 2600
San Diego, CA 92101-3391
Contact Patricia Garcia, Assistant Secretary, (619) 699-5411; fax: (619) 232-8311; e-mail: Info@AckermanFoundation.org or pgarcia@luce.com
Internet http://www.ackermanfoundation.org
Requirements California nonprofits, primarily in San Diego County, are eligible.
Restrictions The foundation does not award grants to religious organizations for religious purposes; individuals; or for brick-and-mortar projects, conferences, symposia, or human medical or biological research.
Areas of Interest Arts, General; Community Development; Cultural Activities/Programs; Education; Food Distribution; Health Care; Homelessness; Social Services; Youth Programs
Sample Awards San Diego Senior Olympics (San Diego, CA)—for Website Online Registration Development, $3500. San ElderHelp of San Diego (San Diego, CA)—for Shared Housing Program, $10,000. Museum of Contemporary Art (San Diego, CA)—for the program Off Broadway: Emerging Artists in Downtown San Diego, $7500.

Adobe Systems Community Relations Grants 40
Adobe Systems Corporation
345 Park Ave
San Jose, CA 95110-2704
Contact Community Relations, (408) 536-3993; fax: (408) 537-6313; e-mail: community_relations@adobe.com
Internet http://www.cfsv.org/adobe.html
Requirements California 501(c)3 nonprofit organizations, organizations with 501(c)3 fiscal sponsors, and public agencies (such as public schools) that benefit residents of Santa Clara and southern San Mateo Counties are eligible.
Restrictions Grants do not support fundraising events (i.e., tickets, raffles, auctions, or tournaments), annual fundraising appeals, agency celebrations, or ongoing fundraising expenses of an organization; sponsorship of workshops, conferences, or conventions; capital campaigns, equipment, or endowment campaigns; building renovation or construction of new facilities; political, fraternal, or religious activities; existing obligations, debts/liabilities, or costs that the agency has already incurred; for-profit schools; individuals; field trips, scholarships, camperships, the like; sports activities, unless part of a larger community effort; governmental entities; or computer hardware.
Areas of Interest Arts; Civic Affairs; Early Childhood Education; Economic Self-Sufficiency; Education; Educational Technology; Family; Literacy; Neighborhoods; Technology; Training and Development; Youth Programs

Akonadi Foundation Anti-Racism Grants 41
Akonadi Foundation
469 9th St, Ste 210
Oakland, CA 94607
Contact Grants Administrator, (510) 663-3867; fax: (510) 663-3860; e-mail: info@akonadi.org
Internet http://www.akonadi.org/application_guidelines.html
Areas of Interest Children and Youth; Children's Literature; Civic Affairs; Civil/Human Rights; Cultural Diversity; Cultural Outreach; Education; Environmental Health; Environmental Programs; Grassroots Leadership; Minorities; Minority Education; Minority Employment; Minority Health; Minority Schools; Minority/Woman-Owned Business; Racism/Race Relations; Social Change; Social Movements
Sample Awards Asian Pacific Environmental Network (Oakland, CA)—to involve Asian-Pacific Islanders in grassroots organizing to fight environmental racism, $20,000 (2001). Ctr for Third World Organizing (Oakland, CA)—for general support, $30,000 (2001). Leadership Excellence (Oakland, CA)—for leadership development for black youths and for critical analysis of racism, $25,000 (2001). Poverty and Race Research Action Council (Washington DC)—to support a civil-rights teaching curriculum, institutes on civil rights, and teacher workshops, $25,000 (2001).

Maurice Amado Foundation Grants 42
Maurice Amado Foundation
3940 Laurel Canyon Blvd, No 809
Studio City, CA 91604

Contact Pam Kaizer, Executive Director, (818) 980-9190; fax: (818) 980-9190; e-mail: pkaizer@mauriceamadofdn.org
Internet http://www.mauriceamadofdn.org
Requirements 501(c)3 organizations in New York and California are eligible. Individuals applying for grants must be affiliated with a tax-exempt organization.
Areas of Interest Children's Museums; Cultural Activities/Programs; Curriculum Development; Education; Jewish Studies; Museums; Music; Publication; Religious Studies
Sample Awards 92nd Street Y (NY)—for operating support, $15,000. American Jewish Historical Society (NY)—for operating support, $10,000.

American Honda Foundation Grants 43
American Honda Foundation
PO Box 2205
Torrance, CA 90509-2205
Contact Program Contact, (310) 781-4090; fax: (310) 781-4270
Internet http://www.hondacorporate.com/community/index.html?subsection=foundation
Requirements An applicant must be a nonprofit, tax-exempt organization that is national in scope, impact, and outreach.
Restrictions The foundation does not consider proposals for service clubs, arts and culture, health and welfare issues, research papers, social issues, medical or educational research, trips, attempts to influence legislation, advocacy, annual funds, hospital operating funds, student exchanges, marathons, sponsorships, political activities, conferences, or fundraising events. An organization may submit only one proposal per year.
Areas of Interest At-Risk Youth; Ecology; Education; Elementary Education; Environmental Programs; Higher Education; Job Training Programs; Junior and Community Colleges; Radio; School-to-Work Transition; Science Education; Secondary Education; Technology; Television; Youth Programs
Sample Awards Children's Health Fund (New York, NY)—to provide medical services to homeless and underprivileged children in New York and other locations nationwide, $50,000.

Amgen Foundation Grants 44
Amgen Foundation
1 Amgen Center Dr, MS 38-3-B
Thousand Oaks, CA 91320
Contact Program Contact, (805) 447-4056 or (805) 447-1000; fax: (805) 447-1010
Internet http://www.amgen.com/community/foundation.html
Requirements 501(c)3 tax-exempt organizations located in Amgen communities are eligible.
Restrictions In general, Amgen does not consider requests for the following: alumni drives and teacher organizations; construction or building improvements; capital campaigns; city/municipal/federal government departments; endowments and foundations; individuals, including scholarships; fundraising activities such as charitable dinners or sporting events; labor unions; municipal and for-profit hospitals; religious, political, fraternal, service or veterans' organizations; professional

sports events or athletes; or civic or cultural organizations that do not serve the areas in which Amgen is located.

Areas of Interest Biology Education; Conservation, Natural Resources; Curriculum Development; Education; Environmental Programs; Health Services Delivery; Literacy; Performing Arts; Remedial Education; Science Education; Social Services; Visual Arts

Sample Awards California Lutheran U (Thousand Oaks, CA)—for the Summer Science Institute, which helps teachers improve science education in middle and high schools, $135,000 (2003).

ARCO Foundation Education Grants 45

ARCO Foundation
151 S Flower St
Los Angeles, CA 90071
Contact Virginia Victorin, (213) 486-3342; fax: (213) 486-0113
Internet http://www.ntlf.com/html/grants/5977.htm
Requirements The foundation is a regional organization funding nonprofit organizations in states where ARCO has facilities and personnel, including Alaska, Arizona, California, Colorado, Nevada, Texas, and Washington. Requests from those states and those nearby should be addressed to the local community affairs managers.
Restrictions The foundation discourages applications from the following: programs not focused on promoting self-sufficiency and economic development of minority populations; historic preservation or urban development projects not tied to neighborhood economic revitalization; proposals from religious organizations; or funding requests from federal, state, county, and municipal agencies, including school districts. The foundation does not generally consider support of hospital building or endowment campaigns, medical equipment, medical research programs, single-issue health organizations, or health services not directed at low-income people.
Areas of Interest Academic Achievement; Business; Disadvantaged (Economically); Education; Engineering; Higher Education; Mathematics Education; Minority Education; Science; Secondary Education
Sample Awards U of Montana (Butte, MT)—to help retain and graduate minority students pursuing engineering degrees, $16,500. $16,500. U of California (Davis, CA)—to help retain and graduate minority students pursuing engineering degrees, $47,000.

Atkinson Foundation Community Grants 46

Atkinson Foundation
1720 Amphlett Blvd, Ste 100
San Mateo, CA 94402
Contact Elizabeth Curtis, Administrator, (650) 357-1101; e-mail: atkinfdn@aol.com
Requirements International grants are awarded to organizations working in the Caribbean, Central America, and Mexico; domestic grants are awarded in San Mateo County, CA. 501(c)3 tax-exempt organizations are eligible but those serving residents of San Mateo County, CA, are given preference.
Restrictions The fund does not make grants to organizations without proof of tax-exempt status; grants to organizations chartered outside the United States; grants, scholarships, or loans to individuals; grants designed to

influence legislation; grants for doctoral study or research; grants for travel to conferences or events; grants for media presentations; donations to annual campaigns or special fund-raising events; sponsorship of sports groups; or grants to national or statewide umbrella organizations.

Areas of Interest Adult and Continuing Education; Alcohol/Alcoholism; Basic Skills Education; Children and Youth; Chronic Illness; Civic Affairs; Conservation, Natural Resources; Counseling/Guidance; Day Care; Disabled; Disadvantaged (Economically); Domestic Violence; Drugs/Drug Abuse; Economic Self-Sufficiency; Economics; Elderly; Family; Health Promotion; Health and Safety Education; Higher Education; Homelessness; Housing; Immigrants; International Programs; Job Training Programs; Latin America; Literacy; Mental Disorders; Nutrition/Dietetics; Rehabilitation/Therapy, Occupational/Vocational; Religion; Secondary Education; Shelters; Social Services; Violent Behavior; Vocational/Technical Education
Sample Awards Pilgrim Baptist Church (San Mateo, CA)—for the pastor's discretionary fund, $3000. Shelter Network of San Mateo County (San Mateo, CA)—for general support of transitional housing facility, $5000. Ctr for Domestic Violence Prevention (San Mateo, CA)—for general support for an emergency shelter, $5000. Coastside Adult Day Health Ctr (CA)—to support a nutrition program for seniors, $5000.

Atkinson Foundation Education Grants 47

Atkinson Foundation
1100 Grundy Ln, Ste 140
San Bruno, CA 94066-3030
Contact Elizabeth Curtis, Administrator, (650) 876-0222; e-mail: atkinfdn@aol.com
Requirements California 501(c)3 tax-exempt organizations are eligible.
Restrictions The foundation awards grants in San Mateo County, CA. The fund does not make grants to organizations without proof of tax-exempt status; grants to organizations chartered outside the United States; grants, scholarships, or loans to individuals; grants designed to influence legislation; grants for doctoral study or research; grants for travel to conferences or events; grants for media presentations; donations to annual campaigns or special fund-raising events; sponsorship of sports groups; or grants to national or statewide umbrella organizations.
Areas of Interest Adult and Continuing Education; At-Risk Youth; Counseling/Guidance; Education; Gifted/Talented Education; Health and Safety Education; Higher Education; Job Training Programs; Junior and Community Colleges; Minority Schools; Religious Studies; Remedial Education; Scholarship Programs, General; Secondary Education; Vocational/Technical Education
Sample Awards Partners in School Innovation (San Francisco, CA)—for a project at Turnball Learning Academy, $15,000. U of California, Cooperative Extension (San Francisco, CA)—for construction in the new Elkus Youth Ranch Ctr, $10,000.

Atkinson Foundation International Grants   48
Atkinson Foundation
17205 Amphlett Blvd, Ste 100
San Mateo, CA 94402
Contact Elizabeth Curtis, Administrator, (650) 357-1101; e-mail: atkinfdn@aol.com
Requirements International grants are awarded to organizations working in the Caribbean, Central America, and Mexico; domestic grants are awarded in San Mateo County, CA. Organizations should contact the foundation by phone prior to applying.
Restrictions The fund does not make grants to organizations without proof of tax-exempt status; grants to organizations chartered outside the United States; grants, scholarships, or loans to individuals; grants designed to influence legislation; grants for doctoral study or research; grants for travel to conferences or events; grants for media presentations; donations to annual campaigns or special fund-raising events; sponsorship of sports groups; or grants to national or statewide umbrella organizations.
Areas of Interest AIDS; Africa; Child Welfare; Churches; Computer Education/Literacy; Disabled; Disadvantaged (Economically); Economic Self-Sufficiency; Education; Elderly; Family Planning; Health Promotion; Homelessness; International Programs; Latin America; Literacy; Reading; Refugees; Social Services; Youth Programs
Sample Awards Community Career Education Ctr (San Mateo, CA)—to upgrade computer training equipment, $4000.

R.C. Baker Foundation Grants   49
R.C. Baker Foundation
PO Box 6150
Orange, CA 92863-6150
Contact Frank Scott, Chairman, (714) 750-8987
Requirements Nonprofit organizations are eligible.
Areas of Interest Crime Prevention; Cultural Activities/Programs; Disabled; Education; Elderly; Fine Arts; Health Care; Higher Education; Hospitals; Hunger; Museums; Religion; Science; Social Services; Youth Programs
Sample Awards Presbyterian Intercommunity Hospital (Whittier, CA)—for operating support, $116,000. YMCA (Los Angeles, CA)—for program support, $20,000. Exeter Christian Services (Exeter, CA)—for operating support, $6000.

Donald R. Barker Foundation Grants   50
Donald R. Barker Foundation
PO Box 936
Rancho Mirage, CA 92270
Contact Nancy Harris, Executive Administrator, (760) 324-2656; fax: (760) 321-8662
Requirements California and Oregon nonprofit organizations are eligible.
Restrictions Grants do not support sectarian religious purposes, federal and tax-dependent organizations, individuals, or endowment funds.
Areas of Interest Arts, General; Children and Youth; Community Development; Conservation, Natural Resources; Health Care; Higher Education; Hospitals; Secondary Education; Social Services

Sample Awards Santa Barbara Zoological Gardens (Santa Barbara, CA), $5000.

K and F Baxter Family Foundation Grants   51
K and F Baxter Family Foundation
PO Box 13053
Berkeley, CA 94712-4053
Contact Stacey Bell, Executive Director, (510) 524-8145; fax: (510) 524-4101; e-mail: E-mail: KFBaxterfound@aol.com
Internet http://www.kfbaxterfoundation.com
Requirements Grants are awarded to nonprofit organizations nationwide. Grants are limited to schools in California's Alameda, Contra Costa, San Francisco, and Los Angeles Counties.
Restrictions Grants do not fund purchasing of buildings or land.
Areas of Interest Child Welfare; Children and Youth; Community Development; Day Care; Education; Elementary Education; Secondary Education; Youth Programs

Bechtel Foundation Grants Program   52
Bechtel Foundation
50 Beale St
San Francisco, CA 94105
Contact Susan Grisso, Foundation Manager, (415) 768-5444; fax: (415) 768-7158; e-mail: foundtn@bechtel.com
Internet http://www.bechtel.com/bechfoun.html
Requirements Tax exempt organizations are eligible to apply.
Restrictions Grants are not made to individuals or to religious organizations. Endowments are not funded.
Areas of Interest Business Education; Children and Youth; Diplomacy; Disabled; Elementary Education; Engineering Education; Environmental Programs; Health Care; Hospitals; Humanities; International Relations; Management Sciences; Mathematics Education; Minority Education; Museums; National Disease Organizations; Performing Arts; Poverty and the Poor; Public Planning/Policy; Science Education; Secondary Education; Social Services; Technology Education; Women; Women's Education

Lowell Berry Foundation Grants   53
Lowell Berry Foundation
3685 Mt Diablo Blvd, Ste 269
Lafayette, CA 94549
Contact Anne Lyons, Office Manager, (925) 284-4427; fax: (925) 284-4332
Requirements 501(c)3 tax-exempt organizations in California may apply.
Restrictions Grants do not support advertising, advocacy orgnizations, individuals, international organizations, political organizations, local and state government agencies, building funds, capital funds, equipment acquisition, or seed money requests.
Areas of Interest Arts, General; Community Development; Cultural Activities; Education; Elderly; Elementary Education; Health Care; Higher Education; Humanities; Infants; Religion; Science; Secondary Education; Social Services; Technology; Women; Youth Programs

Sample Awards East Bay Youth for Christ (CA)—for general operating expenses, $5000. Pre-School Coordinating Council Inc (CA)—for the Therapeutic Infant Care project, $3000.

Burton G. Bettingen Grants   54

Burton G. Bettingen Corporation
9777 Wilshire Blvd, Ste 615
Beverly Hills, CA 90212
Contact Patricia Brown, Executive Director, (310) 276-4115; fax: (310) 476-4693; e-mail: burtonbet@aol.com
Requirements IRS 501(c)3 organizations are eligible. Giving primarily, but not limited to, Southern California.
Restrictions The corporation does not award grants to individuals; for general fund-raising events, dinners, or mass mailings; or to grantmaking organizations.
Areas of Interest Child Abuse; Child Welfare; Children and Youth; Crime Victims; Education; Environmental Programs; Mental Health; Religion; Runaway Youth; Sexual Abuse; Social Services
Sample Awards Childrens Hospital of Los Angeles (Los Angeles, CA)—for capital campaign, $700,000 (2001). Phoenix House (New York, NY)—for general support, $50,000 (2001). Children's Defense Fund (Washington, DC)—for general support, $750,000.

Kathryne Beynon Foundation Grants   55

Kathryne Beynon Foundation
199 S Los Robles Ave, Ste 711
Pasadena, CA 91101-2460
Contact Robert Bannon, Trustee, (626) 584-8800
Requirements 501(c)3 southern California tax-exempt organizations are eligible. Preference is given to requests from Pasadena.
Areas of Interest Alcohol/Alcoholism; Child Welfare; Drugs/Drug Abuse; Education; Rehabilitation/Therapy

Boeckmann Charitable Foundation Grants   56

Boeckmann Charitable Foundation
15505 Roscoe Blvd
North Hills, CA 91343
Contact Herbert Boeckmann II, Chief Executive Officer, (818) 787-3800
Requirements Christian, Evangelical, and Presbyterian nonprofits in California are eligible.
Areas of Interest Broadcast Media; Community Service Programs; Family; Higher Education; Hispanics; International Programs; Private and Parochial Education; Religious Studies; Secondary Education; Social Services; Youth Programs
Sample Awards Church on Way (Van Nuys, CA)—operating support, $300,200. Hispanic Christian Communications Network (Los Angeles, CA)—operating support, $10,000. Valley Interfaith Council (Chatsworth, CA)—operating support, $2000.

David Bohnett Foundation Grants   57

David Bohnett Foundation
2049 Century Park E, Ste 2151
Los Angeles, CA 90067-3123
Contact Michael Fleming, (310) 277-4611; fax: (310) 203-8111; e-mail: mfpfleming@yahoo.com

Internet http://www.bohnettfoundation.org/grants/grantapplication.htm
Requirements Nonprofit organizations are eligible.
Restrictions Grants do not support films, video projects, documentaries, or other productions.
Areas of Interest Animal Rights; Conservation, Natural Resources; Environmental Programs; Fossil Fuels; Gun Control; Homosexuals, Female; Homosexuals, Male; Human/Civil Rights; Media Arts; Transportation; Violent Behavior
Sample Awards Friends of Washoe (Ellensburg, WA)—for animal-language research, $25,000 (2003). Commercial Closet Assoc (New York, NY)—to improve the portrayal of bisexual, gay, lesbian, and transgender people in mainstream advertising, $15,000 (2003). KCRW (Santa Monica, CA)—for general operating support, $50,000 (2003). Women Against Gun Violence (Culver City, CA)—to educate members of the public and policy makers about the financial, human, and public-health costs of gun violence, $20,000 (2003).

Bright Family Foundation Grants   58

Bright Family Foundation
1620 N Carpenter Rd, Bldg B
Modesto, CA 95351
Contact Calvin Bright, President, (209) 526-8242
Requirements Stanislaus County, CA, 501(c)3 tax-exempt organizations within 30 miles of Modesto, CA, are eligible.
Areas of Interest Biomedical Research; Business Education; Children and Youth; Education; Health Care; Higher Education; Medical Education; Religion; Social Services
Sample Awards California Youth Soccer (CA)—$200. Slavic Gospel Assoc (CA)—$7500. Big Valley Grace Church (CA)—$10,000. Ctr for Human Services (CA)—$2500.

Henry W. Bull Foundation Grants   59

Henry W. Bull Foundation
PO Box 2340
Santa Barbara, CA 93120-2340
Contact Janice Gibson, Vice-President & Trustee Officer, Santa Barbara Bank & Trust , (805) 884-7347; fax: (805) 884-1404
Requirements 501(c)3 nonprofits are eligible.
Restrictions Individuals and international organizations are not eligible.
Areas of Interest Arts, General; Disabled; Health Care; Higher Education; Music; Religion

Caddock Foundation Grants   60

Caddock Foundation
1717 Chicago Ave
Riverside, CA 92507
Contact Sue Brinkman, President, (909) 683-5361
Restrictions Grants are not made to individuals.
Areas of Interest Churches; Community Service Programs; Hospitals; International Programs; Jewish Services; Penology/Correctional Institutions and Procedures; Religion; Youth Programs
Sample Awards Set Free Prison Ministries (Riverside CA)—for operating support, $152,000. Grace Evangeli-

cal Society (Roanoke, TX)—for operating support, $40,000.

California Arts Council Organizational Support Program Grants　61
California Arts Council
1300 I St, Ste 930
Sacramento, CA 95814
Contact Scott Heckes, Assistant Chief of Grants Programs, (916) 322-6376; fax: (916) 322-6575; e-mail: sheckes@caartscouncil.com
Internet http://www.cac.ca.gov/programs/description/osp.cfm
Requirements 501(c)3 nonprofit arts producing and presenting organizations located in California are eligible to apply. Applicants must have a demonstrated history of programming arts in the state for at least the past two years and a minimum income of $2000 in its most recently completed fiscal year. All grant recipients must provide a dollar-for-dollar cash match.
Restrictions Out-of-state travel, purchase of equipment, construction, endowments, religious projects, state-local partnership agencies, indirect costs, art therapy, and programs not accessible to the public are not funded.
Areas of Interest Arts Administration; Dance; Interdisciplinary Arts
Sample Awards Oakland Ballet (Oakland, CA)—for organizational support, $42,755.

California Arts Council State-Local Partnerships　62
California Arts Council
1300 I St, Ste 930
Sacramento, CA 95814
Contact Scott Heckes, Assistant Chief of Grants Programs, (916) 322-6376; e-mail: sheckes@caartscouncil.com
Internet http://www.cac.ca.gov/programs/description/slpp.cfm
Requirements Local arts agencies in California are eligible to apply. Local arts agencies are defined as those agencies designated as the State-Local Partner by their local government body (county or city) mandated to foster the development and growth of cultural resources in their communities as identified through a cultural planning process.
Areas of Interest Arts Administration

California Endowment Local Opportunities Fund Grants　63
California Endowment
21650 Oxnard St, Ste 1200
Woodland Hills, CA 91367
Contact Local Opportunities Fund, (800) 449-4149 or (818) 703-3311; fax: (818) 703-4193
Internet http://www.calendow.org/apply/frm_apply.htm
Requirements California nonprofit organizations are eligible. Requests for core operating support will only be considered from organizations with annual operating budgets of less than $500,000 (as determined by financial statements and the annual operating budget submitted with the application).

Areas of Interest Disadvantaged (Economically); Health Care; Health Care Access; Health Promotion; Health Services Delivery
Sample Awards California State U (Fresno, CA)—for the Central Valley Health Policy Institute to conduct research, train leaders, and create graduate-level courses on health policy, $4 million over five years (2003). California Assoc of Health Plans (Sacramento, CA) and California Teachers Assoc (Burlingame, CA)—for the Teachers and Health Plans for Healthy Kids program, which will educate public-school teachers about public health-insurance programs available to low-income children and their families and will work with teachers to devise outreach strategies, $547,000 jointly (2002). Valley Economic Development Ctr (Van Nuys, CA)—for the Healthy Families/Healthy Jobs Initiative, which seeks to develop health-care careers for the predominantly Latino residents of Pacoima, CA, and to improve the delivery of health-care services to the area's residents, $980,000 over three years (2002).

California Wellness Foundation Work and Health Program Grants　64
California Wellness Foundation
6320 Canoga Ave, Ste 1700
Woodland Hills, CA 91367-7111
Contact Grants Administrator, (818) 593-6600; fax: (818) 593-6614
Internet http://www.tcwf.org/grant_programs/grant_programs.htm
Requirements Eligible applicants are California 501(c)3 nonprofit organizations, or organizations with a preapproved fiscal sponsor. An organization should first write a succinct letter of interest (one to two pages) that describes the organization, its leadership, the region and population(s) served, and the activities for which funding is needed, including the amount requested.
Areas of Interest Child/Maternal Health; Consumer Services; Environmental Health; Health Care Access; Health Insurance; Health Planning/Policy; Health Promotion; Health Services Delivery; Medical Education; Occupational Health and Safety; Preventive Medicine; Public Health; Teen Pregnancy; Violent Behavior; Women's Health
Sample Awards San Francisco State U, Graduate Gerontology Program (CA)—for advocacy and leadership-development programs in community-based geriatric-care management, $150,000 over three years (2004). Ma'at Youth Academy (Richmond, CA)—to sustain environmental-health efforts in Richmond, $75,000 (2003). Cambodian Community Development (Oakland, CA)—for violence-prevention services for at-risk Cambodian youths, $60,000 over three years (2003). Sycamores (Pasadena, CA)—for a program that matches youths with mental-health needs who are leaving foster care with mentors who have successfully made a similar transition, $142,000 over three years (2003).

Callaway Golf Company Foundation Grants　65
Callaway Golf Company Foundation
2180 Rutherford Rd
Carlsbad, CA 92008-7328
Contact Director, (760) 930-8686; e-mail: CGC_FOUNDATION@Callawaygolf.com

Internet http://www.callawaygolf.com/en/corporate.
aspx?pid=community
Requirements IRS 501(c)3 nonprofit organizations in
California are eligible.
Restrictions The foundation will not fund applicants
that illegally discriminate on the basis of gender, race,
color, religion, national origin, ancestry, age, marital status, medical condition, or physical disability, either in the
services they provide or in the hiring of staff; or promote
political or particular religious doctrines.
Areas of Interest Disabled; Disadvantaged (Economically); Education; Elderly; Health Care; Mental
Health; Youth Programs

Christensen Fund Grants 66

Christensen Fund
145 Addison Ave
Palo Alto, CA 94301
Contact Grants Administrator, (650) 462-8600 ext
106; e-mail: info@christensenfund.org
Internet http://www.christensenfund.org/index.html
Requirements 501(c)3 nonprofit organizations and
non-USA institutions with nonprofit or equivalent status
in their country of origin are eligible. Partnerships or associations with USA-based nonprofit organizations are
preferred.
Restrictions The fund does not make grants directly to
individuals but rather assists individuals through institutions qualified to receive nonprofit support with which
such individuals are affiliated.
Areas of Interest African Art; Art Conservation; Art
Education; Asian Arts; Biology, Conservation; Curriculum Development; Education; Elementary Education;
Exhibitions, Collections, Performances; Higher Education; Museums; Visual Arts
Sample Awards Cantor Arts Ctr, Stanford U (CA)—for
operating support, $100,000-$150,000 per year for five
years. Honolulu Academy of Arts (HI)—for endowment
support, $5 million.

Clorox Company Foundation Grants 67

Clorox Company Foundation
c/o East Bay Community Foundation, De Domenico
Building, 200 Frank Ogawa Plaza
Oakland, CA 94612
Contact Carmella Johnson, Contribution, (510)
271-2199; fax: (510) 208-4192; e-mail: cloroxfndt@
eastbaycf.org
Internet http://www.clorox.com/company/foundation/
how.html
Requirements Applicants must be charitable 501(c)3
organizations or sponsored by fiscal agents and must be
located in and serving communities where Clorox has
operating facilities (Arkansas, California, Connecticut,
Florida, Georgia, Illinois, Kansas, Kentucky, Maryland,
Mississippi, Missouri, Nevada, New Jersey, Ohio, Oregon, Texas, Vermont, Virginia, West Virginia, and locations in Canada and Puerto Rico).
Restrictions Applicants must not have received a grant
from the foundation during the same fiscal year in which
another grant is sought. The foundation does not favor
funding for benefit/raffle tickets; media production; national conferences, conventions, or meetings; athletic
events or leagues sponsorship; advertising or promotions

sponsorship; fundraising dinners outside the Oakland/
San Francisco Bay area; veterans organizations, except
for programs benefiting the public at large; religious
causes, except for nonsectarian activities available to the
community at large; political parties, organizations, candidates, or issues; association or membership dues; field
trips, tours, and travel; or sponsorship of individuals.
Areas of Interest After-School Programs; Art Educa-
tion; Citizenship; Community Service Programs; Educa-
tion; Elementary Education; Literacy; Mentoring Programs; Minority Education; Remedial Education; Science Education; Secondary Education; Service Delivery
Programs; Volunteers; Youth Programs
Sample Awards Chabot Space and Science Ctr (Oakland, CA)—for education programs that serve approximately 50,000 schoolchildren annually, $300,000 over
three years (2002).

Columbia Foundation Grants Program 68

Columbia Foundation
PO Box 29470
San Francisco, CA 9411194129
Contact Susan Clark, Executive Director, (415)
561-6880; fax: (415) 561-6883; email: info@columbia.
org
Internet http://www.columbia.org
Requirements The foundation considers proposals only
from organizations certified by the IRS as public charities. Priority will be given to applications from the San
Francisco Bay, CA, area. International grants support the
arts in London.
Restrictions The foundation does not customarily provide support for operating budgets of established agencies, recurring expenses for direct services or ongoing
administrative costs, individual fellowships or scholarships, or agencies wholly supported by federated campaigns or heavily subsidized by government funds.
Areas of Interest Arts, General; Civil/Human Rights;
Conflict Resolution; Conservation, Agriculture; Conservation, Natural Resources; Cultural Activities/Pro-
grams; Biodiversity; Cultural Outreach; Death/Mortal-
ity; Disadvantaged (Economically); Economic Development; Environmental Health; Environmental Programs;
Gender Equipty; Fish and Fisheries; Food Distribution;
Homosexuals, Female; Homosexuals, Male; International Relations; Marine Resources; Performing Art;
Peace/Disarmament; Publilc Health; Urban Affairs
Sample Awards 9th Street Media Consortium (San
Francisco, CA)—to purchase a new building in San
Francisco to house several independent media organizations, $100,000 payable over two years (2002). Freedom
to Marry Collaborative (New York, NY)—for a new national initiative to secure civil marriage equality for
same-sex couples, $500,000 payable over five years
(2002). International Society for Ecology and Culture
(Berkeley, CA)—to research, write, produce, and disseminate a California Local Food Report and related educational materials that help inform the public of the social, economic, and ecological benefits of local food systems, $50,000 (2002).

Community Foundation for Monterey County Grants 69

Community Foundation for Monterey County
99 Pacific St, Ste 155A
Monterey, CA 93940
Contact Jackie Wendland, Grants Administrator, (831) 375-9712; fax: (831) 375-4731; e-mail: jackie@cfmco.org
Internet http://www.cfmco.org/grant_over.html
Requirements 501(c)3 tax-exempt organizations in Monterey, CA, may submit applications.
Restrictions The foundation does not make grants to individuals or for annual campaigns, deficit financing, endowments, sectarian religious purposes, dinners, or special events.
Areas of Interest Arts, General; Education; Environmental Programs; Health Care; Neighborhoods; Philanthropy; Restoration and Preservation; Social Services

Community Foundation Silicon Valley Grants 70

Community Foundation Silicon Valley
60 S Market St, Ste 1000
San Jose, CA 95113
Contact Jeff Sunshine, Director of Programs, (408) 278-2200; fax: (408) 278-0280; e-mail: jsunshine@cfsv.org or info@cfsv.org
Internet http://www.cfsv.org/grants_whatwefund.html
Requirements Nonprofit organizations benefiting Santa Clara County and southern San Mateo County, CA, are eligible.
Restrictions In general, the foundation does not consider fundraising events, capital equipment and endowment campaigns, on-going operating expenses, existing debts/obligations, for-profit schools, or individuals.
Areas of Interest Academic Achievement; Arts, General; Community Service Programs; Compensatory Education; Economic Self-Sufficiency; Elementary Education; Health Care; Humanities; Intervention Programs; Neighborhoods; Philanthropy; Scholarship Programs, General; Secondary Education; Social Services; Youth Programs
Sample Awards Child Advocates of Santa Clara and San Mateo Counties (San Jose, CA)—to recruit and train new child-advocacy volunteers, $225,000 over three years (2001). Project H.E.L.P (High Expectations Learning Program) (Sunnyvale, CA)—to expand this early-intervention program that provides high-quality supplemental academic instruction to poorly performing students at public elementary schools in Santa Clara County, CA, $225,0000 over three years (2000).

Compton Foundation Grants Program 71

Compton Foundation
535 Middlefield Rd, Ste 160
Menlo Park, CA 94025
Contact Edith Eddy, Executive Director, (650) 328-0101; fax: (650) 328-0171; e-mail: info@comptonfoundation.org
Internet http://www.comptonfoundation.org/application.html
Requirements The foundation makes grants only to tax-exempt organizations and institutions.
Restrictions Grants will not be made to individuals.

Areas of Interest Arts, General; Civil/Human Rights; Conflict Resolution; Community Development; Cultural Activities/Programs; Environmental Programs; Equal Educational Opportunity; International Education/Training; International Programs; International Relations; Museums; Peace/Disarmament; Population Studies; Regional Planning/Policy; Social Services
Sample Awards Assoc for Conflict Resolution (Washington, DC)—to improve and expand conflict-resolution education in schools and colleges, $50,000 (2003).

S.H. Cowell Foundation Grants 72

S.H. Cowell Foundation
120 Montgomery, Ste 2570
San Francisco, CA 94104
Contact Susan Vandiver, Program Contact, (415) 397-0285; fax: (415) 986-6786; e-mail: info@shcowell.org
Internet http://www.shcowell.org
Requirements Grants are made only to 501(c)3 tax-exempt organizations primarily in northern California.
Restrictions The foundation does not normally make grants to individuals, for start-up of new organizations, for academic or other research, for general support, for annual fund-raising, to governmental agencies, to churches for religious support, to hospitals for medical research or treatment, for conferences, for media projects, or for political lobbying.
Areas of Interest Alcohol/Alcoholism; Children and Youth; Education; Environmental Programs; Family; Family Planning; Hispanic Education; Housing; Job Training Programs; Peace/Disarmament; Population Control; Poverty and the Poor; Private and Parochial Education; Religion; Restoration and Preservation; School-to-Work Transition; Social Services
Sample Awards Affordable Housing Affiliation (Benicia, CA)—to build 12 homes at Hearthstone Village, $130,000 (2001). Garfield Elementary School (Stockton, CA)—award for improved API scores, $10,000 (2001). ArtWorks Downtown (San Rafael, CA)—for capital and operating support, $50,000 (2001).

Crail-Johnson Foundation Grants 73

Crail-Johnson Foundation
222 W Sixth St, Ste 1010
San Pedro, CA 90731
Contact Carolyn Johnson, President, (310) 519-7413; fax: (310) 519-7221; e-mail: Carolyn-Johnson@crail-johnson.org
Internet http://www.crail-johnson.org
Requirements Nonprofit organizations serving the needs of children in California's Orange, Los Angeles, Kern, and Diego Counties and the Denver metropolitan area may submit letters of intent.
Restrictions The foundation does not make grants for religious purposes, graduate and postgraduate education, research, cultural programs, sporting events, dinners, or political activities.
Areas of Interest Adolescent Health; After-School Programs; Basic Skills Education; Child Abuse; Children and Youth; Child/Maternal Health; Curriculum Development; Disabled; Day Care; Disadvantaged (Economically); Domestic Violence; Education; Education

Reform; Educational Technology; Elementary Education; Employment Opportunity Programs; Family; Health Care; Literacy; Mathematics Education; Neighborhoods; Parent Involvement; Problem Solving; Reading Education; Science Education; Secondary Education; School-to-Work Transition; Single-Parent Families; Social Services; Technology; Vocational/Technical Education

Sample Awards Dramatic Results (CA)—to provide its educational arts programs to children of low-income single parents, $15,000. California Academy of Math and Sciences (CA)—for an accelerated curriculum in math and science for underprivileged students, $25,000. Kern Alliance of Business (CA)—for summer jobs for youth in Kern County, $10,000.

Barbara Delano Foundation Grants 74
Barbara Delano Foundation
450 Pacific Ave, 2nd Fl
San Francisco, CA 94133-4640
Contact Stephanie Carnow, Program Assistant, (415) 834-1758; fax: (415) 834-1759; e-mail: bdfoundation@usa.net
Internet http://www.bdfoundation.org
Requirements BDF only accepts proposals for programs outside the United States, primarily in developing countries. BDF only supports research directly related to the implementation of a conservation program.
Areas of Interest Conservation, Natural Resources; Environmental Programs; Wildlife

Walt Disney Company Foundation Grants 75
Walt Disney Company Foundation
500 S Buena Vista St
Burbank, CA 91521-0987
Contact Tillie Baptie, Executive Director, (818) 560-1006; fax: (818) 563-5271
Internet http://disney.go.com/disneyhand/contributions/wdcfoundation.html
Requirements 501(c)3 tax-exempt organizations in California and Florida may apply.
Restrictions Disney will not make grants for scholarships, religious organizations, building campaigns, start-up campaigns, seed purposes, research, loans, conferences, general fund drives, annual charitable appeals, and political purposes.
Areas of Interest Arts, General; Child Welfare; Child/Maternal Health; Cultural Activities/Programs; Dramatic/Theater Arts; Health Services Delivery; Higher Education; Music; Orchestras; Scholarship Programs, General; Urban Areas; Youth Programs
Sample Awards DisneyHand: Survivor Relief Fund—to establish this fund to aid victims of the September 11 terrorist attacks, $5 million (2002). Walt Disney Concert Hall (Los Angeles, CA)—for its capital campaign to build a hall in downtown Los Angeles and to create an endowment that will be used by the California Institute of the Arts for programs, $25 million challenge grant.

DJ and T Foundation Grants 76
DJ and T Foundation
9201 Wilshire Blvd, Ste 204
Beverly Hills, CA 90210
Contact William Prappas, (310) 278-1160; e-mail: WillPrappas@msn.com
Internet http://www.djtfoundation.org
Requirements IRS 501(c)3 nonprofits operating a stationary and/or mobile clinic and nonprofits in the process of creating such a clinic are eligible.
Restrictions The foundation does not underwrite voucher programs or other fees. Grants are not made to individuals.
Areas of Interest Animal Care
Sample Awards Colorado Humane Society (Boulder, CO)—for operating support. Adopt-A-Pet (Columbus, OH)—for operating support. Pasco Animal Welfare Society (FL)—for operating support.

Do Right Foundation Grants 77
Do Right Foundation
852 Fifth Ave, Ste 215
San Diego, CA 92101
Contact James McCrink, President, fax: (619) 233-5634; e-mail: doright@adnc.com
Internet http://www.doright.org/app.html
Requirements Nonprofit 501(c)3 organizations in the United States are eligible.
Restrictions Support is not granted to individuals, schools, or police departments.
Areas of Interest Alcohol/Alcoholism; At-Risk Youth; Compensatory Education; Crime Control; Criminal Behavior; Drugs/Drug Abuse; Employment Opportunity Programs; Government; Law; Parent Education; Violent Behavior; Welfare-to-Work Programs; Women
Sample Awards Broken Connections (East Cleveland, OH)—for a parenting program for women with substance abuse and criminal backgrounds, $7000. Sweetwater Educational Ctr (Sweetwater, FL)—for a tutoring program for at-risk youth, $8000.

Thelma Doelger Charitable Trust Grants 78
Thelma Doelger Charitable Trust
950 Daly Blvd, Ste 300
Daly City, CA 94015-3004
Contact D. Eugene Richard, Trustee, (650) 755-2333
Requirements Nonprofit organizations in the San Francisco Bay area of northern California may submit grant requests.
Restrictions Individuals are not eligible.
Areas of Interest Animal Rights; Elderly; Hospitals; Museums; Zoos
Sample Awards San Francisco Zoo (CA)—for operating support, $100,000. Marin Humane Society (Novato, CA)—for operating support, $70,000.

Carrie Estelle Doheny Foundation Grants 79
Carrie Estelle Doheny Foundation
707 Wilshire Blvd, Ste 4960
Los Angeles, CA 90017
Contact Shirley Bernard, Senior Grants Administrator, (213) 488-1122; fax: (213) 488-1544; e-mail: shirley@dohenyfoundation
Internet http://www.dohenyfoundation.org/dohenyfoundation.htm
Requirements US nonprofit tax-exempt organizations in California are eligible. An application form is required

for submission and may be downloaded from the foundation web site.

Restrictions Grant requests are not considered from individuals or from tax-supported entities. Areas also excluded from consideration include support for individuals, endowment funds, publishing books, television or radio programs, travel funds, advertisement, scholarships, or political purposes in any form.

Areas of Interest Biomedical Research; Catholic Church; Child Welfare; Children and Youth; Disabled; Elderly; Elementary Education; Health Care; Hospitals; Poverty and the Poor; Recreation and Leisure; Religion; Secondary Education

Sample Awards Easter Seals-Southern California (Van Nuys, CA)—to offer scholarships to program participants in the Senior Day Care program, and to provide meals, equipment, and transportation to participants in the Senior Case Management program, $15,000 (2001).

Dreyer's Foundation Large Grants Program   80
Dreyer's Foundation
5929 College Ave
Oakland, CA 94618-1325
Contact Patricia Marino, Large Grants Program, (510) 450-4586; fax: (510) 601-4400; e-mail: kmsua@ dreyers.com
Internet http://www.dreyersinc.com/ dreyersfoundation/index.asp
Requirements Grants are awarded to nonprofit youth-serving organizations and K-12 public education organizations. Priority will be given to programs/projects that support low- and middle-income youth and minority youth.
Restrictions The foundation does not consider funding for raffle tickets/benefit dinners, one-time conventions/meetings, semipro athletic sponsorships, benefit advertising, sectarian religious causes (except for activities open to the public at large), political activities or candidates, or field trips/tours.
Areas of Interest Academic Achievement; After-School Programs; Children and Youth; Elementary Education; Secondary Education; Preschool Education; Poverty and the Poor; Minorities

Joseph Drown Foundation Grants   81
Joseph Drown Foundation
1999 Avenue of the Stars, Ste 1930
Los Angeles, CA 90067
Contact Grants Administrator, (310) 277-4488; fax: (310) 277-4573
Internet http://www.jdrown.org
Requirements California 501(c)3 organizations may apply.
Restrictions The foundation does not provide funds to individuals, endowments, capital campaigns, or annual funds. The foundation does not underwrite annual meetings, conferences, or special events, nor does it fund religious programs or purchase tickets to fund-raising events.
Areas of Interest Alcohol/Alcoholism; Arts, General; Biomedical Research; Cardiology; Community Service Programs; Dropouts; Drugs/Drug Abuse; Education; Education Reform; Health Care; Health Care Access;

Humanities; Pathology; Social Services; Teen Pregnancy; Violent Behavior
Sample Awards HighTechHigh (Los Angeles, CA)—for first-year operating support, 50,000 (2002). UCLA Graduate School of Education and Information Studies (Los Angeles, CA)—for the Governor's Principal Leadership Institute, $75,000 (2002). Cardiac Arrhythmias Research and Education Foundation (Irvine, CA)—to support research in sudden cardiac death, $75,000 (2002). Henry Mancini Institute (Los Angeles, CA)—for support of the Community Outreach Initiative, $15,000 (2002).

East Bay Community Foundation Grants   82
East Bay Community Foundation
200 Frank H. Ogawa Plaza
Oakland, CA 94612
Contact Christina Sutherland, Director of Programs, (510) 836-3223; fax: (510) 836-3287; e-mail: program@eastbaycf.org
Internet http://www.eastbaycf.org/grantmaking/index. html
Requirements IRS 501(c)3 organizations or public agencies that provide services to residents of Alameda or Contra Costa Counties in California and include significant representation of East Bay residents on policy-making boards are eligible.
Restrictions In general, grants are not made for endowments, capital expenditures, annual fund appeals, direct assistance to individuals, religious organizations for religious purposes, fund-raising events and celebrations, and existing obligations.
Areas of Interest Arts, General; Children and Youth; Cultural Activities/Programs; Domestic Violence; Dramatic/Theater Arts; Economic Development; Education; Environmental Programs; Health Promotion; Immigrants; Public Health; Social Services; Volunteers; Youth Programs
Sample Awards West Contra Costa Salesian Boys' Club (Richmond, CA)—for staff for a new gym program, $5000. Southern Alameda County Domestic Violence Law Project—for general operating support, $5000. Experimental Group Young Peoples Theatre (Oakland, CA)—for theater arts classes, $3500. Laotian Educational Council (San Pablo, CA)—for staff and volunteer training, $3500.

eBay Foundation Community Grants   83
eBay Foundation
2145 Hamilton Ave
San Jose, CA 95125
Contact Grants Administrator; e-mail: foundation@ ebay.com or ebayfdn@cfsv.org
Internet http://pages.ebay.com/community/aboutebay/ foundation/grantapp.html
Requirements 501(c)3 nonprofit organizations in communities where eBay has a major employment base, which includes San Jose, CA, and Salt Lake City, UT, are eligible.
Restrictions The foundation will not support government agencies, individuals, organizations with a limited constituency (such as a fraternity or veterans' group), organizations that limit services to one religious group, political parties or causes, or purely social organizations.

Areas of Interest Adult and Continuing Education; Children and Youth; Civic Affairs; Cross-Cultural Studies; Drugs/Drug Abuse; Economic Development; Education; Environmental Programs; Gangs; Job Training Programs; Mental Health; Mentoring Programs; Teacher Education, Inservice; Volunteers

Sample Awards Friends of Farm Drive (San Jose, CA)—for operating support of this organization, which is dedicated to improving the quality of life for residents of a neighborhood rampant with drug dealing and gang activity. U Research Expedition Program (U of California)—for scholarships to send California elementary and high school teachers on UREP trips, where they learn by working with university scientists and local residents in countries around the world, to increase awareness of current events and to foster understanding of different cultures among both students and teachers.

Ecosystem Protection Grants 84

William C. Kenney Watershed Protection Foundation
3030 Bridgeway, Ste 204
Sausalito, CA 94965
Contact Kimery Wiltshire, Director, (415) 332-1363; fax: (415) 332-2250; e-mail: grants@kenneyfdn.org
Internet http://www.kenneyfdn.org/grants.html
Requirements 501(c)3 nonprofit organizations in British Columbia or the Western United States, including Alaska, Arizona, California, Colorado, Idaho, Montana, Nevada, New Mexico, Oregon, Utah, Washington, and Wyoming, are eligible. Organizations must have annual operating budgets under $740,000, collaborate with other groups, be innovative, and produce measurable results.
Restrictions Grants do not support watershed restoration, land acquisition, endowments, research, or legal work.
Areas of Interest Communications; Ecology; Environmental Planning/Policy; Environmental Programs; Information Dissemination; Regional Planning/Policy; Training and Development; Water Resources

Eisner Foundation Grants 85

Eisner Foundation
9401 Wilshire Blvd, Ste 760
Beverly Hills, CA 90212
Contact Program Contact, (310) 777-3640; fax: (310) 777-3644
Internet http://www.eisnerfoundation.org
Requirements California nonprofit organizations serving Los Angeles and Orange Counties are eligible.
Areas of Interest Children and Youth; Elementary Education; Secondary Education
Sample Awards California State U at Northridge, College of Education (CA)—to establish the Center for Teaching and Learning, which will focus on preparing teachers, parents, and clinicians to meet the needs of students with varying learning styles, $7 million (2002). Pediatric and Family Medical Ctr (Los Angeles, CA)—to construct a new building and to remodel its current facilities, $2.5 million (2001).

Fieldstone Foundation Grants 86

Fieldstone Foundation
14 Corporate Plaza
Newport Beach, CA 92660
Contact Janine Mason Barone, Executive Director, (949) 640-9090; fax: (949) 759-5032; e-mail: foundation@fieldstone-homes.com
Internet http://www.fieldstone-homes.com/foundation
Requirements Southern California (Orange, Riverside, San Bernardino, and San Diego Counties) and Salt Lake City, UT, nonprofits are eligible.
Areas of Interest Arts, General; Community Development; Cultural Activities/Programs; Education; Exhibitions, Collections, Performances; Museums; Religion; Science; Social Services
Sample Awards Discovery Science Museum (Santa Ana, CA)—for operating support, $10,000. San Diego Museum of Art (San Diego, CA)—for a biennial exhibition of student art, $20,000 over two years.

Fleishhacker Foundation Grants 87

Fleishhacker Foundation
PO Box 29918
San Francisco, CA 94129-0918
Contact Christine Elbel, Executive Director, (415) 561-5350; fax (415) 561-5345; email: info@fleishhackerfoundation.org
Internet http://www.fleishhackerfoundation.org/grants.html
Requirements Nonprofits in the San Francisco Bay area are eligible.
Restrictions The foundation does not support annual campaigns, deficit financing, matching grants, adult education, special education, programs serving out-of-school youth, social service programs, or remedial programs.
Areas of Interest Art, Experimental; Arts, General; Asian Americans; Dance; Dramatic/Theater Arts; Elementary Education; Fine Arts; Human Learning and Memory; Interdisciplinary Arts; Media Arts; Museums; Music; Private and Parochial Education; Secondary Education; Teacher Education, Inservice; Television; Visual Arts
Sample Awards Fine Arts Museums of San Francisco (San Francisco, CA)—for permanent installation of ancient Mexican Teotihuacan murals at M.H. de Young Museum, $40,000. KQED-TV (San Francisco, CA)—to support the arts programming endowment of the capital campaign, $10,000. Asian American Dance Collective (San Francisco, CA)—for production costs of West Coast Sweep, to commemorate the 50th anniversary of Japanese American internment during World War II, $2500.

Fluor Foundation Grants 88

Fluor Foundation
1 Enterprise Dr
Aliso Viejo, CA 92656-2606
Contact Suzanne Huffmon Esber, Executive Director, (949) 349-6797; fax: (949) 349-7175; e-mail: community.relations@fluor.com
Internet http://www.fluor.com/community/involvement.asp

Requirements Contributions are limited to tax-exempt nonprofit organizations in the areas where Fluor has permanent offices.

Restrictions Support is not given to medical research, sports activities, or promotion of films or television programs.

Areas of Interest Academic Achievement; Civic Affairs; Cultural Activities/Programs; Education; Engineering; Health Care; Higher Education; Mathematics; Science; Social Services

Sample Awards U of California (CA)—for its math, engineering, science achievement program, $25,000. South Carolina Foundation of Independent Colleges (SC)—for program support, $5000.

Forest Lawn Foundation Grants   89

Forest Lawn Foundation
625 Fair Oaks Ave, Ste 360
South Pasadena, CA 91030
Contact Linda Blinkenberg, Program Contact
Requirements Nonprofit organizations in Los Angeles County and Orange County may apply.
Restrictions Grants do not support federated appeals, political purposes, or projects/programs normally funded by the government.
Areas of Interest Disabled; Hospitals; Social Services; Youth Programs
Sample Awards Weingart Center Association (Los Angeles, CA)—for general operating support, $100,000.

Foundation for Deep Ecology Grants   90

Foundation for Deep Ecology
Bldg 1062, Fort Cronkhite
Sausalito, CA 94109
Contact Jerry Mander, Program Director, (415) 229-9339; fax: (415) 229-9340; e-mail: info@deepecology.org
Internet http://www.deepecology.org
Requirements 501(c)3 tax-exempt organizations are eligible.
Restrictions Grants will not be made to support television or video projects, scholarships, curriculum development for K-12 schools, scientific research, or deficit reduction.
Areas of Interest Biodiversity; Conservation, Agriculture; Ecology; Economic Theory; Population Control; Technology Planning/Policy

Friedman Family Foundation Grants   91

Friedman Family Foundation
204 E 2nd Ave, PMB 719
San Mateo, CA 94401
Contact Lisa Kawahara, Grants Administrator, (650) 342-8750; fax: (650) 342-8750; e-mail: fffdn@aol.com
Internet http://www.friedmanfamilyfoundation.org
Requirements California 501(c)3 nonprofit organizations or public entities with a board or advisory group that is reflective of the population or community being served are eligible.
Restrictions The foundation generally does not fund films, videos, conferences, seminars, capital, scholarships, individuals, research, or special or fund-raising events.

Areas of Interest Community Development; Jewish Services; Poverty and the Poor
Sample Awards Shefa Fund (Wyndmoor, PA)—to leverage investments from Jewish institutions and individuals for use by community development financial institutions, $100,000. Juma Ventures (San Francisco, CA)—for general support, $10,000.

Fund for Santa Barbara Grants   92

Fund for Santa Barbara
120 E Jones St, Ste 127
Santa Maria, CA 93454
Contact Fund Administrator, (805) 962-9164; fax: (805) 965-0217; e-mail: email@fundforsantabarbara.org
Internet http://www.fundforsantabarbara.org/apply/apply.htm
Requirements Applications are invited from organizations that are working against discrimination based on race, sex/gender, age, religion, economic status, sexual orientation, physical/mental ability, ethnicity, language, or immigration status; struggling for the rights of workers; promoting self-determination in low-income and disenfranchised communities; promoting international peace and organizing locally for a just foreign policy; working on improving the environment, especially organizing a constituency usually without access or input to environmental concerns; and operating in a democratic manner, responsive to and directed by the constituency being served.
Restrictions Grants do not support projects involved in electoral campaigns on behalf of candidates or parties; private (vs. public) interests; direct labor organizing; projects located outside of Santa Barbara County; projects providing direct services without a social change component; or direct support to individuals, capital ventures, or building improvements.
Areas of Interest Civil/Human Rights; Economic Development; Environmental Health; Environmental Programs; Equal Employment Opportunity; Homosexuals, Female; Homosexuals, Male; Social Change
Sample Awards Committee for Social Justice (CA)—to pay for a Spanish-speaking coordinator to extend their reach, and run workshops and clinics, $3750 (2002). Men Against Rape (CA)—for office supplies, training materials, conference attendance, poster printing, and school outreach expenses, $4000 (2002). Clergy United for Equality of Homosexuals (CA)—for seminars and workshops on biblical oppression and its relief, including models for change for pastors and churches, $3750 (2002).

Gallo Foundation Grants   93

Gallo Foundation
PO Box 1130
Modesto, CA 95353
Contact Ronald Emerzian, (209) 341-3141
Requirements Northern California nonprofits may submit grant requests.
Areas of Interest Community Development; Disabled; Education; Higher Education; Religion; Social Services

David Geffen Foundation Grants 94

David Geffen Foundation
331 N Maple Dr, Ste 200
Beverly Hills, CA 90210
Contact Andy Spahn, Foundation President, (818)
288-7333; fax: (818) 288-7329
Requirements 501(c)3 tax-exempt organizations in Los
Angeles, CA, and New York, NY, may submit letters of
request.
Restrictions Theh foundation generally does not fund
documentaries or other types of audio-publication of
books or magazines.
Areas of Interest AIDS; Arts, General; Civil/Human
Rights; Homosexuals, Male; Jewish Services; Legal Services; Museums
Sample Awards U of California at Los Angeles, School
of Medicine (CA)—for endowment, and to recruit and
retain exemplary physicians and scientists, to create new
programs, and to attract outstanding medical and graduate students pursuing careers in medicine and science,
$200 million (2002).

Carl Gellert and Celia Berta Gellert 95
Foundation Grants

Carl Gellert and Celia Berta Gellert Foundation
1169 Market St, Ste 808
San Francisco, CA 94103
Contact Jack Fitzpatrick, Executive Director, (415)
255-2829
Internet http://home.earthlink.net/~cgcbg
Requirements California 501(c)3 tax-exempt nonprofit
organizations that are not private foundations are eligible.
Restrictions Grants are not awarded to individuals.
Areas of Interest Education; Health Care; Hospitals;
Museums; Philanthropy; Religion; Science
Sample Awards U of San Francisco, School of Business
and Management (CA)—to renovate and add a new wing
to the McLaren Center, home of the School of Business
and Management, $500,000 (2001).

Fred Gellert Family Foundation Grants 96

Fred Gellert Family Foundation
361 Third St, Ste A
San Rafael, CA 94901
Contact Grants Coordinator, (415) 256-5433; fax:
(415) 256-5425; e-mail: foundation@fredgellert.com
Internet http://fdncenter.org/grantmaker/fredgellert
Requirements IRS 501(c)3 organizations are eligible.
Restrictions Grants are not awarded to individuals.
Areas of Interest Art Education; Child Welfare;
Children's Theater; Dance; Disabled; Education; Environmental Programs; Health Care; Hospitals; Libraries;
Marine Sciences; Museums; Performing Arts; Population Control; Public Health; Radio; Recreation and Leisure; Social Services; Wildlife
Sample Awards Marine Science Institute (Redwood
City, CA)—for partial sponsorship of 15 classes in the
Discovery Voyage program, $12,000. Belvedere-Tiburon Library (Tiburon, CA)—toward the construction of the new Belvedere-Tiburon Library,
$25,000. San Francisco Ballet (San Francisco, CA)—for
general operating support, $2000.

GenCorp Foundation Grants 97

GenCorp Foundation
PO Box 15619
Sacramento, CA 95852-0619
Contact Program Contact, (916) 355-3600; e-mail:
gencorp.foundation@gencorp.com
Internet http://www.gencorp.com/foundation.html
Requirements Applicant organizations must be 501(c)3
tax-exempt and be located in one of the following cities
which have GenCorp facilities: Huntsville, AL;
Batesville, AR; Sacramento, CA; Wabash, IN; Lawrence, MA; Farmington Hills, MI; New Haven, MO;
Socorro, NM; Salisbury, NC; and Jonesborough, TN.
Restrictions The foundation generally does not make
contributions to/for individuals; private foundations; social, labor, or veterans organizations; political parties or
candidates; operating expenses of United Way member
agencies; school trips, tours, or athletic equipment; courtesy advertising, benefits, or other fund-raising events;
churches or religious organizations; local or regional
fund-raising events for single-disease organizations; organizations where there is a direct benefit to the foundation trustees, employees, or directors of the corporation;
or for research grants.
Areas of Interest Arts, General; Business Education;
Civic Affairs; Elementary Education; Environmental
Programs; Health Care; Higher Education; Literacy; Parent Involvement; Secondary Education; Social Services;
Space Sciences; Teacher Education
Sample Awards Keep Akron Beautiful (Akron, OH)—
for continued support, $1000. Challenger Ctr for Space
Science Education (Sacramento, CA)—for funding of
space science education at the Sacramento Science Ctr,
$20,000.

Genentech Corporate Contributions Grants 98

Genentech Inc
1 DNA Wy
San Francisco, CA 94080-4990
Contact Contributions Manager, (650) 225-8999; fax:
(650) 225-5795; e-mail: gfbs-d@gene.com
Internet http://www.gene.com/gene/about/community/
corp-contributions.jsp
Requirements National nonprofits and California
nonprofits in south San Francisco or Vacaville are eligible.
Restrictions In general, Genentech does not provide
funding for advertising journals or booklets, alumni
drives, capital improvement or building projects, chairs
or professorships, endowments or foundations, individuals, memorial funds, memberships, political or sectarian
organizations, professional sports events or athletes, religious organizations, scholarships, or yearbooks.
Genentech does not provide funding to any organizations
that discriminate on the basis of age, political affiliation,
race, national origin, ethnicity, gender, disability, sexual
orientation, or religious beliefs.
Areas of Interest Cardiology; Endocrinology; Oncology; Pulmonary Diseases; Science; Science Education
Sample Awards To be distributed among 19 organizations (CA)—for science programs for students in the San
Francisco Bay area, $1 million (2003).

William G. Gilmore Foundation Grants   99

William G. Gilmore Foundation
120 Montgomery St, Ste 1880
San Francisco, CA 94104
Contact Faye Wilson, Executive Director, (415)
546-1400; fax: (415) 391-8732
Requirements California and Oregon nonprofits may
apply.
Areas of Interest AIDS; Arts, General; Community Development; Conservation, Natural Resources; Education; Elderly; Family; Health Care; Social Services;
Youth Programs

Glendale Community Foundation Grants   100

Glendale Community Foundation
PO Box 313
Glendale, CA 91209-0313
Contact Program Contact, (818) 241-8040; fax: (818)
241-8045; e-mail: gcfndn@earthlink.net
Internet http://home.earthlink.net/~gcfndn/grants.html
Requirements Nonprofit, tax-exempt organizations that
serve the Glendale areas (La Crescenta, La Canada
Flintridge, Montrose, and Verdugo City) are eligible.
Restrictions Other than student loans or scholarships,
the foundation generally does not make grants to individuals, funding for religious or political purposes, or for
budget deficits or projects that usually are the responsibility of a public agency.
Areas of Interest Arts, General; Computer Grants; Cultural Activities/Programs; Disaster Relief; Education;
Health Care; Literacy; Nursing; Senior Citizen Programs
and Services; Social Services; Youth Programs
Sample Awards Camp Fire Council of the Foothills
(Glendale, CA)—to purchase a computer and printer,
$1250. VNACare (Glendale, CA)—to purchase
handheld computers for nurses, $3500. YMCA (Glendale, CA)—to purchase computers and peripherals in the
first phase of a two-year technology upgrade, $10,000.

Global Fund for Women Grants   101

Global Fund for Women
1375 Sutter St, Ste 400
San Francisco, CA 94109
Contact Executive Assistant, (415) 202-7640; fax:
(415) 202-8604; e-mail: proposals@
globalfundforwomen.org
Internet http://www.globalfundforwomen.org/3grant
Requirements The board prefers to fund organizations
that demonstrate a clear commitment to women's causes,
are governed by women, have long-term plans to
strengthen the work of their group, and are unlikely to receive support from other funding sources.
Areas of Interest Civil/Human Rights; Communications; Domestic Violence; Economic Development; Education; Homosexuals, Female; Human Reproduction/
Fertility; Law; Leadership; Mass Media; Political Behavior; Poverty and the Poor; Religion; Technology; Violent Behavior; Women
Sample Awards Elgon Free Generation of Girls (Mbale,
Uganda)—to support a group of young women who are
campaigning to end the practice of female genital mutilation, $4000. Lian Shgan Area Women's Coalition (Lian
Shan, China)—to support training and seminars reaching
thousands of village women to expand their skills and ed-

ucation in the areas of culture, law, and technology,
$8000.

Richard and Rhoda Goldman Fund Grants   102

Richard and Rhoda Goldman Fund
1 Lombard St, Ste 303
San Francisco, CA 94111
Contact Robert Gamble, Executive Director, (415)
788-1090; fax: (415) 788-7890; e-mail: info@
goldmanfund.org
Internet http://www.goldmanfund.org
Requirements Nonprofit organizations serving primarily the San Francisco Bay area of California are eligible.
Restrictions The fund does not accept applications for
research or award grants or scholarships for individuals,
conferences, documentary films, or fund-raisers. Unsolicited proposals for support of arts organizations or institutions of primary, secondary, or higher education will
not be accepted.
Areas of Interest Adult and Continuing Education; Basic Skills Education; Children and Youth; Coastal Processes; Conservation, Natural Resources; Education; Elderly; Environmental Programs; Environmental Studies;
Family Planning; Gun Control; Health Care; Jewish
Studies; Literacy; Marine Resources; Oceanography;
Population Studies; Science; Violent Behavior; Youth
Programs
Sample Awards San Francisco Urban Service Project
(CA)—to recruit, train, and employ young adults at 10
organizations that serve disadvantaged children in San
Francisco, $50,000 (2003). Green Course (Tel Aviv, Israel)—to promote environmental involvement and activism by students on college campuses in Israel, $65,000
(2003). National Women's Law Ctr (Washington,
DC)—to protect women's reproductive health care
through advocacy, litigation, and public education,
$100,000 (2003). Violence Policy Ctr (Washington,
DC)—for a public-education campaign on the Federal
Assault Weapons Ban, $200,000 (2003).

Stella B. Gross Charitable Trust Grants   103

Stella B. Gross Charitable Trust
PO Box 1121
San Jose, CA 95108
Contact Gabe Padilla, Trust Administrator, (408)
947-5203 or (408) 998-6867; e-mail: gpadilla@
bankofthewest.com
Requirements Santa Clara County, CA, nonprofits may
apply.
Areas of Interest Arts, General; Biomedical Research;
Catholic Church; Child Psychology/Development; Cultural Activities/Programs; Education; Government;
Health Care; Higher Education; Hospitals; Parent Education; Public Administration; Social Services
Sample Awards Fremont Union High School District
(Fremont, CA)—for the teen parenting program, $4000.
Catholic Charities, Diocese of San Jose (San Jose,
CA)—general support, $10,000.

Josephine S. Gumbiner Foundation Grants   104

Josephine S. Gumbiner Foundation
401 E Ocean Blvd, Ste 503
Long Beach, CA 90802

Contact Grants Administrator, (562) 437-2882; fax: (562) 437-4212; e-mail: jsgf@earthlink.net
Internet http://www.jsgf.gumbiner.com
Requirements Southern California nonprofit organizations are eligible.
Restrictions Grants do not support political campaigns, lobbying efforts, programs that supplant tradition schooling, pass-through organizations, or groups with endowments greater than $5 million.
Areas of Interest Arts; Children and Youth; Day Care; Education; Health Care; Health Promotion; Health Services Delivery; Housing; Women; Recreation and Leisure
Sample Awards Su Casa General (CA)—for operating support, $12,000 (2004). Project Wholeness Wellness B.R.U.C.E.(CA)—for the Say Sistah HIV/AIDS Prevention program $2500 (2004). On Your Feet (CA)—to support a rental assistance and eviction prevention program, $25,000 (2004). L.B. Library Foundation (CA)—for the Family Learning Center, $12,500 (2004).

Evelyn Haas and Walter Haas Jr. Fund Grants   105
Evelyn Haas and Walter Haas Jr. Fund
1 Market, Landmark, Ste 400
San Francisco, CA 94105
Contact Clayton Juan, Grants Administrator, (415) 856-1400; fax: (415) 856-1500; e-mail: sitemaster@ haasjr.org
Internet http://www.haasjr.org
Requirements IRS 501(c)3 organizations in California not classified as private foundations under section 509(a) are eligible. Matching funds are required.
Restrictions The fund will not support organizations that discriminate in their leadership, staffing, service provision, or on the basis of age, political affiliation, or religious belief.
Areas of Interest After-School Programs; Children and Youth; Elderly; Family; Homelessness; Homosexuals, Female; Homosexuals, Male; Hunger; Immigrants; Literature; Native Americans; Neighborhoods; Philanthropy; Refugees; Social Change; Volunteers
Sample Awards San Francisco Adult Day Services Network (CA)—to expand the scope and participation in the Professional Development Institute, which offers training and technical assistance to adult day health centers. $40,000. All Our Families Coalition (CA)—to expand education and support services for lesbian and gay parents, $25,000. Eureka Communities (CA)—to provide leadership training to nonprofit executives in the Bay Area, $50,000.

Miriam and Peter Haas Fund Grants   106
Miriam and Peter Haas Fund
201 Filbert St, 5th Fl
San Francisco, CA 94133
Contact David Thesell, Grants Manager, (415) 296-9249; fax: (415) 296-8842; e-mail: dThesell@ mphf.org
Requirements Nonprofit organizations in the San Francisco Bay area of California may submit grant requests.
Restrictions Individuals are not eligible.
Areas of Interest Art Education; Arts, General; Child Psychology/Development; Education; Environmental

Programs; Family; Health Care; Humanities; Preschool Education; Public Affairs; Public Planning/Policy; Social Services
Sample Awards Child Development Policy Institute Education Fund (CA)—for general operating support, $25,000. Ctr for the Arts, Yerba Buena Gardens (CA)—to support educational and marketing efforts, $100,000. Performing Arts Workshop (CA)—to train a core group of artists to teach creative movements in San Francisco preschools, $10,000.

Walter and Elise Haas Fund Grants   107
Walter and Elise Haas Fund
1 Lombard St, Ste 305
San Francisco, CA 94111-1130
Contact Pamela David, Executive Director, (415) 398-4474
Internet http://www.haassr.org/guidelin.htm
Requirements Organizations in California are eligible to apply.
Restrictions Individuals are ineligible.
Areas of Interest Art Education; Arts, General; Audience Development; Business Ethics; Children and Youth; Civics Education; Conservation, Natural Resources; Dramatic/Theater Arts; Education; Environmental Programs; Ethics; Intervention Programs; Journalism; Journalism Education; Land Use Planning/Policy; Law; Medical Ethics; Parks; Poverty and the Poor; Social Services; Teacher Education, Inservice
Sample Awards Women in Communtiy Service, San Francisco Lifeskills Program (CA)—to expand this program that provides comprehensive life-skills and job-training services to low-income women in San Francisco, $192,000 over three years (2002).

Crescent Porter Hale Foundation Grants   108
Crescent Porter Hale Foundation
655 Redwood Hwy, Ste 301
Mill Valley, CA 94941
Contact Ulla Davis, Executive Director, (415) 388-2333; fax: (415) 381-4799
Requirements Application is open to corporate nonprofit organizations that qualify for tax exemption and can be classified as nonprivate foundations.
Restrictions Individuals are ineligible.
Areas of Interest Art Education; Catholic Church; Disabled; Elderly; Elementary Education; Higher Education; Music Education; Secondary Education; Social Services; Youth Programs

Harden Foundation Grants   109
Harden Foundation
PO Box 779
Salinas, CA 93902
Contact Joseph Grainger, Executive Director, (831) 442-3005; fax: (831) 443-1429
Requirements Nonprofit Monterey County organizations may apply.
Restrictions The foundation does not fund sectarian religious programs, educational projects (except agriculture-related requests), endowments, annual events, conferences, or fund-raising events.
Areas of Interest Aging/Gerontology; Alzheimer's Disease; Animal Care; Arts, General; Community Service

Programs; Elderly; Family; Food Distribution; Single-Parent Families; Social Services; Volunteers; Youth Programs

Sample Awards Boys and Girls Clubs of Monterey County (Seaside, CA)—for youth center at Salinas Sports Complex, $400,000 (2001). Kinship Center (Monterey, CA)—for capital campaign for new building in Salinas, $100,000 (2001). American Red Cross (Monterey, CA)—to upgrade equipment, purchase disaster supplies, and translate and print training materials for educational purposes, $35,000 (2001).

Clarence E. Heller Charitable Foundation   110
Grants

Clarence E. Heller Charitable Foundation
1 Lombard St, Ste 305
San Francisco, CA 94111-1130
Contact Bruce Hirsch, Executive Director, (415) 989-9839; fax: (415) 989-1909; e-mail: info@cehcf.org
Internet http://cehcf.org
Requirements 501(c)3 tax-exempt organizations are eligible.
Areas of Interest Academic Achievement; Agricultural Planning/Policy; Chamber Music; Conservation, Agriculture; Conservation, Natural Resources; Ecology; Education; Elementary Education; Energy; Environmental Education; Environmental Effects; Environmental Planning/Policy; Environmental Programs; Health Care; Music; Music Education; Orchestras; Pesticides; Secondary Education; Sustainable Development; Teacher Education; Toxic Substances
Sample Awards California Public Interest Research Group Charitable Trust (CA)—for research and education programs on pesticide use and sustainable farming practices, $20,000. San Francisco Community Music Ctr (CA)—to support three programs for adults to begin or continue instrument training, $30,000. Classical Philharmonic (CA)—to increase fund-raising capacity, $7500. Land Institute (KS)—for development of a 150-acre farm that uses renewable energy resources, $25,000.

William and Flora Hewlett Foundation   111
Conflict Resolution Grants

William and Flora Hewlett Foundation
525 Middlefield Rd, Ste 200
Menlo Park, CA 94025
Contact Paul Brest, President, (650) 234-4500; fax: (650) 234-4501; e-mail: info@hewlett.org
Internet http://www.hewlett.org
Requirements A letter of inquiry addressed to the president providing a straightforward statement of needs and aspirations for funds should be the initial contact. Applicants who receive favorable responses will be invited to submit formal proposals.
Restrictions Normally the foundation will not consider grants for basic research, capital construction funds, grants in the medical or health-related fields, or general fund-raising drives. It will not make grants to individuals or grants intended directly or indirectly to support candidates for political office or to influence legislation. The foundation does not accept proposals sent via e-mail or fax.

Areas of Interest Conflict/Dispute Resolution; International Programs; Minorities; Native Americans; Public Planning/Policy; Racism/Race Relations
Sample Awards Human Rights Watch (NY)—to respond to discrimination and violence against Arab-Americans, $75,000 (2001). International Crisis Group (Brussels)—to help establish a global terrorism division with offices in the Middle East and in the Pakistan-Afghanistan region, $400,000 (2001).

William and Flora Hewlett Foundation   112
Education Grants

William and Flora Hewlett Foundation
2121 Sand Hill Rd
Menlo Park, CA 94025
Contact Paul Brest, President, (650) 234-4500; fax: (650) 234-4501; e-mail: info@hewlett.org
Internet http://www.hewlett.org
Requirements Elementary and secondary education grants are generally limited to California programs, with primary emphasis on public schools in the San Francisco Bay area. The foundation favors schools, school districts, universities, and groupings of these entities rather than third parties.
Restrictions Requests will not be considered to fund student aid, construction, equipment and computer purchases, education research, basic scientific research, health research, or health education programs.
Areas of Interest African Americans; Area Studies; Business; Citizenship; Communications; Community and School Relations; Education Reform; Educational Administration; Educational Planning/Policy; Elementary Education; Faculty Development; Family; Government; Higher Education; Higher Education, Private; Humanities Education; International Studies; Labor Relations; Leadership; Legal Education; Management; Minority Schools; Publishing Industry; Religious Studies; School-to-Work Transition; Secondary Education; Service Delivery Programs; Teacher Education; Technology; Undergraduate Education
Sample Awards Stanford U (CA)—to establish and endow a program in Islamic studies and to endow a professorship in Islamic studies in the religious-studies department, $2.5 million matching grant and $2 million matching grant, respectively (2003). U of Texas (Austin, TX)—for the Charles A. Dana Center, which conducts research about education policy, $500,000 (2003). Northern Arizona U (AZ)—for programs to increase the recruitment and retention of engineering students and to improve undergraduate teaching in engineering, $1.2 million over four years (2003). American Academy of Arts and Sciences (Cambridge, MA)—to improve data collection about the humanities and American education, to strengthen research on the humanities, and to create new research tools for examining the liberal arts, $750,000 (2003).

William and Flora Hewlett Foundation   113
Environmental Grants

William and Flora Hewlett Foundation
2121 Sand Hill Rd
Menlo Park, CA 94025

Contact Hal Harvey, Program Director, (650) 234-4500 ext 5647; fax: (650) 234-4501; e-mail: info@hewlett.org

Internet http://www.hewlett.org

Requirements Initial contact should be by letter of inquiry addressed to the president providing a straightforward statement of needs and aspirations for support. Applicants who receive favorable responses will be invited to submit formal proposals.

Restrictions The foundation usually does not support proposals in the areas of basic research; capital construction; conferences, symposia, or workshops; environmental education (K-12 or adult); museum facilities, exhibits, or programs; or specific media projects. The foundation does not make awards to individuals, organizations outside the United States, or local land trusts, nor does it support community organizing, advocacy, or litigation.

Areas of Interest Ecology; Economic Development; Environmental Law; Environmental Planning/Policy; Environmental Programs; Environmental Studies; Information Dissemination; Land Management; Regional Planning/Policy; Rural Planning/Policy; Science

Sample Awards Northeast States Ctr for a Clean Air Future (Boston, MA)—to study the economic effects of reducing greenhouse gases from motor vehicles, $1.2 million (2003). U of Virginia, Institute for Environmental Negotiation (Charlottesville, VA)—to coordinate the work of the national Community-Based Collaboratives Research Consortium, $375,000 (2002).

William and Flora Hewlett Foundation Family and Community Development Grants   114

William and Flora Hewlett Foundation
2121 Sand Hill Rd
Menlo Park, CA 94025

Contact Connie Bassett, Grants Administrator, (650) 234-4500; fax: (650) 234-4501; e-mail: info@hewlett.org

Internet http://www.hewlett.org/Grantseekers

Requirements 501(c)3 public charities are eligible.

Restrictions The foundation does not support for-profit corporations or individuals; normally make grants intended to support basic research, capital construction funds, endowment, general fundraising drives, or fundraising events; make grants intended to support candidates for political office, to influence legislation, or to support sectarian or religious purposes; fund endowments or debt reduction; or support annual fundraising campaigns or capital construction.

Areas of Interest Education; Environmental Programs; Performing Arts

Sample Awards Johns Hopkins U (Baltimore, MD)—to create an information-management system to help monitor and evaluate San Francisco-area programs that promote the positive engagement of fathers and male figures in children's lives, $1.4 million (2002). U of Texas (Austin, TX)—for the Lyndon B. Johnson School of Public Affiars, $150,000 (2001). Marin Community Foundation (Larkspur, CA)—for a program that will promote greater positive involvement by noncustodial fathers in the lives of their children, $240,000 over two years (2000).

William and Flora Hewlett Foundation Performing Arts Grants   115

William and Flora Hewlett Foundation
525 Middlefield Rd, Ste 200
Menlo Park, CA 94025

Contact Paul Brest, President, (650) 234-4500; fax: (650) 234-4501; e-mail: info@hewlett.org

Internet http://www.hewlett.org

Requirements The program's geographic focus is the nine California counties that border the San Francisco Bay, with additional limited funding in Santa Cruz and Monterey counties. Letters of inquiry addressed to the president providing a statement of needs and aspirations for support should precede formal applications.

Restrictions Grants are not made for visual or literary arts; humanities; elementary and secondary school programs; college or university proposals; community art classes; folk arts, including crafts and popular music; recreational, therapeutic, and social service arts programs; nor to individuals. The foundation also does not support one-time events such as seminars, conferences, festivals, or cultural foreign exchange programs, nor provide assistance with touring costs for performing companies.

Areas of Interest Arts Administration; Career Education and Planning; Dance; Dramatic/Theater Arts; Film Production; Media Arts; Music, Instrumental; Opera/Musical Theater; Training and Development; Video Production

Sample Awards Northern California Community Loan Fund (San Francisco, CA)—for facility projects of performing-arts groups, $3 million (2003). National Council of the Lewis and Clark Bicentennial (Saint Louis, MO)—for activities, salary support, and a Web site related to the 200th anniversary celebration of the journey across America by explorers Meriwether Lewis and William Clark, $2 million over four years (2003).

William and Flora Hewlett Foundation Population Program Grants   116

William and Flora Hewlett Foundation
2121 Sand Hill Rd
Menlo Park, CA 94025

Contact Program Contact, (650) 234-4500; fax: (650) 234-4501; e-mail: info@hewlett.org

Internet http://www.hewlett.org/Programs/Population

Requirements A letter of inquiry addressed to the president providing a straightforward statement of needs and aspirations for support should be the initial contact (loi&&hewlett.org). Applicants who receive favorable responses will be invited to submit formal proposals.

Restrictions The foundation will not consider support for biomedical research on reproduction, nor will it fund population education programs directed toward the general public.

Areas of Interest Developing/Underdeveloped Nations; Family Planning; Human Reproduction/Fertility; Population Studies; Public Planning/Policy; Teen Pregnancy; Training and Development

Sample Awards Columbia U, Earth Institute (New York, NY)—for research on the role of reproductive health in achieving the United Nations Millennium Devleopment Goals, $500,000 (2003). U of Texas (Austin, TX)—for the Population Research Center, $120,000 (2002).

Colin Higgins Foundation Grants   117

Colin Higgins Foundation
PO Box 29903
San Francisco, CA 94129-0903
Contact Grants Administrator, (415) 561-6323; fax: (415) 561-6401; e-mail: info@colinhiggins.org
Internet http://www.colinhiggins.org/grantmaking
Requirements The foundation only considers organizations with overall budgets under $2 million, or project budgets under $500,000.
Restrictions Grants do not support projects that had previously fallen within its funding priorities, including any organizations or programs based in urban areas (population over 1 million); film and video projects; or organizations with overall budgets of over $2 million, or project budgets over $500,000. The one exception to the exclusion of programs in urban areas is those organizations and projects working with underserved communities (i.e. , communities of color, low-income communities, transgender people, etc.). The foundation does not accept letters of inquiry from universities, schools, individuals, or corporations. It does not support political or legislative activities, endowments, or deficit budgets. Additionally, the foundation does not support capital campaigns, although it will consider requests for capital improvements, and does not award grants to organizations outside the United States.
Areas of Interest AIDS; AIDS Education; AIDS Prevention; HIV; Health Care; Homosexuals, Female; Homosexuals, Male; Rural Areas; Social Change
Sample Awards The AIDS Mastery Fund (New York, NY)—for general support, $15,000 (2001). Archdiocese of San Francisco (CA)—for the Today's Students, Tommorrow's Leaders Program, $2500 (2001). Intersect: The HIV/Violence Against Women Project (New York, NY)—for general support, $5000 (2001). Unity Fellowship Church (Los Angeles, CA)—for the It Starts With Us Outreach Program, $5000 (2001).

Hoffman Foundation Grants   118

Elaine S. Hoffman and H. Leslie Hoffman Foundation
225 S Lake Ave, Ste 1150
Pasadena, CA 91101-3005
Contact J. Kristoffer Popovich, Treasurer, (626) 793-0043
Requirements California organizations serving Pasadena and the Los Angeles areas are eligible.
Areas of Interest Cancer/Carcinogenesis; Elderly; Higher Education; Music; Secondary Education; Youth Programs

H. Leslie Hoffman and Elaine S. Hoffman   119
Foundation Grants

H. Leslie Hoffman and Elaine S. Hoffman Foundation
225 S Lake Ave, Ste 1150
Pasadena, CA 91101
Contact J. Kristoffer Popovich, (626) 793-0043
Requirements California nonprofit organizations are eligible to apply.
Restrictions Individuals are ineligible.
Areas of Interest Cancer/Carcinogenesis; Children and Youth; Education; Elderly; Higher Education; Music; Secondary Education; Social Services Delivery

Homeland Foundation Grants   120

Homeland Foundation
412 N Pacific Coast Hwy, PMB 359
Laguna Beach, CA 92651
Contact Glenda Menges, Grants Administrator, (949) 494-0365
Requirements 501(c)3 nonprofit organizations are eligible.
Restrictions Grants are not awarded to support political campaigns, individuals, scholarships, fellowships, or film or video projects.
Areas of Interest Environmental Programs; Women

Horizons Community Issues Grants   121

Horizons Foundation
870 Market St, Ste 728
San Francisco, CA 94102
Contact Director, (415) 398-2333; fax: (415) 398-4733; e-mail: info@horizonsfoundation.org
Internet http://www.horizonsfoundation.org
Requirements An applicant must: be a nonprofit, 501(c)3 organization, or provide documentation that the organization is sponsored under a fiscal agent umbrella that has 501(c)3 status; request support for a program/activity that benefits LGBT people; request support for a program/organization active in one or more of the identified issue areas; request support for a program/activity within one or more of the nine Bay Area counties, including Alameda, Contra Costa, Marin, Napa, San Francisco, San Mateo, Santa Clara, Solano, Sonoma; and have submitted a final report and financial accounting for past grant(s) received from the foundation.
Restrictions The following are not eligible for support: requests for costs incurred prior to the date of the grant award; requests from government agencies; requests for capital support, including construction and renovation; fundraising or event sponsorship; or projects that directly benefit an individual.
Areas of Interest Arts, General; Children and Youth; Civil/Human Rights; Community Services; Cultural Outreach; Domestic Violence; Dramatic/Theater Arts; Elderly; Family; Homosexuals, Female; Homosexuals, Male; Parent Education; Social Services; Youth Violence
Sample Awards Center for Young Women's Development (San Francisco, CA)—to provide gender-specific, peer-based opportunities for high-risk low-and no-income young woman to build healthier lives and healthier communities, $5000 (2003).

Lucile Horton Howe and Mitchell B. Howe   122
Foundation Grants

Lucile Horton Howe and Mitchell B. Howe Foundation
180 S Lake Ave
Pasadena, CA 91101-2619
Contact Mitchell Howe Jr., President, (626) 792-0514; e-mail: mbromouse@earthlink.net
Requirements Only nonprofit organizations in the Pasadena and San Gabriel, CA, areas are eligible. A brief letter and a copy of the organizations 501(c)3 form are the requirements for application.
Restrictions No restricted grants will be funded by the foundation.

Areas of Interest Biomedical Research; Child Welfare; Drugs/Drug Abuse; Education; Family; Hospitals; Religion; Social Services
Sample Awards Children's Hospital, Pasadena Auxiliary (Los Angeles, CA)—for operating support, $12,000.

Humboldt Area Foundation Grants   123
Humboldt Area Foundation
PO Box 99
Bayside, CA 95524
Contact Lisa Appleton, Grants Administrator, (707) 442-2993; fax: (707) 442-3811; e-mail: hafound@hafoundation.org
Internet http://www.hafoundation.org/grants/haf_grants
Requirements 501(c)3 tax-exempt organizations in Humboldt, Del Norte, and adjacent parts of Trinity and Siskiyou Counties, CA, are eligible.
Restrictions The foundation does not fund projects outside its service area, deferred maintenance, annual operating costs, travel, scholarships and fellowships, or projects that violate nonprofit public laws.
Areas of Interest Civic Affairs; Community Service Programs; Cultural Activities/Programs; Disabled; Education; Health Care; Recreation and Leisure; Safety; Senior Citizen Programs and Services; Social Services; Volunteers; Youth Programs
Sample Awards McKinleyville Community Services (McKinleyville, CA)—toward construction of Community Ctr at Pierson Park, $69,632. Larry McCarty Foundation for Kids (Trinidad, CA)—for the endowment fund, $10,000.

Jaquelin Hume Foundation Grants   124
Jaquelin Hume Foundation
600 Montgomery St, Ste 2800
San Francisco, CA 94111
Contact Gisele Huff, Executive Director, (415) 705-5115
Requirements US 501(c)3 nonprofit organizations may apply.
Restrictions The foundation generally will not consider institutions or organizations primarily supported by tax-derived funding. The foundation will not consider organizations that discriminate on the basis of race, creed, or sex.
Areas of Interest Business; Children and Youth; Civics Education; Economics; Federal Government; Governmental Functions; Values/Moral Education

Audrey and Sydney Irmas Charitable   125
   Foundation Grants
Audrey and Sydney Irmas Charitable Foundation
16830 Ventura Blvd, Ste 364
Encino, CA 91436-2797
Contact Robert Irmas, Administrator, (818) 382-3313; fax: (818) 382-3315; email: robirm@aol.com
Requirements 501(c)3 nonprofit organizations are eligible.
Areas of Interest Arts, General; Cultural Programs/Activities; Drugs/Drug Abuse; Homelessness; Hospitals; Housing; Jewish Services; Religion; Urban Affairs
Sample Awards Meals on Wheels (Santa Monica, CA)—$250. Pasadena Art Alliance (CA)—$400. Arch-

diocese of Los Angeles (CA)—$10,000. Juvenile Diabetes Foundation (New York, NY)—$5000.

James Irvine Foundation Grants   126
James Irvine Foundation
1 Market Pl, Steuart Tower, Ste 2500
San Francisco, CA 94105
Contact Kelly Martin, Grants Manager, (415) 777-2244; fax: (415) 777-0869
Internet http://www.irvine.org
Requirements Grants and program-related investments are limited to charitable uses in California and for the benefit of charities that do not receive a substantial part of their support from taxation or exist primarily to benefit tax-supported entities or agencies of the government.
Restrictions The foundation does not make grants or program-related investments to individuals.
Areas of Interest Arts, General; Career Education and Planning; Chamber Music; Children and Youth; Civic Affairs; Economics; Education; Educational Planning/Policy; Employment Opportunity Programs; Family; Health Care; Higher Education; Homelessness; Jewish Services; Job Training Programs; Marketing; Minorities; Minority Education; Poverty and the Poor; Religion; Statistics; Sustainable Development; Technology; Technology Education
Sample Awards Oakland East Bay Symphony (CA)—to bring together California writers and composers to commission and perform works for the orchestral repertoire, $350,000 over four years (2003). CompuMentor Project (San Francisco, CA)—for technology assistance and training for the Central Valley Partnership for Citizenship, $100,000 (2003. Rainbow Research (Minneapolis, MN)—to evaluate grantees in the Irvine Foundation's organized religion portfolio, $300,000 over two years (2003). Orange County Business Council (Irvine, CA)—for career training and advancement for low-income immigrant residents of Orange County, $150,000 (2003).

Ann Jackson Family Foundation Grants   127
Ann Jackson Family Foundation
PO Box 5580
Santa Barbara, CA 93150-5580
Contact Palmer Jackson, President, (805) 969-2258
Areas of Interest Animal Rights; Child Welfare; Disabled; Health Care; Hospitals; Secondary Education

Jacobs Family Foundation Grants   128
Jacobs Family Foundation
PO Box 740650
San Diego, CA 92174-0650
Contact Jennifer Vanica, Executive Director, (858) 527-6161; fax: (858) 527-6162
Internet http://www.jacobsfamilyfoundation.org
Requirements Nonprofit organizations in California, Lebanon, and the Arab Middle East may apply.
Restrictions The foundation does not make grants for medical services and research, religious activities, political programs, the arts, athletics, bricks and mortar, or to individuals.
Areas of Interest Arab Americans; At-Risk Youth; Cultural Outreach; Economic Development; Education; Entrepreneurship; Family; Leadership; Nonprofit Organi-

zations; Science Education; Technology Education; Youth Programs

J.W. and Ida M. Jameson Foundation Grants — 129
J.W. and Ida M. Jameson Foundation
PO Box 397
Sierra Madre, CA 91025
Contact Les Hugn, President, (626) 355-6973
Requirements California nonprofits may submit applications for grant support.
Areas of Interest Biomedical Research; Catholic Church; Cultural Activities/Programs; Higher Education; Hospitals; Protestant Church; Religious Studies; Theology

George Frederick Jewett Foundation Grants — 130 Program
George Frederick Jewett Foundation
235 Montgomery St, Ste 612
San Francisco, CA 94104
Contact Ann Gralnek, (415) 421-1351; fax: (415) 421-0721; e-mail: tfbjewettf@aol.com
Requirements Preference is given to public charities or nonprivate foundations. The foundation confines its grants largely to requests from eastern Washington and the San Francisco Bay area.
Restrictions Grants do not support advertising; advocacy, athletic, international, religious, political, or veterans organizations; or individuals.
Areas of Interest Arts, General; Conservation, Natural Resources; Cultural Activities/Programs; Education; Elementary Education; Health Care; Health Services Delivery; Higher Education; Humanities; Opera/Musical Theater; Population Studies; Religion; Restoration and Preservation; Secondary Education; Social Services
Sample Awards American U of Beirut (New York, NY)—general support, $15,000. Committee to Restore the Opera House (San Francisco, CA)—for a three-year commitment for restoration of the San Francisco War Memorial Opera House, $120,000.

Walter S. Johnson Foundation Grants — 131
Walter S. Johnson Foundation
525 Middlefield Rd, Ste 160
Menlo Park, CA 94025
Contact Rachel Legree, Grants Administrator, (650) 326-0485; fax: (650) 326-4320; e-mail: rachel@wsjf.org
Internet http://www.wsjf.org
Requirements Proposals are accepted from non-profit organizations throughout Northern California and Washoe County, Nevada.
Restrictions The foundation does not consider proposals for grants to individuals or to religious organizations for sectarian purposes. Funds are not provided for capital projects, organizational deficits, or general operating support.
Areas of Interest Career Education and Planning; Children and Youth; Crisis Counseling; Disaster Relief; Domestic Violence; Education; Education Reform; Family; Family/Marriage Counseling; Homelessness; Housing; Neighborhoods; Parent Education; Poverty

and the Poor; School-to-Work Transition; Teacher Education; Youth Programs
Sample Awards Berkeley Biotechnology Education (CA)— for continuing support of its school-to-career program, $60,000 (2003). Catholic Charities of the East Bay (Oakland, CA)—to create a coordinated continuum of services for youth who are leaving the foster care system, $75,000 (2003). YouthBuild USA (Somerville, MA)—to strengthen its youth-development programs in California, $200,000 (2003).

JoMiJo Foundation Grants — 132
JoMiJo Foundation
170 Oak Dr
San Rafael, CA 94901
Contact Grants Administrator, (415) 721-7397; fax: (415) 721-0916
Internet http://www.jomijo.org
Requirements Small- to medium-sized nonprofit, tax-exempt organizations working in their own communities may apply. Currently the foundation is concentrating on the San Francisco Bay area, Denver, and Chicago. Budgets cannot be over $500,000 per year.
Restrictions Grants do not support large or national nonprofit organizations; scientific or other kinds of research efforts; groups working in the arts; organizations needing to do public relations, or endowment building; nonprofits that run nursing homes; the advancement of religion or organizations associated with religious educational outlets; hospitals and health organizations; capital campaigns and other efforts for bricks and mortar; individuals without any connection to a 501(c)3, including scholarships; efforts that produce video, or support acquisition of technology or access to technology such as web sites; governmental entities of any kind, including public schools; or emergency funds.
Areas of Interest At-Risk Youth; Children and Youth; Disadvantaged (Economically); Environmental Programs; Human/Civil Rights; Grassroots Leadership; Minorities; Social Change; Women

Henry J. Kaiser Family Foundation Grants — 133
Henry J. Kaiser Family Foundation
2400 Sand Hill Rd
Menlo Park, CA 94025
Contact Diane Rowland, Executive Vice President, (415) 854-9400; fax: (415) 854-4800
Internet http://www.kff.org
Requirements Grants in response to unsolicited proposals are made only to governmental agencies and to private organizations with IRS 501(c)3 tax-exempt status.
Restrictions The foundation does not award grants to individuals. Support is not given to ongoing general operating expenses, indirect costs, capital campaigns, annual appeals or other fundraising events, construction, purchase or renovation of facilities, or equipment purchases.
Areas of Interest AIDS; Broadcast Media; Civil/Human Rights; Communications; Conservation, Natural Resources; Environmental Programs; Governmental Functions; HIV; Health Care Access; Health Care Administration; Health Planning/Policy; Hispanics; Homosexuals, Female; Homosexuals, Male; Human Reproduction/Fertility; Immigrants; International Programs; Mi-

nority Health; Poverty and the Poor; Print Media; Public Health; Security

Sample Awards Alliance for Justice (Washington, DC)—for general operating support, $600,000 over three years (2003). U of Florida, Tropical Conservation and Development Program (Gainesville, FL)—for a community-based conservation and training program for organizations working in protected areas of Colombia and Ecuador, $240,000 over three years (2003). U of California at Los Angeles (CA)—for the Network on Youth Mental Health Care, $5 million over four years (2003). Ctr for Defense Information (Washington, DC)—for policy research and advocacy on nuclear-weapons systems and their vulnerabilities, $650,000 over three years (2003).

Koret Foundation Grants 134

Koret Foundation
33 New Montgomery St, Ste 1090
San Francisco, CA 94105-4509
Contact Irving Cramer, Executive Director, (415) 882-7740; fax: (415) 882-7775; e-mail: koret@koretfoundation.org
Internet http://www.koretfoundation.org
Requirements Applicant must first submit a one- to three-page preliminary letter briefly outlining the project or need for which support is being requested; the population(s) and geographic area(s) to be served; the proposed starting date and duration of grant-supported activities; an outline of the budget including all funding sources; highlights of organization's experience in the program or service area; list of board of directors; and IRS tax-exempt letter verifying applicant's 501(c)3 status.
Restrictions Grants will not be made for direct support, scholarships, or loans to individuals; for general fund drives, annual appeals, or endowments; for emergency funding, debt retirement, or deficits; for indirect or overhead costs; to fiscal agents soliciting funds for projects or programs not conducted by the applicant; to organizations in support of propaganda or activities to influence legislation; to projects of sectarian/fraternal/religious/veteran/military organizations whose principal benefit is for their own members or adherents; or to grantees who have not fulfilled terms and conditions of a previous award.
Areas of Interest Community Service Programs; Cultural Activities/Programs; Cultural Diversity; Economic Development; Education; Elementary Education; Higher Education; Israel; Jewish Services; Public Planning/Policy; Religion; Secondary Eucation; Security; Training and Development; Youth Programs
Sample Awards Stern Grove Festival Assoc (San Francisco, CA)—for concert sponsorship, $75,000 over three years (2003). United Way Silicon Valley (San Jose, CA)—for its 2003 campaign, $25,000 (2003). Oakland Military Institute (CA)—for a remedial-reading program at this new charter school, $90,000 (2003). Camp Tawonga (San Francisco, CA)—to renovate a building at this Jewish camp, $75,000 (2003).

Herbert and Gertrude Latkin Charitable Foundation Grants 135

Herbert and Gertrude Latkin Charitable Foundation
PO Box 2340
Santa Barbara, CA 93120-2340
Contact Janice Gibbons, (805) 564-6211
Requirements California nonprofit organizations serving Santa Barbara County are eligible.
Areas of Interest Aging/Gerontology; Animal Care; Child Abuse; Critical Care Medicine; Elderly; Family; Health Care; Social Services

Thomas and Dorothy Leavey Foundation Grants 136

Thomas and Dorothy Leavey Foundation
10100 Santa Monica Blvd, Ste 610
Los Angeles, CA 90067
Contact Kathleen Leavey McCarthy, Chair, (323) 551-9936
Requirements The foundation gives primarily in southern California.
Areas of Interest Biomedical Research; Catholic Church; Higher Education; Hospitals; Secondary Education
Sample Awards Georgetown U (Washington, DC)—for the new Southwest Quadrangle, which will include a residence hall for students, a new home for the university's Jesuit community, a modern dining hall, and underground parking, $5 million.

Liberty Hill Foundation Grants 137

Liberty Hill Foundation
2121 Cloverhill Blvd, Ste 113
Santa Monica, CA 90404
Contact James Williams, (310) 453-3611; fax: (310) 453-7806; e-mail: jwilliams@libertyhill.org
Internet http://www.libertyhill.org/grant/home.html
Requirements Los Angeles County, CA, grassroots, proactive, community organizations that are committed to diversity, with a record of leadership development through a democratic process, are eligible.
Restrictions The foundation does not fund social service providers that do not have a strong community organizing component, projects directed at constituencies outside Los Angeles County, individual efforts, film projects, groups that received foundation funding in the previous funding cycle, direct union organizing, nor businesses or profit-making ventures. Liberty Hill generally does not fund travel expenses, equipment purchases, or research.
Areas of Interest Civic Affairs; Community Development; Environment; Environmental Programs; Homosexuals, Female; Homosexuals, Male; Human Rights; Social Change
Sample Awards Jewish Vocational Services (Los Angeles, CA)—for a program that trains disabled people to operate coffee carts and to pursue careers in the coffee-service industry, $12,500 (2003). New Directions (Los Angeles, CA)—for a catering business and a cafeteria at the Veterans Administration campus that will provide jobs and job training, $20,000 (2003). Pueblo Nuevo Enterprises (Los Angeles, CA)—to purchase equipment for this employee-owned janitorial service, $20,000 (2003). Tia Chucha's Cafe Cultural (Los Angeles, CA)—for general operating support of this book-

store, cafe, art gallery, and computer center seving Latinos in northern Los Angeles, $25,000 (2003).

Louis R. Lurie Foundation Grants 138

Louis R. Lurie Foundation
555 California St, Ste 5100
San Francisco, CA 94104
Contact Nancy Terry, Administrator, (415) 392-2470
Internet http://fdncenter.org/grantmaker/lurie
Requirements Nonprofits serving the metropolitan Chicago area and the San Francisco Bay area are eligible for grant support.
Areas of Interest Arts, General; Children's Museums; Community Service Programs; Education; Health Care; History Education
Sample Awards Chicago Children's Museum (IL)—for museum relocation, $25,000. Chicago Metro History Education Ctr (IL)—for general operating support, $1000.

Miranda Lux Foundation Grants 139

Miranda Lux Foundation
57 Post St, Ste 510
San Francisco, CA 94104-5020
Contact Kenneth Blum, Executive Director, (415) 981-2966
Requirements Grants are awarded in San Francisco, CA.
Restrictions Support will not be given to individuals or for annual campaigns, emergency funds, deficit financing, building or endowment funds, land acquisition, renovations, research, publications, or loans.
Areas of Interest Adult and Continuing Education; Basic Skills Education; Children and Youth; Employment Opportunity Programs; Job Training Programs; Junior and Community Colleges; Literacy; Preschool Education; Reading; Vocational/Technical Education
Sample Awards Arriba Juntos Ctr (San Francisco, CA)—to support the Youth at Work program, $25,000. Youth Assistance Assoc (San Francisco, CA)— for the Auto Technician program, $17,500. YMCA, Embarcadero Branch (San Francisco, CA)—to support an employment readiness training program, $10,000.

Maddie's Fund Grant 140

Maddie's Fund
2223 Santa Clara Ave, Ste B
Alameda, CA 94501
Contact Grants Administrator, (510) 337-8989; fax: (510) 337-8988; e-mail: info@maddies.org
Internet http://www.maddies.org/grant/index.html
Requirements Eligible to apply are California 501(c)3 nonprofit animal welfare organizations that have a no-kill policy in place or a plan to establish one within two or three years and a timeline for eliminating the deaths of all adoptable animals in their area.
Areas of Interest Animal Behavior/Ethology; Animal Care; Animals as Pets; Poverty and the Poor; Veterinary Medicine
Sample Awards Western U of Health Sciences' College of Veterinary Medicine (CA)—to develop the Maddie's Shelter Medicine Program, which will integrate the no-kill philosophy and methods into the college's core curriculum for veterinary student. provide medical consultation and other services to animal shelter. and make clinical experiences at no-kill shelters a significant component of the college's program, $1.25 million over five years (2002).

Margoes Foundation Grants 141

Margoes Foundation
57 Post St, Ste 510
San Francisco, CA 94104
Contact John Blum, Principal Manager, (415) 981-2966; fax: (415) 981-5218; e-mail: margoesfdn@aol.com
Requirements California nonprofits are eligible, with preference given to the San Francisco Bay area.
Restrictions Grants are not awarded to agencies supported by federated campaigns or to individuals.
Areas of Interest Adolescents; Africa; Asia; Cardiology; Dental Education; Independent Living Programs; Mental Disorders; Minority Education; Rehabilitation/Therapy, Emotional/Social; Scholarship Programs, General; Youth Programs
Sample Awards Community Music Center (San Francisco, CA)—for financial aid, $10,000. U of the Pacific (Stockton, CA)—to increase minority enrollment in the predentistry undergraduate programs, $20,000 over two years. Fred Finch Youth Ctr (Oakland, CA)—for salary support of a part-time counselor for a transitional independent living program for older adolescents and young adults with severe emotional problems, $15,000.

MAZON Grants: A Jewish Response to Hunger 142

MAZON: A Jewish Response to Hunger
1990 S Bundy Dr, Ste 260
Los Angeles, CA 90025-5232
Contact Grants Administrator, (310) 442-0020; fax: (310) 442-0030; e-mail: mazonmail@mazon.org
Internet http://www.mazon.org/pages/grantmaking.html
Requirements US nonprofit organizations that meet program criteria may apply.
Restrictions MAZON does not make grants to groups that proselytize or place any religious requirements on service; have national name recognition; are principally focused on homelessness; charge individuals for food; or are government entities, professional associations, job training programs, or grantmaking organizations. Capital grants for building projects are not eligible for support. Prepared and perishable food programs are not eligible unless they are in their first two years of operation. MAZON does not fund holiday meal programs.
Areas of Interest Africa; Education; Emergency Programs; Food Banks; Food Distribution; Hispanics; Hunger; Nutrition/Dietetics; Poverty and the Poor; Public Planning/Policy; Service Delivery Programs
Sample Awards 28 nonprofit organizations nationwide—for their work to relieve hunger in the United States, $110,500 divided (2002).

Alletta Morris McBean Charitable Trust Grants 143

Alletta Morris McBean Charitable Trust
400 S El Camino Real, Ste 777
San Mateo, CA 94402-1724

Contact Charlene Kleiner, (650) 558-8480; fax: (650) 558-8481; e-mail: McBeanproperties@worldnet.att.net
Requirements Rhode Island tax-exempt organizations in Newport and Aquidneck Island are eligible.
Areas of Interest Conservation, Natural Resources; Environmental Programs; Exhibitions, Collections, Performances; Land Management; Restoration and Preservation
Sample Awards Foundation for Newport (RI)—for general operating support, $70,000. Preservation Society of Newport County (RI)—$500,000.

MCF Human Needs Grants 144
Marin Community Foundation
5 Hamilton Landing, Ste 200
Novato, CA 94949
Contact Grants Administrator, Awards Administrator, (415) 464-2500; fax:(415) 464-2555; e-mail: MCF@marincf.org
Internet http://www.marincf.org
Requirements The applicant must be a public or nonprofit organization. The proposed project must be conducted either in Marin County or benefit the residents of Marin County. Projects with regional or multicounty benefits may be funded only in proportion to the extent that they benefit the Marin County community.
Restrictions Ineligible activities include for-profit purposes, basic research, the start-up of new nonprofit organizations that duplicate existing programs or services or undertake services that can be more effectively provided by other organizations, and grants to individuals.
Areas of Interest Arts, General; Community Development; Community Service Programs; Conservation, Agriculture; Curriculum Development; Disabled; Education; Elderly; Environmental Programs; Philanthropy; Religion; Social Services; Teacher Education, Inservice; Training and Development; Transportation
Sample Awards Marin Theatre Co (Mill Valley, CA)—for its productions of class and contemporary plays, $118,000 (2002). Bolinas Community Land Trust (CA)—to transform a vacant bakery in downtown Bolinas into six affordable rental units, $300,000 (2002). Marin Community Clinic (Greenbrae, CA)—to expand its medical and healthcare services for uninsured and low-income residents of Marin County, $680,000 over three years (2002). Ecumenical Assoc for Housing (San Rafael, CA)—to build 34 transitional-housing units for low-income residents who have faced domestic violence, homelessness, mental and physical disabilities, and other difficulties, $2 million grant and loan (2002).

McKay Foundation Grants 145
McKay Foundation
303 Sacramento St, 4th Fl
San Francisco, CA 94111
Contact Robert McKay, Executive Director, (415) 288-1313 or 288-1320; fax: (415) 288-1320; e-mail: info@mckayfund.org
Internet http://www.mckayfund.org/guidelines.html
Restrictions The foundation does not fund direct service programs, capital expenditures, research, or scholarships.
Areas of Interest Asian Americans; Civil/Human Rights; Economic Development; Environmental Health; Immigrants; Leadership; Natural Resources; Racism/Race Relations; Sex Roles; Women

McKesson Foundation Grants 146
McKesson Corporation
1 Post St
San Francisco, CA 94104
Contact Marcia Argyris, Community Relations and President, (415) 983-9478; fax: (415) 983-7590; e-mail: marciaargyris@mckesson.com
Internet http://community.mckesson.com/wt/home.php
Requirements 501(c)3 tax-exempt organizations are eligible.
Restrictions Grants are not made to endowment campaigns, individuals or individual scholarships, religious organizations for religious purposes, political causes or campaigns, advertising in charitable publications, research studies or health organizations concentrating on one disease.
Areas of Interest Arts, General; At-Risk Youth; Audience Development; Children and Youth; Creative Writing; Cultural Activities/Programs; Education; Emergency Programs; Family; Health Services Delivery; Juvenile Delinquency; Literature; Performing Arts; Recreation and Leisure; School Health Programs; Social Services; Youth Programs
Sample Awards LA Theater Work (CA)—for a project that creates hands-on performing arts and literary workshops aimed at finding a positive outlet for the aggression of 3000 at-risk and incarcerated youths, $7500. Massachusetts Coalition for School-Based Health Ctrs (MA)—to hire a coordinator and to continue providing school-based health care, $125,000 over three years.

Catherine L. and Robert O. McMahan 147
Foundation Grants
Catherine L. and Robert O. McMahan Foundation
PO Box 221580
Carmel, CA 93922
Contact Neal McMahan, CEO, (831) 625-6444
Requirements Nonprofit organizations serving Monterey County, CA, are eligible.
Areas of Interest Arts, General; Conservation, Natural Resources; Cultural Activities/Programs; Education; Health Care; Restoration and Preservation; Social Services; Youth Programs
Sample Awards Guide Dogs for the Blind (San Rafael, CA)—for general support, $2500.

Milken Family Foundation Grants 148
Milken Family Foundation
1250 Fourth St, Sixth Fl
Santa Monica, CA 90401-1353
Contact Dr. Julius Lesner, Executive Vice President, (310) 570-4800; fax: (310) 570-4801; email: admin@mff.org
Internet http://www.mff.org/index.taf
Requirements Grants are made to California 501(c)3 tax-exempt organizations in the greater Los Angeles area. Grant recipients must have the financial potential to sustain the program for which funding is sought following the period of foundation support.
Restrictions Grants are not made directly to individuals.

Areas of Interest Biomedical Research; Cancer/ Carcinogenesis; Community and School Relations; Education; Educational Planning/Policy; Epilepsy; Family; Health Care; Health Promotion; Leadership; Parent Involvement; Social Services; Teacher Attitudes; Teacher Education

Sample Awards To be distributed among 100 educators nationwide—for the Milken Educator Awards, which honor outstanding elementary and secondary teachers, principals, and other education professionals, $2.5 million (2003).

Dan Murphy Foundation Grants　　149
Dan Murphy Foundation
PO Box 711267
Los Angeles, CA 90071
Contact Grants Administrator, (213) 623-3120
Areas of Interest Churches; Education; Health Care; Religion; Religious Welfare Programs
Sample Awards Council of Major Superiors of Women Religious (Washington, DC)—for general operating support, $150,000. Notre Dame High School of Sherman Oaks (CA)—for a matching grant for the capital campaign, $350,000. Thomas Aquinas College (Santa Paula, CA)—for the scholarship endowment fund, $545,511.

Myers Family Foundation Grants　　150
Myers Family Foundation
2376 Hermitage Rd
Ojai, CA 93023-9634
Contact William Myers, Trustee, (805) 646-8195; fax: (805) 646-3830
Requirements 501(c)3 nonprofit organizations are eligible. Giving is primarily made in California.
Areas of Interest Arts, General; Churches; Cultural Activities/Programs; Education; Family; Hospitals

NationsBank/Bank of America Foundation　　151 Grants
NationsBank/Bank of America Foundation
PO Box 37000, Department 3246
San Francisco, CA 94137
Contact Tracy Boyce, (704) 386-5476; e-mail: tracy. boyce@nationsbank.com
Internet http://www.bankofamerica.com/foundation
Requirements 501(c)3 nonprofit organizations with operating budgets of $50,000 or less in the following states are eligible: Arkansas, Arizona, California, Florida, Georgia, Iowa, Idaho, Illinois, Kansas, Maryland, Missouri, North Carolina, New Mexico, Oklahoma, Oregon, South Carolina, Tennessee, Texas, Virginia, Washington, and the District of Columbia.
Restrictions Organizations that receive United Way support are not eligible.
Areas of Interest Business Development; Business Education; Child Psychology/Development; Clinics; Community Development; Consumer Services; Economic Development; Education; Elementary Education; Health Care; Higher Education; Housing; Minorities; Minority Schools; Minority/Woman-Owned Business; Poverty and the Poor; Preschool Education; Regional Planning/ Policy; Secondary Education; Small Businesses; Social Services; Teacher Education; Wetlands

Sample Awards Benedict College (Columbia, SC)—to support teacher education programs at affiliate schools of the United Negro College Fund, $50,000 (1999). United Health Services (Arcata, CA)—for Health Village, a health clinic that combines traditional and modern medicine and includes a community gathering center and restoration of a major wetlands, $100,000. United Way of Anchorage (AK)—for regional planning, $50,000.

Nissan Foundation Grants　　152
Nissan North America Inc
PO Box 191
Gardena, CA 90248-0191
Contact Terri Hernandez, Program Contact, (310) 771-5594; fax: (310) 516-7967; e-mail: dierdre. dickerson@nissan-usa.com
Internet http://www.nissandriven.com/insideNissan/ CorporateOutreach/0,9396,,00.html#AS1341
Requirements The foundation supports programs in Southern California, South Central Mississippi, and Middle Tennessee only.
Areas of Interest Community Development; Economic Development; Job Training Programs

Kenneth T. and Eileen L. Norris Foundation　153 Grants
Kenneth T. and Eileen L. Norris Foundation
11 Golden Shore, Ste 450
Long Beach, CA 90802
Contact Savannah Gerringer, Grants Administrator, (562) 435-8444; fax: (562) 436-0584; e-mail: savannah@ktn.org
Internet http://www.norrisfoundation.org/grant_ funding.html
Requirements Grants are awarded to organizations in southern California.
Areas of Interest Arts, General; Biomedical Research; Citizenship; Cultural Activities/Programs; Dance; Disabled; Dramatic/Theater Arts; Environmental Programs; Food Banks; Health Care Access; Higher Education, Private; Law Enforcement; Museums; Orchestras; Private and Parochial Education; Science; Secondary Education; Youth Programs
Sample Awards Los Angeles Regional Foodbank (Los Angeles, CA)—for general operating support, $10,000.

Northrop Grumman Foundation Grants　　154
Northrop Grumman Foundation
1840 Century Park E, MS 131/CC
Los Angeles, CA 90067
Contact Grants Administrator, (888) 478-5478
Internet http://www.northropgrumman.com/com_rel/ community_main.html
Requirements Grants are limited to tax-exempt organizations.
Restrictions Grants are not made to groups with unusually high fund-raising expenses; fraternal, political, or labor organizations; religious organizations for religious purposes; individuals; or endowments.
Areas of Interest Business Administration; Business Education; Civic Affairs; Computer Grants; Computer Software; Cultural Activities/Programs; Curriculum Development; Engineering Education; Health Care; Hospitals; International Organizations; Preschool Education;

Science Education; Social Services; Technology Education; Transportation; Youth Programs

Sample Awards U of Nevada (Las Vegas, NV)—to purchase computer equipment and software for the Transportation Research Ctr, $30,000. California State U at Long Beach (Long Beach, CA)—for curriculum development in software engineering, $10,000.

Bernard Osher Foundation Grants 155

Bernard Osher Foundation
909 Montgomery St, Ste 300
San Francisco, CA 94133
Contact Patricia Tracy-Nagle, Executive Administrator, (415) 861-5587; fax: (415) 677-5868; e-mail: nagle@osherfoundation.com
Requirements California 501(c)3 organizations are eligible to apply with preference given to those serving Alameda and San Francisco Counties.
Restrictions Individuals are ineligible.
Areas of Interest Arts, General; Dental Education; Education; Humanities; Jewish Services; Nursing Education; Social Services; Vocational/Technical Education
Sample Awards University of California (Berkeley, CA)—for Incentive Awards Program, providing scholarships for financially disadvantaged students, $700,000.

Pacific Life Foundation Grants 156

Pacific Life Foundation
700 Newport Center Dr
Newport Beach, CA 92660
Contact Brenda Hardwig, Program Contact, (949) 219-3787; fax: (949) 219-7614; e-mail: info@PacificLife.com
Internet http://www.pacificlife.com/About+Pacific+Life/Foundation+or+Community
Requirements Contributions are made primarily in areas with large concentrations of Pacific Life employees: generally, Orange County, California, and the Greater Phoenix, Arizona area. Some California statewide and national organizations also receive support.
Restrictions The foundation does not support individuals; political parties, candidates, and organizations; professional associations; veterans' and labor organizations; social or athletic clubs; sectarian or denominational religious organizations; or organizations receiving United Way funding.
Areas of Interest AIDS; Arts, General; Child Abuse; Civic Affairs; Community Service Programs; Cultural Activities/Programs; Cultural Diversity; Day Care; Education; Environmental Programs; Health Care; Minorities; Parent Education; Poverty and the Poor; Social Services; Youth Programs
Sample Awards California Child Care Resource and Referral Network (CA)—to support the TrustLine Statewide Education and Public Relations Campaign, $90,000. Parent Institute for Quality Education (CA)—to provide parent instruction for nearly 4000 parents of elementary school students throughout Orange County, $50,000. Orange County Human Relations Council (CA)—to support a comprehensive program to improve intergroup relations on school campuses, $135,000.

PacifiCare Health Systems Foundation Grants 157

PacifiCare Health Systems Foundation
P O Box 25186
Santa Ana, CA 92799
Contact Program Contact, (714) 825-5233
Internet http://www.pacificare.com/commonPortal/application?origin=hnav_bar.jsp&event=bea.portal.framework.internal.portlet.event&pageid=ContentDisplay&portletid=contentdisplay&wfevent=link.viewarticle&navnode=Foundation.1
Requirements IRS 501(c)3 nonprofit organizations serving residents of PacifiCare regions in Arizona, California, Colorado, Kentucky, Nevada, Ohio, Oklahoma, Oregon, Texas, and Washington are eligible.
Restrictions The foundation will not consider grants for arts/cultural programs, associations, annual campaigns, associations—professional/technical, capital campaigns, challenge/matching grants, hosting/supporting conferences, individual support, private foundations, programs that promote religious doctrine, research, scholarships, or sponsorship of special events.
Areas of Interest Academic Achievement; Child Abuse; Children and Youth; Community Development; Counseling/Guidance; Crime Control; Elderly; Elementary Education; Family; Food Distribution; Health Care; Health Care Access; Health Promotion; Housing; Job Training Programs; Literacy; Mental Health; Secondary Education; Social Services; Youth Programs
Sample Awards Casa de Esperanza (Green Valley, AZ)—to provide intergenerational community programming for children and the elderly, $10,000. Escape Family Resource Ctr (Houston, TX)—for a school-based child abuse prevention and family support program, $10,000.

David and Lucile Packard Foundation Grants 158

David and Lucile Packard Foundation
300 Second St, Ste 200
Los Altos, CA 94022
Contact Carol Larson, VP and Director of Foundation Programs, (650) 948-7658; fax: (650) 948-5793; e-mail: inquiries@packfound.org
Internet http://www.packfound.org/index.cgi?page=program
Requirements Grant proposals are accepted only from tax-exempt, charitable organizations.
Restrictions Grants are not given to individuals or for endowment funds, religious purposes, or the purchase of computer equipment.
Areas of Interest Art Conservation; Children and Youth; Conservation, Natural Resources; Deserts and Arid Zones; Education; Employment Opportunity Programs; Ethics; Family; Fellowship Programs, General; Films; Food Distribution; Government; Job Training Programs; Mass Media; Minority Schools; Neighborhoods; Nonprofit Organizations; Organizational Theory and Behavior; Philanthropy; Population Studies; Reading Education; Restoration and Preservation; Science Education; Shelters; Social Stratification/Mobility; Training and Development; Welfare-to-Work Programs; Youth Programs
Sample Awards Arts Council Silicon Valley (San Jose, CA)—to establish an arts and cultural Web site serving

Silicon Valley, $100,000 (2004). New England Aquarium (Boston, MA)—for the Aldo Leopold Leadership Program that teaches academic environmental scientists how to explain complex scientific issues to the news media, policy makers, and the public, $1.5 million over three years (2003).

Packard Foundation Children, Families, and Communities Program—Economic Security Grants   159
David and Lucile Packard Foundation
300 Second St, Ste 200
Los Altos, CA 94022
Contact Program Officer, (650) 948-7658
Internet http://www.packard.org/index.cgi?page=childimp#economic
Requirements Eligible applicants are 501(c)3 nonprofit organizations.
Areas of Interest Career Education and Planning; Children and Youth; Employment Opportunity Programs; Family; Food Banks; Homeless Shelters; Homelessness; Hunger; Information Dissemination; Mentoring Programs; Poverty and the Poor; Public Planning/Policy; Rural Areas; School Food Programs; Social Stratification/Mobility; Volunteers; Welfare Reform; Welfare-to-Work Programs
Sample Awards Institute for Women's Policy Research (Washington, DC)—to study the well-being of children who live in low-income, single-mother families, and to examine how children's circumstances relate to the economic and work lives of single mothers, $200,000 over two years (2001).

Lucile Packard Foundation for Children's Health Grants   160
Lucile Packard Foundation for Children's Health
770 Welch Rd, Ste 350
Palo Alto, CA 94304
Contact Grants Administrator, (650) 497-8365;
e-mail: grants@lpfch.org
Internet http://www.lpfch.org/grantmaking
Requirements Nonprofit organizations and public agencies providing healthcare services to children in California's San Mateo and Santa Clara Counties are eligible.
Restrictions Grants do not support annual fund appeals; basic biomedical research; for-profit organizations; fundraising sponsorships; individuals; political activities, lobbying, or support of candidates for political office; private foundations 509(a); or religious organizations for religious purposes.
Areas of Interest Adolescent Health; Adolescents; Children and Youth; Mental Health
Sample Awards Concern for the Poor (San Jose, CA)—for the San Jose Family Shelter, which provides emergency shelter and support services for up to 35 homeless families with children, $100,000 over two years (2002). Gilroy Family Resource Ctr (Gilroy, CA)—for an after-school youth-development program that serves at-risk students attending Gilroy's two middle schools, $200,000 over three years (2002). KidPower, TeenPower, FullPower International (Santa Cruz, CA)—for workshops that teach children how to handle bully situations, stranger interactions, and inappropriate physical contact, and that provide caregivers with training activities so that they can reinforce these safety skills at home, $110,000 over two years (2002). Mid-Peninsula Boys and Girls Club (San Mateo, CA)—for the San Mateo County Smart Moves Collaborative, designed to help adolescents learn skills that can enable them to act responsibly and make positive life decisions, $142,000 over two years (2002).

George B. Page Foundation Grants   161
George B. Page Foundation
PO Box 1299
Santa Barbara, CA 93102-1299
Contact John Erickson, Trustee
Requirements Santa Barbara, CA, 501(c)3 tax-exempt organizations are eligible.
Areas of Interest Children and Youth; Poverty and the Poor; Restoration and Preservation

Pajaro Valley Community Health Grants   162
Pajaro Valley Community Health Trust
85 Nielson St
Watsonville, CA 95076
Contact Ciel Benedetto, Program Director/Grants Manager, (831) 761-5695; fax: (831) 763-6084; e-mail: info@pvhealthtrust.org
Internet http://www.pvhealthtrust.org
Requirements California 501(c)3 organizations, organizations with 501(c)3 fiscal sponsors, and school-based health programs in the primary service area consisting of zip codes 95076, 95019, and 95004, in the communities of Watsonville, Pajaro, Freedom, and Aromas are eligible.
Areas of Interest Alcohol/Alcoholism; Child/Maternal Health; Children and Youth; Conflict/Dispute Resolution; Dental Education; Dental Health and Hygiene; Drugs/Drug Abuse; Farm and Ranch Management; Health Care; Obesity; Oral Health and Hygiene; Periodontal Disorders; Preventive Dentistry; Violence in Schools; Violent Behavior
Sample Awards Ctr for Community Advocacy (Watsonville, CA)—to expand the Promotores de Salud program to include indigenous Mexican farm workers, $15,000 (2003). Family Services Assoc of the Pajaro Valley (Watsonville, CA)—to explain and provide mental-health services to farmworker families, $10,000 (2003). Salud Para la Gente (Watsonville, CA)—to develop and expand its dental-services program, $30,000 (2003). Pajaro Valley Prevention and Student Assistance (Watsonville, CA)—for a school-based violence-prevention and conflict-resolution program, $15,000 (2003).

Parker Foundation Grants   163
Parker Foundation
4365 Executive Dr, Ste 1100
San Diego, CA 92121-2133
Contact Robbin Powell, Assistant Secretary, (858) 677-1460; fax: (858) 677-1477
Requirements 501(c)3 San Diego County, CA, nonprofit organizations are eligible.
Restrictions Grants are not made to individuals nor is grant support given to religious organizations for denominational programs.

Areas of Interest AIDS; Children and Youth; Community Development; Museums; Performing Arts; Visual Arts

Sample Awards Neurosciences Institute (La Jolla, CA)—for its campaign for endowment and research operations, $50,000 (2001).

Ralph M. Parsons Foundation Grants   164
Ralph M. Parsons Foundation
1055 Wilshire Blvd, Ste 1701
Los Angeles, CA 90017
Contact Wendy Hoppe, Executive Director, (213) 482-3185; fax: (213) 482-8878
Internet http://www.rmpf.org
Requirements IRS 501(c)3 tax-exempt organizations located in Los Angeles County are eligible. (Applicant higher education institutions are not limited to this geographic area.)
Restrictions IRS 509(a) private foundations are ineligible. Funding generally is not favored for general fund-raising events, dinners, or mass mailings; direct aid to individuals; conferences, seminars, workshops, etc.; sectarian, religious, or fraternal purposes; endowment; federated fund-raising appeals; programs for which substantial support from government or other sources is available; nor support of candidates for political office or to influence legislation.
Areas of Interest AIDS; Children and Youth; Civic Affairs; Computer Grants; Cultural Activities/Programs; Elderly; Engineering Education; Equipment/Instrumentation; Family; Health Care; Hepatitis; Higher Education; Homosexuals, Female; Homosexuals, Male; Science Education; Technology Education; Women; Youth Programs
Sample Awards California Polytechnic State U at San Luis Obispo (CA)—to purchase a shake table, which is usesd to simulate earthquakes in order to develop stronger building structures, $250,000 (2001). California Institute of Technology (Pasadena, CA)—to purchase computer equipment for the study of protein structure, function, and design at the Biomolecular Structures Laboratory, $2 million. Hepatitis Experimental Therapeutics Group (Los Angeles, CA)—for research on chronic hepatitis B and C, $500,000.

Edwin W. Pauley Foundation Grants   165
Edwin W. Pauley Foundation
5670 Wilshire Blvd, Ste 1450
Los Angeles, CA 90036
Contact Grants Administrator, (323) 954-3131
Requirements California nonprofit organizations are eligible.
Restrictions Grants are not made to individuals.
Areas of Interest Children and Youth; Higher Education; Marine Sciences; Youth Programs
Sample Awards Pomona College (Claremont, CA)—to endow a professorship in environmental analysis, $1.5 million (2002).

Ann Peppers Foundation Grants   166
Ann Peppers Foundation
PO Box 50146
Pasadena, CA 91115-0146
Contact Jack Alexander, Secretary, (626) 449-0793

Requirements Southern California 501(c)3 nonprofits, colleges, and universities are eligible. Preference is given to requests from Los Angeles County.
Areas of Interest Cultural Activities/Programs; Disabled; Education; Elderly; Health Care; Health Promotion; Higher Education; Housing; Social Services; Social Services Delivery
Sample Awards Pepperdine University (Malibu, CA)—for scholarships, $35,000 (2002). Huntington Hospital, Senior Care Network (Pasadena, CA)—for operating support, $10,000 (2002). Marymount College (Rancho Palos Verdes, CA)—for scholarships, $10,000 (2002).

Evert B. and Ruth Finley Person Foundation 167 Grants
Evert B. and Ruth Finley Person Foundation
1400 N Dutton Ave, Suite 12
Santa Rosa, CA 95401-4644
Contact Evert Person, Trustee, (707) 545-3136; fax: (707) 575-5778
Requirements 501(c)3 nonprofit organizations in northern California may apply.
Areas of Interest Community Development; Engineering; Health Care; Higher Education; Journalism; Music; Religion; Science Education

Patricia Price Peterson Foundation Grants   168
Patricia Price Peterson Foundation
555 California St, 11th Fl
San Francisco, CA 94104
Contact Rudolph Peterson, Director, (415) 622-6011; fax: (415) 622-5388
Requirements California nonprofit organizations serving the San Francisco Bay area are eligible.
Areas of Interest Conservation, Natural Resources; Environmental Programs; Science Education

Ploughshares Fund Grants   169
Ploughshares Fund
Fort Mason Ctr, Bldg B, Ste 330
San Francisco, CA 94123
Contact Executive Director, (415) 775-2244; fax: (415) 775-4529; e-mail: proposals@ploughshares.org
Internet http://www.ploughshares.org/grants.php?a=2&b=0&c=0
Requirements US and international nonprofit organizations and individuals may apply.
Areas of Interest International Trade and Finance; Mass Media; New Independent States; Nuclear Safety; Nuclear Science Education; Peace/Disarmament; Public Planning/Policy; Radio

Lewis Preston Fund for Girls Education   170 Grants
Global Fund for Women
1375 Sutter St, Ste 400
San Francisco, CA 94109
Contact Executive Assistant, (415) 202-7640; fax: (415) 202-8604; e-mail: proposals@globalfundforwomen.org
Internet http://www.globalfundforwomen.org
Requirements Eligible organizations are schools, teacher training and curriculum programs, locally based

community organizations, nongovernmental organizations, local women's associations, and coalitions focused on the education of girls.

Areas of Interest Africa; Elementary Education; Language Arts Education; Mathematics Education; Nonprofit Organizations; Reading Education; Science Education; Girls' Education; Poverty and the Poor; South Asia; Teacher Education; Writing/Composition Education

Ralph's-Food 4 Less Foundation Grants 171

Ralph's-Food 4 Less Foundation
PO Box 54143
Los Angeles, CA 90054
Contact Executive Director, (310) 884-6205
Internet http://www.ralphs.com/corpnewsinfo_charitablegiving_art5.htm
Requirements Southern California nonprofits may apply.
Restrictions Individuals are ineligible for grant support.
Areas of Interest Arts, General; Cultural Activities/Programs; Disaster Relief; Education; Health Care; Hospitals; Housing; Neighborhoods; Recreation and Leisure; Youth Programs
Sample Awards Habitat for Humanity (CA)—for operating support, $78,000. DARE America (CA)—for operating support, $400,000. Boy Scouts of America (CA)—for operating support, $5000. Children's Hospital of Los Angeles (CA)—for operating support, $2500.

Righteous Persons Foundation Grants 172

Righteous Persons Foundation
2800 28th St, Ste 105
Santa Monica, CA 90405
Contact Rachel Levin, Program Officer, (310) 314-8393; fax: (310) 314-8396
Requirements US 501(c)3 nonprofits are eligible.
Restrictions Grants are not awarded to support endowments, capital campaigns, building funds, university faculty chairs, individual synagogues or day schools, research, or the publication of books or magazines.
Areas of Interest Jewish Services; Jewish Studies; Religion; Youth Programs; Curriculum Development; Civil/Human Rights; History; Television; Arts, General; Cultural Heritage Preservation
Sample Awards Raoul Wallenberg Committee of the United States (New York, NY)—to help bring its A Study of Heroes curriculum to additional US schools and communities, $20,000 matching grant over two years. Anti-Defamation League (Los Angeles, CA)—for its Stop the Hate Program, $50,000 matching grant. Clark U (Worcester, MA)—to support a doctoral fellow in its program on the history of the Holocaust, $60,000. Jewish Television Network (Los Angeles, CA)—to produce a television program on Jewish art and culture, $50,000.

San Diego Foundation Grants 173

San Diego Foundation
1420 Kettner Blvd, Ste 500
San Diego, CA 92101
Contact Program Officer, (619) 235-2300; fax: (619) 239-1710; e-mail: info@sdfoundation.org
Internet http://www.sdfoundation.org/grant
Requirements IRS 501(c)3 organizations located in San Diego County, CA, are eligible.

Restrictions Generally grants are not awarded for support of existing debts and deficits; individuals; scholarships and fellowships; performances, conferences, festivals, workshops, seminars, and other short-term events; capital/endowment campaigns or fund-raisers; religious or political purposes; and organizations outside of the county.
Areas of Interest AIDS Prevention; Arts, General; Citizenship; Cultural Activities/Programs; Cultural Diversity; Economic Development; Education; Environmental Programs; Health Care; Homosexuals, Female; Homosexuals, Male; Housing; Intervention Programs; Job Training Programs; Mental Health; Preventive Medicine; Social Services; Veterinary Medicine; Youth Programs; Zoos
Sample Awards Linda Vista Health Care Ctr (San Diego, CA)—for the Multi-Ethnic Teen AIDS Prevention project, $10,000. Zoological Society of San Diego (San Diego, CA)—for a mobile veterinary clinic, $10,000.

San Francisco Foundation Grants 174

San Francisco Foundation
225 Bush St, Ste 500
San Francisco, CA 94104-4224
Contact Grants Coordinator, (415) 733-8500; fax: (415) 477-2783; e-mail: rec@sff.org
Internet http://www.sff.org/grantmaking/documents/GrantGuidelines.doc
Requirements Grants are made to nonprofit organizations in Alameda, Contra Costa, Marin, San Francisco, and San Mateo Counties of California.
Restrictions The foundation generally does not fund projects outside the Bay Area community; long-term operating support; medical, academic, or scientific research; religious activities (religious institutions may apply for nonsectarian programs); direct assistance to individuals; or conferences or one-time events.
Areas of Interest AIDS; Arts, General; Art Education; Children and Youth; Civic Affairs; Civil/Human Rights; Ecology; Economic Development; Education; Elementary Education; Environmental Health; Environmental Programs; Familiy; Health Services Delivery; Homosexuals, Female; Homosexuals, Male; Housing; Humanities; Neighborhoods; Nonprofit Organizations; Organizational Theory and Behavior; Philanthropy; Photography; Problem Solving; Public Health; Social Services Delivery; Urban Affairs; Workforce Development
Sample Awards AIDS Project East Bay (Oakland, CA)—to strengthen its ability to provide HIV/AIDS education, prevention, and direct services, $20,000 (2003). American Cancer Society of San Francisco (CA)—to recruit volunteers to drive people with cancer to medical appointments, $25,000 (2003). Bay Area Emergency Preparedness (San Francisco, CA)—to prepare vulnerable elderly and disabled people and their home-care providers for emergencies, $20,000 (2003). Homeless Prenatal Program (San Francisco, CA)—to help homeless children and families gain access to mental-health treatment, $60,000 (2003).

Charles Schwab Corporation Foundation Grants 175

Charles Schwab Corporation Foundation
101 Montgomery St, 26th Fl, MS SF120KNY-28
San Francisco, CA 94104
Contact Elinore Robey, Senior Manager, (877) 408-5438; fax: (415) 636-3262; e-mail: CIS@Schwab.com
Requirements Nonprofit organizations in Charles Schwab communities nationwide are eligible.
Restrictions The foundation does not award grants to support fund-raising events, religious projects, lobbying, cause-related marketing, capital campaigns, seed funding, higher education, hospitals, or medical research.
Areas of Interest Art Education; Arts, General; Civic Affairs; Disabled; Disadvantaged (Economically); Elementary Education; Environmental Education; Environmental Programs; Family; Health Care; Homelessness; Minorities; Museums; Science Education; Secondary Education; Social Services; Sports; Youth Programs; Zoos
Sample Awards US Ski Team Foundation (Park City, UT)—for the disabled ski team sponsorship program, $150,000. San Francisco Museum of Modern Art (San Francisco, CA)—for general support, $40,000. East Bay Zoological Society (Oakland, CA)—for the Ctr for Science and Environmental Education program, $20,000.

Seventh Generation Fund Grants 176

Seventh Generation Fund
PO Box 4569
Arcata, CA 95518
Contact Program Director, (866) 335-7113; fax: (707) 825-7639; email: of7gen@pacbell.net
Internet http://www.7genfund.org/we_help.html
Requirements 501(c)3 (and organizations with 501(c)3 fiscal sponsors) focused in the Native American community are eligible. Mini-grant applicants need not have 501(c)3 status.
Areas of Interest Arts; Cultural Programs/Activities; Environmental Health; Environmental Law; Environmental Programs; Native Americans; Sustainable Development

Sisters of Saint Joseph Healthcare Foundation Grants 177

Sisters of Saint Joseph Healthcare Foundation
440 S Batavia St
Orange, CA 92868-3998
Contact Sidney Yeaman, Director, (714) 633-8121 ext 7119; fax: (714) 744-3164
Internet http://www.sistersofstjosephorange.com/healthfoundpurp.html
Requirements Southern California, Humbolt County, and San Francisco bay area nonprofits are eligible.
Restrictions The Foundation does not fund direct support to individuals, annual fund drives, or capital campaigns.
Areas of Interest Children and Youth; Economically Disadvantaged; Health Care Access; Health Promotion; Health and Safety Education; Health Services Delivery; Homeless; Homeless Shelters; Mental Health; Religion; Social Services Delivery; Violent Behavior

Sample Awards AIDS Services Foundation Orange County (Irvine, CA)—to fund a full-time mental health counselor for monolingual Latinos affected by HIV/AIDS, $59,277 (2003). Alliance Medical Center (Healdsburg, CA)—to increase mental health services for medically underserved Latino patients, $39,200 (2003). Assistance League of Santa Ana (Santa Ana, CA)—to provide funding for the dentist's stipend at the Dental Center which provides low-cost dental care to low-income elementary and high school students, $45,000 (2003). Boys and Girls Club of Laguna Beach (Laguna Beach, CA)—to provide staffing for the School Readiness Program and to support the nutrition program at the Even Start Preschool, $15,000 (2003).

Skoll Foundation Silicon Valley Grants 178

Skoll Foundation
60 S Market St, Ste 1000
San Jose, CA 95113
Contact Grants Administrator, (408) 278-2200; fax: (408) 278-0280; e-mail: grants@skollfund.org
Internet http://www.skollfoundation.org
Requirements Nonprofit organizations must have been nominated or invited to apply.
Areas of Interest Entrepreneurship; Social Change
Sample Awards Accion International (Boston, MA)—to develop model technology to streamline microcredit lending to help low-income women around the world run small businesses, $75,000 (2003). Benetech (Palo Alto, CA)—to support research and development for technologies benefiting humanity, $50,000 (2003). Grameen Foundation USA (WA)—to promote development of the microfinance industry in Pakistan, $50,000 (2003). U of Oxford (England)—to create the Skoll Centre on Social Entrepreneurship at the Said Business School and to support the Skoll World Forum on Social Entrepreneurship, $7.7 million (2003).

May and Stanley Smith Trust Grants 179

May and Stanley Smith Trust
720 Market St, Ste 250
San Francisco, CA 94102
Contact Dale Matheny, (415) 391-0292
Restrictions Grants are not made to individuals.
Areas of Interest Children and Youth; Disabled; Disadvantaged (Economically); Education; Elderly; Social Services; Social Services Delivery; Visual Impairments

James L. Stamps Foundation Grants 180

James L. Stamps Foundation
2000 E 4th St, Ste 230
Santa Ana, CA 92705-3814
Contact Delores Boutault, Manager, (714) 568-9740
Requirements Southern California nonprofit organizations may apply.
Areas of Interest Higher Education; Private and Parochial Education; Protestant Church; Religious Studies
Sample Awards Azusa Pacific U (CA)—for furniture and shelving for its new theology library, $100,000 (2003).

Harry and Grace Steele Foundation Grants 181

Harry and Grace Steele Foundation
441 Old Newport Blvd, Ste 301
Newport Beach, CA 92663
Contact Elizabeth Steele, Secretary, (949) 631-0418
Requirements IRS 501(c)3 tax-exempt organizations in Orange County, CA, are eligible.
Restrictions Grants are not made to individuals.
Areas of Interest Animals for Assistance/Therapy; Biotechnology; Clinics; Fine Arts; Higher Education; Hospitals; Population Control; Religion; Scholarship Programs, General; Secondary Education; Youth Programs
Sample Awards Traveler's Aid Society (Garden Grove, CA)—for an additional case worker, $50,000. Canine Companions for Independence (Rancho Santa Fe, CA)—for training of working dogs, $12,000. Chapman U—for renovation of the biotechnology laboratory, $200,000.

Sidney Stern Memorial Trust Grants 182

Sidney Stern Memorial Trust
PO Box 893
Pacific Palisades, CA 90272
Contact Marvin Hoffenberg, (310) 459-2117
Areas of Interest Children and Youth; Civil/Human Rights; Community Development; Disabled; Education; Health Care; Native Americans; Science; Social Services

Levi Strauss Foundation Grants Programs 183

Levi Strauss Foundation
PO Box 7215, 1155 Battery St
San Francisco, CA 94111
Contact Theresa Fay-Bustillos, Executive Director, (415) 501-6579; fax: (415) 501-6575; e-mail: lsf@levi.com
Internet http://www.levistrauss.com/responsibility/foundation/guidelines.htm
Requirements Giving is on a national basis with emphasis on areas of company operations. Agencies receiving funding must be accredited charitable organizations or public entities and have boards or advisory groups that reflect the population or communities being served.
Restrictions The company does not fund projects by individuals or for political, sectarian, or religious purposes; tickets for dinners or other special events; requests for sponsorships; or courtesy advertising. Research and conferences are generally not considered for funding unless they are an integral part of a larger effort that the company is supporting. The foundation does not accept unsolicited proposals.
Areas of Interest AIDS; AIDS Counseling; AIDS Education; AIDS Prevention; Children and Youth; Civil/Human Rights; Cultural Diversity; Disadvantaged (Economically); Economic Development; Employment Opportunity Programs; HIV; Health Care; Health and Safety Education; Hispanics; Homosexuals, Female; Homosexuals, Male; International Education/Training; Job Training Programs; Leadership; Microenterprises; Peace/Disarmament; Poverty and the Poor; Preventive Medicine; Racism/Race Relations; Risk Factors/Analysis; Violent Behavior; Youth Violence; Women
Sample Awards DKP Produaies S/C LTDA (Sao Paulo, Brazil)—to support a Brazilian cultural fair of activities

and lectures discussing and promoting AIDS prevention, $5000. Oak Cliff YMCA (Dallas, TX)—to fund the SOAR program, aimed to help children at low-performing schools excel in academics, $5000. Citizens' Scholarship Foundation of America (Saint Peter, MN)—for the Families of Freedom Scholarship Fund, to provide undergraduate scholarships for the spouses and children of people injured or killed as a result of the September 11 terrorist attacks, $500,000.

Streisand Foundation Grants 184

Streisand Foundation
2800 28th St, Ste 105
Santa Monica, CA 90405
Contact Margery Tabankin, Executive Director, (310) 535-3767; fax: (310) 314-8396; e-mail: stfnd@aol.com
Internet http://www.barbrastreisand.com/bio_streisand_foundation.html
Requirements 501(c)3 nonprofits and California projects in the Los Angeles area are eligible.
Restrictions Grants are not made to individuals nor do they support start-up organizations, endowments, or capital campaigns.
Areas of Interest AIDS; Children and Youth; Civil/Human Rights; Economics; Homosexuals, Female; Homosexuals, Male; Peace/Disarmament; Public Planning/Policy; Voter Educational Programs; Women; Youth Programs
Sample Awards Crossroads Community Foundation (Santa Monica, CA)—to support free quality arts and enrichment programming for children at Walgrove Elementary School in Venice, CA, $5000 (2000). Women Against Gun Violence (Culver City, CA)—to galvanize support for the reduction and prevention of gun violence, $5000 (2000). League of Conservation Voters Education Fund (Washington, DC)—to help grassroots environmental organizations motivate their members to be involved in the decision-making process, $20,000 (2000).

Stuart Foundation Grants 185

Stuart Foundation
50 California St, Ste 3350
San Francisco, CA 94111-4735
Contact Stephanie Titus, Grants Manager, (415) 393-1551; fax: (415) 393-1552
Internet http://www.stuartfoundation.org/how.html
Requirements The foundation supports programs serving California and Washington.
Restrictions The foundation does not make grants to support political activities, endowments, building campaigns, fundraising events, material acquisition, or operating funds.
Areas of Interest Child Welfare; Children and Youth; Citizenship; Classroom Instruction; Conflict/Dispute Resolution; Curriculum Development; Education; Educational Evaluation/Assessment; Educational Planning/Policy; Family; Foster Care; Middle School Education; Reading Education; Scholarship Programs, General; Secondary Education; Teacher Education; Technology; Training and Development
Sample Awards California State U (Fullerton, CA)—for the second year of a program that provides scholarships to students who are leaving foster-care placements, $324,495 (2000). West Ed (San Francisco, CA)—to de-

velop a comprehensive program combining case methods with curriculum, assessments, and a teacher network to enable teachers to teach middle school and high school students reading skills, $200,000.

Morris Stulsaft Foundation Grants 186
Morris Stulsaft Foundation
100 Bush St, Ste 825
San Francisco, CA 94104-3911
Contact Joseph Valentine, Executive Director, (415) 986-7117; fax: (415) 986-2521; e-mail: Stulsaft@aol. com
Internet http://www.stulsaft.org/approvedgrants.html
Requirements Nonprofits in California counties, including Alameda, Contra Costa, Marin, San Francisco, Santa Clara, and San Mateo, are eligible.
Restrictions Grants do not support individuals, deficit funding, emergency funding, endowments, fundraising, or special events/benefit dinners.
Areas of Interest After-School Programs; Children and Youth; Cultural Activities/Programs; Dance; Education; Health Care; Hispanics; Minorities; Poverty and the Poor; Recreation and Leisure; Social Services; Sports
Sample Awards Dance Palace (CA)—toward dance scholarships for low-income Latino children, $2500. Fort Milky Adventures Rope Course (CA)—to purchase and upgrade equipment for the Ropes Course, $5000. National Junior Tennis League of San Francisco (CA)—to expand summer after-school program for low-income minority children and youth, $7500.

Sun Microsystems Community Development Grants 187
Sun Microsystems Foundation
901 San Antonio Rd, MS PAL1-462
Palo Alto, CA 94303
Contact Andrea Gooden, Executive Director, Sun Foundation, (303) 272-2354; e-mail: corpaffrs@corp. sun.com
Internet http://www.sun.com/aboutsun/comm_invest/ giving/foundation.
html;$sessionid$0IIBBRHWZEYJJAMTA1LU4GQ
Requirements Although the foundation funds nonprofit organizations nationwide and internationally; primary focus is made in the southern San Francisco Bay area in California, the Merrimack Valley in Massachusetts, and the West Lothian District of Scotland are eligible.
Areas of Interest Business Development; Disadvantaged (Economically); Dropouts; Employment Opportunity Programs; Job Training Programs; Leadership; Secondary Education; Youth Programs
Sample Awards WGBH Educational Foundation (Boston, MA)—for the Digital Innovation Fund, which provides information-systems hardware and equipment to support WGBH's Web site, $2 million. Freemont Union High School (Sunnyvale, CA)—for a college readiness program, $13,894. Ctr for Employment Training (San Jose, CA)—for its Youth Development Initiative, $50,000.

S. Mark Taper Foundation Grants 188
S. Mark Taper Foundation
12011 San Vicente Blvd, Ste 400
Los Angeles, CA 90049

Contact Raymond Reister, Executive Director, (310) 476-5413; fax: (310) 471-4993; e-mail: rreisler@ smtfoundation.org
Requirements 501(c)3 nonprofit organizations in California are eligible for grant support.
Areas of Interest AIDS; Arts, General; Children and Youth; Disabled; Domestic Violence; Economic Development; Education; Employment Opportunity Programs; Environmental Programs; Health Care; Housing; Hunger; Immigrants; Independent Living Programs; Teen Pregnancy; Visual Impairments; Women; Academic Achievement; Disadvantaged (Economically); Shelters; Homelessness; Pregnancy
Sample Awards College Bound (Cerritos, CA)—to operate and expand a Saturday academic program that prepares underrepresented high school students for college, $50,000 (2001). Summerbridge LA (Los Angeles, CA)—for general operations of this tuition-free, year-round academic-enrichment program for disadvantaged seventh- and eighth-grade students, $10,000 (2001). Dress-4-Success (Panorama City, CA)—to provide low-income individuals with appropriate clothing for job interviews, $10,000 (2001). Elizabeth House (Pasadena, CA)—for salary support of a case manager at this shelter for homeless, abandoned, or abused pregnant women, $25,000 (2001).

Thornton Foundation Grants 189
Thornton Foundation
523 W Sixth St, Ste 636
Los Angeles, CA 90014
Contact Charles Thornton Jr., President, (213) 629-3867
Requirements California nonprofit organizations are eligible.
Areas of Interest Arts, General; Cultural Activities/Programs; Higher Education; Secondary Education

Three Guineas Fund Grants 190
Three Guineas Fund
525 Brannan St, Ste 208
San Francisco, CA 94107
Contact Grants Administrator, (415) 348-1581; fax: (415) 348-1584; e-mail: info@3gf.org
Internet http://www.3gf.org/index.html
Requirements 501(c)3 tax-exempt organizations and organizations with a fiscal agent with that status are eligible.
Restrictions The fund does not make grants to support direct service projects, unless they are of strategic interest as potentially scalable models; scholarship programs; film production; fundraising events; conferences; or individuals.
Areas of Interest Women's Education; Women's Employment

Threshold Foundation Grants 191
Threshold Foundation
PO Box 29903
San Francisco, CA 94129-0903
Contact Foundation Administrator, e-mail: tholdgrants@tides.org
Internet http://www.thresholdfoundation.org

Requirements Organizations with 501(c)3 tax exempt status are eligible. Occasionally, 501(c)4 lobbying organizations are funded.

Restrictions Grants do not support emergency or discretionary funding.

Areas of Interest Homosexuals, Female; Homosexuals, Male; Public Planning/Policy; Social Change

Sample Awards Lambi Fund of Haiti (Haiti)—for field support and training to small economic development project that are conceived and implemented by peasant, women's, or community associations and are designed to become self-sustaining within 18 months, $20,000. About Face Theatre Collective—general support for this collective of artists who, regardless of their sexuality, are committed to the creation of performances that examine and participate in the development of gay and lesbian lives, histories and experiences, $5000.

Tides Foundation Grants 192

Tides Foundation
PO Box 29903
San Francisco, CA 94129-0903
Contact Idelise Malave, Executive Director, (415) 561-6359; fax: (415) 561-6401; e-mail: imalave@ tides.org
Internet http://www.tidesfoundation.org/index_tf.cfm
Requirements Nonprofit organizations are eligible. Preference is given to nonprofits engaged in grassroots organizing.
Restrictions Tides does not accept requests from universities, schools, individuals, or corporations; nor for capital campaigns, endowments, or film production.
Areas of Interest Arts, General; Civic Affairs; Civil/Human Rights; Conservation, Natural Resources; Cultural Activities/Programs; Death Penalty; Drugs/Drug Abuse; Economics; Environmental Programs; Homosexuals, Female; Homosexuals, Male; International Relations; Native Americans; Public Planning/Policy; Women

Times Mirror Foundation Grants Program 193

Times Mirror Foundation
202 W 1st St
Los Angeles, CA 90053
Contact Michelle Williams, Executive Director, (213) 237-3945; fax: (213) 237-2116
Internet http://www.timesmirrorfoundation.org
Requirements The foundation's geographical area is restricted to Southern California (Los Angeles, Orange, Ventura, San Bernardino and Riverside counties); Stamford, Greenwich and Hartford, Connecticut; and Allentown, Pennsylvania, and Queens and Long Island, New York. An applicant organization must include evidence of 501(c)3 status when requesting funds.
Restrictions The foundation will not consider grants for production costs of films, videos, or television programs; religious or fraternal purposes; publications; conferences; or to individuals.
Areas of Interest Arts, General; Children and Youth; Civic Affairs; Civil/Human Rights; Community Service Programs; Cultural Activities/Programs; Dramatic/Theater Arts; Education; Elementary Education; Journalism; Literacy; Preschool Education; Social Services

Sample Awards Mount Baldy United Way (Rancho Cucamonga, CA)—for a community service program, $10,000 (2003). Town Hall Los Angeles (CA)—for its program series Who's Saving America's Kids?, $25,000 (2003). Food Share (Oxnard, CA)—for its capital development plan, $75,000 (2003). El Centro de Accion Social (Pasadena, CA)—for after-school tutorials and early-childhood literacy and education programs, $25,000 (2003).

Union Bank of California Foundation Grants 194

Union Bank of California Foundation
200 Pringle Ave, Ste 200
Walnut Creek, CA 94596
Contact Bob McNeely, (415) 230-4592
Requirements Nonprofits in company-operating areas are eligible, including San Diego, San Francisco, Los Angeles, Anaheim, Berkeley, Del Mar, Fresno, Irvine, Mission Grove, Pasadena, Sacramento, Salinas, San Jose, Santa Ana, and Torrance, CA.
Restrictions The foundation does not support individuals, political groups, organizations receiving a majority of funding from United Way, or groups with limited membership. Grants do not support advertising.
Areas of Interest Cancer/Carcinogenesis; Community Development; Cultural Activities/Programs; Disaster Relief; Economic Development; Economic Self-Sufficiency; Elementary Education; Health Care; Higher Education; Homelessness; Housing; Minorities; Parent Education; Performing Arts; Preschool Education; Secondary Education; Social Services; Youth Programs
Sample Awards American Red Cross-San Diego/Imperial Counties Chapter (San Diego, CA)—for relief efforts related to the recent widespread wildfires in California, $75,000 (2003). Eden Housing (Hayward, CA)—for summer youth-enrichment programs at low-cost housing complexes in the San Francisco Bay area, $20,000 (2003).

Until There's a Cure Foundation Grants 195

Until There's a Cure Foundation
560 Mountain Home Rd
Redwood City, CA 94062
Contact Grants Administrator, (800) 888-6845 or (650) 332-3200; fax: (650) 332-3210; e-mail: grants@ utac.org
Internet http://www.utac.org
Requirements 501(c)3 nonprofit US organizations are eligible for grant support.
Restrictions The foundation does not make grants for: for walk-a-thons, tournaments, or special events; to organizations with religious affiliations, unless the program is open to the entire community without regard to religious beliefs; for costs already incurred by an organization; or to fund general administration expenses of an organization rather than for specific projects and programs
Areas of Interest AIDS; AIDS Education; AIDS Prevention; Community Service Programs; Health Care; Health Policy/Planning; Health and Health Services; HIV; Vaccines; Youth Programs
Sample Awards AIDS Service Agency of North Carolina (NC)—$9000. AIDS Task Force Greater Cleveland (Cleveland, OH)—$41,818. AIDS Walk At-

lanta (Atlanta, GA)—$15,000. Wisconsin AIDS Fund (WI)—$40,000.

Valley Foundation Grants 196
Valley Foundation
16450 Los Gatos Blvd, Ste 210
Los Gatos, CA 95032-5594
Contact Program Contact, (408) 358-4545; fax: (408) 358-4548; e-mail: admin@valley.org
Internet http://www.valley.org
Requirements Nonprofit organizations in Santa Clara County, CA, may submit applications.
Restrictions The foundation avoids grants that provide more than one-fourth of an organization's total budget in a 12-month period, usually expecting community and applicant commitment to a project through cost sharing.
Areas of Interest Arts, General; Biomedical Research; Education; Educational Programs; Elderly; Employment Opportunity Programs; Food Banks; Health Care; Health and Health Services; Medical Research; Poverty and the Poor
Sample Awards California Institute for Medical Research (CA)—to fund capital improvements, $98,465. Foundation for Hope (CA)—to support expansion of employment services, $45,000. Second Harvest Food Bank (CA)—to support construction of the new food distribution center, $50,000.

Wayne and Gladys Valley Foundation Grants 197
Wayne and Gladys Valley Foundation
1939 Harrison St, Ste 510
Oakland, CA 94612-3532
Contact Michael Desler, Executive Director, (510) 466-6060; fax (510) 466-6067; e-mail: info@wgvalley.org
Requirements California nonprofits in Alameda, Contra Costa, and Santa Clara Counties are eligible.
Areas of Interest Biomedical Research; Business Education; Education; Engineering; Family; Health Care; Higher Education; Libraries, Academic; Religion; Science; Social Services; Technology Education; Youth Programs
Sample Awards Dominican U of California (San Rafael, CA)—for a new science and technology center, $2.25 million (2004). Oregon State U (Corvallis, OR)—to expand the animal hospital at the College of Veterinary Medicine, $5 million (2004).

Vanguard Public Foundation Grant Funds 198
Vanguard Public Foundation
383 Rhode Island St, Ste 301
San Francisco, CA 94103
Contact Grants Director, (415) 487-2111; fax: (415) 487-2124; e-mail: grants@vanguardsf.org
Internet http://www.vanguardsf.org
Requirements Vanguard funds new or existing organizations involved in direct organizing or advocacy that are based in northern California (i.e., all counties north of Monterey). At the time a grant is made, an organization must either be tax-exempt or have a fiscal sponsor.
Restrictions Vanguard does not fund capital campaigns or equipment purchase; organizations involved in direct services, research, or education, unless the proposed project clearly has an organizing component and cannot be supported within the general program budget; production costs for film; out-of-state travel; one-time conferences or events not integrally related to ongoing organizing; organizations with access to traditional funding sources and budgets of over $200,000 (unless the project for which funds are requested is unlikely to attract support because of its risky or controversial character); and costs already incurred.
Areas of Interest Civil/Human Rights; Community Development; Education; Equal Educational Opportunity; Equal Employment Opportunity; Homosexuals, Female; Homosexuals, Male; Poverty and the Poor; Racism/Race Relations; Sexism; Women
Sample Awards Global Fund for Women (CA)—for general operating support, $11,000. Cannery Workers' Assoc (CA)—for community development, $8000. National Coalition of Education Activists (CA)—for general operating support, $8075.

Warsh-Mott Legacy Grants 199
Warsh-Mott Legacy Foundation
469 Bohemian Hwy
Freestone, CA 95472
Contact Program Contact, (707) 874-2942; fax: (707) 874-1734; e-mail: inquiries@csfund.org
Internet http://www.csfund.org/procedures.html
Restrictions Grants do not support endowments, capital funds, or film/video projects.
Areas of Interest Agricultural Management; Biotechnology; Economic Development; Elementary Education; Environmental Health; Food Safety; International Economics; Pesticides; School Health Programs; Toxic Substances
Sample Awards U of Texas, School of Public Health (Houston, TX)—for study of dioxins and effects on public health, $20,000. Council for Responsible Genetic (Boston, MA)—for general support, $30,000. Nevada Outdoor Recreation Assoc (Carson City, NV)—to purchase equipment), $20,000.

Wilbur Foundation Grants 200
Wilbur Foundation
PO Box 3370
Santa Barbara, CA 93130-3370
Contact Gary Ricks, President, fax: (805) 563-1082; e-mail: grants@wilburfoundation.org
Internet http://www.wilburfoundation.org
Requirements Tax-exempt nonprofit organizations that reflect a concern for historical continuity and studies of a traditional nature may apply.
Restrictions Except for resident fellowships, no grants are made to individuals, and the foundation does not consider grants for general building purposes.
Areas of Interest History; Humanities; Literature; Philosophy; Religion

Women's Foundation Grants 201
Women's Foundation
340 Pine St, Ste 302
San Francisco, CA 94104
Contact Grants Administrator, (415) 837-1113; fax: (415) 837-1144; e-mail: info@twfusa.org
Internet http://www.twfusa.org/apply_ga.html

Requirements To be considered for a grant, organizations must work with low-income women and girls in California.

Restrictions The foundation does not fund capital improvements, endowments, loans, individuals, debt reduction, expenses that accrued prior to the date of the grant award, or fundraising events.

Areas of Interest Girls; Disabled; Homosexuals, Female; Familial Abuse; Female; Health Care; Human/Civil Rights; Immigrants; Leadership; Sex Roles; Violent Behavior; Women; Women's Health

Sample Awards Alaide Foppa (Mexicali, Mexico)—to coordinate government agencies and nonprofit groups working to analyze legislation, educate policy makers, and train women to advocate women's reproductive health and rights at local and federal levels in Mexico, $12,500 (2003). Asian Immigrant Women Advocates (Oakland, CA)—for community organizing, litigation, and policy advocacy related to the rights of women working in the electronics industry, $30,000 (2003). Clinica de la Raza (Oakland, CA)—for health-education services at three California high schools, $22,500 (2003). Women's Health Rights Coalition (Oakland, CA)—for advocacy efforts, activist organizing, hotlines, and operating expenses including rent, salary support, and supplies, $22,500 (2003).

Wood-Claeyssens Foundation Grants 202
Wood-Claeyssens Foundation
PO Box 30586
Santa Barbara, CA 93130-0586
Contact Pierre Claeyssens, President, (805) 966-0543; fax: (805) 966-1415
Requirements California nonprofit organizations serving Santa Barbara and Ventura Counties are eligible.
Restrictions Grants do not support tax-supported educational institutions; government-funded organizations; religious organizations, or political organizations; individuals; or medical research.
Areas of Interest Civil/Human Rights; Disabled; Dramatic/Theater Arts; Family; Health Care; Hospitals; Music; Performing Arts; Social Services; Visual Arts; Youth Programs

Colorado

Anschutz Family Foundation Grants 203
Anschutz Family Foundation
555 17th St, Ste 2400
Denver, CO 80202
Contact Sue Anschutz-Rodgers, Executive Director, (303) 293-2338; fax: (303) 299-1235; e-mail: info@anschutzfamilyfoundation.org
Internet http://www.anschutzfamilyfoundation.org/info.htm
Requirements Nonprofit organizations in Colorado may apply.
Restrictions Grants are not awarded to support capital projects, endowments, political campaigns, graduate and postgraduate research, religious organizations, special events, conferences, or trips.
Areas of Interest Children's Museums; Disadvantaged (Economically); Elderly; Family; Health Care; Home-

lessness; Job Training Programs; Literacy; Religion; Volunteers; Women's Employment; Youth Programs
Sample Awards U of Colorado Hospital (Denver, CO)—to construct a new hospital, $30 million (2001). Adult Learning Source (Denver, CO)—to support literacy training and the training of volunteer tutors, $5000. Children's Museum of Denver (Denver, CO)—for general operating support, $5000. Women's Bean Project (Denver, CO)—for job training and support for homeless women, $5000.

Aspen Valley Community Foundation Grants 204
Aspen Valley Community Foundation
110 E Hallam St, Ste 126
Aspen, CO 81611
Contact Tamara Tormohlen, Director of Programs, (970) 925-9300; fax: (970) 920-2892; e-mail: tamara@avcfoundation.org
Internet http://www.avcfoundation.org/programs.html
Requirements The foundation supports 501(c)3 organizations that enhance the quality of life in Aspen, Snowmass, the Roaring Fork Valley, and other nearby areas on the Western Slope of Colorado. The service area is generally limited to organizations located in and whose work primarily serves the citizens of Pitkin and Garfield Counties and the Basalt/El Jebel area of Eagle County.
Restrictions The foundation does not consider grants for projects that have been completed or that will be held prior to the allocations decisions; deficits, retirement of debt, or endowments; religious purposes; political campaigns or organizations that publicly take political positions; medical research; organizations primarily supported by tax-derived funding; or conduit organizations. The foundation does not give priority to applications for hospital equipment; conferences; sports/recreational groups; civic, environmental, or media projects; or arts and culture groups.
Areas of Interest Children and Youth; Citizenship; Cultural Diversity; Economic Self-Sufficiency; Education; Faculty Development; Family; Health Care; Problem Solving; Shelters; Social Services; Volunteers
Sample Awards The Buddy Program (Aspen, CO)—to support mentoring programs for at-risk youth, $20,000. Roaring Fork Family Resource Centers (Glenwood Springs, CO)—to support the start-up of a new Family Resource Center, $50,000. Glenwood Springs Soccer Club (CO)—to purchase equipment to maintain the new soccer fields at the Gates Soccer Complex, $2500 matching grant. Advocate Safehouse Project (CO)—general operating support, $10,000.

Bacon Family Foundation Grants 205
Bacon Family Foundation
PO Box 4010
Grand Junction, CO 81502
Contact Program Contact, c/o Wells Fargo Bank, (970) 257-4880; fax: (970) 243-0579
Requirements Colorado nonprofit organizations are eligible. Preference will be given to requests from western Colorado.
Areas of Interest Arts, General; Community Development; Cultural Activities/Programs; Economic Develop-

ment; Education; Environmental Programs; Food Distribution; Health Care; Hospitals; Housing; Literacy; Parks; Recreation and Leisure; Religion; Social Services Delivery; Youth Programs

Boettcher Foundation Grants 206

Boettcher Foundation
600 17th St, Ste 2210 S
Denver, CO 80202
Contact Timothy Schultz, President, (303) 534-1937; e-mail: grants@boettcherfoundation.org
Internet http://www.boettcherfoundation.org/Grants_home_page.htm
Requirements Capital projects must have 50 percent of fund-raising completed before requesting support. Organizations must be Colorado-based.
Restrictions Grants are not made to individuals or for endowment funds.
Areas of Interest Adult and Continuing Education; Basic Skills Education; Business Education; Cultural Activities/Programs; Education; Health Care; Higher Education; Hospitals; Jewish Services; Libraries; Literacy; Private and Parochial Education; Reading; Religious Studies; Scholarship Programs, General; Secondary Education; Social Services; Theology
Sample Awards Johnson and Wales U (Denver, CO)—for renovations and restoration at its Park Hill Campus, $100,000 (2003).

Bohemian Foundation Pharos Fund Grants 207

Bohemian Foundation
103 W Mountain Ave
Fort Collins, CO 80524
Contact Grants Administrator, (970) 482-4642; fax: (970) 482-6139; e-mail: info@bohemianfoundation.org
Internet http://www.bohemianfoundation.org
Requirements Colorado 501(c)3 tax-exempt organizations in Fort Collins are eligible.
Restrictions Grants do not support political campaigns or specific legislative issues; activities that have a specific religious purpose; endowments, except in rare cases; for-profit organizations; individual team requests; discriminatory programs; requests for individuals; debt reduction; fundraising events; tuition-based private schools; multiyear requests; and multiprogram requests.
Areas of Interest Children and Youth; Community Development; Community Outreach Programs; Community Service Programs; Education; Elementary Education; Family; Nonprofit Organizations; Public Affairs; Public Planning/Policy; Secondary Education; Service Delivery Programs; Youth Programs
Sample Awards Colorado State U (CO)—for the University Center for the Arts, an academic facility for programs in music, theater, and dance, and to renovate an athletic stadium, $20.1 million (2003).

Brett Family Foundation Grants 208

Brett Family Foundation
1123 Spruce St
Boulder, CO 80302
Contact Peggy Driscoll, Executive Director, (303) 442-1200; fax: (303) 442-1221; e-mail: info@brettfoundation.org

Internet http://www.brettfoundation.org
Requirements Proposals are accepted from organizations serving the communities of Boulder County and public policy initiatives serving the state of Colorado. The foundation generally funds 501(c)3 tax-exempt groups.
Restrictions The foundation rarely funds large, public charities.
Areas of Interest Child Welfare; Children and Youth; Community Development; Disadvantaged (Economically); Education; Elementary Education; Higher Education; Poverty and the Poor; Public Planning/Policy; Secondary Education; Service Delivery Programs; Social Services; Social Services Delivery
Sample Awards Boulder County AIDS Project (CO)—to support AIDS education and prevention programs, $10,000 (2002). Colorado Youth Program (CO)—for operating support, $10,000 (2002). Thorne Ecological Institute (CO)—for expansion of environmental education efforts, $10,000 (2002). Bell Policy Ctr (CO)—for operating support, $100,000 (2002).

Temple Hoyne Buell Foundation Grants 209

Temple Hoyne Buell Foundation
1666 S University Blvd, Ste B
Denver, CO 80210
Contact Grants Manager and Program Officer, (303) 744-1688; e-mail: info@buellfoundation.org
Internet http://www.buellfoundation.org/granttypes.htm
Requirements Nonprofit organizations in Colorado may apply.
Restrictions Grants do not support advertising, athletic groups, individuals, international organizations, religious or political projects, special events, past operating deficits, debt retirement, litigation, medical programs, multiyear awards, testimonial events, annual campaigns, endowments, membership drives, or conferences.
Areas of Interest Child Psychology/Development; Children and Youth; Education; Family; Literacy; Parenting Education; Preschool Education

Castle Rock Foundation Grants 210

Castle Rock Foundation
4100 E Mississippi Ave, Ste 1850
Denver, CO 80246
Contact Grants Administrator, (303) 388-1683; fax: (303) 388-1684; e-mail: generalinfo@castlerockfdn.org
Internet http://www.castlerockfoundation.org
Requirements US 501(c)3 organizations are eligible.
Restrictions Grants requests from human service agencies, museums, organizations primarily supported by tax-derived funding, endowments, scientific or medical research, publications or media projects, churches, debt retirement, special events, or individuals will be denied.
Areas of Interest Business; Civil/Human Rights; Government; Leadership; Religion
Sample Awards American Battle Monuments Commission (Arlington, VA)—for general operating support, $200,000 (2002). Global Futures (San Francisco, CA)—to support a public education campaign, $50,000 (2002). Boy Scouts of America, Denver Area Council (CO)—for the Inner City Scouting program, $250,000 (2002).

Chamberlain Foundation Grants   211

Chamberlain Foundation
501 N Main St, Ste 222
Pueblo, CO 81003
Contact Foundation Chair, David Shaw, c/o Shaw and Quigg, Attorneys, (719) 543-8596; fax: (719) 543-8599
Requirements 501(c)3 Pueblo, CO, nonprofit organizations are eligible.
Restrictions Grants do not support individuals; conferences; political activities; religious organizations whose services are limited to members; veteran, labor, fraternal, athletic, or social clubs; national health agencies concerned with specific diseases or health issues; operating expenses for United Way-supported organizations; publications, advertising campaigns, or travel expenses.
Areas of Interest Arts, General; Cultural Activities/Programs; Education; Religion; Science

Chinook Fund Grants   212

Chinook Fund
2418 W 32nd Ave
Denver, CO 80218
Contact DeQuan Mack, Program Coordinator, (303) 455-6905; fax: (303) 477-1617; e-mail: dlmack@ chinookfund.org
Internet http://www.chinookfund.org
Requirements Applicants do not have to be tax-exempt, but the activities for which funds are sought must fit within the IRS eligibility requirements for 501(c)3 organizations.
Restrictions Groups with annual budgets over $350,000 are not eligible for grants. Groups whose purpose is to provide direct services are generally not funded.
Areas of Interest Cultural Activities/Programs; Cultural Diversity; Cultural Identity; Disabled; Homosexuals, Female; Homosexuals, Male; Leadership; Minorities; Political Behavior; Poverty and the Poor; Public Policy/Planning; Race/Race Relations; Social Change; Social Stratification/Mobility
Sample Awards Jobs with Justice (Englewood, CO)—to create a series of educational forums and hearings on the growing unemployment rate in Colorado, develop programs to better serve displaced workers, and develop strategies to create jobs, $7000 (2002). Two Spirit Society of Denver (CO)—to confront and combat issues of homophobia, racism, and cultural oppression toward the Native American, non-Native, gay, lesbian, bisexual, and transgender communities, $3000 (2002). Domestic Violence Initiative for Women with Disabilities (CO)—to provide support and intervention for disabled women who are victims/survivors of domestic violence and abuse, $3000 (2002).

Colorado Council on the Arts Grants for   213
Artists and Organizations

Colorado Council on the Arts
750 Pennsylvania St
Denver, CO 80203-3699
Contact Renee Bovee, Acting Executive Director, (303) 866-2723; e-mail: renee.bovee@state.co.us
Internet http://www.coloarts.state.co.us/default.asp
Requirements The council will consider proposals from Colorado artists, organizations, and community partners that meet the following eligibility criteria: an individual artist who has been a full-time resident of Colorado for at least three years prior to application deadline; an organization that has been in existence in Colorado for at least three years and is a nonprofit, tax-exempt organization, or an agency of government; or a partnership of two or more individually identified entities (the lead of which must meet one of the previously stated eligibility criteria) that undertake a shared project that requires combining capital and human resources.
Restrictions A dollar-for-dollar cash match is required on all projects, regardless of the size the grant request.
Areas of Interest Artists' Fellowships; Arts Administration; Audience Development; Education; Economics

Colorado Interstate Gas Grants   214

Colorado Interstate Gas Company
PO Box 1087
Colorado Springs, CO 80944
Contact Mel Scott, Public Relations, (719) 420-3039; e-mail: Mel.Scott@ElPaso.com
Internet http://www.cigco.com
Requirements Colorado, Wyoming, Texas, Utah, and Kansas 501(c)3 tax-exempt organizations where the company has pipelines are eligible.
Areas of Interest Air Pollution; Child Psychology/Development; Civic Affairs; Cultural Activities/Programs; Elementary Education; Environmental Programs; Health Care; Higher Education; Minorities; Secondary Education; Social Services; Volunteers; Youth Programs

Colorado Trust Grants   215

Colorado Trust
1600 Sherman St
Denver, CO 80230-1200
Contact Grants Administrator, (888) 847-9140 or (303) 837-1200; fax: (303) 839-9034; e-mail: Rachel@ coloradotrust.org
Internet http://www.coloradotrust.org
Areas of Interest Education; Employment Opportunity Programs; Environmental Programs; Family; Health Care Access; Health Care Economics; Health Services Delivery; Human Development; Immunization Programs; Nonprofit Organizations; Social Services
Sample Awards West Regional Mental Health (Craig, CO)—for suicide-prevention programs, $150,000 over three years (2003). Suicide Prevention Partnership-Pikes Peak Region (Colorado Springs, CO)—for suicide-prevention programs, $150,000 over three years (2003).

Community Foundation Serving Boulder   216
County Grants

Community Foundation Serving Boulder County
1123 Spruce St
Boulder, CO 80302
Contact Grants Administrator, (303) 442-0436; fax: (303) 415-1542 ; e-mail: info@commfound.org
Internet http://www.commfound.org/grants/index.html
Requirements Colorado 501(c)3 nonprofit organizations serving the Boulder area are eligible.

Areas of Interest Arts, General; Civic Affairs; Community Development; Education; Environmental Programs; Health Care; Homosexuals, Female; Homosexuals, Male; Human Services; Nonprofit Organizations; Social Services

Sample Awards Colorado Music Festival (CO)—$7500. Meals on Wheels of Boulder (CO)—$2100. Legal Aid Foundation of Colorado (CO)—$2000. Redwood Day School (CO)—$35,000.

Adolph Coors Foundation Grants   217
Adolph Coors Foundation
4100 E Mississippi Ave, Ste 1850
Denver, CO 80246
Contact Program Contact, (303) 388-1636; fax: (303) 388-1684; e-mail: generalinfo@acoorsfdn.org
Internet http://www.coorsfoundation.org
Requirements Only tax-exempt, nonprofit organizations in or benefiting Colorado that do not also receive tax money are eligible to apply.
Restrictions Individuals are ineligible. The foundation does not support preschools or day-care centers.
Areas of Interest Beverages, Alcoholic; Beverages, Non-alcoholic; Culinary Arts; Disabled, Accessibility for; Economic Self-Sufficiency; Food Management; Health Care; Higher Education; Inner Cities; Jewish Services; Mental Disorders; Minorities; Religion; Secondary Education; Youth Programs
Sample Awards U of Denver (CO)—for the center for the performing arts, $1 million.

The Crowell Trust Grants   218
Henry P. Crowell and Susan C. Crowell Trust
1880 Office Club Pointe, Ste. 2200
Colorado Springs, CO 80920
Contact Paul Nelson, Executive Director, (719) 272-8300; fax: (719) 272-8305; e-mail: info@crowelltrust.org
Internet http://www.crowelltrust.org/apply.asp
Restrictions Grants are not awarded to individuals or for endowments or research.
Areas of Interest Religion

Denver Foundation Grants   219
Denver Foundation
950 S Sherman St, Ste 200
Denver, CO 80246
Contact Jim Casey, Grants Manager, (303) 300-1790; e-mail: jcasey@denverfoundation.org
Internet http://www.denverfoundation.org/800/Discretionary%20Grant%20Guidelines.PDF
Requirements Application is open to tax-exempt, nonprofit charitable organizations serving the residents of Adams, Arapahoe, Boulder, Denver, Douglas, and Jefferson Counties of Colorado.
Restrictions The foundation generally does not fund annual membership or affiliation campaigns, dinners, or special events; capital fund campaigns until 85 percent of the total campaign goal has been met; or conferences, symposiums, or workshops.
Areas of Interest Academic Achievement; Architecture; Arts, General; Children and Youth; Civic Affairs; Cultural Activities/Programs; Disabled; Economic Development; Education; Educational/Public Television;

Food Banks; Health Care; Homelessness; Housing; Natural History; Nonprofit Organizations; Nutrition/Dietetics; Runaway Youth; School-to-Work Transition; Social Services; Sports

Sample Awards Denver Ctr for Performing Arts (CO)—for drama workshops, $10,000 (2003). Colorado Parent and Child Foundation (Denver, CO)—for general operating support, $20,000 (2003). Urban League of Metropolitan Denver (CO)—for the academic-enhancement center, $15,000 (2003). Goodwill Industries (Denver, CO)—for the School to Work Program, $10,000 (2003).

John G. Duncan Trust Grants   220
John G. Duncan Trust
PO Box 5825
Denver, CO 80217
Contact Yvonne Baca, Wells Fargo Bank, (303) 293-5324
Requirements IRS 501(c)3 organizations in Colorado are eligible.
Restrictions Individuals are ineligible.
Areas of Interest Education; Health Care; Religion; Youth Programs

El Pomar Foundation Awards and Grants   221
El Pomar Foundation
10 Lake Circle
Colorado Springs, CO 80906
Contact Executive Office, (719) 633-7733 or (800) 554-7001; fax: (719) 577-7010; e-mail: grants@elpomar.org
Internet http://www.elpomar.org/grant2.html
Requirements The foundation makes grants to 501(c)3 nonprofit Colorado organizations and for activities that take place within the state.
Restrictions Proposals will be denied for deficits, debt elimination, endowments, films or other media projects, research or studies, groups that do not have fiscal responsibility for a proposed project, travel, conferences, camp programs or other seasonal activities, individual religious congregations, or efforts to influence legislation.
Areas of Interest Arts, General; Children and Youth; Community Service Programs; Dental Health and Hygiene; Disabled; Disaster Relief; Education; Environmental Programs; Health Care; Humanities; Leadership; Libraries, Public; Nonprofit Organizations; Recreation and Leisure; Rural Areas; Senior Citizen Programs and Services; Social Services; Sports; Youth Programs
Sample Awards Four Miles Historical Park (Denver, CO)—to construct a visitors center on the history of Denver, $50,000 (2003). Saint Paul Catholic Church (Colorado Springs, CO)—to construct a community center, $333,333 (2003). Pikes Peak Hospice and Palliative Care (Colorado Springs, CO)—for a new system for managing patient information, $75,000 (2003). Colorado Assoc of Nonprofit Organizations (Denver, CO)—for general operating support for statewide nonprofit programs, $20,000 (2003).

Gill Foundation Grants   222
Gill Foundation
2215 Market St, Ste 205
Denver, CO 80205

Contact Cristina Arnal, Grants Manager, (303) 292-4455; fax: (303) 292-2155; e-mail: grantsmanager@gillfoundation.org
Internet http://www.gillfoundation.org
Requirements IRS 501(c)3 organizations are eligible to apply. The foundation primarily supports gay, lesbian, bisexual, transgender, and HIV/AIDS organizations.
Areas of Interest AIDS; AIDS Education; Arts, General; Civil/Human Rights; HIV; Homosexuals, Female; Homosexuals, Male; Mass Media; Public Planning/Policy; Radio; Social Services; Technology Planning/Policy
Sample Awards National Assoc of People With AIDS (Washington, DC)—for programs related to HIV/AIDS, $15,000 (2003). Human Rights Campaign Foundation (Washington, DC)—for programs supporting lesbian, gay, bisexual, and transgender people, $100,000 (2003). Gay and Lesbian Fund of Colorado (CO)—for leadership-development activities, $26,500 distributed among seven organizations (2003). AIDS Resource Ctr of Wisconsin (Milwaukee, WI)—for HIV/AIDS prevention and human services programs, $60,000 (2003).

Mabel Y. Hughes Charitable Trust Grants 223
Mabel Y. Hughes Charitable Trust
1740 Broadway, MC 7300-483
Denver, CO 80274
Contact Judy Dowling, c/o Wells Fargo Bank, (720) 947-6725
Requirements Colorado nonprofit organizations are eligible.
Restrictions Grants do not support conferences, individuals, or ticket purchases for benefits.
Areas of Interest Community Development; Cultural Activities/Programs; Education; Health Care; Hospitals; Museums; Social Services; Youth Programs

A.V. Hunter Trust Grants 224
A.V. Hunter Trust
650 S Cherry St, Ste 535
Denver, CO 80246
Contact Sharon Siddons, Executive Director, Board of Trustees, (303) 399-5450; fax: (303) 399-5499; e-mail: sharonsiddons@avhuntertrust.org
Internet http://avhuntertrust.org
Requirements Applications are considered from charitable 501(c)3 nonprofit Colorado-based organizations or projects or endeavors located in Colorado. The trust will consider only one request from an organization during any 12-month period.
Restrictions Grants are not awarded for scholarships. Generally, the trustees will not consider grants or loans to individuals; developmental or start-up funds; research; publications, films, or other media projects; capital campaigns or capital acquisitions; scholarship aid; grants to cover deficits or retirement of debt; grants to purchase tickets for fund-raising events; or endowments. Proposals are not accepted by fax.
Areas of Interest Children and Youth; Counseling/Guidance; Day Care; Domestic Violence; Elderly; Gangs; Poverty and the Poor; Transportation
Sample Awards Safehouse for Battered Women—to support a counseling program for children, $15,000. Human Services, Inc—for program support $70,000. Colo-

rado Christian Home—to support transportation of children to a day-treatment program, $6500. Open Door Youth Gang Alternatives—for program support, $20,000.

Johns Manville Fund Grants 225
Johns Manville Fund
PO Box 5108
Denver, CO 80217-5108
Contact Community Relations Manager, (303) 978-3863; fax: (303) 978-2108
Internet http://www.jm.com/corporate/jmfund/index.shtml
Requirements States and provinces with JM communities are Arizona, Arkansas, California, Colorado, Florida, Georgia, Illinois, Indiana, Kentucky, Maine, Maryland, Mississippi, New Jersey, New York, Ohio, Oklahoma, Ontario, Pennsylvania, South Carolina, Tennessee, Texas, Virginia, Washington, and West Virginia.
Restrictions The fund does not support religious activities (nonreligious activities of faith-based groups are eligible), hospitals, special events, or private education.
Areas of Interest Arts, General; Education; Health Care; Social Services; Volunteers

Helen K. and Arthur E. Johnson Foundation 226 Grants
Helen K. and Arthur E. Johnson Foundation
1700 Broadway, Ste 1100
Denver, CO 80290-1718
Contact Stan Kamprath, Vice President and Executive Director, (800) 232-9931 or (303) 861-4127; fax: (303) 861-0607; e-mail: johnsonfoundation@cs.com
Requirements IRS 501(c)3 tax-exempt organizations serving Colorado residents may apply.
Restrictions The foundation does not make loans or fund endowments, fund conferences or give scholarships to individuals, or make multiple-year grants or award grants more frequently than once in any 12-month period.
Areas of Interest Civic Affairs; Community Service Programs; Cultural Activities/Programs; Education; Health Care; Senior Citizen Programs and Services; Social Services; Youth Programs
Sample Awards Little Sisters of the Poor (Denver, CO)—for heating and air conditioning system, $250,000 (2002). Educare Colorado (Denver, CO)—for program support, $100,000 (2002).

Carl W. and Carrie Mae Joslyn Trust Grants 227
Carl W. and Carrie Mae Joslyn Charitable Trust
PO Box 1699, Trust Department
Colorado Springs, CO 80942
Contact Sue Laabs, Vice President and Trust Officer, Bank One (719) 227-6448; fax: (719) 227-6448
Requirements Nonprofit organizations in El Paso County, CO, are eligible.
Restrictions Grants are not made to individuals or for research, scholarships, fellowships, loans, or matching gifts.
Areas of Interest Aging/Gerontology; Children and Youth; Disabled; Education; Elderly; Health Care; Hearing Impairments; Hospices; Rehabilitation/Therapy; Visual Impairments

Sample Awards Colorado School for the Deaf and Blind (Colorado Springs, CO)—for equipment and dormitory furnishings, $18,330. Junior Achievement of Colorado Springs (CO)—for materials, $1000. Pikes Peak Hospice (Colorado Springs, CO)—for respiratory equipment, $2800. Goodwill Industries of Colorado Springs (CO)—for the endowment fund, $1800.

Kenneth King Foundation Grants 228

Kenneth King Foundation
900 Pennsylvania St
Denver, CO 80203-3163
Contact Program Contact, (303) 832-3200; fax: (303) 832-4176; e-mail: jfritsch@kennethkingfoundation.org
Internet http://www.kennethkingfoundation.org
Requirements Colorado 501(c)3 nonprofit organizations are eligible. Organizations that received more than $1500 in the previous year should contact the office by phone or e-mail before submitting a proposal.
Restrictions Capital requests will not be considered.
Areas of Interest Agriculture; Arts, General; Civic Affairs; Community Development; Cultural Activities/Programs; Disabled; Disadvantaged (Economically); Elementary Education; Environmental Programs; Health Care; Higher Education; International Programs; Public Affairs; Religion; Secondary Education; Social Services Delivery; Technology; Women

Livingston Memorial Foundation Grants 229

Livingston Memorial Foundation
2815 Townsgate Rd, Ste 200
Westlake Village, CO 91361
Contact Laura McAvoy, (805) 495-7489; e-mail: lmcavoy@jdplaw.com
Requirements California nonprofit organizations serving Ventura County are eligible.
Restrictions Grants are not awarded to individuals or for projects normally financed from government sources, conferences, seminars, workshops, exhibits, travel, or publication.
Areas of Interest Health Care Access; Health Insurance; Health Services Delivery

J.M. McDonald Foundation Grants Program 230

J.M. McDonald Foundation
PO Box 3219
Evergreen, CO 80437
Contact Donald McJunkin, President, (303) 674-9300; fax (303) 674-9216
Requirements New York organizations classified as IRS 509(a) tax-exempt are eligible to apply.
Restrictions Grants are not made to individuals, or for seminars, workshops, endowment funds, fellowships, travel, exhibits, or conferences.
Areas of Interest Child/Maternal Health; Children and Youth; Day Care; Disabled; Education; Elderly; Higher Education; Hospitals; Juvenile Delinquency; Mental Retardation; Poverty and the Poor; Visual Impairments; Youth Programs
Sample Awards Nazareth College (Rochester, NY)—for its capital campaign, which includes the purchase of new property, construction, and the renovation of existing buildings, $30,000 (2003).

Monfort Family Foundation Grants 231

Monfort Family Foundation
Box 337300
Greeley, CO 80633
Contact Dave Evans, (970) 454-1357
Requirements Colorado nonprofits, primarily in Weld County, are eligible.
Areas of Interest Agriculture; Arts, General; Biomedical Research; Business Education; Cultural Activities/Programs; Education; Entrepreneurship; Health Care; Technology
Sample Awards U of Northern Colorado, College of Business Administration (Greeley, CO)—to bring nationally prominent business leaders to campus to teac. to create a technology cente. and to establish an entrepreneurship institute, a lecture series, and an instruction-improvement fund, $10.5 million (1999).

Needmor Fund Grants 232

Needmor Fund
1840 Folsom St, No 110
Boulder, CO 80302
Contact Charles Shuford, Executive Director, (303) 449-5801; e-mail: needmor@aol.com
Internet http://fdncenter.org/grantmaker/needmor
Requirements Nonprofit community-based organizations may apply for support.
Restrictions Grants do not support individuals, capital funds, scholarships, fellowships, deficit financing, replacement of lost government funding, land acquisition, purchase of buildings or equipment, publications, media, films, TV or radio productions, computer projects, or university research. Nonprofits with access to traditional funding sources generally are denied support.
Areas of Interest Churches; Civil/Human Rights; Education; Employment Opportunity Programs; Food Distribution; Grassroots Leadership; Health Care; Homosexuals, Female; Homosexuals, Male; Migrant Labor; Political Behavior; Poverty and the Poor; Safety; Shelters; Social Services
Sample Awards Congregations United for Community Action (Saint Petersburg, FL)—for operating support, $20,000. Congregations Allied for Community Improvement (Saint Louis, MO)—for operating support, $9333. Farmworkers Self-Help Inc (Dade City, FL)—for operating support, $20,000. Greater Columbus Community Shares (Columbus, OH)—for operating support, $20,000.

Piton Foundation Grants 233

Piton Foundation
370 17th St, Ste 5300
Denver, CO 80202
Contact Jeanette Montoya, (303) 572-1727; fax: (303) 628-3839; e-mail: info@piton.org
Internet http://www.piton.org/default.asp?nav_id=8
Requirements Colorado organizations are eligible for grants. Scholarship applicants must be residents of Colorado, Wyoming, Utah, Montana, North Dakota, or South Dakota.
Restrictions Grants do not support basic research, long-range support, debt reduction, building or endowment funding, or media projects.

Areas of Interest Citizenship; Civic Affairs; Economic Development; Education Reform; Family; Neighborhoods

Qwest Foundation Grants—Economic Development　　234

Qwest Foundation
1801 California St, 50th Fl
Denver, CO 80202
Contact Qwest Foundation, (303) 896-1266; e-mail: Qwest.Foundation@qwest.com
Internet http://www.qwest.com/about/company/sponsorships/foundation/innovative_Uses.html
Requirements Eligible are 501(c)3 nonprofit organizations located in the Qwest service areas.
Restrictions The foundation is unable to fund: direct grants or scholarships to individuals; political organizations; sectarian religious activities; capital campaigns, chairs, or endowments; private foundations or pass-through organizations; general operating funds for single-disease health groups; goodwill advertising; or organizations that receive 3 percent or more of funds from United Way.
Areas of Interest Adult and Continuing Education; Economic Development; School-to-Work Transition; Workforce Development

Qwest Foundation Grants—Education　　235

Qwest Foundation
1801 California St, 50th Fl
Denver, CO 80202
Contact Qwest Foundation, (303) 896-1266; e-mail: Qwest.Foundation@qwest.com
Internet http://www.qwest.com/about/company/sponsorships/foundation/investing.html
Requirements Eligible are 501(c)3 nonprofit organizations located in the Qwest service area.
Restrictions The foundation is unable to fund direct grants or scholarships to individuals; political organizations; sectarian religious activities; capital campaigns, chairs, or endowments; private foundations or pass-through organizations; general operating funds for single-disease health groups; goodwill advertising; or organizations that receive 3 percent or more of funds from United Way.
Areas of Interest Computer Grants; Educational Technology; Elementary Education; Minority Education; Native American Education; Preschool Education; Secondary Education; Technology; Volunteers

Qwest Foundation Grants—Community　　236

Qwest Foundation
1801 California St, 50th Fl
Denver, CO 80202
Contact QWest Foundation, e-mail: Qwest.Foundation@qwest.com
Internet http://www.qwest.com/about/company/sponsorships/foundation/improving.html
Requirements Eligible are 501(c)3 nonprofit organizations located in the Qwest service area.
Restrictions The foundation is unable to fund direct grants or scholarships to individuals; political organizations; sectarian religious activities; capital campaigns, chairs, or endowments; private foundations or pass-through organizations; general operating funds for single-disease health groups; goodwill advertising; or organizations that receive 3 percent or more of funds from United Way.
Areas of Interest Community Development; Economic Development; Nonprofit Organizations

Rose Community Foundation Grants　　237

Rose Community Foundation
600 S Cherry St, Ste 1200
Denver, CO 80246
Contact Grants Manager, (303) 398-7400; fax: (303) 398-7430; e-mail: rcf@rcfdenver.org
Internet http://www.rcfdenver.org/RCF.grants_sect.htm
Requirements Colorado 501(c)3 tax-exempt organizations serving Adams, Arapahoe, Boulder, Denver, Douglas, and Jefferson Counties are eligible.
Areas of Interest Alzheimer's Disease; Children and Youth; Economic Development; Education; Elderly; Elementary Education; Family; Jewish Services; Literacy; Native Americans; Public Health; Recreation and Leisure; Regional Planning/Policy
Sample Awards Volunteers of America (Denver, CO)—for programs to help older adults live independently, $150,000 partial challenge grant (2004). Creating Caring Communities (Denver, CO)—to help schools promote democracy and justice, $15,000 (2004). Doctors Care (Littleton, CO)—to provide health care to low-income, uninsured, and underinsured people, $20,000 (2004). Rocky Mountain Rabbinical Council (Denver, CO)—to expand and publicize an Introduction to Judaism course, $20,000 challenge grant (2004).

Schlessman Family Foundation Grants　　238

Schlessman Family Foundation
1301 Pennsylvania St, Ste 800
Denver, CO 80203-5015
Contact Patricia Middendorf, Treasurer, (303) 831-5683; fax: (303) 831-5676; e-mail: sffoundation@qwest.net
Internet http://www.schlessmanfoundation.org
Requirements Colorado nonprofits in the greater Denver area are eligible to receive grant support.
Areas of Interest Adult and Continuing Education; Cultural Activities/Programs; Disabled; Education; Food Distribution; Higher Education; Hospices; Religion; Social Services; Urban Areas; Youth Programs
Sample Awards Urban Ministries (CO)—for operating support, $6000. Adult Learning Source (CO)—for operating support, $7500. Greeley Meals on Wheels (CO)—for operating support, $2000. Hospice of Metro Denver (CO)—for operating support, $3000.

Schramm Foundation Grants　　239

Schramm Foundation
800 Grant St, Ste 404
Denver, CO 80203
Contact Gary Kring, President, (303) 797-6718
Requirements Colorado 501(c)3 nonprofit organizations are eligible. Preference is given to requests from the Denver area.
Restrictions Grants do not support advertising, advocacy organizations, individuals, international organiza-

tions, political organizations, religious organizations, school districts, special events, or veterans organizations.

Areas of Interest Arts, General; Civic Affairs; Children and Youth; Community Development; Elderly; Elementary Education; Health Care; Higher Education; Housing; Humanities; Medical Research; Public Affairs; Science; Social Services Delivery; Technology; Women

Sample Awards U of Denver (CO)—to renovate Spruce Hall of the Graduate School of Social Work, $100,000 (2002).

Storage Tek Foundation Grants 240

Storage Tek Foundation
One Storage Tek Dr
Louisville, CO 80028-4307
Contact Community Relations Manager, (303) 661-2461 or (800) 877-9220; e-mail: communityrelations@storagetek.com
Internet http://www.storagetek.com/company/ community_outreach/storagetek_foundation.html
Requirements Colorado nonprofits may submit letters of request.
Areas of Interest Arts, General; Computer Grants; Cultural Activities/Programs; Higher Education; Mathematics Education; Science; Science Education; Technology
Sample Awards Robert E. Loup Jewish Community Ctr (Denver, CO)—for a computer laboratory, $18,000.

Ruth and Vernon Taylor Foundation Grants 241

Ruth and Vernon Taylor Foundation
518 17th St, Ste 1670
Denver, CO 80202
Contact Friday Green, Trustee, (303) 893-5284
Requirements Organizations located in Colorado, Illinois, Montana, New Jersey, New York, Pennsylvania, Texas, or Wyoming are eligible.
Restrictions Grants are not awarded to individuals.
Areas of Interest Arts, General; Civic Affairs; Education; Environmental Programs; Health Care; Humanities; Public Affairs; Social Services

Telluride Foundation Community Grants 242

Telluride Foundation
620 Mountain Village Blvd, Ste 2B
Telluride, CO 81435
Contact Grants Administrator, (970) 728-8717; fax: (970) 728-9007
Internet http://www.telluridefoundation.org/ communitygrants.html
Requirements 501(c) tax-exempt organizations (and organizations with 501(c)3 fiscal sponsors) serving San Miguel County are eligible.
Restrictions Grants will not be awarded for building/ renovation, capital campaigns, debt reduction or retiring past operating deficits, fellowships or other grants to individuals, loans, publications (i.e., annual reports), litigation, political campaigns, economic development, or endowment funds.
Areas of Interest Arts, General; Children and Youth; Community Development; Community Outreach Programs; Community Service Programs; Cultural Activities/Programs; Education; Health Care; Sports

Sample Awards MountainFilm (Telluride, CO)—for programs for high-school students, $10,000 (2003). Ucompahgre Medical Ctr (Norwood, CO)—to purchase an X-ray machine, $25,000 (2003). Telluride Ski and Snowboard Club (CO)—for operating support, $12,500 (2003). Telluride Historical Museum (CO)—for operating support, $10,000 (2003).

Yampa Valley Community Foundation 243 Grants

Yampa Valley Community Foundation
PO Box 774965, 701 Yampa St, Bear River Ctr
Steamboat Springs, CO 80477
Contact Grants Administrator, (970) 879-8632; fax: (970) 871-0431; e-mail: brooke@yvcf.org
Internet http://www.yvcf.org/grantmaking.htm
Requirements Nonprofit organizations in Steamboat Springs, CO, may apply.
Restrictions The foundation does not make grants for debt reduction, endowments, political, or religious purposes.
Areas of Interest Community Development

Connecticut

Aetna Foundation Grants 244

Aetna Incorporated
151 Farmington Ave
Hartford, CT 06156
Contact Kellie Miller, Program Officer, (800) 273-6382 or (860) 273-0123; fax: (860) 273-4764; e-mail: aetnafoundation@aetna.com
Internet http://www.aetna.com/foundation/main_ guidelines.htm
Requirements Applicants must be 501(c)3 public charities or units of government and must be located in the United States.
Restrictions The foundation does not provide funding for capital drives, endowment funds, debt reduction, private secondary or elementary schools, annual operations of colleges and universities, medical research, political activities, religious groups, scholarships, sporting events, or fund-raising dinners.
Areas of Interest Asthma; Cardiovascular Diseases; Child/Maternal Health; Civic Affairs; Disaster Relief; Elderly; Employment Opportunity Programs; Health Care; Health Promotion; Higher Education; Immunization Programs; Jewish Services; Minority Education; Social Services; Women's Health
Sample Awards American Red Cross (Charlestown, WV)—general support for the Red Cross disaster relief operation in West Virginia, $10,000 (2002). Barnes Jewish Hospital (Saint Louis, MO)—for audio-visual equipment to allow for a multi-media classroom used to train health-care preofessionals, $10,000 (2002). Capital Region Workforce Development Board (Hartford, CT)—to support work experience and private-sector placement, $15,000 (2002). Amistad Foundation (Hartford, CT)—to support the 11th annual Juneteenth celebration, $7500 (2002).

Barnes Group Foundation Grants 245

Barnes Group Foundation
123 Main St
Bristol, CT 06010
Contact Program Officer, (603) 627-3870
Requirements 501(c)3 tax-exempt organizations in the United States (with a focus on Connecticut, Massachusetts, Maine, New Hampshire, Rhode Island, and Vermont) are eligible.
Restrictions Individuals and religious organizations are ineligible.
Areas of Interest Community Development; Environmental Programs; Higher Education

Beinecke Foundation Grants 246

Beinecke Foundation
8 Sound Shore Dr - Ste 120
Greenwich, CT 06830
Contact John Robinson, President, (203) 861-7314
Internet http://www.career.cornell.edu/students/grad/fellowships/beinecke.app.html
Requirements Nonprofits in New York and Connecticut are eligible.
Restrictions Grants are not awarded to individuals or for endowments, capital costs, renovation, equipment, conferences, publications, and media projects.
Areas of Interest Arts, General; Conservation, Natural Resources; Cultural Activities/Programs; Environmental Programs; Family Planning; Higher Education; Legal Education; Libraries; Medical Education; Museums; Religion; Restoration and Preservation; Secondary Education; Youth Programs; Zoos
Sample Awards Connecticut Fund for the Environment (CT)—for operating support, $5000. Boys Club of New York (NY)—for operating support, $2000.

J. Walton Bissell Foundation Grants 247

J. Walton Bissell Foundation
1 Cityplace, 25th Fl
Hartford, CT 06103-3408
Contact J.D. Anthony Jr., President, (860) 275-0136; fax: (860) 275-0343
Requirements Grants are awarded to 501(c)3 charitable organizations in Connecticut, Massachusetts, New Hampshire, and Vermont that are not private foundations.
Restrictions Grants are not awarded to support campaigns or endowment funding, nor are they awarded to individuals.
Areas of Interest Arts, General; Disabled; Elderly; Higher Education; Hospitals; Secondary Education; Visual Impairments; Youth Programs

Community Foundation for Greater New Haven Grants 248

Community Foundation for Greater New Haven
70 Audubon St
New Haven, CT 06510
Contact Etha Henry, Vice President for Programs, (203) 777-2386; fax: (203) 787-6584; e-mail: contactus@cfgnh.org
Internet http://www.cfgnh.org/page9075.cfm
Requirements IRS 501(c)3 nonprofit organizations in the greater New Haven area, which includes the area from Wallingford to Long Island Sound, shoreline communities from Milford to Madison, and towns in the lower Naugatuck Valley, are eligible.
Restrictions Grants are not made to support religious activities, lobbying, or travel. Only in rare instances does the foundation support research projects, publications, scholarship programs, or single event/activities.
Areas of Interest Children and Youth; Dramatic/Theater Arts; Education; Health Care; Horticulture; Restoration and Preservation, Structural/Architectural; Social Services
Sample Awards Saint Rose Parish (CT)—support for maintenance and improvements to a garden used by residents of the area as a tool to teach science to children attending Saint Rose School. Long Wharf Theater (New Haven, CT)—to refurbish and expand this 32-year-old theater, $500,000. LEAP (New Haven, CT)—to support the Community Gardens Spring program, $31,050.

Daphne Seybolt Culpeper Memorial Foundation Grants 249

Daphne Seybolt Culpeper Memorial Foundation
PO Box 206, 129 Musket Ridge Rd
Norwalk, CT 06852-0206
Contact Nicholas Nardi, (203) 762-3984
Requirements Nonprofits in Connecticut and Florida are eligible.
Restrictions Grants are not made to individuals.
Areas of Interest Social Services
Sample Awards AIDS Project New Haven (New Haven, CT)—for general support, $35,000 (2002). Center for the Arts at Mizner Park (Boca Raton, FL)—for annual campaign, $10,000 (2002).

Fairfield County Community Foundation Grants 250

Fairfield County Community Foundation
523 Danbury Rd
Wilton, CT 06897
Contact Jeanette Allam, Program Contact, (203) 563-3604; fax (203) 834-9996; e-mail: jallam@fccfoundation.org
Internet http://www.fcfoundation.org/page3809.cfm
Requirements Nonprofit organizations in Fairfield County, CT, are eligible.
Restrictions The foundation does not provide funds for religious or political purposes, deficit financing, annual giving, capital, or endowment funds.
Areas of Interest Adult and Continuing Education; Arts, General; Basic Skills Education; Children and Youth; Community Development; Computer Education/Literacy; Cultural Activities/Programs; Economic Development; Environmental Programs; Family; Health Care; Job Training Programs; Literacy; Museums; Social Services; Vocational/Technical Education; Youth Programs
Sample Awards Lockwood-Mathews Mansion Museum (Norwalk, CT)—partial support of a project to establish a comprehensive visitor orientation program, $9000. Domus Foundation (Stamford, CT)—to create an ongoing fund to support youth services organizations as public support declines, $30,000 challenge grant. Mercy Learning Ctr (Bridgeport, CT)—to support the establishment of a computer-instructor position, $15,000. Long

Island Sound Keeper Fund (Norwalk, CT)—to supplement a federal grant for a vessel pump-out program, $8500.

Fisher Foundation Grants 251
Fisher Foundation
36 Brookside Blvd
West Hartford, CT 06107
Contact Beverly Boyle, Executive Director, (860) 570-0221; fax: (860) 570-0225
Requirements Nonprofits in the greater Hartford, CT, area are eligible.
Areas of Interest Adult and Continuing Education; Economic Development; Elementary Education; Employment Opportunity Programs; Health Care; Housing; Preschool Education; Social Services

Hartford Foundation for Public Giving Grants 252
Hartford Foundation for Public Giving
85 Gillett St
Hartford, CT 06105-2643
Contact Christopher Hall, Director of Programs, (860) 548-1888; fax: (860) 524-8346; e-mail: hfpg2@hfpg.org
Internet http://www.hfpg.org/html/grants.shtml
Requirements The foundation distributes available funds to charitable organizations serving the residents of the Capitol Region. The geographic area served by the foundation includes Hartford and 29 surrounding towns in Connecticut, including Andover, Avon, Bloomfield, Bolton, Burlington, Canton, East Granby, East Hartford, East Windsor, Ellington, Enfield, Farmington, Glastonbury, Granby, Hebron, Manchester, Marlborough, Newington, Rocky Hill, Simsbury, Somers, South Windsor, Suffield, Tolland, Vernon, West Hartford, Wethersfield, Windsor, and Windsor Locks.
Restrictions The foundation does not make grants for sectarian or religious activities; directly to individuals; endowments or memorials; direct or grassroots lobbying; or conferences, research, or informational activities on topics that are primarily national or international in perspective. Grants are not made to liquidate obligations incurred at a previous date; federal, state, or municipal agencies or departments supported by taxation; or one-time events.
Areas of Interest Arts, General; Cultural Activities/Programs; Education; Health Care; Higher Education; Housing; Neighborhoods; Nonprofit Organizations; Opera/Musical Theater; Social Services
Sample Awards Saint Joseph College (West Hartford, CT)—to upgrade its quarter-mile running track and interior playing field, $300,000 (2002).

Carl J. Herzog Foundation Grants 253
Carl J. Herzog Foundation
321 Railroad Ave
Greenwich, CT 06836-0788
Contact Peter Bentley, President, (203) 629-2424
Areas of Interest Biomedical Research; Dermatology; Hospitals; Medical Education
Sample Awards Prosthetics Research Foundation (Seattle, WA)—for medical research, $50,000. Bridgeport Area Foundation (Bridgeport, CT)—for medical research, $25,000.

Huisking Foundation Grants 254
Huisking Foundation
PO Box 369
Botsford, CT 06404-0368
Contact Frank Huisking, Treasurer, (203) 426-8618
Areas of Interest Animal Care; Catholic Church; Higher Education, Private; Hospitals; Private and Parochial Education; Religious Welfare Programs; Scholarship Programs, General; Secondary Education
Sample Awards KITSAP Humane Society (OR)—for operating support, $1000. Georgetown U, Alumni Fund, (Washington, DC)—for the scholarship fund, $6000.

International Paper Company Foundation Grants 255
International Paper Company Foundation
400 Atlantic St
Stamford, CT 06921
Contact Phyllis Epp, (203) 541-8000; fax: (203) 541-8309; e-mail: comm@ipaper.com
Internet http://www.internationalpaper.com/our_world/philanthropy/outreach.html
Requirements Tax-exempt 501(c)3 nonprofit organizations are eligible to apply.
Restrictions Grants are not awarded to individuals.
Areas of Interest Arts, Genearl; Cultural Activities/Programs; Cancer/Carcinogenesis; Children and Youth; Civic Affairs; Curriculum Development; Health Care; Minority Education; Minorities; Science; Elementary Education; Environmental Programs; Secondary Education; Higher Education; Minority Education; Social Services Delivery; Women
Sample Awards National Council on Economics Education (New York, NY)—to promote economics education and understanding among students and adults, $140,000.

International Paper Grants 256
International Paper Corporation
400 Atlantic St
Stamford, CT 06921
Contact Brenda Lee, Foundation Grant Reviewer, (203) 541-8589
Internet http://www.internationalpaper.com/our_world/philanthropy/index.asp
Requirements 501(c)3 nonprofit educational, civic, cultural, and social welfare organizations in company-operating areas in Alabama, Florida, Georgia, Maine, Michigan, Minnesota, New York, North Carolina, Ohio, South Carolina, and Texas are eligible.
Areas of Interest Arts, General; Civic Affairs; Community Service Programs; Conservation, Natural Resources; Cultural Activities/Programs; Education; Environmental Education; Health Care; Hospitals; Libraries; Museums; Oncology; Public Broadcasting; Public Planning/Policy; Social Services; Volunteers
Sample Awards Museum of East Texas (TX)—to support expansion and renovation, $15,000. Buck Memorial Library (ME)—to support its capital campaign, $7500. Decatur General Hospital (AL)—to support the oncology center, $20,000.

Kaman Corporate Giving Program Grants   257
Kaman Corporation
PO Box 1
Bloomfield, CT 06002
Contact Russell Jones, Vice President, (860)
243-6308; fax: (860) 243-6365
Requirements Nonprofits in the greater Hartford region
of Connecticut are eligible.
Restrictions Grants do not support endowment funds,
recipients of state grants, agencies receiving funds from
the United Way/Combined Health Appeal, or galas and
events.
Areas of Interest Children and Youth; Disabled; Drugs/
Drug Abuse; Health Care; Mental Health

Loctite Corporate Contributions Program   258
Loctite Corporation
1001 Trout Brook Crossing
Rocky Hill, CT 06067
Contact Corporate Contributions Administrator, (860)
571-5100; e-mail: info@loctite.com
Requirements Connecticut, Ohio, and Puerto Rico
nonprofits may apply.
Areas of Interest Arts, General; Chemistry; Elementary
Education; Engineering; Fine Arts; Health Care; Higher
Education; Mathematics Education; Neighborhoods;
Science; Science Education; Secondary Education;
Technology; Technology Education; Youth Programs
Sample Awards Trinity College (Hartford, CT)—to
help establish the Math, Science, and Technology Mag-
net High School Resource Ctr, a part of the Trinity
Heights neighborhood revitalization program, $1 mil-
lion.

MassMutual Foundation for Hartford   259
    Grants
MassMutual Foundation for Hartford
140 Garden St, H356
Hartford, CT 06154
Contact Ronald Copes, Executive Director, (860)
987-2085
Requirements Grants are limited to Connecticut
tax-exempt organizations.
Restrictions No support for sectarian groups; political,
fraternal, labor, or veterans' organizations; or federated
drives outside the local area. No grants to individuals (including direct scholarships), or for endowment funds,
deficit financing, emergency funds, publications, land
acquisition, fellowships, capital fund drives outside the
local area, or goodwill advertising.
Areas of Interest Alternative Medicine; Education;
Health Care; Health Care Assessment; Health Care Economics; Health Services Delivery; Health and Safety Education; Higher Education; Housing; Middle School Education; Neighborhoods; Preventive Medicine; Scholarship Programs, General; Secondary Education; Social
Services; Women's Education
Sample Awards Connecticut Assoc for Human Services
(CT)—for operating support, $5000. Connecticut
Housing Investment Fund (CT)—for operating support,
$4000. Hartford College for Women (CT)—for financial
aid for Hartford Public High School graduates, $3000.

Katharine Matthies Foundation Grants   260
Katharine Matthies Foundation
777 Main St
Hartford, CT 06115
Contact Marjorie Alexandre Davis, Associate
Vice-President, Fleet National Bank, (860) 952-7405
Internet http://electronicvalley.org/matthies/index.
html
Requirements Connecticut 501(c)3 nonprofit organizations serving Seymour, Ansonia, Derby, Oxford,
Shelton, and Bacon Falls are eligible. Preference is given
to requests from Seymour.
Restrictions Grants do not support advertising, advo-
cacy organizations, colleges and universities, individu-
als, international organizations, political organizations,
special events, or state and local government agencies.
Areas of Interest Arts, General; Civic Affairs; Community Development; Cultural Activities/Programs; Elderly; Public Affairs; Elementary Education; Secondary
Education; Environmental Programs; Minorities; Job
Training Programs; Health Care; Housing; Humanities;
Religion; Social Services; Women; Youth Programs
Sample Awards City of Ansonia (CT)—to purchase a
mass disaster alarm system, $9000 (2003). Birmingham
Group Health Services (CT)—to support the Valley Sub-
stance Abuse Action Council program, $54,420 (2003).

Meriden Foundation Grants   261
Meriden Foundation
Michaels Bldg, Webster Plz
Waterbury, CT 06702
Contact Jeffrey Otis, c/o Webster Trust Co, (203)
578-2450
Requirements Connecticut nonprofit organizations in
the Meriden-Wallingford area are eligible.
Areas of Interest Arts, General; Children and Youth;
Civic Affairs; Health Care; Higher Education; Hospitals;
Religion; Religious Welfare Programs; Social Services;
Social Services Delivery; Youth Programs
Sample Awards Childrens Medical Ctr of Connecticut
(Hartford, CT)—for general operating support, $21,540.
Yale U, School of Law (New Haven, CT)—to support
the annual fund, $43,080. Gaylord Hospital
(Wallingford, CT)—for general support, $21,540.

Edward S. Moore Foundation Grants   262
Edward S. Moore Foundation
47 Arch St
Greenwich, CT 06830
Contact John W. Cross III, President, (203) 629-4591
Requirements Nonprofits in Connecticut and New York
may submit proposals.
Restrictions Grants are not awarded to individuals or for
deficit financing, publications, or conferences.
Areas of Interest Children and Youth; Cultural Activ-
ities/Programs; Education; Hospitals; Museums; Opera/
Musical Theater; Religion; Youth Programs
Sample Awards Children's Aid Society (New York,
NY)—$50,000. Metropolitan Opera (New York, NY)—
$35,000. Stamford Hospital Foundation (Stamford,
CT)—$430,000.

Newman's Own Inc Grants 263

Newman's Own Inc
246 Post Rd E
Westport, CT 06880
Contact Director, (203) 222-7278; fax: (203) 227-5630
Internet http://www.newmansown.com/5_good.html
Requirements IRS 501(c)3 nonprofits are eligible for grant support.
Areas of Interest Alcohol/Alcoholism; Arts, General; Children and Youth; Disabled; Drugs/Drug Abuse; Education; Elderly; Elementary Education; Family; Food Banks; Health Care; Higher Education; Housing; Literacy; Philanthropy; Secondary Education; Social Services; Sports; Wildlife

Northeast Utilities Environmental Community Grant Program 264

Northeast Utilities
PO Box 5563
Hartford, CT 06102-5563
Contact Theresa Hopkins-Staten, Chairman of the Board and President, (860) 721-4063; fax: (860) 721-4331; e-mail: hopkit@nu.com
Internet http://www.cl-p.com/community/partners/grants/nufoundation.asp
Requirements Nonprofits in company-operating areas in Connecticut, Massachusetts, and New Hampshire are eligible.
Areas of Interest Adults; Children and Youth; Ecology, Aquatic; Environmental Education; Environmental Programs; Grassroots Leadership; Solid Waste Disposal; Wildlife; Youth Programs
Sample Awards Bristol, NH—for a program for troubled youth to install a summer camp septic system, $1000. Connecticut—to an ecology club to study vernal pools in their town, $610.

Olin Corporation Charitable Trust Grants 265

Olin Corporation Charitable Trust
PO Box 4500, 501 Merritt 7
Norwalk, CT 06856-4500
Contact Carmella Piacentini, Administrator, (203) 750-3301
Internet http://www.olin.com/about/charitable.asp
Requirements Support is directed primarily to communities where Olin has a major employee presence including AL, CT, GA, IL, IN, NY, and TN.
Restrictions Grants are not awarded to individuals or for endowments.
Areas of Interest Business Education; Computer Technology; Conservation, Natural Resources; Drugs/Drug Abuse; Environmental Education; Environmental Studies; Health Care; Higher Education; Hospices; Hospitals; Housing; Safety; Science Education; Technology Education; Volunteers; Wildlife; Women; Youth Programs
Sample Awards Thirteen communities in Olin operating areas—for education programs, with a focus on computer technology and science education, $242,137 divided.

Emily Hall Tremaine Foundation Grants 266

Emily Hall Tremaine Foundation
290 Pratt St
Meriden, CT 06450
Contact Stewart Hudson, President, (203) 639-5544; fax: (203) 639-5545; e-mail: info@tremainefoundation.org
Internet http://www.tremainefoundation.org
Requirements Education-related nonprofits may apply for grant support.
Restrictions No grants are awarded to individuals or for building funds, research, or experimental demonstrations.
Areas of Interest Arts, General; Design Arts; Elementary Education; Environmental Programs; Learning Disabilities; Religion; Secondary Education
Sample Awards Baltimore Museum of Art (MD)—for awards to reward curatorial innovation and experimentation that challenge audiences and expand the boundaries of contemporary art, $100,000 (2001). Institute of Contemporary Art (Philadelphia, PA)—for an exhibition entitled Against Design: Art for Modern Living, $100,000. Aldrich Museum of Contemporary Art (Ridgefield, CT)—for an exhibition entitled Faith: The Impact of Judeo-Christian Religion on Art at the Millennium, $100,000.

Trinity Conference Center Meeting Spirit Grants 267

Trinity Conference Center
79 Lower River Rd
West Cornwall, CT 06796
Contact Jon Denn, Co-Director, (860) 672-1000; fax: (860) 672-6968; e-mail: triconfcen@aol.com
Internet http://www.trinitywallstreet.org/center/sgrants/index.html
Requirements 501(c)3 nonprofit organizations are eligible.
Areas of Interest Arts, General; Children and Youth; Education; Environmental Programs; Family; Human Services; Natural Resources; Philanthropy; Psychology; Religion; Science; Senior Citizen Programs and Services

TWS Foundation Grants 268

TWS Foundation
323 Railroad Ave
Greenwich, CT 06830-6306
Contact Thomas Smith, Trustee
Requirements Nonprofit organizations, primarily in Connecticut, New York, Rhode Island, and Texas, are eligible.
Areas of Interest Arts and Culture; Community Development; Education; Health and Health Services; Health Care; Higher Education; Human Services; Public Policy/Planning; Social Services; Social Services Delivery
Sample Awards National Center for Policy Analysis (Dallas, TX)—$200,000. Westerly Hospital Foundation (Westerly, RI)—$100,000. Philharmonic-Symphony Society of New York (New York, NY)—$10,000.

Union Carbide Foundation Grants 269

Union Carbide Foundation
39 Old Ridgebury Rd, L-4
Danbury, CT 06817-0001

Contact Grants Administrator, (203) 794-2000
Internet http://www.dow.com/ucc/index.htm
Requirements Nonprofits in company-operating areas in Connecticut, West Virginia, New Jersey, Louisiana, and Texas may apply.
Areas of Interest African Americans; Business Education; Civic Affairs; Elementary Education; Environmental Programs; Health Care; Higher Education; Hispanics; Mathematics Education; Minorities; Native Americans; Science Education; Secondary Education; Social Services; Technology; Women
Sample Awards PhD Project (Montvale, NJ)—to attract successful African American, Hispanic American, and American Indian businesspeople to teaching careers at business schools where they can serve as role models for underrepresented students, $50,000.

R.T. Vanderbilt Trust Grants 270
R.T. Vanderbilt Trust
30 Winfield St
Norwalk, CT 06855
Contact Gloria Kallas, Trustee, (203) 853-1400
Areas of Interest Conservation, Natural Resources; Cultural Activities/Programs; Education; Hospitals; Restoration and Preservation

Xerox Foundation Grants 271
Xerox Foundation
PO Box 1600, 800 Long Ridge Rd
Stamford, CT 06904
Contact Joseph Cahalan, Vice President, (203) 968-3445; fax: (203) 968-3330
Internet http://www.xerox.com/Static_HTML/xerox_foundation/en_US/xerox_foundation.html?Xcntry=USA&Xlang=en_US
Requirements Grants are made only to 501(c)3 and 509(a) organizations.
Restrictions The foundation declines requests to support individuals; capital grants (new construction or renovation); endowments or endowed chairs; organizations supported by United Way, unless permission has been granted by United Way to a member agency to conduct a capital fund drive or a special benefit; political organizations or candidates; religious or sectarian groups; or municipal, county, state, federal, or quasi-government agencies.
Areas of Interest Business; Community Development; Civic Affairs; Cultural Activities/Programs; Education; Education and Work; Homosexuals, Female; Homosexuals, Male; Information Science/Systems; Leadership; Management Sciences; Minority Education; Scholarship Programs, General; Science; Science Education; Technology; Technology Education; Volunteers
Sample Awards Monroe Community College (Rochester, NY)—for workforce training and development, $1.75 million over five years.

Delaware

Borkee-Hagley Foundation Grants 272
Borkee-Hagley Foundation
PO Box 4590
Wilmington, DE 19807

Contact Henry Silliman Jr., President, (302) 652-8616
Requirements Delaware nonprofits are eligible to apply.
Restrictions No support for specific churches or synagogues. Grants are not made to individuals.
Areas of Interest Social Services; Family; Children and Youth; Religion; Environmental Programs; Arts, General; Hospices
Sample Awards Artistic Productions Inc (Hockessin, DE)—$1000. Delaware Hospice (Wilmington, DE)—$13,000. Better Life Outreach Ministries (Newport, DE)—$5000. Children and Families First (Wilmington, DE)—$13,000.

Crestlea Foundation Grants 273
Crestlea Foundation
100 W Tenth St, Ste 1109
Wilmington, DE 19801
Contact Stephen Martinenza, Secretary-Treasurer, (302) 654-2477
Requirements Delaware nonprofits are eligible.
Areas of Interest Community Development; Conservation, Natural Resources; Health Care; Higher Education; Housing; Public Affairs; Secondary Education; Social Services
Sample Awards Episcopal Community Services (DE)—for operating support. Academy of Music (DE)—for operating support.

Delaware State Arts Council General Operating Support Grants 274
Delaware State Arts Council
820 N French St, Carvel State Office Bldg
Wilmington, DE 19801
Contact Gwen Henderson, Grants Manager, (302) 577-8282; e-mail: Gwen.Henderson@state.de.us or delarts@state.de.us
Internet http://www.artsdel.org/guide/fy04guide.pdf
Requirements Nonprofit, tax-exempt organizations in Delaware are eligible to apply. Applicants must be dedicated to maintaining a standard of high-quality artistic programming and administrative excellence; have a stable functioning board of directors that meets at least quarterly; have a paid professional staff that carries out the policies established by the board and an office designated as a place of business; and be designated by the council as eligible to apply in this category. Organizations categorized by DDA as primary institutions must have been incorporated in the state for at least four years at the time of application with the promotion, production, and/or teaching of the arts as their primary purpose.
Areas of Interest Art Education; Arts Administration

Delaware State Arts Council Opportunity Grants—Artists and Arts Organizations 275
Delaware State Arts Council
820 N French St, Carvel State Office Bldg
Wilmington, DE 19801
Contact Gwen Henderson, Grants Manager, (302) 577-8282; fax: (302) 577-6561; e-mail: Gwen.Henderson@state.de.us or delarts@state.de.us
Internet http://www.artsdel.org/information.shtml
Requirements Delaware nonprofits may apply.

Restrictions Conferences that are considered a part of the organization's membership requirement or obligation and annual conferences in the organization's discipline or (in some cases) other specific areas of arts administration are not eligible for funding.
Areas of Interest Artists' Fellowships; Arts Administration; Mentoring Programs; Training and Development; Conferences

DuPont Corporate Contributions Program 276
Grants

E.I. DuPont de Nemours and Company
PO Box 80016, Barley Mill Plaza 16/2150
Wilmington, DE 19880-0016
Contact Sylvia Banks, (302) 773-2731; fax: (302) 774-7321; e-mail: info@dupont.com
Internet http://www1.dupont.com/NASApp/dupontglobal/corp/index.jsp?GXHC_gx_session_id_=cc7c51c7cda4b1f0&GXHC_lang=en_US&GXHC_ctry=US&page=/content/US/en_US/social/outreach/index.html
Requirements The corporation gives primarily in company-operating areas. Within the United States, locations include Billings, MT; Glen Rock, NJ; Houston and La Porte, TX; Pittsburgh, PA; and Manati, Puerto Rico. Company-operating areas abroad include Argentina, Australia, Belgium, Brazil, Canada, Colombia, France, Germany, Hong Kong, Indonesia, Italy, Japan, Korea, Mexico, the Netherlands, New Zealand, Singapore, Spain, Switzerland, the United Kingdom, and Venezuela.
Restrictions DuPont does not support US nonprofit organizations not eligible for support under federal IRS code; disease-specific organizations; endowments; fraternal and veterans groups; individuals; political organizations and campaigns; sectarian organizations whose programs are limited to members of one religious group; and organizations that discriminate based on age, race, religion, color, gender, disability, national origin, ancestry, ancestry, marital status, sexual orientation, or veteran status
Areas of Interest At-Risk Youth; Business Education; Child/Maternal Health; Children and Youth; Cultural Activities/Programs; Economic Development; Education; Elementary Education; Engineering Education; Environmental Education; Environmental Programs; Health Care; Homelessness; Higher Education; Hospitals; Libraries; Life Sciences; Literacy; Museums; Performing Arts; Physical Sciences; Science; Secondary Education; Social Services; Teen Pregnancy

Good Samaritan Inc Grants 277

Good Samaritan Inc
600 Center Mill Rd
Wilmington, DE 19807
Contact Edmund Carpenter II, President, (302) 654-7558; fax: (302) 654-2376
Requirements 501(c)3 nonprofit organizations are eligible.
Restrictions Grants do not support individuals, conferences, or building funds.
Areas of Interest Dyslexia; Higher Education; Biomedical Research; Spain; Criminal Justice; Environmental Programs

Raskob Foundation for Catholic Activities 278
Grants

Raskob Foundation for Catholic Activities
PO Box 4019
Wilmington, DE 19807
Contact Maureen Horner, Grants Management, (302) 655-4440; fax: (302) 655-3223
Internet http://www.rfca.org/grantinfo.htm
Requirements Roman Catholic organizations listed in the Kenedy Directory of Official Catholic Organizations may apply.
Areas of Interest Catholic Church; Disadvantaged (Economically); Emergency Services; Health Care; Hospitals; Rehabilitation/Therapy; Social Services; Training and Development
Sample Awards Missionary Vehicle Assoc-USA (Washington, DC)—for general operating expenses, $3000. Portsmouth Abbey School (Portsmouth, RI)—for renovation and expansion of a dormitory as part of capital campaign to go co-ed, $12,500. Saint Mary's Hospital (Tucson, AZ)—to purchase rehabilitation equipment, $20,000.

District Of Columbia

AED New Voices Fellowship Program 279

Academy for Educational Development
1825 Connecticut Ave NW, Ste 744
Washington, DC 20009-5721
Contact Program Officer, (202) 884-8607; fax: (202) 884-8400; e-mail: newvoice@aed.org
Internet http://www.aed.org/newvoices
Requirements 501(c)3 nonprofit organizations that reflect diverse educational, cultural, and experiential backgrounds are eligible. Potential fellows should have completed an undergraduate or graduate degree or have comparable education, skills, and relevant experience.
Restrictions Groups with budgets of more than $5 million are not eligible.
Areas of Interest AIDS; HIV; Human/Civil Rights; International Trade and Finance; International Relations; Leadership; Migrants; Peace/Disarmament; Race/Race Relations; Reproduction; Women's Rights

Arca Foundation Grants 280

Arca Foundation
1308 19th St, NW
Washington, DC 20036
Contact Donna Edwards, Program Contact, (202) 822-9193; fax: (202) 785-1446; e-mail: grants@arcafoundation.org
Internet http://www.arcafoundation.org
Requirements The foundation accepts proposals from 501(c)3 and 509(a) tax-exempt organizations.
Restrictions The foundation does not fund organizations that provide direct social services, scholarship funds or scholarly research, capital projects or endowments, individuals, or government programs. Proposals received via fax or email will not be considered.
Areas of Interest Campaign Finance Reform; Central America; Civil/Human Rights; Cuba; Government; International Relations; Leadership; Public Health; Public Planning/Policy

Sample Awards Public Justice Foundation of Texas (Austin, TX)—for research, advocacy, and outreach to citizens and the news media about the campaign-finance system in Texas, $50,000 (2002). Youth Advocate Program International (Washington, DC)—to complete and distribute a publication on child slavery, $10,000 (2002). Cuba Policy Foundation (Washington, DC)—to educate the public about US policy toward Cuba through research, analysis, and dissemination of materials, $450,000 partial matching grant (2002). South Africa Development Fund (Boston, MA)—for the Treatment Action Campaign for AIDS Education, and for a grant fund that supports public-policy programs in South Africa, $40,000 (2002).

Bender Foundation Grants   281
Bender Foundation
1120 Connecticut Ave NW, Ste 1200
Washington, DC 20036
Contact Julie Bender Silver, President, (202) 828-9000; fax: (202) 785-9347
Requirements Grants are made to organizations and institutions in Maryland and Washington, DC. An applicant should initially send a brief letter of intent. Full proposals are by invitation.
Restrictions Grants are not made to individuals.
Areas of Interest Aging/Gerontology; Children and Youth; Elderly; Environmental Programs; Health Care; Higher Education; Jewish Services; Museums; Parent Education; Religion; Social Services; Youth Programs
Sample Awards Jewish National Fund (Silver Spring, MD)—general support, $10,000. US Holocaust Memorial Museum (Washington, DC)—general support, $1500. YMCA of Metropolitan Washington (Washington, DC)—general support, $1000.

Morris and Gwendolyn Cafritz Foundation   282 Grants
Morris and Gwendolyn Cafritz Foundation
1825 K St NW, Ste 1400
Washington, DC 20006
Contact Anne Allen, Executive Director, (202) 223-3100; fax: (202) 296-7567; e-mail: aallen@ cafritzfoundation.org or grantscoord@ cafritzfoundation.org
Internet http://www.cafritzfoundation.org/guide.htm
Requirements Nonprofits in the District of Columbia, Maryland, and Virginia may apply.
Restrictions Grants are not made to individuals or for emergency funds, deficit financing, capital, endowment, or building funds.
Areas of Interest Arts, General; Breast Cancer; Cancer Detection; Catholic Church; Community Service Programs; Children and Youth; Cultural Activities/Programs; Education; Elderly; Episcopal Church; Family; Health Care; Health and Safety Education; Hispanics; Humanities; Jewish Studies; Philanthropy; Religion
Sample Awards National Family Caregivers Assoc (Kensington, MD)—to hire a part-time representative who will work as part of its Caregiver Community Action Network, $25,000 (2002). Women's Business Ctr (Washington, DC)—to provide self-employment training to low-income parents in Washington, $20,000 (2001). Marymount U (Arlington, VA)—to study the ef-

fect of health-education programs on breast-cancer screening practices among elderly Hispanic women, $22,450.

Campaign for Human Development Grants   283
United States Conference of Catholic Bishops
3211 Fourth St NE
Washington, DC 20017-1194
Contact Program Contact, (202) 541-3213 or (202) 541-3000
Internet http://www.nccbuscc.org/cchd/grant.htm
Requirements Funds are only allocated to projects of 501(c)3 tax-exempt, incorporated organizations.
Restrictions General classifications that will not be considered for funding include direct service projects (e.g., day care centers, recreation programs, community centers, emergency shelters, etc.); projects controlled by local, state, or federal government or educational or ecclesiastical bodies; research projects, surveys, planning and feasibility studies, etc.; projects sponsored by organizations that at present receive substantial sums from other private or public funding agencies; individually owned, for-profit businesses; or projects engaged in partisan political activities.
Areas of Interest Agriculture; Business Development; Catholic Church; Economic Development; Employment Opportunity Programs; Human Development; Labor Relations; Minorities; Political Science; Poverty and the Poor; Problem Solving; Religion; Small Businesses; Training and Development
Sample Awards Farm Labor Organizing Committee (Toledo, OH)—for operating support, $60,000. Citizens Coal Council (Washington, DC)—to provide groups with technical assistance in strategic planning and to conduct training workshops, $50,000. Washington Interfaith Sponsoring Committee (Washington, DC)—to hire an organizer, $50,000. Worker Ownership Resource Ctr (Geneva, NY)—to encourage small-business development that creates jobs in low-income minority communities of upstate New York, $75,000.

CNCS Foster Grandparent Projects Grants   284
Corporation for National and Community Service
1201 New York Ave NW
Washington, DC 20525
Contact Ruth Archie, Foster Grandparent Program, National Senior Service Corps, (202) 606-5000 ext 289; e-mail: rarchie@cns.gov
Internet http://www.seniorcorps.org/research/ overview_fgp01.html
Requirements Grants are made only to state and local government agencies and private nonprofit organizations.
Restrictions Volunteers are not to supplant hiring or displace employed workers or impair existing contracts for service. No agency supervising volunteers shall request or receive compensation for services of the volunteers. Volunteers are not to be involved in and funds are not to be used for religious activities, labor or antilabor organization, lobbying, or partisan or nonpartisan political activities.
Areas of Interest Children and Youth; Education; Food Distribution; Health Care; Infants; Poverty and the Poor;

Preschool Education; Social Services; Transportation; Volunteers

Naomi and Nehemiah Cohen Foundation Grants 285

Naomi and Nehemiah Cohen Foundation
PO Box 73708
Washington, DC 20056
Contact Alison McWilliams, Associate Director, (202) 234-5454; fax: (202) 234-8797; e-mail: NNCF@erols. com
Areas of Interest Community Service Programs; Education; Jewish Services; Peace/Disarmament; Religion; Finance; Community Development
Sample Awards Jewish Federation of Greater Washington (Rockville, MD)—for the United Jewish Endowment Fund's annual campaign, $4 million (2001). Shefa Fund (Wyndmoor, PA)—to leverage investments from Jewish institutions and individuals for use by community development financial institutions, $360,000 (1999). United Jewish Appeal Federation (Rockville, MD)—operating support, $200,000.

Community Foundation for the National Capital Region Competitive Grants 286

Community Foundation for the National Capital Region
1201 15th St NW, Ste 420
Washington, DC 20005
Contact Miriam Liepold, Program Officer, (202) 263-4769; fax: (202) 955-8084; email: mliepold@ cfncr.org
Internet http://www.cfncr.org/page13847.cfm
Requirements 501(c)3 nonprofits in the metropolitan Washington region, including the District of Columbia, northern Virginia, and suburban Maryland may submit letters of inquiry. Applicants must represent a neighborhood, citywide, or regional coalition effort, with one nonprofit organization serving as project sponsor.
Areas of Interest Arts, General; Children and Youth; Civic Affairs; Communications; Community Development; Cultural Activities/Programs; Education; Family; Health Care Assessment; Homosexuals, Female; Homosexuals, Male; Leadership; Managed Care; Minority Health; Municipal Government; Neighborhoods; Public Administration; Regional Planning/Policy; Urban Affairs; Violent Behavior
Sample Awards Nine nonprofit organizations (Washington, DC)—for awards through the Bridge Builders Fund, which supports projects that promote communication and understanding between the lesbian, gay, and bisexual populations and other city residents, $60,000 divided. George Washington U (Washington, DC)—for the Ctr for Excellence in Municipal Management, $150,000. Henry Ford Health System (Troy, MI)—to develop a set of standards for measuring the quality of health care provided to minority patients in managed-care plans, $179,464.

Department of Education American Overseas Research Centers 287

Department of Education
Smithsonian Institution, 1100 Jefferson Dr, SW
Washington, DC 20560

Contact Cheryl Gibbs, (202) 502-7634; e-mail: cheryl. gibbs@ed.gov
Internet http://www.ed.gov/programs/iegpsaorc/index. html
Requirements Eligible applicants are consortia of US-based, nonprofit IHEs that have a permanent presence in the host country; 501(c)3 organizations; and organizations that receive more than 50 percent of their funding from public or private US sources.
Areas of Interest Area Studies; Higher Education; International Education/Training; International Exchange Programs; International Studies

DHHS Individual Development Accounts for Refugees Project Grants 288

Department of Health and Human Services
370 L'Enfant Promenade SW
Washington, DC 20447
Contact Program Contact, Office of Refugee Resettlement, (202) 205-2589
Internet http://www.os.dhhs.gov/grants/index.shtml
Requirements Eligible applicants include states and private, nonprofit organizations.
Areas of Interest Counseling/Guidance; Economic Self-Sufficiency; Education; Family; Finance; Homeownership; Poverty and the Poor; Refugees

District of Columbia Commission on the Arts City Arts Grants 289

District of Columbia Commission on the Arts and Humanities
410 Eighth St NW, 5th Fl
Washington, DC 20004
Contact Lionell Thomas, Program Contact, (202) 724-5613; fax: (202) 727-4135; TDD: (202) 727-3148; e-mail: lionell.thomas@dc.gov or dcart@dc.gov
Internet http://dcarts.dc.gov
Requirements Grants and awards are made to individuals and nonprofit 501(c)3 organizations based in the District of Columbia.
Areas of Interest Arts, General; Creative Writing; Cultural Diversity; Disabled; Disadvantaged (Economically); Films; Literature; Music; Visual Arts

Lois and Richard England Family Foundation Grants 290

Lois and Richard England Family Foundation
PO Box 11582
Washington, DC 20008
Contact Margaret Siegel, Program Director, (202) 244-4636; fax: (202) 244-9566; e-mail: engfmfnd@ mail.clark.net
Internet http://fdncenter.org/grantmaker/england/ guide.html
Requirements The foundation supports programs in the Washington, DC, metropolitan area, and for targeted programs to enhance Jewish life and causes locally, nationally, and internationally.
Areas of Interest AIDS; AIDS Education; AIDS Prevention; Art Education; Arts, General; Civil/Human Rights; Community Outreach Programs; Cultural Activities/Programs; Dance; Disadvantaged (Economically); Economic Self-Sufficiency; Education; Elementary Education; Employment Opportunity Programs; Family;

Gifted/Talented Education; Hispanics; Independent Living Programs; Israel; Jewish Services; Nonprofit Organizations; Peace/Disarmament; Poverty and the Poor; Preschool Education; Religious Pluralism; Secondary Education; Social Services; Training and Development; Youth Programs

Sample Awards Washington AIDS Partnership (Washington, DC)—to support AIDS prevention, education, and treatment, $10,000. New Israel Fund (Washington, DC)—to make small grants to nonprofit organizations in Israel, $15,000. Washington Ballet (Washington, DC)—for its educational programs, $10,000. Latin American Youth Ctr (Washington, DC)—for general operating support, $102,750.

John Edward Fowler Memorial Foundation Grants

291

John Edward Fowler Memorial Foundation
1725 K St NW, Ste 1201
Washington, DC 20006
Contact Richard Lee, President, (202) 728-9080; fax: (202) 728-9082
Internet http://fdncenter.org/grantmaker/fowler
Requirements Organizations in Washington, DC, and its close Maryland and Virginia suburbs are eligible.
Restrictions Grants are not made outside the metropolitan Washington, DC, area, or to/for national health organizations; government agencies; medical research; public school districts; or arts (except for intensive arts-in-education programs that directly benefit at-risk youth).
Areas of Interest Adolescent Health; Art Education; At-Risk Youth; Children and Youth; Citizenship; Elderly; Food Distribution; Grassroots Leadership; Health Care; Homelessness; Hunger; Independent Living Programs; Job Training Programs; Leadership; Literacy; Medical Programs; Mentoring Programs; Poverty and the Poor; Preschool Education; Religious Studies; Social Services; Youth Programs
Sample Awards Archbishop Carroll High Scool—for a van for the students' social service program, $28,000 (2001). Carlos Rosario International Career Ctr—for education and citizenship courses, $10,000 (2001). Casa del Pueblo—for an afterschool program, $10,000 (2001). Ctr for Artistry in Teaching—for a summer student and teacher enrichment project, $15,000 (2001).

HUD Supportive Housing Program Grants

292

Department of Housing and Urban Development
451 Seventh St SW
Washington, DC 20410
Contact John Garrity, Director, Office of Special Needs Assistance Programs, (202) 708-4300; e-mail: John_Garrity@hud.gov
Internet http://www.hud.gov/offices/cpd/homeless/programs/shp/index.cfm
Requirements States, local governments, other governmental entities; Native American tribes; private nonprofit organizations; and public, nonprofit community mental health associations are eligible to apply.
Areas of Interest Homelessness; Housing; Supportive Housing Programs

Kiplinger Foundation Grants Program

293

Kiplinger Foundation
1729 H St NW
Washington, DC 20006
Contact Andrea Wilkes, Secretary, (202) 887-6559; e-mail: foundation@kiplinger.com
Requirements Organizations with IRS 501(c)3 status in the greater Washington, DC area are eligible.
Restrictions The foundation does offer money for seed grants nor does it support scholarships.
Areas of Interest Arts, General; Civic Affairs; Cultural Activities/Programs; Disadvantaged (Economically); Education; Health Care; Higher Education; Secondary Education; Social Services; Youth Programs

Charles G. Koch Charitable Foundation Grants

294

Charles G. Koch Charitable Foundation
1450 G St NW, Ste 445
Washington, DC 20005-2001
Contact Kelly Young, Vice President, (202) 393-2354; fax: (202) 393-2355
Areas of Interest Business; Economics; Educational Planning/Policy; History; Organizational Theory and Behavior; Philosophy; Political Economics; Political Science; Public Planning/Policy; Volunteers
Sample Awards George Mason U (Fairfax, VA)—to recruit faculty members, and for programs in experimental economics, $3 million (2001).

Jacob and Charlotte Lehrman Foundation Grants

295

Jacob and Charlotte Lehrman Foundation
1027 33rd St NW, 2nd Fl
Washington, DC 20007
Contact Robert Lehrman, Vice President, (202) 338-8400; fax: (202) 338-8405; e-mail: info@lehrmanfoundation.org
Requirements Grants are made primarily to organizations in the greater metropolitan Washington, DC, area.
Restrictions Grants are not made to individuals.
Areas of Interest Biomedical Research; Elderly; Fellowship Programs, General; Health Care; Jewish Services; Recreation and Leisure; Refugees; Religion; Scholarship Programs, General; Science; Social Services; Vocational/Technical Education

J. Willard and Alice S. Marriott Foundation Grants

296

J. Willard and Alice S. Marriott Foundation
PO Box 150
Washington, DC 20058
Contact Anne Gunsteens, fax: (301) 380-8957; e-mail: anne.gunsteens@marriott.com
Restrictions Individuals are ineligible.
Areas of Interest Education; Health Care; Higher Education; Social Sciences
Sample Awards Western Governors U (Salt Lake City, UT)—to provide online courses to students located throughout the United States and in five foreign countries, $25,000 (2001). Johnson and Wales U—for scholarships in the hospitality-management program, $2 million (2001).

William G. McGowan Charitable Fund Grants   297

William G. McGowan Charitable Fund
PO Box 40515
Washington, DC 20016-0515
Contact Bernard Goodrich, Executive Director, (301) 320-8570; fax: (301) 320-8627; e-mail: goodric@aol.com or info@mcgowanfund.org
Internet http://www.mcgowanfund.org/guidelines.html
Requirements Nonprofit organizations in the following states and cities are eligible: central and northern California; Chicago; Dallas, Houston, and San Antonio, TX; District of Columbia and its Virginia suburbs; Chicago; metropolitan Kansas City, western New York; and northeast Pennsylvania.
Restrictions The fund does not support multiyear grants; accept requests online; or fund art or theatrical activities, building funds, church renovation campaigns, or endowments.
Areas of Interest Biomedical Research; Business Administration; Business Education; Cancer/Carcinogenesis; Children and Youth; Education; Health Care; Poverty and the Poor; Prostate Gland; Safety; Scholarship Programs, General; Urban Areas; Youth Violence
Sample Awards Foundation for the National Archives (Washington, DC)—for the National Archives Experience, which will make important American documents accessible to the public and teach visitors about the value of archives, $5 million (2003). Dominican U, Graduate School of Business and Information Systems (River Forest, IL)—for one full-tuition, graduate scholarships, $21,000 (2002). U of Notre Dame (IN)—to provide one full-tuition scholarships in the Master of Business Administration program at the Mendoza College of Business, $21,000 (2002).

Eugene and Agnes E. Meyer Foundation Grants   298

Eugene and Agnes E. Meyer Foundation
1400 16th St NW, Ste 360
Washington, DC 20036
Contact Julie Rogers, President, or Katherine Freshley, Senior Program Officer, (202) 483-8294; fax: (202) 328-6850; e-mail: meyer@meyerfdn.org or kfreshley@meyerfdn.org
Internet http://www.meyerfoundation.org
Requirements Eligibility includes 501(c)3 nonprofit organizations located in and primarily serving the Washington, DC, region, which is defined as: District of Columbia; the Maryland counties of Montgomery, Prince George's, Calvert, Charles, and Saint Mary's; and the Virginia counties of Arlington, Fairfax, Loudoun, Prince William, and Stafford and cities of Alexandria, Falls Church, Manassas, and Manassas Park, VA.
Restrictions The foundation does not make grants to individuals, for projects that are primarily sectarian in nature, for capital campaigns or endowment drives, or for scientific and medical research. Funding is not provided to projects outside the Washington, DC, metropolitan area.
Areas of Interest Accounting; Arts, General; Civil/Human Rights; Community Service Programs; Dramatic/Theater Arts; Education; Family; Health Care; Housing;

Humanities; Law; Mental Health; Neighborhoods; Nonprofit Organizations; Youth Programs
Sample Awards Theatre Downtown, Washington Stage Guild (Washington, DC)—for general operating support, $20,000. Empower Program (Washington, DC)—to support local youth-services programs, $20,000. Community Family Life Services (Washington, DC)—to revamp and document its financial accounting and reporting systems, $10,000. Independent Sector (Washington, DC)—for its conference program, $10,000.

Moriah Fund Grants   299

Moriah Fund
1634 I St NW, Ste 1000
Washington, DC 20006
Contact Program Contact, (202) 783-8488; fax: (202) 783-8499; e-mail: info@moriahfund.org
Internet http://www.moriahfund.org/grants/index.htm
Restrictions Grants do not support political campaigns, private foundations, arts organizations, medical research, or individuals.
Areas of Interest Cultural Diversity; Government; Community Development; Conservation, Natural Resourcese; Education; Environmental Programs; International Programs; Disadvantaged (Economically); Housing; Family Planning; Conservation, Natural Resources; Ecology; Women's Health; Human Reproduction/Fertility
Sample Awards Ctr for Community Change (Washington, DC)—for general support, including work on welfare reform and public housing, $70,000. Washington Regional Assoc of Grantmakers (Washington, DC)—for Community Development Support Collaborative, to revitalize and stabilize low-income, distressed neighborhoods in the District of Columbia, $60,000. Shefa Fund, Tzedek Economic Development Campaign, (Philadelphia, PA)—for matching grant for Local Tzedek Challenge Fund, which facilitates increased investment by Jewish communal organizations in institutions that finance efforts to revitalize low-income communities, $55,000.

NFF Community Assistance Program Grants 300

National Forest Foundation
2715 M St NW, Ste 100
Washington, DC 20007
Contact Alexandra Kenny, Conservation Programs Officer, (202) 298-6740; fax: (202) 298-6758; e-mail: akenny@natlforests.org
Internet http://www.natlforests.org/consp_05_cap.html
Areas of Interest Community Outreach Programs; Conservation, Natural Resources; Environmental Programs; Forestry/Forest Sciences; Forestry and Woodlands; Recreation and Leisure; Water Resources; Water Resources, Environmental Impacts; Waterways and Harbors; Wildlife

NNEDVF/Altria Doors of Hope Program   301

National Network to End Domestic Violence Fund
660 Pennsylvania Ave SE, Ste 303
Washington, DC 20003
Contact Grants Administrator, (202) 543-5566; fax: (202) 543-5626; e-mail: altriadoorsofhope@nnedv.org

Internet http://www.altria.com/responsibility/04_05_02_04_00_DOH_Main.asp

Requirements Eligible organizations must have a primary mission which includes the provision of direct services to survivors of domestic violence; provide shelter and/or legal advocacy services to survivors of domestic violence; be a US based non-profit, non-governmental, tax-exempt organization; have been in operation for a minimum of three years with an organization budget greater than or equal to $250,000; and have nondiscrimination policies that include ethnicity, race, religious creed, national origin, disability, sexual orientation, marital status, age, and gender.

Restrictions Applications will only be accepted through the online RFP.

Areas of Interest Community Outreach Programs; Domestic Violence; Hospitals; Legal Services; Mental Disorders; Minorities; Safety; Shelters; Training and Development

Sample Awards Hmong American Friendship Association (Milwaukee, WI)—to provide group facilitators, education groups in the workplace, and domestic violence training for Hmong elders, $24,000. Susquehanna Valley Women in Transition (Lewisburg, PA)—to implement and teach a curriculum of safe living and violence prevention to group home residents with mental disabilities, $19,000.

OCS Urban and Rural Community Economic Development (CED) Grants   302

Office of Community Services
370 L'Enfant Promenade SW
Washington, DC 20447
Contact Carol Watkins, Director, (202)401-5282
Internet http://www.acf.hhs.gov/programs/ocs

Requirements For operational, predevelopment grants and partnerships with HBCUs, private, locally initiated, nonprofit community development corporations governed by a board consisting of low income residents of the community and business and civic leaders may apply. For development grants, eligible applicants are organizations that received predevelopment grants from OCS. For administration and management expertise activities, eligible applicants are OCS-funded grantees that have completed several successful projects. For training and technical assistance programs, private nonprofit organizations that operate on a national basis and have significant and relevant experience in working with CDCs are eligible. Eligible applicants for rural community development activities are multistate, regional private nonprofit organizations that can provide training and technical assistance to small, rural communities in meeting their community facility needs.

Areas of Interest Business Development; Community Development; Economic Development; Education; Employment Opportunity Programs; Management; Minority Schools; Poverty and the Poor; Rural Areas; Training and Development; Urban Areas; Wastewater Treatment; Water Resources

Partnership Enhancement Program (PEP) Grants   303

National Tree Trust
1120 G St NW, Ste 770
Washington, DC 20005
Contact Jacqueline Bentz, Program Director, (800) 846-8733; e-mail: jbentz@nationaltreetrust.org or info@nationaltreetrust.org
Internet http://www.nationaltreetrust.org/index.cfm?cid=75000

Requirements To be eligible, the applying organization must: be a currently certified 501(c)3 nonprofit organization located within the United States; have been in existence for a minimum of two years; demonstrate that tree planting, maintenance, and education are components of the organization; and be volunteer based.

Areas of Interest Education; Forests and Woodlands; Training and Development

Prince Charitable Trusts District of Columbia Grants   304

Prince Charitable Trusts
816 Connecticut Ave NW
Washington, DC 20006
Contact Diane Glover, Grants Manager, (202) 728-0646; fax: (202) 466-4726; e-mail: info@princetrusts.org
Internet http://www.fdncenter.org/grantmaker/prince/dc_interest.html

Requirements Nonprofit organizations in Washington, DC, are eligible.

Areas of Interest After-School Programs; Art Education; Arts, General; Career Education and Planning; Community Development; Cultural Programs/Activities; Disadvantaged (Economically); Economic Development; Emergency Programs; Environmental Health; Environmental Programs; Families; Food Distribution; Health Personnel/Professions; Health Promotion; Health Services Delivery; Environmental Programs; Families; Housing; Medical Programs; Neighborhoods; Poverty and the Poor; Rural Areas; Youth Programs

Public Welfare Foundation Grants   305

Public Welfare Foundation
1200 U St NW
Washington, DC 20009
Contact Teresa Langston (Health, Disadvantaged Elderly), Adisa Douglas (Population and Reproductive Health), Dana Alston (Environment), Rebecca Davis (Community Support), Neil Stanley (Disadvantaged Youth), (202) 965-1800; fax: (202) 265-8851; e-mail: general@p
Internet http://www.publicwelfare.org/about/about.asp

Requirements Nonprofit organizations and, in certain cases, organizations without 501(c)3 status, may apply for grant support. Eligible exceptions are listed in the guidelines (available upon request).

Restrictions Grants will not be made to individuals or for religious purposes, building funds, capital improvements, endowments, scholarships, graduate work, foreign study, conferences, seminars, publications, research, workshops, consulting services, annual campaigns, or deficit financing.

Areas of Interest AIDS; African Americans; Churches; Community Service Programs; Criminal Justice; Disaster Relief; Elderly; Environmental Programs; Grassroots Leadership; HIV; Hazardous Wastes; Health Care; Human Reproduction/Fertility; Hunger; Native Americans; Population Studies; Religion; Vocational/Technical Education; Youth Programs

Sample Awards Lambi Fund of Haiti (Washington, DC)—for general operating support, $50,000 (2003). Disabled Rights Action Committee (Salt Lake City, UT)—for the Our Homes Not Nursing Homes project, $40,000 (2003). Georgetown Public Policy Institute (Washington, DC)—for the Senior Fellow Program, $150,000 (2003). Research Action Information Network for the Bodily Integrity of Women (New York, NY)—for the African Immigrant Women Program, $45,000 (2003).

Luther I. Replogle Foundation Grants 306

Luther I. Replogle Foundation
1 Dupont Circle NW, Ste 700
Washington, DC 20036-1133
Contact Grants Administrator, (202) 955-0688; fax (202) 467-0790; e-mail: info@lirf.org
Internet http://www.lirf.org
Requirements 501(c)3 nonprofits in Chicago, IL; Minneapolis, MN; Palm Beach County, FL; and Washington, DC, are eligible. Preference is given to organizations with small or modest operating budgets
Areas of Interest Arts, General; After-School Programs; Archaeology; Archaeology Education; Art Education; At-Risk Youth; Charter Schools; Children and Youth; Cultural Activities; Education; Elementary Education; Geography; Geography Education; Homelessness; Housing; Inner Cities; Migrant Labor; Migrants; Poverty and the Poor; Science Education; Secondary Education; Service Delivery Programs; Shelters; Youth Programs
Sample Awards John Carter Brown Library (Providence, RI)—for the conservation of maps and globes, $5000 (2002). Jobs for Youth (Chicago, IL), $2500 (2002). Planned Parenthood of Chicago (IL)—to support teen-pregancy prevention, $7500 (2002). Wayne Bush, United States Department of State (Washington, DC)—recipient of the 2001 Luther I. Replogle Award for Management Improvement, $5000 (2002).

Hattie M. Strong Foundation Grants 307

Hattie M. Strong Foundation
1620 Eye St, Ste 700
Washington, DC 20006
Contact Judith Cyphers, Grants Director, (202) 331-1619; fax: (202) 466-2894; e-mail: hmsf@hmstrongfoundation.org
Internet http://www.hmstrongfoundation.org
Requirements Nonprofit organizations serving the Washington, DC, metropolitan area may apply.
Restrictions The foundation does not make grants for buildings, endowments, equipment, research, conferences, special events, benefits, activities designed to educate the general public, and programs with a national or international scope.
Areas of Interest Academic Achievement; Basic Skills Education; Gifted/Talented Education; Job Training Programs; Literacy; Reading; Remedial Education; Vo-

cational/Technical Education; Adult and Continuing Education
Sample Awards Campagna Ctr (Alexandria, VA)—to support the Reading Specialist Program for first- to third-grade students at Mount Vernon Elementary School, $6000. Carlos Rosario Adult and Career Ctr (Washington, DC)—for general support to expand this adult education program, $6500.

Wallace Global Fund Grants 308

Wallace Global Fund
1990 M St NW, Ste 250
Washington, DC 20036
Contact Catherine Cameron, Executive Director, (202) 452-1530; fax: (202) 452-0922; e-mail: tkroll@wgf.org
Internet http://www.wgf.org/grants_finances.html
Requirements Interested applicants are encouraged to submit a concept paper of three pages or less before submitting a full proposal.
Restrictions Grants are not made to: individuals; universities; for-profit organizations; endowments; capital fund projects; scholarships; conferences; books or magazines; building construction; or travel (not including project-related travel). The fund does not support film or video projects, the acquisition of land, or grants intended to support candidates for political office.
Areas of Interest Consumer Behavior; Economic Development; Economic Theory; Environmental Economics; Environmental Law; Environmental Planning/Policy; Environmental Programs; Forestry Management; Globalization; Human Reproduction/Fertility; International Programs; Population Control; Population Studies; Public Planning/Policy; Social Measurement and Indicators; Sustainable Development
Sample Awards Rainforest Action Network—for the Old Growth Campaign, aimed at shifting the forest products industry away from old growth wood and toward sustainable alternatives, $40,000. Advocates for Youth—support for Standing Up for Research-Based Approaches to Adolescent Sexual Health, $30,000 over six months.

Washington Post Contributions Program 309 Grants

Washington Post Educational Foundation
1150 15th St NW
Washington, DC 20071
Contact Eric Grant, Director of Community Affairs and Contributions, (202) 334-6834; fax: (202) 334-5609
Internet http://washpost.com/community/charities/contributions.shtml
Restrictions Funding is not available for individuals; national or other organizations whose programs do not directly serve Washington-area needs; religious organizations for religious purposes; fraternal, membership, or veterans organizations or athletic teams; volunteer fire/emergency services, or similar groups; political action or advocacy groups; multiyear grants; challenge grants; third-party fund-raising efforts; conferences; research; or start-up projects. Applications are not accepted.

Areas of Interest Arts, General; Civic Affairs; Community Service Programs; Disabled; Education; Health Care; Poverty and the Poor; Social Services

Florida

Anthony R. Abraham Foundation Grants 310
Anthony R. Abraham Foundation
6600 SW 57th Ave
Miami, FL 33143
Contact Anthony Abraham, Chair, (305) 665-2222
Requirements Florida nonprofit organizations are eligible.
Restrictions Grants are not made to individuals.
Areas of Interest Biomedical Research; Catholic Church; Children and Youth; Churches; Education; Hospitals; Religion; Social Services; Youth Programs
Sample Awards Catholic Near East Welfare Assoc (New York, NY)—operating support, $100,195.

Ruth Anderson Foundation Grants 311
Ruth Anderson Foundation
2555 Ponce de Leon Blvd, Ste 320
Coral Gables, FL 33134
Contact Ruth Admire, (305) 444-6121; fax: (305) 444-5508
Requirements Miami Dade County 501(c)3 tax-exempt organizations are eligible.
Restrictions Grants are not awarded to individuals.
Areas of Interest AIDS; Alcohol/Alcoholism; Children and Youth; Community Development; Cultural Activities/Programs; Drugs/Drug Abuse; Education; Elderly; Environmental Programs; Health Care; Homelessness; Housing; Philanthropy; Public Education; Service Delivery Program; Social Services

Scott B. and Annie P. Appleby Trust Grants 312
Scott B. and Annie P. Appleby Trust
PO Box 2018
Sarasota, FL 34230
Contact Program Contact
Requirements The foundation funds those in the District of Columbia, Florida, and Georgia.
Areas of Interest Child Welfare; Cultural Activities/Programs; Higher Education

Frank Stanley Beveridge Foundation Grants 313
Frank Stanley Beveridge Foundation
301 Yamato Rd, Ste 1130
Boca Raton, FL 33431
Contact Philip Caswell, President, (800) 600-3723 or (561) 241-8388; fax: (561) 241-8332; e-mail: administrator@beveridge.org
Internet http://www.beveridge.org/index.cfm?fuseaction=gfc
Requirements Applicants must be 501(c)3 nonprofit organizations or foundations in Massachusett's Hampden and Hampshire Counties.
Restrictions Grants do not support units of government including federal, state, county and municipal agencies, schools, colleges, universities and hospitals and their foundations; foreign organizations or for foreign expenditure; organizations that are located outside the geographically approved area of giving; other private foundations excluding private operating foundations; private educational institutions not attended by members of the Beveridge Family; or federated drives and their foundations including Catholic Charities, United Jewish Appeal, and the United Way.
Areas of Interest Animal Rights; Arts, General; Biomedical Research; Children and Youth; Civil/Human Rights; Community Development; Conservation, Natural Resources; Crime Prevention; Curriculum Development; Disabled; Education; Employment Opportunity Programs; Exhibitions, Collections, Performances; Film Production; Food Banks; Health Care; Housing; Land Use Planning/Policy; Mental Health; Publication; Recreation and Leisure; Religion; Safety; Science; Social Services; Video Production; Women; Youth Programs
Sample Awards Christ Church Cathedral—$25,000 (2002). Early Childhood Ctrs of Greater Springfield Inc—$35,000 (2002. Friends of the Chicopee Public library—$25,000 (2002). Hospice by the Sea Inc—$50,000 (2002).

Chatlos Foundation Grants Program 314
Chatlos Foundation
PO Box 915048
Longwood, FL 32791-5048
Contact William Chatlos, President, (407) 862-5077
Internet http://www.chatlos.org/Guidelines.htm
Requirements Applicants must be US tax-exempt, nonprofit organizations that provide services in the following areas: bible colleges, religious causes, medical concerns, liberal arts colleges, and social concerns. Proposals must include cover letter, specific request, tax-exemption letter, and budget. If proposal is to be considered at board level, additional information will be requested.
Restrictions The foundation will not accept requests from individual church congregations, individuals, organizations in existence for less than two years as indicated by IRS tax-exempt letter of determination, for education below the college level, for medical research projects, or for support of the arts.
Areas of Interest Civic Affairs; Computer Grants; Distance Learning; Equipment/Instrumentation; Health Care; Humanities Education; Religion; Religious Studies
Sample Awards Baptist Bible College of Pennsylvania (Clarks Summit, PA)—for a distance learning program, $50,000. Ozark Christian College (Joplin, MI)—for an academic computing laboratory, $30,000.

Cobb Family Foundation Grants 315
Cobb Family Foundation
255 Aragon Ave, Ste 333
Coral Gables, FL 33134
Contact Charles Cobb Jr., (305) 441-1700; fax: (305) 445-5674
Requirements Nonprofit organizations in Florida are eligible to apply.
Areas of Interest Community Development; Higher Education; Libraries; Protestant Church; Recreation and Leisure; Secondary Education; Zoos

Dade Community Foundation Grants 316

Dade Community Foundation
200 S Biscayne Blvd, Ste 2780
Miami, FL 33131-2343
Contact Cristina Prado, Program Associate, (305) 371-2711; fax: (305) 371-5342; e-mail: cristina. prado@dadecommunityfoundation.org
Internet http://www.dadecommunityfoundation.org/ Site/programs/overview.jsp
Requirements IRS 501(c)3 nonprofit organizations in Dade County, FL, are eligible.
Restrictions Grants to government agencies are made on a very restricted basis. Grants are not made to individuals or for memberships, fundraising events, or memorials.
Areas of Interest Adolescent Health; Adult and Continuing Education; AIDS; AIDS Education; AIDS Prevention; Arts, General; Basic Skills Education; Child Abuse; Child Welfare; Cultural Activities/Programs; Cultural Diversity; Death/Mortality; Economic Development; Elementary Education; Environmental Programs; Eye Diseases; Health Care; Health Insurance; HIV; Homelessness; Hospices; Immigrants; Legal Education; Mural Painting; Neighborhoods; Nonprofit Organizations; Racism/Race Relations; Refugees; Religion; Religious Welfare Programs; School Health Programs; Secondary Education; Smoking Behavior; Social Services; Tobacco; Volunteers
Sample Awards American Red Cross of Greater Miami and the Keys (FL)—to increase the number of public high schools in Miami and Dade County that have peer-based HIV/AIDS health-education groups, through the South Florida Community AIDS Partnership, $10,000 (2003). Community-Jail Linkage Coalition (Miami, FL)—to coordinate HIV education, prevention, and testing services in Dade County jails and to connect inmates with community services upon their release, through the South Florida Community AIDS Partnership, $30,000 (2003).

Darden Restaurants Foundation Grants 317

Darden Restaurants Foundation
PO Box 593330
Orlando, FL 32859-3330
Contact Patty DeYoung, Program Contact, (407) 245-5213; fax: (407) 245-4462; e-mail: pdeyoung@ darden.com
Internet http://www.dardenusa.com/community/ grant_request_form.html
Requirements US nonprofit organizations are eligible.
Restrictions Grants do not support religious or non-exempt organizations; individuals; one-time, short-term events; advertising; team sponsorships; or athletic scholarships.
Areas of Interest Arts, General; Children and Youth; Cultural Activities/Programs; Environmental Programs; Family; Food Distribution; Housing; Literacy; Social Services; Training and Development
Sample Awards Warrington College of Business (Gainesville, FL)—to establish an endowment to support diversity and business ethics, $1.22 million (2001). Pennsylvania State U, School of Hotel, Restaurant, and Recreation Management (University Park, PA)—to establish the Darden Hospitality Student Leadership Endowment Fund, and for the Penn State Hotel and Restaurant Society Endowment Fund, $50,000 (2001).

Dunspaugh-Dalton Foundation Grants 318

Dunspaugh-Dalton Foundation
1533 Sunset Dr, Ste 150
Coral Gables, FL 33143-5700
Contact William Lane Jr, (305) 668-4192; fax: (305) 668-4247
Requirements US nonprofit organizations are eligible. The foundation primarily supports programs in California, Florida, and North Carolina.
Restrictions Individuals are not eligible.
Areas of Interest Civic Affairs; Cultural Activities/Programs; Elementary Education; Health Care; Higher Education; Hospices; Hospitals; Secondary Education; Social Services; Youth Programs
Sample Awards Barry U—for program support, $1.5 million over five years. Bertha Abess Children's Ctr (Miami, FL)—for operating support, $3000.

Alfred I. DuPont Foundation Grants 319

Alfred I. DuPont Foundation Inc
4600 Touchton Rd E, Bldg 200, Ste 120
Jacksonville, FL 32246
Contact Rosemary Cusimano Wills, Secretary, (904) 232-4123
Requirements Nonprofit organizations in the southeastern US are eligible. Preference is given to those in Florida.
Areas of Interest Biomedical Research; Education; Elderly; Health Care; Higher Education
Sample Awards Gulf Coast Community College Fdn (Panama City, FL)—for operating support, $50,000. Dreams Come True of Jacksonville (Jacksonville, FL)— for operating support, $10,000.

Jessie Ball Dupont Fund Grants 320

Jessie Ball Dupont Fund
1 Independent Dr, Ste 1400
Jacksonville, FL 32202-5011
Contact Dr. Sherry P. Magill, President, (904) 353-0890 or (800) 252-3452; fax: (904) 353-3870; e-mail: smagill@dupontfund.org
Internet http://www.dupontfund.org/grants/ grantmaking.asp
Requirements Applying organizations must have received a contribution from Mrs. DuPont between the five-year period of January 1, 1960, and December 31, 1964.
Areas of Interest Arts, General; Churches; Cultural Activities/Programs; Disaster Relief; Education; Health Care; Museums; Poverty and the Poor; Religion; Restoration and Preservation; Social Services; Volunteers
Sample Awards Auburn U (AL)—for an architecture-education program, $56,200 (2003). U of North Carolina at Chapel Hill (NC)—for research on successful relationships between government agencies and nonprofit organizations, $138,975 (2003). U of Richmond (VA)—to establish an interdisciplinary summer student-faculty research project, $125,000 (2003). Virginia Foundation for Independent Colleges (Richmond, VA)—to coordinate environmental-study activities of member colleges and universities focusing on water quality in Virginia, $104,550 (2003).

Eckerd Corporation Foundation Grants 321
Eckerd Corporation
8333 Bryan Dairy Rd
Largo, FL 33777
Contact Tami Alderman, Administrator, (727)
395-7091; fax: (727) 395-7934; e-mail: service@
eckerd.com
Internet http://www.eckerd.com/content.asp?content=
company/news/presscontact
Requirements Nonprofit organizations in company operating areas are eligible.
Restrictions Grants do not support athletic groups, political organizations, religious organizations, school districts, schools, state or local government agencies, individuals, deficit financing, equipment or land acquisition,
renovation projects, research, publications, or conferences.
Areas of Interest Children and Youth; Community Development; Cultural Activities/Programs; Health Care;
Education; Higher Education; Hospices; Hospitals;
Women

Florida Arts Council Quarterly Grant 322
Assistance Program
Florida Department of State Division of Cultural Affairs
1001 DeSoto Park Dr
Tallahassee, FL 32301-4555
Contact Dr. Gaylen Phillips, Grants Administrator,
(850) 245-6482; fax: (850) 245-6497; TTY: (850)
488-5779
Internet http://www.florida-arts.org/grants/qa/index.
htm
Requirements Florida nonprofit, tax-exempt organizations are eligible. Matching requirements are dollar-for-dollar, and up to 50 percent of applicant match
may be in kind.
Areas of Interest Arts Administration

Florida Arts Council Underserved Arts 323
Communities Assistance Program
Florida Department of State Division of Cultural Affairs
1001 DeSoto Park Dr
Tallahassee, FL 32301
Contact Dr. Gaylen Phillips, Grants Administrator,
(850) 245-6482; fax: (850) 245-6497; TTY: (850)
488-5779
Internet http://www.florida-arts.org/grants/uacap/
index.htm
Requirements An organization must qualify as a political subdivision of a municipal, county, or state government in Florida; or be a nonprofit, tax-exempt Florida
corporation.
Restrictions Grants are for administrative purposes
only, not for artistic programs.
Areas of Interest Arts Administration

Florida Arts Organizations Grants—Visual 324
Arts
Florida Department of State Division of Cultural Affairs
1001 DeSoto Park Dr
Tallahassee, FL 32301
Contact Melissa Ray, Program Contact, (850)
245-6487; fax: (850) 245-6497; e-mail: mray@dos.
state.fl.us
Internet http://www.florida-arts.org/grants/csg/index.
htm
Requirements An organization must qualify as a political subdivision of a municipal, county, or state government in Florida; or be a nonprofit, tax-exempt Florida
corporation. Accreditation by the American Association
of Museums, though not required, is encouraged for museum applicants. A dollar-for-dollar match is required,
and 25 percent in kind is allowed.
Restrictions Organizations applying for general program support may not apply for a specific project grant.
Arts organizations that have been incorporated for less
than one year are not eligible for general program support.
Areas of Interest Art Appreciation; Arts Administration; Exhibitions, Collections, Performances; Junior and
Community Colleges; Museums; Publication; Visual
Arts
Sample Awards Miami-Dade Community College,
Wolfson Galleries (FL)—for exhibition support,
$12,607. Pensacola Museum of Art (Pensacola, FL)—
for season support, $14,622.

Florida Department of State Cultural 325
Support Grants
Florida Department of State Division of Cultural Af-
fairs
1001 DeSoto Park Dr
Tallahassee, FL 32301-4555
Contact Melissa Ray, Arts Administrator, Bureau of
Grant Services, (850) 245-6487; e-mail: mray@dos.
state.fl.us
Internet http://www.florida-arts.org/grants/csg/index.
htm
Requirements Nonprofit organizations in Florida are el-
igible.
Areas of Interest Children's Museums; Cultural Activ-
ities/Programs; Dramatic/Theater Arts; Museums;
Sample Awards Young at Art of Broward (Broward,
FL)—for general support, $39,862. Miami Children's
Museum (Miami, FL)—for operating support, $45,617.

Lucy Gooding Charitable Foundation Trust 326
Lucy Gooding Charitable Foundation Trust
PO Box 37347
Jacksonville, FL 32236-7349
Contact Bonnie Smith, Trustee, (904) 786-4796; fax:
(904) 786-4796; e-mail: bhsmith@bellsouth.net
Requirements Florida 501(c)3 nonprofit organizations
serving the Jacksonville area are eligible.
Areas of Interest Child Welfare; Disabled; Children and
Youth; Disadvantaged (Economically); Homelessness;
Hospices

Leo Goodwin Foundation Grants 327
Leo Goodwin Foundation
800 Corporate Dr, Ste 510
Fort Lauderdale, FL 33334-3621
Contact Helen Furia, Secretary-Treasurer, (954)
491-2000
Requirements Nonprofit organizations are eligible.

Restrictions Individuals are not eligible.
Areas of Interest Cancer/Carcinogenesis; Child Welfare; Education; Hospitals; Mental Health; Youth Programs

Greenburg-May Foundation Grants 328
Greenburg-May Foundation
PO Box 54-5816
Miami Beach, FL 33154
Contact Isabel May, President, (305) 864-8639
Requirements Nonprofit organizations in southern Florida and New York are eligible.
Restrictions Grants are not given to individuals or for endowment funds, special projects, publications, or conferences, and generally not for scholarships and fellowships.
Areas of Interest Aging/Gerontology; Cancer/Carcinogenesis; Cardiovascular Diseases; Hospitals; Jewish Services; Neurology; Opera/Musical Theater
Sample Awards Miami Jewish Home and Hospital for the Aged (Miami, FL)—$75,200. Greater Miami Opera (Miami, FL)—$4,220.

Knight Community Partners Grants 329
John S. and James L. Knight Foundation
Wachovia Financial Ctr, Ste 3300, 200 S Biscayne Blvd
Miami, FL 33131-2349
Contact Joe Ervin, Community Partners Program Director, (305) 908-2600
Internet http://www.knightfdn.org/default.asp?story=cpp/index.html
Requirements Nonprofit organizations and institutions are eligible. The proposed project must serve at least one of the following target areas: Long Beach or San Jose, CA; Boulder, CO; Boca Raton, Bradenton, Miami, or Tallahassee, FL; Columbus, Macon, or Milledgeville, GA; Fort Wayne or Gary, IN; Wichita, KS; Lexington, KY; Detroit, MI; Duluth or Saint Paul, MN; Biloxi, MS; Charlotte, NC; Akron, OH; Philadelphia or State College, PA; Columbia or Myrtle Beach, SC; and Aberdeen, SD. Applicant organizations may be located outside of the project target area.
Areas of Interest Arts, General; Children and Youth; Civic Affairs; Community Development; Cultural Activities/Programs; Disaster Relief; Economic Development; Education; Family; Housing; Jewish Services
Sample Awards Florida International U (Miami, FL)—to survey residents of Miami's Overtown and East Little Havan neighborhoods and sections of Broward County, FL, regarding their thoughts on economic development, law enforcement, neighborhood safety, and other issues, $95,800 (2003). One Economy Corp (Washington, DC)—to provide 100 low-income families in Miami and San Jose, CA, with computers, Internet access, and technology training, $750,000 (2003). Jewish Family and Children's Service of Long Beach-West Orange County (Long Beach, CA)—to train 60 parents to help improve the academic performance of their children, who attend Lee and Willard Elementary Schools in West Long Beach, CA, $31,600 (2003).

Pinellas County Grants 330
Pinellas County Community Foundation
PO Box 205
Clearwater, FL 33757-0205
Contact Grants Administrator, (727) 446-0058; fax: (727) 446-0948; e-mail: tom1pccf@aol.com
Internet http://fdncenter.org/grantmaker/pinellas/discret.html
Requirements Florida nonprofit organizations serving Pinellas County are eligible.
Restrictions Grants do not support individuals, endowments, research, scholarships, fellowships, or matching gifts.
Areas of Interest Social Services; Disabled; Mental Health; Child Abuse; Sexual Abuse; Education; Job Training Programs; Economic Self-Sufficiency; Homelessness; Poverty and the Poor; Single-Parent Families; Children and Youth; Elderly; Playgrounds; Housing
Sample Awards Partners in Self Sufficiency (FL)—to assist 53 single-parent families in becoming self-supporting, through school or job training, $8000. Homeless Emergency Project (FL)—for furniture for three apartments, $8300. Alpha A Beginning (FL)—to construct an equipped playground, decks, family picnic area at a transitional housing complex, $5000.

Publix Super Markets Charities Grants 331
Publix Super Markets Charities
PO Box 407
Lakeland, FL 33802-0407
Contact Director, Community Affairs, (863) 680-5339
Internet http://www.publix.com
Requirements Florida nonprofits are eligible.
Areas of Interest Community Development; Disabled; Higher Education; Social Services; Youth Programs

Rayonier Foundation Grants 332
Rayonier Foundation
50 N Laura St, Ste 1900
Jacksonville, FL 32202
Contact Jay Fredericksen, Vice-President, (904) 357-9100
Requirements Nonprofit organizations in Florida, Georgia, and Washington are eligible.
Areas of Interest Alcohol/Alcoholism; Children and Youth; Community Development; Disabled; Disadvantaged (Economically); Drugs/Drug Abuse; Economics; Education; Engineering; Environmental Health; Environmental Programs; Family; Health Care; Hospitals; Libraries; Medical Programs; Mental Health; Minorities; Performing Arts; Recreation and Leisure; Science; Social Services; Social Services Delivery; Technology; Volunteers; Women

Paul E. and Klare N. Reinhold Foundation Grants 333
Paul E. and Klare N. Reinhold Foundation
1845 Town Center Blvd, Ste 105
Orange Park, FL 32003
Contact Eileen Chisholm, (904) 269-5857; fax: (904) 269-8382; e-mail: echisholm@reinhold.net
Internet http://www.reinhold.org/html/guidelines.htm
Requirements 501(c)3 tax-exempt organizations in Florida's Clay County are eligible.

Restrictions Grants do not support advertising for fund-raising campaigns, tickets, debt reduction, endowments, or basic operating costs.

Areas of Interest Art Appreciation; Art Education; Children and Youth; Computer Grants; Health Care; Music Appreciation; Music Education; Playgrounds; Public Affairs; Religion; Sports

Sample Awards Clay County Habitat For Humanity, Inc (FL)—to supplement a Capacity Building Grant to help pay the Executive Director's salary, $20,000 (2002). Alzheimer's Assoc (FL)—to support Caregiver Education By enhancing the resource library, $3000 (2002). Christ Episcopal Church Building Fund (FL)—dedication of family/gathering room in honor of Thomas E. Camp, III, $50,000 (2002). Keystone Heights Elementary School FL)—for additional supplies for Project Playground, $500 (2002).

Ryder System Charitable Foundation Grants 334
Ryder System Charitable Foundation, Inc
3600 NW 82nd Ave
Miami, FL 33166
Contact Grants Administrator, (305) 500-3031
Requirements Organizations in California, Florida, Georgia, Michigan, Missouri, Ohio, and Texas are eligible to apply.
Areas of Interest Children and Youth; Community Development; Crisis Counseling; Cultural Activities/Programs; Disadvantaged (Economically); Economic Development; Elementary Education; Equipment/Instrumentation; Higher Education; Housing; Minority Education; Minority Employment; Private and Parochial Education; Secondary Education; Social Services Delivery; Volunteers

Ted Arison Family Foundation Grants   335
Ted Arison Family Foundation USA, Inc.
3655 NW 87th Ave
Miami, FL 33178-2428
Contact Maddy Rosenburg, (305) 599-2600
Requirements Funding is primarily for New York nonprofits.
Areas of Interest Arts, General; Cultural Activities/Programs; Cultural Outreach; Education; Film Production; Human Services; International Education/Training; International Relations; International Studies; Jewish Services; Middle East; Music
Sample Awards Performing Arts Center Foundation of Greater Miami (Miami, FL)—for operating support, $3,333,333. American Committee for Tel Aviv Foundation (New York, NY)—for Tel Aviv Foundation Israel Arison Art Campus, $123,500. Kartemquin Educational Films (Chicago, IL)—for film, Is Jerusalem Burning, $90,000. American Friends of Keshet Eilon (New York, NY)—for scholarships for Violin Master Course, $40,000.

Robert Lee Turner Foundation Grants   336
Robert Lee Turner Foundation
311 S Flagler Dr, Ste 1005
Palm Beach, FL 33401
Contact Robert Turner, Trustee, (561) 655-0755
Areas of Interest Private and Parochial Education; Religion; Recreation and Leisure; Religious Studies

Lillian S. Wells Foundation Grants   337
Lillian S. Wells Foundation
600 Sagamore Rd
Fort Lauderdale, FL 33301-2215
Contact Barbara Van Fleet, (954) 462-8639
Requirements Nonprofit organizations in Chicago, IL; Fort Lauderdale, FL; and Washington, DC; area are eligible.
Areas of Interest Art Appreciation; Art Education; Biomedical Research

**Whitehall Foundation Neurobiology   338
   Research Grants**
Whitehall Foundation
PO Box 3423
Palm Beach, FL 33480
Contact Program Director, (561) 655-4474; fax (561) 655-4978; e-mail: email@whitehall.org
Internet http://www.whitehall.org
Requirements Accredited US institutions are eligible. The foundation prefers to support scientists at the beginning of their career and those senior scientists who have maintained productivity. The principal investigator must hold no less than the position of assistant professor or the equivalent.
Areas of Interest Behavioral Sciences; Biomedical Research; Brain; Immune System; Life Sciences; Neurobiology; Primatology; Sensory System
Sample Awards Daniel Pollen, U of Massachusetts (MA)—for research on the cerebral integration in the primate visual system, $40,000 of three-year grant. Richard Ivry, U of California (CA)—for research on the role of the cerebellum in temporal processing, $24,000 final payment on three-year grant. Paul Black, Boston U (Boston, MA)—to support research on brain-immune system interactions, $130,020 final payment on three-year grant.

Wilson-Wood Foundation Grants   339
Wilson-Wood Foundation
3665 Bee Ridge Rd, Ste 302
Sarasota, FL 34233-1056
Contact Program Contact, (941) 921-2856
Requirements Nonprofit Florida organizations in the Manatee and Sarasota area may apply for grant support.
Restrictions Organizations outside of the United States are ineligible, as are private foundations. In addition, grants are not made to individuals or for endowment funds, deficit financing, travel, research, fund-raising, or multiyear funding.
Areas of Interest Adult and Continuing Education; Basic Skills Education; Education; Health Care; Housing; Immigrants; Literacy; Minorities; Social Services; Women; Youth Programs

Georgia

AEC Trust Grants   340
AEC Trust
191 Peachtree St, 24th Fl, GA 8023
Atlanta, GA 30303
Contact Susanna Adams, fax: (404) 332-1389

Requirements 501(c)3 nonprofit organizations in the communities of Boulder, CO; Gainesville, FL; Atlanta, GA; Amherst, MA; and Green Bay, WI, are eligible.
Restrictions Grants do not support individuals, international organizations, political organizations, religious organizations, school districts, special events/benefit dinners, state and local government agencies, United Way agencies, national public charities, endowments, sponsorships, or annual fund campaigns.
Areas of Interest AIDS; Arts, General; Community Development; Cultural Activities/Programs; Elementary Education; Environmental Programs; Health Care; Higher Education; Social Services; Women

Atlanta Foundation Grants 341
Atlanta Foundation
191 Peachtree St, MC 1102
Atlanta, GA 30303
Contact Ben Boswell, c/o Wachovia Bank of Georgia NA, (404) 332-6074; e-mail: grantinquiriesga@ wachovia.com
Internet http://www.wachovia.com/corp_inst/ charitable_services/0,,4269_3296,00.html
Requirements Nonprofit organizations in Georgia's DeKalb and Fulton Counties may apply for grant support.
Restrictions Grants are not awarded to individuals or for scholarships, fellowships, or loans.
Areas of Interest Adult and Continuing Education; Arts, General; Basic Skills Education; Cultural Activities/Programs; Education; Family; Health Care; Higher Education; Housing; Literacy; Performing Arts; Recreation and Leisure; Social Services; Youth Programs

Atlanta Women's Foundation Grants 342
Atlanta Women's Foundation
The Hurt Bldg, Ste 401
Atlanta, GA 30303
Contact DiShonda Hughes, Program Contact, (404) 577-5000 ext 5; fax: (404) 589-0000; e-mail: dhughes@atlantawomen.org
Internet http://awf.techbridge.org/grants/grants.asp
Requirements Southern nonprofits are eligible.
Restrictions Grants are not awarded for endowments, debt reduction, religious groups, building funds, or large equipment (e.g., vehicles).
Areas of Interest Civil/Human Rights; Economics; Homelessness; Mental Health; Poverty and the Poor; Rape/Sexual Abuse; Violent Behavior; Women; Women's Employment; Women's Health
Sample Awards Alternate Life Paths (Atlanta, GA)— for support services and emergency, transitional, and group housing for homeless girls, $15,000 (2003). Flint Circuit Council on Family Violence (McDonough, GA)—to provide mental-health services, shelter, and job-placement and relocation assistance to women experiencing domestic violence, $15,000 (2003). Fulton County Juvenile Justice Fund (Atlanta, GA)—for an emergency safe house for girls and teenagers who are victims of sexual exploitation, $20,000 (2003). International Women's House (Decatur, GA)—to provide emergency housing and mental-health services to refugee and immigrant battered women, $10,000 (2003).

BellSouth Corporation Charitable 343
  Contributions
BellSouth Corporation
1155 Peachtree St NE
Atlanta, GA 30309
Contact Corporate Contributions, (404) 927-7417; e-mail: grants.manager@bellsouth.com
Internet http://www.bellsouthfoundation.org
Requirements Nonprofit organizations in the BellSouth nine-state service area are eligible, including Alabama, Florida, Georgia, Kentucky, Louisiana, Mississippi, North Carolina, South Carolina, and Tennessee.
Areas of Interest Arts, General; Children and Youth; Community Development; Community Service Programs; Conservation, Natural Resources; Cultural Programs/Activities; Service Delivery Program; Social Services Delivery
Sample Awards High Museum of Art (Atlanta, GA)— for expansion costs, $50,000 (2003). Georgia Conservancy (Atlanta, GA)—for general support, $10,000 over two years (2003). Salvation Army (Atlanta, GA)—for program support, $25,000 (2003). NewTwon Macon Terminal Station)GA)—to revitalize the downtown area of Macon, $12,500 (2003).

Callaway Foundation Grants 344
Callaway Foundation
PO Box 790
La Grange, GA 30241
Contact Program Contact, (706) 884-7348; fax: (706) 884-0201
Requirements Georgia nonprofit organizations are eligible. Preference is given to requests from La Grange, GA, and Troup County.
Areas of Interest Churches; Community Development; Community Service Programs; Education; Elderly; Elementary Education; Health Care; Higher Education; Hospitals; Humanities; Libraries; Religion; Secondary Education
Sample Awards La Grange College (GA)—to endow its Callaway campus, which includes an auditorium, tennis courts, athletic field, and a multipurpose athletic and educational building, $5.75 million (2002).

Fuller E. Callaway Foundation Grants 345
Fuller E. Callaway Foundation
PO Box 790
LaGrange, GA 30241
Contact H. Speer Burdette, General Manager, (706) 884-7348; fax: (706) 884-0201; e-mail: hsburdette@ callaway-foundation.org
Requirements Nonprofit organizations and individuals in LaGrange and Troup County, GA, are eligible for support.
Areas of Interest Education; Health Care; Higher Education; Religion; Social Services; Youth Programs
Sample Awards First Baptist Church of Fannin Street (LaGrange, GA)—for permanent improvements, $267,296.

Camp Younts Foundation Grants 346
Camp Younts Foundation
PO Box 4655
Atlanta, GA 30302

Contact Bobby Worrell, Executive Director, (757) 562-3439

Requirements Nonprofit organizations in Florida, Georgia, North Carolina, and Virginia may request grant support.

Areas of Interest Health Care; Higher Education; Hospitals; Protestant Church; Secondary Education; Social Services; Youth Programs

Sample Awards Virginia Baptist General Board (Richmond, VA)—for operating support, $40,000. Saint Edwards School (Bon Air, VA)—for operating support, $25,000.

Chatham Valley Foundation Grants   347

Chatham Valley Foundation
191 Peachtree St NE, 22nd Fl
Atlanta, GA 30308
Contact Susanna Adams, c/o Wachovia Charitable Services, (404) 332-5106

Requirements Nonprofit organizations in the greater metropolitan Atlanta, GA, area are eligible.

Areas of Interest Cancer/Carcinogenesis; Crime Prevention; Cultural Activities/Programs; Education; Health Care; Higher Education; Homelessness; Jewish Services; Law Enforcement; Museums; Nursing Homes; Performing Arts; Social Services

Sample Awards Anti-Defamation League of B'nai B'rith (Atlanta, GA)—for operating support, $10,000.

Coca-Cola Foundation Grants   348

Coca-Cola Foundation
PO Box Drawer 1734
Atlanta, GA 30301
Contact Helen Smith-Price, Executive Director, (800) 438-2653 or (404) 676-2568; fax: (404) 676-8804
Internet http://www2.coca-cola.com/citizenship/foundation_guidelines.html

Requirements IRS 501(c)3 nonprofits are eligible.

Restrictions The foundation does not make grants to individuals, religious endeavors, political or fraternal organizations, or organizations without 501(c)3 status.

Areas of Interest African Americans; Allergy; Business Education; Classroom Instruction; Disaster Relief; Dropouts; Economics Education; Education; Elementary Education; Food Consumption; Food Sciences; Health Care; Higher Education; Higher Education, Private; Human Learning and Memory; International Education/Training; International Exchange Programs; International Relations; International Studies; Mentoring Programs; Minority Education; Minority Schools; Nutrition Education; Political Science Education; Private and Parochial Education; Scholarship Programs, General; Secondary Education; Teacher Education, Inservice; Youth Programs

Sample Awards Ohio State U (Columbus, OH)—for scholarships for women seeking undergraduate, graduate, and professional degrees who have financial limitations and family obligations, and for research on gender, $400,000 and $100,000, respectively (2003). Duke U, Terry Sanford Institute of Public Policy (Durham, NC)—for the Multimedia and Instructional Technology Center at the institute's new facility, $1 million (2003). American Red Cross, Liberty Fund (Washington, DC)—to provide disaster-relief services to victims of the September 11 terrorist attacks, $6 million (2002). John F. Kennedy Ctr for the Performing Arts (Washington, DC)—for its long-term plans to develop interactive, educational programs, $1 million over five years (2002).

Robert and Polly Dunn Foundation Grants   349

Robert and Polly Dunn Foundation
PO Box 723194
Atlanta, GA 31139
Contact Karen Wilbanks, Executive Director, (404) 816-2883; fax: (404) 816-2883

Areas of Interest Child Psychology/Development; Youth Programs

Fraser-Parker Foundation Grants   350

Fraser-Parker Foundation Grants
50 Hurt Plz, Ste 850
Atlanta, GA 30303
Contact John Stephenson, Executive Director, (404) 658-9066

Areas of Interest Education; Higher Education; Hospitals; Religion

Georgia Council for the Arts Organizational   351
Grants

Georgia Council for the Arts
260 14th St, Ste 401
Atlanta, GA 30318-5793
Contact Martine Collier, Community Arts Development Manager, 404-685-2796; fax: 404-685-2788; e-mail: mcollier@gaarts.org
Internet http://www.web-dept.com/gca/resources_forms.asp#

Requirements Georgia nonprofits are eligible.

Areas of Interest Arts Administration; Arts and Culture; Art, General; Dance; Museums; Visual Arts

Sample Awards Cobb County (GA)—for the Georgia Ballet, $2500. Muscogee County (GA)—for The Columbus Museum, $68,616.

Georgia-Pacific Grants   352

Georgia-Pacific Foundation
133 Peachtree St NE, 39th Fl
Atlanta, GA 30303
Contact Curley Dossman Jr., President, (404) 652-4182; fax: (404) 749-2754
Internet http://www.gp.com/center/community/grantprocess.html

Requirements Nonprofit organizations in Georgia-Pacific communities are eligible, including Alabama, Arkansas, California, Florida, Georgia, Kentucky, Maine, Massachusetts, Michigan, Mississippi, New York, North Carolina, Ohio, Oklahoma, Oregon, Pennsylvania, South Carolina, Virginia, Washington, West Virginia, and Wisconsin.

Restrictions Grants do not support bail-out funds for emergency aid for general operations, political or religious causes, goodwill advertising, sporting events, general support for United Way agencies, ticket purchase, medical and nursing schools, named academic chairs, social sciences or health sciences programs, and travel.

Areas of Interest Civic Affairs; Conservation, Natural Resources; Environmental Programs; Health Care;

Higher Education; Housing; Literacy; Parks; Scholarship Programs, General; Social Services Delivery; Vocational/Technical Education

Sample Awards Nature Conservancy (Arlington, VA)—to conserve specific sites in Alabama, Florida, and Georgia and for critical conservation projects in other states, $3 million over three years.

Georgia Power Foundation Grants   353
Georgia Power Foundation
241 Ralph McGill Blvd, NE, Bin 10230
Atlanta, GA 30308-3374
Contact Susan Carter, Executive Director, (404) 506-6784; fax: (404) 506-1485; e-mail: gpfoundation@southernco.com
Requirements The foundation makes grants to tax-exempt organizations that seek to improve the quality of life for Georgia's residents.
Restrictions Grants are not awarded to private secondary schools or religious organizations.
Areas of Interest AIDS; Audience Development; Cultural Activities/Programs; Education; Elderly; Environmental Programs; Health Care; Homelessness; Performing Arts; Racism/Race Relations; Visual Arts
Sample Awards Georgia State University (Atlanta, GA)—for operating support, $100,000. United Way of Metropolitan Atlanta (Atlanta, GA)—for operating support, $1,546,500 (2002). Robert W. Woodruff Arts Center (Atlanta, GA)—for capital support $250,000 2002).

John H. and Wilhelmina D. Harland   354
Charitable Foundation Grants
John H. and Wilhelmina D. Harland Charitable Foundation
2 Piedmont Ctr, Ste 106
Atlanta, GA 30305
Contact John Conant, Secretary, (404) 264-9912; e-mail: harland@randomc.com
Requirements Grant support is available to nonprofit organizations in Georgia, with emphasis on the metropolitan Atlanta area.
Restrictions Grants are not awarded to individuals.
Areas of Interest Adult and Continuing Education; Arts, General; Basic Skills Education; Child Welfare; Churches; Community Development; Cultural Activities/Programs; Disabled; Higher Education; Homelessness; Literacy; Museums; Religion; Social Services; Youth Programs
Sample Awards Boys and Girls Clubs of Metropolitan Atlanta (Atlanta, GA)—for the Harland Club Teen Ctr, $50,000. Atlanta Union Mission (Atlanta, GA)—for facility renovations, $48,000. Howard Schools (Atlanta, GA)—for property acquisition, $48,000.

Sartain Lanier Family Foundation Grants   355
Sartain Lanier Family Foundation
25 Puritan Mill, 950 Lowery Blvd
Atlanta, GA 30318
Contact Mark Riley, Director, (404) 564-1259; fax: (404) 564-1251; e-mail: info@lanierfamilyfoundation.com
Internet http://www.lanierfamilyfoundation.org/grant.html

Restrictions Grants are made only in the southeastern United States with the majority of recipients being located in Georgia and specifically the Atlanta metro area. The foundation does not make grants for individuals; churches or religious organizations for projects that primarily benefit their own members; partisan political purposes; tickets to charitable events or dinners, or to sponsor special events or fundraisers.
Areas of Interest Arts; Community Development; Elementary Education; Environment; Health and Health Services; Higher Education; Human Services; Secondary Education; Social Services Delivery
Sample Awards Vanderbilt University (Nashville, TN)—for operating support, $700,000. Westminster Schools (Atlanta, GA)—for operating support, $100,000. Whitefoord Community Program (Atlanta, GA)—for operating support, $50,000.

Rich Foundation Grants   356
Rich Foundation
11 Piedmont Ctr, Ste 204
Atlanta, GA 30305
Contact Anne Poland Berg, Grant Consultant, (404) 262-2266
Requirements Nonprofit organizations in the Atlanta, GA, area are eligible for grant support.
Areas of Interest AIDS; Cardiovascular Diseases; Community Development; Cultural Activities/Programs; Dramatic/Theater Arts; Higher Education; Homelessness; Hospitals; Performing Arts; Social Services; Youth Programs

Sapelo Foundation Grants   357
Sapelo Foundation
1712 Ellis St, 2nd Fl
Brunswick, GA 31520
Contact Phyllis Bowen, (912) 265-0520; fax: (912) 254-1888; e-mail: info@sapelofoundation.org
Internet http://www.sapelofoundation.org/grants.html
Requirements Georgia 501(c)3 nonprofit organizations are eligible.
Areas of Interest Economic Development; Education Reform; Environmental Health; Environmental Programs; Housing; Judicial/Law Administration; Labor Relations; Microenterprises; Pollution; Pollution Control; Racism/Race Relations; Rural Areas; Water Pollution

Scientific-Atlanta Foundation Grants   358
Scientific-Atlanta Foundation
5030 Sugarloaf Pkwy
Lawrenceville, GA 30044
Contact Grant Proposals
Internet http://www.scientificatlanta.com/aboutus/S-A-Foundation.htm
Requirements 501(c)3 nonprofit organizations are eligible.
Restrictions The foundation does not award grants to individuals in the form of scholarships or other direct support; political causes or candidates; religious organizations, theological functions, or church-sponsored programs limited to church members, unless engaged in activities that benefit the entire community; or athletic organizations.

Areas of Interest Arts & Culture; Civic Affairs; Community Service Programs; Cultural Activities/Programs; Education; Health Care; Health Services Delivery; Mathematics Education; Science Education;

Edna Wardlaw Charitable Trust Grants 359
Edna Wardlaw Charitable Trust
PO Box 4655, MC 217
Atlanta, GA 30302-4655
Contact Danah Craft, (404) 827-6921
Areas of Interest Children and Youth; Conservation, Natural Resources; Cultural Activities/Programs; Environmental Health; Health Care; Homelessness; Human Reproduction/Fertility; Peace/Disarmament; Social Services; Social Services Delivery; Youth Programs
Sample Awards National Coalition for the Homeless (Washington, DC)—for general operating support, $6000 (2000). Ctr for Democratic Renewal and Education (Atlanta, GA)—for general operating support, $40,000 (2000). Ecology Action of the Mid-Peninsula (Willits, CA)—for general operating support, $25,000 (2000). Peace House (Ashland, OR)—for general operating support, $5000 (2002).

Gertrude and William C. Wardlaw Fund 360
  Grants
Gertrude and William C. Wardlaw Fund
PO Box 4655, MC 217
Atlanta, GA 30302
Contact Danah Craft, Secretary
Requirements Georgia nonprofit organizations are eligible.
Areas of Interest Community Development; Cultural Activities/Programs; Education; Health Care; Higher Education; Hospitals; Youth Programs

Hawaii

Alexander and Baldwin Foundation Grants 361
Alexander and Baldwin Foundation
822 Bishop St
Honolulu, HI 96813
Contact Kris Okutani, Program Contact, (808) 525-6641; fax: (808) 525-6677; e-mail: kokutani@abinc.com
Internet http://www.alexanderbaldwin.com/abf/index.htm
Requirements The foundation gives funding to nonprofit organizations on a national level in A&B operating communities with an emphasis on California and Hawaii.
Restrictions Grants are not awarded to support United Way agencies for operating support, individuals, events, travel expenses, or scholarships.
Areas of Interest Arts, General; Community Development; Cultural Outreach; Education; Environmental Programs; Social Services; Social Services Delivery

Atherton Family Foundation Grants 362
Atherton Family Foundation
1164 Bishop St, Ste 800
Honolulu, HI 96813

Contact Lissa Schiff, Private Foundation Services Officer, (808) 566-5524; fax: (808) 521-6286; e-mail: foundations@hcf-hawaii.org
Internet http://www.Athertonfamilyfoundation.org
Requirements Hawaii nonprofit organizations are eligible.
Areas of Interest Arts, General; Computer Grants; Cultural Activities/Programs; Domestic Violence; Education; Environmental Programs; Health Care; Humanities; Protestant Church; Religion; Social Services; Theology
Sample Awards La Pietra-Hawaii School for Girls (Honolulu, HI)—for capital campaign, $112,000. Le Jardin Academy (HI)—to purchase computer network equipment, $5000. Hawaii State Committee on Family Violence (HI)—for general operating support, $4000.

Harold K. L. Castle Foundation Grants 363
Harold K. L. Castle Foundation
146 Hekili St, Ste 203
Kailua, HI 96734
Contact Christine Plunkett, Program Manager, (808) 263-7072; fax: (808) 261-6918; e-mail: cplunkett@castlefoundation.org
Internet http://www.castlefoundation.org
Requirements Nonprofit 501(c)3 organizations in Hawaii and government agencies may apply.
Areas of Interest Arts, General; Cultural Activities/Programs; Environmental Programs; Health Services Delivery; Private and Parochial Education; Reading; Religion; Restoration and Preservation, Structural/Architectural; Science; Social Services; Sports; Technology; Youth Programs
Sample Awards Honolulu Academy of Arts (HI)—for the second payment toward repair of the roof on the historic main building, $200,000. Blanch Pope Elementary School (HI)—toward the Success for All reading program, $50,000. Lanikai Canoe Club (HI)—for second year start-up operating support, $5000.

Samuel N. and Mary Castle Foundation 364
  Grants
Samuel N. and Mary Castle Foundation
733 Bishop St, Ste 1275
Honolulu, HI 96813
Contact Alfred Castle, Executive Director, (808) 522-1101; fax: (808) 522-1103; e-mail: acastle@aloha.net
Internet http://www.fdncenter.org/grantmaker/castle
Requirements Hawaii nonprofit organizations may apply.
Areas of Interest Art Education; Arts, General; Children and Youth; Education; Environmental Programs; Exhibitions, Collections, Performances; Family; Health Care; Health Promotion; Higher Education; Religion; Science Education
Sample Awards Saint Mark Lutheran School (Kaneohe, HI)—for a security system and classroom furniture, $15,000 (2003). Honolulu Symphony (HI)—for its Youth Music Education program, $20,000 (2003). YMCA of Honolulu (HI)—for its capital campaign, $250,000 (2003). Haili Christian School (Hilo, HI)—to improve the playground and purchase sports equipment, $10,000 (2003).

Cooke Foundation Grants 365
Cooke Foundation Ltd
1164 Bishop St, Ste 800
Honolulu, HI 96813
Contact Program Officer, (808) 566-5524; e-mail:
foundations@hcf-hawaii.org
Internet http://www.cookefdn.org
Requirements Grant making is limited to the state of
Hawaii.
Restrictions Grants are not made to individuals,
churches, or religious organizations, or for endowment
funds, scholarships, or fellowships.
Areas of Interest Arts, General; Cultural Activities/Programs; Dance; Education; Elderly; Environmental Programs; Health Care; History; Humanities; Social Services; Youth Programs
Sample Awards Maui Community Arts and Cultural Ctr
(HI)—to support the capital campaign to complete construction, $10,000. Honolulu Dance Theatre (HI)—for a
ballet performance, $2500. Kauai Historical Society
(HI)—to support the lecture series, $2500. Honolulu
Academy of Arts (HI)—annual grant, $100,000.

Mary D. and Walter F. Frear Eleemosynary 366
Trust Grants
Mary D. and Walter F. Frear Eleemosynary Trust
PO Box 3170
Honolulu, HI 96802-3170
Contact Paula Boyce, Grants Administrator, c/o
Pacific Century Trust, (808) 538-4944; fax: (808)
538-4647
Requirements Grant applications are accepted from
qualified tax-exempt charitable organizations in Hawaii.
Restrictions Grants are not made to individuals, nor for
endowments, reserve purposes, deficit financing, or
travel.
Areas of Interest Religion; Philanthropy; Science; Literature; Education; Economic Self-Sufficiency; Citizenship; Civic Affairs; Youth Programs; Education; Music;
Dramatic/Theater Arts; Reading; Parks
Sample Awards Daughters of Hawaii (HI)—to support
capital projects at Queen Emma Summer Palace, $3000.
Manoa Valley Theatre (HI)—to support the community
outreach program, $2250. Hospice Hawaii (HI)—for bereavement support groups, $4000. Alzheimer's Assoc
(HI)—toward start-up costs of the respite care center,
$5000.

Hawaii Community Foundation Grants 367
Hawaii Community Foundation
1164 Bishop St, Ste 800
Honolulu, HI 96813
Contact Kelvin Taketa, President, (808) 537-6333;
fax: (808) 521-6286; e-mail: hcf@pixi.com
Internet http://www.hawaiicommunityfoundation.org
Requirements Hawaii 501(c)3 tax-exempt organizations that are not private foundations are eligible.
Restrictions Requests for support of annual campaigns,
deficit financing, or land acquisition are denied.
Areas of Interest Community Development; Education;
Health Care; Neighborhoods; Social Services
Sample Awards Chamber Music Hawii (HI)—for general operating support, $15,000 (2001). Waimanalo
Health Ctr (HI)—for general operating support, $60,000

(2001). Catholic Charities of the Diocese of Honolulu
(HI)—for general operating support, $5000 (2001).

Hawaii Community Foundation Medical 368
Research Grants
Hawaii Community Foundation
1164 Bishop Street
Honolulu, HI 96813
Contact Christine Sunada, Grants Manager, (808)
537-6333; fax: (808) 521-6286; e-mail: csunada@
hcf-hawaii.org or grantsinfo@hcf-hawaii.org
Internet http://www.hawaiicommunityfoundation.org/
grants/browse.php?categoryID=23
Requirements IRS 501(c)3 organizations serving Hawaii's people and its environment are eligible.
Restrictions The foundation does not fund endowments,
emergency support, individuals (except certain programs), large major capital projects, ongoing support, tuition aid programs, or deficit funding.
Areas of Interest Alzheimer's Disease; Cancer/
Carcinogenesis; Cardiovascular Diseases; Diabetes;
Health Services Delivery; Mental Health; Pulmonary
Diseases
Sample Awards Waimanalo Health Ctr (HI)—operating support, $60,000. Mental Health Assoc (HI)—operating support, $14,000.

G.N. Wilcox Trust Grants 369
G.N. Wilcox Trust
PO Box 3170
Honolulu, HI 96802-3170
Contact Program Contact, c/o Pacific Century Trust,
(808) 538-4944; fax: (808) 538-4647; e-mail:
pboyce@boh.com or emoniz@boh.com
Requirements Giving is limited to Hawaii, with emphasis on the island of Kauai.
Restrictions Grants are not awarded to support government agencies (or organizations substantially supported
by government funds), individuals, or for endowment
funds, research, deficit financing, or student aid in scholarships or loans.
Areas of Interest Adult and Continuing Education; Alzheimer's Disease; Basic Skills Education; Crime Prevention; Cultural Activities/Programs; Education; Elderly;
Environmental Programs; Family; Health Care; Hospitals; Juvenile Delinquency; Literacy; Performing Arts;
Protestant Church; Public Broadcasting; Radio; Social
Services; Volunteers; Youth Programs
Sample Awards Save our Seas (HI)—to support scholarships for youth to participate in the Second Annual
Clean Oceans Conference, $2954. Church of the Crossroads (HI)—to support the capital campaigns for renovations, $10,000. Hawaii Public Radio (HI)—to support
the membership challenge grant, $3000.

Idaho

Albertson's Charitable Giving Grants 370
Albertson's Inc
PO Box 20
Boise, ID 83726
Contact Community Relations, (208) 395-6200; fax:
(208) 395-4382

Internet http://www.albertsons.com/abs_
inthecommunity
Requirements Tax-exempt organizations in Arizona, Arkansas, California, Colorado, Delaware, Florida, Georgia, Idaho, Illinois, Indiana, Iowa, Kansas, Louisiana, Maine, Maryland, Massachusetts, Michigan, Minnesota, Mississippi, Missouri, Montana, Nebraska, Nevada, New Hampshire, New Jersey, New Mexico, North Dakota, Oklahoma, Oregon, Pennsylvania, South Dakota, Tennessee, Texas, Utah, Vermont, Washington, Wisconsin, and Wyoming are eligible.
Restrictions Contributions cannot be made to churches or religious organizations for purposes of religious advocacy.
Areas of Interest Academic Achievement; Diseases; Education; Food Distribution; Health Care; Health Promotion; Health Services Delivery; Higher Education; Hunger; Nutrition; Social Services; Youth Programs
Sample Awards Northwest Nazarene College (Nampa, ID)—to assist 20 teachers from three public school districts and one private school to work toward national board certification, $151,787.

AMI Semiconductors Corporate Grants   371
AMI Semiconductors
2300 Buckskin Rd
Pocatello, ID 83201
Contact Terri Timberman, Senior Vice President, Human Resources, (208) 233-4690 ext 6601; fax: (208) 234-6795 or (208) 234-6796
Internet http://www.amis.com/about
Restrictions The company does not support political or lobbying groups.
Areas of Interest Business Education; Economic Development; Elderly; Health Care Economics; Performing Arts; Social Services

Boise Cascade Corporation Contributions   372
   Grants
Boise Cascade Corporation
PO Box 50
Boise, ID 83728-0001
Contact Corporate Contributions, (208) 384-6161; fax: (208) 384-7189; e-mail: bcweb@bc.com
Internet http://www.bc.com/corporate/community.
html
Requirements US 501(c)3 nonprofit organizations in company-operating areas may apply.
Restrictions The corporation will not support areas where the corporation has minimal or no operations; individuals, private foundations, or international organizations; trips, athletic teams, scholarships, or sports vehicle sponsorships; or religious, fraternal, social, labor, or veterans organizations.
Areas of Interest Cultural Activities/Programs; Education; Environmental Programs

CHC Foundation Grants   373
CHC Foundation
PO Box 1644
Idaho Falls, ID 83403-1644
Contact Ralph Isom, President, (208) 522-2368
Requirements 501(c)3 southeastern Idaho nonprofit organizations may apply.

Areas of Interest Children and Youth; Community Development; Conservation, Natural Resources; Social Services
Sample Awards Tautphaus Park Zoo Animal Health Care Center—for building a hospital/quarantine facility for zoo animals, $250,000 (2001).

Idaho Community Foundation Grants   374
Idaho Community Foundation
210 W State St
Boise, ID 83702
Contact Grants Administrator, (208) 342-3535; fax: (208) 342-3577; e-mail: info@idcomfdn.org
Internet http://www.idcomfdn.org/grants.htm
Requirements Idaho nonprofit organizations are eligible.
Restrictions Grants do not support religious or political activities, individuals, deficit financing, fundraising, or endowments.
Areas of Interest Arts, General; Children and Youth; Community Development; Cultural Activities/Programs; Education; Environmental Programs; Family; Health Care; Health Services Delivery; Music; Public Affairs

Illinois

Abbott Laboratories Fund Grants   375
Abbott Laboratories Fund
100 Abbott Park Rd
Abbott Park, IL 60064-3500
Contact Cindy Schwab, Vice President, (847) 937-7075; fax: (847) 935-5051
Internet http://abbott.com/citizenship/fund/fund.
shtml#apply
Requirements Grants are made to tax-exempt organizations in company operating areas in Arizona, California, Illinois, Kansas, Massachusetts, Michigan, New Jersey, New York, North Carolina, Ohio, Puerto Rico, Texas, and Virginia, and Utah.
Restrictions Grants will be made only to associations and organizations and not directly to individuals. Contributions will not be made to purely social organizations; political parties or candidates; sectarian religious institutions; for social events, meetings, symposiums or conferences; or advertising journals, booklets, etc.
Areas of Interest Allied Health Education; Animal Care; Disaster Relief; Education; Health Care; Hospitals; Medical Education; Museums; Nursing Education; Social Services; Youth Programs
Sample Awards American Veterinary Medical Foundation (Schaumburg, IL)—to provide care for injured seaRch-rescue dogs, as well as animals of victims of the September 11 terrorist attacks, $10,000. Kenosha Public Museum (Kenosha, WI)—for its capital campaign, $100,000.

Actuarial Foundation Advancing Student   376
   Achievement Grants
Actuarial Foundation
475 N Martingale, Ste 600
Schaumburg, IL 60173

Contact Grants Administrator, (847) 706-3535; fax: (847) 706-3599; e-mail: ASA@ActFdn.org
Internet http://www.actuarialfoundation.org/grant/index.html
Requirements US and Canadian local groups or organizations are eligible. Collaboration among school systems, local actuarial clubs, corporations, and other stakeholders in education is encouraged.
Areas of Interest Insurance/Actuarial Science; Mathematics Education; Mentoring Programs

Alberto Culver Corporate Contributions Grants 377
Alberto Culver
2525 Armitage Ave
Melrose Park, IL 60160
Contact Nancy Shields, Corporate Communications, (708) 450-3000; fax: (708) 450-3435
Internet http://www.alberto.com
Requirements The company prefers to make small donations to a large number of grantees and fund groups where employees volunteer.
Restrictions Grants are not awarded to support United Way affiliates, religious groups, preschools, K-12 schools, tax-supported colleges, projects that duplicate other efforts, and multiyear commitments.
Areas of Interest Animal Care; Arts, General; Civic Affairs; Cultural Activities/Programs; Disabled; Disadvantaged (Economically); Health Care; Higher Education; Minorities; Rehabilitation/Therapy; Social Services; Training and Development; Women; Youth Programs

Andrew Family Foundation Grants 378
Andrew Family Foundation
14628 John Humphrey Dr
Orland Park, IL 60462
Contact Kim Lumiquinga
Requirements Organizations in Arizona, Illinois, Nevada, and Texas are eligible.
Restrictions The foundation does not make grants to individuals or for scholarships or loans.
Areas of Interest Children and Youth; Education; Hospitals; Human Learning and Memory; Music; Science; Social Services; Sports
Sample Awards Knox College (Galesburg, IL)—for the Harley Knosher Natatorium Project, $55,000. Northwestern U (Evanston, IL)—for the Learning Dynamic Laboratory, $30,000. Hope Childrens Hospital (Oak Lawn, IL)—to purchase beds and bedding, $25,000. Sherwood Conservatory of Music (Chicago, IL)—for construction of a new building, $25,000.

Bank One Foundation Grants 379
Bank One Foundation
1 Bank 1 Plaza, Ste 0308
Chicago, IL 60670
Contact James Donovan, (312) 407-8052
Requirements Giving limited to the metropolitan Chicago, IL, area.
Restrictions No support for fraternal or religious organizations; preschool, elementary, or secondary education; public agencies; or United Way/Crusade of Mercy-supported agencies. No grants to individuals, or for emergency funds, deficit financing, land acquisition,

research, publications, conferences, or multiyear operating pledges; no loans (except for program-related investments).
Areas of Interest Art Education; Arts, General; Civic Affairs; Community Development; Cultural Activities/Programs; Education; Educational Instruction Programs; Environmental Programs; Higher Education; Public Affairs
Sample Awards Columbia College Chicago (IL)—to start arts-education programs at four public elementary schools in Chicago, $200,000 (2003).

Barr Fund Grants 380
Barr Fund
8000 Sears Tower
Chicago, IL 60606
Contact Donald Lubin, President, c/o Sonnenschein, Nath & Rosenthal, (312) 876-8000
Requirements Illinois nonprofits are eligible.
Restrictions Individuals are not eligible.
Areas of Interest Children and Youth; Crisis Counseling; Higher Education; Jewish Services; Jewish Studies; Mental Health; Orchestras; Social Services

Baxter International Foundation Grants 381
Baxter International Foundation
1 Baxter Pkwy
Deerfield, IL 60015
Contact Patricia Morgan, Executive Director, (847) 948-4604
Internet http://www.baxter.com/investors/citizenship/foundation/index.html
Requirements Nonprofits in the United States, Europe, Latin America, and Mexico, with some emphasis on Chicago and Puerto Rico, are eligible.
Restrictions In general, the foundation does not make grants to capital and endowment campaigns; disease-specific organizations; educational institutions (except in instances where a grant would help to achieve other goals, such as increasing the skills and availability of health care providers); hospitals; individuals; fraternal, veterans, or religious organizations; or organizations for contributions for advertising space, tickets to dinners and fund-raising events, and promotional materials.
Areas of Interest Child/Maternal Health; Cultural Outreach; Education; Health Care; Health Education; International Programs; Social Services Delivery
Sample Awards Community Service Assoc (New Providence, NJ)—for a dedicated medical emergency fund, $10,000. Women's Transitional Living Ctr (Orange County, CA)—to provide routine health screenings and physicals for children living in the shelter, $25,000. Fox Cities Community Clinic (Menasha, WI)—to provide free health care to low-income, uninsured residents, $25,000.

Bersted Foundation Grants 382
Bersted Foundation
231 S LaSalle St
Chicago, IL 60697
Contact M.Catherine Ryan, (312) 828-1785
Requirements Illinois tax-exempt organizations in DeKalb, DuPage, Kane, and McHenry Counties are eligible.

Restrictions Grants do not support religious houses of worship, institutions of higher education, endowment funds, or deficit financing.

Areas of Interest Children and Youth; Community Development; Environmental Programs; Family; Health Care; Homelessness; Mental Health; Parks; Recreation and Leisure; Social Services

Sample Awards Aurora Foundation (IL)—for general support, $50,000. South East Assoc for Special Parks and Recreation (Downers Grove, IL)—for general support, $5000.

William Blair and Company Foundation Grants 383

William Blair and Company Foundation
222 W Adams St
Chicago, IL 60606
Contact David Coolidge III, Vice President, (312) 236-1600
Requirements Illinois nonprofit organizations are eligible.
Areas of Interest Arts, General; Catholic Church; Civic Affairs; Community Development; Cultural Activities/ Programs; Elementary Education; Health Care; Higher Education; Jewish Services; Public Affairs; Secondary Education; Social Services; Youth Programs
Sample Awards Chicago Botanic Garden (Glencoe, IL)—for general support, $10,000. Commercial Club Foundation (Chicago, IL)—for general support, $25,000.

Blowitz-Ridgeway Foundation Early Childhood Development Research Award 384

Blowitz-Ridgeway Foundation
1 Northfield Plaza, Ste 528
Northfield, IL 60093
Contact Megan Wilson, Administrator, (847) 446-1010; fax: (847) 446-6318; email: megan@ blowitzridgeway.org
Internet http://www.blowitzridgeway.org/information/ information.html
Requirements Applicants must be classified as 501(c)3 by the IRS.
Restrictions Grants will not be made for religious or political purposes, nor generally for the production or writing of audio-visual materials.
Areas of Interest Education; Educational Programs; Health Care; Health Education; Medical Programs; Medical Research; Mental Health; Social Science Education; Social Sciences
Sample Awards Catholic Charities, Diocese of Joliet (IL)—for support of its Back to School Fairs in DuPage and Will counties, which provide low-income families with immunizations and services, $10,000 (2003). Children's Memorial Hospital/Northwestern U, Dr. Emerick (IL)—for a research project which will study the mechanisms of growth failure in children with different forms of liver disease, $63,700 (2003). Cabrini-Green Tutoring Program (IL)—for general operating support of its tutoring programs, $5000 (2003). Science and Arts Academy (IL)—for scholarships of varying amounts to help economically disadvantaged, gifted students attend its school, $10,500 (2003).

Blowitz-Ridgeway Foundation Grants 385

Blowitz-Ridgeway Foundation
1 Northfield Plaza, Ste 528
Northfield, IL 60093
Contact Megan Wilson, Administrator, (847) 446-1010; fax: (847) 446-6318; e-mail: brf_mcw@ sbcglobal.net
Internet http://fdncenter.org/grantmaker/blowitz
Requirements 501(c)3 nonprofit organizations in Illinois who offer services to people who lack resources to provide for themselves may apply.
Restrictions Grants will not be awarded to government agencies or to organizations that subsist mainly on third-party funding and have demonstrated no ability or expended little effort to attract private funding. Grants will not be made for religious or political purposes or for the production or writing of audio-visual materials.
Areas of Interest AIDS; Adolescent Health; Adolescent Psychiatry; Adolescent Psychology; Alternative Medicine; Child/Maternal Health; Children and Youth; Education; Emergency Programs; HIV; Health Care; Pediatrics; Psychiatry; Psychology; Shelters; Social Sciences
Sample Awards The Night Ministry (IL)—for continued support of its Open Door youth emergency shelter, $10,000. Rehabilitation Institute of Chicago (IL)—for continued support of its Pediatric Free Care program, $18,000. AIDS Alternative Health Project (IL)—for its psychological services program for men and women with HIV and AIDS, $7500.

Helen V. Brach Foundation Grants 386

Helen V. Brach Foundation
55 W Wacker Dr, Ste 701
Chicago, IL 60601
Contact Raymond Simon, President, (312) 372-4417; fax: (312) 372-0290
Requirements Although 501(c)3 nonprofits from across the nation are eligible, giving is primarily made in the Midwest and California, Massachusetts, Ohio, Pennsylvania, and South Carolina.
Restrictions Grants are not made to individuals or to organizations outside the United States. Typically grants are not made in excess of 10 percent of a group's operating budget, which automatically excludes start-up grants.
Areas of Interest Animal Rights; Catholic Church; Child Welfare; Children and Youth; Education; Emergency Programs; Health Care; Homelessness; Job Training Programs; Literature; Parent Education; Philanthropy; Religion; Safety; Scholarship Programs, General; Science; Shelters; Teen Pregnancy; Women
Sample Awards Zoological Society of Florida (Miami, FL)—to purchase dinosaur and bird artifacts to be used in an educational program called Are Birds Really Dinosaurs?, $20,000 (2003).

Brunswick Foundation Grants 387

Brunswick Foundation
1 N Field Ct
Lake Forest, IL 60045
Contact Carol Stame, President, (847) 735-4467
Internet http://www.brunswickcorp.com
Requirements IRS 501(c)3 organizations in Alabama, Arizona, Connecticut, Florida, Georgia, Illinois, Indi-

ana, Kentucky, Louisiana, Maryland, Michigan, Minnesota, Mississippi, Nebraska, North Carolina, Oklahoma, Oregon, South Carolina, Tennessee, Texas, Washington, and Wisconsin are eligible.

Restrictions Grants are not made to religious organizations for religious purposes; for any form of political activity; to veterans groups, fraternal orders, or labor groups; for loans of any kind; or for trips, tours, dinners, tickets, or advertising.

Areas of Interest Conservation, Natural Resources; Environmental Programs; Higher Education; Parks; Recreation and Leisure; Volunteers; Water Resources

Sample Awards Grand Valley State U (Allendale, MI)—for the fresh water research program, $50,000. Texas Department of Parks and Wildlife (Austin, TX)—for capital support, $50,000.

Burlington Northern Santa Fe Foundation Grants 388

Burlington Northern Santa Fe Foundation
5601 W 26th St
Cicero, IL 60804
Contact Richard Russack, President, (708) 924-5615; fax: (708) 924-5657
Requirements 501(c)3 organizations located in Schaumburg, IL, and communities where the corporation operates, including 28 states and two Canadian provinces, are eligible to apply.
Areas of Interest Arts, General; Civic Affairs; Cultural Activities/Programs; Fire Prevention; Health Care; Higher Education; Higher Education, Private; Hospitals; Law Enforcement; Libraries; Museums; Native American Education; Performing Arts; Public Affairs; Scholarship Programs, General; Social Services
Sample Awards United Way of Metro Tarrant County (Fort Worth, TX)—for the capital campaign, $100,000.

Leo Burnett Company Charitable Foundation Grants 389

Leo Burnett Company Charitable Foundation
35 Wacker Dr
Chicago, IL 60601
Contact Chris Kimball, (312) 220-5959; fax: (312) 220-3299; e-mail: belief@leoburnett.com
Internet http://www.leoburnett.com
Requirements Illinois nonprofit organizations are eligible.
Areas of Interest At-Risk Youth; Environmental Programs; International Programs; Literacy; Wildlife

Carylon Foundation Grants 390

Carylon Foundation
2500 W Arthington
Chicago, IL 60612-4108
Contact Marcie Mervis, Trustee, (312) 666-7700
Areas of Interest Health Care; Higher Education; Hospitals; International Programs; Museums; Religion; Science
Sample Awards Rush-Presbyterian-Saint Lukes Medical Center (Chicago, IL)—for educational programs, $25,000 (1999). Holocaust Museum (Chicago, IL)—for operating support, $220,500. Weizmann Institute of Science (Palm Beach, FL)—for operating support, $10,000.

Caterpillar Foundation Grants 391

Caterpillar Foundation
100 NE Adams St
Peoria, IL 61629
Contact Maryann Morrison, Manager, (309) 675-4464
Internet http://www.cat.com
Restrictions Grants do not support fraternal organizations, religious organizations for religious purposes, political activities, individuals, United Way organizations, ticket purchase, or advertising for fund-raising benefits.
Areas of Interest Churches; Critical Care Medicine; Disabled; Elderly; Environmental Programs; Health Promotion; Health and Safety Education; Housing; Preventive Medicine; Public Health; Teen Pregnancy; Violent Behavior; Volunteers; Youth Programs
Sample Awards Illinois Nature Conservancy (IL)—for conservation activities along the Illinois River, $625,000 over five years (2001).

Chicago Board of Trade Foundation Grants 392

Chicago Board of Trade Foundation
141 W Jackson Blvd, Ste 600-A
Chicago, IL 60604
Contact Grants Administrator, (312) 435-3456; fax: (312) 341-3306
Internet http://www.cbot.com/cbot/www/page/ 0,1398,10+12,00.html
Requirements Nonprofit organizations in a 75-mile radius of the metropolitan Chicago, IL, area may apply for grant support.
Restrictions Support is not given to hospitals or foundations. Loans and program-related investments will also be denied.
Areas of Interest Adult and Continuing Education; Arts, General; Basic Skills Education; Cancer/ Carcinogenesis; Child Psychology/Development; Children and Youth; Communications; Cultural Activities/Programs; Health Care; Higher Education; Libraries; Literacy; Mass Media; Mental Health; Minorities; Museums; Rehabilitation/Therapy; Science Education; Technology Education; Visual Impairments; Wildlife
Sample Awards Kent State U (Kent, OH)—to coordinate research symposia on derivative markets and instruments, $1.2 million (2002).

Chicago Community Trust Grants 393

Chicago Community Trust
111 E Wacker Dr, Ste 1400
Chicago, IL 60601
Contact Program Contact, (312) 616-8000; fax: (312) 616-7955; email: info@cct.org
Internet http://www.cct.org/grantsseekers/ grantguidelines/index.html
Requirements Trust funds support 501(c)3 charitable organizations that serve residents of Cook County, IL. In general, grant requests from organizations that do not directly serve this geographic area will not be considered.
Restrictions The trust generally will not make grants for scholarships, individuals, religious purposes, endowments, or operating support of government agencies.
Areas of Interest Alternative Modes of Education; Art Education; Arts, General; Community Development; Criminal Justice; Dance; Education; Elementary Educa-

tion; Employment Opportunity Programs; Environmental Health; Food Distribution; High School Education; Health Promotion; Housing; Humanities; Juvenile Law; Leadership; Literacy; Nonprofit Organizations; Violent Behavior

Sample Awards ARK (Chicago, IL)—for the 2003 James Brown IV Award of Excellence for Outstanding Community Service, $50,000 (2003). Chicago Metropolitan Battered Women's Network (IL)—for a training institute for case workers, allied professionals, and others working in health care, law enforcement, and legal advocacy, $35,000 (2002). Chicago Dance Medium (IL)—for its Dance Legacy Project, which enables young dancers to learn from modern-dance masters in Chicago, $25,000 (2002).

Chicago Sun Times Charity Trust Grants 394

Chicago Sun Times Charity Trust
401 N Wabash Ave, Rm 326
Chicago, IL 60611
Contact Patricia Dudek, Client and Community Services, (312) 321-3000; fax: (312) 321-2278; e-mail: pdudek@hollingerintl.com
Requirements IRS 501(c)3 organizations serving the Chicago, IL, metropolitan area are eligible.
Restrictions The trust does not make grants to individuals, religious organizations for religious purposes, scholarships or fellowships, medical research or national health agency drives, or to political activities.
Areas of Interest Arts, General; Cultural Activities/Programs; Education; Literacy; Social Services

Chicago Title and Trust Company 395 Foundation Grants

Chicago Title and Trust Company Foundation
410 N Michigan Ave
Chicago, IL 60611
Contact Eileen Hughes, c/o Miami Corp, Treasurer, (312) 223-2911
Requirements Nonprofit organizations serving Chicago, IL, may apply.
Areas of Interest Cultural Activities/Programs; Economic Development; Higher Education; Job Training Programs; Literacy; Neighborhoods

Chicago Tribune's Corporate Contributions 396 Grants

Chicago Tribune Corporation
435 N Michigan Ave, 2nd Fl
Chicago, IL 60611-4041
Contact Community Relations, (312) 222-4300; fax: (312) 222-3751; e-mail: ctcommunityrelations@tribune.com
Internet http://www.chicagotribune.com/extras/comrel/guidectf.html
Requirements Grants are made to Chicago-area tax-exempt organizations.
Restrictions Grants are not made to individuals nor for fund-raising events.
Areas of Interest Architecture; Civic Affairs; Conservation, Natural Resources; Cultural Activities/Programs; Education; Health Care; Intellectual Freedom; Journalism; Minority Employment; Youth Programs

Sample Awards Westside Baptist Ministers' Conference (Chicago, IL)—for its youth development center, $10,000 and 12 computers. Chicago Architecture Foundation (Chicago, IL)—for educational programs for youths, $10,000.

Clarcor Foundation Grants 397

Clarcor Foundation
PO Box 7007, 2323 6th St
Rockford, IL 61125
Contact David Lindsay, Chairman, (815) 962-8867; fax: (815) 962-0417
Requirements Tax-exempt organizations in company-operating areas in Rockford, IL; Louisville, KY; Kearney and Gothenburg, NE; Cincinnati, OH; Oklahoma, and Lancaster, PA; are eligible.
Restrictions Grants are not made to support individuals, endowment funds, research, scholarships, fellowships, or loans.
Areas of Interest Arts, General; Civic Affairs; Crime Prevention; Cultural Activities/Programs; Dramatic/Theater Arts; Education; Health Care; Libraries; Library Automation; Social Services; Youth Programs
Sample Awards Boys & Girls Assoc of Rockford (IL)—to support the Crime Prevention program, $3000. New American Theater (Rockford, IL)—for educational outreach, $6000. Lancaster Theological Seminary (Lancaster, PA)—to fund creation of a computerized card catalog system, $2500. Boy Scouts of America (Kearney, NE)—to support the annual campaign, $1000.

CNA Foundation Grants 398

CNA Foundation
CNA Plaza, 15 S
Chicago, IL 60685
Contact Karen Harrigan, Program Officer, (312) 822-4985
Internet http://www.cna.com/about_cna/shtml/community.shtml
Requirements IRS 501(c)3 tax-exempt organizations are eligible.
Restrictions Grants are not made to/for individuals; political causes, candidates, or organizations; veterans, labor, alumni, military, athletic clubs, or social clubs; sectarian organizations or denominational religious organizations; capital improvement or building projects; endowed chairs or professorships; United Way-affiliated agencies; or national groups whose local chapters have already received support.
Areas of Interest Arts, General; Civic Affairs; Community Development; Cultural Activities/Programs; Disabled; Disadvantaged (Economically); Education; Elderly; Gifted/Talented Education; Health Care; Minorities; Social Services; Women; Youth Programs

Coleman Foundation Grants 399

Coleman Foundation Inc
575 W Madison, Ste 4605
Chicago, IL 60661
Contact Michael Hennessy, President, (312) 902-7120; fax: (312) 902-7124; e-mail: coleman@colemanfoundation.org
Internet http://www.colemanfoundation.org/index1.html

Requirements Nonprofits across the Midwest are eligible. Preference is given to requests from Illinois and Chicago.

Restrictions The program does not fund for-profit businesses, individuals, individual scholarships, ad books, tickets, equipment purchases (including computer hardware or software), or advertising.

Areas of Interest Business Education; Cancer/Carcinogenesis; Catholic Church; Disabled; Education; Entrepreneurship; Exhibitions, Collections, Performances; Housing; Infectious Diseases/Agents; Methodist Church; Museums; Natural History; Presbyterian Church; Religion; Urban Areas

Sample Awards Educated Eats (Chicago, IL)—for program evaluation and curriculum development, $25,000 (2003). Urban Gateways (Chicago, IL)—for the Arts Options Program, $11,000 (2003). Benedictine College (Atchison, KS)—for the Entrepreneurship Camp for high-school students, $23,000 (2003). Chicago Economic Development Council (IL)—for Web-site development and program support, $10,000 (2003).

Comer Foundation Grants   400
Comer Foundation
2 N LaSalle St
Chicago, IL 60602
Contact Stephanie Comer, President
Restrictions Individuals are ineligible for grant support.
Areas of Interest AIDS; AIDS Education; Arts, General; Career Education and Planning; Children and Youth; Cultural Activities/Programs; Cultural Outreach; Drug Education; Drugs/Drug Abuse; Family; Health Care; Homelessness; Humanities; Job Training Programs; Shelters; Social Services

Community Foundation of Central Illinois   401
  Grants
Community Foundation of Central Illinois
331 Fulton St, Ste 310
Peoria, IL 61602
Contact Michelle Moestue, Program Officer, (309) 674-8730; fax: (309) 674-8754; e-mail: michelle@communityfoundationci.org
Internet http://www.communityfoundationci.org/grant_guidelines.asp
Requirements Nonprofit organizations within a 50-mile radius of Peoria, IL are eligible.
Restrictions The foundation will not fund annual campaigns, individuals, or endowments, or make grants for sectarian religious purposes.
Areas of Interest Adult and Continuing Education; Arts, General; Basic Skills Education; Community Service Programs; Elementary Education; Family; Health Care; Humanities; Literacy; Scholarship Programs, General; Secondary Education; Social Services

Community Memorial Foundation Grants   402
Community Memorial Foundation
15 Spinning Wheel Rd, Ste 326
Hinsdale, IL 60521
Contact Program Contact, (630) 654-4729; fax: (630) 654-3402; e-mail: info@cmfdn.org
Internet http://www.cmfdn.org/guidelines.html

Requirements 501(c)3 organizations located in the Illinois communities of Argo, Bridgeview, Broadview, Brookfield, Burr Ridge, Clarendon Hills, Countryside, Darien, Downers Grove, Hickory Hills, Hinsdale, Hodgkins, Indian Head Park, Justice, La Grange, La Grange Park, Lyons, McCook, North Riverside, Oak Brook, Riverside, Stickney, Summit, Westchester, Western Springs, Westmont, Willow Springs, and Willowbrooks may apply.

Restrictions Grants are not awarded to individuals, sectarian or religious organizations, or for purposes to influence legislation or other political activities.

Areas of Interest Aging/Gerontology; Business; Education; Family; Government; Language; Nonprofit Organizations; Service Delivery Programs; Speech Pathology; Youth Programs

Sample Awards All Saints Episcopal Church & First Congregational Church (Western Springs, IL)—to establish a program to match volunteers with service opportunities, with a particular focus on older adults, $19,750 (2000). Parent & Community Network (Western Springs, IL) —to sponsor a conference and workshops on relevant issues to parents of children in School District 204 and feeder schools, $5,000 (2000). Boy Scouts of America-Des Plaines Valley Council (La Grange, IL)—for general operating support, $10,000 challenge grant.

Crossroads Fund Seed Grants   403
Crossroads Fund
3411 W Diversity Ave, Ste 20
Chicago, IL 60647
Contact Inhe Choi, Program Director, (773) 227-7676; fax: (773) 227-7790; e-mail: inhe@crossroadsfund.org or info@crossroadsfund,org
Internet http://www.crossroadsfund.org/seedfund.html
Requirements Community organizations in the Chicago metropolitan area, including northwestern Indiana, with annual expenses under $150,000 in the last completed fiscal year are eligible.
Restrictions The fund does not support organizations that are involved in electoral campaigns; contribute substantially to support lobbying at the federal, state, or local levels; or support private, in contrast to public, interest.
Areas of Interest Arts, Social Services; Civil/Human Rights; Economics; Grassroots Leadership; Minorities; Public Affairs; Public Policy/Planning; Racism/Race Relations; Social Change; Social Movements; Social Services
Sample Awards Beyondmedia Education—to create media for progressive organizing with a focus on girls' activism and women's incarceration, $7000 (2003). Illinois Coalition Against the Death Penalty—to facilitate a coalition of organizations in setting a common strategy for death penalty abolition in Illinois, capitalizing on momentum from recent commutation of death row inmates, $7000 (2003). Westside Ministers Coalition—for leadership development and organizing among Westside residents, to bring positive community change through a range of intergenerational projects and partnerships, $4500 (2003).

Crossroads Technical Assistance Program Grants 404

Crossroads Fund
3411 W Diversey, Ste 20
Chicago, IL 60647
Contact Inhe Choi, Program Director, (773) 227-7676; fax: (773) 227-7790; e-mail: inhe@crossroadsfund.org or info@crossroadsfund.org
Internet http://www.crossroadsfund.org/techassist. html
Requirements Community-based organizations in the Chicago metropolitan area, including northwestern Indiana, that have annual expenses under $150,000, and that have been in operation for at least 3 years are eligible.
Restrictions The fund does not support organizations that are involved in electoral campaigns; contribute substantially to support lobbying at the federal, state, or local levels; or support private, in contrast to public, interest.
Areas of Interest Arts, Social Services; Civil/Human Rights; Economics; Grassroots Leadership; Minorities; Public Affairs; Public Policy/Planning; Racism/Race Relations; Social Change; Social Movements; Social Services

Arie and Ida Crown Memorial Grants 405

Arie and Ida Crown Memorial
222 N LaSalle St, Ste 2000
Chicago, IL 60601
Contact Susan Crown, President, (312) 236-6300; fax: (312) 984-1499; e-mail: AICM@crown-Chicago.com
Requirements Nonprofit organizations in Chicago and Cook County, IL, may apply for grant support.
Restrictions Grants are not made to support individuals, conference expenses, film projects, government programs (50 percent government funded), or research projects.
Areas of Interest Civic Affairs; Cultural Activities/Programs; Education; Health Care; Inner Cities; International Relations; Jewish Services

Patrick and Anna M. Cudahy Fund Grants 406

Patrick and Anna M. Cudahy Fund
1007 Church St, Ste 414
Evanston, IL 60201
Contact Program Contact, (847) 866-0760; fax: (847) 475-0679
Internet http://www.cudahyfund.org
Requirements Nonprofit organizations in Chicago, IL, and Wisconsin are eligible to apply.
Areas of Interest Arts, General; Education; Environmental Programs; International Programs; International and Comparative Law; Social Services; Youth Programs
Sample Awards Art Institute of Chicago (IL)—for general operating support, $10,000. Council for the Spanish Speaking (Milwaukee, WI)—for the summer youth program, $7500. Milwaukee Christian Ctr (Milwaukee, WI)—for the Elderly Independent Living program, $10,000. Josephinum High School (Chicago, IL)—for scholarship support, $15,000.

Doris and Victor Day Foundation Grants 407

Doris and Victor Day Foundation Grants
1705 Second Ave, Ste 424
Rock Island, IL 61201
Contact Program Contact, (309) 788-2300; fax: (309) 788-3298; e-mail: info@dayfoundation.org
Internet http://www.dayfoundation.org/guide.htm
Requirements Illinois and Iowa nonprofit organizations may apply.
Areas of Interest Child Abuse; Education; Food Distribution; Health Care; History; Muscular Dystrophy; Museums; Shelters
Sample Awards Iowa Medical Aid Fund (IA)—for medical aid to women, $35,000 (2003). Muscular Dystrophy Assoc (IL)—for program support $2000. Child Abuse Council (IL)—for operating support, $3500. Putnam Museum of History (IL)—for operating support, $1000.

John Deere Foundation Grants 408

John Deere Foundation
1515 River Dr
Moline, IL 61265
Contact Foundation Administrator, (309) 748-7955; fax: (309) 748-7953; e-mail: ChristisonJudyA@ JohnDeere.com
Internet http://www.deere.com/en_US/compinfo/ johndeere_foundations/contributions_index. html?sidenavstate=000000000001
Requirements Nonprofit organizations in company-operating areas are eligible, including the following states: Alabama, Organizations in Connecticut, Georgia, Illinois, Indiana, Iowa, Michigan, Minnesota, New Hampshire, Oklahoma, Pennsylvania, Virginia, and Wisconsin are eligible to apply. Also eligible to apply are organizations and institutions of national or international scope that reflect the foundation's concerns.
Restrictions The foundation does not provide support for individuals, dinners or special events, fraternal organizations, good-will advertising, or political or lobbying groups.
Areas of Interest Civic Affairs; Cultural Activities/Programs; Developing/Underdeveloped Nations; Education; Health Care; Higher Education; International Programs; Libraries, Academic; Safety; Social Services
Sample Awards Wartburg College (Waverly, IA)—to expand and remodel the college's Robert and Sally Vogel Library, $100,000. Western Illinois U (Macomb, IL)—for the new regional center, $500,000.

Gaylord and Dorothy Donnelley Foundation 409 Grants

Gaylord and Dorothy Donnelley Foundation
35 E Wacker Dr, Ste 2600
Chicago, IL 60601-2102
Contact Grants Manager, (312) 977-2700; fax: (312) 977-1686; e-mail: gddf@gddf.org
Internet http://www.gddf.org/grant/process.asp
Requirements IRS 501(c)3 organizations serving the Chicago region or the South Carolina low country are eligible.
Restrictions The foundation usually will not support requests for individuals; endowments or capital campaigns; fund-raising events; publications, films, or videos; eradication of deficits or loans; conferences; or religious purposes.
Areas of Interest Arts, General; Child Abuse; Conservation, Natural Resources; Cultural Activities/Pro-

grams; Education; Environmental Programs; Hispanics; History; Social Services

Sample Awards Child Abuse Prevention Services (Chicago, IL)—for the Latino outreach initiative, $5000. DuPage Environmental Awareness Ctr (Chicago, IL)—for general operating support, $5000. South Carolina Historical Society (SC)—for general operating support, $12,000.

R.R. Donnelley Corporate Contributions Program   410

R.R. Donnelley & Sons Company
77 W Wacker Dr
Chicago, IL 60601
Contact Susan Levy, (312) 326-8102; fax: (312) 326-8262; e-mail: susan.levy@rrd.com
Internet http://www.rrdonnelley.com/cportal/public/home/aboutus/communityrelations/community_involvement.jsp
Requirements Grants are made to nonprofit US organizations and not to individuals. Application consists of a short proposal containing a description of the organization, its activities, and its clients; a clear statement of the amount requested; and an explanation of what is to be accomplished with the assistance. Applicant is also asked to submit a copy of the IRS letter of tax exemption, a list of board members, and an audited financial statement.
Restrictions The company does not contribute printing; make grants to individuals or to religious organizations; make grants for television, radio, film or video; or make grants for specific diseases, clinical care, or medical research or equipment.
Areas of Interest Children and Youth; Cultural Activities/Programs; Curriculum Development; Health Care; Literacy; Public Planning/Policy

Evanston Community Foundation Grants   411

Evanston Community Foundation
1007 Church St, Ste 108
Evanston, IL 60201
Contact Sara Schastok, Executive Director, (847) 492-0990; fax: (847) 492-0904; e-mail: info@evcommfdn.org
Internet http://www.evcommfdn.org/grant_making.htm
Requirements IRS 501(c)3 organizations serving the Evanston, IL, community are eligible.
Areas of Interest Arts, General; Children and Youth; Community Development; Community and School Relations; Education; Family; Health Care; Housing; Leadership; Neighborhoods
Sample Awards Evanston Youth Bank (Evanston, IL)—for Northwestern University Undergraduate Leadership Program, $1000 (2003).

Field Foundation of Illinois Grants   412

Field Foundation of Illinois, Inc
200 S Wacker Dr, Ste 3860
Chicago, IL 60606
Contact Danelle Williams, Program Contact, (312) 831-0910; fax: (312) 831-0961; e-mail: DWilliams@fieldfoundation.org
Internet http://www.fieldfoundation.org

Requirements Applicants must reside in Illinois. Proposals should include a cover letter summarizing why foundation support is sought, a brief history and background of the applicant organization/agency, a budget for the applicant's current financial year and most recent audited financial statement, a list of board members and their affiliations, and an IRS determination letter.
Restrictions Grants will not be made to or for United Way of Chicago member agencies for regular operating support; medical research or national health agency appeals; propaganda organizations or committees whose efforts are aimed at influencing legislation; conferences, seminars, or meetings; fund-raising events or advertising; appeals for religious purposes; other granting agencies or foundations; operating support of neighborhood health centers or clinics, day care centers for children, or small cultural groups; endowments; or individuals. Operating support is generally limited from one to three years.
Areas of Interest Adult and Continuing Education; Basic Skills Education; Conservation, Natural Resources; Cultural Activities/Programs; Education Reform; Elementary Education; Environmental Programs; Health Care; Leadership; Literacy; Public Affairs; Public Planning/Policy; Secondary Education; Social Services; Urban Affairs; Volunteers; Women; Youth Programs
Sample Awards Boys Club of Bellwood and Hillside—to support the club's building expansion program, $10,000. Metropolitan Planning Council—to provide partial funding for the Health Care project, $7500. Chicago Panel on Public School Policy and Finance—to support the Monitoring School Reform in Chicago project, $16,500. Chicago Foundation for Women—to support a new women's leadership development initiative, $5000. Friends of the Chicago River—as a matching grant payment to establish a full-time public policy and planning position, $7500.

Lloyd A. Fry Foundation Grants   413

Lloyd A. Fry Foundation
120 S LaSalle St, Ste 1950
Chicago, IL 60603
Contact Unmi Song, Executive Director, (312) 580-0310; fax: (312) 580-0980; e-mail: jdseltzer@fryfoundation.org
Internet http://www.fryfoundation.org/guidelines.html
Requirements Grants are made only to tax-exempt organizations and are rarely made to organizations outside the Chicago metropolitan area.
Restrictions Grants are not made to individuals, governmental bodies, tax-supported educational institutions, or for fund-raising benefits.
Areas of Interest Arts, General; Civic Affairs; Cultural Activities/Programs; Education; Food Distribution; HIV; Health Care; Health Promotion; Job Training Programs; Men; Photography; Social Services; Welfare-to-Work Programs
Sample Awards Small Schools Coalition (Chicago, IL)—for general operating support, $25,000. Resource Ctr (Chicago, IL)—for the Perishable Food Recovery program, $10,000. Art Institute of Chicago (IL)—for acquisitions in the department of photography, $5000. Better Existence with HIV (Evanston, IL)—for the Healthier Men 2000 Education Outreach program,

$10,000. Jobs for Youth (Chicago, IL)—for the Welfare-to-Work model, $45,000. Abraham Lincoln Ctr (Chicago, IL)—for a job-training and placement program for welfare recipients, $80,000.

GATX Corporation Grants Program 414

GATX Corporation
500 W Monroe
Chicago, IL 60661
Contact Jesse Kane, Supervisor of Community Affairs, (312) 621-6222; fax: (312) 499-7219; e-mail: communityaffairs@gatx.com
Internet http://www.gatx.com/common/about/community/about.asp
Requirements Eligible to apply are nonprofit 501(c)3 tax-exempt organizations located in company-operating areas and that serve the economically disadvantaged.
Restrictions Grants are not awarded to individuals, political organizations, religious organizations, private foundations, capital campaigns, endowment funds, health research, national organizations, or for fund-raisers.
Areas of Interest Arts, General; At-Risk Youth; Civic Affairs; Culinary Arts; Cultural Activities/Programs; Disabled; Education; Family; Health Care; Homelessness; Hunger; Minorities; Music Education; Poverty and the Poor; Public Planning/Policy; Reading; Recreation and Leisure; Social Services
Sample Awards Suzuki-Orff School for Young Musicians (Chicago, IL)—for the Clap, Sing, and Read program, which uses music to promote reading skills among at-risk children, $15,000. Chicago Anti-Hunger Federation (Chicago, IL)—for the Oliver's Kitchen Employment Training Program, which provides culinary training to formerly homeless and low-income individuals, $20,000. National Lekotek Ctr (Evanston, IL)—to provide learning and recreational services for disabled children in Chicago's West Humboldt Park neighborhood, as well as supportive services for their parents, $19,534.

Girl's Best Friend Foundation Grants 415

Girl's Best Friend Foundation
900 N Franklin, Ste 210
Chicago, IL 60610
Contact Robin Dixon, Program Officer, (312) 266-2842; fax: (312) 266-2972; e-mail: robin@girlsbestfriend.org or contact@girlsbestfriend.org
Internet http://www.girlsbestfriend.org/apply/index.html
Requirements Letters of intent will be accepted from 501(c)3 nonprofits for projects that serve or have a direct impact on girls living in the Chicago metropolitan area including Cook, DuPage, Kane, Lake, McHenry, and Will counties.
Restrictions Organizations with budgets that exceed $650,000 may apply only for technical assistance and/or collaborative action research grants. The foundation generally does not fund individuals, capital campaigns, debt reduction, scholarships, or government or religious organizations.
Areas of Interest Career Education and Planning; Construction Management; Cultural Diversity; Grassroots Leadership; Jewish Services; Juvenile Delinquency; Mental Health; Public Planning/Policy; Women; Women's Employment; Youth Violence
Sample Awards Beyondmedia Education (Chicago, IL)—to expand a program that provides media workshops for a diverse group of girls and young women, $14,000 (2002). Chicago Women in Trades (IL)—for the Aspiring Tradeswomen program, which serves girls enrolled in high-school vocational classes, $15,000 (2002). Family Planning of Western Illinois (IL)— to expand a leadership-development program for girls ages 11 to 17 in Galesburg, $15,000 (2002). Literature for All of Us (Evanston, IL)—for general support of this program, which offers book groups for young women and girls throughout metropolitan Chicago, $14,000 (2002).

Grand Victoria Foundation Grants 416

Grand Victoria Foundation
60 S Grove Ave
Elgin, IL 60120
Contact Grants Administrator, (847) 289-8575; fax: (847) 289-8576; e-mail: info@grandvictoriafdn.org
Internet http://www.grandvictoriafdn.org
Requirements For local projects, nonprofit organizations must be operating in Kane, DuPage, Lake, McHenry, Kendall, Will, Winnebago, DeKalb, or suburban Cook Counties. Regional project applicants must be operating in the Chicago metropolitan area. Statewide project applicants must be operating in Illinois and engaged in child care, land use and protection, and/or workforce development efforts that impact a substantial portion of Illinois.
Restrictions Grants are not available to support endowments, fundraising events, debt or deficit reduction, political campaigns, religious purposes, individuals, taxing bodies to accomplish programs that fall within the normal scope of their responsibilities, or research or planning projects unless they are a well-integrated step to program implementation.
Areas of Interest Air Pollution; Child Welfare; Children and Youth; Economic Development; Education; Environmental Health; Housing; Environmental Programs; Job Training Programs; Land Management; Neighborhoods; Water Pollution; Youth Programs
Sample Awards Housing Opportunity Development Corp (Wilmette, IL)—to purchase and restore housing for low- and moderate-income people who live and/or work in the Northeastern Illinois region, $40,000 (2003). Environmental Law and Policy Ctr (Chicago, IL)—two-year general operating grant, $100,000 (2003). Garfield Park Conservatory Alliance (Chicago, IL)—two-year grant in renewed support of youth education programs, $25,000 (2003). Elgin Children's Chorus (Elgin, IL)—Elgin Grantworks general program, $8000 (2003).

Harris Bank Foundation Grants Program 417

Harris Bank Foundation
PO Box 755, 111 W Monroe St
Chicago, IL 60690
Contact Donna Streibich, Treasurer, (312) 461-5834; fax: (312) 293-4702
Requirements Grants are given only to tax-exempt organizations located in the Chicago metropolitan area. A proposal should include a statement of the proposed pro-

ject; project budget and potential funding sources; background information about the organization; evidence of tax-exempt status; and current, audited financial statements.

Restrictions Grants are not made for or to political activities, individuals, individual sectarian or religious organizations, fraternal organizations, nor for testimonial drives, advertisements in souvenir or program books, or raffle tickets.

Areas of Interest Art Appreciation; Arts Administration; Business Development; Career Education and Planning; Civic Affairs; Cultural Activities/Programs; Disabled; Drugs/Drug Abuse; Education; Educational/Public Television; Fine Arts; Health Care Access; Health Services Delivery; Higher Education, Private; Housing

Sample Awards Art Institute of Chicago (IL)—for general operating support, $14,000. YMCA of Metropolitan Chicago (IL)—for Duncan YMCA renovation and expansion, $10,000. Habitat for Humanity Uptown Chicago (IL)—for general operating support, $10,000.

Household International Corporate Giving Program Grants 418

Household International Corporate Giving Program
2700 Sanders Rd
Prospect Heights, IL 60070
Contact Contributions Administrator, (847) 564-6010; fax: (847) 564-7094; e-mail: communityrelations@household.com
Internet http://www.household.com/corp/hioc_community_commit.jsp
Requirements Nonprofit organizations in corporate operating areas are eligible.
Restrictions The corporation does not make direct grants to schools, hospitals, or single-disease research organizations.
Areas of Interest Basic Skills Education; Children and Youth; Civic Affairs; Disabled; Economic Development; Economics Education; Education; Family; Health Care; Housing; Job Training Programs; Shelters; Social Services
Sample Awards Beacon Light Community Housing Development Organization (Hampton, VA)—for money-management classes for low- and middle-income people, $109,000 (2003). Catholic Charities Community Development Corp (Saint Petersburg, FL)—to provide homeownership and financial education to low- and moderate-income adults, and for a program to teach youths about budgeting and investing, $215,000 (2003). Vecinos Unidos (Dallas, TX)—for educational courses for low- and middle-income Latinos buying homes, $60,950 (2003). FAIM Economic Development Corp (Dallas, TX)—for a money-management and credit-education program for members of African-American churches and other Dallas residents, $114,000 over two years (2003).

Illinois Arts Council Local Arts Agencies Program Grants 419

Illinois Arts Council
100 W Randolph St, Ste 10-500
Chicago, IL 60601-3298
Contact Public Information Office, (312) 814-6750 or (800) 237-6994; fax: (312) 814-1471; TTY: (312) 814-4831; e-mail: info@arts.state.il.us
Internet http://www.state.il.us/agency/iac/Guidelines/guidelines.htm
Requirements Nonprofit organizations must be chartered in the state of Illinois.
Areas of Interest Arts Administration

Illinois Arts Council Multidisciplinary Program Grants 420

Illinois Arts Council
100 W Randolph St, Ste 10-500
Chicago, IL 60601-3298
Contact Public Information Office, (312) 814-6750 or (800) 237-6994; fax: (312) 814-1471; TTY: (312) 814-4831; e-mail: info@arts.state.il.us
Internet http://www.state.il.us/agency/iac/Guidelines/guidelines.htm
Requirements Nonprofit organizations must be chartered in the state of Illinois.
Areas of Interest Arts, General

Illinois Arts Council Music Program Grants 421

Illinois Arts Council
100 W Randolph St, Ste 10-500
Chicago, IL 60601-3298
Contact Public Information Office, (312) 814-6750 or (800) 237-6994; fax: (312) 814-1471; TTY: (312) 814-4831; e-mail: info@arts.state.il.us
Internet http://www.state.il.us/agency/iac/Guidelines/guidelines.htm
Requirements Nonprofit organizations must be chartered in the state of Illinois.
Areas of Interest Band Music; Chamber Music; Jazz; Music; Music, Vocal; Opera/Musical Theater; Orchestras

Illinois Arts Council Theater Program Grants 422

Illinois Arts Council
100 W Randolph St, Ste 10-500
Chicago, IL 60601-3298
Contact Public Information Office, (312) 814-6750 or (800) 237-6994; fax: (312) 814-1471; TTY: (312) 814-4831; e-mail: info@arts.state.il.us
Internet http://www.state.il.us/agency/iac/Guidelines/guidelines.htm
Requirements Nonprofit organizations must be chartered in the state of Illinois.
Areas of Interest Children's Theater; Dramatic/Theater Arts

Illinois Tool Works Foundation Grants 423

Illinois Tool Works Foundation
3600 W Lake Ave
Glenview, IL 60025-5811
Contact Mary Ann Mallahan, Director, (847) 724-7500; fax: (847) 657-4505; e-mail: mmallahan@itw.com
Internet http://www.itwinc.com/itw_foundation.html
Requirements Applicant organizations must be located in Illinois to be eligible.

Areas of Interest Arts, General; Children and Youth; Community Development; Crime Prevention; Cultural Activities/Programs; Education; Employment Opportunity Programs; Family; Higher Education; Industry; Mathematics Education; Museums; Neighborhoods; Orchestras; Performing Arts; Professional Associations; Public Affairs; Public Planning/Policy; Restoration and Preservation; Science; Science Education; Senior Citizen Programs and Services; Social Services; Vocational/Technical Education; Youth Programs

Sample Awards United Way/Crusade of Mercy (Chicago, IL)—for annual campaign, $638,482 (2002). Museum of Science and Industry (IL)—to support Campaign 2000, $200,000. Chicago Symphony Orchestra (IL)—for continued support, $25,000.

Joyce Foundation Grants 424

Joyce Foundation
70 W Madison, Ste 2750
Chicago, IL 60602
Contact Mary O'Connell, Communications Officer, (312) 782-2464; fax: (312) 782-4160; e-mail: info@joycefdn.org
Internet http://www.joycefdn.org/guidelines/guideintro.html
Requirements Applications should be made only by organizations that can demonstrate their tax-exempt status and that can supply complete financial information and permit the results of a grant to be audited. Preference is given to nonprofit organizations that are based, or have a program, in Illinois, Indiana, Iowa, Michigan, Minnesota, Ohio, or Wisconsin.
Restrictions The foundation generally does not support capital projects, endowment campaigns, religious activities, direct services, or scholarships.
Areas of Interest Biotechnology; Campaign Finance Reform; Conservation, Agriculture; Conservation, Natural Resources; Cultural Activities/Programs; Cultural Diversity; Curriculum Development; Economic Development; Education; Education Reform; Elementary Education; Employment Opportunity Programs; Fossil Fuels; Great Lakes; Gun Control; Hazardous Wastes; Mathematics Education; Poverty and the Poor; Public Health; Science Education; Secondary Education; Training and Development; Transportation; Urban Areas; Urban Education; Violent Behavior; Water Pollution; Welfare-to-Work Programs
Sample Awards Citizens for a Better Environment (Milwaukee, WI)—for board and professional-development activities, $20,000 (2002). Chicago Historical Society (Chicago, IL)—for an exhibit on adolescence based on extensive oral histories culled from a diverse group of young Chicago residents, $375,000 (2002). Ctr for Voting and Democracy (Takoma Park, MD)—to organize, educate, and mobilize people in favor of restoring Illinois's multi-member House legislative districts, $70,000 over two years (2002). Johns Hopkins U (Baltimore, MD)—for continued support of the Bloomberg School of Public Health's Center for Gun Policy and Research, $600,000 (2002).

Mayer and Morris Kaplan Family Foundation Grants 425

Mayer and Morris Kaplan Family Foundation
1780 Green Bay Rd, Ste 205
Highland Park, IL 60035
Contact Jason Heeney, Executive Director, (847) 926-8350; e-mail: Jheeney@kapfam.com
Requirements Illinois nonprofit organizations are eligible.
Restrictions Grants are generally not given to sectarian institutions; purchase of tickets to testimonial events or goodwill advertising; medical, scientific, or academic research; individuals, films, or funding of meetings; capital and endowment campaigns, building and equipment acquisition, or fund-raising drives; health care institutions; national health, welfare, education, or cultural organizations; or an institution more than once during the fiscal year.
Areas of Interest Arts, General; Civic Affairs; Education; Inner Cities; Jewish Services; Museums; Social Services

Donald P. and Byrd M. Kelly Foundation Grants 426

Donald P. and Byrd M. Kelly Foundation
701 Harger Rd
Oak Brook, IL 60523
Contact Laura McGrath, Treasurer
Requirements Nonprofit organizations are eligible. Illinois nonprofits, with an emphasis on Chicago, receive preference.
Areas of Interest Adult and Continuing Education; Education; Elementary Education; Higher Education; Minorities; Preschool Education; Secondary Education
Sample Awards Big Shoulders Fund (Chicago, IL)—for general operating support, $25,000. Foundation Fighting Blindness (Hunt Valley, MD)—for general operating support, $76,191. Robert Crown Ctr for Health Education (Hinsdale, IL)—for general operating support, $12,500. Museum of Science and Industry (Chicago, IL)—for general operating support, $30,000.

Kenny's Kids Grants 427

Kenny's Kids
1212 W Lill St
Chicago, IL 60614
Contact Nicholas Pontikes, President
Requirements Nonprofits in company operating areas of Illinois are eligible.
Restrictions No support for private foundations, schools (public or private), or corporations. Grants are not made to individuals, or for political campaigns, film, video, or audio productions.
Areas of Interest Child Welfare

MacArthur Fund for Arts and Culture 428

Richard H. Driehaus Foundation
203 N Wabash Ave, Ste 1800
Chicago, IL 60601
Contact MacArthur Fund for Arts and Culture, (312) 641-5772; fax: (312) 641-5736; e-mail: driehausfoundation@ameritech.net
Internet http://www.macfound.org/programs/gen/dh_macfund.htm

Restrictions This program is not intended for arts education programs. Nor is it intended, for professional theater and dance companies with operating budgets of less than $150,000; those companies should visit the MacArthur Foundation website to review the guidelines for the Small Theater and Dance Group Funding Program.
Areas of Interest Art Appreciation; Arts, General; Cultural Activities/Programs; Interdisciplinary Arts; Media Arts; Museums; Performing Arts; Visual Arts
Sample Awards Marin Corp Productions (Chicago, IL)— in support of the television documentary Lila's Hope, $50,000 (2003).

John D. and Catherine T. MacArthur Foundation Community Initiatives Program Grants 429
John D. and Catherine T. MacArthur Foundation
140 S Dearborn St, Ste 1100
Chicago, IL 60603
Contact Office of Grants Management, Research, and Information, (312) 726-8000; fax: (312) 920-6258; TDD: (312) 920-6285; e-mail: 4answers@macfdn.org
Internet http://www.macfdn.org/programs
Areas of Interest Arts, General; Civic Affairs; Community Development; Cultural Programs; Education; Higher Education; Urban Areas
Sample Awards Metropolitan Alliance of Congregations (Chicago, IL)—for leadership training designed to encourage broader civic participation in regional decision-making, $75,000 (2003). Chicago Housing Authority (IL)—to plan several public-housing developments, $310,000 (2003). Art Institute of Chicago (IL)—for general operating support, $400,000 over five years (2003). Metropolitan Caucus (Chicago, IL)—to help develop solutions to key issues affecting the six-county metropolitan Chicago area, including education, the environment and health, housing, and transportation, $1.3 million (2003).

Robert R. McCormick Tribune Foundation Grants Programs 430
Robert R. McCormick Tribune Foundation
435 N Michigan Ave, Ste 770
Chicago, IL 60611
Contact Mark Hallett, Senior Program Officer, (312) 222-3512; fax: (312) 222-3523; e-mail: mhallett@tribune.com
Internet http://www.rrmtf.org/mtf/mtfinfo.htm
Requirements The foundation funds education programs in the Chicago metropolitan area only. Community programs are funded in Anaheim; Atlanta; Chicago; Cleveland; Denver; El Paso; Escondido; Fort Lauderdale; Los Angeles; Manhattan, KS; New York; Newport News, VA; Orlando; and Phoenix.
Areas of Interest Community Development; Economic Development; Education; Educational Administration; Hispanics; Intellectual Freedom; Journalism; Leadership; National Security; Parent Education; Philanthropy; Preschool Education; Teacher Education
Sample Awards Asian American Federation of New York (NY)—for the Disaster Relief Workforce Development Initiative, $400,000 (2002). Catholic Charities of the Archdiocese of New York (NY)—to provide case-management services and emergency cash assis-

tance to immigrant and low-wage workers who lost their jobs as a result of the September 11th terrorist attacks, $500,000 (2002). U of Chicago (IL)—to establish a professorship dedicated to the study of urban issues, to create full-tuition scholarships, and to support activities linking the university with the city, including internships, workshops, and policy briefings for city officials, $5 million (2002). Structured Employment Economic Development Corp (New York, NY)—to provide grants, loans, and other assistance to small businesses in lower Manhattan that were affected by the attacks on the World Trade Center, $425,000 (2002).

Colonel Stanley R. McNeil Foundation Grants 431
Colonel Stanley R. McNeil Foundation
231 S LaSalle St
Chicago, IL 60697-0246
Contact Charles Slamar, Jr. Vice- President, Bank of America, (312) 828-8028
Requirements Illinois nonprofit organizations serving the Chicago metropolitan area are eligible.
Areas of Interest Child Welfare; Education; Health Care; Youth Programs

Motorola Foundation Grants 432
Motorola Foundation
1303 E Algonquin Rd
Schaumburg, IL 60196
Contact Linda Tucker, Executive Director, (847) 576-6200; fax: (847) 576-3997
Internet http://www.motorola.com/MotorolaFoundation
Requirements All grants are made to 501(c)3 tax-exempt organizations.
Restrictions Grants may not be made to individuals, private foundations, benefit events or ads, specific disease organizations, United Way agencies (other than capital), higher education capital drives, endowments, research, sectarian/denominational religious organizations, or fraternal organizations.
Areas of Interest Arts, General; Civic Affairs; Communications; Community Development; Criminal Justice; Cultural Activities/Programs; Cultural Diversity; DNA; Electronics/Electrical Engineering; Elementary Education; Environmental Programs; Higher Education; Libraries; Mathematics Education; Museums; Public Broadcasting; Public Planning/Policy; Science Education; Secondary Education; Social Services
Sample Awards North Carolina A&T State U (NC)— for a computer-engineering laboratory, $400,000.

New Prospect Foundation Grants 433
New Prospect Foundation
1603 Orrington Ave, Ste 1880
Evanston, IL 60201
Contact Paul Lehman, Director, (847) 328-2288
Requirements Priority is given to requests from the Chicago metropolitan area.
Restrictions Grants do not fund the arts, higher education, individuals, capital or endowment requests, basic research, scholarships, fellowships, or loans.
Areas of Interest Abortion; Central America; Civil/Human Rights; Economic Development; Education Re-

form; Employment Opportunity Programs; Health Care; Health Planning/Policy; Housing; Inner Cities; Israel; Jewish Services; Neighborhoods; Social Services; Urban Areas

Sample Awards Shefa Fund (Wyndmoor, PA)—to leverage investments from Jewish institutions and individuals for use by community-development financial institutions, $180,000.

Northern Trust Company Charitable Trust and Corporate Giving Program   434

Northern Trust Company
50 S LaSalle St, Ste M-5
Chicago, IL 60675
Contact Dawn McGovern, Program Contact, (312) 444-4059
Internet http://www.northerntrust.com/aboutus/community/charitable/index.html
Requirements Nonprofit organizations in Illinois are eligible. A proposal should include a short cover letter, an operating budget for the current year, a copy of the agency's most recent audited financial statement, a list of members of the agency's governing board, a list of Chicago-based corporate and foundation contributors and amounts each has contributed in the last calendar year, and a letter from the IRS indicating tax-exempt status.
Areas of Interest Alcohol/Alcoholism; Arts, General; Business Development; Civic Affairs; Community Development; Cultural Activities/Programs; Domestic Violence; Drugs/Drug Abuse; Education; Employment Opportunity Programs; Health Care; Health Care Access; Health Care Economics; Health Services Delivery; Homelessness; Hunger; Industry; Inner Cities; Job Training Programs; Literacy; Mental Health; Minority Education; Neighborhoods; Parent Involvement; Poverty and the Poor; Social Services; Teen Pregnancy
Sample Awards Parents United for Responsible Education (Chicago, IL)—for operating support, $5000. Chicago Reporter (Chicago, IL)—for operating support, $3000.

Frank E. and Seba B. Payne Foundation Grants   435

Frank E. Payne and Seba B. Payne Foundation Grants
231 S LaSalle St
Chicago, IL 60697
Contact M. Catherine Ryan, c/o Bank of America, (312) 828-1785
Requirements Nonprofit organizations in the greater Chicago, IL, metropolitan area and in Pennsylvania are eligible.
Restrictions Grants are not made to individuals.
Areas of Interest AIDS; Animal Care; Children and Youth; Cultural Activities/Programs; Education; Hospitals

Peoples Energy Corporation Grants   436

Peoples Energy Corporation
130 E Randolph Dr
Chicago, IL 60601
Contact Community Contributions, (312) 240-4000; fax: (312) 240-4389
Internet http://www.pecorp.com
Requirements Organizations in Illinois are eligible.
Restrictions Contributions will not be made to individuals; organizations that discriminate by race, color, creed, or national origin; political organizations or campaigns; organizations whose prime purpose is to influence legislation; religious organizations for religious purposes; agencies owned and operated by local, state, or federal governments; or for trips or tours, or special-occasion or goodwill advertising.
Areas of Interest Civic Affairs; Community Development; Cultural Activities/Programs; Health Care; Higher Education; Neighborhoods; Social Services

Albert Pick Jr. Fund Grants   437

Albert Pick Jr. Fund
30 N Michigan Ave, Ste 1002
Chicago, IL 60602-3402
Contact Cleopatra Alexander, Program Consultant, (312) 236-1192
Requirements Only Illinois organizations may apply.
Restrictions Funds will not be provided for reduction or liquidation of debts, religious purposes, endowments, long-term commitments, building programs, individuals, political purposes, or advertising/program books.
Areas of Interest Civic Affairs; Community Development; Cultural Activities/Programs; Education; Health Care; Radio; Social Services; Youth Programs
Sample Awards Chicagoland Radio Information Service (Chicago, IL)—for operating support, $2500. Youth Service project (Chicago, IL)—for program support, $5000. Girl Scouts of Chicago (Chicago, IL)—for program support, $6500.

Playboy Foundation Grants   438

Playboy Foundation
680 N Lake Shore Dr
Chicago, IL 60611
Contact Cleo Wilson, Executive Director, (312) 373-2437 or (312) 751-8000; fax: (312) 751-2818; email: giving@playboy.com
Internet http://www.playboyenterprises.com/foundation
Restrictions The foundation will not consider religious programs, individual needs, capital campaigns, endowments, scholarships, or fellowships; social services, including residential care, clinics, treatment, or recreation programs; national health, welfare, educational, or cultural organizations, or their state affiliates; or government agencies or projects.
Areas of Interest AIDS; Abortion; Civil/Human Rights; Film Production; Government; HIV; Homosexuals, Female; Homosexuals, Male; Human Reproduction/Fertility; Intellectual Freedom; Journalism; Minorities; Poverty and the Poor; Public Planning/Policy; Sexual Behavior; Social Change; Women
Sample Awards Population Council—for research to find an alternative abortifacient to RU 486. AIDS Legal Referral Panel—to support its policy work on issues affecting women with HIV/AIDS. Student Press Law Ctr—for general operating support for work with high school and college journalists. KCTS-TV/Florentine Films—for production costs of Defending Everybody: A History of the American Civil Liberties Union.

Prince Charitable Trusts Chicago Grants 439

Prince Charitable Trusts
300 W Madison St, Ste 1900
Chicago, IL 60606
Contact Chicago Grants, (312) 419-8700; fax: (312)
419-8558; e-mail: info@prince-trusts.org
Internet http://www.fdncenter.org/grantmaker/prince/
chicago.html
Requirements Chicago nonprofit organizations are eligible.
Areas of Interest Arts, General; Child/Maternal Health;
Children and Youth; Cultural Activities/Programs; Education; Education Reform; Emergency Services; Environmental Planning/Policy; Environmental Programs;
Health Care; Health Insurance; Health Personnel/Professions; Parent Involvement; Parks; Social Services Delivery; Teen Pregnancy

Prince Charitable Trusts Grants 440

Prince Charitable Trusts
303 W Madison St, Ste 1900
Chicago, IL 60606
Contact Sharon Robison, Grants Manager, (312)
419-8700; fax: (312) 419-8558; e-mail: srobison@
prince-trusts.org
Internet http://www.fdncenter.org/grantmaker/prince
Requirements IRS 509(a) or 501(c)3 organizations in
Illinois, the District of Columbia, and Rhode Island are
eligible.
Areas of Interest Adoption; Arts, General; Children and
Youth; Children's Museums; Clinics; Cultural Activities/Programs; Disadvantaged (Economically); Elementary Education; Environmental Programs; Family;
Grassroots Leadership; Health Care; Hispanics; Homelessness; Hospitals; Minorities; Neighborhoods; Regional Planning/Policy; Secondary Education; Social
Services
Sample Awards Latin American Youth Ctr (Washington, DC)—for operating support, $20,000. Chicago
Childrens Museum (Chicago, IL)—for operating support, $10,000. Ocease State Adoption Resource Exchange (Providence, RI)—for operating support,
$10,000.

Prince Charitable Trusts Rhode Island 441
Grants

Prince Charitable Trusts
303 W Madison St, Ste 1900
Chicago, IL 60606
Contact Sharon Robison, Grants Manager, (312)
419-8700; e-mail: srobison@prince-trusts.org
Internet http://fdncenter.org/grantmaker/prince/ri.html
Requirements Rhode Island 509(a) or 501(c)3 nonprofit
organizations are eligible.
Areas of Interest After-School Programs; Arts, General; Cultural Activities/Programs; Disadvantaged (Economically); Education; Elementary Education; Emergency Services; Environmental Planning/Policy; Environmental Programs; Families; Health Insurance; Parks;
Secondary Education; Social Services; Social Services
Delivery; Women's Health

Quaker Oats Company Grants 442

Quaker Oats
PO Box 049001, Community Relations, #07-05
Chicago, IL 60604-9001
Contact Susan Ball, Executive Director, (312)
222-7377; fax: (312) 222-8323
Internet http://www.quakeroats.com/qfb_Community/
GivingGuidelines.cfm
Requirements Nonprofits with 501(c)3 status, including schools, school districts, and colleges and universities, in communities nationwide where Quaker Oats
maintains facilities are eligible to receive grant support.
Restrictions Grants are not made to individuals, religious organizations, elected officials, or for advertising.
Areas of Interest Developmentally Disabled; Elementary Education; Family; Health Care; Health Promotion;
Higher Education; Housing; Hunger; Minority Education; Nutrition/Dietetics; Secondary Education
Sample Awards Misericordia Heart of Mercy (Chicago,
IL)—to implement a healthy-lifestyles program for developmentally disabled residents, $25,000. U of North
Carolina (Chapel Hill, NC)—for a nutrition program,
$25,500. Rush-Presbyterian-Saint Lukes Medical Ctr
(Chicago, IL)—for its nutrition program, $25,000.

Michael Reese Health Trust Grants 443

Michael Reese Health Trust
20 N Wacker Dr, Ste 760
Chicago, IL 60606
Contact Dorothy Gardner, President, (312) 726-1008;
fax (312) 726-2797; e-mail: programs@healthtrust.net
Internet http://fdncenter.org/grantmaker/health/guide.
html
Requirements Nonprofit organizations operating in the
metropolitan Chicago area are eligible.
Restrictions Grants do not support capital needs (i.e.,
building construction/renovation, vehicles, and equipment), endowments, fund-raising events, individuals,
scholarships or debt reduction.
Areas of Interest Health Promotion; Health Services
Delivery; Preventive Medicine; Public Health

Relations Foundation Grants 444

Relations Foundation
205 N Wabash, Ste 1800
Chicago, IL 60601
Contact Iris Kreig, (312) 647-5765
Requirements Illinois nonprofit organizations are eligible. Grants are awarded primarily in Chicago.
Areas of Interest Civic Affairs; Education

Rice Foundation Grants 445

Rice Foundation
8600 Gross Point Rd
Skokie, IL 60077-2151
Contact Peter Nolan, (847) 581-9999
Requirements Illinois nonprofit organizations are eligible.
Areas of Interest Civic Affairs; Higher Education; Hospitals; Libraries; Medical Education; Youth Programs

Sara Lee Foundation Grants 446
Sara Lee Foundation
3 First National Plaza
Chicago, IL 60602-4260
Contact Robin Tryloff, Executive Director, (312) 558-8448; fax: (312) 419-3192
Internet http://www.saraleefoundation.org/funding/focus.cfm
Requirements IRS 501(c)3 nonprofit organizations in Illinois that have been in existence for at least two years at the time of application and that are located in a community where a Sara Lee Corporation division has facilities are eligible.
Restrictions Grants do not support individuals; organizations with a limited constituency, such as fraternities or veterans groups; organizations that limit their services to members of one religious group, or those whose services propagate religious faith or creed, including churches, seminaries, bible colleges, and theological institutions; political organizations or those having the primary purpose of influencing legislation or promoting a particular ideological point of view; elementary and secondary schools, either private or public; units of government or quasi-governmental agencies; or hospitals and health organizations concentrating their research and/or treatment in one area of human disease.
Areas of Interest Adult and Continuing Education; Arts, General; Basic Skills Education; Child Psychology/Development; Cultural Activities/Programs; Disabled; Education; Employment Opportunity Programs; Food Safety; Homelessness; Housing; Hunger; Leadership; Libraries; Literacy; Scholarship Programs, General; Women; Youth Programs
Sample Awards Steppenwolf Theatre Co (Chicago, IL)—for its campaign to build endowment and to support key programs, $1 million (2001).

Seabury Foundation Grants 447
Seabury Foundation
1111 N Wells St, Ste 503
Chicago, IL 60610
Contact Grants Administrator, (312) 587-7146; fax: (312) 587-7332; e-mail: seabury@seaburyfoundation.org
Requirements Chicago, IL, nonprofit organizations are eligible.
Areas of Interest Child Psychology/Development; Children and Youth; Disabled; Hospitals

Solo Cup Foundation Grants 448
Solo Cup Foundation
1700 Old Deerfield Rd
Highland Park, IL 60035
Contact Ronald Whaley, Secretary/Treasurer, (847) 831-4800
Requirements Illinois nonprofit organizations are eligible.
Areas of Interest Health Care; Health Care Access; Higher Education; Hospitals; Human Services; Religion; Religious Welfare Programs
Sample Awards La Rashida Children's Hospital (Chicago, IL)—for a capital campaign to modernize and upgrade its inpatient facility, $1 million. Immaculate Conception Church (Chicago, IL)—for restoration project, $85,000. Congregation of the Passion (Chicago, IL)—for general support, $50,000.

Square D Foundation Grants 449
Square D Foundation
1415 S Roselle Rd
Palatine, IL 60067
Contact Harry Wilson, Secretary, (847) 397-2600
Requirements 501(c)3 tax-exempt organizations in company operating locations are eligible, including Bakersfield, CA; Clearwater, FL; Schiller Park, IL; Huntington and Peru, IN; Cedar Rapids, IA; Crestview Hills, Florence, and Lexington, KY; Columbia, MO; Lincoln, NE; Asheville, Monroe, and Raleigh, NC; Dublin, Middletown, and Oxford, OH; Mechanicsburg, PA; Columbia, SC; Memphis and Smyrna, TN; Dallas, TX; and Milwaukee and Oshkosh, WI.
Restrictions Grants are not made to religious organizations for religious purposes, political groups and organizations, labor unions and organizations, organizations making requests by telephone, organizations listed by the US attorney general as subversive, or to individuals.
Areas of Interest Arts, General; Civic Affairs; Cultural Activities/Programs; Education; Equipment/Instrumentation; Health Services Delivery; Higher Education; Scholarship Programs, General; Social Services Delivery

Irvin Stern Foundation Grants 450
Irvin Stern Foundation
116 W Illinois St, Ste 2E
Chicago, IL 60610
Contact Jeffrey Epstein, (312) 321-9402; e-mail: info@irvinstern.org
Internet http://www.irvinstern.org/guidelines.html
Requirements The foundation makes grants to tax-exempt organizations with preference given to Chicago and New York City metropolitan areas.
Restrictions Grants are not awarded to individuals or for building funds or research.
Areas of Interest Chronic Illness; Civic Affairs; Community Development; Grassroots Leadership; Health Promotion; Jewish Services; Neighborhoods; Social Services Delivery; Urban Affairs; Vocational/Technical Education

United Airlines Foundation Education Grants 451
United Airlines Foundation
PO Box 66100
Chicago, IL 60666
Contact Caryn Cross, fax: (708) 700-7345; e-mail: uafoundation@ual.com
Internet http://www.united.com/page/article/0,,1367,00.html
Requirements Nonprofits and school districts in Boston, MA; Chicago, IL; Denver, CO; Los Angeles and San Francisco, CA; New York, NY; Miami, FL; and Seattle, WA are eligible.
Restrictions The foundation does not support capital grants, in-kind donations, or development campaigns.
Areas of Interest Career Education and Planning; Civic Affairs; Community and School Relations; Compensatory Education; Cultural Activities/Programs; Cultural

Outreach; Elementary Education; Mentoring Programs; Middle School Education; Museums; School-to-Work Transition; Secondary Education

Frederick S. Upton Foundation Grants 452
Frederick S. Upton Foundation
1 Bank One Plz, Ste IL1-0111
Chicago, IL 60670-0111
Contact Trust Administrator, fax: (269) 982-0323; e-mail: supton@qtm.net
Requirements Grants are awarded to Illinois and Michigan nonprofits.
Areas of Interest Arts, General; Children and Youth; Cultural Activities/Programs; Education; Higher Education; Religion; Youth Programs
Sample Awards Nature Conservancy (East Lansing, MI)—for general support, $5000 (2001).

USG Foundation Grants 453
USG Foundation
125 S Franklin St
Chicago, IL 60606
Contact Harold Pendexter, Program Contact, (312) 606-4297; fax: (312) 606-5316
Areas of Interest Arts, General; Cultural Activities/Programs; Government; Health Care; Higher Education; Hospitals; Public Administration; Public Planning/Policy; Social Services; Youth Programs
Sample Awards Child Welfare League of America (Washington, DC)—to conduct the Positive Parenting for Homeless Families of Young Children program, $100,000.

Visiting Nurse Foundation Grants 454
VNA Foundation
20 N Wacker, Ste 3118
Chicago, IL 60606
Contact Robert DiLeonardi, Executive Director, (312) 214-1521; fax: (312) 214-1529
Internet http://www.vnafoundation.net
Requirements Nonprofit organizations in Cook, Lake, McHenry, DuPage, Kane, and Willare counties of Illinois eligible.
Restrictions No grants are made to individuals.
Areas of Interest Cancer/Carcinogenesis; Community Service Programs; Health and Health Services; Health Care Access; Health Promotion; Hospices; Intervention, Types of (Health/Safety/Medical); Nursing; Preventive Medicine; School Health Programs
Sample Awards Horizon Hospice (IL)—for hospice care for cancer patients unable to pay for care, $33,000. U of Illinois at Chicago, College of Nursing (IL)—to support its school-based health center at Carrie Jacobs Bond Elementary School in Chicago's Englewood community, $45,521.

W.P. and H.B. White Foundation Grants 455
W.P. and H.B. White Foundation
540 Frontage Rd, Ste 3240
Northfield, IL 60093
Contact M. Margaret Blandford, Executive Director, (847) 446-1441

Requirements Only Illinois organizations are eligible to apply.
Areas of Interest Adult and Continuing Education; Elementary Education; Health Care; Higher Education; Preschool Education; Social Services
Sample Awards Austin Career Education Ctr (Chicago, IL)—for operating support, $12,000. Greater Chicago Food Depository (Chicago, IL)—for operating support, $20,000. Roosevelt U (Chicago, IL)—for program support, $10,000.

Wieboldt Foundation Grants 456
Wieboldt Foundation
53 W Jackson Blvd, Ste 838
Chicago, IL 60604
Contact Carmen Prieto, Associate Director, (312) 786-9377; fax: (312) 786-9232; e-mail: info@wieboldt.org
Internet http://www.wieboldtfoundation.org/guidelines_general.htm
Requirements Nonprofit organizations in low-income areas in Chicago, IL may submit grant proposals.
Restrictions The foundation generally does not fund individuals, studies and research, conferences, capital development, or direct or social service programs.
Areas of Interest Community Development; Community Outreach Programs; Community Service Programs; Educational Programs; Human Services; Job Training Programs; Leadership; Legal Services; Neighborhoods; Poverty and the Poor; Public Affairs; Public Planning/Policy; Racism/Race Relations; Women

Woods Fund of Chicago Grants 457
Woods Fund of Chicago
360 N Michigan Ave, Ste 1600
Chicago, IL 60601
Contact Sally Gonzalez, Grants and Operations Manager, (312) 782-2698; fax: (312) 782-4155; fax: info@woodsfund.org
Internet http://www.woodsfund.org/File_1043643135130
Requirements The fund makes grants to tax-exempt organizations working to enhance life for all people in the metropolitan Chicago area and to improve opportunities for its least advantaged residents.
Restrictions Areas not eligible for grant review include business or economic development, capital campaigns, endowments, fundraising, advertising, health care organizations, housing construction/rehabilitation, medical and scientific research, individual public and private schools, religious programs, residential care, counseling, clinics, recreational programs, social welfare agencies, and scholarships.
Areas of Interest Arts; Citizenship; Community Development; Community and School Relations; Cultural Activities/Programs; Economic Development; Education Reform; Family; Governmental Functions; Legal Services; Neighborhoods; Public Planning/Policy
Sample Awards North Lawndale Employment Network (Chicago, IL)—for advocacy and policy work in behalf of ex-inmates and development of job-training programs and a booklet that directs ex-prisoners to government and nonprofit services, $103,000 over two years (2002).

Woodward Governor Company Charitable Trust Grants 458

Woodward Governor Company Charitable Trust
5001 N Second St
Rockford, IL 61125-7001
Contact Pam Johnson, Chair, Contributions Committee
Requirements Only Colorado, Illinois, and Wisconsin organizations are eligible to apply.
Restrictions Grants are not awarded to individuals or for endowment funds, research, scholarships, fellowships, special projects, publications, conferences, loans, or matching gifts.
Areas of Interest Adult and Continuing Education; Arts, General; Basic Skills Education; Community Development; Cultural Activities/Programs; Economic Development; Health Care; Homelessness; Hospices; Immigrants; Juvenile Delinquency; Literacy; Minorities; Museums; Social Services; Vocational/Technical Education

Indiana

John W. Anderson Foundation Grants 459

John W. Anderson Foundation
402 Wall St
Valparaiso, IN 46383
Contact William Vinovich, Vice Chair, (219) 462-4611
Requirements Nonprofit Indiana organizations in Lake and Porter Counties are eligible.
Restrictions Grants are not generally made for start-up costs, endowment funds, deficit financing, or loans.
Areas of Interest Higher Education; Youth Programs
Sample Awards Ball State University Foundation (Muncie, Indiana)—for operating support, $100,000. Boys and Girls Club of Porter County (Valparaiso, IN)—$614,000.

Ball Brothers Foundation Grants 460

Ball Brothers Foundation
PO Box 1408
Muncie, IN 47308
Contact Douglas Bakken, Executive Director, (765) 741-5500; fax: (765) 741-5518; e-mail: doug.bakken@ballfdn.org
Requirements Indiana nonprofit institutions and organizations are eligible.
Restrictions Grants will not be made to individuals, to booster organizations, for direct scholarships to individuals, or for services that the community-at-large should normally underwrite (e.g., roads, bus transportation, etc.).
Areas of Interest Adult and Continuing Education; Basic Skills Education; Community Development; Cultural Activities/Programs; Cultural Outreach; Elementary Education; Health Care; Higher Education; Literacy; Museums; Secondary Education; Social Services
Sample Awards Muncie Center for the Arts (Muncie, IN)—for general operating support, $15,000. Ball State U (Muncie, IN)—for the university's museum, $2 million and artwork valued at $8 million. Minnetrista Cultural Foundation (IN)—for general support, $2.6 million.

Clowes Fund Grants 461

Clowes Fund Inc
320 N Meridian, Ste 316
Indianapolis, IN 46204
Contact Elizabeth Casselman, Program Manager, (800) 943-7209 or (317) 833-0144; fax: (317) 833-0145; e-mail: staff@clowesfund.org
Internet http://www.clowesfund.org
Requirements Nonprofit organizations in northern New England and the metropolitan Indianapolis, IN; Boston, MA; and metropolitan Seattle, WA, areas are eligible.
Restrictions The fund does not make grants to individuals or for publications, conferences, videos, or seminars. No grants are made to organizations in foreign countries. No grants are made for programs promoting specific religious doctrine. The fund will not accept unsolicited proposals from any organization for operating support. The fund will not accept unsolicited proposals of any sort from colleges and universities.
Areas of Interest Art Education; Art, General; Classroom Instruction; Education; Fine Arts; Higher Education; Immigrants; Medical Education; Performing Arts; Refugees; Secondary Education; Social Services; Workforce Development
Sample Awards Northwest Chamber Orchestra (Seattle, WA)—for operating support, $10,000 (2003). Massachusetts Maritime Academy (Buzzards Bay, MA)—to modernize the electrical-machinery laboratory, $80,000 (2003). Case Western Reserve U, School of Medicine (Cleveland, OH)—to establish the Endowment for Innovations in Medical Education, $1 million (2003). Training Inc (Indianapolis, IN)—for scholarships for career-training programs, $12,000 (2003).

Olive B. Cole Foundation Grants 462

Olive B. Cole Foundation
6207 Constitution Dr
Fort Wayne, IN 46804
Contact Maclyn Parker, President, (212) 436-2182
Requirements Indiana nonprofit organizations are eligible to apply.
Areas of Interest Arts, General; Cultural Activities/Programs; Higher Education; Hospitals; Public Affairs; Youth Programs

Community Foundation of Muncie and Delaware County Grants 463

Community Foundation of Muncie and Delaware County
PO Box 807
Muncie, IN 47308
Contact Roni Johnson, Executive Director, (765) 747-7181; fax: (765) 289-7770; e-mail: commfound@cfmdin.org
Internet http://www.cfmdin.org
Requirements 501(c)3 tax-exempt organizations in Muncie and Delaware County, IN, are eligible.
Restrictions The foundation does not make grants to individuals or for religious purposes, budget deficits, endowments, or projects normally the responsibility of a public agency.
Areas of Interest Community Development; Cultural Activities/Programs; Economic Development; Educa-

tion; Horticulture; Neighborhoods; Parks; Philanthropy; Scholarship Programs, General
Sample Awards Aultshire Neighborhood Assoc (Muncie, IN)—for materials used in revitalizing their neighborhood community park, $2000. Munsyana Garden Club (Muncie, IN)—to support a garden-planting program in the Munsayana and Parkview apartment areas, $350.

Cummins Foundation Grants 464
Cummins Foundation
500 Jackson St
Columbus, IN 47201
Contact Gayle Dudley Nay, (812) 377-3114; fax: (812) 377-7897
Internet http://www.cummins.com/na/pages/en/whoweare/foundation.cfm
Requirements Support for local projects is made only in communities where the company has manufacturing facilities (such as Jamestown, NY; Charleston, SC; Rocky Mount, NC; Memphis and Cookeville, TN; Lake Mills, IA; Minneapolis, MN; and El Paso, TX). Contact program staff for complete list of eligible areas. International contributions are made through foreign subsidiaries.
Restrictions Grants and loans will not be awarded to individuals nor for the start-up of business.
Areas of Interest Arts, General; Business Education; Community Development; Education; Engineering; Health Care; Leadership; Minorities; Poverty and the Poor; Secondary Education; Women; Youth Programs
Sample Awards Advancing Minorities Interest in Engineering (IN)—for operating support, $7500.

Foellinger Foundation Grants 465
Foellinger Foundation
520 E Berry St
Fort Wayne, IN 46802
Contact Cheryl Taylor, President, (219) 422-2900; fax: (219) 422-9436; email: cherylt@foellinger.org
Requirements Indiana organizations are eligible to apply.
Restrictions The foundation does not fund scholarships, travel assistance, religious groups, public or private elementary or secondary schools, sponsorships, special events, advertising, or endowments.
Areas of Interest After-School Programs; Arts, General; Children and Youth; Community Development; Disabled; Education; Elderly; Health Care; Higher Education; Humanities; Public Broadcasting; Recreation and Leisure; Social Services; Transportation; Youth Programs
Sample Awards Public Broadcasting of Northeast Indiana (IN)—for general operating support. Arthur J. Blaising Social Services (IN)—for its after-school program and its 10-week summer day camp, $75,585. Turnstone (IN)—for a transportation program that serves elderly and disabled people, $187,500 over 18 months. Taylor U—for the Allen County Postsecondary Education Consortium, $219,690 over two years.

Health Foundation of Greater Indianapolis 466 Grants
Health Foundation of Greater Indianapolis
342 Massachusetts Ave
Indianapolis, IN 46204
Contact Phyllis Tisdale-Yager, Program Officer, (317) 630-1805; fax: (317) 630-1806; e-mail: pty@thfgi.org
Internet http://www.THFGI.org
Requirements Grants are awarded to neighborhood-based service centers in Indiana's Marion County and the seven contiguous counties of Boone, Hamilton, Hancock, Hendricks, Johnson, Morgan and Shelby.
Areas of Interest AIDS Education; Allied Health Education; Child/Maternal Health; Dental Health and Hygiene; Domestic Violence; Family; Family Planning; HIV; Health Care; Health Promotion; Infants; Medical Education; Elderly; Minorities; Nursing Education; Nutrition/Dietetics; Pediatrics; Smoking Behavior; Social Services; Teen Pregnancy; Tobacco; Women
Sample Awards Community Wealth (Indianapolis, IN)—to produce a public-service announcement on HIV/AIDS, $10,000 (2003). Morgan County Coordinated Aging Services (Indianapolis, IN)—for an outreach program for elderly people, $20,000 (2003). Prevent Blindness (Inidanapolis, IN)—to expand its vision screening and education program to five additional schools, $20,000 (2003). CICOA the Access Network (Indianapolis, IN)—to provide emergency financial assistance to elderly people in need of food, housing, or medical care, $30,000 (2003).

Indianapolis Foundation Grants 467
Indianapolis Foundation
615 N Alabama St, Ste 119
Indianapolis, IN 46204
Contact Grants Director, (317) 634-2423; fax: (317) 684-0943; e-mail: info@cicf.org
Internet http://www.indyfund.org/grant
Requirements Only Indiana organizations are eligible to apply.
Restrictions The foundation does not make grants to individuals or to organizations for sectarian or religious purposes, contribute to endowments, provide long-term funding, or postevent or after-the-fact situations.
Areas of Interest Children and Youth; Civic Affairs; Cultural Activities/Programs; Disabled; Education; Elderly; Environmental Programs; Family; Health Care; Legal Education; Philanthropy; Social Services
Sample Awards Indiana U-Purdue U (Indianapolis, IN)—to endow a chair in philanthropy at the Ctr on Philanthropy, $1 million. Indiana U, School of Law (IN)—for a new law school facility, $250,000. Greater Indianapolis Progress Committee (IN)—for general operating support, $25,000.

Journal Gazette Foundation Grants 468
Journal Gazette Foundation
701 S Clinton
Fort Wayne, IN 46802-1883
Contact Richard Inskeep, President, (219) 424-5257
Requirements Indiana nonprofit organizations are eligible. Preference is given to requests from northeastern Indiana.

Areas of Interest Education; Higher Education; Hospitals; Social Services

Sample Awards Lincoln Museum (Fort Wayne, Indiana)—for operating support, $6000.

Eli Lilly & Company Foundation Grants Program   469
Eli Lilly & Company Foundation
Lilly Corporate Ctr
Indianapolis, IN 46285
Contact Thomas King, President, (317) 276-3177; fax: (317) 277-2025
Internet http://www.lilly.com/about/social/foundation/cash/index.html
Restrictions Grants do not support individuals; endowments; debt reduction; religious or sectarian programs for religious purposes; bands or fraternal, labor, athletic, or veterans organizations; political contributions; beauty or talent contests; fundraising activities related to individual sponsorship; conferences or media productions; nonaccredited education groups; or memorials.
Areas of Interest Civic Affairs; Dentistry; Diabetes; Health Care; International Education/Training; International Programs; Medical Education; Medicine, History of; Performing Arts; Pharmacy; Preventive Medicine; Restoration and Preservation, Structural/Architectural; Social Services
Sample Awards Purdue U (West Lafayette, IN)—to construct a facility for the department of computer science, $150,000 (2003). Hoosier Veterans Assistance Foundation (Indianapolis, IN)—for the Veterans Integrated Services Training for Achievement Center, which will provide services to war veterans who suffer from substance abuse, $100,000 (2003). CDC Foundation (Atlanta, GA)—to train 28 international scientists from both developed and developing countries in the detection of, and response to, threats of infectious disease, approximately $2 million over four years (2002).

Lilly Endowment Educational Leadership Grants   470
Lilly Endowment Inc
2801 N Meridian St
Indianapolis, IN 46208
Contact Sue Ellen Walker, Communications Associate, (317) 924-5471; fax: (317) 926-4431
Requirements Only Indiana organizations are eligible to apply.
Areas of Interest Adult and Continuing Education; Classroom Instruction; Education Reform; Educational Administration; Educational Technology; Leadership; Literacy; Theology; Training and Development; Volunteers
Sample Awards Spelman College (Atlanta, GA)—to implement programs focused on religion and spirituality, $2 million over five years (2002). Corp for Educational Technology (Indianapolis, IN)—to upgrade My Target, an online assessment tool for Indiana teachers and administrators, $33,000 (2002). County School Corp of Brown County (Nashville, IN)—for an education and career-development resource center, $3,998 million (2002). Goshen College (IN)—for a program in two counties to improve early childhood development, curriculums for K-12 students, adult education, and cross-cultural awareness, $9.993 million (2002).

Lilly Endowment Giving Indiana Funds for Tomorrow Grants   471
Lilly Endowment Inc
2801 N Meridian St
Indianapolis, IN 46208
Contact Program Office, (317) 924-5471; fax: (317) 926-4431
Requirements Only Indiana organizations are eligible to apply.
Areas of Interest Community Development
Sample Awards Community foundations throughout Indiana (IN)—for unrestricted use, operating funds, or both, through the GIFT Initiative, $189 million (2002). Indiana Grantmakers Alliance Foundation (Indianapolis, IN)—to provide technical assistance to the GIFT Initiative, $504,364 (2002). Community Ctrs of Indianapolis (IN)—for transitional support, $1 million. Lawrence County Community Foundation (Bedford, IN)—for program support, $130,000.

Lilly Endowment Grants Program   472
Lilly Endowment Inc
2801 N Meridian St
Indianapolis, IN 46208-0068
Contact Sue Ellen Walker, Communications Associate, (317) 924-5471; fax: (317) 926-4431
Requirements Applicant should send a letter describing credentials of organization, project proposed, and amount of funding requested.
Restrictions The endowment does not consider applications for health care and biological science projects, mass media initiatives, endowments or endowed chairs, libraries, building campaigns, K-12 schools, or general operations.
Areas of Interest African Americans; Arts, General; Cultural Activities/Programs; Disaster Relief; Dropouts; Education; Faculty Development; Higher Education; Housing; Human Genome; Leadership; Men; Minority Education; Minority Schools; Poverty and the Poor; Public Planning/Policy; Religion; Religious Studies; Theology; Transportation; Utilities; Youth Programs
Sample Awards Salvation Army (Alexandria, VA)—to help military personnel in Iraq and their families pay for medicine, rent, utilities, and other basic living expenses, $3 million (2003). Indianapolis Neighborhood Resource Ctr (IN)—for neighborhood development activities, $240,000 (2002). Federalist Society for Law and Public Policy Studies (Washington, DC)—for general operating support, $262,500 (2002). Indianapolis Urban League (IN)—for the Kwanzaa Christmas program, $25,000 (2002).

Lilly Endowment Indiana Camp Ministries Enhancement Program Grants   473
Lilly Endowment Inc
2801 N Meridian St
Indianapolis, IN 46208
Contact Sue Ellen Walker, (317) 924-5471; fax: (317) 926-4431
Requirements Christian denominations, congregations, and other religious organizations that own and operate

camps in Indiana are eligible. The camps should serve more than one congregation.
Areas of Interest Children and Youth; Leadership; Recreation and Leisure; Religion; Religious Studies
Sample Awards Purdue Research Foundation (West Lafayette, Indiana)—for Purdue Discovery Park, $25,647,959. Indianapolis-Marion County Public Library Foundation (Indianapolis, Indiana)—for capital campaign, $25,250,000.

Lilly Endowment National Clergy Renewal Grants   474

Lilly Endowment Inc
PO Box 88068, 2801 N Meridian St
Indianapolis, IN 46208
Contact National Clergy Renewal Program, (317) 916-7302; fax: (317) 926-4431; e-mail: clergyrenewal@yahoo.com
Internet http://www.clergyrenewal.org
Requirements A Christian congregation whose ordained pastor has a master of divinity degree is eligible.
Restrictions The program for Indiana congregation continues, so Indiana pastors are ineligible for the national program.
Areas of Interest Churches
Sample Awards For the Clergy Renewal Program—to be distributed among churches and congregations throughout the United States, $3,134,304 (2002).

Lumina Foundation for Education Grants   475

Lumina Foundation for Education
30 S Meridian St, Ste 700
Indianapolis, IN 46204-3503
Contact Gloria Ackerson-Seats, Coordinator of Grant Programs and Special Projects, (317) 951-5704; fax: (317) 951-5063
Internet http://www.luminafoundation.org/grants/grants.shtml
Requirements IRS 501(c)3 or 509(a)(1, 2 or 3) tax-exemp organizations and public school organizations are eligible.
Restrictions The foundation will not award grants that support corporate sponsorships and fundraising events; fund partisan political or lobbying efforts; or provide direct support for individuals, including scholarships or institutional scholarship funds.
Areas of Interest Academic Achievement; Adult and Continuing Education; Communications; Educational Administration; Educational Planning/Policy; Higher Education; Leadership; Mass Media; Public Planning/Policy
Sample Awards Indianapolis Downtown (IN) and Keep Indianapolis Beautiful (IN)—for general operating support, $10,000 each (2003). Indiana U-Purdue U Indianapolis (IN)—to develop programs designed to increase the academic success of African-American and Latino first-year students enrolled in introductory courses, $100,000 over three years (2003). Indiana U, Ctr on Philanthropy (IN)—to advance philanthropic study and practice, $10,000 (2003). Assoc for the Study of Higher Education (MO)—for fellowships to support dissertation research on the broad topics of financial aid, student retention and success, and adult learners and learning, $100,000 (2003).

Martin Foundation Grants   476

Martin Foundation
500 Simpson Ave
Elkhart, IN 46515
Contact Geraldine Martin, Chairperson & President, (219) 295-3343
Requirements Applications are not required but applicants should submit a copy of an IRS determination letter, amount of funding requested, and detailed information about how a project will be sustained once foundation support is completed.
Areas of Interest Conservation, Natural Resources; Cultural Activities/Programs; Education; Environmental Programs; Literacy; Public Affairs; Women; Youth Programs
Sample Awards Massachusetts Institute of Technology (Cambridge, MA)—for continued support for commitment of Graduate Fellows, $950,000 (2000). University of California (Berkeley, CA)—for Geraldine Fitzgarrald Martin Fellowship, $30,000 (2000). Elkhart Literacy Network (IN)—for operating support.

McMillen Foundation Grants   477

McMillen Foundation
6610 Mutual Dr
Fort Wayne, IN 46825-4236
Contact Grants Administrator, (219) 484-8631
Requirements Indiana nonprofit organizations are eligible. Preference will be given to Fort Wayne requests.
Restrictions Support is not given for churches or religious groups.
Areas of Interest Children and Youth; Community Development; Education; Health Care; Recreation and Leisure

Nicholas H. Noyes Jr. Memorial Foundation Grants   478

Nicholas H. Noyes Jr. Memorial Foundation
1950 E Greyhound Pass, No 18
Carmel, IN 46033-7730
Contact Kelly Mills, Assistant Secretary, (317) 844-8009; fax: (317) 844-8099
Internet http://www.noyesfoundation.org
Areas of Interest Arts, General; Children and Youth; Cultural Activities/Programs; Disadvantaged (Economically); Elementary Education; Family; Health Care; Higher Education; Hospitals; Museums; Performing Arts; Secondary Education; Social Services; Youth Programs

Nina Mason Pulliam Charitable Trust Grants   479

Nina Mason Pulliam Charitable Trust
135 N Pennsylvania St, Ste 1200
Indianapolis, IN 46204
Contact Grants Administrator, (317) 231-6075; fax: (317) 231-9208
Internet http://www.ninapulliamtrust.org
Requirements Primary consideration is given to 501(c)3 charitable organizations that serve the communities of Indianapolis and metropolitan Phoenix. Secondary consideration is given to the states of Indiana and Arizona. National organizations whose programs benefit

these priority areas and/or benefit society as a whole are considered on an occasional basis.

Restrictions Grants are not awarded for international purposes or academic research. Grants are not awarded to individuals, sectarian organizations for religious purposes, or to nonoperating private foundations except in extraordinary circumstances.

Areas of Interest Arts, General; Children and Youth; Civic Affairs; Conservation, Natural Resources; Cultural Activities/Programs; Disabled; Education; Elderly; Environmental Programs; Family; Health Care; Higher Education; Horticulture; Inner Cities; Mental Disorders; Nonprofit Organizations; Secondary Education; Vision; Visual Impairments; Wildlife; Women

Sample Awards Arizona Humane Society (Phoenix, AZ)—to develop a crisis-response program for animal-welfare organizations throughout Arizona, $48,000 (2004). Writers Ctr of Indianapolis (IN)—for the Institute of Writing and Creativity, which serves minority middle- and high-school students and creative-writing teachers, $45,000 (2004). African Community International (Indianapolis, IN)—to provide health care and health education for African immigrants and refugees, $55,000 (2004). NPower Indiana (Indianapolis, IN)—to provide customized technology-consulting services to nine nonprofit groups, $30,000 (2004).

M.E. Raker Foundation Grants   480
M.E. Raker Foundation
6207 Constitution Dr
Fort Wayne, IN 46804
Contact John Hogan, President, (219) 436-2182
Requirements Indiana nonprofit organizations are eligible. Emphasis is given to requests from Fort Wayne.
Areas of Interest Children and Youth; Education; Higher Education; Religion; Secondary Education
Sample Awards Nature Conservancy (Indianapolis, IN)—for seedlings along Fish Creek, $32,000 (2001). Turnstone Center for Disabled Children and Adults (Fort Wayne, IN)—for equipment, $10,000 (2001).

Iowa

AmerUs Group Charitable Foundation   481
Grants
AmerUs Group Charitable Foundation
699 Walnut St
Des Moines, IA 50309
Contact Jonna La Toure, Community Relations, (515) 557-3910
Internet http://www.amerus.com/about/community.html
Requirements Nonprofit organizations in central Iowa are eligible to apply.
Restrictions Grants do not support athletic organizations, conferences, goodwill advertising, endowments, fellowships, festival participation, fraternal organizations, hospital or health care facilities, individual K-8 schools, political parties, religious groups for religious programs, social organizations, and trade or professional associations.
Areas of Interest Civil/Human Rights; Community Development; Conservation, Natural Resources; Elemen-

tary Education; Higher Education; Hospices; Libraries, Public; Medical Education; Minorities; Public Planning/Policy; Religious Studies; Secondary Education; Theology; Visual Arts; Youth Programs; Business; Children and Youth; Family

Sample Awards American Institute of Business (Des Moines, IA)—$5000 (2001). Children and Families of Iowa (Des Moines, IA)—$18,000 (2001). Iowa National Heritage Foundation (IA)—$2500 (2001). Young Women's Resource Ctr (IA)—$2500 (2001).

Diana, Princess of Wales Memorial Fund   482
Grants
Diana, Princess of Wales Memorial Fund (United States)
PO Box 494, 27 Westwood Dr
Estherville, IA 51334-0494
Contact Grants Administrator, (712) 362-5400; fax: (712) 362-5401; e-mail: info@usdianafund.org
Internet http://www.usdianafund.org
Requirements Eligible are 501(c)3 nonprofit organizations that work in the areas listed.
Restrictions The fund will not support government agencies, schools, colleges, or hospitals (unless part of a collaborative project); disease-specific organizations; rapid response to emergency situations or humanitarian aid; promotion of religious beliefs; academic research; or projects that have received support through the United Kingdom branch of the fund.
Areas of Interest At-Risk Youth; Crisis Counseling; Disabled; Domestic Violence; Drugs/Drug Abuse; Eating Disorders; Family; HIV; Hispanics; Homelessness; Homosexuals, Female; Homosexuals, Male; Injury; Leadership; Preventive Medicine; Recreation and Leisure; Safety; Sexual Behavior; Teen Pregnancy; Youth Violence
Sample Awards Latino Community Development Agency (Oklahoma City, OK)—to provide recreational activities to disabled Hispanic youths and their families, $25,000. Santa Fe Rape Crisis Ctr (Santa Fe, NM)—for a prevention, safety-skills, and education program for youths that seeks to eliminate hate-motivated violence, $20,000. Jacksonville Area Sexual Minority Youth Network (Jacksonville, FL)—to develop leadership skills among lesbian, gay, and bisexual teenagers in northeastern Florida and southeastern Georgia, $25,000.

Iowa Arts Council Operational Support   483
Grants for Major and Mid-Size Arts
Organizations
Iowa Arts Council
600 E Locust, Capitol Complex
Des Moines, IA 50319
Contact Bruce Williams, Program Contact, (515) 281-4406; e-mail: Bruce.Williams@iowa.gov
Internet http://www.iowaartscouncil.org/guidebook/gb20.htm
Requirements Organizations must be located and incorporated in Iowa, federally tax-exempt, and must have had an annual cash operating budget of between $50,000 and $250,000 (for midsize) for at least three years before filing an application. Applicant organizations must be unattached to an educational institution, must operate year-round, and must have at least one professional staff member.

Restrictions Organizations requesting operational support are not eligible to apply for project grants.
Areas of Interest Arts Administration

Maytag Corporation Foundation Grants 484
Maytag Corporation Foundation
PO Box 39, 403 W 4th St N
Newton, IA 50208—0039
Contact Michele Walstrom, Manager, Community Relations and Foundation, (641) 787-6357; fax: (641) 787-8170
Internet http://www.maytag.com/mths/our_company/default.jsp?partner=none
Requirements Nonprofit organizations in Arkansas, Iowa, Illinois, Ohio, South Carolina, and Tennessee are eligible.
Restrictions Grants are not awarded to individuals, religious organizations, health organizations (single disease), fraternal organizations, political or lobbying organizations, goodwill advertising, fundraising dinners, or member agencies of United Way.
Areas of Interest Arts, General; Business Education; Community Development; Children and Youth; Community Service Programs; Cultural Activities/Programs; Economics Education; Family; Higher Education; Performing Arts; School-to-Work Transition; Secondary Education; Visual Arts; Youth Programs
Sample Awards El Paso Community College (TX)—$25,000. Herrin City Library (IL)—$50,000. 100 Black Men of Bradley County (TN)—$15,000. Parents as Teachers (IA)—$10,000.

F. Maytag Family Foundation Grants 485
Fred Maytag Family Foundation
PO Box 366
Newton, IA 50208
Contact Ellen Bergeron, Administrator, (641) 791-0395
Internet http://www.maytag.com/mths/our_company/default.jsp
Requirements Nonprofit organizations in Iowa may apply.
Restrictions Grants are not awarded to individuals or for emergency funds, deficit financing, endowments, scholarships, fellowships, demonstration projects, publications, or conferences.
Areas of Interest Arts, General; Cancer/Carcinogenesis; Cultural Activities/Programs; Disabled; Education; Family Planning; Health Care; Higher Education; Public Affairs; Social Services

Mid-Iowa Health Foundation Grants 486
Mid-Iowa Health Foundation
550 39th St, Ste 104
Des Moines, IA 50312
Contact Kathryn Bradley, Executive Director, (641) 277-6411; fax: (515) 271-7579; e-mail: bradleymihf@aol.com
Requirements Organizations with nonprofit, tax-exempt status under IRS codes in Polk, IA, and contiguous counties are eligible.
Restrictions The foundation does not provide grants for direct aid to individuals, religious programs, political organizations or projects, or dinners or tickets.

Areas of Interest Alcohol/Alcoholism; Child/Maternal Health; Children and Youth; Chronic Illness; Disabled; Drugs/Drug Abuse; Elderly; Health Services Delivery; Poverty and the Poor; Youth Programs
Sample Awards Drake University (Des Moines, IA)—for capital support of the Knapp Recreation and Sports Arena, $10,000.

Pioneer Hi-Bred Community Grants 487
Pioneer Hi-Bred International Inc
400 Locust St, Ste 800
Des Moines, IA 50309-2340
Contact Grants Administrator, (515) 248-4800; fax: (515) 248-4999; e-mail: community.investment@pioneer.com
Internet http://www.pioneer.com/pioneer_info/corporate/us_guidelines.htm
Requirements Nonprofit organizations are eligible. All requests should be directed to the Pioneer Hi-Bred office within the local area. Otherwise, send to the contact listed. Pioneer does not respond favorably to verbal requests.
Restrictions Grants are not made to individuals, religious or political organizations that promote a particular doctrine, elected officials, company marketing or advertising, or organizations where there is a conflict of interest with Pioneer Hi-Bred.
Areas of Interest Education; Elementary Education; Environmental Programs; Farm and Ranch Management; Land Use Planning/Policy; Rural Health Care; Safety; Secondary Education; Water Resources; Higher Education; Environmental Health; Occupational Health and Safety
Sample Awards U of Iowa Foundation (Iowa City, IA)—to create a professorship in rural safety and health within the College of Public Health's Institute for Rural and Environmental Health and Department of Occupational and Environmental Health, $500,000.

Principal Financial Group Foundation Grants 488
Principal Financial Group Foundation Inc
711 High St
Des Moines, IA 50392-0150
Contact Laura Sauser, Community Investment Consultant, (515) 247-7227; fax: (515) 246-5475
Internet http://www.principal.com/about/giving/grant.htm
Requirements 501(c)3 tax-exempt organizations in company operating locations may apply.
Restrictions Proposals for athletic groups, conferences, endowments, fellowships, festivals, fraternal organizations, health care facility fund drives, libraries, or religious groups are denied.
Areas of Interest Adult and Continuing Education; Arts, General; Basic Skills Education; Cultural Activities/Programs; Education; Environmental Programs; Exhibitions, Collections, Performances; Health Care; Performing Arts; Recreation and Leisure; Social Services; Tourism; Vocational/Technical Education

Transamerica Foundation Grants   **489**
AEGON Transamerica Foundation
4333 Edgewood Rd, NE
Cedar Rapids, IA 52499
Contact Program Director, (319) 398-8852
Internet http://www.transamerica.com
Requirements Nonprofit organizations are eligible.
Restrictions The foundation will not make contributions to organizations that are exclusively religious.
Areas of Interest Children and Youth; Exercise; Family; Food Preparation; Health Care; Health Promotion; Homelessness; Housing; Nutrition/Dietetics; Sports; Stress
Sample Awards San Francisco Unified School District (CA)—to provide health screenings, nutrition and cooking classes, physical and athletic activities, stress management workshops, and other health promotion activities for children at Lawton Alternative School and their families, $1 million (1999).

Kansas

Baughman Foundation Grants   **490**
Baughman Foundation
PO Box 1356
Liberal, KS 67905-1356
Contact Carol Feather-Francis, President, (316) 624-1371
Requirements Nonprofit organizations in southwest Kansas, the Oklahoma panhandle, and southeast Colorado are eligible.
Areas of Interest Civic Affairs; Community Development; Higher Education; Youth Programs

Hutchinson Community Foundation Grants   **491**
Hutchinson Community Foundation
PO Box 298
Hutchinson, KS 67504-0298
Contact Lynette Lacy, President, (316) 663-5293; fax: (316) 663-9277; e-mail: info@hutchcf.org
Requirements Nonprofit organizations in Kansas, including 501(c)3 nonprofits, advocacy organizations, colleges and universities, religious organizations, school districts, schools, and state and local government agencies, are eligible.
Restrictions The foundation generally will not award scholarships to students, operating budgets for established organizations, or support of sectarian religious purposes.
Areas of Interest Arts, General; Children and Youth; Civil/Human Rights; Community Development; Education; Elementary Education; Health Care; Higher Education; Hospices; Housing; Mental Health; Preschool Education; Secondary Education; Social Services

Kansas Arts Commission Operational   **492**
    Support for Arts and Cultural
    Organizations
Kansas Arts Commission
700 SW Jackson, Jayhawk Tower, Ste 1004
Topeka, KS 66603

Contact Raena Miller, Grants Administrator, (785) 296-4089; fax: (785) 296-4989; email: raena@arts.state.ks.us
Internet http://arts.state.ks.us/grant_program2001.html
Requirements Applicants must be residents of Kansas.
Areas of Interest Art Education; Arts Administration; Performing Arts; Touring Arts Programs

Kansas Health Foundation Grants   **493**
Kansas Health Foundation
309 E Douglas
Wichita, KS 67202-3475
Contact Grants Manager, (800) 373-7681 or (316) 262-7676; fax: (316) 262-2044; e-mail: info@khf.org
Internet http://www.kansashealth.org/grants/recognition_grants.jsp
Requirements Kansas 501(c)3 nonprofit organizations are eligible.
Restrictions The foundation does not support clinical or medical research; contributions to capital campaigns; organizations that practice discrimination by race, color, creed, sex, age or national origin; operating deficits or retirement of debt; endowment programs; construction projects or real estate acquisitions; political projects of any kind; and vehicles, such as vans or buses, or emergency medical services equipment.
Areas of Interest Child/Maternal Health; Family; Health Care Assessment; Health Planning/Policy; Health Promotion; Health and Safety Education; Mentoring Programs; Preventive Medicine; Primary Care Services; Public Health; Rural Health Care; Senior Citizen Programs and Services; Space Sciences; Youth Violence
Sample Awards Challenger Learning Ctr Foundation (Wellington, KS)—to develop the center, which will provide educational opportunities that simulate actual space missions, $100,000. Exploration Place (Wichita, KS)—to support a program that offers hands-on activities for children and adults that explore public and individual health issues, $2.3 million. Family Life Ctr (Columbus, KS)—to recruit and train senior citizens to care for sick children while their parents are working, $17,524. Menninger Foundation (Topeka, KS)—for a violence-prevention program for elementary school children that uses teenagers as mentors, $24,580.

Fred C. and Mary R. Koch Foundation   **494**
    Grants Program
Fred C. and Mary R. Koch Foundation
PO Box 2256
Wichita, KS 67201-2256
Contact Roger Ramseyer, Program Contact, (316) 828-2646; e-mail: RamseyeR@kochind.com
Internet http://www.kochind.com/community/default.asp
Requirements The foundation supports nonprofit, tax-exempt organizations and institutions in communities that have Koch employees and facilities: Kansas, Minnesota, Texas, Oklahoma, Louisiana, and Alberta, Canada.
Restrictions Grants are not made to individuals.
Areas of Interest Children's Museums; Civil/Human Rights; Economic Self-Sufficiency; Economics; Educa-

tion; Environmental Programs; Family; Parks; Problem Solving; Science; Science Education; Social Services
Sample Awards Exploration Place (Wichita, KS)—for interactive, family-oriented educational programs for visitors to this science center, children's museum, and park, $500,000.

Powell Family Foundation Grants   **495**
Powell Family Foundation
4350 Shawnee Mission Pkwy, Ste 280
Fairway, KS 66205
Contact Grants Administrator, (913) 236-0003; fax: (913) 262-0058
Requirements Nonprofits in Missouri are eligible.
Restrictions The foundation does not support welfare or social services programs.
Areas of Interest Arts, General; Children and Youth; Civic Affairs; Environmental Programs; Humanities; Neighborhoods
Sample Awards Pembroke Hill School (Kansas City, MO)—for endowment support, $75,000.

Ethel and Raymond F. Rice Foundation   **496**
   Grants
Ethel and Raymond F. Rice Foundation
700 Massachusetts St
Lawrence, KS 66044
Contact James Paddock, President, (785) 841-9961
Requirements 501(c)3 nonprofit organizations and colleges and universities, school districts, and schools in Kansas are eligible.
Areas of Interest Arts, General; Cultural Activities/Programs; Elderly; Elementary Education; Environmental Programs; Higher Education; Secondary Education; Social Services; Youth Programs

Sprint Foundation Grants   **497**
Sprint Foundation
2330 Shawnee Mission Pkwy
Westwood, KS 66205
Contact David Thomas, Executive Director, (913) 624-3343; fax: (913) 624-3490
Internet http://www.sprintproposals.com
Requirements 501(c)3 organizations in Atlanta, Boston, Chicago, Dallas, Kansas City, Las Vegas, Los Angeles, New York City, Orlando, San Francisco and the District of Columbia are eligible; however, these areas are subject to change. Support of national organizations with a broad sphere of interests will be considered on a case-by-case basis. The foundation's geographic focus is primarily domestic.
Restrictions Organizations generally excluded from the foundation's grantmaking activities include political, religious, fraternal, labor, and veterans organizations; hospitals; and neighborhood associations. No grants are made to individuals.
Areas of Interest Adult and Continuing Education; Alcohol Education; Arts, General; Basic Skills Education; Business Education; Classroom Instruction; Communications; Community Service Programs; Cultural Activities/Programs; Cultural Outreach; Drug Education; Economics Education; Education; Education Reform; Higher Education; Leadership; Literacy; Museums; Per-

forming Arts; Technology; Textiles; Visual Arts; Youth Programs
Sample Awards American Red Cross, National Disaster Relief Fund (Washington, DC)—to provide support services to victims of the September 11 terrorist attacks, $500,000. Prairie View A&M U (TX)—to build a Broadband Data laboratory and supporting curriculum, $600,000.

Topeka Community Foundation Grants   **498**
Topeka Community Foundation
PO Box 4525, 1315 SW Arrowhead Dr
Topeka, KS 66604
Contact Chandler Moenius, President, (785) 272-4804; fax: (785) 273-2467; e-mail: tcf@ cjnetworks.com
Requirements Grants are awarded to Topeka and Shawnee County, KS, nonprofit organizations.
Restrictions Grants are not awarded to religious organizations for religious purposes or for scientific, medical, or academic research.
Areas of Interest Alcohol/Alcoholism; Arts, General; Children and Youth; Community Development; Cultural Activities/Programs; Drugs/Drug Abuse; Education; Environmental Programs; Family; Preschool Education; Public Affairs; Scholarship Programs, General

Westar Energy Foundation Grants   **499**
Westar Energy Foundation
818 Kansas Ave
Topeka, KS 66612
Contact Cynthia McCarvel, President, (785) 575-1544; fax: (785) 785-6399
Requirements Nonprofit organizations in company-operating areas of Kansas are eligible to apply.
Areas of Interest Children and Youth; Education; Employment Opportunity Programs; Energy; Environmental Education; Environmental Programs; Federal Government; Health Care; Local Government; Senior Citizen Programs and Services; State Government
Sample Awards Exploration Place (Wichita, KS)—for its capital campaign, and for the Season of Creativity exhibit, $100,000 and $40,000, respectively.

Kentucky

James Graham Brown Foundation Grants   **500**
James Graham Brown Foundation
4350 Brownsboro Rd, Ste 200
Louisville, KY 40207
Contact Dodie McKenzie, (502) 896-2440; fax: (502) 896-1774; e-mail: mason@brownfoundation.com
Internet http://www.jgbf.org
Requirements Nonprofit organizations in Kentucky may apply.
Restrictions Grants are not awarded to support private foundations, the performing arts, national organizations, political activities, elementary or secondary schools, or individuals.
Areas of Interest Catholic Church; Civic Affairs; Computer Science; Disabled; Health Care; Higher Education; Jewish Services; Libraries; Mathematics Education;

Museums; Science Education; Social Services; Technology Education; Youth Programs

Sample Awards Bellarmine U (Louisville, KY)—to endow student scholarships, $1 million (2003). U of Louisville (KY)—for cancer research and care at the Louisville Medical Center, $15 million partial challenge grant (2002).

CE and S Foundation Grants 501

CE and S Foundation
1650 National City Tower
Louisville, KY 40202
Contact Bruce Maza, Executive Director, (502) 583-0546; fax: (502) 583-7648; e-mail: bruce@ cesfoundation.com
Internet http://www.cesfoundation.com/grantmaking. html
Requirements Nonprofit organizations are eligible to apply.
Restrictions The foundation does not provide support individuals or for medical research.
Areas of Interest Archives; Art Education; Churches; Community Service Programs; Emergency Services; English Education; Health Care; Higher Education; Hospitals; International Programs; Minority Education; Religion; Religious Studies; Theology; Urban Areas; Urban Planning/Policy
Sample Awards City U of New York, Graduate School and U Ctr (NY)—for fellowships for minority doctoral students, $1 million. United Board for Christian Higher Education in Asia (New York, NY)—to train young archivists at the Tibet Autonomous Regional Archives in Lhasa, and to provide English-language training for Tibetans living in China's Qinghai Province, $40,000. United Board for Christian Higher Education in Arts (New York, NY)—program support in Cambodia and Vietnam, $32,900. Auburn Theological Seminary (New York, NY)—for surveys on theological education, $25,000.

Community Foundation of Louisville Grants 502

Community Foundation of Louisville
325 W Main St, Ste 1110, Waterfront Plaza
Louisville, KY 40202
Contact Alexandra Spoelker, Director of Grants, (502) 585-4649; fax: (502) 587-7484; e-mail: alexs@ cflouisville.org
Internet http://www.cflouisville.org/page13464.cfm
Requirements Only Kentucky non-profit organizations are eligible to apply. For the community grants, programs must serve populations in Algonquin, California, Chickasaw, Limerick, Old Louisville, Park DuValle, Park Hill, Parkland, Phoenix Hill, Portland, Russell, Shawnee, Shelby Park, Smoketown, or South Louisville neighborhoods.
Areas of Interest African Americans; Children and Youth; Community Development; Family; Health Promotion; Health and Safety Education; Law Enforcement; Mentoring Programs; Music, Vocal; Poverty and the Poor
Sample Awards West Louisville Boys Choir (Louisville, KY)—for operating support, $25,000. Big Brothers and Big Sisters of Kentuckiana (Louisville, KS)—to enable police officers to provide weekly educa-

tional, mentorship, and safety programs at Coleridge-Taylor Elementary School and King Elementary School, $10,000. Health Promotion Schools of Excellence (Louisville, KY)—to promote healthy behavior for K-12 students at 10 schools, $25,000 matching grant.

V.V. Cooke Foundation Grants 503

V.V. Cooke Foundation
PO Box 202
Pewee Valley, KY 40056-0202
Contact Theodore Merhoff, Executive Director, (502) 241-0303; e-mail: cookefdn@bellsouth.net
Requirements Grants are awarded to nonprofit organizations in Kentucky.
Restrictions Grants are not awarded to individuals or for general endowment funds, scholarships, fellowships, or loans.
Areas of Interest Baptist Church; Children and Youth; Education; Higher Education; Medical Education; Religion
Sample Awards Campbellsville U (Campbellsville, KY), Cumberland College (Williamsburg, KY), and Georgetown College (Georgetown, KY)—to raise funds for student financial aid and for capital projects, $90,000 jointly.

Cralle Foundation Grants 504

Cralle Foundation
620 W Main St, Ste 320
Louisville, KY 40202
Contact James Crain Jr., Executive Director, (502) 581-1148; fax: (502) 581-1937
Requirements Nonprofit organizations in Kentucky are eligible.
Areas of Interest Children and Youth; Community Development; Education; Higher Education; Social Services
Sample Awards Bellarmine College (Louisville, KY)—to construct a new student activities center, $500,000.

Kentucky Arts Council Community Arts 505
Development Program Grants

Kentucky Arts Council
300 W Broadway
Frankfort, KY 40601-1950
Contact Daniel Strauss, Arts Program Branch Manager, (888) 833-2787 (ext 4809); e-mail: chris. harp@mail.state.ky.us; Daniel Strauss, Arts Program Branch Manager, (888) 833-2787 ext 4804; fax: (502) 564-2839; voice/TDD: (502) 564-3757; e-mail: Dan. Strauss@ky.gov
Internet http://www.state.ky.us/agencies/arts/guide/ prog7/ca_gdl.html
Requirements The program will provide technical assistance to new or emerging arts organizations in Kentucky to gradually increase organizational development and maturity over a five-year period. Organizations need not be incorporated as a nonprofit, tax-exempt entity in their first year, but must have applied for this status by year two and secured such status by year three. Other eligible organizations include those which provide some arts programming (not year-round); organizations with budgets of $50,000 or more; and local arts agencies and discipline-based arts organizations (such as community

theaters, visual art leagues, dance companies, etc.) with budgets under $50,000. Cash matches are required at every level of funding; amounts vary.

Restrictions Funds cannot be used for deficits, capital expenditures, or major purchases of equipment.

Areas of Interest Arts Administration; Dance; Dramatic/Theater Arts; Neighborhoods; Visual Arts

Kentucky Arts Council Organizational Support—Arts Development Grants   506

Kentucky Arts Council
300 W Broadway
Frankfort, KY 40601
Contact Dan Strauss, Branch Program Manager, (888) 833-2787 ext 4804; fax: (502) 564-2839; e-mail: dan. strauss@mail.state.ky.us
Internet http://www.kyarts.org/guide/prog2/gos1_gdl. html
Requirements Kentucky nonprofit arts organizations committed to providing arts programs and services to the public are eligible to apply. First-time organizations applying to the program must contact the program manager listed prior to making application. All applicants with operating expenses greater than or equal to $150,000 during their most recently completed fiscal year must submit an audit for that period.
Restrictions Not eligible are internal programs of academic institutions and state or other agencies supported primarily with state or federal funds. Applicants to the Challenge or Community Arts programs are not eligible.
Areas of Interest Arts Administration

Kentucky Arts Council Organizational Support—Challenge Grants   507

Kentucky Arts Council
300 W Broadway
Frankfort, KY 40601-1980
Contact Dan Strauss, Branch Program Manager, (888) 833-2787 ext 4804; fax: (502) 564-2839; e-mail: dan. strauss@mail.state.ky.us
Internet http://www.state.ky.us/agencies/arts/guide/ prog2/cg_gdl.html
Requirements Kentucky nonprofit arts organizations committed to providing arts programs and services to the public are eligible to apply. First-time organizations applying to the program must contact the program manager listed prior to making application. All applicants with operating expenses greater than or equal to $150,000 during their most recently completed fiscal year must submit an audit for that period.
Restrictions Not eligible are internal programs of academic institutions and state or other agencies supported primarily with state or federal funds. Applicants to the Arts Development or Community Arts programs are not eligible.
Areas of Interest Arts Administration

Kentucky Arts Council Organizational Technical Assistance Grants   508

Kentucky Arts Council
300 W Broadway
Frankfort, KY 40601

Contact Daniel Strauss, Arts Program Branch Manager, (888) 833-2787 ext 4804; fax: (502) 564-2839; voice/TDD: (502) 564-3757; e-mail: dan. strauss@mail.state.ky.us
Internet http://artscouncil.ky.gov/gtprogs.htm
Requirements Kentucky arts organizations that are current Kentucky Arts Council grantees or applicants may apply. Applicants must match the KAC grant dollar-for-dollar in cash.
Restrictions In-kind contributions are not eligible as matching funds.
Areas of Interest Arts Administration; Management; Training and Development

Norton Foundation Grants   509

Norton Foundation
4350 Brownsboro Rd, Ste 133
Louisville, KY 40207
Contact Lucy Crawford, Executive Director, (502) 893-9549; fax: (502) 896-9378; e-mail: nortfound@ aol.com
Requirements Nonprofit organizations in the metropolitan Louisville, KY, area may submit applications.
Restrictions Individuals and private foundations are ineligible.
Areas of Interest Adult and Continuing Education; Basic Skills Education; Disadvantaged (Economically); Elementary Education; Family; Immigrants; Literacy; Minorities; Preschool Education; Secondary Education; Social Services; Youth Programs

Louisiana

Charles T. Beaird Foundation Grants   510

Charles T. Beaird Foundation
330 Marshall St, Ste 1112
Shreveport, LA 71101
Contact Grants Administrator, (318) 221-8276; fax: (318) 221-5993; e-mail: BeairdP@aol.com or info@ beairdfoundation.org
Internet http://www.beairdfoundation.org
Requirements Nonprofit organizations in, or projects that take place in, the Shreveport, LA, area are eligible. Requests from other areas, if they have the potential to be replicated in the Shreveport area, may be considered.
Areas of Interest Community Outreach Programs

Joe W. and Dorothy Dorsett Brown Foundation Grants   511

Joe W. and Dorothy Dorsett Brown Foundation
320 Hammond Hwy, Ste 500
Metairie, LA 70005
Contact D.P. Spencer, President, (504) 834-3433
Internet http://www.thebrownfoundation.org
Requirements Louisiana and Mississippi nonprofit organizations, with a focus on South Louisiana, the New Orleans area, and the Mississippi Gulf Coast, are eligible. Service Learning grant applications are available yearly to sixth through 12th grades in the following parishes: Orleans, Jefferson, Plaquemines, Saint Bernard, Saint Charles, Tangipahoa, Saint James, Saint John, Saint Tammany, and Washington.

Areas of Interest Biomedical Research; Community and School Relations; Community Development; Education; Health Promotion; Health Services Delivery; Higher Education; Homeless; Hospitals; Housing; Religion; Social Services Delivery

**Coughlin-Saunders Foundation Grants   512
   Program**
Coughlin-Saunders Foundation
1412 Centre Ct, Ste 202
Alexandria, LA 71301
Contact Ed Crump Jr., Grants Administrator, (318) 487-4332; fax: (318) 487-7339; e-mail: csfoundation@ kricket.net
Requirements 501(c)3 tax-exempt organizations in central Louisiana may apply.
Restrictions Grants are not made to individuals.
Areas of Interest Art Education; Arts, General; Building Grants; Education; Emergency Programs; Equipment/Instrumentation; Museums; Religion; Social Services

Collins C. Diboll Private Foundation Grants 513
Collins C. Diboll Private Foundation
201 Saint Charles Ave, 50th Fl
New Orleans, LA 70170-5100
Contact Donald Diboll, Chair, (504) 582-8103
Requirements Louisiana nonprofit organizations are eligible.
Restrictions Individuals are not eligible for grants.
Areas of Interest Business; Catholic Church; Education; Higher Education; Health Care; Historic Preservation; Kidney Diseases and Disorders; Museums; Protestant Church; Sports; Youth Programs
Sample Awards Alton Ochsner Medical Foundation (New Orleans, LA)—for Golden Jubilee/Initiative Campaign, $100,000. New Orleans Museum of Art (New Orleans, LA)—$100,000. Junior Achievement of New Orleans (New Orleans, LA)—$35,000. Preservation Resource Ctr of New Orleans (New Orleans, LA)—for renovations, $11,000.

Huie-Dellmon Trust Grants   514
Huie-Dellmon Trust
PO Box 330
Alexandria, LA 71309
Contact Richard Crowell Jr., Trustee
Requirements Central Louisiana nonprofit organizations are eligible.
Areas of Interest Child Abuse; Higher Education; Hospitals; Libraries; Museums; Protestant Church; Secondary Education
Sample Awards Boy Scouts of America (Alexandria, LA)—for child abuse programs, $35,210. First United Methodist Church (LA)—for operating support, $10,000. Southern Forest Heritage Museum (LA)—for operating support, $25,942.

**Louisiana State Arts Council General   515
   Operating Support Program**
Louisiana State Arts Council and Division of the Arts
PO Box 44247
Baton Rouge, LA 70804

Contact Program Officer, Major Art Institutions, (225) 342-8180; fax: (225) 342-8173; e-mail: arts@crt.state. la.us
Internet http://www.crt.state.la.us/arts/state_art_grant/ gos.htm
Requirements Louisiana nonprofit 501(c)3 organizations are eligible. Applicants for both Level One and Level Two funding must have been incorporated as an arts producing and programming organization for at least three years prior to the application deadline; have an independent governing board empowered to formulate policies and execute programs; have significant educational outreach for children and adults; provide a full season of 26 weeks or more of public programming to include production or exhibitions, educational activities, outreach programs, and free public performances; have produced at least one free community performance during the preceding year; and provided with the application a complete copy of an independent financial audit for the organization's prior year if such audit has not been previously submitted. In addition, Level One applicants must provide a copy of the organization's long-range plan with application. Level Two applicants must provide a three-year, long-range plan with their application addressing the following areas: artistic program, educational outreach, fund raising and development, personnel/staff development, financial development, and marketing. Grants must be matched by cash reflected in the operating budget approved by the organization's governing board.
Restrictions Grants will not be made to fund exhibitions or productions by children or students in grades K-12 or performances or exhibitions primarily for student audiences. In addition, the program does not support projects that pay children or students in grades K-12 or in undergraduate degree programs. Applicants for these grants are not eligible to apply for funding under the project assistance program.
Areas of Interest Art Education; Arts Administration; Exhibitions, Collections, Performances; Finance; Fund-Raising; Marketing; Personnel Training and Development

**Louisiana State Arts Council Local Arts   516
   Agency Level One Program Grants**
Louisiana State Arts Council and Division of the Arts
PO Box 44247
Baton Rouge, LA 70804
Contact Program Officer, Local Arts Agencies, (225) 342-8180; fax: (225) 342-8173; e-mail: arts@crt.state. la.us
Internet http://www.crt.state.la.us/arts/state_art_grant/ laa.htm
Requirements Louisiana 501(c)3 nonprofit organizations may apply. In addition, Level One applicants must be officially designated by the municipal or parish governing body with jurisdiction over the service area to act on its behalf as the local arts agency; have at least one full-time, paid professional staff member; have a governing board with the responsibility and the legal power to set agency policy; have had annual operating revenues of $100,000 or more for the preceding fiscal year; provide, with the application, a complete copy of an independent financial audit for the organization's prior year (if such

audit has not previously been submitted); and provide a copy of the current community cultural plan.

Areas of Interest Arts Administration; Local Government

Louisiana State Arts Council Local Arts Agency Level Two Program Grants   517

Louisiana State Arts Council and Division of the Arts
PO Box 44247
Baton Rouge, LA 70804

Contact Program Officer, Local Arts Agencies, (225) 342-8180; fax: (225) 342-8173; e-mail: arts@crt.state.la.us

Internet http://www.crt.state.la.us/arts/state_art_grant/laa.htm

Requirements Louisiana 501(c)3 nonprofit organizations may apply. In addition, Level Two applicants must be officially designated by the municipal or parish governing body with jurisdiction over the service area to act on its behalf as the local arts agency; have a governing board with the responsibility and the legal power to set agency policy; have had annual operating revenues of not more than $100,000 for the preceding fiscal year; and provide a copy of current community cultural plans.

Areas of Interest Arts Administration; Municipal Government

Maine

George P. Davenport Trust Fund Grants   518

George P. Davenport Trust Fund
55 Front St
Bath, ME 04530

Contact J. Franklin Howe, Treasurer, (207) 443-3431

Requirements Nonprofit organizations serving Bath, ME, are eligible.

Restrictions Grants are not awarded for continuing support, annual campaigns, deficit financing, equipment, programs, research, demonstration projects, or publications.

Areas of Interest Community Development; Education; Health Care; Higher Education; Religion; Scholarship Programs, General

Sample Awards Salvation Army (Bath, ME)—for program support, $17,000. U of Maine (Orono, ME)—for scholarships, $10,750.

Fore River Foundation Grants   519

Fore River Foundation
PO Box 7525
Portland, ME 04112-7525

Contact Mary Gamage, Foundation Manager

Requirements Nonprofit organizations may apply; preference is given to those organizations in Maine.

Areas of Interest Arts, General; Conservation, Natural Resources; Cultural Activities/Programs; Education; History; Music; Restoration and Preservation; Wildlife

Sample Awards Portland Concert Assoc (Portland, ME)—for operating support, $5000. Concord Academy (Concord, MA)—for general operating support, $30,000.

Hannaford Charitable Foundation Grants   520

Hannaford Charitable Foundation
PO Box 1000
Portland, ME 04104

Contact Grants Administrator, c/o Citizens Scholarship Foundation of America, (800) 213-9000

Internet http://www.hannaford.com/community/index.htm

Requirements Nonprofit organizations are eligible, with preference given to requests in Maine and New Hampshire.

Areas of Interest Arts, General; Children and Youth; Community Development; Cultural Activities/Programs; Education; Environmental Programs; Neighborhoods; Scholarship Programs, General; Social Services

Libra Foundation Grants   521

Libra Foundation
PO Box 17516
Portland, ME 04112-8516

Contact Elizabeth Flaherty, (207) 879-6280; fax: (207) 879-6281

Internet http://www.librafoundation.org

Requirements Maine 501(c)3 nonprofits and nonprofits serving the state may apply.

Restrictions Individuals are ineligible.

Areas of Interest Environmental Programs; Genetics; Higher Education; Philanthropy; Religion; Youth Programs

Sample Awards New England Forestry Foundation (Groton, MA)—to purchase the largest forestland easement in US history, which will protect 762,192 acres in Maine from development, $2 million (2001). Jackson Laboratory (Bar Harbor, ME)—to construct facilities for genetics research and education, $1 million (2000).

Morton-Kelly Charitable Trust Grants   522

Morton-Kelly Charitable Trust
10 Free St, Box 4510
Portland, ME 04112

Contact Michael Quinlan, Secretary & Clerk, (207) 775-7271; fax: (207) 775-7935; e-mail: mquinlan@jbgh.com

Requirements Maine nonprofit organizations are eligible.

Areas of Interest Arts, General; Cultural Activities/Programs; Education; Environmental Programs; Restoration and Preservation; Vocational/Technical Education

Orchard Foundation Grants   523

Orchard Foundation
PO Box 2587
Portland, ME 04116

Contact Executive Director, (207) 799-0686; fax: (207) 799-0686; e-mail: orchard@maine.rr.com

Internet http://home.maine.rr.com/orchard

Requirements The foundation focuses Massachusetts, Maine, New Hampshire, New York, Vermont, Connecticut, and Rhode Island. The foundation accepts letters of inquiry from groups in those seven states as well as from national groups with regional offices or projects in the area.

Restrictions Grants are not made to individuals or for endowments, annual or capital campaigns, religious programs, any religion-affiliated organization, conference participation/travel unrelated to current foundation grant, research efforts unrelated to advocacy interests of the foundation, scholarships, fellowships, building projects, equipment needs, film and video projects, land acquisition, animal hospitals/rehabilitation centers, or groups that focus on specific diseases or conditions. Loans are not made.

Areas of Interest Air Pollution; Biodiversity; Campaign Finance Reform; Child Welfare; Children and Youth; Environmental Programs; Family; Forest Ecology; Literacy; Pollution Control; Pregnancy; Reproduction; Toxic Substances; Water Pollution

Sample Awards New England Forestry Foundation (Groton, MA)—to purchase the largest forestland easement in US history, which will protect 762,192 acres in Maine from development, $35,000 (2001).

Simmons Foundation Grants 524

Simmons Foundation
1 Canal Plaza
Portland, ME 04112
Contact Suzanne McGuffey, Treasurer, (207) 774-2635
Requirements Maine nonprofits are eligible.
Restrictions Individuals are ineligible.
Areas of Interest Arts, General; Children and Youth; Computer Grants; Cultural Activities/Programs; Health Care; Higher Education; Networking (Computers); Nursing Education; Social Services; Visual Impairments; Women
Sample Awards U of Southern Maine, School of Nursing (Portland, ME)—for scholarships, $5000. Maine Ctr for the Blind and Visually Impaired (Portland, ME)—for a computer network, $6000.

Maryland

American Society for Parenteral and Enteral 525 Nutrition Research Grants

American Society for Parenteral and Enteral Nutrition
8630 Fenton St, Ste 412
Silver Spring, MD 20910
Contact Research Programs Manager, (301) 587-6315; fax: (301) 587-2365; e-mail: aspen@nutr.org
Internet http://www.nutritioncare.org
Requirements Applicants are encouraged from the fields of medicine, dietetics, nursing, and pharmacy.
Areas of Interest Biomedicine; Nursing; Nutrition/Dietetics; Pharmacology

Clayton Baker Trust Grants 526

Clayton Baker Trust
2 E Read St, Ste 100
Baltimore, MD 21202
Contact Program Contact, (410) 837-3555; fax: (410) 837-7711
Requirements Nonprofit organizations in Maryland are eligible to apply.
Restrictions Grants do not support the arts, research, higher educational institutions, individuals, building construction/renovation, or endowment funding.

Areas of Interest Children and Youth; Disadvantaged (Economically); Environmental Programs; Gun Control; Population Control

Baltimore Community Foundation Grants 527

Baltimore Community Foundation
2 E Read St
Baltimore, MD 21202
Contact Dion Cartwright, Program Contact, (410) 332-4171; fax: (410) 837-4701; e-mail: dcartwright@bcf.org or grants@bcf.org
Internet http://www.bcf.org/grants.html
Requirements 501(c)3 tax-exempt organizations in the greater Baltimore region are eligible.
Restrictions The foundation does not usually make grants for annual fund campaigns; operating support, except for start-up; religious or sectarian purposes; campaigns for capital to which the foundation can contribute no more than a small fraction of the total need; or individuals.
Areas of Interest After-School Programs; Art Education; Arts, General; Children and Youth; Community Development; Cultural Activities/Programs; Elderly; Environmental Programs; Family; Health Care; Housing; Mental Health; Minorities; Neighborhoods; Public Administration; Social Services; Volunteers; Youth Programs
Sample Awards Downtown Partnership (Baltimore, MD)—for marketing expenses for Vivat, a festival celebrating Russian culture, $15,000 (2003). Advocates for Children and Youth (Baltimore, MD)—for advocacy work related to the Maryland Children's Action Network, $45,000 over three years (2003). Connexions Community Leadership Academy (Baltimore, MD)—for start-up expenses of this school, $25,000 (2003). Community Law Ctr (Baltimore, MD)—to recruit and train volunteer lawyers to help neighborhoods handle vacant and nuisance properties, $20,000 (2003).

Helen and Merrill Bank Foundation Grants 528

Helen and Merrill Bank Foundation
Baronet Rd
Owings Mills, MD 21117
Contact Herbert Bank, (410) 363-6767
Requirements Nonprofit organizations in Florida and Maryland are eligible.
Areas of Interest Disabled; Hospitals; Jewish Services; Museums; Performing Arts; Private and Parochial Education; Religion; Women
Sample Awards Raymond F. Kravis Ctr for the Performing Arts (West Palm Beach, FL)—for operating support, $79,150. Temple Israel (Boston, MA)—for operating support, $45,000.

Jacob and Hilda Blaustein Foundation 529 Grants

Jacob and Hilda Blaustein Foundation
10 E Baltimore St, Ste 1111
Baltimore, MD 21202
Contact Betsy Ringel, Executive Director, (410) 347-7201; fax: (410) 347-7210; e-mail: info@blaufund.org
Internet http://www.blaufund.org/foundations/jacobandhilda_f.html

Requirements Nonprofit organizations of the Christian and Jewish faiths located in Maryland are eligible.

Restrictions Grants are not made to individuals or to unaffiliated schools.

Areas of Interest Children and Youth; Civil/Human Rights; Communinty Development; Community Service Programs; Family; Government Functions; Governmental Function; Health Care; Health Promotion; Higher Education; Hospitals; International Programs; Israel; Jewish Services; Mental Health; Public Policy/Planning; Training and Development

Sample Awards Shefa Fund (Wyndmoor, PA)—to leverage investments from Jewish institutions and individuals for use by community development financial institutions, $200,000. Johns Hopkins Medical Institutions (Baltimore, MD)—to help construct a cancer research building at the Johns Hopkins Oncology Ctr, $10 million. Sinai Hospital (Baltimore, MD)—$100,000. Institute for Christian-Jewish Studies (Baltimore, MD)—$80,000.

Alex Brown and Sons Charitable Foundation Grants 530

Alex Brown and Sons Charitable Foundation
1 South St
Baltimore, MD 21202
Contact Margaret Preston, Secretary, c/o Deutsche Bank Alex Brown Inc
Requirements 501(c)3 tax-exempt organizations in Maryland are eligible.
Restrictions No support for private schools or churches. Grants are not made to individuals.
Areas of Interest Arts, General; Civic Affairs; Education; Humanities; Medicine, Internal; Science
Sample Awards Baltimore Symphony Orchestra (MD)—for discretionary use, $1 million (2002). Johns Hopkins Hospital (Baltimore, MD)—for discretionary use, $1 million (2002). Baltimore Zoo (MD)—for discretionary use, $1 million (2002).

Eugene B. Casey Foundation Grants 531

Eugene B. Casey Foundation
800 S Frederick Ave, Ste 100
Gaithersburg, MD 20877-1701
Contact Betty Brown Casey, (301) 948-4595
Requirements Nonprofits in Maryland or the District of Columbia are eligible to apply.
Areas of Interest Higher Education; Community Service Programs; Government; Hospitals; Private and Parochial Education; Religion; Catholic Church; Forests and Woodlands; Performing Arts
Sample Awards Duke Ellington School of the Arts (Washingtion, DC)—for Denyce Graves Endowment Fund, $100,000. Round House Theater (Silver Spring, MD)—for general support, $15,000. Government of the District of Columbia (Washington, DC)—to be split evenly, with half going to build a mayoral mansion in the Foxhall neighborhood of Northwest Washington, and the rest to plant new trees and maintain and restore damaged trees throughout the District of Columbia, $100 million.

Clark Charitable Foundation Grants 532

Clark Charitable Foundation
7500 Old Georgetown Rd, 15th Fl
Bethesda, MD 20814
Contact Courtney Clark Pastrick, Secretary, (301) 657-7166
Areas of Interest Arts, General; Community Development; Higher Education; Social Services

Clark-Winchcole Foundation Grants 533

Clark-Winchcole Foundation
3 Bethesda Metro Ctr, Ste 550
Bethesda, MD 20814
Contact Vincent Burke, President, (301) 654-3607
Requirements Only nonprofit organizations in the District of Columbia are eligible to apply.
Areas of Interest Cultural Activities/Programs; Disabled; Health Care; Higher Education; Hospitals; Religion; Youth Programs
Sample Awards District of Columbia College Access Program (DC)—for general operating support, $100,000. Washington Theater Awards Society (Washington, DC)—for program support, $35,000. First Baptist Church of the City of Washington, DC (Washington, DC)—for a community ministries program, $30,000.

Constellation Energy Group and Baltimore Gas and Electric Corporate Contributions 534

Constellation Energy Group and Baltimore Gas and Electric Company Foundation
PO Box 1475, 750 E Pratt St
Baltimore, MD 21203-1475
Contact Malinda Small, Corporate Contributions Committee, (410) 234-7481; fax: (410) 234-7471; e-mail: corporate.contributions@constellation.com
Internet http://www.constellation.com/about/community.asp
Requirements The company makes charitable donations to 501(c)3 tax-exempt, nonprofit organizations in Maryland, where the company has significant business interests.
Restrictions The company does not contribute to churches for religious causes, sports teams, organizations that actively oppose the company's position on issues, nor does it support health research programs or activities.
Areas of Interest Adult and Continuing Education; Cancer/Carcinogenesis; Child Psychology/Development; Civic Affairs; Community Development; Cultural Activities/Programs; Disaster Relief; Environmental Programs; Health Care; Homosexuals, Female; Homosexuals, Male; Hospitals; Leadership; Minority Education; Preschool Education; Religion; Social Services
Sample Awards Johns Hopkins U (Baltimore, MD)—to renovate the Peabody Institute of Music, $1 million (2003). Pride of Baltimore (MD)—for sponsorship of 25-Years-of-Pride event, $5000 (2002). American Red Cross Calvert County (MD)—support for victims in Calvert and Charles Counties of April 29, 2002 toronado, $10,000 (2002. Baltimore's Festival of the Arts (MD)—sponsorship of ARTSCAPE's 21st annual celebration, $7500 (2002).

DHHS Allied Health Project Grants   535
Department of Health and Human Services
5600 Fishers Ln, Parklawn Bldg
Rockville, MD 20857
Contact Young Song, Program Contact, (301)
443-3353; fax: (301) 443-0162; e-mail: ysong@hrsa.
gov
Internet http://bhpr.hrsa.gov/grants/applications/
htmlapps/allhlth.htm
Requirements Schools, universities, or other educational entities including public or nonprofit private entities that provide for allied health personnel education and training and are located in a state, the District of Columbia, Puerto Rico, Northern Mariannas, Virgin Islands, Guam, American Samoa, Republic of Palau, Republic of the Marshall Islands, or the Federal States of Micronesia may apply.
Restrictions Grant funds may not be used for construction of facilities, acquisition of land, foreign travel, or support of students.
Areas of Interest Allied Health Education; Curriculum Development; Minority Education

DHHS Health Centers Grants for Migratory   536
  and Seasonal Farmworkers
Department of Health and Human Services
4350 East-West Hwy
Bethesda, MD 20814
Contact Migrant Health Branch, Division of Health Center Management, (301) 594-4420; Grants Management Officer, Bureau of Primary Health Care, (301) 594-4235
Internet http://aspe.os.dhhs.gov/cfda/p93246.htm
Requirements Any public or nonprofit private entity may apply. Preference will be given to applications submitted by community-based organizations that are representative of the populations to be served.
Restrictions For-profit organizations are ineligible.
Areas of Interest Environmental Health; Family; Migrant Health Centers; Migrants; Primary Care Services; Training and Development

Dresher Foundation Grants   537
Dresher Foundation
4940 Campbell Blvd, Ste 110
Baltimore, MD 21236
Contact Grants Administrator, (410) 931-9050; fax: (410) 931-9052
Requirements Maryland nonprofit organizations located in Hartford County are eligible.
Areas of Interest Disadvantaged (Economically); Education; Elementary Education; Homelessness; Protestant Church; Religious Welfare Programs; Secondary Education; Social Services Delivery; Youth Programs
Sample Awards Johns Hopkins U (Baltimore, MD)—to establish a professorship in cardiac surgery in the department of medicine, $2 million (2003).

Carl M. Freeman Foundation Grants   538
Carl M. Freeman Foundation
18330 Village Mart Dr, 2nd Fl
Olney, MD 20832
Contact Cheryl Kagan, Executive Director, (240) 779-8000; fax: (240) 779-8180; e-mail: cheryl@freemanfoundation.org
Internet http://www.freemancompanies.com
Requirements 501(c)3 tax-exempt organizations in Maryland and the District of Columbia are eligible. Nonsectarian religious programs also are eligible.
Areas of Interest Arts, General; Education; Literature; Philanthropy; Religion; Science

Corina Higginson Trust Grants   539
Corina Higginson Trust
3400 Bryan Point Rd
Accokeek, MD 20607
Contact Wilton Corkern Jr., Trustee, (301) 283-2113; fax (301) 283-2049
Requirements 501(c)3 District of Columbia, Maryland, and Virginia nonprofit organizations are eligible.
Restrictions Grants do not support individuals, religious organizations, medical or health-related programs, endowment funds, or scholarship funds.
Areas of Interest Education; Social Services

Howard County Community Foundation   540
  Grants
Columbia Foundation/Howard County Community Foundation
10221 Wincopin Cir, Ste G-15
Columbia, MD 21044-2624
Contact Barbara Lawson, Executive Director, (410) 730-7840; fax: (410) 997-6021; e-mail: info@columbiafoundation.org
Internet http://www.columbiafoundation.org/grants/index.html
Requirements Howard County, MD, nonprofit organizations are eligible.
Restrictions Grants do not support individuals, sectarian religious purposes, annual campaigns, deficit financing, land acquisition, medical research, or endowments.
Areas of Interest Arts, General; Children and Youth; Civic Affairs; Community Development; Education; Family; Music; Social Services

Keith Campbell Foundation for the   541
  Environment Grants
Keith Campbell Foundation for the Environment
210 W Pennsylvania Ave, Ste 770
Towson, MD 21204
Contact Keith Campbell, President, (410) 825-0545, ext 103
Requirements Maryland 501(c)3 tax-exempt organizations are eligible. The majority of grants are awarded in the Baltimore area.
Areas of Interest Children and Youth; Cultural Activities/Programs; Social Services Delivery

Marion I. and Henry J. Knott Foundation   542
  Grants Program
Marion I. and Henry J. Knott Foundation
3904 Hickory Ave
Baltimore, MD 21211-1834
Contact Gregory Cantori, Executive Director, (410) 235-7068; fax: (410) 889-2577; e-mail: knott@knottfoundation.org

Internet http://knottfoundation.org
Requirements Funding is limited to 501(c)3 organizations serving Baltimore City and the following counties in Maryland: Allegheny, Anne Arundel, Baltimore, Carroll, Frederick, Garrett, Harford, Howard, and Washington.
Restrictions The following will not be funded: organizations that have not been in operation for at least one year, scholarships, public education/public sector agencies, pro-choice activities, individuals, annual giving, political activities, one-time only events/seminars/workshops, legal services, environment, medical research, day care centers, endowment funds for arts/humanities, national/local chapters for specific diseases, agencies that redistribute grant funds to other nonprofits, or government agencies that form 501(c)3 nonprofits to fund public sector projects.
Areas of Interest Art Education; Biology; Catholic Church; Chemistry; Criminal Justice; Cultural Activities/Programs; Elementary Education; Health Care; Physical Sciences; Physics; Private and Parochial Education; Religion; Secondary Education; Social Services Delivery; Sports
Sample Awards Goodwill Industries of the Chesapeake (Baltimore, MD)—for its programs to help former prisoners reenter society, $30,000 (2003). Archbishop Curley High School (Baltimore, MD)—to replace windows in the friary, $50,000 (2003). Episcopal Social Ministries (Baltimore, MD)—to expand the drug-rehabilitation program in Collington Square, $32,221 (2003). Younglife Baltimore Urban (MD)—for the Midnight Madness basketball program, $15,000 (2003).

John J. Leidy Foundation Grants 543
John J. Leidy Foundation
201 E Baltimore St, Ste 1420
Baltimore, MD 21202
Contact Grants Administrator, (410) 727-4136; fax: (410) 625-0253; e-mail: leidyfd@attglobal.net
Requirements IRS tax-exempt organizations are eligible.
Restrictions The foundation does not award grants, scholarships, fellowships, loans, prizes, or similar benefits to individuals. Grants do not support political organizations, special events, or benefit dinners.
Areas of Interest Arts, General; Civic Affairs; Cultural Activities/Programs; Health Care; Higher Education; Social Services
Sample Awards Chesapeake Ctr for Youth—for education program support, $1000. Maryland Historical Society—for program support, $1000. Ctr for Poverty Solutions—operating support for the food pantry, $25,000.

Marpat Foundation Grants 544
Marpat Foundation
PO Box 1769
Silver Spring, MD 20915-1769
Contact Joan Koven, Secretary/Treasurer; e-mail: jkoven@marpatfoundation.org
Internet http://fdncenter.org/grantmaker/marpat/2004guide.html
Requirements Nonprofits in the Washington, DC, area are eligible.

Restrictions Grants are not made to support individuals, endowments, or projects or organizations for weapons development.
Areas of Interest Academic Achievement; After-School Programs; American Studies; Counseling/Guidance; Cultural Activities/Programs; Education; English as a Second Language; Family; Family Planning; Food Distribution; Health Care; Higher Education; International Programs; Leadership; Libraries; Mentoring Programs; Museums; Natural Sciences; Photography; Religion; Restoration and Preservation; Science; Shelters; United States History; Women
Sample Awards Indochinese Community Ctr (Washington, DC)—to provide family support services, mentoring, leadership training, and academic enrichment for 250 Vietnamese youth and a comprehensive after-school program that provides daily English classes and tutoring for 80 children, $10,000. National Museum of Women in the Arts (New York, NY)—for the first major traveling retrospective of photographer Sarah Charlesworth, $7500.

J.P. Morgan Chase Foundation Awards for 545
Excellence in Workforce Development
Grants
Enterprise Foundation
10277 Wincopin Circle, Ste 500
Columbia, MD 21044
Contact Bahar Babaturk, Program Content, (410) 772-2428; e-mail: bbabaturk@enterprisefoundation.org
Internet http://www.enterprisefoundation.org/resources/Trainingconf/conferences/workforceConference/workforceconference.asp
Requirements 501(c)3 nonprofit organizations or Native American tribes that provide employment services for low-income people; are members of the Enterprise network (nonprofits can apply online at no cost); and have placed and retained at least 30 people for six months of employment between January 2001 and June 30, 2002.
Areas of Interest Economic Opportunity Programs; Economically Disadvantaged; Employment Opportunity Programs; Job Training Programs; Poverty and the Poor
Sample Awards Transitional Work Corporation (Philadelphia, PA)—$15,000 (2003). Project QUEST (San Antonio, TX)—$15,000 (2003). Larkin Street Youth Services (San Francisco, CA)—$15,000 (2003).

NCI Cancer Biology Research Grants 546
National Cancer Institute
6130 Executive Blvd, Executive Plaza N
Bethesda, MD 20892
Contact Dr. John Sogn, Deputy Director, Division of Cancer Biology, (301) 435-5225; Leo Buscher Jr., Grants Management Officer, (301) 496-7753
Internet http://www.nci.nih.gov/researchfunding
Requirements The awardee will be a university, college, hospital, public agency, nonprofit research institution, or for-profit organization that submits an application and receives a grant for support of research by a named principal investigator.
Areas of Interest Cancer/Carcinogenesis; Immunology; Nutrition/Dietetics; Oncology

William and Charlotte Parks Foundation for 547 Animal Welfare Grants
William and Charlotte Parks Foundation
700 Professional Dr
Gaithersburg, MD 20879
Contact Donna Pease, fax: (301) 548-7726; e-mail: info@parksfoundation.org
Internet http://www.parksfoundation.org
Requirements 501(c)3 tax-exempt organizations are eligible. A non-US applicant must be registered as a charitable organization in the home country.
Restrictions Grants will not normally be awarded to improve animal health, for local spay/neuter assistance, to save endangered species, to rehabilitate wildlife, or to support political candidates. Grants focused on the conservation or protection of wild animal populations will not be funded. Grants will not ordinarily be made to organizations with an annual income of more than $1 million or a large asset base, with the exception of institutions of higher learning.
Areas of Interest Animal Care; Animal Research Policy; Animal Rights; Animal Welfare; Population Control; Veterinary Medicine

T. Rowe Price Associates Foundation Grants 548
T. Rowe Price Associates Foundation
100 E Pratt St, 8th Fl
Baltimore, MD 21202
Contact Christine Stein, Program Director, (410) 345-3603; fax: (410) 345-2848
Requirements Although not limited to, giving is primarily made in the metropolitan Baltimore, MD, area.
Restrictions No support provided for religious or political organizations; hospitals or health care providers; recreational sports leagues and sports related fundraisers; private foundations; or grants to individuals.
Areas of Interest Arts and Culture; Civic Affairs; Community and Civic; Community Development; Education; Higher Education; Human Services; Secondary Education; Social Services
Sample Awards Maryland Institute College of Art (Baltimore, MD)—for unrestricted support, $30,000. Baltimore Symphony Orchestra (Baltimore, MD)—for unrestricted support, $30,640. YMCA of Metropolitan Phoenix (Phoenix, AZ)—for civic and community purposes, $5000.

Rathmann Family Foundation Grants 549
Rathmann Family Foundation
1290 Bay Dale Dr
Arnold, MD 21012
Contact Rick Rathmann, (410) 349-2376; fax: (410) 349-2377
Requirements Grants are awarded to organizations in the San Francisco Bay, CA area; Annapolis, MD; Seattle, WA; Philadelphia, PA: and metropolitan Minneapolis/Saint Paul, MN.
Restrictions Grants are not awarded to/for private foundations; religious organizations for religious activities; civil rights; social action; advocacy organizations; fraternal groups; political purposes; mental health counseling; individuals; or fundraisers, media events, public relations, annual appeals, or propaganda.

Areas of Interest Arts, General; Children and Youth; Curriculum Development; Education; Environmental Programs; Health Care; Mathematics Education; Medical Education; Patient Care and Education; Scholarship Programs, General; Science Education
Sample Awards U of Washington, School of Medicine (Seattle, WA)—to endow a chair in patient-centered clinical education, $1.5 million.

Rollins-Luetkemeyer Foundation Grants 550
Rollins-Luetkemeyer Foundation
105 W Chesapeake Ave, Ste 109
Towson, MD 21204
Contact President, (410) 296-4800
Requirements Maryland nonprofit organizations, with preference given to the Baltimore area, are eligible.
Areas of Interest Education; Early Childhood Education; Elementary Education; Health; Health Care; Hospitals; Protestant Church; Religion; Social Services Delivery
Sample Awards McDonogh School (Owings Mills, MD)—for student scholarships and salary support for faculty members, $20 million challenge grant (2004).

Thomas B. and Elizabeth M. Sheridan 551 Foundation Grants
Thomas B. and Elizabeth M. Sheridan Foundation
11350 McCormick Rd, Executive Plz II, Ste 704
Hunt Valley, MD 21031
Contact James Sinclair, President, (410) 771-0475
Requirements Nonprofit organizations in the greater Baltimore, MD, area are eligible.
Restrictions Grants are not awarded to individuals, for employee matching gifts, or for loans.
Areas of Interest Arts and Culture; Biology Education; Chemistry Education; Cultural Activities/Programs; Education; Higher Education; Physics Education; Private and Parochial Education; Secondary Education
Sample Awards Notre Dame Preparatory School (Towson, MD)—to renovate its biology, chemistry, and physics laboratories, as part of its capital campaign, $50,000. Baltimore Symphony Orchestra (Baltimore, MD)—$126,000. Gilman School (Baltimore, MD)—$103,000. Contemporary Museum (Baltimore, MD)—$10,000.

Alvin and Fanny Blaustein Thalheimer 552 Foundation Grants
Alvin and Fanny Blaustein Thalheimer Foundation
10 E Baltimore St, Ste1111
Baltimore, MD 21202
Contact Betsy Ringel, Executive Director, (410) 347-7103; fax: (410) 347-7210; e-mail: info@blaufund.org
Internet http://www.blaufund.org/foundations/alvinandfanny_f.html
Requirements Only Maryland organizations are eligible to apply.
Restrictions Grants are not made to individuals.
Areas of Interest Arts, General; Audience Development; Cultural Programs/Activities; Families; Health Promotion; Health Services Delivery
Sample Awards Mercy Medical Ctr (Baltimore, MD)—for general operating support, $10,000. Baltimore Mu-

seum of Art (Baltimore, MD)—for general operating support, $62,500. Maryland/Israel Economic Development Ctr (Baltimore, MD)—for general operating support, $17,500.

Town Creek Foundation Grants 553
Town Creek Foundation
121 N West St
Easton, MD 21601
Contact Christine Shelton, Executive Director, (410) 763-8171; fax: (410) 763-8172; e-mail: info@ towncreekfdn.org
Internet http://www.towncreekfdn.org/tcfsite/tguides.html
Requirements IRS 501(c)3 tax-exempt organizations are eligible. Social service grants are limited to nonprofits in Talbot County, MD.
Restrictions The foundation does not fund programs outside of North America, nor does it make grants to individuals, primary and secondary schools, hospitals, health care institutions, or religious organizations; or for endowment, capital and building fund campaigns, or the purchase of land or buildings. It does not make grants in general to colleges or universities or for research, scholarship programs, conferences, the publication of books and periodicals, or visual or performing arts projects.
Areas of Interest Civic Affairs; Conventional Warfare; Defense Studies; Economics; Educational/Public Television; Environmental Law; Environmental Programs; Governmental Functions; Journalism; Peace/Disarmament; Public Broadcasting; Radio

Harry and Jeanette Weinberg Foundation 554 Grants
Harry and Jeanette Weinberg Foundation
7 Park Center Ct
Owings Mills, MD 21117
Contact Grants Administrator, (410) 654-6900
Restrictions Grants are not awarded to institutions of higher education or museums.
Areas of Interest Aging/Gerontology; Disabled; Disadvantaged (Economically); Food Distribution; Social Services Delivery
Sample Awards Metropolitan Career Ctr (Philadelphia, PA)—for general operating support of its work with low-income and unemployed people, $330,000 over three years (2004). Strive (New York, NY)—to strengthen and expand its job training and placement network, and for endowment, $5 million challenge grant (2003).

Massachusetts

Azadoutioun Foundation Grants 555
Azadoutioun Foundation
10 Madison Ave
Groveland, MA 01834
Contact Laurie LeBlanc, (978) 374-5504; fax: (978) 521-9204; e-mail: lleblanc9498C@aol.com
Restrictions Grants are not made to individuals.
Areas of Interest Adult and Continuing Education; Basic Skills Education; Economic Development; Environ-

mental Programs; International Programs; Literacy; Reading; Social Services

Paul and Edith Babson Foundation Grants 556
Paul and Edith Babson Foundation
50 Congress St, Ste 832
Boston, MA 02109-4017
Contact Elizabeth Nichols, Grants Administrator, (617) 523-8368; fax: (617) 523-8949; e-mail: pebabsonfdn@babsonfoundations.org
Internet http://www.babsonfoundations.org
Requirements IRS 501(c)3 tax-exempt organizations in Massachusetts are eligible.
Restrictions Films, videos, conferences, and fund-raising events will not be supported.
Areas of Interest Conservation, Natural Resources; Counseling/Guidance; Economic Development; Entrepreneurship; Exercise; Family; Health Services Delivery; Higher Education; Hospitals; Music; Opera/Musical Theater; Private and Parochial Education; Recreation and Leisure; Restoration and Preservation; Scholarship Programs, General; Secondary Education; Social Services; Urban Areas; Youth Programs
Sample Awards Boston Lyric Opera (Boston, MA)—for operating support, $10,000. Steppingstone Foundation—for operating support, $5000. Urban Health Project, Harvard Medical School (Cambridge, MA)—for operating support, $3000.

Lloyd G. Balfour Foundation Grants 557
Fleet Investment Management
75 State St
Boston, MA 02109
Contact Kerry Herlihy Sullivan, Director, (617) 434-4846; e-mail: kerry_h_sullivan@fleet.com
Internet http://www.fleet.com/about_ inthecommunity_balfouroverview.asp
Requirements IRS 501(c)3 organizations in Massachusetts and the New England area eligible.
Areas of Interest Academic Achievement; Education; Elementary Education; Higher Education; Minority Education; Secondary Education; Youth Programs

Boston Foundation Grants Program 558
Boston Foundation
75 Arlington St, 10th Fl
Boston, MA 02116
Contact Grants Administrator, (617)338-1700; e-mail: info@tbf.org
Internet http://www.tbf.org/Fund/Fund-L1.asp
Requirements Grants are made only to tax-exempt organizations in Massachusetts.
Restrictions The committee does not consider more than one proposal from the same organization within a 12-month period. Grants are not made for annual operations not linked to a specific strategy, capital campaigns, city or state governments, conferences, endowments, equipment, publications, private or parochial schools, religion, replacement of lost government funds, research, scholarships, or travel.
Areas of Interest AIDS; Adult and Continuing Education; African Americans; Arts, General; Basic Skills Education; Churches; Community Outreach Programs; Cultural Activities/Programs; Disabled; Elderly; Ele-

mentary Education; Employment Opportunity Programs; Environmental Programs; Family; Health Care; Homelessness; Housing; Immigrants; Juvenile Delinquency; Literacy; Minorities; Nature Centers; Nutrition/ Dietetics; Opera/Musical Theater; Preschool Education; Reading; Recreation and Leisure; Secondary Education; Social Services; Women; Youth Programs

Sample Awards New Boston Pilot Middle School Design Team (MA)—$50,000 (2003). Charles River Conservancy (MA)—$20,000 (2003). Trinity Church (MA)—$25,000 (2003). Stop Handgun Violence (MA)—$20,000 (2003).

Boston Foundation Initiative to Strengthen Arts and Cultural Service Organizations 559
Boston Foundation
75 Arlington St, 10th Fl
Boston, MA 02116
Contact Ann McQueen, (617)338-2773; e-mail: mcq@tbf.org
Internet http://www.tbf.org/fund/fund-L2.asp?id=1607
Requirements 501(c)3 nonprofit agencies that provide services to artists and/or cultural nonprofits within the greater Boston service area are eligible.
Areas of Interest Arts
Sample Awards American Composers Forum, Boston Area Chapter, (MA)—to implement a strategic plan, $7000 (2003). Cultural Access Consortium (MA)—to work with five theater companies to develop and implement access strategies, $20,000 (2003). StageSource (MA)—to enhance current and launch new professional development and job resource programs for theater artists, $15,000 (2003). The Art Connection (MA)—to frame works of art, facilitating donations from and placements to less affluent artists and nonprofit agencies, $10,000 (2003).

Boston Globe Foundation Grants 560
Boston Globe Foundation
PO Box 55819
Boston, MA 02205
Contact Leah Bailey, (617) 929-2895; e-mail: foundation@globe.com
Internet http://bostonglobe.com/community/foundation/index.stm
Requirements Only nonprofit Massachusetts organizations in Boston, Cambridge, Somerville, and Chelsea are eligible.
Areas of Interest Arts, General; Children and Youth; Civic Affairs; Community Service Programs; Cultural Activities/Programs; Education; Environmental Programs; Family; Health Care; Humanities; Literacy; Youth Programs

Boston Women's Fund Grants 561
Boston Women's Fund
14 Beacon St, Ste 805
Boston, MA 02108
Contact Grants Administration, (617) 725-0035 ext 3007; fax: (617) 725-0277; e-mail: Catherine@bostonwomensfund.org
Internet http://www.bostonwomensfund.org/grantinfo.html

Requirements Applicant must be a Boston-area group with an organizational budget of less than $150,000 per year.
Areas of Interest Children and Youth; Disabled; Economic Development; Elderly; Homosexuals, Female; Minorities; Poverty and the Poor; Service Delivery Programs; Social Change; Women

Alexander H. Bright Charitable Trust Grants 562
Alexander H. Bright Charitable Trust
88 Broad St
Boston, MA 02110
Contact Solange Bell, c/o The Boston Family Office, (617) 227-2676 or (617) 624-0800
Requirements Northeast US nonprofits are eligible. Preference is given to requests from Massachusetts.
Areas of Interest Children and Youth; Education; Environmental Law; Environmental Programs; Migratory Animals and Birds; Social Services; Wildlife
Sample Awards Massachusetts Audubon Society (Lincoln, MA)—for general operating support, $3000 (2002). Conservation Law Foundation (Boston, MA)—for general operating support, $2500 (2002). New England Wildlife Center (Hingham, MA)—for general operating support, $12,000 (2002).

Cabot Corporation Foundation Grants Program 563
Cabot Corporation Foundation
2 Seaport Ln, Ste 1300
Boston, MA 02210
Contact Dorothy Forbes, Executive Director, (617) 342-6002; fax: (617) 342-6320; e-mail: dorothy_forbes@cabot-corp.com
Internet http://w1.cabot-corp.com/controller.jsp?N=21+4294966792&entry=
Requirements The foundation supports only nonprofit 501(c)3 tax-exempt organizations in Georgia, Illinois, Louisiana, Massachusetts, Pennsylvania, Texas, and West Virginia. Modest support is available for international organizations that qualify under US tax regulations.
Restrictions Contributions are not made to individuals, political organizations, religious institutions (except for projects that are open to individuals without regard to religious preference), advertising, dinner-table sponsorship, or fraternal organizations.
Areas of Interest Arts, General; Children's Museums; Education; Environmental Education; Literacy; Science; Science Education; Technology
Sample Awards Gilbertsville Elementary School (PA)—to enhance science curriculum with LEGO products and training materials, $3700. Pact Malaysia (Malaysia)—to support literacy programs in Malaysia, $5000. Children's Hands-On Art Museum (MA)—equipment grant, $2500.

Cambridge Community Foundation Grants 564
Cambridge Community Foundation
99 Bishop Richard Allen Dr
Cambridge, MA 02139

Contact Robert Hurlbut Jr., Executive Director, (617) 576-9966; fax: (617) 876-8187; e-mail: cambridgecf@ igc.org

Restrictions Support is not provided for municipal, state, or federal agencies. Grants for individuals, scholarships, research studies, conferences, films, capital fund drives, or loans are not eligible.

Areas of Interest Alcohol/Alcoholism; Cultural Activities/Programs; Curriculum Development; Domestic Violence; Drugs/Drug Abuse; Education; Gender Equity; Health Care; Housing; Intervention Programs; Juvenile Delinquency; Penology/Correctional Institutions and Procedures; Social Services; Volunteers; Women

Sample Awards Homeowners Rehab Inc—for operating support. East End House—to support domestic violence education, $5000. Adolescent Consultation Services—to support substance abuse prevention and intervention services for court-involved youth and their families, $5000.

Bushrod H. Campbell and Adah F. Hall Charity Fund Grants 565

Bushrod H. Campbell and Adah F. Hall Charity Fund
111 Huntington Ave at Prudential Ctr
Boston, MA 02199-7613
Contact Brenda Taylor, c/o Palmer & Dodge, (617) 239-0556; fax: (617) 227-4420
Requirements Tax-exempt organizations located within Boston and neighboring communities and US tax-exempt organizations devoted to population control are eligible.
Restrictions Grants are not awarded to individuals.
Areas of Interest Biomedical Research; Elderly; Health Care; Hearing Impairments; Hospitals; Population Control; Visual Impairments

CarEth World Peace and Justice Grants 566

CarEth Foundation
264 N Pleasant St, 2nd Fl
Amherst, MA 01002
Contact Grants Administrator, (413) 256-0349; fax: (413) 256-3536
Internet http://www.funder.org/grantmaking/careth
Restrictions The foundation does not consider requests for conferences, fund-raising events, capital improvements, human rights organizations, relief aid, research, groups based outside the United States, schools, or film/video projects. Due to a high number of virus-infected proposals, the foundation is unable to accept any e-mailed proposals at this time. The foundation does not accept faxed proposals either, so please allow time for mailing your proposal to us so that we receive it by the deadline.
Areas of Interest Civil/Human Rights; Economics; Government; Middle East; Peace/Disarmament; Political Behavior; Public Relations; Social Stratification/Mobility; Youth Programs
Sample Awards Americans for Peace Now—to promote the peace process in the Middle East, $6000. Ctr for Media and Democracy—to expose the influence of the public relations industry on public discourse, $6000. Share the Wealth—for education on the increasing gap between the wealthy and everyone else and its implica-

tions for US democracy, $8000. Peaceworkers—for third-tier peacekeeping missions, $8000.

Chahara Foundation Grants 567

Chahara Foundation
4 Copley Pl
Boston, MA 02116-6504
Contact Program Contact, (617) 247-1580; fax: (617) 247-7177; e-mail: carol@chahara.org
Internet http://www.chahara.org
Requirements Nonprofit organizations run by and for lower-income women in the greater Boston, MA, area are eligible.
Areas of Interest Community Development; Women

Chestnut Hill Charitable Foundation, Inc Grants 568

Chestnut Hill Charitable Foundation, Inc
27 Boylston St
Chestnut Hill, MA 02167-1700
Contact Kay Kilpatrick, Director Corporate Giving, (617) 630-2415
Requirements Nonprofit organizations in the greater Boston, MA, area may submit letters of request.
Restrictions Grants are not awarded to support individuals or political or religious organizations.
Areas of Interest AIDS; Arts, General; Cancer/Carcinogenesis; Cardiovascular Diseases; Child Psychology/Development; Children and Youth; Computer Education/Literacy; Computer Software; Cultural Activities/Programs; Diabetes; Education; Hospitals; Humanities; Museums; Neighborhoods; Philanthropy; Poverty and the Poor; Preschool Education; Pulmonary Diseases; Social Services; Visual Arts; Youth Programs
Sample Awards Leslie Berg, U of Massachusetts Medical Ctr (Worcester, MA)—for the Chestnut Hill Award for Excellence in Medical Research, administered by the Medical Foundation, in Boston, $15,000 (2003).

Jessie B. Cox Charitable Trust Grants 569

Jessie B. Cox Foundation
60 State St
Boston, MA 02109-1899
Contact Donor Services Office, Hemenway and Barnes, (617) 227-7940 ext 775; e-mail: scs@hembar.com
Internet http://hemenwaybarnes.com/privatesrv/jbcox/cox.html
Requirements New England nonprofit organizations are eligible.
Restrictions The trust does not normally provide support for buildings, equipment, or land purchases; endowments, scholarship funds, or fundraising activities; loans to charitable organizations; or deficits or normal operating budgets or where the trust may become the organization's predominant source of support.
Areas of Interest Academic Achievement; Art Education; Conservation, Natural Resources; Disadvantaged (Economically); Education; Environmental Health; Environmental Programs; Health Care; Health Promotion; Health Services Delivery; Performing Arts; Philanthropy; Visual Arts

Fred Harris Daniels Foundation Grants   570
Fred Harris Daniels Foundation
c/o Fleet Private Client Group, 100 Front St
Worcester, MA 01608
Contact Fred Daniels, President
Requirements Only Massachusetts organizations may apply.
Restrictions Grants are not awarded to individuals or for deficit financing, seed money, or loans.
Areas of Interest Adult and Continuing Education; Basic Skills Education; Biomedical Research; Botanical Gardens; Family; Health Services Delivery; Higher Education; Hospitals; Libraries; Literacy; Marine Sciences; Mental Disorders; Museums; Music; Protestant Church; Restoration and Preservation; Science; Secondary Education; Social Services
Sample Awards Bancroft School (Worcester, MA)—for general support, $45,000. New England Science Ctr, Rutland House (Worcester, MA)—for repairs, $20,000. Tower Hill Botanic Garden (Boylston, MA)—for general support, $30,000.

Eastern Bank Charitable Foundation Grants 571
Eastern Bank Charitable Foundation
1 Eastern Pl, 195 Market St
Lynn, MA 01901
Contact Laura Kurzrok, Foundation Corrdinator, (781) 598-7888; fax: (978) 740-6329; e-mail: Lkurzrok@ easternbk.com
Internet http://www.easternbank.com/a_charitable_ foundation.html
Requirements Nonprofit organizations operating in northeastern Massachusetts communities served by Eastern Bank are eligible for funding.
Restrictions Recipients of major gifts generally will be considered ineligible to reapply for a major gift for a period of three years.
Areas of Interest Children and Youth; Community Service Programs; Cultural Activities/Programs; Education; Emergency Programs; Health Care; Nursing; Volunteers
Sample Awards Special Children's Outing Committee (MA)—charitable support, $1000. Northeastern U (MA)—pledge payment, $2000. Visiting Nurse Assoc Foundation (MA)—program support, $1000.

Ruth H. and Warren A. Ellsworth   572
   Foundation Grants
Ruth H. and Warren A. Ellsworth Foundation
370 Main St, 12th Fl, Ste 1250
Worcester, MA 01608
Contact Sumner Tilton Jr., Trustee, (508) 798-8621
Requirements Nonprofits in the Worcester, MA, area are eligible.
Restrictions Grants are not awarded to individuals or for endowment funds, scholarships, fellowships, research, publications, conferences, matching gifts, or loans.
Areas of Interest Arts, General; Children and Youth; Community Development; Counseling/Guidance; Education; Family; Health Care; Higher Education; Hospitals
Sample Awards Childrens Friend (Worcester, MA)—for Putting Kids First capital campaign, $100,000

(2001). American Antiquarian Society (Worcester, MA)—for capital campaign, $20,000 (2001).

Essex County Community Foundation   573
   Grants
Essex County Community Foundation
45 Salem Rd
Topsfield, MA 01983-2112
Contact Grants Administrator, (978) 887-8876; fax: (978) 887-8454; e-mail: info@eccf.org
Internet http://www.eccf.org/grants/index.html
Requirements Massachusetts 501(c)3 organizations offering programs and services in Essex County communities and, in some cases, agencies of local or state government are eligible. Organizations with a pending application for 501(c)3 status, and new or informal groups with a qualified fiscal sponsor, are also considered.
Restrictions Discretionary grants are not awarded to individuals; for political purposes; for sectarian or religious purposes; for debt or deficit reduction; or for activities that have already taken place or expenses incurred prior to the grant award date. The following purposes are not a priority for support and thus generally grants are not awarded: to support major capital campaigns for buildings, land acquisition, or endowment; as general operating support to established organizations (more than three years); to support academic research or program development feasibility studies; for travel out of the region; or to state and local government agencies.
Areas of Interest Arts, General; Community Service Programs; Cultural Activities/Programs; Education; Environmental Programs; Health Promotion; Youth Programs

Charles H. Farnsworth Trust Grants   574
Charles H. Farnsworth Trust
95 Berkeley St, Ste 201
Boston, MA 02116
Contact Grants Administrator, (617) 451-0049, ext 702; e-mail: research@tmfnet.org
Requirements Only nonprofits in Massachusetts are eligible to apply.
Areas of Interest Elderly; Health Care; Nutrition/Dietetics; Supportive Housing Programs

FleetBoston Financial Foundation Grants   575
FleetBoston Financial Foundation
100 Federal St, MADE 10018A
Boston, MA 02110
Contact Kerry Herlihy Sullivan, Director, Foundation & Philanthropic Services, Fleet National Bank, (617) 434-4846; e-mail: Kerry_H_Sullivan@fleet.com
Internet http://www.fleet.com/aboutfleet/community/ relatedlinks/grants.html
Requirements Charitable support focuses on nonprofits in states where Fleet Bank operates, including Connecticut, Maine, Massachusetts, New Hampshire, New Jersey, New York, eastern Pennsylvania, and Rhode Island.
Restrictions The foundation does not support individuals; religious, fraternal, political, or veterans organizations; national organizations, including state and local chapters; organizations that are not open to the general public; annual funds of hospitals, colleges, universities, grade schools, or high schools; trips, tours, or confer-

ences; scientific or medical research; or deficit spending or debt liquidation.

Areas of Interest Arts, General; Audience Development; Education Reform; Business Development; Business Education; Children and Youth; Community Development; Disadvantaged (Economically); Economic Development; Education; Employment Opportunity Programs; Entrepreneurship; Families; Homeless Shelters; Homelessness; Homeownership; Housing; Humanities; Job Training Programs; Leadership; Literacy; Mentoring Programs; Microenterprises; Public Education; Poverty and the Poor; School-to-Work Transition; Social Services; Youth Programs

Francis A. and Jacquelyn H. Harrington   576
Foundation Grants
Francis A. and Jacquelyn H. Harrington Foundation
370 Main St, 12th Fl
Worcester, MA 01608
Contact Sumner Tilton Jr., Trustee, (508) 798-8621
Requirements The foundation provides grants to 501(c)3 tax-exempt organizations that are based in the Worcester, MA, area.
Areas of Interest Cultural Activities/Programs; Education; Health Care
Sample Awards Bancroft School (Worcester, MA)—for building new Lower and Middle School facilit. and new science classrooms, $100,000.

Haymarket People's Fund Grants   577
Haymarket People's Fund
42 Seaverns Ave
Boston, MA 02130
Contact Tommie Hollis-Younger Grants Coordinator, (617) 522-7676; fax: (617) 522-9580; e-mail: Tommie@haymarket.org
Internet http://www.haymarket.org/grants.htm
Requirements Both incorporated organizations (with or without established 501(c)3 status) and unincorporated organizations may apply. Applicants must conduct work within New England (Connecticut, Maine, Massachusetts, New Hampshire, Rhode Island, and Vermont).
Restrictions Grants do not support social services if they do not demonstrate some organizing strategies to challenge the systems that lead to oppression; alternative business (food co-ops and alternative schools, for example); organizations with access to traditional or mainstream funding sources, including those with significant government and/or corporate funding and those with relatively large budgets; government agencies; individuals, or individual projects, such as graduate research or fellowships; or other grantmaking foundations.
Areas of Interest Economic Development; Grassroots Leadership; Peace/Disarmament

High Meadow Foundation Grants   578
High Meadow Foundation
Main St
Stockbridge, MA 01262
Contact Jane Fitzpatrick, Chair, (413) 298-5565; fax: (413) 298-4058
Requirements Western Massachusetts 501(c)3 tax-exempt organizations in Berkshire County are eligible.

Areas of Interest Cultural Activities/Programs; Dramatic/Theater Arts; Music; Performing Arts

Hyams Foundation Grants   579
Hyams Foundation
175 Federal St, 14th Fl
Boston, MA 02110
Contact Susan Perry, Grants Administrator, (617) 426-5600 ext 307; fax: (617) 426-5696; e-mail: sperry@hyamsfoundation.org
Internet http://www.hyamsfoundation.org
Requirements Massachusetts 501(c)3 charitable organizations are eligible. The foundation will give priority to programs that have a substantial impact on low-income neighborhoods/populations in Boston, Cambridge, Chelsea, Lynn, and Somerville.
Restrictions Grants do not support advertising, athletic groups, colleges and universities, international organizations, political organizations, school districts, schools, special events/benefit dinners, state and local government agencies, municipal or federal agencies, religious purposes, individuals, endowments, hospitals for capital funds, conferences, scholarships, national or regional organizations, or film production.
Areas of Interest Citizenship; Crime Prevention; Cultural Diversity; Disadvantaged (Economically); Economic Development; Education; Employment Opportunity Programs; English as a Second Language; Family; Homelessness; Housing; Immigrants; Intervention Programs; Minorities; Neighborhoods; Nonprofit Organizations; Refugees; Urban Areas; Violent Behavior; Youth Programs
Sample Awards Urban Revival (Boston, MA)—to support general operating expenses, $17,500. Committee for Boston Public Housing (Boston, MA)—to support crime and violence prevention coalition-building in four Boston neighborhoods, $59,083. Project Life (Boston, MA)—to support a bilingual intervention program for families in Mission Hill, $12,500.

Island Foundation Grants   580
Island Foundation
589 Mill St
Marion, MA 02738
Contact Julie Early, Executive Director, (508) 748-2809; fax: (508) 748-0991; e-mail: islandfdn@earthlink.net
Requirements Nonprofit organizations in Maine, Massachusetts, and Rhode Island are eligible for grant support.
Restrictions Grants do not support individuals, international organizations, religious organizations, special events, benefit dinners, or political campaigns.
Areas of Interest Ecology, Aquatic; Education; Environmental Programs; Social Services; Solar Studies; Wastewater Treatment
Sample Awards Woods Hole Oceanographic Institution (Woods Hole, MA)—to support research on solar aquatic systems, $231,000. Coalition for Buzzards Bay (Buzzards Bay, MA)—for the protection of Buzzards Bay, $45,000.

Henry P. Kendall Foundation Grants 581

Henry P. Kendall Foundation
176 Federal St
Boston, MA 02110
Contact Jennifer Patrick, Associate Program Officer,
(617) 951-2525; fax: (617) 443-1977
Internet http://www.kendall.org/prior.htm
Restrictions Grants do not support endowments or capital fund campaigns, land acquisition, television and film projects, fellowships, basic scientific research, building construction or maintenance, equipment, debt reduction, or conferences unrelated to current foundation institutional grants. Nor does the foundation normally fund waste clean-ups, toxics or air/water pollution prevention or pollution monitoring initiatives, individual land trusts, or species-specific preservation efforts.
Areas of Interest Climatology; Conservation, Natural Resources; Environmental Programs; Land Management; Water Resources, Management/Planning
Sample Awards Alaska Conservation Foundation (Anchorage, AK)—to create a strategic transition fund dedicated to strengthening and expanding efforts to build a popular majority for conservation values—terrestrial and marine—throughout Alaska over the next two decades, $100,000. Earth Day Network (Seattle, WA)—to support preparatory organizing efforts in New England for Earth Day 2000, $35,000. Montana Wilderness Assoc (Helena, MT)—for general support to advance the protection of public wildlands and naturally functioning ecosystems in the Montana portion of the Yellowstone to Yukon landscape, $40,000.

Merck Family Fund Grants 582

Merck Family Fund
303 Adams St
Milton, MA 02186
Contact Jenny Russell, Executive Director, (617) 696-3580; fax: (617) 696-7262; e-mail: merck@merckff.org
Internet http://www.merckff.org
Requirements US tax-exempt organizations are eligible.
Restrictions The foundation does not generally support academic research or books. It does not fund endowments, debt reduction, annual fund-raising campaigns, capital construction, the purchase of equipment, the acquisition of land, film or video projects, or political candidates.
Areas of Interest Ecology; Environmental Health; Environmental Programs; Forests and Woodlands; Land Use Planning/Policy; Neighborhoods; Pollution Control; Social Change; Solid Waste Disposal; Sustainable Development; Urban Planning/Policy; Water Resources; Wetlands; Youth Programs
Sample Awards Audubon South Carolina (Harleyville, SC)—to support the land protection program in Four Holes Swamp area of Edisto River Basin, $25,000 (2003). Ctr for Land and People (San Francisco, CA)—to support two leadership retreats for land conservation activists, $10,000 (2003). Franklin Park Coalition (Franklin Park, MA)—for general support, $30,000 (2003). Northwest Bronx Community and Clergy Coalition (Bronx, NY)—to support Sistas and Brothas United, $35,000 (2003).

Millipore Foundation Grants 583

Millipore Foundation
290 Concord Rd
Billerica, MA 01821-7037
Contact Charleen Johnson, Executive Director, (978) 715-1268; fax: (978) 715-1385; e-mail: Charleen_Johnson@millipore.com
Internet http://www.millipore.com/corporate/milliporefoundation.nsf/foundationhome
Requirements 501(c)3 tax-exempt organizations are eligible.
Areas of Interest Biochemistry; Chemistry; Cultural Activities/Programs; Engineering; Health Care; Industry; Inner Cities; Minority Education; Public Planning/Policy; Social Services; Youth Programs

NEFA National Dance Project Grants 584

New England Foundation for the Arts
266 Summer St, 2nd Fl
Boston, MA 02210
Contact Expeditions Grants, (617) 951-0010; fax: (617) 951-0016; e-mail: info@nefa.org
Internet http://www.nefa.org/grantprog/ndp/ndp_prod_grant_app.html
Requirements Production grants are awarded to dance projects based on nominations received from presenters, artists, artist managers, and agents.
Restrictions Artists receiving production grants in any given season are not eligible to apply for production grant support in the following season.
Areas of Interest Cultural Activities/Programs; Cultural Diversity; Cultural Outreach; Dance
Sample Awards For touring grants that support the presentation of dance works nationwide, $825,329 to be divided among 24 contemporary-dance companies (2002).

New England Biolabs Foundation Grants 585

New England Biolabs Foundation
32 Tozer Rd
Beverly, MA 01915
Contact Martine Kellett, Executive Director, (978) 927-2404; fax: (508) 921-1350; e-mail: kellett@nebf.org
Internet http://www.nebf.org/application.html
Requirements The foundation makes grants to grassroots organizations, emerging support groups, and other charitable organizations, generally nonprofits with revenue under $3 million. International projects located in Cambodia, Cameroon, the Caribbean (not Haiti, Cuba, the US Virgin Islands, or the Dominican Republic), Central America (not Mexico, Costa Rica, Panama or Belize), Guatemala (funding environmental education projects for students and/or teachers), Ghana (environmental projects only), Tanzania, Madagascar, Papua New Guinea, South America (not Argentina, Brazil, Fr. Guiana, Suriname, Uruguay, Columbia, or Venezuela), Viet Nam, and Zimbabwe will be considered. Under certain provisions, individuals also may be eligible.
Restrictions Grants are not awarded to support religious activities, specific animal protection, services for the elderly or the disabled, projects normally funded by major agencies, or art projects outside the immediate community. Grants do not support capital endowment or build-

ing funds, fellowships, movies or videos, scholarships, or conferences.

Areas of Interest Arts, General; Biodiversity; Conservation, Agriculture; Conservation, Natural Resources; Developing/Underdeveloped Nations; Economic Development; Education; Environmental Programs; Estuarine Sciences; Forestry Management; Inner Cities; Marine Sciences; Sustainable Development; Women; Youth Programs; Youth Violence

Sample Awards Artcorps (Boston, MA)—to support inner city teens art design in Boston, $20,000. A Woman's Voice—to prevent female circumcision in young girls in Kenya, $5000. Lesson One (Peabody, MA)—for violence prevention programs in elementary schools in Peabody, MA, $7500. Idea Wild (Fort Collins, CO)—to continue a biodiversity and conservation program in Latin America, $5000.

Peace Development Fund Grants   586
Peace Development Fund
Box 1280, 44 N Prospect St
Amherst, MA 01004
Contact Program Director, (413) 256-8306 ext 110; fax: (413) 256-8871; e-mail: grants@peacefund.org
Internet http://www.peacefund.org/grant/-grnntrn.htm
Requirements Nonprofit organizations within the United States and its territories may submit requests.
Restrictions The fund does not support individuals, academic institutions, research projects, conferences and other single events, or production of audio-visual materials.
Areas of Interest Civil/Human Rights; Cultural Activities/Programs; Economic Development; Education; Environmental Effects; Environmental Programs; Fund-Raising; Grassroots Leadership; International Relations; Military Sciences; Minorities; Organizational Theory and Behavior; Peace/Disarmament; Political Behavior; Racism/Race Relations; Sexism; Social Change; Women; Youth Programs
Sample Awards Piedmont Peace Project (Kannapolis, NC)—to support a one-year strategic planning process to define an alternative model of economic development, $6500. Appalachian Women's Alliance (Floyd, VA)—start-up funds to hire three local organizers to work in the communities of Clinchco, $5700.

Harold Whitworth Pierce Charitable Trust   587
    Grants
Harold Whitworth Pierce Charitable Trust
50 Congress St, Ste 832
Boston, MA 02109
Contact Elizabeth Nichols, (617) 523-8368; fax: (617) 523-8949; e-mail: piercetrust@nichols-pratt.com
Requirements 501(c)3 tax-exempt organizations in the Boston, MA, area are eligible.
Restrictions Grants do not support scholarships, individuals, fund-raising events or training, films, videos, travel, or advocacy.
Areas of Interest Environmental Programs; Parks

Polaroid Fund Grants Program   588
Polaroid Fund
75 Arlington St
Boston, MA 02116

Contact Corey Davis, Grants Manager, (617) 338-2521; fax: (617) 338-1606; e-mail: cld@tbf.org
Internet http://www.polaroid.com/company_info/fund.jsp
Requirements The foundation supports nonprofit organizations whose work benefits Massachusetts communities where Polaroid operates, in particular Boston, Cambridge, Greater New Bedford, and Waltham. Requests for funding should be submitted on organizational letterhead and should include a grant application, brief history of the program, description of the population served, outline of the program or project for which support is requested, annual budget for the specific project, latest audited financial statement, and a copy of the IRS tax-exemption letter. In lieu of this information, Polaroid will accept the AGM common proposal format. A request for Polaroid photographic equipment should be submitted in letter form on organizational letterhead and include an outline of the program, description of the population served, specific account of the role instant photography will play in the program, and a general statement regarding how much equipment is required. An IRS letter is not required. Organizations that qualify will be contacted directly by staff personnel.
Restrictions The foundation does not make contributions for research or for purchasing advertisements, tables or tickets at dinners, or other functions; does not provide cameras or film for any fund-raising activities, nor for prizes, raffles, photo booths, fairs, conferences, or similar activities; and does not usually make more than one grant to an organization in any calendar year. Grants are not made to individuals.
Areas of Interest Children and Youth; Computer Education/Literacy; Computer Grants; Disabled; Economic Development; Economic Self-Sufficiency; Higher Education; Minority Education; Neighborhoods; Photography; School-to-Work Transition
Sample Awards Community Economic Development Ctr of Southeastern Massachusetts (New Bedford, MA)—to maintain ongoing functioning of the computer centers and to introduce new training programs, $15,000. Nemasket Group (Fairhaven, MA)—for a school-to-work program for students with severe disabilities, $20,000.

A.C. Ratshesky Foundation Grants   589
A.C. Ratshesky Foundation
77 Summer St, 8th Fl
Boston, MA 02110
Contact Michealle Larkins, Program Officer, (617) 426-7172 ext 302; fax: (617) 426-5441; e-mail: ratsheskyfoundation@grantsmanagement.com
Internet http://www.grantsmanagement.com/ratshesky.html
Requirements Boston area nonprofits may apply.
Restrictions Grants are not awarded to individuals or for continuing support, annual campaigns, general endowments, deficit financing, land acquisition, scientific or other research, publications, conferences, or loans.
Areas of Interest Arts, General; Children and Youth; Cultural Activities/Programs; Disadvantaged (Economically); Education; Jewish Services; Religion; Religious Welfare Programs; Social Services Delivery

Sample Awards Women's Institute for Housing and Economic Development (Boston, MA)—for operating support, $1000. Hebrew Rehabilitation Ctr for Aged (Roslindale, MA)—for ESL course staff, $2000. Dorchester Counseling Ctr (Boston, MA)—for a program for three- to five-year-old children of substance abusers, $2500. Aquinas College (Newton, MA)—for day care teacher training program for the disadvantaged, $2000.

Raytheon Company Corporate Contributions Program   590

Raytheon Company
141 Spring St
Lexington, MA 02421
Contact Corporate Contributions Program, (781) 860-2753; fax: (781) 860-2999; e-mail: corporatecontributions@raytheon.com
Internet http://www.raytheon.com/community
Requirements Nonprofit groups near company facilities may apply.
Areas of Interest Air Pollution; Arts Administration; Day Care; Disabled; Disaster Relief; Education; Elderly; Elementary Education; Engineering Education; Environmental Economics; Family; Health Services Delivery; Higher Education; Libraries; Mathematics; Mathematics Education; Minorities; Museums; Nonprofit Organizations; Regional Planning/Policy; Science; Science Education; Secondary Education; Teacher Education; Technology Education; Water Pollution; Women; Youth Programs
Sample Awards Exploration Place (Wichita, KS)—to support the capital campaign, $300,000 (2002). Air Force Memorial Commission—to support the design, construction, and dedication of the Air Force Memorial in Washington, DC, $200,000 (2002). American Battle Monuments Commission—for the National World War II Memorial, $120,000 (2002). Youth Tech Entrepreneurs—to support operating expenses, $25,000 (2002).

Resist Inc Priority Grants   591

Resist Inc
259 Elm St
Somerville, MA 02144
Contact Grants Administrator, (617) 623-5110; e-mail: resistinc@igc.apc.org
Internet http://www.resistinc.org
Requirements Organizations with a budget of approximately $125,000 or less may apply for a one-year grant.
Restrictions Resist does not fund social service or research projects; legal defense costs or lawsuit projects; material aid campaigns; tours, trips, or travel expenses; individuals; projects located outside the United States; the production of films, videos, or radio projects; publications, media, or cultural projects not directly connected to a progressive organizing campaign; capital campaigns, capital projects or endowments; organizations with access to traditional sources of funding; and other foundations or grant giving organizations.
Areas of Interest Social Change

Rogers Family Foundation Grants   592

Rogers Family Foundation
PO Box 100
Lawrence, MA 01842
Contact Irving Rogers Jr., Trustee, (978) 685-1000
Requirements Nonprofit organizations in the Lawrence, MA, area are eligible, including Methuen, Andover, and Haverhill, MA; and southeastern New Hampshire.
Restrictions Grants are not made to individuals or for endowment funds, research, scholarships, fellowships, or matching gifts.
Areas of Interest Community Development; Higher Education; Hospitals; Religion; Secondary Education; Social Services; Youth Programs

William E. and Bertha E. Schrafft Charitable Trust Grants   593

William E. and Bertha E. Schrafft Charitable Trust
One Boston Pl, 34th Fl
Boston, MA 02108-4408
Contact Karen Faulkner, Executive Director, (617) 457-7327; e-mail: funding@schrafftcharitable.org
Internet http://www.schrafftcharitable.org
Requirements Grants are awarded to nonprofit organizations in Massachusetts, with emphasis on the Boston area.
Restrictions Grants are not awarded to individuals or for matching gifts, seed money, emergency funds, or deficit financing.
Areas of Interest Disadvantaged (Economically); Education; Youth Programs
Sample Awards Huntington Theatre (MA)—for operating support, $15,000. Crittenton Hastings House (MA)—to support the Young Fathers Program, $10,000. Castle School (MA)—for building renovations, $10,000.

Gardiner Howland Shaw Foundation Grants 594

Gardiner Howland Shaw Foundation
10 Lincoln Rd, 2nd Fl
Foxboro, MA 02035
Contact Thomas Coury, Executive Director, (781) 455-8303; fax: (781) 433-0980; e-mail: ghsfound@aol.com
Requirements Nonprofit Massachusetts organizations are eligible.
Restrictions The foundation does not support capital requests, the arts, endowments, grants to individuals, or scholarships.
Areas of Interest Crime Control; Criminal Justice; Domestic Violence; Education; Employment Opportunity Programs; Juvenile Correctional Facilities; Juvenile Delinquency; Penology/Correctional Institutions and Procedures; Prison Reform; Public Planning/Policy; Rehabilitation/Therapy; Training and Development; Women
Sample Awards Crime and Justice Foundation (Boston, MA)—for general operating support, $25,000. Springfield Employment Resource Ctr (Springfield, MA)—to support an employment and training program for female offenders, $17,500. Citizen's Training Group (Boston, MA)—to support summer job services to juvenile offenders, $5000.

Richard and Susan Smith Family Foundation Grants 595

Richard and Susan Smith Family Foundation
1280 Boylston St, Ste 100
Chestnut Hill, MA 02467
Contact David Ford, Executive Director, (617) 278-5209; fax: (617) 278-5250; e-mail: dford@ smithfamilyfoundation.net
Requirements Massachusetts nonprofit organizations serving the greater Boston area are eligible.
Restrictions Grants do not support political activities; religious activities; individuals; or requests for deficit financing or endowment funds.
Areas of Interest Arts, General; Children and Youth; Cultural Activities/Programs; Cultural Outreach; Disadvantaged (Economically); Education; Elementary Education; Higher Education; Homelessness; Hospitals; Minorities; Museums; Secondary Education; Service Delivery Programs; Social Services Delivery
Sample Awards Steppingstone Foundation (Boston, MA)—to increase the number of children from inner-city Boston who receive rigorous academic preparation and support services, $1 million challenge grant over five years (2003).

Staples Foundation for Learning Grants 596

Staples Foundation for Learning
500 Staples Dr 4 W
Framingham, MA 01702
Contact Grants Administrator, fax: (508) 253-9600
Internet http://www.staplesfoundation.org
Requirements 501(c)3 nonprofit organizations are eligible.
Restrictions Contributions do not support the following: individuals; educational loans; organizations that discriminate on the basis of race, religion, creed, gender, or national origin; international organizations; travel expenses or fees to conferences or conventions; political organizations; books, research papers, or articles in professional journals; medical research projects or medical procedures for individuals; religious organizations, unless they are engaged in a significant project that benefits a broad base of the community; fraternal organizations, veterans' organizations, professional associations, and similar membership groups; or public or commercial broadcasting programs.
Areas of Interest At-Risk Youth; Children and Youth; Disadvantaged (Economically); Elementary Education; Job Training Programs; Secondary Education; Youth Programs
Sample Awards Educational Network of Artists in Creative Theater (New York, NY)—for a drama and education program in New York City Public Schools, $10,000 (2003). Horizons (Atlanta, GA)—for a summer program for children, $10,000 (2003). Los Angeles Educational Partnership (CA)—for the Career Academies Program at inner-city high schools, $10,000 (2003). See Forever Foundation (Washington, DC)—for a job-training program for at-risk teenagers, $10,000 (2003).

State Strategies Fund Grants 597

State Strategies Fund
264 North Pleasant St
Amherst, MA 01002
Contact Amy Clough, Grants Manager, (413) 256-0349 ext 12; e-mail: aclough@proteusfund.org
Internet http://www.funder.org/grantmaking/ssf/ grant_guidelines
Areas of Interest Campaign Finance Reform; Civic Affairs; Community&Civic; Disadvantaged (Economically); Grassroots Leadership; Political Behavior; Public Affairs; Taxes and Taxation
Sample Awards Alabama Organizing Project (AL)—to support Greater Birmingham Ministries, $35,000 (2002). Citizen Action Illinois (IL)—to support the Public Action Foundation, $40,000 (2002). New York Community Leadership Institute (NY)—$30,000 (2002). Wisconsin Citizen Action (WI)—$50,000 (2002).

State Street Foundation Grants 598

State Street Foundation
225 Franklin St, 12th Fl
Boston, MA 02110
Contact Grants Administrator, (617) 664-1937; e-mail: gabowman@statestreet.com
Internet http://www.statestreet.com/company/ community_affairs/global_philanthropy/overview.html
Requirements 501(c)3 organizations that are not private foundations and are located in Alameda, Los Angeles, and San Francisco, CA; Connecticut; Florida; Atlanta, GA; Illinois; Boston and the Cape Cod, MA, area; Saint Louis and Kansas City, MO; New Hampshire; New Jersey; and New York are eligible.
Restrictions The foundation does not make grants for scholarships or fellowships; research projects; emergency cash flow, deficit spending, or debt liquidation situations; seed money/start-up programs; trips, tours, and transportation expenses; or films or videos.
Areas of Interest Civic Affairs; Education; Employment Opportunity Programs; Health Care; Housing; Job Training Programs; Neighborhoods; Nonprofit Organizations; Philanthropy; Social Services; Youth Programs
Sample Awards 114 nonprofit organizations in nine countries—for programs and services related to arts and culture, civic improvement, education, health and human services, neighborhood revitalization, vocational training, and youths, $3.1 million divided (2002).

Abbot and Dorothy H. Stevens Foundation Grants 599

Abbot and Dorothy H. Stevens Foundation
PO Box 111
North Andover, MA 01845
Contact Elizabeth Beland, Administrator, (978) 688-7211; fax: (978) 686-1620; e-mail: 74722.2637@ compuserve.com
Requirements Massachusetts 501(c)3 tax-exempt organizations serving the greater Lawrence and Merrimack Valley are eligible.
Restrictions Grants do not support national organizations, state or federal agencies, individuals, annual campaigns, deficit financing, exchange programs, internships, professorships, scholarships, or fellowships.

Areas of Interest Arts, General; Community Development; Community Service Programs; Education; Religion; Youth Programs

Nathaniel and Elizabeth P. Stevens Foundation Grants 600

Nathaniel and Elizabeth P. Stevens Foundation
PO Box 111
North Andover, MA 01845
Contact Elizabeth Beland, Administrator, (978) 688-7211; fax: (978) 686-1620; e-mail: 74722,2637@ compuserve.com
Requirements Massachusetts 501(c)3 tax-exempt organizations serving the greater Lawrence and Merrimack Valley are eligible.
Restrictions Grants do not support national organizations, state or federal agencies, individuals, annual campaigns, deficit financing, exchange programs, internships, professorships, scholarships, or fellowships.
Areas of Interest Arts, General; Community Service Programs; Cultural Activities/Programs; Education; Religion; Youth Programs

Stride Rite Philanthropic Foundation Grants 601

Stride Rite Corporation
191 Spring St
Lexington, MA 02420-9191
Contact Charitable Giving Program, (617) 824-6000; e-mail: diversity_committee@striderite.com
Internet http://www.striderecorp.com/pages/ corporate/community_service.asp
Requirements 501(c)3 tax-exempt nonprofit organizations in Indiana, Kentucky, and Massachusetts that serve the needs of children and families are eligible.
Restrictions The review committee will not consider funding requests for conferences, film production, scholarships, travel, loans, research projects, curriculum development, publications, national organizations, construction projects, day care programs, and advertising. Grants are not awarded to individuals, medical institutions, individual public or private schools, religious organizations, or political organizations.
Areas of Interest After-School Programs; Children and Youth; Education; Family; Health Care; Inner Cities; Intervention Programs; Recreation and Leisure

TJX Foundation Grants 602

TJX Foundation
770 Cochituate Rd, Rte 1E
Framingham, MA 01701
Contact Christine Strickland, Foundation Manager, (508) 390-3199; fax: (508) 390-2091; e-mail: Christy_ Strickland@TJX.com
Requirements IRS 501(c)3 tax-exempt organizations are eligible.
Restrictions The foundation will not fund individuals, political organizations, publications, cash reserves, seed money/start-up projects, endowments, religious groups, public policy research, travel grants, environmental issues, education loans, international organizations, film/ photography, conferences/seminars, unrestricted grants, fellowships, or advocacy.

Areas of Interest Arts, General; Children and Youth; Civic Affairs; Cultural Activities/Programs; Education; Family; Health Care; Health Promotion; Housing; Job Training Programs; Mental Health; Poverty and the Poor; Shelters; Social Services

George R. Wallace Foundation Grants 603

George R. Wallace Foundation
1 Exchange Pl
Boston, MA 02109-2881
Contact Nancy Keller, (617) 570-1735
Requirements Organizations in Florida and Massachusetts are eligible to apply.
Restrictions Grants will not be awarded to individuals or for scholarships, fellowships, or loans.
Areas of Interest Churches; Education; Higher Education; Minorities; Museums; Orchestras; Philanthropy
Sample Awards Philharmonic Ctr for the Arts (Naples, FL)—for general operating support, $105,000. Walnut Hill School (Natick, MA)—for program support, $53,000.

Edwin S. Webster Foundation Grants 604

Edwin S. Webster Foundation
c/o Grants Management Associates, 77 Summer St, 8th Fl
Boston, MA 02110
Contact Program Contact, (617) 426-7172; fax: (617) 426-5441; e-mail: philanthropy@grant.management. com
Requirements Grantees must provide evidence of their tax-exempt status. Requests for grants must be submitted in letter form. Funding is confined primarily to the New England area.
Restrictions Grants are not made to organizations outside the United States or to individuals.
Areas of Interest Biomedical Research; Cultural Activities/Programs; Education; Hospitals; Minorities; Youth Programs

Michigan

Arcus Foundation Grants 605

Arcus Foundation
303 N Rose St, Ste 300
Kalamazoo, MI 49007-3846
Contact Linda May, Executive Director, (269) 373-4373; e-mail: info@arcusfoundation.org
Internet http://www.arcusfoundation.org
Requirements Nonprofit organizations are eligible.
Areas of Interest Animal Care; Animal Rights; Cultural Activities/Programs; Cultural Diversity; Cultural Outreach; Environmental Health; Environmental Programs; Homosexuals, Female; Homosexuals, Male; Youth Programs
Sample Awards Primate Rescue Ctr (Nicholasville, KY)—for general operating support, $40,000 over two years (2003). Bach Festival Society of Kalamazoo (MI)—for educational outreach, $20,000 (2003). YWCA of Kalamazoo (MI)—for capital improvements and projects, $10,000 (2003). Rainbow Train (Seattle, WA)—to train health and social-service providers who

serve older gay, lesbian, bisexual, and transgender clients, $50,000 over two years (2003).

ArvinMeritor Foundation Grants 606
ArvinMeritor Foundation
2135 W Maple Rd
Troy, MI 48084
Contact Laura Bochenek Powell, (248) 435-1000; fax: (248) 435-9946; e-mail: laura.bochenek@arvinmeritor.com
Internet http://www.arvinmeritor.com/community/community.asp
Requirements Nonprofit 501(c)3 organizations should submit a one- to two-page letter outlining the purpose and needs of the program, its budget, duration, goals, leadership, and amount requested.
Restrictions Grants are not awarded to individuals or religious organizations or for endowments, scholarships, fellowships, or matching gifts.
Areas of Interest Arts, General; Cancer/Carcinogenesis; Civic Affairs; Community Service Programs; Cultural Activities/Programs; Elementary Education; Engineering Education; Health Care; Higher Education, Private; History; Museums; National Disease Organizations; Opera/Musical Theater; Performing Arts; Professional Associations; Scholarship Programs, General; Science; Science Education; Secondary Education; Sports; Technology Education; Training and Development; Visual Arts; Youth Programs
Sample Awards Dana Farber Cancer Institute (MA)—for building support, $5000. Columbus Area Arts Council (IN)—for operating support, $7000. Michigan Opera Theatre (MI)—for operating support, $1000. Tennessee Foundation for Independent Colleges (TN)—for operating support, $1000.

Berrien Community Foundation Grants 607
Berrien Community Foundation
2900 South State St, Ste 2 East
Saint Joseph, MI 49085
Contact Anne McCausland, Program Manager, (616) 983-3304; fax: (616) 983-4939; email: amccausland@qtm.net
Internet http://www.berriencommunity.org
Requirements Nonprofit organizations in Berrien County, MI, may apply.
Restrictions Grants are not made for support of religious purposes, consulting services, deficit financing, annual fund drives, or technical assistance.
Areas of Interest Adult and Continuing Education; Arts, General; Basic Skills Education; Children and Youth; Cultural Activities/Programs; Disabled; Education; Elderly; Elementary Education; Environmental Programs; Family; Health Care; Homelessness; Humanities; Literacy; Museums; Philanthropy; Public Affairs; Restoration and Preservation; Secondary Education; Youth Programs

Besser Foundation Grants 608
Besser Foundation
123 N Second Ave
Alpena, MI 49707-2801
Contact J. Richard Wilson, President, (989) 354-4722; fax: (517) 354-8099; e-mail: bessfdtn@freeway.net

Requirements Only nonprofits in Michigan may apply.
Restrictions Grants are not made to individuals.
Areas of Interest Adult and Continuing Education; Africa; Arts, General; Civic Affairs; Cultural Activities/Programs; Education; Health Care; International Programs; Religion; Social Services; Vocational/Technical Education
Sample Awards Albion College (Albion, MI)—for the scholarship fund, $2800. Alpena Community College (Alpena, MI)—for operating expenses of an adult vocational center, $24,000. World Relief (Detroit, MI)—toward cost of shipping medical supplies to Third World countries, $2000.

Guido A. and Elizabeth H. Binda Foundation 609 Grants
Guido A. and Elizabeth H. Binda Foundation
124 S Minges Rd
Battle Creek, MI 49017
Contact Elizabeth Binda, President
Requirements Nonprofit organizations in Battle Creek and southwestern Michigan may request grant support.
Areas of Interest Adult and Continuing Education; Alcohol/Alcoholism; Architecture; Arts, General; Basic Skills Education; Community Development; Cultural Activities/Programs; Drugs/Drug Abuse; Education; Literacy; Religion; Social Services
Sample Awards Literacy Council of Calhoun County (Battle Creek, MI)—for general support, $5000. United Arts Council of Calhoun County (Battle Creek, MI)—for a school program, $7500. U of Michigan, School of Architecture (Ann Arbor, MI)—for a foreign study program, $10,000.

Community Foundation for Southeastern 610 Michigan Grants
Community Foundation for Southeastern Michigan
333 W Fort St, Ste 2010
Detroit, MI 48226-3134
Contact Mark Neithercut, Vice President, Programs, (313) 961-6675; fax: (313) 961-2886; e-mail: cfsem@cfsem.org
Internet http://www.cfsem.org/grants/guide.htm
Requirements 501(c)3 nonprofit organizations in the seven Michigan counties, including Livingston, Macomb, Montclair, Monroe, Oakland, Washtenaw, and Wayne, are eligible.
Restrictions Normally, grants will not be made for buildings or equipment, general operating support (except in the first few years of an organization's existence), endowments, sectarian religious programs, fund-raising campaigns, grants to individuals, conferences and annual meetings, or projects outside the seven-county region.
Areas of Interest Adolescents; Arts, General; Children and Youth; Civic Affairs; Cultural Activities/Programs; Economic Development; Education; Emergency Services; Grief; Health Care; Mental Health; Nonprofit Organizations; Scholarship Programs, General; Senior Citizen Programs and Services; Smoking Behavior; Social Services; Technology; Tobacco; Trauma; Volunteers
Sample Awards City of Dearborn (MI)—to plan and design an extended greenway, $89,000 (2003). HP Devco (Highland Park, MI)—to retain and attract businesses in Highland Park, $22,000 (2003). Care House (Mount

Clemens, MI)—for a program that provides medical examinations for young victims of physical and sexual abuse, $20,000 (2002). Forgotten Harvest (Southfield, MI)—to expand a program that delivers fresh food to low-income elderly people, pregnant women, and young children, $70,530 (2002).

Community Foundation of Greater Flint Grants   611

Community Foundation of Greater Flint
502 Church St
Flint, MI 48502-1206
Contact Program Contact, (810) 767-8270; fax: (810) 767-0496; e-mail: commfoundationgreaterflint@CFgf.org
Internet http://www.cfgf.org/grants.htm
Requirements IRS 501(c)3 organizations with programs of direct relevance to the residents of Genesee County, MI, are eligible. Types of support include general operating support.
Restrictions Grants will not be made to individuals. In general, requests for sectarian religious purposes, budget deficits, routine operating expenses of existing organizations, litigation, endowments, and other capital fund drives or projects are not funded.
Areas of Interest Arts, General; Career Education and Planning; Children and Youth; Community Service Programs; Education; Engineering; Environmental Programs; Ethics; Health Care; Humanities; Mathematics; Philanthropy; Poverty and the Poor; Science; Social Services; Women's Employment
Sample Awards GMI Engineering and Management Institute (Flint, MI)—for a program to help interest young women in careers in engineering, mathematics, and science, $18,860.

Consumers Energy Foundation   612

Consumers Energy
1 Energy Plz, Rm EP8-210
Jackson, MI 49201
Contact Carolyn Bloodworth, Secretary/Treasurer, (517) 788-0432; fax: (517) 788-2281; e-mail: foundation@consumersenergy.com
Internet http://www.consumersenergy.com/welcome.htm
Requirements Michigan 501(c)3 organizations are eligible.
Restrictions Contributions are not made to individuals, including individual scholarships; organizations to which contributions are not tax deductible; organizations that practice discrimination on the basis of sex, age, height, weight, etc.; those whose operating activities are already supported by the United Way; political organizations and campaigns; religious organizations for religious purposes; or labor or veterans organizations, fraternal orders, or social clubs.
Areas of Interest Arts, General; Business Education; Civic Affairs; Computer Education/Literacy; Cultural Activities/Programs; Curriculum Development; Economics Education; Education; Education Reform; Engineering Education; Environmental Programs; Family; Health Services Delivery; Higher Education; Mathematics Education; Minority Education; Physical Sciences Education; Political Science Education; Scholarship

Programs, General; Science Education; Service Delivery Programs; Social Services Delivery; Women's Education
Sample Awards Spring Arbor College (MI)—for a new library, $40,000. College Fund/UNCF (MI)—for scholarships for Michigan students, $20,000.

Detroit Edison Foundation Grants   613

Detroit Edison Foundation
2000 Second Ave, 1046 WCB
Detroit, MI 48226
Contact Karla Hall, Secretary, (313) 235-9416; e-mail: hallk@detroitedison.com
Internet http://www.dteenergy.com/community/foundation/apply.html
Requirements IRS 501(c)3 tax-exempt organizations serving residents of the Detroit Edison and MichCon service areas in Michigan are eligible.
Restrictions Grants are generally not made to/for individuals or families; political parties, organizations, or activities; religious organizations for religious purposes; basic research; labor or veterans organizations, fraternal orders, and social clubs; conventions, conferences, seminars, and travel; public service or congratulatory advertising in benefit programs or convention souvenir booklets; national or international organizations, unless services provided directly benefit residents of Detroit Edison's service area; or benefit fund-raising events for organizations that are already receiving foundation support either directly or through United Way.
Areas of Interest Arts, General; Children and Youth; Civic Affairs; Cultural Activities/Programs; Disadvantaged (Economically); Diversity; Education; Environmental Programs; Family; Health Care; History; Housing; Leadership; Nonprofit Organizations; Poverty and the Poor; Social Services
Sample Awards Detroit Historical Society (MI)—to support an education program for fourth and fifth graders that focuses on the participation of Detroit-area residents in the Underground Railroad movement, $11,600. Detroit Institute of the Arts (MI)—for its capital campaign, $750,000 over five years. Habitat for Humanity of Michigan (Lansing, MI)—to construct homes for low-income people and to provide services to its affiliates, $350,000 over three years. Wayne State U, Merrill-Palmer Institute (Detroit, MI)—to develop innovative programs designed to improve the quality of life of disadvantaged children and families, $10,000.

Richard and Helen DeVos Foundation Grants   614

Richard and Helen DeVos Foundation Grants
PO Box 230257
Grand Rapids, MI 49523-0257
Contact Ginny Vander Hart, Foundation Director, (616) 643-4700
Requirements Nonprofit organizations in western Michigan and central Florida are eligible to apply.
Restrictions Individuals are ineligible.
Areas of Interest Arts, General; Business Education; Churches; Community Outreach Programs; Education; Family; Health Care; Management; Public Planning/Policy; Religion; Social Services; Sports

Sample Awards U of Central Florida (Orlando, FL)—to create a graduate program in sports business management, $2.5 million (2000). Coral Ridge Presbyterian Church (Fort Lauderdale, FL)—to support Evangelism Explosion International, $900,000. Butterworth Foundation (Grand Rapids, MI)—general operating support, $2.015 million. Focus on the Family (Colorado Springs, CO)—general operating support, $1 million.

Herbert H. and Grace A. Dow Foundation Grants 615

Herbert H. and Grace A. Dow Foundation
1018 W Main St
Midland, MI 48640-4292
Contact Margaret Ann Riecker, President, (989) 631-3699; fax: (989) 631-0675; email: info@hhdowfdn.org
Internet http://www.hhdowfdn.org
Requirements Only organizations in Michigan are eligible to apply.
Restrictions The foundation does not make direct grants to individuals, provide loan funds, or make grants to students for scholarships.
Areas of Interest Chemistry; Civic Affairs; Community Development; Conservation, Natural Resources; Cultural Activities/Programs; Curriculum Development; Equipment/Instrumentation; Higher Education; Recreation and Leisure; Religion; Science; Social Services
Sample Awards Mackinac Ctr for Public Policy (Midland, MI)—for education-policy projects, including publication of Michigan Education Report, a quarterly journal, $967,700 over three years (2003).

Ford Motor Company Fund Grants Program 616

Ford Motor Company Fund
1 American Rd
Dearborn, MI 48121
Contact Sandra Ulsh, President, (888) 313-0102 or (313) 248-4745; fax: (313) 337-6680
Internet http://www.ford.com
Restrictions Grants are not made directly to individuals or for endowments, debt reduction, private schools, United Way-supported organizations, animal rights organizations, religious organizations for sectarian purposes, vehicle donation, fraternal organizations, political contributions, day-to-day business operations, non US-based charities, fellowships, loans, profit-making enterprises, labor groups, beauty or talent contests, or fundraising.
Areas of Interest Africa; Art Education; Arts, General; Asia; Business; Career Education and Planning; Civic Affairs; Community Development; Conservation, Natural Resources; Curriculum Development; Economics; Education; Employment Opportunity Programs; Engineering Education; Fellowship Programs, General; Gifted/Talented Education; Health Care; Hospitals; Humanities; Human/Civil Rights; International Relations; Landscape Architecture/Design; Latin America; Mathematics Education; North America; Public Planning/Policy; Restoration and Preservation, Structural/Architectural; Safety; Scholarship Programs, General; Science Education; Social Services; Technology; Youth Programs

Sample Awards U of Pittsburgh (PA)—to establish the Institute for Human Security, which will address contemporary challenges to human freedoms and international security, including civil war, environmental degradation, forced and slave labor, genocide, global epidemics, and nalnutrition, $2.25 million (2002). National Park Foundation (Washington, DC)—for planning to help reduce the traffic congestion in and around the Great Smoky Mountains National Park, $70,000 (2002).

Fremont Area Community Foundation Grants 617

Fremont Area Community Foundation
PO Box B
Fremont, MI 49412
Contact Jeff Jahr, Program Officer, (616) 924-5350; fax: (616) 924-5391; e-mail: jjahr@tfacf.org
Internet http://www.tfaf.org/grants/require.html
Requirements Michigan 501(c)3 organizations in Newaygo County are eligible.
Restrictions The foundation typically does not fund requests for endowments, contingencies, reserves, or deficit financing.
Areas of Interest After-School Programs; Alzheimer's Disease; Arts, General; Community Development; Cultural Activities/Programs; Domestic Violence; Education; Health Care; Orchestras; Social Services
Sample Awards Arts Center for Newaygo County, Fremont, MI, For community contributions for construction of Dogwood Center for the Performing Arts, $943,773. Grand Rapids Symphony Society (Grand Rapids, MI)—for performances at schools in Newaygo County, $10,000. Newaygo County Sheriffs Department (White Cloud, MI)—for staff support of a team to respond to domestic-violence calls, $15,437.

General Motors Foundation Grants Support Program 618

General Motors Foundation
300 Renaissance Ctr, MC 482-C27-D76
Detroit, MI 48265
Contact Deborah Dingell, (313) 665-0824
Internet http://www.gm.com/company/gmability/community/guidelines/index.html
Requirements Nonprofit, tax-exempt organizations and institutions are eligible to apply.
Restrictions The foundation generally does not contribute to individuals; capital campaigns and operating budgets of medical-related facilities; US hospitals and health care institutions; religious organizations; endowments; political parties or candidates; or conferences, workshops, or seminars not directly related to GM's business interests.
Areas of Interest Arts, General; Business Development; Business Education; Cancer/Carcinogenesis; Cancer Detection; Cultural Activities/Programs; Education; Energy; Environmental Programs; Health Care; Hispanic Education; Management Sciences; Native American Education; Public Planning/Policy
Sample Awards Pierre Chambon, College de France (Paris, France) and Ronald Evans, Salk Institute for Biological Studies (La Jolla, CA)—to honor their contributions to the diagnosis, prevention, and treatment of cancer, $250,000 jointly (2003).

Hudson Webber Foundation Grants 619

Hudson Webber Foundation
333 W Fort St, Ste 1310
Detroit, MI 48226
Contact David Egner, Foundation President, (313) 963-7777
Requirements The foundation concentrates its giving within Detroit. Grants are made to educational institutions and neighborhood organizations. Programs in communities outside of Detroit within the Wayne, Oakland, and Macomb tricounty area of southeastern Michigan are assigned considerably lower priority.
Restrictions Grants are not made for endowments, fund-raising social events, conferences, or exhibits. The foundation does not provide grants to individuals.
Areas of Interest Arts, General; Community Development; Counseling/Guidance; Crime Prevention; Cultural Programs; Economic Development; Environmental Programs; Hospitals; Law Enforcement; Museums; Urban Areas
Sample Awards Vanguard Community Development Corp (Detroit, MI)—for revitalization efforts in the New Center East, Milwaukee Junction neighborhood, $120,000 (2002). Wayne State U (Detroit, MI)—for predevelopment activities associated with a mixed-use development complex on Detroit's Woodward Avenue, $120,000 (2002). Michigan Opera Theatre (Detroit, MI)—for the Dance Theatre of Harlem residency program and for performances by the Alvin Ailey American Dance Theater, $100,000 over two years (2002).

Jackson County Community Foundation 620
Grants

Jackson County Community Foundation
One Jackson Sq, Ste 110-A
Jackson, MI 49201
Contact Jan Maino, Program Officer, (517) 787-1321; fax: (517) 787-4333; e-mail: info@jacksoncf.org
Internet http://www.jacksoncf.org/grants.htm
Requirements The foundation makes grants to Jackson County, Michigan nonprofit, tax-exempt organizations.
Restrictions Grants will not be made to organizations that deny equal access to their programs, services, or employment on the basis of sex, sexual preference, age, height, weight, marital status, race, religion, creed, color, national origin, ancestry, disability, handicap, or veteran status.
Areas of Interest Academic Achievement; Arts, General; Children and Youth; Classroom Instruction; Community Development; Cultural Activities/Programs; Economic Development; Education; Elementary Education; Grassroots Leadership; Health Promotion; Leadership; Minorities; Neighborhoods; Private and Parochial Education; Public Education; Secondary Education; Teacher Education; Tobacco; Youth Programs
Sample Awards Jackson High School (Jackson, MI)—to refurbish the planetarium and for the teacher's fund, $11,000. Michigan Theater Ctr (Detroit, MI)—for renovations, $25,000. Family Health Ctr (Kalamazoo, MI)—for operating support, $40,000.

Jewish Fund Grants 621

Jewish Fund
6735 Telegraph Rd
Bloomfield, MI 48303-2030
Contact Jodee Fishman Raines, Director, The Jewish Fund, (248) 203-1487; fax: (248) 645-7879; e-mail: raines@jfmd.org
Internet http://www.thisisfederation.org/who
Requirements Michigan 501(c)3 nonprofit organizations that serve the Jewish and/or Detroit communities are eligible.
Areas of Interest Child/Maternal Health; Elderly; Health Care; Health Care Access; Health Promotion; Health Services Delivery; Jewish Services

Kalamazoo Foundation Grants 622

Kalamazoo Foundation
151 S Rose St, Ste 332
Kalamazoo, MI 49007
Contact Program Contact, (616) 381-4416; fax: (616) 381-3146; e-mail: info@kalfound.org
Internet http://www.kalfound.org/page8490.cfm
Requirements Kalamazoo, MI, organizations recognized (or in the process of applying for recognition) under IRS code 501(c)3 are encouraged to contact foundation staff before submitting a request to determine eligibility.
Restrictions Generally, the foundation does not provide funding for debt retirement, endowments, individuals, travel for individuals or groups, religious organizations for religious purposes, meetings, conferences, publications, films, or television and radio programming.
Areas of Interest Alcohol/Alcoholism; Drugs/Drug Abuse; Economic Development; Education; Family; Health Care; Hispanics; Homelessness; Housing; Museums; Reading; Shelters; Writing/Composition Education
Sample Awards Hispanic American Council—to establish the Family Reading Program to increase English reading and writing skills of Hispanic parents, $40,000. Kalamazoo Valley Community College—to assist with the construction of a new public museum, $2 million. Emergency Shelter Coordinating Council—to support implementation of a strategy for identifying and providing treatment for substance abusers within homeless shelters, $42,000. Vine Ventures—to support the purchase and rehabilitation of 10 units for rental to low-income Vine residents, $40,000.

La-Z-Boy Foundation Grants 623

La-Z-Boy Foundation
1284 N Telegraph Rd
Monroe, MI 48162
Contact Donald Blohm, Administrator, (734) 242-1444; fax: (734) 457-2005
Internet http://www.la-z-boy.com
Requirements 501(c)3 nonprofit charities are eligible. Grants are awarded primarily in communities of company operations, including Siloam Springs, AR; Redlands, CA; Monroe, MI; Neosho, MO; Newton and Leland, MS; Lincolnton, NC; Florence, SC; Dayton, TN; and Tremonton, UT.
Areas of Interest Civic Affairs; Education; Health Care; Hospitals; Philanthropy; Restoration and Preservation

McGregor Fund Grants 624

McGregor Fund
333 W Fort St, Ste 2090
Detroit, MI 48226
Contact C. David Campbell, President, (313)
963-3495; fax: (313) 963-3512; e-mail: info@
mcgregfund.org
Internet http://www.mcgregorfund.org/guideline.html
Requirements Organizations in the metropolitan Detroit, MI, area, are eligible. Requests will be considered
from organizations located elsewhere for programs or
projects that significantly benefit the metropolitan De-
troit area (city of Detroit and Wayne, Oakland, and
Macomb Counties).
Restrictions The fund discourages proposals for student
scholarships, travel, seminars, conferences, workshops,
film or video projects, as well as disease-specific organi-
zations and their local affiliates.
Areas of Interest Art Education; Arts & Culture; Child
Abuse; Community Service Programs; Early Childhood
Education; Education; Emergency Programs; Faculty
Development; Family; Food Distribution; Health Care;
Higher Education; Higher Education, Private; Hospitals;
Housing; Humanities; Job Training Programs; Science;
Social Sciences; Youth Programs
Sample Awards Otterbein College, Ctr for Teaching
and Learning (Westerville, OH)—for a program through
which a cross-disciplinary group of students and profes-
sors meet regularly, and for accompanying profes-
sional-development activities, $100,000 (2003). Wayne
State U (Detroit, MI)—for design improvements as part
of the renovation of its conference center, $2.5 million
(2002).

Metro Health Foundation Grants 625

Metro Health Foundation
333 W Fort St, Ste 1370
Detroit, MI 48226-3134
Contact Theresa Sondys, Program Contact, (313)
965-4220; fax: (313) 965-3626; e-mail:
metrohealthfdn@aol.com
Requirements Nonprofit organizations in the metropolitan tri-county Detroit, MI, area are eligible to apply.
Restrictions Grants do not support advertising, advocacy organizations, athletic groups, individuals, international organizations, political organizations, special
events, benefit dinners, or state or local government
agencies.
Areas of Interest Children and Youth; Elderly; Health
Care; Higher Education; Social Services; Women

Michigan Arts Organization Development 626
   Program Grants

Michigan Council for Arts and Cultural Affairs
PO Box 30705, 702 W Kalamazoo
Lansing, MI 48909-8205
Contact Program Coordinator, (517) 241-4011; fax:
(517) 241-3979; e-mail: artsinfo@michigan.gov
Internet http://www.michigan.gov/hal/
0,1607,7-160-18833_18834_18842—,00.html
Requirements Professional arts-producing organizations in Michigan that meet the following criteria may
apply development program: have produced or presented
in each of the three fiscal years prior to the date of appli-

cation; have an operating budget under $250,000 at the
time of application; have administrative and artistic staff
sufficient to satisfy program requirements; and have either an audit or review of financial statements prepared
by an independent certified public accountant. Organizations that have successfully completed multiyear busi-
ness/strategic plans through this program or completed a
planning process within the past two years may apply for
implementation grants.
Restrictions No part of the net earnings may benefit a
private individual.
Areas of Interest Arts Administration

Michigan Community Arts Agencies Services 627
   Program Grants

Michigan Council for Arts and Cultural Affairs
525 W Ottawa
Lansing, MI 48909-8205
Contact Betty Boone, Executive Director, (517)
241-4011; TTY: (517) 373-1592; fax: (517) 241-5979;
e-mail: bboone@Michigan.gov
Internet http://www.michigan.gov/hal/
0,1607,7-160-18833_18834_18840-59474—,00.html
Requirements Eligible to apply are local Michigan arts
agencies and regional or statewide service organizations,
which are defined as public or private nonprofit councils,
commissions, societies, or organizations that, by their
charters and operating policies, are publicly accountable
to provide financial and/or service support for the arts in
the communities that they serve. Applicants must provide a cash match of at least 50 percent of the grant
amount requested. The remainder of the match requirement may be in any combination of cash and/or in-kind
contributions.
Restrictions No part of the net earnings may benefit a
private individual. Funding may not exceed one-third of
a project's total cost. State funds may not be used as a
match. The same matching funds may not be utilized in
more than one project application.
Areas of Interest Arts Administration; Cultural Activ-
ities/Programs

Charles Stewart Mott Foundation 628
   Anti-Poverty Program

Charles Stewart Mott Foundation
503 S Saginaw St, Ste 1200
Flint, MI 48502-1851
Contact Office of Proposal Entry, (810) 238-5651;
fax: (810) 766-1753; e-mail: infocenter@mott.org
Internet http://www.mott.org/programs/poverty.asp
Requirements Nonprofits and K-12 organizations are
eligible to apply. A proposal may be submitted by a
church-based or similar organization if the project falls
clearly within program guidelines and is intended to
serve as broad a segment of the population as the program of a comparable nonreligious organization.
Areas of Interest Advertising; After-School Programs;
Economic Development; Economic Self-Sufficiency;
Education; Law; Leadership; Poverty and the Poor; Religion
Sample Awards Accion USA (Boston, MA)—to gain
additional financing for its credit and business training
programs for small-business owners, $50,000 (2004).
Ctr for Law and Social Policy (Washington, DC)—to

promote state welfare programs that are most able to improve the economic well-being of low-income families, $400,000 over two years (2004). National League of Cities Institute (Washington, DC)—to promote alternative education for vulnerable and out-of-school youths, $300,000 over three years (2004). Public/Private Ventures (Philadelphia, PA)—for Working Ventures, which seeks to improve the practice of workforce development, $500,000 (2004).

Charles Stewart Mott Foundation Grants 629

Charles Stewart Mott Foundation
1200 Mott Foundation Bldg
Flint, MI 48502-1851
Contact Office of Proposal Entry, (810) 238-5651; fax: (810) 766-1753; e-mail: infocenter@mott.org
Internet http://www.mott.org/programs/programs.asp
Requirements Only 501(c)3 organizations are eligible, including schools and school districts.
Restrictions Grants are not made to/for individuals; religious activities or programs that serve, or appear to serve, specific religious groups or denominations; or local projects outside the Flint area unless the projects are part of a national demonstration or foundation-planned network of grants that have clear and significant implications for replication in other communities.
Areas of Interest Children and Youth; Civic Affairs; Classroom Instruction; Community and School Relations; Community Development; Education; Education Reform; Environmental Programs; Europe, Central; Europe, Eastern; Family; Health Care; International Programs; Leadership; New Independent States; Poverty and the Poor; Problem Solving; Public Planning/Policy; Russia; South Africa; Volunteers
Sample Awards Court Street Village Nonprofit Housing Corp (Flint, MI)—for salary support of a staff person to organize Flint residents to engage in community-revitalization projects, $22,581 (2004). Interhemispheric Resource Ctr (Silver City, NM)—for research on international trade arrangements, $150,000 over two years (2004). Nature Conservancy (Arlington, VA)—to begin or expand freshwater-conservation efforts in the Great Lakes region and the Southeast, $75,000 (2004). South Africa National Anti-Discrimination Forum (Braamfonstein, South Africa)—to develop the National Action Plan Against Racism and Racial Discrimination for South Africa, $125,000 (2004).

Nokomis Foundation Grants 630

Nokomis Foundation
161 Ottawa NW, Ste 305-C
Grand Rapids, MI 49503
Contact Kymberly Mulhern, President, (616) 451-0267; fax: (616) 451-9914; e-mail: kmulhern@nokomisfoundation.org
Internet http://www.nokomisfoundation.org/whathow.htm
Requirements Giving primarily in the greater Grand Rapids, MI, area; limited support for national organizations.
Restrictions The foundation does not provide funding to individuals or to religious organizations for religious purposes, and does not normally fund scholarships, fellowships, medical research, capital requests, endowments, or attendance at conferences. Support is rarely provided for capital expenditures (e.g., building renovations, new equipment, or endowments).
Areas of Interest Community Service Programs; Education; Health Care; Women
Sample Awards Pathfinder Resources/One-Way House (Grand Rapids, MI)—for the Family Restoration program expansion, $20,000. Women Matter Grand Rapids (Grand Rapids, MI)—for general operating support, $15,000.

Sage Foundation Grants 631

Sage Foundation
PO Box 1919
Brighton, MI 48116
Contact Melissa Sage Fadim, Grants Administrator
Areas of Interest Arts, General; Catholic Church; Civic Affairs; Community Development; Cultural Activities/Programs; Elementary Education; Public Affairs; Secondary Education

Skillman Foundation Grants Program 632

Skillman Foundation
600 Renaissance Ctr, Ste 1700
Detroit, MI 48243
Contact Grants Administrator, (313) 393-1185; fax: (313) 393-1187; e-mail: dlaskie@skillman.org
Internet http://www.skillman.org
Requirements The applicant organization must be tax exempt and may not be a 509(a) private foundation. The foundation's primary geographic area of focus is the Detroit metropolitan area, comprising Wayne, Macomb, and Oakland Counties.
Restrictions The foundation does not award grants directly to individuals or provide loans of any kind; nor does it support sectarian religious activities, political lobbying, political advocacy, legislative activities, endowments, annual fund drives, basic research, or support of past operating deficits. Support is not granted to organizations that discriminate against people because of age, race, color, creed, or sex.
Areas of Interest Adults; After-School Programs; Arts, General; At-Risk Youth; Children and Youth; Civic Affairs; Community Development; Cultural Activities/Programs; Day Care; Disabled; Education; Health Promotion; Jewish Services; Parent Education; Poverty and the Poor; Safety; Social Services
Sample Awards Heat and Warmth Fund (Detroit, MI)—to provide emergency heating assistance to poor families in Michigan's Macomb, Oakland, and Wayne Counties, $200,000 (2003). United Negro College Fund (Fairfax, VA)—to provide scholarships at 39 historically black colleges and universities, $90,000 (2003). Council of Michigan Foundations (Grand Haven, MI)—for salary support of a foundation liaison with the executive branch of the State of Michigan, $50,000 over two years (2003). Benjamin E. Mays Male Academy Assoc (Detroit, MI)—to expand its after-school program to boys and girls in the school's East Detroit neighborhood, in collaboration with surrounding churches, $75,000 (2003).

Steelcase Foundation Grants 633

Steelcase Foundation
PO Box 1967, CH43
Grand Rapids, MI 49501
Contact Susan Broman, Executive Director, (616) 246-4695; fax (616) 475-2200; email: sbroman@ steelcase.com
Internet http://www.steelcase.com
Requirements Nonprofits in Athens, AL; Orange County, CA; western Michigan; Asheville, NC; and Markham, ON are eligible.
Restrictions Grants do not support churches or programs with substantial religious overtones of a sectarian nature; individuals; endowment; or conferences and seminars.
Areas of Interest AIDS; Alcohol/Alcoholism; Disabled; Drugs/Drug Abuse; Education; Health Care; Intervention Programs; Mental Health; Social Services; Violent Behavior; Youth Programs

Taubman Endowment for the Arts 634

Taubman Endowment for the Arts
200 E Long Lake Rd, Ste 300
Bloomfield Hills, MI 48304
Contact Fred Henshaw, Executive Director, (248) 258-7207; fax: (248) 258-7476
Restrictions Grants are not made to individuals.
Areas of Interest Arts, General; Museums; Orchestras
Sample Awards Smithsonian Institute (Washington, DC)—for general operating support, $12,000. Detroit Symphony Orchestra Hall (Detroit, MI)—for general operating support, $2000.

Taubman Foundation Grants Program 635

Taubman Foundation
200 E Long Lake Rd, Ste 300
Bloomfield Hills, MI 48304
Contact Fred Henshaw, Executive Director, (248) 258-7207; fax: (248) 258-7476
Requirements 501(c)3 tax-exempt organizations are eligible. Giving is primarily made in Michigan.
Restrictions Grants are not made to individuals.
Areas of Interest Higher Education; Medical Research
Sample Awards Brown U (Providence, RI)—program support, $200,000. Michigan Partnership for New Education (East Lansing, MI)—program support, $97,000. United States Department of Education (Washington, DC)—program support, $10,000.

Thompson-McCully Foundation Grants 636

Thompson-McCully Foundation
225 N Sheldon Rd
Plymouth, MI 48170
Contact John Ziraldo, Executive Director, (734) 453-6412; fax: (734) 453-6475
Requirements Individuals and nonprofit organizations in the metropolitan Detroit, MI, area are eligible.
Areas of Interest Disadvantaged (Economically); Homeless Shelters; Homelessness; Housing; Poverty and the Poor
Sample Awards HOPE (Detroit, MI)—for its student loan program that allows participants to borrow against their future earnings in order to pay tuition expenses, $1. 2 million (2002). Big Brothers Big Sisters of Metropolitan Detroit (MI)—to provide school-based mentor programs for children and youths in Detroit, $100,000 (2001).

Weatherwax Foundation Grants 637

Weatherwax Foundation
PO Box 1111, 245 W Michigan Ave, 4th Fl
Jackson, MI 49204
Contact Maria Dotterweich, Executive Director, (517) 787-2117; fax: (517) 787-2118
Internet http://www.lib.msu.edu/harris23/grants/ wfbrochu.htm
Requirements Giving primarily in Hillsdale, Lenawee, and Jackson counties, MI.
Restrictions No grants to individuals; or for computer purchases.
Areas of Interest Art Education; Arts and Culture; Civic Affairs; Education; Health Care; Higher Education; Human Services; Museums; Science Education; Social Services
Sample Awards Albion College (MI)—for music facility renovation, $125,000. Michigan Theatre (MI)—for restoration, strategic planning, and executive search, $27,500. Family Service and Children's Aid (MI)—for general operating support and neighborhood outreach activities, $45,491.

Whirlpool Foundation Grants 638

Whirlpool Foundation
2000 N M-63
Benton Harbor, MI 49022
Contact Barbara Hall, (616) 923-5580; fax: (616) 925-0154
Internet http://www.whirlpoolcorp.com/social_ responsibility/whirlpoolfoundation/grants.asp
Requirements 501(c)3 tax-exempt organizations in Whirlpool communities are eligible, including Fort Smith, AK; Evansville, LaPorte, and W Lafayette, IN; Benton Harbor, MI; Oxford, MS; Clyde, Findlay, Greenville, and Marion, OH; Tulsa, OK; Knoxville, LaVergne, and Nashville, TN; and McAllen, TX.
Restrictions Grants will not be made to individuals; for-profit organizations; political causes; religious-related organizations; social, labor, veterans, or fraternal organizations; athletic associations and events; fund-raising benefits; United Way agencies seeking general operating support; or national groups whose local chapters have already received support.
Areas of Interest Adult and Continuing Education; Basic Skills Education; Cancer/Carcinogenesis; Counseling/Guidance; Cultural Diversity; Cultural Outreach; Family; Foreign Languages Education; Job Training Programs; Parent Education; Scholarship Programs, General; Technology Education
Sample Awards Lake Michigan College (MI)—for the center for technical training, $1 million over four years. Gilda's Club (New York, NY)—to educate families about the value of social and emotional support when family members are living with cancer, $200,000 over two years.

Whiting Foundation Grants   **639**
Whiting Foundation
901 Citizens Bank Bldg
Flint, MI 48502
Contact Program Contact, (810) 767-3600
Areas of Interest At-Risk Youth; Cancer/
Carcinogenesis; Children and Youth; Disabled; Education; Elderly; Health Care; Mental Health; Poverty and
the Poor; Religious Studies; Values/Moral Education
Sample Awards Boy Scouts of America (Flint, MI)—to
support an at-risk youth program, $6000. Community
Foundation of Greater Flint (Flint, MI)—for Operation
Brush-Up, $2500.

Minnesota

Elmer L. and Eleanor J. Andersen   **640**
   Foundation Grants
Elmer L. and Eleanor J. Andersen Foundation
2424 Territorial Rd
Saint Paul, MN 55114
Contact Mari Oyanagi Eggum, Foundation
Administrator, (651) 642-0127; fax: (651) 645-4684;
e-mail: eandefdn@mtn.org
Requirements Minnesota nonprofit organizations are
eligible.
Areas of Interest Civic Affairs; Cultural Activities/Programs; Education; Environmental Programs; Urban
Areas

Andersen Foundation Grants   **641**
Andersen Foundation
100 Fourth Ave N
Bayport, MN 55003-1096
Contact Mary Gillstrom, Assistant Secretary, (651)
439-5150
Requirements 501(c)3 tax-exempt organizations are eligible. Giving is on a national basis although preference
is given to requests from Minnesota.
Restrictions The foundation does not make grants to institutions that receive federal funding.
Areas of Interest Aging/Gerontology; Alcohol/Alcoholism; Animal Rights; Arts Administration; Arts, General; Cancer/Carcinogenesis; Cardiovascular Diseases;
Child Welfare; Churches; Clinics; Cultural Activities/
Programs; Domestic Violence; Drugs/Drug Abuse; Education; Educational/Public Television; Elementary Education; Family; Health Care; Higher Education; Kidney
Diseases and Disorders; Libraries; Mental Health; Minority Education; Performing Arts; Public Broadcasting;
Radio; Religion; Religious Studies; Restoration and
Preservation; Secondary Education; Social Services;
Special Education; Vision
Sample Awards Dallas Baptist U (TX)—to construct a
chapel building, $250,000 (2003).

Hugh J. Andersen Foundation Grants   **642**
Hugh J. Andersen Foundation
342 Fifth Ave N, White Pine Bldg
Bayport, MN 55003
Contact Brad Kruse, (651) 439-1557 or (888)
439-9508; fax: (651) 439-9480; e-mail: hjafdn@srinc.
biz

Internet http://www.scenicriver.org/hja/index.html
Requirements Minnesota nonprofits in Saint Croix Valley-Washington County, MN; Saint Paul, MN; and
Pierce, Polk, and Saint Croix Counties, WI are eligible.
Areas of Interest Alcohol/Alcoholism; Arts, General;
Children and Youth; Civic Affairs; Community Development; Cultural Activities/Programs; Disabled, Accessibility for; Domestic Violence; Drugs/Drug Abuse;
Family; Health Care; Housing; Literacy; Museums; Public Broadcasting; Social Services Delivery

Athwin Foundation Grants   **643**
Athwin Foundation
5200 Wilson Rd, Ste 307
Minneapolis, MN 55424
Contact Bruce Bean, Trustee, (612) 915-6165; fax:
(612) 915-6148
Requirements Tax-exempt organizations in the Twin
Cities area of Minnesota and Claremont, CA are eligible.
Restrictions Grants do not support individuals, scholarships, fellowships, or loans.
Areas of Interest Arts, General; Children's Museums;
Education; Health Care; Higher Education; Humanities
Sample Awards Claremont McKenna College (CA)—
for program support, $30,000. Minnesota Children's
Museum (Saint Paul, MN)—to support the capital campaign, $5000.

Beim Foundation Grants   **644**
Beim Foundation
333 Washington Ave N, Ste 300
Minneapolis, MN 55401
Contact Grants Administrator, (612) 373-7087;
e-mail: contact@beimfoundation.org
Internet http://www.beimfoundation.org/guide.html
Requirements Minnesota and upper Midwest
tax-exempt organizations may apply.
Restrictions The foundation does not fund individuals;
private foundations; political organizations or campaigns; religious organizations, including schools, except for secular human service activities; memberships,
subscriptions, tickets for benefits, etc.; or organizations
that have as a substantial part of their purpose, the influencing of legislation.
Areas of Interest Animal Care; Arts, General; Biomedical Research; Conservation, Natural Resources; Cultural
Activities/Programs; Education; Environmental Programs; Fund-Raising; Government; Social Services;
Wildlife; Women

James Ford Bell Foundation Grants   **645**
James Ford Bell Foundation
1818 Oliver Ave S
Minneapolis, MN 55405
Contact Diane Neimann, Executive Director, (612)
377-8400; fax: (612) 377-8407
Internet http://www.users.uswest.net/~famphiladv/
jamesfordbell.htm
Requirements Minnesota 501(c)3 tax-exempt organizations are eligible. Preference is given to requests from the
Twin Cities area.
Restrictions No grants are made directly to individuals,
nor for scholarships, fellowships, or political campaigns.
No funding is available to units of local government. The

Foundation does not respond to requests for memberships, annual appeals, or special events and fundraisers.

Areas of Interest Adult and Continuing Education; Arts, General; Basic Skills Education; Children and Youth; Community Development; Conservation, Natural Resources; Cultural Activities/Programs; Disabled; Disadvantaged (Economically); Environmental Education; Environmental Programs; Family; Higher Education; Immigrants; Literacy; Minorities; Museums; Preschool Education; Private and Parochial Education; Population Control; Social Services; Wildlife; Women; Youth Programs

Sample Awards Saint David's School (MN)—general support, $15,000. Delta Research Station (MN)—to support waterfowl research, $30,000. Harriet Tubman Women's Shelter (MN)—to support the capital campaign, $20,000.

Bemis Company Foundation Grants   646
Bemis Company Foundation
222 S 9th St, Ste 2300
Minneapolis, MN 55402
Contact G.H. Seashore, (612) 376-3093 or (612) 376-3007; e-mail: ajkirchner@bemis.com
Requirements IRS 501(c)3 tax-exempt organizations in states in which the company facilities are located are eligible.
Restrictions The foundation will not make grants to individuals or to organizations for religious or political purposes, either for lobbying efforts or campaigns.
Areas of Interest Arts, General; Civic Affairs; Domestic Violence; Education; Museums; Personnel Training and Development; Science
Sample Awards Regional Domestic Abuse Services (Neenah, WI)—$50,000. Science Museum of Minnesota (MN)—$260,000. YMCA of Metropolitan Minneapolis (MN)—$25,000.

Best Buy Children's Foundation Grants   647
Best Buy Children's Foundation
PO Box 9448
Minneapolis, MN 55440-9448
Contact Community Relations Department, (952) 947-2650; fax: (612) 947-2693; e-mail: communityrelations@bestbuy.com
Internet http://communications.bestbuy.com/communityrelations/default.asp
Requirements Eligible applicants are 501(c)3 nonprofit organizations in communities with Best Buy stores with projects that address the foundation's mission.
Restrictions The foundation typically will not make grants to fraternal organizations or social clubs; units of government or quasi-governmental agencies; labor organizations or political campaigns; organizations designed primarily for lobbying; for-profit organizations or travel programs; fundraising dinners, testimonials, or similar events; support of operating or advertising expenses; individual requests for aid; religious organizations for religious purposes; third-party fundraising organizations; or causes or programs unrelated to the foundation's funding priorities.
Areas of Interest Curriculum Development; Education; Scholarship Programs, General; Technology; Technology Education; Youth Programs

Sample Awards American Film Institute (Los Angeles, CA)—for the Screen Education Center, which teaches students to use digital cameras and computer editing systems, $250,000 (2003).

F.R. Bigelow Foundation Grants   648
F.R. Bigelow Foundation
55 E Fifth St, 600 5th St Ctr
Saint Paul, MN 55101-1797
Contact Paul Verret , Secretary, (651) 224-5463; fax: (651) 224-8123; e-mail: inbox@frbigelow.org
Internet http://www.frbigelow.org
Requirements IRS 501(c)3 organizations in the greater Saint Paul, MN, metropolitan area are eligible, including Ramsey, Wahington, and Dakota Counties.
Restrictions Normally, the foundation will not act as the only source of financial support for a project, make annual grants, support sectarian religious programs, make grants to individuals, make ongoing or open-ended grants, or support medical research.
Areas of Interest Adult and Continuing Education; Arts, General; Basic Skills Education; Children and Youth; Community and School Relations; Education; Health Care; Humanities; Literacy; Neighborhoods; Social Services
Sample Awards Minnesota Minority Education Partnership (MN)—to expand a collaborative effort to increase success of students of color in county school districts, $30,000 (2002). Lauj Youth Society of Minnesota (MN)—to provide Hmong youths with in-school and home tutoring, $30,000 (2002). Saint Peter Claver Catholic Church (MN)—for start-up expenses for their elementary school library, $25,000 (2002).

Blandin Foundation Grants   649
Blandin Foundation
100 N Pokegama Ave
Grand Rapids, MN 55744
Contact Grant Administrator, (877) 882-2257 or (218) 326-0523; fax: (218) 327-1949; e-mail: bfinfo@blandinfoundation.org
Internet http://www.blandinfoundation.org/grants/index.html
Requirements Minnesota nonprofits and local collaborations that strengthen rural communities are eligible to apply.
Restrictions Grants do not support organizations not located in Minnesota; capital campaigns for construction, renovation, equipment purchase, or endowments outside the Grand Rapids/Itasca County area; religious activities; medical research; publications, films, or videos; travel grants for individuals or groups; camping programs; ordinary government services; individuals, except the Grand Rapids/Itasca County Blandin Educational Awards Program; political activities to influence legislation; or general operating funds outside the Grand Rapids/Itasca County area.
Areas of Interest Academic Achievement; Children and Youth; Community Service Programs; Community and School Relations; Cultural Activities/Programs; Economic Development; Education; Elementary Education; Environmental Programs; Family; Higher Education; Housing; Leadership; Rural Areas; Safety; Secondary Education; Service Delivery Programs; Youth Programs

Sample Awards Minnesota Diversified Industries (Saint Paul, MN)—to purchase equipment for its Grand Rapids, MN, plant, $240,000 (2003). Arrowhead Economic Opportunity Agency (Grand Rapids, MN)—for the Adult Scholarship Program, $120,500 (2003). Northern Itasca Health Care Ctr (Big Fork, MN)—for the Community Parish Nurse Project, $60,000 over five years (2003). Itasca Community Television (Grand Rapids, MN)—for program and operating support, $60,000 (2003).

Otto Bremer Foundation Grants 650
Otto Bremer Foundation
445 Minnesota St, Ste 2250
Saint Paul, MN 55101-2107
Contact Lynda Miner, Grants Manager, (651) 227-8036 or (888) 291-1123; fax: (651) 312-3665; e-mail: obf@bremer.com
Internet http://fdncenter.org/grantmaker/bremer/guideln.htm
Requirements Private nonprofit or public 501(c)3 tax-exempt organizations whose beneficiaries are residents of Minnesota, Montana, North Dakota, or northwestern Wisconsin are eligible.
Restrictions Grants are rarely awarded to support annual fund drives; benefit events; camps; economic development; medical research; building endowments other than for the development of community foundations; theatrical productions including motion pictures, books, or other artistic or media projects; or sporting activities.
Areas of Interest Catholic Church; Children and Youth; Civic Affairs; Community Development; Domestic Violence; Economic Development; Education; Equipment/Instrumentation; Family; Health Care; Hispanics; Homelessness; Housing; Immigrants; Jewish Studies; Medical Education; Mental Health; Methodist Church; Nonprofit Organizations; Philanthropy; Poverty and the Poor; Racism/Race Relations; Religion; Rural Areas; Sexual Abuse; Social Services Delivery
Sample Awards Youth Leadership (Minneapolis, MN)—to restructure congregational services and develop sustainable training programs, $60,000 over three years (2003). Productive Alternatives (Fergus Falls, MN)—to provide services to people with disabilities who have barriers to employment, $50,000 over three years (2003). Bosnian Women's Network (Brooklyn Park, MN)—to support immigrant women and their families, $60,000 over three years (2003). Mental Health Resources (Saint Paul, MN)—for supportive housing for homeless single adults, $15,000 (2003).

Bush Foundation Grants 651
Bush Foundation
332 Minnesota St, E-900 First National Bank Bldg
Saint Paul, MN 55101
Contact Program Contact, (651) 227-0891; fax: (651) 297-6485; e-mail: info@bushfound.org
Internet http://www.bushfound.org
Areas of Interest Alcohol Education; Arts, General; Communications; Drug Education; Education; Educational Administration; Faculty Development; Gangs; Health Planning/Policy; Health Services Delivery; Homelessness; Humanities; Job Training Programs; Leadership; Library Automation; Literature; Minority Schools; Native Americans; Philanthropy; Regional Planning/Policy; Public Broadcasting; Religion; Religious Studies; Religious Welfare Programs; Rural Health Care; Science; Science Education; Social Services; Women's Education; Youth Programs
Sample Awards Clark Atlanta U (Atlanta, GA)—for a faculty-development program, $150,000 (2004). Valley City State U (Valley City, ND)—to assess student learning and strengthen faculty instructional skills, $150,000 (2004).

Bush Foundation Regional Arts Development 652
    Program Grants
Bush Foundation
332 Minnesota St, E 900
Saint Paul, MN 55101
Contact Grants Administrator, (651) 227-0891; fax: (651) 297-6485; e-mail: info@bushfoundation.org
Internet http://www.bushfoundation.org/programs/Arts_Humanities.htm#radp
Requirements Minnesota, North Dakota, and South Dakota arts organizations that create or present performing, visual, media, or literary arts; have at least a five-year programming history; have average annual operating expenses of at least $250,000 during the three most recently completed fiscal years; operate year-round programs, rather than sponsor one-time events such as festivals or programs that operate only in the summer; pay artists a reasonable salary or fee, rather than involve volunteers in artistic activity; and produce, present, or develop arts programs for the public, rather than provide services for other arts organizations.
Restrictions Government agencies and public and private educational institutions are not eligible, nor are public broadcasting entities such as nonprofit radio or television stations.
Areas of Interest Arts, General; Literature; Media Arts; Performing Arts; Visual Arts
Sample Awards Bismarck/Mandan Orchestral Assoc (Bismarck, ND)—to develop and implement a fundraising plan, $14,786 (2003). Minnesota Dance Theatre and School (Minneapolis, MN)—to develop and produce dance works, $40,000 (2003). Northern Clay Ctr (Minneapolis, MN)—for operating support, $300,000 (2003). Theater Mu (Minneapolis, MN)—to improve the artistic quality of its productions, $56,000 (2003).

Patrick and Aimee Butler Family 653
    Foundation Grants
Patrick and Aimee Butler Family Foundation
332 Minnesota, Ste E-1420
Saint Paul, MN 55101-1369
Contact Kerrie Blevins, Foundation Director, (651) 222-2565; fax: (651) 222-2566; e-mail: kerrieb@butlerfamilyfoundation.org
Internet http://www.butlerfamilyfoundation.org/guidelines.htm
Requirements Minnesota nonprofits are eligible to apply.
Restrictions The foundation does not fund criminal justice, economic development or education, work or vocational programs, films or videos, health care, hospitals, medical research, elementary or secondary education, and music or dance.

Areas of Interest Arts, General; Civic Affairs; Community Service Programs; Cultural Activities/Programs; Environmental Programs; Family; Higher Education; Land Use Planning/Policy; Literacy; Philanthropy; Religion; Social Services; Youth Programs

Sample Awards Minnesota Land Trust (Minneapolis, MN)—support for land preservation and education, $3000. Minnesota Project (Saint Paul, MN)—for operating support, $3000. College of Saint Catherine (Saint Paul, MN)—to support the capital campaign, $100,000. Catholic Charities (Minneapolis, MN)—for operating support, $5000.

Cargill Inc Corporate Giving Grants 654
Cargill Foundation
PO Box 5650
Minneapolis, MN 55440
Contact Stacey Smida, Grants Administrator, (952) 742-4311; fax: (952) 742-7224; e-mail: stacey_smida@cargill.com
Internet http://www.cargill.com/commun/found.htm
Requirements 501(c)3 and 509(a) nonprofit organizations in in the Twin Cities metropolitan area that serve a significant proportion of people from Minneapolis and its northern and western suburbs are eligible.
Restrictions The foundation does not provide seed money or start-up funds for new organizations; grants are rarely made to organizations without a full year of operation. Contributions are not made to political organizations or campaigns, organizations designed primarily for lobbying or advocacy, religious organizations for direct religious activities, endowment campaigns, fraternal organizations, travel by groups or individuals, advertising, telephone solicitations, or individuals and their projects.
Areas of Interest Academic Achievement; Business Administration; Cultural Diversity; Education; Ethics; Family; Higher Education; Life Skills Training; Values/Moral Education; Youth Programs
Sample Awards Children's Theatre Co (Minneapolis, MN)—for the capital campaign, $2.5 million (2003). MacPhail Ctr for Music (Minneapolis, MN)—for the capital campaign, $100,000 (2003). Minneapolis Central Public Library (MN)—for the capital campaign, $1 million (2003).

Carolyn Foundation Grants 655
Carolyn Foundation
901 Marquette Ave, Ste 2630
Minneapolis, MN 55402
Contact Cindy Mellin, Foundation Administrator, (612) 596-3266; fax: (612) 338-2084; e-mail: CMellin@carolynfoundation.org or carolyn@winternet.com
Internet http://www.carolynfoundation.org/guidelines.html
Requirements IRS 501(c)3 nonprofit organizations in Minnesota and Connecticut may apply for the community grants. All 501(c)3 organizations are eligle for the enviromental grants.
Restrictions Grants are not awarded to individuals, political organizations or candidates, veterans' organizations, fraternal societies or orders, annual fund drives, umbrella organizations, or to deficits already incurred. The foundation does not generally make grants to reli-

gious organizations for religious purposes or to organizations in support of operations carried on in foreign countries.
Areas of Interest Arts; Children and Youth; Child Welfare; Cultural Activities/Programs; Disadvantaged (Economically); Education; Environmental Programs; Health Care; Renewable Energy Sources; Social Services; Water Resources
Sample Awards Minnesota Public Radio (Saint Paul, MN)—$15,000. Planned Parenthood of Minnesota (Saint Paul, MN)—$45,000. School Volunteers for New Haven (New Haven, CT)—$50,000. Women of Nations (Saint Paul, MN)—$30,000.

Central Minnesota Community Foundation 656 Grants
Central Minnesota Community Foundation
101 S 7th Ave, Ste 200
Saint Cloud, MN 56301
Contact Susan Lorenz, Program Officer, (877) 253-4380 or (320) 253-4380; fax: (320) 240-9215
Internet http://www.communitygiving.org/about_us_cm_6.php4
Requirements The primary geographic focus of the foundation includes Benton, Sherburne, and Stearns Counties, but grants also are made to organizations located in rural central Minnesota counties. IRS 501(c)3 organizations are eligible, but applicants not meeting this requirement may apply through a fiscal agent.
Restrictions The foundation will not fund individuals, endowments, medical research, capital campaigns to which the foundation can contribute no more than a tiny fraction of the total need, debt retirement or deficit financing, dollar-for-dollar replacement of government funding that has been reduced or eliminated, religious organizations for direct religious activities, political organizations or political campaigns, fraternal organizations, societies or orders, telephone solicitations, national fundraising efforts, or grants for travel.
Areas of Interest Cultural Activities/Programs; Cultural Diversity; Cultural Heritage Preservation; Public Planning/Policy; Volunteers

Charity Inc Grants 657
Charity Inc
PO Box 21055
Minneapolis, MN 55421-0055
Contact Deanna Hulme, Grants Administrator, c/o Totino's (612) 576-6979
Requirements Minnesota 501(c)3 tax-exempt organizations are eligible.
Restrictions The foundation does not provide grants to individuals.
Areas of Interest Catholic Church; Children and Youth; Churches; Community Development; Domestic Violence; Education; Elementary Education; Family; Higher Education; Recreation; Secondary Education; Social Services Delivery

Albert W. Cherne Foundation Grants 658
Albert W. Cherne Foundation
PO Box 975
Minneapolis, MN 55440

Contact Sara Ribbens, President, (612) 944-4378; fax: (952) 944-4399

Requirements Grants support nonprofit organizations primarily in the five-county metropolitan area of Minneapolis and Saint Paul, MN.

Restrictions Grants do not support veterans, fraternal, or labor organizations; religious purposes; conduit organizations; civil rights/social action groups; mental health counseling; specific-disease organizations; housing programs; individuals; capital improvements; or endowment funds.

Areas of Interest Adult and Continuing Education; At-Risk Youth; Basic Skills Education; Children and Youth; Disabled; Family Planning; Literacy; Social Services

Sample Awards Planned Parenthood of Minnesota (Saint Paul, MN)—to support a high-risk youth program, $5000. Loring Nicollet-Bethlehem Community Ctrs (Minneapolis, MN)—to support adult education and literacy programs, $12,000. YMCA, Greater Lake County Family (Waukegan, IL)—for a dining hall, $75,000.

COMPAS Community Art Program Grants 659
COMPAS
304 Landmark Center, 75 W Fifth St
Saint Paul, MN 55102-1414
Contact John Mentzos, (651) 292-3287; fax: (651) 292-3258; e-mail: john@compas.org
Internet http://www.compas.org/pages/communityart.html

Requirements Any group, organization, or individual is eligible to apply. All proposed activities must occur within the cities of St. Paul and/or Minneapolis.

Restrictions Grants do not support capital improvements, mortgage payments, property purchase, or building construction; deficit financing; administrative costs unrelated to the CAP sponsored project; fundraising events; or projects that result in lobbying for particular legislation, promoting of a particular religious belief, are discriminatory, or in any way violate federal, state or local laws.

Areas of Interest Arts and Culture; Arts, Social Services; Community Development; Community Outreach Programs; Cross-Cultural Studies; Social Change

COMPAS General Fund Grants 660
COMPAS
304 Landmark Center, 75 W Fifth St
Saint Paul, MN 55102-1414
Contact John Mentzos, Grant Allocations Director, (651) 292-3287; fax: (651) 292-3258; e-mail: jeff@compas.org
Internet http://www.compas.org/pages/generalfundover.html

Requirements Minnesota 501(c)3 organizations located in or serving the 12 county Twin Cities metro area are eligible.

Areas of Interest Arts and Culture; Art Education; Arts, Social Services; Community and School Relations; Community Development; Community Outreach Programs; Education; Human Services; Neighborhoods

COMPAS Medtronic Arts Access Program 661
Grants
COMPAS
304 Landmark Center, 75 W Fifth St
Saint Paul, MN 55102-1414
Contact John Mentzos, Grant Allocations Director, (651) 292-3287; fax: (651) 292-3258; e-mail: john@compas.org
Internet http://www.compas.org/pages/medtronicoverview.html

Requirements Minnesota nonprofit arts organizations in Anoka, Dakota, Hennepin, Ramsey, Scott, Washington, and Wright counties are eligible.

Restrictions Grants will not support: capital improvements, mortgage payments, property purchases, or building construction; deficit financing; administrative costs unrelated to the project supported by the grant; fundraising events; and projects which result in lobbying for particular legislation, promoting of a particular religious belief, are discriminatory, or in any way that violate federal, state or local laws.

Areas of Interest Arts and Culture; Art Education; Art, General; Artists in Residence; Arts, Social Services; Community and School Relations; Community Development; Community Outreach Programs; Economically Disadvantaged; Families; Mentoring Programs; Social Services

Edwin W. and Catherine M. Davis 662
Foundation Grants
Edwin W. and Catherine M. Davis Foundation
332 Minnesota St, Ste 2100
Saint Paul, MN 55101-1394
Contact Bette Moorman, President, (651) 228-0935; fax: (651) 228-0776
Requirements US nonprofit organizations are eligible.
Areas of Interest Arts, General; Elderly; Environmental Programs; Higher Education; Housing; Mental Health; Music; Religion; Social Services; Youth Programs
Sample Awards International Dyslexia Association (Baltimore, MD)—for scholarships, $20,000.

Roger L. and Agnes C. Dell Charitable Trust 663
II Grants
Roger L. and Agnes C. Dell Charitable Trust II
PO Box 64713
Saint Paul, MN 55164-0713
Contact Richard Hefte, c/o U.S. Bank, N.A., Tax Services, (651) 244-0941
Requirements Minnesota 501(c)3 tax-exempt organizations in Fergus Falls and the surrounding area are eligible.
Restrictions Individuals are not eligible for grants.
Areas of Interest Arts, General; Children and Youth; Cultural Activities/Programs; Education; Human Services; Jewish Services; Youth Programs
Sample Awards YMCA (Fergus Falls, MN)—for general support, $50,000. Fergus Falls Center for the Arts (Fergus Falls, MN)—for general support, $17,500. William Mitchell College of Law (Saint Paul, MN)—for scholarships, $9,000

Deluxe Corporation Foundation Grants   **664**
Deluxe Corporation Foundation
PO Box 64235
Saint Paul, MN 55164-0235
Contact Jennifer Anderson, Director of Foundations, (651) 483-7842; e-mail: jenny.anderson@deluxe.com
Internet http://www.deluxe.com/dlxab/deluxe-foundation-guidelines.jsp
Requirements Nonprofit organizations in Deluxe Corporation communities located in Alabama, Arizona, California, Colorado, Illinois, Indiana, Kansas, Minnesota, New Jersey, New York, North Carolina, Ohio, Pennsylvania, Texas, and Utah are eligible.
Restrictions The foundation does not generally award grants to seminars, conferences, workshops, fund-raisers, and other events; individuals; primary or secondary schools; publicly funded colleges or universities; national organizations; religious organizations; organizations designed primarily for lobbying; endowments; research projects; tours and travel expenses; start-up organizations; athletic events; sponsorships; long-term housing; community theater and music groups; civic organizations; libraries; or zoos.
Areas of Interest Cultural Activities/Programs; Education; Literacy; Social Services; Social Services Delivery

Duluth-Superior Area Community   **665**
    Foundation Grants
Duluth-Superior Area Community Foundation
227 W First St, 618 Missabe Bldg
Duluth, MN 55802
Contact Program Contact, (218) 726-0232; fax: (218) 726-0257; e-mail: info@dsacommunityfoundation.com
Internet http://www.dsacommunityfoundation.com
Requirements Applicant organizations must be 501(c)3 tax-exempt and located in or provide service to residents within the seven counties of northeastern Minnesota (Aitkin, Carlton, Cook, Itasca, Koochiching, Lake, and Saint Louis) and/or the two counties of northwestern Wisconsin (Douglas and Bayfield).
Restrictions The foundation does not make grants for the following: endowment, religious organizations for direct religious activities, medical research, debt retirement, individuals (except scholarships), political organizations or campaigns, tickets for benefits, telephone solicitations, fund-raising, and organizations that have as a substantial part of their purpose the influencing of legislation.
Areas of Interest Arts, General; Civic Affairs; Domestic Violence; Education; Environmental Programs; Museums; Public Broadcasting; Public Planning/Policy; Radio; Small Businesses; Social Services; Women
Sample Awards AM Chisholm Museum—for operating support, $2097. Minnesota Public Radio—to support program underwriting, $780. Advocates against Domestic Abuse—to support services to battered women, $2500. Patt's House Cleaning—to support small-business education, $400.

EcoLab Inc Lifeline for Children at Risk   **666**
    Education Grant Program
EcoLab Inc
370 Wabasha St
St Paul, MN 55102
Contact Grants Administrator, (651) 293-2658

Internet http://www.ecolab.com/CompanyProfile/Foundation/default.asp
Requirements Eligible to apply are public schools and school districts in the communities where EcoLab has facilities. These communities are: Atlanta, GA; Beloit, WI; Garland, TX; Hebron, OH; Joliet, IL; Memphis, TN; San Jose, CA; Woodbridge, NJ; Grand Forks, ND; and Saint Paul, MN. Applicants are required to submit proposals on a company application form.
Areas of Interest At-Risk Youth; Counseling/Guidance; Curriculum Development; Educational Psychology; Elementary Education; Family; Social Work; Teacher Education, Inservice

EcoLab Inc Quest for Excellence in   **667**
    Education
EcoLab Inc
370 Wabasha St
St Paul, MN 55102
Contact Grants Adminstrator, (651) 293-2658
Internet http://www.ecolab.com/companyprofile/foundation/default.asp
Requirements Eligible to apply are public schools and school districts in the communities where EcoLab has facilities. These communities are: Atlanta, GA; Beloit, WI; Garland, TX; Hebron, OH; Joliet, IL; Memphis, TN; San Jose, CA; Woodbridge, NJ; Grand Forks, ND; and St Paul, MN. Applicants are required to submit proposals on a company application form.
Areas of Interest Art Education; Business; Classroom Instruction; Communications; Computer Science; Curriculum Development; Mathematics; Natural Sciences; Physical Sciences; Social Sciences; Vocational/Technical Education

Edwards Memorial Trust Grants   **668**
Edwards Memorial Trust
c/o U.S. Bank, PO Box 64713
Saint Paul, MN 55164-0713
Contact Cheryl Nelson, (651) 244-0924; fax: (651) 244-4267
Requirements Minnesota 501(c)3 tax-exempt organizations in the greater Saint Paul area are eligible.
Areas of Interest Child/Maternal Health; Children and Youth; Crisis Counseling; Disabled; Health Care; Health Insurance; Hospitals; Mental Health; Preventive Medicine; Social Services

H.B. Fuller Company Foundation Grants   **669**
H.B. Fuller Co
PO Box 64683, 1200 Willow Lake Blvd
Saint Paul, MN 55164-0683
Contact Naida Kissner, (651) 236-5217
Internet http://www.hbfuller.com/About_Us/Community/000110.shtml#P0_0
Requirements 501(c)3 organizations serving the communities where the company has operations are eligible. Organizations incorporated in countries other than the United States must qualify for tax-exempt status according to US tax regulations and comply with national and/or state charity laws.
Restrictions Grants will not be made to support individuals; religious, fraternal, or veterans' organizations in most cases; political/lobbying organizations; travel; ba-

sic or applied research; disease-specific organizations; or courtesy or public service advertisements.

Areas of Interest Arts, General; Children's Theater; Community Development; Education; Environmental Programs; Health Care; Humanities; Immigrants; International Education/Training; Literacy Refugees; Social Services; Volunteers; Youth Programs

Sample Awards Children's Theater Comp—for education and outreach initiatives, $5000. English Learning Ctr for Immigrant and Refugee Families—for a youth program, $5000.

General Mills Foundation Grants 670

General Mills Foundation
PO Box 1113
Minneapolis, MN 55440
Contact Chris Shea, President, (612) 540-7890; fax: (763) 764-4114; e-mail: mills999@mail.genmills.com
Internet http://www.generalmills.com/corporate/about/community/#Foundation
Requirements US and Canadian charitable 501(c)3 and 509(a) nonprofits in communities where General Mills operates (California, Colorado, Florida, Georgia, Idaho, Illinois, Iowa, Minnesota, Michigan, Montana, Massachusetts, Missouri, Nevada, New Mexico, New York, Ohio, Pennsylvania, Texas, and Wisconsin) are eligible. Proposals should be by letter with adequate documentation including specific details of the project, evidence of its need, evidence that the people proposing the project are able to carry it to completion, an evaluating method, a brief description of the organization requesting support, a specific budget, and an audited financial statement and the most recent Form 990.
Restrictions The foundation does not make grants to individuals; religious organizations for religious purposes; political campaigns; organizations designed primarily for lobbying; for-profit organizations; support travel, either by groups or individuals; national or local campaigns to eliminate or control specific diseases; basic or applied research, including, but not limited to, science, medicine, engineering, or energy; recreation or athletic events; testimonial dinners or fund-raisers; or to underwrite scholarships or advertising.
Areas of Interest Academic Achievement; Arts, General; Children and Youth; Churches; Cultural Activities/Programs; Education; Elementary Education; Emergency Services; Family; Food Distribution; Health Care; Health Promotion; Job Training Programs; Literacy; Nutrition/Dietetics; Organizational Theory and Behavior; Performing Arts; Preventive Medicine; Safety; Scholarship Programs, General; Secondary Education; Visual Arts; Zoos
Sample Awards Hispanic Assoc of Colleges and Universities (San Antonio, TX)—to promote Hispanics' success in higher education and careers, $25,000 (2003).

Graco Foundation Grants 671

Graco Foundation
88 11th Ave NE
Minneapolis, MN 55413
Contact Robert Mattison, Vice President, (612) 623-6684; fax: (612) 623-6944

Requirements IRS 501(c)3 organizations in company-operating areas (including California, Colorado, Georgia, Illinois, Michigan, Minnesota, and South Dakota) may apply.
Restrictions Grants are not awarded to support political campaigns, individuals, religious organizations for religious purposes, fund-raising events, travel, fraternal organizations, or disease research.
Areas of Interest Business; Economic Self-Sufficiency; Education; Employment Opportunity Programs; Ethics; Minority Education; Neighborhoods; Social Services; Vocational Counseling; Youth Programs
Sample Awards Minneapolis Neighborhood Employment Network—for operating support, $3000. United Negro College Fund—for scholarships, $5000. City Inc—for renovations of its north Minneapolis facility, $125,000.

Grotto Foundation Project Grants 672

Grotto Foundation
332 Minnesota St, W-1050 First National Bank Bldg
Saint Paul, MN 55101-1312
Contact Sarah Marquardt, Grants Manager, (651) 225-0777; fax: (651) 225-0752; e-mail: info@grottofoundation.org
Internet http://www.grottofoundation.org
Requirements Minnesota 501(c)3 nonprofits may submit grant applications.
Restrictions Policy precludes grants being awarded for capital fund projects, travel, publication of books or manuscripts, undergraduate research projects, or grants to individuals.
Areas of Interest Asian Americans; Children and Youth; Dental Health and Hygiene; Economic Development; Education; Health Care; Homosexuals, Female; Homosexuals, Male; Immigrants; Leadership; Minorities; Native Americans; Refugees; Social Services; Sports; Youth Programs
Sample Awards W. Harry Davis Leadership Institute (Minneapolis, MN)—for the African American Youth Leadership Training Initiative, $4500. Girl Scout Council of Saint Croix Valley (MN)—for a volleyball program for Asian American girls, $3000. Mankato State U (MN)—for a dental health program for Native Americans, $2467.

Honor the Earth Grants 673

Honor the Earth
2104 Stevens Ave S
Minneapolis, MN 55404
Contact Executive Director, (800) 327-8407 or (612) 879-7529; fax: (612) 278-7162; e-mail: honorearth@earthlink.net
Internet http://honorearth.org/grantees/guidelines.html
Requirements Native American individuals or organizations may apply.
Areas of Interest Environmental Law; Environmental Programs; Hazardous Wastes; Land Management; Native Americans; Political Behavior; Training and Development; Wildlife
Sample Awards Eyak Rainforest Preservation Fund (Cordova, AK)—for operating support, $5000.

Emma B. Howe Memorial Foundation Grants 674

Emma B. Howe Memorial Foundation
821 Marquette Ave, A200 Foshay Tower
Minneapolis, MN 55402
Contact Patti Marsh Cagle, Grants Administrator ,
(612) 672-3837; fax: (612) 672-3868; e-mail:
pmarshcagle@mplsfoundation.org
Internet http://www.mplsfoundation.org/grants/
guidelines.htm
Requirements Grants are made only to organizations
that are located in and/or provide service in Minnesota.
Restrictions Support is not provided for religious organizations for religious purposes, or political, veterans, or
fraternal organizations. Grants are not awarded to individuals, nor for capital or federated fund drives, operating budgets, scholarships, conferences, deficit financing,
courtesy advertising, tickets, or national fund-raising ef-
forts.
Areas of Interest Adult and Continuing Education; Af-
ter-School Programs; Biomedical Research; Cancer/
Carcinogenesis; Cardiovascular Diseases; Children and
Youth; Chronic Illness; Diagnosis, Medical; Disabled;
Economic Self-Sufficiency; Education; Family; Health
Services Delivery; Land Use Planning/Policy; Native
Americans; Poverty and the Poor; Preventive Medicine;
Public Planning/Policy; Recreation and Leisure
Sample Awards Kids in Distressed Situations (KIDS)—
(New York, NY)—to provide donated products to
low-income children and families in the Minneapolis
area through Bridging Inc, $75,000 over three years
(2002).

HRK Foundation Grants 675

HRK Foundation
345 Saint Peter St, Ste 1200
Saint Paul, MN 55102-1639
Contact Kathleen Fluegel, Foundation Director, (866)
342-5475 or (612) 293-9001; fax: (612) 298-0551;
e-mail: Heidi@hrkfoundation.org or
HRKFoundation@HRKGroup.com
Internet http://www.hrkfoundation.org/grants/index.
htm
Requirements The foundation makes grants only to
qualified IRS 501(c)3 organizations that specifically
benefit people in the area surrounding Bayport and Saint
Paul, MN, and western Wisconsin.
Restrictions The foundation does not make loans or provide grants to individuals.
Areas of Interest AIDS; Child/Maternal Health;
Children and Youth; Drug Education; Health Care; Neu-
rology
Sample Awards American Red Cross, Saint Croix Valley Chapter (Stillwater, MN)—for general operating
support, $3000. A Chance to Grow (Minneapolis,
MN)—to support the EEG neurofeedback program,
$1000. Minnesota DARE (Saint Paul, MN)—for work-
books for the drug education and prevention program,
$1000.

International Multifoods Community Connection Grants 676

International Multifoods
110 Cheshire Ln, Ste 300
Minnetonka, MN 55305
Contact Karen Anderson, Communications Specialist ,
(952) 594-3568; fax: (952) 594-3304; e-mail: info@
multifoods.com
Internet http://www.multifoods.com
Requirements Nonprofit 501(c)3 organizations may apply if they are located in Multifoods communities nationwide and comply with state charities laws.
Restrictions Multifoods does not contribute to individuals; sectarian/denominational religious organizations,
unless the funds are for nonsectarian community purposes; political/lobbying organizations; industry, trade,
or professional associations memberships; organizations
receiving more than 25 percent of their operating support
from the United Way or government agencies; or to medical research, treatment, or equipment.
Areas of Interest Arts, General; Community Development; Education; Social Services; Youth Programs
Sample Awards Junior Achievement—$1500. Boys
and Girls Club—$2500. Youth Trust—$2500.

Jerome Foundation Grants 677

Jerome Foundation
125 Park Square Ct, 400 Sibley St
Saint Paul, MN 55101-1928
Contact Cynthia Gehrig, President, (800) 995-3766 or
(651) 224-9431; fax: (651) 224-3439; e-mail: info@
jeromefdn.org
Internet http://www.jeromefdn.org
Requirements Artists and nonprofit, tax-exempt organizations in Minnesota and New York are eligible. Projects
with total budgets of $200,000 or less are eligible.
Restrictions Grants are not made for building funds or
endowments. Students are ineligible.
Areas of Interest Art Criticism; Artists' Fellowships;
Artists in Residence; Arts, General; Choreography;
Dance; Dramatic/Theater Arts; Film Production; Humanities; Interdisciplinary Arts; Media Arts; Music; Performance Art; Video Production; Visual Arts; Exhibitions, Collections, Performances
Sample Awards Creative Time (New York, NY)—to
help emerging artists present art installations and projects throughout New York, $10,000 (2003). Foundation
for Independent Artists (New York, NY)—to enable an
independent choreographer to create new work, $12,000
(2003). James Sewell Ballet (Minneapolis, MN)—for
the Ballet Works Program for emerging choreographers
in Minnesota and New York City, $11,600 (2003). Aaron
Davis Hall (Harlem, NY)—to commission work by
emerging artists, $85,000 over two years to Performance
Space 122 (2003).

Jostens Foundation Community Grants 678

Jostens Foundation
5601 American Blvd W
Minneapolis, MN 55437
Contact Mary Klimek, (952) 830-3235; fax: (952)
897-4116; e-mail: foundation@jostens.com
Internet http://www.jostens.com/company/
community/index.asp

Requirements Nonprofit organizations with 501(c)3 status are eligible. The foundation gives priority to organizations where Jostens facilities and employees are located and gives priority to nonprofit organizations that involve Jostens employees.

Restrictions In general, grants are not made to support educational institutions or for scholarships, political organizations, churches or religious groups, fund-raising events, or endowment funds.

Areas of Interest Children and Youth; Education; Family; Health Promotion; Nonprofit Organizations; Social Services

Land O'Lakes Foundation Mid-Atlantic   679
Grants Program

Land O'Lakes Foundation
PO Box 64150
Saint Paul, MN 55164-0150
Contact Bonnie Bassett, Executive Director, (651) 481-2222; fax: (651) 481-2000; e-mail: Bbbass@landolakes.com or MLAtkins-Sakry@landolakes.com
Internet http://www.foundation.landolakes.com/mida_desc.asp
Requirements 501(c)3 community organizations serving Land O'Lakes dairy communities in Maryland, New Jersey, New York, Pennsylvania, and Virginia are eligible.
Restrictions Grants will not be awarded for the following purposes: scholarship funds, gifts or fund raisers for individuals, or non-public church use.
Areas of Interest Arts, General; Children and Youth; Civic Affairs; Cultural Activities/Programs; Health Care; Education; Humanities; Hunger; Public Affairs; Rural Areas; Science; Social Services; Water Supply; Youth Programs

Mardag Foundation Grants   680

Mardag Foundation
600 Fifth St Ctr, 55 Fifth St E
Saint Paul, MN 55101
Contact Paul Verret, Secretary, (612) 224-5463; fax: (651) 224-8123; e-mail: inbox@mardag.org
Internet http://www.mardag.org
Requirements Minnesota 501(c)3 tax-exempt organizations are eligible. The geographic focus of the grantmaking is the East Metro area of Ramsey, Washington, and Dakota counties, as well as greater Minnesota.
Restrictions Normally the foundation will not fund grants for the West Metro area; individuals; annual grants; events, development offices or officers, medical research, conservation, and scholarship programs; or sectarian religious programs.
Areas of Interest Adult and Continuing Education; Arts, General; Basic Skills Education; Children and Youth; Domestic Violence; Education; Elderly; Elementary Education; Literacy; Shelters; Women; Youth Programs
Sample Awards Central Minnesota Task Force on Battered Women (MN)—to help finance construction of a new shelter, $75,000. Women's Coalition (Duluth, MN)—to construct an emergency shelter for battered women and their children, $50,000. Girl Scout Council of the Saint Croix Valley (Saint Paul, MN)—for its capital campaign, $100,000.

McKnight Foundation Grants   681

McKnight Foundation
600 TCF Tower, 121 S Eighth St
Minneapolis, MN 55402
Contact Sara Whitehead, (612) 333-4220; fax: (612) 332-3833; e-mail: info@mcknight.org
Internet http://www.mcknight.org
Requirements Eligible applicants must be tax-exempt, nonprofit organizations in Minnesota that are not private foundations.
Restrictions Examples of areas not supported by grants include mental health or disabilities, except for services to enhance parents' capacity to nurture their children; chemical dependency treatment; services for seniors; and health. In addition to these program areas, grants do not support scholarships or other types of assistance for individuals; attendance at or travel to conferences or costs related to conferences; travel, except when related to other McKnight support of an organization; scientific research outside established McKnight research programs; endowments, except in rare cases; or activities that have a specific religious purpose.
Areas of Interest Arts, General; Children and Youth; Community Development; Environmental Programs; Families
Sample Awards Minnesota Ctr for Book Arts (Minneapolis, MN)—for operating support, $165,000 (2003). Communities Investing in Families (Taylor Falls, MN)—for training programs for low-income workers, $250,000 (2003). Cloverleaf Youth Partnership (Wadena, MN)—to renovate a building and start a youth-run cyber-cafe business, $57,000 (2003). Minnesota Land Trust (Saint Paul, MN)—to increase land- and water-protection efforts along the hedwaters of the Mississippi River, $50,000 (2003).

Medtronic Foundation Full Life Patient   682
Partnership Program—Heart Rescue
Grants

Medtronic Foundation
710 Medtronic Pkwy, LC110
Minneapolis, MN 55432-5604
Contact Grants Administrator, (763) 505-2646; fax: (763) 505-2648
Internet http://www.medtronic.com/foundation/heartrescue.html
Requirements National and local nonprofit organizations and government agencies that provide education, training, and awareness programs related to sudden cardiac death, early defibrillation, and early intervention are eligible.
Restrictions The foundation does not support individuals, including scholarships for individuals; religious groups for religious purposes; fund-raising events or activities, social events or goodwill advertising; reimbursable health treatment or scientific research; general support of educational institutions; long-term counseling or personal development; lobbying, political, or fraternal activities; or programs that receive support from United Way of the Minneapolis area.
Areas of Interest Cardiovascular Diseases; Education; Health and Safety Education; Training and Development

Minnesota Mutual Foundation Grants 683

Minnesota Mutual Foundation
400 Robert St N
Saint Paul, MN 55101-2098
Contact Lori Koutsky, Manager, (651) 665-3501; fax:
(651) 665-3551
Internet http://www.minnesotamutual.com/about/
community.asp
Requirements IRS 501(c)3 nonprofit organizations primarily in the twin cities of Saint Paul and Minneapolis,
MN, where the company and foundation are headquar-
tered, are eligible.
Restrictions Grants are not awarded to individuals or for
benefits, trips, tours, political activities, or religious ser-
vices/groups.
Areas of Interest Cultural Activities/Programs; Employment Opportunity Programs; Higher Education; Job
Training Programs; Social Services
Sample Awards Junior Achievement (MN)—$7000
(2001. Habitat for Humanity (MN)—$5000 (2001). IN-
ROADS (MN)—$3900 (2001).

Minnesota State Arts Board Institutional 684 Support Grants

Minnesota State Arts Board
400 Sibley St, Ste 200
Saint Paul, MN 55101-1928
Contact Kimberly Travis Hocker, (651) 215-1616 or
(800) 866-2787; fax: (651) 215-1602; TTY: (651)
215-6235; e-mail: kimberly.hocker@arts.state.mn.us
Internet http://www.arts.state.mn.us/grants/
institutional_support.htm
Requirements Nonprofit, tax-exempt arts-producing or
arts service organizations that have been in existence for
at least two years, are incorporated in Minnesota, have at-
tained annual operating expenses of at least $128,000,
and have at least one paid professional staff member are
eligible to apply.
Restrictions Institutions of primary, secondary, and
higher education; public broadcasting organizations; libraries; and civic organizations such as chambers of
commerce and community service agencies are not eligible to apply.
Areas of Interest Arts, General

Ordean Foundation Grants 685

Ordean Foundation
501 Ordean Bldg, 424 W Superior St
Duluth, MN 55802
Contact Stephen Mangan, Executive Director, (218)
726-4785; fax: (218) 726-4848; e-mail: ordean@
computerpro.com
Requirements 501(c)3 organizations serving residents
of Duluth, Hermantown, and Proctor, MN, and the town-
ships contiguous to Duluth in Saint Louis County, are eligible.
Areas of Interest Children and Youth; Disabled; Drugs/
Drug Abuse; Education; Elderly; Food Distribution;
Health Care; Juvenile Delinquency; Mental Disorders;
Poverty and the Poor; Social Services
Sample Awards Salvation Army (Duluth, MN)—for
operating support. Damiano Ctr (Duluth, MN)—to support the soup kitchen.

I.A. O'Shaughnessy Foundation Grants 686

I.A. O'Shaughnessy Foundation Inc
332 Minnesota St, Ste W1271
Saint Paul, MN 55101
Contact Gayle Watson, (651) 222-2323; e-mail:
iaoshaughnessyFD@Qwest.net
Areas of Interest Catholic Church; Churches; Cultural
Activities/Programs; Education; Higher Education; Music; Performing Arts; Religion; Secondary Education
Sample Awards College of Santa Fe (NM)—to construct a center to house the college's creative writing program, $150,000 (2002).

Pentair Education and Community 687 Programs

Pentair Foundation
90 S 7th St, 36th Fl
Saint Paul, MN 55402
Contact Michelle Murphy, Manager, c/o Wells Fargo
Center, (651) 636-7920; fax: (612) 486-2759
Internet http://www.pentair.com
Requirements Nonprofit organizations, including
schools and school districts, in communities where
Pentair has a presence may apply. For information on eli-
gible locations, contact the company.
Areas of Interest Alternative Modes of Education; Art
Education; Career Education and Planning; Community
Development; Crisis Counseling; Disabled; Education;
Job Training Programs; Mental Disorders;
School-to-Work Transition; Youth Programs

Piper Jaffray Companies Community 688 Support Grants

Piper Jaffray Companies Foundation
800 Nicollet Mall, Ste 800
Minneapolis, MN 55402
Contact Program Contact, (612) 342-5501; fax: (612)
342-6085; e-mail: tbonner@pjc.com
Internet http://www.piperjaffray.com/info3.aspx?id=
220
Requirements IRS 501(c)3 organizations located in the
Minneapolis/Saint Paul metropolitan area should submit
requests directly to the foundation. Organizations located outside the Minneapolis/Saint Paul metropolitan
area should submit requests to the nearest Piper Jaffray
office for forwarding to the foundation. Offices are located in communities in Arizona, California, Colorado,
Idaho, Illinois, Iowa, Kansas, Kentucky, Minnesota,
Missouri, Montana, Nebraska, Nevada, North Dakota,
Ohio, Oregon, South Dakota, Tennessee, Utah, Washington, Wisconsin, and Wyoming.
Restrictions Requests will not be considered from
newly formed nonprofit organizations; individuals;
teams; religious, political, veterans, or fraternal organizations; or organizations working to treat or eliminate
specific diseases. Support is not available for basic or applied research, travel, event sponsorship, benefits or tickets, or to eliminate an organization's operating deficit.
Areas of Interest Adult and Continuing Education;
Arts, General; Career Education and Planning; Child
Psychology/Development; Citizenship; Civic Affairs;
Cultural Activities/Programs; Domestic Violence; Elementary Education; Family; Higher Education; Hospitals; Housing; Job Training Programs; Parent Education;

Private and Parochial Education; Secondary Education; Youth Programs

Sample Awards Abbott Northwestern Hospital Park House (Minneapolis, MN)—for capital support. CARE Foundation (Plymouth, MN)—for general operating support. United Way of the Minneapolis Area (Minneapolis, MN)—for operating support.

Carl and Eloise Pohlad Family Foundation Grants   689

Carl and Eloise Pohlad Family Foundation
60 S Sixth St, Ste 3900
Minneapolis, MN 55402
Contact Marina Lyon, (612) 661-3910; fax: (612) 661-3715; e-mail: mlyon@pohadfamilycharities.org
Internet http://www.pohladfamilycharities.org
Requirements Minnesota nonprofits are eligible.
Restrictions Individuals are not eligible.
Areas of Interest Arts, General; Cultural Activities/Programs; Economic Development; Education; Environmental Programs; Health Care; Housing; Social Services; Sports; Youth Programs
Sample Awards Abbott Northwestern Hospital (Minneapolis, MN)—to construct a cardiology hospital, $3 million (2003).

RBC Dain Rauscher Foundation Grants   690

RBC Dain Rauscher Foundation
60 S 6th St.
Minneapolis, MN 55402-4422
Contact Sherry Koster, Foundation Program Manager, (612) 371-2765; fax: (612) 371-7933; e-mail: sherry.koster@rbcdain.com
Internet http://www.rbcdain.com/communityinvolvement
Requirements Organizations in Arizona, California, Illinois, Iowa, Kansas, Louisiana, Minnesota, Montana, Nebraska, North Dakota, Oklahoma, Oregon, South Dakota, Texas, Utah, Washington, and Wyoming are eligible.
Areas of Interest Arts, General; Disadvantaged (Economically); Economic Self-Sufficiency; Economics Education; Education; Elementary Education; Family; Minority Education; Secondary Education; Social Services

Saint Paul Companies Foundation Grants   691

Saint Paul Companies
385 Washington St, MC 514D
Saint Paul, MN 55102-1396
Contact Ronald McKinley, Community Affairs, (651) 310-2623; Deb Anderson, Community Affairs, (651) 310-7875 or (800) 328-2189
Internet http://www.stpaul.com/wwwcorporate/content/Communities/full_guidelines.asp
Areas of Interest Art Education; Arts; Child Psychology/Development; Community Development; Cultural Activities/Programs; Disadvantaged (Economically); Economic Opportunity Programs; Education; Inner Cities; Leadership; Neighborhoods; Nonprofit Organizations
Sample Awards Artrain USA (Ann Arbor, MI)—for a touring art exhibition entitled Native Views: Influences on Modern Culture, $50,000 (2003). Canadian Council for Aboriginal Business (Canada)—to develop a portal website and expand economic and community development programs throughout Canada, $2000 (2002). Family Housing Fund of Minneapolis and Saint Paul (MN)—for the Public Education Initiative, which develops, disseminates, and advocates around materials on affordable housing through the Twin Cities metropolitan area, $150,000 (2002). Minnesota Private Colleg Fund (MN)—for the Urban Education Scholarship program, which provides support for 22 Minnesota students of color committed to a career in urban teaching, $200,000 (2002).

Saint Paul Foundation Grants   692

Saint Paul Foundation
600 Fifth St Ctr, 55 Fifth St E
Saint Paul, MN 55101
Contact Program Contact, (800) 875-6167 or (651) 224-5463; fax: (651) 224-8123; e-mail: inbox@saintpaulfoundation.org
Internet http://saintpaulfoundation.org/grantseekers/guidelines
Requirements Minnesota 501(c)3 tax-exempt organizations are eligible.
Areas of Interest Adult and Continuing Education; Basic Skills Education; Career Education and Planning; Cultural Activities/Programs; Education; Literacy; Opera/Musical Theater; Philanthropy; Racism/Race Relations; Religion
Sample Awards Culture Incorporated (Saint Paul, MN)—for operating support, $10,000 (2003). Great River Greening (Saint Paul, MN)—for the River Steward Program, $23,625 (2003). Home/Block Nurse Program (Saint Paul, MN)—for the Senior Care Community Partnership Program, $50,000 (2003). Volunteers of America of Minnesota (Saint Paul, MN)—to purchase furniture and appliances for the Women's Recovery Center, $20,000 (2003).

Star Tribune Foundation Grants   693

Star Tribune Foundation
425 Portland Ave
Minneapolis, MN 55488-0002
Contact Sandra Fleitman, Foundation Coordinator, (612) 673-7051; fax: (612) 673-7847; e-mail: sfleitman@startribune.com
Internet http://www.startribune.com/company/ic/home/community/foundation.htm
Requirements 501(c)3 tax-exempt organizations in Minneapolis, MN are eligible to apply.
Restrictions As a general rule, support will not be made to/for organizations whose objectives are principally related to health and medicine, substance abuse, rehabilitation, and research; religious programs; international programs; political programs; individuals; subsidized publications or films; conferences; travel; advertising; fund-raising events; or general operating support.
Areas of Interest Career Education and Planning; Civic Affairs; Community Development; Creative Writing; Cultural Activities/Programs; Cultural Diversity; Dramatic/Theater Arts; Economic Self-Sufficiency; Family; Family Planning; Intellectual Freedom; Job Training Programs; Journalism; Mass Media; Neighborhoods; Parent Education; Publishing Industry; Urban Areas; Youth Programs

Sample Awards Big Brothers/Big Sisters of Greater Minneapolis (Minneapolis, MN)—to support a capital campaign for a new headquarters building, $10,000. Club Fed (Minneapolis, MN)—to create positive alternative activities for youth in northern Minneapolis, $5000. Old Highland Neighborhood Assoc (MN)—to support neighborhood and community development, $500.

Supervalu Inc Grants 694

Supervalu Inc
PO Box 990
Minneapolis, MN 55440
Contact Grants Administrator, (612) 828-4000; fax: (612) 828-4403
Internet http://www.supervalu.com/community/comm_application.html
Requirements 501(c)3 nonprofit organizations in company operating areas are eligible.
Restrictions Grants generally do not support: individuals; travel or research expenses; fees for participation in competitive programs; organizations that receive more than 30 percent of their funding from the United Way; capital campaigns; veteran, fraternal or labor organizations; lobbying, political, or religious programs; or organizations that are not tax-exempt under section 501(c)3 of the IRS tax code.
Areas of Interest After-School Programs; Art Education; Arts, General; Business Education; Cooperative Education; Educational Instruction Programs; Disabled; Economics Education; Education; Employment Opportunity Programs; Higher Education; Hunger; Job Training Programs; Leadership; Minorities; Nutrition/Dietetics; Political Science Education; School-to-Work Transition; Social Services; Urban Areas; Youth Programs; Zoos

Target Foundation Grants 695

Target Foundation
33 S Sixth St, CC-28Y
Minneapolis, MN 55402
Contact Grants Administrator, (612) 696-6098
Internet http://target.com/targetcorp_group/community/foundation.jhtml
Requirements 501(c)3 nonprofit organizations in the Minneapolis/Saint Paul metropolitan area are eligible.
Restrictions The foundation does not make grants to individuals or to religious groups for religious purposes; usually support national ceremonies, memorials, conferences, fundraising dinners, testimonials, or other similar events; usually support health, recreation, therapeutic programs; living subsidies; or care of disabled persons.
Areas of Interest Art in Public Places; Arts, General; At-Risk Youth; Cultural Activities/Programs; Exhibitions, Collections, Performances; Family; Social Services Delivery

James R. Thorpe Foundation Grants 696

James R. Thorpe Foundation
333 Washington Ave N, Ste 322
Minneapolis, MN 55401
Contact Edith Thorpe, President, (612) 373-9484

Requirements Giving is limited to 501(c)3 tax exempt organizations in Hennepin County, MN, with emphasis on Minneapolis.
Restrictions Grants do not support advertising, athletic groups, colleges and universities, individuals, international organizations, political organizations, school districts, special events/benefits, state and local government agencies, endowments, fundraising events, or seminars and conferences.
Areas of Interest Arts, General; Children and Youth; Civic Affairs; Cultural Activities/Programs; Education; Health Care; Medicine, Internal; Public Affairs; Research Participation

US Bank Foundation Grants 697

US Bank Foundation
800 Nicollet Mall, 23rd Fl
Minneapolis, MN 55402
Contact Teresa Bonner, Charitable Giving, (612) 303-0737
Internet http://www.usbank.com/about/community_relations/grant_guidelines.html
Requirements Nonprofit organizations in company-operating locations are eligible, including Colorado, Illinois, Iowa, Kansas, Minnesota, Montana, Nebraska, North Dakota, South Dakota, Wisconsin, and Wyoming.
Restrictions The foundation does not award grants to fraternal organizations, merchant associations, chamber memberships or programs, or 501(c)4 or 6 organizations; fundraising events or sponsorships; private foundations; organizations outside US Bancorp communities; programs operated by religious organizations for religious purposes; political organizations; individuals; travel and related expenses; endowment campaigns; deficit reduction; or organizations receiving primary funding from United Way.
Areas of Interest Art Education; Arts and Culture; At-Risk Youth; Cultural Activities/Programs; Economic Development; Economic Opportunity Programs; Economic Self-Sufficiency; Education; Elementary Education; Housing; Human Services; Mentoring Programs; Neighborhoods; Secondary Education; Social Services Delivery; Welfare-to-Work Programs; Workforce Development

Women's Foundation of Minnesota Grants 698

Women's Foundation of Minnesota
155 Fifth Ave S, Ste 900
Minneapolis, MN 55401
Contact Liz Johnson, (888) 337-5010; (612) 337-5010; fax: (612) 337-0404; e-mail: Liz@wfmn.org
Internet http://www.wfmn.org
Requirements Minnesota grassroots and established organizations operated by and for women and/or girls are eligible.
Restrictions Grants do not support individuals, capital or endowment campaigns, political campaigns, or religious programs or activities.
Areas of Interest Social Change; Women
Sample Awards Alliance of Early Childhood Professionals (Minneapolis, MN)—for the Child Care Workers Organizing project, $15,000. Ctr for True Economic Progress (Saint Paul, MN)—for general support,

$40,000 over two years. Minesota Coalition Against Sexual Assault (Minneapolis, MN)—for the Sexual Violence Justice Institute, $15,000. Pro-Choice Resources (Minneapolis, MN)—to support the Communities of Color Outreach Pilot program, $10,000.

Mississippi

Gulf Coast Community Foundation Grants   699
Gulf Coast Community Foundation
PO Box 1899
Gulfport, MS 39502
Contact Dickie Roberts, (228) 868-1563; fax: (228) 868-4999, E-mail: gccf@bellsouth.net
Internet http://www.charityadvantage.com/gulfcoastfoundation
Requirements Mississippi nonprofits in Harrison, Hancock, Jackson, Pearl River, and Stone Counties may apply.
Restrictions Grants do not support governmental agencies, private foundations, religious organizations for religious purposes, athletic programs, school band drives, or capital drives.
Areas of Interest Arts, General; Civic Affairs; Cultural Activities/Programs; Education; Scholarship Programs, General; Health; Recreation and Leisure; Social Services

Phil Hardin Foundation Grants   700
Phil Hardin Foundation
1921 24th Ave
Meridian, MS 39301
Contact C. Thompson Wacaster, (601) 483-4282; fax: (601) 483-5665; e-mail: info@philhardin.org
Internet http://www.philhardin.org
Requirements Applicants must either be based in Mississippi or the project must benefit Mississippi, depending on the program. Contact program staff for eligibility.
Areas of Interest Arts, General; Children and Youth; Economic Development; Education; Education Reform; Educational Planning/Policy; Elementary Education; Fellowship Programs, General; Higher Education; Leadership; Performing Arts; Secondary Education
Sample Awards Meridian Foundation (MS)—to endow the Riley Education and Performing Arts Center, $2.5 million (2002).

Elizabeth M. Irby Foundation Grants   701
Elizabeth M. Irby Foundation
PO Box 1819
Jackson, MS 39215
Contact Stuart Irby, President, (601) 989-1811
Requirements Mississippi nonprofit organizations may apply.
Restrictions Individuals are ineligible.
Areas of Interest Arts, General; Churches; Cultural Activities/Programs; Elementary Education; Higher Education; Religion; Secondary Education; Social Services

Midsouth Foundation Grants   702
Midsouth Foundation
1230 Raymond Rd, Box 700
Jackson, MS 39204

Contact Grants Administrator, (601) 355-8167; fax: (601) 355-6499; e-mail: kshields@fndmidsouth.org
Internet http://www.fndmidsouth.org/grants/grants.asp
Requirements Nonprofits in Arkansas, Louisiana, and Mississippi are eligible.
Areas of Interest Children and Youth; Day Care; Disabled; Economic Development; Education; Education Reform; Family; Higher Education; Job Training Programs; Nonprofit Organizations; Parent Education; Poverty and the Poor
Sample Awards All Our Children (West Memphis, AR)—to aid low-income residents in community resource development, $10,000. Christian Children's Fund (Jackson, MS)—to strengthen a statewide child care advocacy organization, $60,000. East Arkansas Private Industry Council (West Memphis, AR)—to provide personal development training for parents, $10,000.

Mississippi Arts Commission Arts-Based   703
Community Development Program
Grants
Mississippi Arts Commission
239 N Lamar St, Ste 207
Jackson, MS 39201
Contact Beth Batton, 601-359-6546
Internet http://www.arts.state.ms.us/grants_abcd.html
Requirements Applicants must reside in Mississippi.
Areas of Interest Art Appreciation; Arts, General; Audience Development; Community Development; Arts Administration; Training and Development; Planning/Policy Studies; Regional Planning/Policy

Mississippi Arts Commission Arts in   704
Education Program Grants
Mississippi Arts Commission
239 N Lamar St, Ste 207
Jackson, MS 39201
Contact Wendy Shenefelt McCurtis, Arts in Education Program Director, 601-359-6037; e-mail: wshenefelt@arts.state.ms.us
Internet http://www.arts.state.ms.us/grants_education.html
Requirements Applicants must reside in Mississippi.
Areas of Interest Art Education; Curriculum Development; Elementary Education; Secondary Education

Missouri

Ameren Corporation Community Grants   705
Ameren Corporation
PO Box 66149
Saint Louis, MO 63166-6149
Contact Otis Cowan, Manager of Community Relations, (314) 554-4740; fax: (314) 554-2888; e-mail: ocowan@ameren.com
Internet http://www.ameren.com/community/adc_cm_NonProfitGrants.asp
Requirements Illinois and Missouri tax-exempt organizations in AmerenUE and AmerenCIPS service areas are eligible.
Restrictions Grants do not support individuals or political, religious, fraternal, veteran, social, or similar groups. Ameren cannot donate electric or natural gas service.

Areas of Interest Arts, General; Children and Youth; Community Development; Cultural Activities/Programs; Elderly; Environmental Programs; Family; Jewish Services; Science and Technology; Social Services Delivery
Sample Awards Abraham Lincoln Presidential Library & Museum, $125,000 (2002. Jewish Federation, $7000 (2002. Saint Vincent DePaul Society, Alton—$5000 (2002). Saint Louis Zoo—$35,000 (2002).

Anheuser-Busch Foundation Grants 706
Anheuser-Busch Foundation
1 Busch Pl
Saint Louis, MO 63118-1852
Contact Jayne Nicholson, Charitable Contributions, (314) 577-2000; fax: (314) 557-3251
Internet http://www.anheuser-busch.com/publications
Requirements 501(c)3 tax-exempt organizations in Fairfield, Los Angeles, and San Diego, CA; Fort Collins, CO; District of Columbia; Jacksonville, Orlando, and Tampa, FL; Cartersville, GA; Saint Louis, MO; Newark, NJ; Baldwinsville, NY; Cleveland and Columbus, OH: Langhorne, PA; San Antonio, TX; and Merrimac, VA, are eligible.
Restrictions Grants are not made to individuals; political, social, fraternal, religious, or athletic organizations; or hospitals for operating funds.
Areas of Interest Children and Youth; Community Development; Community Service Programs; Cultural Activities/Programs; Cultural Outreach; Education; Education Reform; Environmental Programs; Health Care; Health Care Access; Health Promotion; Minorities; Minority Education; Minority Health; Social Services; Social Services Delivery
Sample Awards Marine Corps Heritage Foundation (Quantico, VA)—for its campaign to build a national museum devoted to the Marine Corps, $500,000 (2004). U of California at Davis (CA)—to help build a food-science laboratory at the Robert Mondavi Institute for Wine and Food Science, $5 million challenge grant (2002). Saint Louis Science Ctr (MO)—to expand science-education programs for people of all ages, including mathematics, science, and technology programs in hundreds of area schools and school districts, $2.3 million over five years (2002). U of California at Davis (CA)—to help build a food-science laboratory facility as part of the new Robert Mondavi Institute for Wine and Food Science, $5 million challenge grant (2002).

Boeing-McDonnell Foundation Grants 707
Boeing-McDonnell Foundation
PO Box 516, M/C S100 1510
Saint Louis, MO 63166
Contact Karen A. Bedell, President, fax: (314) 232-7654
Internet http://www.boeing.com/companyoffices/aboutus/community/charitable.htm
Requirements Missouri 501(c)3 nonprofits in the Saint Louis area are eligible.
Restrictions The foundation generally will not consider requests from or for political organizations or programs; sectarian, denominational, fraternal, social, religious, labor, or similar organizations; individuals; loans or investment funds; advertisements; university/labor affili-

ates; or fund-raisers, benefits, dinners, or sporting events.
Areas of Interest Arts, General; Business Education; Civic Affairs; Cultural Activities/Programs; Community Outreach Programs; Elementary Education; Engineering Education; Environmental Programs; Leadership; Minority Education; Public Broadcasting; Science Education; Secondary Education

Butler Manufacturing Company Foundation Grants 708
Butler Manufacturing Company Foundation
PO Box 419917
Kansas City, MO 64141-0917
Contact Foundation Administrator, (816) 968-3208; fax: (816) 968-3211; e-mail: blfay@butlermfg.org
Internet http://www.butlermfg.com/faq/foundationguidelines.pdf
Requirements Applicants must be nonprofit institutions meeting the human needs of society in the greater Kansas City area and other communities where employees reside.
Areas of Interest Arts, General; Disadvantaged (Economically); Dramatic/Theater Arts; Education; Health Care; Higher Education; Job Training Programs; Minorities; Neighborhoods; Philanthropy; Scholarship Programs, General; Social Services; Youth Programs
Sample Awards Missouri Repertory Theatre (MO)—for project support, $5000. Kansas City Neighborhood Alliance (MO)—for operating support, $5000.

Deaconess Foundation Grants 709
Deaconess Foundation
211 N Broadway, Ste 1260
Saint Louis, MO 63102
Contact Rev. Jerry Paul, President, (314) 436-8001; fax: (314) 436-5352; e-mail: jerryp@deaconess.org or info@deaconess.org
Internet http://www.deaconess.org/grantmaking.phtml
Requirements Nonprofit groups and organizations in the metropolitan Saint Louis area are eligible for funding. Organizations should send a one- to two-page letter of intent that should include name of organization, mission, and history; purpose for which the organization is seeking funding; health issues that will be addressed; description of who will be served; anticipated outcomes; other participating organizations; amount of funding requested; time frame; and contact person's name, address, and phone and fax numbers.
Areas of Interest Child/Maternal Health; Health Promotion; Inner Cities; Poverty and the Poor; Preventive Medicine; Religion
Sample Awards Faith in Action, Eden United Church of Christ (Edwardsville, MO)—for operating support. Frazer Health Ctr (Saint Louis, MO)—for operating support.

Caleb C. and Julia W. Dula Educational and Charitable Foundation Grants 710
Caleb C. and Julia W. Dula Educational and Charitable Foundation
112 S Hanley Rd
Saint Louis, MO 63105

Contact James Mauze, (314) 726-2800; fax: (314) 863-3821
Requirements Grants are given to support projects of tax-exempt organizations.
Restrictions Support is not available to individuals.
Areas of Interest Arts, General; Child Welfare; Community Development; Elderly; Health Care; Humanities; Libraries; Museums; Religion; Restoration and Preservation, Structural/Architectural

Emerson Charitable Trust Grants   711
Emerson Charitable Trust
PO Box 4100, 8000 W Florissant
Saint Louis, MO 63136
Contact Jo Ann Harmon, Senior Vice President, (314) 553-2000; fax: (314) 553-1605
Areas of Interest Community Service Programs; Cultural Activities/Programs; Engineering Education; Higher Education; Social Services; Youth Programs

Enterprise Rent-A-Car Foundation Grants   712
Enterprise Rent-A-Car Foundation
600 Corporate Park Dr
Saint Louis, MO 63105-4211
Contact Jo Ann Kindle, President, (314) 512-2754; fax: (314) 512-4754
Requirements Nonprofit organizations involving Enterprise employees, their families, and customers are eligible.
Areas of Interest Disabled; Education; Social Services; Youth Programs
Sample Awards Harris-Stowe State College—for the business-administration program, $1 million (2002). Washington U (Saint Louis, MO)—to endow undergraduate scholarships and financial assistance for minority and other student's, as part of the university's campaign, $25 million (2001).

Francis Families Foundation Grants   713
Francis Families Foundation
800 W 47th St, Ste 717
Kansas City, MO 64112
Contact Lyn Knox, Program Officer, (816) 531-0077
Internet http://www.francisfoundation.org/guidelines.htm
Requirements The applying entity must be tax-exempt under the IRS code and geographically located within the greater Kansas City area (60 mile radius).
Restrictions The foundation does not make grants to individuals.
Areas of Interest Art Education; Arts Administration; Arts, General; Child Psychology/Development; Cultural Activities/Programs; Higher Education; Youth Programs
Sample Awards Child and youth development programs and organizations (Kansas City, KS)—$1.3 million total. Art and cultural programs and organizations (Kansas City, KS)—$265,428 total.

Gateway Foundation Grants   714
Gateway Foundation
720 Olive St, Ste 1977
Saint Louis, MO 63101

Contact Christy Fox, Administrator, (314) 241-3337; e-mail: gwf1977@aol.com
Internet http://www.gateway-foundation.org
Restrictions The foundation does not award grants for general operating support or endowment drives.
Areas of Interest Arts, General; Cultural Activities/Programs; Dance; Dramatic/Theater Arts; Education; Higher Education; Parks; Playgrounds; Transportation

Catherine Manley Gaylord Foundation   715
Grants
Catherine Manley Gaylord Foundation
1015 Locust St, Ste 500
Saint Louis, MO 63101
Contact Donald Fahey, Manager-Trustee, (314) 421-0181; fax: (314) 241-2258
Requirements Saint Louis metropolitan area 501(c)3 nonprofit organizations may apply.
Areas of Interest Adult and Continuing Education; Basic Skills Education; Community Development; Education; Equipment/Instrumentation; Philanthropy; Religion; Scholarship Programs, General

GenAmerica Foundation Grants   716
GenAmerica Foundation
700 Market St
Saint Louis, MO 63101
Contact Sheryl Endicott, Contributions Consultant, (314) 444-0434; fax: (314) 444-0681; e-mail: cendicott@genam.com
Internet http://www.genamerica.com
Requirements Missouri nonprofit organizations serving the greater Saint Louis metropolitan area are eligible.
Areas of Interest Arts, General; Education; Social Services
Sample Awards Young Audiences of Saint Louis (Saint Louis, MO)—for general support, $25,000 (2002). Arts and Education Council of Greater Saint Louis (Saint Louis, MO)—for general support, $11,000 (2002).

Hallmark Corporate Foundation Grants   717
Hallmark Corporate Foundation
PO Box 419580, Mail Drop 323
Kansas City, MO 64141-6580
Contact Karen Bartz, Senior Program Officer, (816) 545-6906
Internet http://www.hallmark.com/hmk/Website/AboutHallmark/ah_4.jsp?BV_SessionID=@@@@1820986222.1078250531@@@@&BV_EngineID=jadcjkedmdffbedcfchchm.0&CONTENT_KEY=SUPPORTING_OUR_COMMUNITY&CONTENT_TYPE=TOP_PAGE&fromPage=%2fWebsite%2fAboutHallmark%2fah_4.jsp%3fCONTENT_
Requirements Support is limited to the Kansas City, MO, area and communities where major Hallmark facilities are located, including Enfield, CT; Columbus, GA; Metamora, IL; Lawrence, Leavenworth, and Topeka, KS; Liberty, MO; and Center, TX.
Restrictions Grants are not awarded to/for individuals, veterans groups, athletic groups, labor groups, social clubs, endowment funds, debt reduction, travel, conferences, scholarly research, charitable advertisements, or mass media campaigns.

Areas of Interest Adult and Continuing Education; Arts, General; Basic Skills Education; Civic Affairs; Education; Health Care; Humanities; Literacy; Social Services
Sample Awards Society of Illustrators (New York, NY)—for Student Scholarship Competition, $68,000.

H&R Block Foundation Grants   **718**
H&R Block Foundation
4400 Main St
Kansas City, MO 64111
Contact Grants Administrator, (816) 932-8324; fax: (816) 753-1585
Internet http://www.hrblockfoundation.org/grants/index.html
Requirements 501(c)3 tax-exempt organizations are eligible. Major emphasis is placed on support of activities in the Kansas City metropolitan area.
Restrictions Except in most unusual circumstances, the foundation does not make grants to individuals or businesses; publications; projects for which the foundation must exercise expenditure responsibility; single-disease agencies; travel or conferences; historic preservation; or telethons, dinners, advertising, or other fundraising events.
Areas of Interest Arts, General; Community Development; Cultural Activities/Programs; Health Services Delivery; Social Services; Social Services Delivery

Ewing Marion Kauffman Foundation Grants 719
Ewing Marion Kauffman Foundation
4801 Rockhill Rd
Kansas City, MO 64110-2046
Contact Paul Carttar, Program Operations, (816) 932-1000; fax: (816) 932-1100; e-mail: info@emkf.org
Internet http://www.emkf.org/pages/49.cfm
Requirements The foundation only funds programs within the United States. The majority of education grants go to organizations within the Kansas City metropolitan area. The foundation's entrepreneurship efforts fund programs and activities nationally and within the Kansas City area.
Restrictions The foundation does not fund requests from individuals, political, social, fraternal, or arts organizations, and capital campaigns or construction projects; endowments, special events, or international programs; loans, start-up expenses, or seed capital funding for private businesses or scholarships requested by individuals; institutions that discriminate on the basis of race, creed, gender, national origin, age, disability, or sexual orientation in policy or in practice; organizations engaged in sectarian religious activities, political lobbying, or legislative activities; programs targeted for people with a specific physical, medical, or psychological condition; or medical research or profit-making enterprises.
Areas of Interest Business Development; Career Education and Planning; Child Psychology/Development; Economic Self-Sufficiency; Employment Opportunity Programs; Entrepreneurship; Leadership; Mathematics Education; Philanthropy; Public Planning/Policy; School-to-Work Transition; Science Education; Technology Education
Sample Awards U of Illinois at Urbana-Champaign (IL)—to create an interdisciplinary entrepreneur-

ship-education program, $4.5 million challenge grant (2003). Fifty-two US colleges and universities—to develop, expand, or enhance entrepreneurship-education programs, $2.3 million (2003). U of Health Sciences—for a comprehensive health-screening program for elementary-school students in the Raytown and Hickman Mills School Districts and slected schools in the Kansas City, MO, School District, $125,000 (2003).

Kellwood Foundation Grants   **720**
Kellwood Foundation
600 Kellwood Pkwy
Chesterfield, MO 63017
Contact Terri Wise, Secretary & Treasurer, (314) 576-3431; fax: (314) 576-3439
Requirements Giving is primarily made to the greater St. Louis, MO, area.
Areas of Interest Civic Affairs; Cultural Activities/Programs; Education; Emergency Programs; Health Services Delivery; Literature; Performing Arts; Philanthropy; Science; Social Sciences; Youth Programs
Sample Awards Central Institute for the Deaf (Saint Louis, MO)—for endowment, $10,000 (2002). Girl Scouts of the USA (Saint Louis, MO)—for program support, $3000. American Red Cross (Saint Louis, MO)—for operating support, $10,000.

Laclede Gas Charitable Trust Grants   **721**
Laclede Gas Charitable Trust
720 Olive St, Rm 1517
Saint Louis, MO 63101
Contact Mary Kullman, Secretary; fax: (314) 421-1979; e-mail: mkullman@lacledegas.com
Internet http://www.lacledegas.com/about/cs_charitable.htm
Requirements Contributions are limited to those organizations located in the company's service area. Contact program staff for locations.
Restrictions The trust does not support individuals, churches and sectarian organizations, political organizations, or veterans groups.
Areas of Interest Arts, General; Civic Affairs; Community Development; Cultural Activities/Programs; Education; Social Services; Youth Programs

Millstone Foundation Grants   **722**
Millstone Foundation
7701 Forsyth Blvd, Ste 925
Saint Louis, MO 63105-1842
Contact I.E. Millstone, President or Colleen Millstone, Director, (314) 961-8500
Requirements Missouri tax-exempt organizations are eligible. Preference is given to requests from Saint Louis.
Areas of Interest Education; Higher Education; Israel; Jewish Services; Social Services

Missouri Arts Council Community Arts   **723**
    Program Grants
Missouri Arts Council
111 N Seventh St, Ste 105
Saint Louis, MO 63101-2188
Contact Julie Hale, (314) 340-6845; fax: (314) 340-7215; e-mail: julie.hale@ded.mo.gov

Internet http://www.missouriartscouncil.org/html/funding.shtml

Requirements Applicants must be nonmetropolitan community arts councils and other local arts coordinating agencies in Missouri, must be nonprofit and tax-exempt, and must be governed by citizen boards. Organizations can request arts agency administration support only in conjunction with project support; funds are not available for arts agency administration only.

Areas of Interest Architecture; Art Education; Arts Administration; Dance; Dramatic/Theater Arts; Folk/Ethnic Arts; Literature; Media Arts; Music; Rural Areas; Visual Arts

Missouri Housing Trust Fund Grants   724

Missouri Housing Trust Fund
3435 Broadway
Kansas City, MO 64111-2415
Contact Valori Sanders, (816) 759-7226; e-mail: vsanders@mhdc.com
Internet http://www.mhdc.com/housing_trust_fund/index.htm

Requirements Any Missouri developers or nonprofit organizations involved in housing, community service, or community or economic development may apply. Applicants must demonstrate prior, successful housing experience and have the financial capacity to successfully complete and operate the housing and/or service proposed. Provider of services must have qualified and trained staff, and a successful recording of providing the proposed services.

Areas of Interest Community Service Programs; Economic Development; Family; Homelessness; Housing; Poverty and the Poor

Sample Awards The Kitchen Inc (Springfield, MO)—for general operating support, $100,000. Economic Security of the Southwest Area (Joplin, MO)—for general operating support, $96,690. The Haven of Grace (Saint Louis, MO)—for general operating support, $25,000.

Jeannette L. Musgrave Foundation Grants   725

Jeannette L. Musgrave Foundation
4035 S Fremont
Springfield, MO 65804
Contact Joe Clark, Chairperson, (417) 883-5348; fax: (417) 883-8961

Requirements 501(c)3 tax-exempt organizations and colleges, univiersities, and schools in Missouri may apply.

Areas of Interest Alcohol/Alcoholism; Children and Youth; Civic Affairs; Drugs/Drug Abuse; Education; Elderly; Elementary Education; Exhibitions, Collections, Performances; Higher Education; Housing; Public Affairs; Public Broadcasting; Religion; Secondary Education; Social Services Delivery

Oppenstein Brothers Foundation Grants   726

Oppenstein Brothers Foundation
PO Box 13095
Kansas City, MO 64199-3095
Contact Sheila Rice, Program Officer, (816) 234-8671
Requirements Nonprofit organizations in the metropolitan Kansas City, MO, area may submit grant proposals.

Restrictions Grants are not awarded to support individuals, annual campaigns, scholarships, fellowships, medical equipment, or endowment funds.

Areas of Interest AIDS; Adult and Continuing Education; Arts, General; Basic Skills Education; Cultural Activities/Programs; Disabled; Elderly; Elementary Education; Family Planning; Health Care; Higher Education; Homelessness; Hospitals; Jewish Services; Jewish Studies; Juvenile Delinquency; Mental Disorders; Minorities; Museums; Performing Arts; Preschool Education; Secondary Education; Social Services; Vocational/Technical Education; Volunteers; Youth Programs

Sample Awards Arts Partners Fund (Kansas City, MO)—for program support. Children's Mercy Hospital (Kansas City, MO)—for program support.

Pulitzer Foundation Grants   727

Pulitzer Foundation
900 N Tucker Blvd
Saint Louis, MO 63101-1069
Contact Alan Silverglat, Secretary/Treasurer, (314) 340-8440

Requirements Missouri tax-exempt organizations in the Saint Louis metropolitan area are eligible.

Restrictions Grants do not support individuals, international organizations, or religious organizations.

Areas of Interest Arts, General; Education; Higher Education; Music

J.B. Reynolds Foundation   728

J.B. Reynolds Foundation
PO Box 219139
Kansas City, MO 64141-6139
Contact Program Contact

Requirements 501(c)3 organizations in the Kansas City, MO, area may submit applications.

Areas of Interest Arts, General; Biomedical Research; Community Development; Higher Education; Humanities; Social Services

Joseph H. and Florence A. Roblee   729
Foundation Grants

Joseph H. and Florence A. Roblee Foundation
PO Box 14737
Saint Louis, MO 63178
Contact Emily Cohen, (314) 961-4493; fax: (314) 961-2116; e-mail: jfroblee@swbell.net

Requirements Nonprofit organizations in Saint Louis, MO; Miami, FL; Dallas, TX; Chapel Hill and Greenville, NC; and Boston, MA, may submit grant applications.

Restrictions Support is not given to individuals or for annual campaigns, research, or loans.

Areas of Interest Adult and Continuing Education; Alcohol/Alcoholism; Basic Skills Education; Citizenship; Crime Prevention; Cultural Outreach; Disadvantaged (Economically); Drugs/Drug Abuse; Education Reform; Homelessness; Literacy; Minorities; Racism/Race Relations; Religion; Teacher Education; Violent Behavior; Women; Youth Programs

Saint Louis Rams Foundation Grants 730
Saint Louis Rams Foundation
1 Rams Way
Saint Louis, MO 63045
Contact Coordinator, (314) 516-8788; fax: (314) 770-0392
Internet http://www.stlouisrams.com/Community
Requirements Nonprofits in the metropolitan Saint Louis, MO, area, including southern Illinois and eastern Missouri, are eligible. Preference is given to organizations that partner with other local nonprofits and offer creative approaches for more than grants (i.e., personnel involvement or in-kind support) and ways the Rams can participate.
Restrictions Capital grants are rarely given.
Areas of Interest Arts, General; Education; Fund-Raising; Health Care; Leadership; Literacy; Mental Retardation; Mentoring Programs; Recreation and Leisure; Science; Sports; Youth Programs; Zoos

Sosland Foundation Grants 731
Sosland Foundation
4800 Main St, Ste 100
Kansas City, MO 64112
Contact Dr. Debbie Sosland-Edelman, Executive Director, (816) 756-1000; fax: (816) 756-0494
Requirements Metropolitan Kansas City, MO, 501(c)3 nonprofit organizations are eligible.
Restrictions Individuals are ineligible.
Areas of Interest Arts, General; Arts and Culture; Civic Affairs; Cultural Activities/Programs; Education; Secondary Education; Government Functions; Health Care; Higher Education; Hospitals; Human Services; Jewish Services; Music; Performing Arts; Public Administration; Restoration and Preservation; Social Services
Sample Awards William Jewell College (Liberty, MO)—to renovate Jewell Hall, $50,000.

Montana

Charles M. Bair Family Trust Grants 732
Charles M. Bair Family Trust
PO Box 20678
Billings, MT 59115
Contact Grants Administrator, c/o US Bank, Tax Department
Requirements Montana nonprofit organizations are eligible, with emphasis on Yellowstone, Meagher and Wheatland counties.
Restrictions Funding is not provided for: churches, conventions, or associations of churches; individuals; conferences; symposiums; or for fundraising events.
Areas of Interest Arts, General; Civic Affairs; Cultural Activities/Programs; Higher Education; Hospitals; Human Services; Museums; Performing Arts; Social Services; Youth Programs

Cinnabar Foundation Grants 733
Cinnabar Foundation
PO Box 5088
Helena, MT 59604
Contact James Posewitz, c/o Holmes and Turner, (406) 449-2795; fax: (406) 449-9985; e-mail: cinnabar@mt.net
Requirements Idaho, Montana, and Wyoming nonprofit organizations may apply.
Areas of Interest Conservation, Natural Resources; Environmental Programs; Wildlife

Lippard-Clawiter Foundation Grants 734
Lippard-Clawiter Foundation
PO Box 1605
Great Falls, MT 59403
Contact Rodney Thorne, Secretary-Treasurer, (406) 727-0888
Requirements Chouteau County, MT, nonprofits are eligible.
Restrictions Individuals are ineligible.
Areas of Interest Children and Youth; Community Development; Recreation and Leisure
Sample Awards Chouteau County Fair Board (Fort Benton, MT)—for renovation of fair ground buildings and for chairs, $25,000 (2000). Chouteau County Free Library Foundation (Fort Benton, MT)—for installation of elevator, $15,000 (2000).

Montana Arts Council Cultural and Aesthetic Project Grants 735
Montana Arts Council
PO Box 202201, 316 N Park Ave, Ste 252
Helena, MT 59620
Contact Director of Organizational Services, (406) 444-6430; fax: (406) 444-6548; e-mail: mac@state.mt.us
Internet http://www.art.state.mt.us/orgs/orgs_c&a.htm
Requirements Any person, association, or representative of a governing unit in Montana including, but not limited to, state, regional, county, city, town, or Indian tribal governments may submit an application. Examples of eligible applicants are county art or historical museums, public libraries, public educational institutions or school districts, state agencies, city arts commissions or parks and recreation departments, and tribal cultural or education committees.
Areas of Interest Archaeology; Archives; Children and Youth; Disabled; Elderly; Exhibitions, Collections, Performances; Folklore and Mythology; History; Literature; Media Arts; Minorities; Performing Arts; Restoration and Preservation; Rural Areas; Visual Arts; Women

Montana Arts Council Organizational Excellence Grants 736
Montana Arts Council
316 N Park Ave, Ste 252
Helena, MT 59620
Contact Kristin Han Burgoyne, Grants Director, (406) 444-6430; fax: (406) 444-6548; e-mail: khan@state.mt.us
Internet http://www.art.state.mt.us/orgs/orgs_excellence.htm
Requirements Nonprofit organizations and units of government in Montana are eligible to apply.
Restrictions Grant funds may not be used to fund permanent capital expenditures; purchase equipment, art, or ar-

tifacts; establish or develop a cash reserve; establish or add to a permanent endowment; or reduce a deficit.
Areas of Interest Arts Administration

Montana Community Foundation Grants   737
Montana Community Foundation
101 N Last Chance Gulch, Ste 211
Helena, MT 59601
Contact Grants Officer, (406) 443-8313 or (800) 443-8314; fax: (406) 442-0482; e-mail: ryaeger@mtcf.org
Internet http://www.mtcf.org
Requirements The applicant program or project to be funded must be for charitable purposes, serve the people of Montana, and not discriminate on the basis of race, religion, sex, age, or national origin when employing staff or providing services.
Restrictions The foundation will not make grants for religious purposes or lobbying. The foundation will place a lower priority on requests for endowment funds, capital campaigns, annual campaigns, debt retirement, or requests for funding from public agencies for mandated services.
Areas of Interest After-School Programs; Arts, General; Conservation, Natural Resources; Cultural Activities/Programs; Economic Development; Education; Elderly; Health Care; Orchestras; Social Services; Volunteers; Youth Programs
Sample Awards Child Care Connections (Bozeman, MT)—for a year-long match of 50 college-age volunteers and senior citizens, including training, follow-up, and monitoring, $2000. Helena Symphony Society (Helena, MT)—to continue the youth symphony program and increase youth participation in Lewis and Clark County, $2500. Community After School Activities (Billings, MT)—to purchase equipment and resource library materials for a new after-school care program, $1000.

Montana Power Foundation Grants   738
Montana Power Foundation
40 E Broadway
Butte, MT 59701-9394
Contact Bill Cain, (406) 497-2602; fax: (406) 497-2451; e-mail: bcain@mtpower.com
Internet http://www.mtpower.com
Requirements Montana nonprofits in the service area of the power company and its subsidiaries may submit grant requests.
Restrictions Health and human services funding does not support national health organizations, medical equipment purchases, or research.
Areas of Interest Civic Affairs; Conservation, Natural Resources; Cultural Activities/Programs; Elementary Education; Health Care; Higher Education; Leadership; Mathematics Education; Public Health; Safety; Scholarship Programs, General; Science Education; Secondary Education; Social Services; Youth Programs; Senior Citizen Programs and Services; Museums; Libraries; Performing Arts; Fish and Fisheries; Wildlife
Sample Awards Butte Family YMCA (Butte, MT)—operating support, $27,500. Montana Race for the Cure (Helena, MT)—program support, $2000.

Sands Memorial Foundation Grants   739
Sands Memorial Foundation
306 3rd Ave Ste 201
Havre, MT 59501
Contact LuAnn McLain, Executive Director, (406) 265-4271; fax: (406) 265-4271; e-mail: smf@hi-line.net
Requirements Montana nonprofit organizations may apply.
Restrictions Individuals are ineligible.
Areas of Interest Animal Care

Dennis and Phyllis Washington Foundation   740 Grants
Dennis and Phyllis Washington Foundation
PO Box 16630
Missoula, MT 59808-6630
Contact Russell Ritter, President, (406) 523-1320; e-mail: lpaulson@washcorp.com
Internet http://www.dpwfoundation.org
Requirements 501(c)3 nonprofit organizations in communities across Montana and the West are eligible. Preference is given to organizations that have low administrative expenses.
Restrictions Grants do not support religious organizations for religious purposes; veteran or fraternal organizations; national health organizations and programs; travel expenses; conferences and symposiums; general endowment funds; pperating expenses for tax-supported groups; Sponsorships; or fundraising activities such as auctions, dinners, advertising, etc.
Areas of Interest Alcohol/Alcoholism; Children and Youth; Community Service Programs; Disadvantaged (Economically); Domestic Violence; Drugs/Drug Abuse; Elderly; Elementary Education; Family; Health Care; Health Services Delivery; Higher Education; Hospitals; Housing; Quality of Life; Secondary Education; Shelters; Social Services Delivery; Women; Youth Programs
Sample Awards Horatio Alger Assoc (Alexandria, VA)—to provide college scholarships for students from Montana who plan to attend the U of Montana, $1 million over four years (2003).

Nebraska

Abel Foundation Grants   741
Abel Foundation
PO Box 80268
Lincoln, NE 68501-0268
Contact J. Ross McCown, Vice President, (402) 434-1212
Requirements Nebraska nonprofit organizations are eligible. Preference is given to requests from Licoln, NE, and the state's southeastern area.
Areas of Interest Churches; Conservation, Natural Resources; Environmental Programs; Higher Education; Religion; Social Services; Social Services Delivery

ConAgra Foundation Grants   742
ConAgra Foundation
1 ConAgra Dr
Omaha, NE 68102-5001

Contact Lynne Phares, Corporate Relations Department CC-304, (402) 595-4000; fax: (402) 595-4595
Internet http://www.conagra.com/leadership/community_foundation.jsp
Requirements Eligible organizations must have been in existence for at least one year, have 501(c)3 tax-exempt status, and be located in California, Colorado, Illinois, Minnesota, Nebraska, or Wisconsin.
Restrictions The foundation does not support individuals; fundraising and testimonial events/dinners; organizations with a limited constituency, such as clubs, fraternal, athletic, or social organizations; religious organizations for religious endeavors; travel or tours; advertising; K-12 education institutions; radio or TX programming; emergency operating support; or for-profit organizations.
Areas of Interest Arts, General; Children and Youth; Civic Affairs; Cultural Activities/Programs; Education; Health Care; Hunger; International Programs; Nutrition/ Dietetics; Social Services

Cooper Foundation Grants 743
Cooper Foundation
211 N 12th St, Ste 304
Lincoln, NE 68508-1411
Contact Grants Administrator, (402) 476-7571; fax: (402) 476-2356; e-mail: info@cooperfoundation.org
Internet http://www.cooperfoundation.org
Requirements Nebraska 501(c)3 organizations are eligible.
Restrictions Grants will not be made to support individuals, endowments, private foundations, businesses, proposals devoted to health issues, or proposals of a religious nature.
Areas of Interest Arts, General; Children and Youth; Curriculum Development; Economic Development; Education; Environmental Programs; Family; Humanities; International Relations; Parks; Performing Arts; Social Services; Undergraduate Education
Sample Awards Meadowlark Music Festival (Lincoln, NE)—for its 2003 and 2004 classical-music festivals, $10,000 (2003). Nature Conservancy-Nebraska Chapter (Omaha, NE)—for salary support of a coordinator focusing on the rare saline wetlands in Nebraska's Lancaster and Saunders Counties, $15,000 (2003). First Plymouth Preschool and Discovery Days (Lincoln, NE)—to develop a curriculum that advances young children's visual and spatial skills, $29,200 (2003). Sunrise Equi'Therapy (Eagle, NE)—for general operating support of this therapeutic riding program, $10,000 (2003).

Peter Kiewit Foundation Grants 744
Peter Kiewit Foundation
8805 Indian Hills Dr, Ste 225
Omaha, NE 68114
Contact Lynn Wallin Ziegenbein, Executive Director, (402) 344-7890; fax: (402) 344-8099
Requirements Nonprofit organizations in Rancho Mirage, California; western IA; Nebraska; and Sheridan, Wyoming are eligible.
Restrictions Grants are not awarded to support elementary or secondary schools, churches, or religious groups.

Grants are not awarded to individuals (except for scholarships), or for endowment funds or annual campaigns.
Areas of Interest Arts, General; Community Development; Cultural Activities/Programs; Education; Health Care; Higher Education; Public Administration; Rural Areas; Social Services; Youth Programs
Sample Awards U of Nebraska Medical Ctr (Omaha, NE)—for the proposed Research Center of Excellence, $17.5 million (2001).

Lincoln Community Foundation Grants 745
Lincoln Community Foundation
215 Centennial Mall S, Ste 200
Lincoln, NE 68508
Contact Program Contact, (402) 474-2345; fax: (402) 476-8532; e-mail: lcf@lcf.org
Internet http://www.lcf.org
Requirements IRS 501(c)3 organizations serving the Lincoln, NE, area are eligible.
Restrictions Grants are not awarded to individuals, and requests are generally not considered for religious purposes, political purposes, endowments, programs outside the Lincoln/Lancaster County area, routine operating expenses, large capital expenditures, budget deficits, and projects with future annual commitments.
Areas of Interest Arts, General; Civic Affairs; Cultural Activities/Programs; Economic Development; Education; Emergency Programs; Environmental Education; Health Care; History Education; Preschool Education; Social Services
Sample Awards 7th Street Loft Consortium (Lincoln, NE)—to develop a capital campaign, $11,500 (2003). Good Neighbor Community Ctr (Lincoln, NE)—for salary support of a part-time coordinator responsible for resource development and volunteer management, $14,000 (2003). Lincoln Literacy Council (Lincoln, NE)—for a program that promotes greater parental involvement in their children's education and activities, $14,736 (2003).

Nebraska Arts Council Basic Support Grants 746
Nebraska Arts Council
3838 Davenport St
Omaha, NE 68131-2329
Contact Elaine Buescher, Grants Manager, (800) 341-4067 or (402) 595-2122; fax: (402) 595-2334; e-mail: ebuescher@nebraskaartscouncil.org
Internet http://www.nebraskaartscouncil.org/NAC_Programs/NACPRGMS.HTM
Requirements Nebraska nonprofit, tax-exempt organizations that dedicate 51 percent or more of their budget to producing or sponsoring arts events or to providing arts services are eligible. In addition, if applying organizations are not currently participating in a community challenge grant program, they must have done so three years prior to application in this category.
Areas of Interest Arts Administration; Volunteers

Phelps County Community Foundation Grants 747
Phelps County Community Foundation
701 Fourth Ave, Ste 2A
Holdrege, NE 68949

Contact Julene Schoen, Executive Director, (308) 995-6847; fax: (308) 995-2146
Requirements Grants are made to 501(c)3 nonprofit organizations in Nebraska and sometimes to governmental agencies for capital expenditures and/or capital improvements within Phelps County.
Restrictions Grants are not made to individuals, to support political activities, to support operating expenses of well-established organizations or public service agencies, to established or new endowment funds, for travel or related expenses for individuals or groups, for operating support of governmental agencies, to religious groups for religious purposes, to profit-making enterprises, or to agencies serving a populace outside of Phelps County. In addition, grants are not made to support annual fund drives or to eliminate previously incurred deficits.
Areas of Interest Citizenship; Community Development; Cultural Activities/Programs; Education; Elderly; Health Care; Libraries; Social Services; Volunteers
Sample Awards Methodist Memorial Homes (Holdrege, NE)—to purchase a new whirlpool bath, $4000. Young at Heart Senior Ctr (Bertrand, NE)—to purchase appliances, $500. City of Holdrege (Holdrege, NE)—to replace welcome signs, $1400. Public Library System (Holdrege, NE)—to assist with renovation costs, $6000.

Union Pacific Foundation Grants Program   748
Union Pacific Corporation
1416 Dodge St, Rm 802
Omaha, NE 69179
Contact Union Pacific Foundation, (402) 271-5600; fax: (402) 271-5477; e-mail: upf@up.com
Internet http://www.up.com/found/grants.shtml
Requirements The foundation will accept only online applications; printed copies of the application are not available and will not be accepted. Grants are made to institutions located in communities served by Union Pacific Corporation and its operating company Union Pacific Railroad Company.
Restrictions Grants will not be given to organizations that are not tax-exempt; specialized national health organizations; political organizations; organizations engaged in influencing legislation; religious organizations that are sectarian or denominational in purpose; veterans organizations; labor groups, social clubs, fraternal organizations, or individuals. United Way-affiliated organizations may apply only for capital projects that have received written approval from United Way.
Areas of Interest Arts Administration; Arts, General; Children and Youth; Cultural Activities/Programs; Dance; Environmental Programs; Health Care; Higher Education, Private; Hospitals; Land Management; Museums; Opera/Musical Theater; Orchestras; Performing Arts; Rehabilitation/Therapy; Social Services; Water Resources, Management/Planning; Youth Programs

Woods Charitable Fund Grants   749
Woods Charitable Fund
PO Box 81309
Lincoln, NE 68501
Contact Pam Baker, (402) 436-5971; fax: (402) 436-4128; e-mail: pbaker@woodscharitable.org

Internet http://www.woodscharitable.org/grants.html
Requirements Eligible applicants are 501(c)3 organizations that serve Lincoln, NE.
Restrictions Grants are not awarded to support individual needs, endowments, scholarships or fellowships, fund-raising benefits or program advertising, religious programs, capital projects in health care institutions, or medical and scientific research.
Areas of Interest Arts, General; Children and Youth; Civic Affairs; Community Service Programs; Cultural Activities/Programs; Day Care; Domestic Violence; Education; Elderly; Family; Hispanics; Immigrants; Performing Arts; Public Planning/Policy; Refugees; Shelters; Single-Parent Families; Violent Behavior; Women; Youth Programs; Youth Violence
Sample Awards Indian Ctr (Lincoln, NE)—to distribute food to disadvantaged children and elderly peole in Lincoln and Lancaster County, NE, $20,000 partial challenge grant (2003). Lincoln Interfaith Council (NE)—to strenthen the African Multicultural Community Center, $10,000 (2003). United Methodist Ministries (Lincoln, NE)—for Equity in Nebraska, a public-education and litigation program to advance the legal rights of low-income victims of injustice, $10,000 (2003). Cedar's Youth Services (Lincoln, NE)—to build a community center that will offer programs in early-childhood development, English as a second language, health services, and job training, $50,000 (2003).

Nevada

Cord Foundation Grants   750
Cord Foundation
1 E First St
Reno, NV 89501
Contact William Bradley, Trustee, (775) 323-0373
Requirements Nonprofit organizations are eligible but giving is primarily in the northern NV area.
Restrictions The foundation does not support general fund-raising events, memorial campaigns, deficit fundings, conferences, dinners, or mass mailings.
Areas of Interest Arts, General; Community Service Programs; Education; Higher Education; Legal Education; Medical Education; Military Sciences; Performing Arts; Religion; Social Services; Visual Arts; Youth Programs
Sample Awards George Washington U (Washington, DC)—for the medical school and law school, $100,000. Nevada Self-Help Foundation (Reno, NV)—for administrative support, $30,500. Saint Johns Military Academy (Delafield, WI)—for operating and enhancement support, $50,000.

Gabelli Foundation Grants   751
Gabelli Foundation
165 W Liberty St
Reno, NV 89501-1915
Contact Mario Gabelli, c/o Avansino, Melarkey, and Knobel, (702) 333-0360
Areas of Interest Fine Arts; Higher Education; Hospitals; Museums; Secondary Education
Sample Awards Nevada Museum of Art (Reno, NV)—for operating support, $1000. Boston College (Chestnut

Hill, MA)—for the building fund, $120,000. Roger Williams U (Bristol, RI)—for operating support, $10,000.

Nevada Community Foundation Grants   752
Nevada Community Foundation
1850 E Sahara Ave, Ste 207
Las Vegas, NV 89104
Contact Lou Gamage, President, (702) 892-2326; fax: (702) 892-8580; e-mail: lou@nevadacf.org
Internet http://www.nevadacf.org
Requirements Las Vegas, NV, nonprofits are eligible.
Areas of Interest Adult and Continuing Education; Alcohol/Alcoholism; Basic Skills Education; Children and Youth; Citizenship; Community Development; Drugs/Drug Abuse; Elderly; Family; Health Care; Immigrants; Literacy; Mental Health; Public Administration; Public Affairs; Women; Youth Programs

Nevada State Council on the Arts   753
   Community Arts Development Grants
Nevada State Council on the Arts
716 N Carson St, Ste A
Carson City, NV 89701
Contact Robin Hodgkin, Community Arts Development Coordinator, (775) 687-7109; fax: (775) 687-6688; e-mail: rahodgki@clan.lib.nv.us
Internet http://dmla.clan.lib.nv.us/docs/arts/comm/commarts.htm
Requirements Any Nevada-based nonprofit, tax-exempt community organization, or local government entity (Developing Communities); or nonprofit tax-exempt rural performing arts presenter or significant arts organizations (Developing Arts Organizations) that wishes to expand programming or solve organizational community issues may apply.
Areas of Interest Arts Administration; Audience Development; Rural Areas; Urban Areas

Nevada State Council on the Arts   754
   Established Organizational Support Grants
Nevada State Council on the Arts
716 N Carson St, Ste A
Carson City, NV 89703
Contact Grants Program Coordinator, (775) 687-6680; fax: (775) 687-6688
Internet http://dmla.clan.lib.nv.us/docs/arts
Requirements Applicants must be Nevada tax-exempt, nonprofit organizations with at least three years of professional programming providing the resident communities with a regular schedule of activities, such as exhibits, theater or concert seasons, community service programs, educational programs, specialized touring activities, and training programs; have an operating cash budget over $300,000 in the last fiscal year; have a three-year plan; and have paid professional staff and established season's services.
Areas of Interest Art Education; Arts Administration; Community Service Programs; Dramatic/Theater Arts; Exhibitions, Collections, Performances; Performing Arts; Touring Arts Programs

Nevada State Council on the Arts Large   755
   Organizational Support Grants
Nevada State Council on the Arts
602 N Curry St, Capitol Complex
Carson City, NV 89703
Contact Grants Program Coordinator, (775) 687-6680; fax: (775) 687-6688
Internet http://dmla.clan.lib.nv.us/docs/arts
Requirements Applicants must be Nevada tax-exempt, nonprofit organizations and public institutions that have completed two years of effective programming and have an operating cash budget over $100,000.
Areas of Interest Arts Administration; Training and Development

Nevada State Council on the Arts Partners in   756
   Excellence Grants
Nevada State Council on the Arts
716 N Carson St, Ste A
Carson City, NV 89701
Contact Grants Program Coordinator, (775) 687-6680; fax: (775) 687-6688
Internet http://dmla.clan.lib.nv.us/docs/arts/grants/grantsg.pdf
Requirements Applicants must be Nevada tax-exempt, nonprofit organizations with at least two years of effective programming, including at least one year with a paid staff, and an operating cash budget over $25,001.
Areas of Interest Arts Administration

Nevada State Council on the Arts Small   757
   Organization Support
Nevada State Council on the Arts
716 N Carson St, Ste A
Carson City, NV 89701
Contact Kellie O'Donnell, Grants Program Coordinator, (775) 687-6680; fax: (775) 687-6688; e-mail: kjodonne@clan.lib.nv.us
Internet http://dmla.clan.lib.nv.us/docs/arts/grants/grantsprog.htm
Requirements Applicants must be Nevada tax-exempt, nonprofit organizations and public institutions that have completed two years of effective programming and have an operating cash budget under $25,000.
Areas of Interest Arts Administration

William N. and Myriam Pennington   758
   Foundation Grants
William N. and Myriam Pennington Foundation
441 W Plumb Ln
Reno, NV 89509
Contact Kent Green, Foundation Manager, (775) 333-9100
Requirements Nevada nonprofits may apply for grant support.
Areas of Interest Biomedical Research; Cancer/Carcinogenesis; Children and Youth; Disadvantaged (Economically); Education; Elderly; Health Care
Sample Awards Assistance League of Reno-Sparks (Reno, NV)—for general support, $15,000. U of Nevada, Department of Speech Pathology (Reno, NV)—for equipment, $17,500.

Ray Foundation Mental Health and Substance Abuse Prevention Grants   759
Ray Foundation
2241 Park Place, Ste A1
Minden, NV 89423
Contact Program Contact, (775) 782-8337
Requirements Youth agencies in the Pacific Northwest are eligible to apply.
Restrictions Grants are not made to individuals or for deficit funding, and no support is given to religious organizations unless they are requesting funds for a community project.
Areas of Interest Alcohol/Alcoholism; Aviation; Children and Youth; Drugs/Drug Abuse; Fine Arts; Higher Education; History; Mental Health; Preventive Medicine; Sports; Youth Programs

Southwest Gas Corporation Foundation Grants   760
Southwest Gas Corporation
PO Box 98510
Las Vegas, NV 89193-8510
Contact Suzanne Farinas, (702) 876-7247; fax: (702) 876-7037
Internet http://www.swgas.com
Requirements Nonprofit organizations in Arizona; San Bernardino County, CA; and Nevada may apply.
Areas of Interest Arts, General; Community Development; Community Service Programs; Cultural Activities/Programs; Education; Elderly; Elementary Education; Environmental Programs; Health Care; Higher Education; Secondary Education; Social Services; Social Services Delivery; Women; Youth Programs
Sample Awards Phoenix Art Museum (Phoenix, AZ)—for general support, $3000. Boys and Girls Clubs (Tucson, AZ)—for general support, $1000. Community Food Bank (Phoenix, AZ)—for general support, $3500.

New Hampshire

Barker Foundation Grants   761
Barker Foundation
PO Box 328
Nashua, NH 03061-0328
Contact Allan Barker, Treasurer
Requirements New Hampshire nonprofit organizations are eligible.
Areas of Interest Children and Youth; Education; Health Care; Hospitals; Scholarship Programs, General; Social Services

Norwin S. and Elizabeth N. Bean Foundation Grants   762
Norwin S. and Elizabeth N. Bean Foundation
37 Pleasant St
Concord, NH 03301-4005
Contact Nike Speltz, Senior Program Officer, (603) 225-6641; fax: (603) 225-1700
Requirements Applications are accepted from nonprofit 501(c)3 organizations and municipal and public agencies serving the communities of Manchester and Amherst, NH. Priority consideration is given to organizations operating primarily in those two communities;

however, the foundation will consider applications from statewide or regional organizations that provide a substantial and documented level of service to those communities.
Restrictions The foundation does not make grants to individuals or provide scholarship aid.
Areas of Interest Arts, General; Community Development; Education; Environmental Studies; Equipment/Instrumentation; Health Care; Humanities; Restoration and Preservation; Social Services

Alexander Eastman Foundation Grants   763
Alexander Eastman Foundation
37 Pleasant St
Concord, NH 03301-4005
Contact Donna Dunlop, (603) 225-6641
Requirements Nonprofit organizations serving Derry, Londonderry, Windham, Chester, Hampstead, and Sandown, NH, are eligible.
Areas of Interest Dental Health and Hygiene; Health Care Access; Health Care Assessment; Health Promotion; Parent Education
Sample Awards Londonderry School District (NH)—to support a dental hygiene program, $31,708. Upper Room Education for Parenting (NH)—to support the Tips program, $20,000. Seacoast HealthNet (NH)—for general support, $1000.

Fuller Foundation Grants   764
Fuller Foundation
PO Box 479
Rye Beach, NH 03871
Contact John Bottomley, Executive Director, (603) 964-6998; e-mail: atfuller@aol.com
Internet http://www.fullerfoundation.org
Requirements Nonprofits in the Boston, MA, area and the immediate seacost region of New Hampshire are eligible.
Restrictions Grants do not support individuals, seed money, publications, capital projects, United Way-funded organizations, or conferences and seminars.
Areas of Interest Alcohol/Alcoholism; Animal Care; Art Education; Arts, General; At-Risk Youth; Dramatic/Theater Arts; Drugs/Drug Abuse; Environmental Education; Leadership; Museum Education; Opera/Musical Theater; Orchestras; Performing Arts; Recreation and Leisure; Tobacco; Veterinary Medicine; Wildlife

Healthy New Hampshire Foundation Grants 765
Healthy New Hampshire Foundation
14 Dixon Ave
Concord, NH 03301
Contact Sandi Van Scoyoc, Executive Director, (603) 229-3260; fax: (603) 229-3259
Requirements New Hampshire nonprofit organizations are eligible.
Areas of Interest Children and Youth; Community Outreach Programs; Education; Health Care; Health Insurance; Health Promotion; Service Delivery Programs
Sample Awards Home Health and Hospice Care (Nashua, NH)—to support an outreach program for uninsured children, $10,000. North Country Health Consortium (NH)—for health insurance for small busi-

nesses, $35,361. Community Health Access Network (Newmarket, NH)—to support chronic-disease education programs, $34,433.

Oleonda Jameson Trust Grants 766

Oleonda Jameson Trust
1 Eagle Sq, PO Box 3550
Concord, NH 03302-3550
Contact Malcolm McLane, Trustee, (603) 224-2381; fax: (603) 224-2318
Requirements New Hampshire nonprofit organizations are eligible. Requests from Concord nonprofits receive preference.
Restrictions Grants do not support endowments.
Areas of Interest Arts, General; Children and Youth; Community Development; Cultural Activities/Programs; Health Care; Housing; Internet; Social Services

New Hampshire State Council on the Arts 767
Professional Advancement Grants

New Hampshire State Council on the Arts
2 1/2 Beacon St, 2nd Fl
Concord, NH 03301-4974
Contact Yvonne Stahr, Assistant Director, (603) 271-0791; e-mail: ystahr@nharts.state.nh.us
Internet http://www.nh.gov/nharts/grantsandservices/index.html
Requirements Eligible applicants include New Hampshire nonprofit organizations, arts organizations seeking assistance to incorporate in the state within the next 12 months, and cultural facilities seeking planning assistance. Applicants who have not received funding through this program previously are given preference. Preference will also be given to smaller community arts organizations with all volunteer or part-time staff in particular need of assistance.
Restrictions These grants may not be used to produce or present specific arts events or to produce marketing, fund-raising or education materials. Nor may grants be used for independent contractors that the organization hires on an ongoing basis such as an accountant, grant writer, advertising firm, or lawyer on retainer. No organization or individual may receive more than one Professional Advancement grant per year.
Areas of Interest Architecture; Arts Administration; Audience Development; Planning/Policy Studies; Scholarship Programs, General; Training and Development

Putnam Foundation Grants 768

Putnam Foundation
PO Box 323
Keene, NH 03431-0323
Contact David Putnam, Senior Treasurer, (603) 352-2448
Requirements New Hampshire nonprofit organizations serving the Monadnock region are eligible.
Areas of Interest Civic Affairs; Conservation, Natural Resources; Cultural Activities/Programs; Ecology; Education; Environmental Programs; History; Public Affairs
Sample Awards Saint James Episcopal Church (NH)—for general operating support, $100,000. YMCA of Cheshire County, for general operating support,

$20,000. Historical Society of New Hampshire (NH)—for general operating support, $10,000.

New Jersey

Russell Berrie Foundation Grants 769

Russell Berrie Foundation
111 Bauer Dr
Oakland, NJ 07436-3192
Contact Susan Strunk, Administrative Director, (201) 337-9000; fax: (201) 405-7907
Internet http://www.russberrie.com/foundation.html
Requirements Christian, Jewish, and Roman Catholic organizations in New Jersey are eligible.
Areas of Interest Biomedical Research; Cancer/Carcinogenesis; Health Care; Higher Education; Hospitals; International Programs; Israel; Jewish Studies; Long-Term Care; Private and Parochial Education; Rehabilitation/Therapy; Religion; Religious Studies; Social Services; Youth Programs
Sample Awards Columbia U, Naomi Berrie Diabetes Ctr (New York, NY)—for research on cellular therapy as a potential treatment for diabetes, $12 million (2003). William Paterson U (Wayne, NJ)—to create the Institute for Professional Selling at the university's College of Business, which will develop professional and academic programs for undergraduate students and sales professionals, $5 million maximum over five years (2002).

Bildner Family Foundation Grants 770

Bildner Family Foundation
293 Eisenhower Pkwy, Ste 150
Livingston, NJ 07039
Contact Allen Bildner, President
Restrictions The foundation does not support private foundations or individuals.
Areas of Interest Arts, General; Food Banks; Health Care; Health Promotion; Hospitals; Jewish Services; Performing Arts; Theater
Sample Awards Rutgers, (New Brunswick, NJ)—for general support, $162,197. Bergen Community College (Paramus, NJ)—to develop the Center for the Study of International Understanding, $225,000 (2002).

Black United Fund of New Jersey Grants 771

Black United Fund of New Jersey
132 S Harrison St
East Orange, NJ 07018
Contact Sondra Clark, President, (973) 676-5283; fax: (973) 672-5030; e-mail: info@bufnj.org
Internet http://www.bufnj.org
Requirements New Jersey 501(c)3 nonprofit, tax-exempt agencies, community-based organizations, and schools are eligible.
Areas of Interest AIDS Education; African Americans; Alcohol/Alcoholism; Arts, General; Cultural Activities/Programs; Drugs/Drug Abuse; Education; Family; Health Care; Homelessness; Housing; Leadership; Recreation and Leisure; Social Services Delivery; Teen Pregnancy; Youth Programs

Mary Owen Borden Foundation Grants 772

Mary Owen Borden Foundation
160 Hodge Rd
Princeton, NJ 08540-3014
Contact Thomas Borden, Executive Director, (609) 252-9492; fax: (609) 252-9472; e-mail: tborden@ibm.net
Internet http://fdncenter.org/grantmaker/borden/guide.html
Requirements New Jersey nonprofits in Monmouth and Mercer Counties are eligible.
Areas of Interest Alcohol/Alcoholism; Arts, General; At-Risk Youth; Conflict/Dispute Resolution; Conservation, Natural Resources; Counseling/Guidance; Cultural Activities/Programs; Day Care; Disadvantaged (Economically); Drugs/Drug Abuse; Education; Environmental Programs; Family; Family Planning; Health Care; Housing; Juvenile Delinquency; Youth Programs
Sample Awards Young Scholars' Institute (Trenton, NJ)—to support after-school, Saturday, and summer programs for more than 200 students (K-12), $18,500. Union Industrial Home (Trenton, NJ)—to provide residential care for young unwed mothers and their children, and support a program for young fathers, $14,000. Peace Action Education Fund (Princeton, NJ)—to provide conflict resolution training to Trenton youth, $12,500.

Bunbury Company Grants 773

Bunbury Company
2 Railroad Pl
Hopewell, NJ 08525
Contact Grants Administrator, (609) 333-8800; fax: (609) 333-8900
Internet http://www.bunburycompany.org/grant-guidelines.html
Requirements New Jersey nonprofit organizations in Burlington, Camden, Hunterdon, Mercer, Middlesex, Monmouth, Ocean, and Somerset Counties are eligible. Emphasis will be given to organizations located in Mercer County.
Areas of Interest Arts, General; Children and Youth; Disadvantaged (Economically); Ecology; Environmental Health; Environmental Programs; Families

Campbell Soup Foundation Grants 774

Campbell Soup Foundation
1 Campbell Pl, Box 60D
Camden, NJ 08103-1799
Contact Wendy Milanese, Grant Administrator, (856) 342-6423; fax: (856) 541-8185; e-mail: wendy_milanese@campbellsoup.com
Internet http://www.campbellsoupcompany.com/community_center.asp
Requirements Grants are limited to 501(c)3 tax-exempt organizations in New Jersey. The foundation encourages grant requests for projects that anticipate funding from other sources and that would not rely on the foundation for total support.
Restrictions Grants are not made to individuals or to organizations based outside the United States and its possessions.
Areas of Interest Children and Youth; Community Development; Equipment/Instrumentation; Family;

Homeownership; Scholarship Programs, General; Volunteers
Sample Awards Joseph's Carpenter Society (Camden, NJ)—to support the Campbell Soup Homeowners Academy, which teaches skills needed to own a home, $100,000.

Cape Branch Foundation Grants 775

Cape Branch Foundation
5 Independence Way
Princeton, NJ 08540
Contact Dorothy Frank, c/o Danser, Balaam and Frank, (609) 987-0300; fax: (609) 452-1024
Requirements New Jersey nonprofit organization are eligible.
Areas of Interest Conservation, Natural Resources; Education; Museums; Secondary Education; Water Resources; Wetlands
Sample Awards Edison Wetlands Assoc (Edison, NJ)—for the Raritan River project, $10,000.

Capezio/Ballet Makers Inc Grants and 776 Awards

Capezio/Ballet Makers Inc
1 Campus Rd
Totowa, NJ 07512
Contact Grants and Program Director, (973) 595-9000 ext 203; fax: (973) 595-0341
Internet http://www.capeziodance.com/about.htm?foundation
Requirements Organizations must provide evidence of nonprofit status in their letters of application.
Restrictions Awards are not made to individuals, companies, schools, or organizations for which dance is not a major priority.
Areas of Interest Dance; Scholarship Programs, General

Cowles Charitable Trust Grants 777

Cowles Charitable Trust
PO Box 219
Rumson, NJ 07760
Contact Gardner Cowles III, President, (732) 936-9826
Requirements Nonprofit organizations may apply for grant support. Grants are awarded primarily along the Eastern Seaboard.
Areas of Interest AIDS; Adult and Continuing Education; Arts, General; Basic Skills Education; Civil/Human Rights; Cultural Activities/Programs; Education; Environmental Programs; Family Planning; Higher Education; Hospitals; Leadership; Literacy; Medical Education; Museums; Performing Arts; Preschool Education; Racism/Race Relations; Secondary Education; Social Services

CRH Foundation Grants 778

CRH Foundation
175 N Woodland St
Englewood, NJ 07631
Contact Susan Harris, Secretary, (201) 568-9300; fax: (201) 568-6374

Requirements US 501(c)3 nonprofit organizations may apply.

Areas of Interest Cancer/Carcinogenesis; Health Care; Jewish Services; Poverty and the Poor; Religion; Social Services

Sample Awards United Jewish Community (River Edge, NJ)—$4000 (1999). New York Times Neediest Cases (New York, NY)—$1000 (1999). American Cancer Society (Atlanta, GA)—$1000 (1999).

Danellie Foundation Grants   779
Danellie Foundation
PO Box 376
Marlton, NJ 08053
Contact Daniel Cheney, President, (856) 810-8320
Requirements Nonprofit organizations in New Jersey are eligible to apply.
Restrictions Grants are not made to individuals or for university capital campaigns or scholarship funds.
Areas of Interest Churches; Community Outreach Programs; Education; Health Care; Housing; International Programs; Methodist Church; Poverty and the Poor; Religion; Scholarship Programs, General

Geraldine R. Dodge Foundation Grants   780
   Program
Geraldine R. Dodge Foundation
PO Box 1239, 163 Madison Ave
Morristown, NJ 07962-1239
Contact David Grant, Executive Director, (973) 540-8442; fax: (973) 540-1211; e-mail: info@grdodge. org
Internet http://www.grdodge.org/guidelines.html
Requirements The foundation awards grant to 501(c)3 nonprofits primarily in New Jersey, New England, and Middle Atlantic states.
Restrictions Grants are not made to individuals or for the support of religion, higher education, health, international programs, conduit organizations, capital projects, deficit financing, or endowment funds.
Areas of Interest Animal Care; Animal Rights; Animals for Assistance/Therapy; Arts, General; Elementary Education; Environmental Programs; Hearing Impairments; Public Affairs; Secondary Education; Veterinary Medicine; Visual Impairments; Wildlife
Sample Awards George Street Playhouse (New Brunswick, NJ)—for the New Works Initiative and Education program, $175,000 (2003). Mid Atlantic Arts Foundation (Baltimore, MD)—for New Jersey artists and organizations to participate in the Artists Residency Program, $75,000 (2003). Saint Hubert's Animal Welfare Ctr (Madison, NJ)—to produce a special newsletter and to transport and store excess dog food donated to search-and-rescue dogs involved in rescue efforts following the September 11 attacks, $5000 (2002). National Public Radio (Washington, DC)—for expanded and special programming related to September 11, $50,000 (2002).

Fund for New Jersey Grants   781
Fund for New Jersey
94 Church St, Ste 303
New Brunswick, NJ 08901

Contact Mark Murphy, Executive Director, (732) 220-8656; fax: (732) 220-8654; e-mail: info@ fundfornj.org
Internet http://www.fundfornj.org/app_guide.html
Requirements 501(c)3 tax-exempt organizations are eligible. Proposals are not accepted via e-mail.
Restrictions The fund does not accept proposals for support of individuals nor for capital projects such as acquisition, renovation, or equipment. The fund is unable to support day care centers, drug treatment programs, arts programs, health care delivery, or scholarships.
Areas of Interest AIDS; Aquariums; Higher Education, Private; Public Planning/Policy; Science; Transportation; Urban Areas; Urban Planning/Policy
Sample Awards Isles Inc (Trenton, NJ)—to encourage citizens and community leaders in New Jersey's Mercer region to address education, housing, land-use, and tax-reform issues, $25,000 (2003). Stony Brook-Millstone Watershed Assoc (Pennington, NJ)—for projects to combat sprawl, including the development of a model for managing municipal water resources, $70,000 (2003). New Jerseyans for a Death Penalty Moratorium, New Jersey Assoc (NJ)—to educate citizens and government leaders about concerns surrounding the use of capital punishment, $50,000 (2003). Regional Plan Assoc (New York, NY)—to advocate a new train tunnel that would provide access to the East Side of Manhattan, $25,000 (2003).

Honeywell Foundation Grants   782
Honeywell Foundation
101 Columbia Rd
Morristown, NJ 07962
Contact Andre Lewis, Vice President and Executive Director, (973) 455-5876; fax: (612) 951-0433
Internet http://www.honeywell.com/about/foundation. html
Requirements Nonprofit organizations in company-operating areas are eligible. Areas include Arizona, Florida, Illinois, Minnesota, and New Mexico.
Restrictions Grants do not support individuals, church-related programs, special interest groups (such as labor or veterans) unless activity benefits entire community, political organizations, or for international organizations.
Areas of Interest Aging/Gerontology; Cultural Activities/Programs; Education; Health Care; Higher Education; International Programs; Scholarship Programs, General; Social Services; Youth Programs

Huber Foundation Grants   783
Huber Foundation
PO Box 277
Rumson, NJ 07760
Contact Lorraine Barnhart, Executive Director, (908) 933-7700
Requirements US nonprofits, including advocacy groups, hospitals, legal defense groups, family planning agencies, educational organizations, universities, and women's groups may submit grant applications.
Restrictions The foundation will not consider grants to individuals, foreign organizations, capital campaigns, scholarships, endowment funds, research, international projects, or film productions.

Areas of Interest Family Planning; Human Reproduction/Fertility; Population Control

Sample Awards Planned Parenthood Federation of America (New York, NY)—for general support and Responsible Choices Campaign, $700,000. Feminist Majority Foundation (Arlington, VA)—for the National Clinic Access Project, $100,000. Planned Parenthood of Northern New England (Williston, VT)—for general support, $90,000.

Janx Foundation Grants 784

Janx Foundation
PO Box 187, 178 Devon Rd
Essex Fells, NJ 07021
Contact Grants Administrator, c/o Janx Partners LP; e-mail: janxfoundation@aol.com
Internet http://fdncenter.org/grantmaker/janx
Requirements The foundation limits its giving to grant proposals from organizations located in the greater New York/New Jersey metropolitan area.
Areas of Interest Education; Training and Development; Urban Areas; Youth Programs

Johnson & Johnson Grants Program 785

Johnson & Johnson
1 Johnson & Johnson Plaza
New Brunswick, NJ 08933
Contact Laura Bauer, Project Director, (229) 928-1234; fax: (229) 931-2663; e-mail: laura@rci.gsw.edu
Internet http://www.jnj.com/community/contributions/programs/JohnsonJohnsonCaregiversProgram.htm
Requirements Grants are awarded to nonprofit and tax-exempt local, national, and international organizations and institutions.
Restrictions Grants are not awarded to individuals, for deficit funding, capital or endowment funds, demonstration projects, or publications.
Areas of Interest Addictions; Alcohol/Alcoholism; Biomedical Research; Child/Maternal Health; Drugs/Drug Abuse; Education; Employment Opportunity Programs; Family; Health Care; Health Care Access; Health Services Delivery; Health and Safety Education; Higher Education; Job Training Programs; Leadership; Management Sciences; Minority Education; Preschool Education; Preventive Medicine; Teacher Education
Sample Awards Easter Seals Arkansas (LIttle Rock, AR)—to expand its Early Head Start Program for at-risk children, $25,000 (2003). Easter Seals Children's Development Ctr (Rockford, IL)—for a project that helps parents and staff members understand how sensory experiences affect children's behavior, $25,000 (2003). Easter Seals New Hampshire (Manchester, NH)—to provide in-home medical rehabilitation, including assistive technology and advocacy services, $30,000 (2003).

Karma Foundation Grants 786

Karma Foundation
18 Upper Brook Dr
North Brunswick, NJ 08902
Contact Dina Karmazin Elkins, Executive Director, (818) 760-6545; fax: (818) 760-6777; e-mail: info@karmafoundation.org

Internet http://www.karmafoundation.org
Requirements National and international nonprofit organizations are eligible.
Restrictions Grants do not support travel expenses for bands or sports teams, political or lobbying activities, advertising for fundraising events, litigation, charter schools, or loans.
Areas of Interest AIDS; Arts, General; Cultural Activities/Programs; Disaster Relief; Education; Food Banks; Health Care; International Programs; Jewish Services; Literacy; Social Services
Sample Awards Wheaton Village—to purchase a computerized collection management system and to train personnel at the Museum of AmericanGlass, $15,900 (2001). Children's Hospital of Los Angeles (CA)—for medical equipment for the emergency transport team, $18,081 (2001). First Concern (Somerset, NJ)—to refurbish the kitchen and laundry room, $25,000 (2001). National Jewish Medical and Research Ctr—for asthma research, $10,000 (2001).

F.M. Kirby Foundation Grants 787

F.M. Kirby Foundation
PO Box 151, 17 DeHart St.
Morristown, NJ 07963-0151
Contact S. Dillard Kirby, Executive Director, (973) 538-4800
Internet http://www.fdncenter.org/grantmaker/kirby
Requirements North Carolina, New Jersey, and Pennsylvania tax-exempt organizations are eligible.
Restrictions Grants are not made to individuals or to public foundations, for loans, or to underwrite fund-raising activities and benefits.
Areas of Interest Alzheimer's Disease; Arts, General; Biomedical Research; Business Education; Cerebral Palsy; Child/Maternal Health; Civic Affairs; Dramatic/Theater Arts; Education; Epilepsy; Health Care; Hospitals; Humanities; Public Affairs; Public Planning/Policy; Religion; Social Services; Youth Programs
Sample Awards Wake Forest U (Winston-Salem, NC)—to construct a wing at the Wayne Calloway School of Business and Accountancy, $5 million (2000). Children's Hospital of Boston, Division of Neuroscience (Boston, MA)—for research on cerebral palsy, epilepsy, Alzheimer's disease, and other diseases and degenerative disorders, $2 million (1999). Carolina Theatre (Durham, NC)—for general operating support, $40,000.

Lucent Technologies Foundation Grants 788

Lucent Technologies Foundation
600 Mountain Ave, Rm 6F4
Murray Hill, NJ 07974
Contact Program Contact, (908) 582-7906; e-mail: foundation@lucent.com
Internet http://www.lucent.com/social/home.html
Requirements Giving is on a national basis with an emphasis on Arizona and Illinois are eligible to apply.
Areas of Interest Arts Administration; Arts, General; Child/Maternal Health; Children and Youth; Civic Affairs; Cultural Activities/Programs; Dramatic/Theater Arts; Drug Education; Economic Development; Educational Technology; Elementary Education; Emergency Programs; Engineering Education; Family; Health Care; Libraries; Literacy; National Disease Organizations; Or-

chestras; Performing Arts; Safety; Secondary Education; Social Services; Youth Programs

Merck Company Foundation Grants   789

Merck Company Foundation
PO Box 100 (WSIAF-35)
Whitehouse Station, NJ 08889-0100
Contact Foundation Administrator, (908) 423-2042; fax: (908) 423-1987
Internet http://www.merck.com
Requirements Operating support of health and social service agencies is reserved for Merck communities and generally directed through annual contributions to United Way.
Restrictions Grants are not made to political, labor, fraternal, or veterans organizations; sectarian groups; or to individuals. Except within foundation programs, grants are not given for elementary/secondary education, scholarships, fellowships, research, publications, conferences/seminars/symposia, and travel.
Areas of Interest Diagnosis, Medical; Disaster Relief; Health Care; Health Care Administration; Health Care Economics; Health Planning/Policy; Higher Education; International Education/Training; Medical Education; Neuroscience; Pediatrics; Pharmacology; Preventive Medicine; Public Planning/Policy; Science Education
Sample Awards American Red Cross (Washington, DC)—for relief efforts related to the recent widespread wildfires in California, $100,000 (2003). American Red Cross, Liberty Fund (Washington, DC), and the September 11th Fund (New York, NY)—to provide disaster-relief services to victims of the September 11th attacks, $5 million divided (2002).

National Starch and Chemical Foundation   790
Grants

National Starch and Chemical Foundation
10 Finderne Ave
Bridgewater, NJ 08807
Contact Carmen Ortiz, (908) 685-5201; e-mail: carmen.ortiz@nstarch.com
Internet http://news.nationalstarch.com/NewsStory.asp?newsItemId=214
Requirements Nonprofits in company operating areas such as Georgia, Illinois, Indiana, Missouri, North Carolina, New Jersey, Pennsylvania, South Carolina, and Tennessee may apply.
Areas of Interest Children and Youth; Higher Education; Hospitals

NJSCA General Operating Support Grants   791

New Jersey State Council on the Arts
PO Box 306, 225 W State St
Trenton, NJ 08625
Contact Program Director, (609) 292-6130; fax: (609) 989-1440; TDD: (609) 633-1186; e-mail: njsca@arts.sos.state.nj.us
Internet http://www.njartscouncil.org/program2.html
Requirements To be eligible, an applicant must be a 501(c)3 nonprofit organization or a unit of government in New Jersey, have been in existence and active for at least two years at the time of application, have a board of directors, have a clearly articulated mission relating to the arts, and demonstrate that the organization or project

is multiregional or statewide in impact. Matching funds are required.
Areas of Interest Arts Administration; Dance; Dramatic/Theater Arts; Orchestras
Sample Awards American Repertory Ballet Comp (Middlesex)—for dance general operating support, $250,000. Haddonfield Symphony Society (Camden)—for music general operating support, $177,915. Paper Mill Playhouse—for theater general operating support, $1.05 million.

NJSCA Local Arts Program Grants   792

New Jersey State Council on the Arts
20 W State St, CN 306
Trenton, NJ 08625-0306
Contact Steven Runk, Director of Programs and Services, (609) 292-6130; fax: (609) 989-1440; TDD: (609) 633-1186; e-mail: steve@arts.sos.state.nj.us
Internet http://www.njartscouncil.org/program2.html
Requirements To be eligible, an applicant must be a 501(c)3 nonprofit organization or unit of government in New Jersey, have been in existence and active for at least two years at the time of application, have a board of directors, have a clearly articulated mission relating to the arts, and demonstrate that the organization or project is multiregional or statewide in impact.
Areas of Interest Cultural Diversity; Folk/Ethnic Arts; Arts Administration; Leadership
Sample Awards Cumberland County Cultural and Heritage Commission (Cumberland County)—for a local arts program, $150,320. Middlesex County Cultural and Heritage Commission (Middlesex County)—for a local arts program, $177,730. Monmouth County Arts Council Inc (Monmouth County)—for a local arts program, $192,339.

Prudential Foundation Grants Program   793

Prudential Foundation
751 Broad St
Newark, NJ 07102-3777
Contact Gabriella Morris, President, (973) 802-7354; fax: (973) 367-6635; e-mail: community.resources@prudential.com
Internet http://www.prudential.com
Requirements Tax-exempt nonprofit organizations are eligible. Priority in order of preference goes to programs in Newark and surrounding communities; Los Angeles, CA; Jacksonville, FL; Atlanta, GA: Minneapolis, MN; Philadelphia, PA; and Houston, TX. Third priority are national programs that can be implemented or replicated in the above cities.
Areas of Interest Biomedicine; Business; Children and Youth; Community Service Programs; Conservation, Natural Resources; Cultural Activities/Programs; Disadvantaged (Economically); Ecology; Economics; Education; Elderly; Employment Opportunity Programs; Equipment/Instrumentation; Family; Health Care; Inner Cities; Journalism; Law; Leadership; Long-Term Care; Men; Mentoring Programs; Minorities; Neighborhoods; Public Affairs; Retirement; Training and Development; Urban Affairs; Volunteers; Welfare-to-Work Programs; Youth Programs
Sample Awards Meld (Minneapolis, MN)—for group-based parent support and education activities for

disadvantaged families in North Minneapolis who are making the move from welfare to work, $35,000 (2003). National Urban League (New York, NY)—to promote economic independence among African Americans through job training and placement, housing assistance, and other services, $1.5 million over three years (2002). Bank Street College of Education (New York, NY)—to create two early-childhood demonstration schools in Newark, NJ, and for professional development training for paraprofessionals and other staff members at the Quitman Street Community School, $260,000 (2002). Trust for Public Land (New York, NY)—for its Newark CitySpaces program, which develops school playgrounds and community parks in underserved Newark, NJ, neighborhoods, $900,000 over three years (2002).

Fannie E. Rippel Foundation Grants 794

Fannie E. Rippel Foundation
180 Mount Airy Rd, Ste 200
Basking Ridge, NJ 07920
Contact Edward Probert, President, (908) 766-0404; e-mail: rippel@attglobal.net
Internet http://fdncenter.org/grantmaker/rippel/index.html
Requirements Organizations, associations, institutions, and hospitals in the Northeast are eligible.
Restrictions Grants are not awarded to individuals.
Areas of Interest Alternative Medicine; Cancer/Carcinogenesis; Cardiovascular Diseases; Elderly; Genetics; Hospitals; Medical Informatics; Preventive Medicine; Rural Health Care; Women's Health
Sample Awards Fox Chase Cancer Ctr (Philadelphia, PA)—for two new scientific facilities devoted to bioinformatics and genomics, $350,000. Jackson Laboratory (Bar Harbor, ME)—for genetics research on cancer and heart disease, $300,000.

Schering-Plough Foundation Grants 795

Schering-Plough Foundation
2000 Galloping Hill Rd
Kennilworth, NJ 07033-0530
Contact Christine Fahey, Assistant Secretary, (908) 298-7232; fax: (908) 298-7349
Internet http://www.sch-plough.com/schering_plough/corp/foundation_grant.jsp
Requirements Applying organizations must be 501(c)3 tax-exempt. National organizations are eligible to apply.
Restrictions Grants are not made to individuals.
Areas of Interest Allied Health Education; Biomedical Research; Cultural Activities/Programs; Arts and Culture; Educational Programs; Disaster Relief; Equipment/Instrumentation; Health, Allied Fields; Health Care; Health Services Delivery; Higher Education; Hospitals; Medical Education; Medical Pharmacy; Pharmacy Education; Public Policy; Science Education; Secondary Education; Social Services
Sample Awards New Jersey Institute of Technology (Newark, NJ)—to enhance its master's degree program in pharmaceutical engineering, $250,000 (2002).

Schumann Center for Media and Democracy, Inc Grants 796

Schumann Center for Media and Democracy, Inc
33 Park St
Montclair, NJ 07042
Contact Lynn Welhorsky, Vice President & Administrator, (973) 783-6660; fax: (973) 783-7553
Internet http://www.undueinfluence.com/schumann_foundation.htm
Restrictions The foundation does not encourage applications for capital campaigns, annual giving, endowment, or direct support of individuals.
Areas of Interest Campaign Finance Reform; Citizenship; Environmental Studies; Government; Grassroots Leadership; Journalism; Public Affairs; Scholarship Programs, General; Television
Sample Awards Wesleyan U (CT)—for a professorship in environmental studies, $3 million. Alverno College (Milwaukee, WI)—for the Caroline Mark Scholarship Endowment Fund, $1 million. Foundation for National Progress (San Francisco, CA)—to fund a senior editor at Mother Jones magazine and to develop TV outlets for investigative journalism, $150,000.

Schumann Fund for New Jersey Grants 797

Schumann Fund for New Jersey
21 Van Vleck St
Montclair, NJ 07042
Contact Barbara Reisman, Executive Director, (973) 509-9883; fax: (973) 509-1149; e-mail: breisman@worldnet.att.net
Internet http://fdncenter.org/grantmaker/schumann
Requirements IRS 501(c)3 tax-exempt nonprofit organizations located in New Jersey are eligible.
Restrictions The fund does not accept applications for capital campaigns, annual giving, endowment, direct support of individuals, and local programs in counties other than Essex.
Areas of Interest Academic Achievement; Children and Youth; Conservation, Natural Resources; Economic Development; Education; Educational Planning/Policy; Environmental Programs; Family; Land Use Planning/Policy; Parks; Poverty and the Poor; Preschool Education; Public Planning/Policy; Social Services; Urban Areas; Wildlife
Sample Awards Thomas Edison State College (Trenton, NJ)—for the John S. Watson Institute for Public Policy, $30,000. New Jersey Conservation Foundation (Far Hills, NJ)—to create urban parks and to provide technical expertise to nonprofit and government groups working on land conservation and open space planning issues in Newark, Camden, and the Arthur Kill Watershed, $25,000.

Victoria Foundation Grants 798

Victoria Foundation
946 Bloomfield Ave, 2nd Fl
Glen Ridge, NJ 07028
Contact Catherine McFarland, Executive Officer, (973) 748-5300; fax: (973) 748-0016; e-mail: CatherineMcFarland@victoriafoundation.org
Internet http://www.victoriafoundation.org
Requirements The foundation funds 501(c)3 tax-exempt organizations in New Jersey.

Areas of Interest Education; Elementary Education; Environmental Programs; Family; Leadership; Minorities; Neighborhoods; Nonprofit Organizations; Racism/Race Relations; Secondary Education; Urban Planning/Policy; Youth Programs

Sample Awards Bank Street College of Education (New York, NY)—to develop two New Beginnings demonstration schools and at least six demonstration classrooms in two primary schools in Newark, NJ, $350,000 (2003).

New Mexico

Albuquerque Community Foundation Grants   799

Albuquerque Community Foundation
PO Box 36960
Albuquerque, NM 87176-6960
Contact Grant Review Committee, (505) 883-6240; e-mail: acf@albuquerquefoundation.org
Internet http://www.albuquerquefoundation.org
Requirements IRS 501(c)3 organizations based in Albuquerque, NM, are eligible. Proposals are reviewed on the basis of the following priorities: impact, innovation, leverage, management, and nonduplication.
Restrictions Grants are generally not made to or for individuals, political or religious purposes, debt retirement, payment of interest or taxes, annual campaigns, endowments, emergency funding, to influence legislation or elections, scholarships, awards, or to private foundations and other grantmaking organizations.
Areas of Interest Arts, General; Cultural Activities/Programs; Disabled; Disadvantaged (Economically); Education; Environmental Programs; Health Care; International Exchange Programs; Jewish Services; Museums; Restoration and Preservation; Scholarship Programs, General; Social Services
Sample Awards U of New Mexico Art Museum (NM)—to produce an illustrated handbook on its collections, $40,000. Heritage Education Resources (NM)—for general operating support, $10,000. Jewish Community Ctr of Greater Albuquerque (NM)—for its building fund, $10,000. Armand Hammer United World College (NM)—for a scholarship for a student from Poland, $20,000.

FHL Foundation Grants   800

FHL Foundation
PO Box 27650
Albuquerque, NM 87125
Contact Grants Administrator, (505) 247-2400; fax (505) 247-2300; e-mail: fhlfound@thuntek.net
Internet http://www.fhlfoundation.com
Requirements New Mexico nonprofit organizations are eligible.
Restrictions Grants are not made to individuals.
Areas of Interest Animal Care; Child Abuse; Fund-Raising; Service Delivery Programs; Sexual Abuse

Max and Anna Levinson Foundation Grants   801

Max and Anna Levinson Foundation
PO Box 6309
Santa Fe, NM 87502-6309
Contact Charlotte Talberth, Executive Director, (505) 995-8802; fax: (505) 995-8982; e-mail: info@levinsonfoundation.org
Internet http://www.levinsonfoundation.org/Bhow2.html
Restrictions Grants generally are not awarded to organizations with annual budgets in excess of $500,000. Grants do not support building programs, capital or endowment funds, expansion of existing services, fellowships or scholarships, matching gifts, programs serving local communities, or travel.
Areas of Interest Agricultural Planning/Policy; Agriculture; Alternative Fuels; Biodiversity; Civil/Human Rights; Community Development; Conflict/Dispute Resolution; Cultural Outreach; Economic Development; Environmental Health; Environmental Programs; Health Care; International Programs; Israel; Jewish Services; Violent Crime; Youth Programs

J. F. Maddox Foundation Grants   802

J. F. Maddox Foundation
PO Box 2588
Hobbs, NM 88241-2588
Contact Grants Administrator, (505) 393-6338; fax: (505) 397-7266
Internet http://www.jfmaddox.org
Requirements Nonprofit organizations and governmental agencies seeking grants for the explicit benefit of southeast New Mexico are eligible.
Restrictions Grants are not made to individuals, for the express benefit of an individual, or to other private foundations.
Areas of Interest Arts, General; Children and Youth; Community Development; Cultural Programs/Activities; Economic Development; Education; Education Reform; Elderly; Family; Social Services Delivery; Youth Programs
Sample Awards College of Southwest (Hobbs, NM)—for operating costs and capital improvements, $15 million over five years (2003).

McCune Charitable Foundation Grants   803

McCune Charitable Foundation
345 E Alameda St
Santa Fe, NM 87501-2229
Contact Frances Sowers, (505) 983-8300; fax: (505) 983-7887; e-mail: fsowers@swcp.com or info@nmmccune.org
Internet http://www.nmmccune.org
Requirements Nonprofit organizations in New Mexico, with emphasis on northern New Mexico, may submit applications.
Restrictions Grants are not awarded to individuals or to support endowments.
Areas of Interest Adult and Continuing Education; Alcohol/Alcoholism; Archaeology; Arts, General; Basic Skills Education; Child Psychology/Development; Community Development; Conservation, Natural Resources; Crime Prevention; Cultural Activities/Programs; Dental Health and Hygiene; Disadvantaged (Eco-

nomically); Drugs/Drug Abuse; Education; Elderly; Elementary Education; Environmental Programs; Family Planning; Health Care; Higher Education; History; Homelessness; Homosexuals, Female; Homosexuals, Male; Hospices; Housing; Juvenile Delinquency; Libraries; Literacy; Museums; Native Americans; Performing Arts; Public Affairs; Restoration and Preservation; Rural Planning/Policy; Secondary Education; Social Services; Visual Arts; Vocational/Technical Education; Wildlife; Women; Youth Programs

Sample Awards La Familia Medical Ctr (Santa Fe, NM)—for construction of a new medical and dental facility, $60,000. Hospice Ctr (Santa Fe, NM)—for support of the Rural Hospice program, $60,000. Big Brothers/Big Sisters of Santa Fe (Santa Fe, NM)—to support group activities, $40,000.

Native American Housing Development Capacity Building Grants 804

AMERIND Risk Management Corporation
6201 Uptown Blvd, Ste 100
Albuquerque, NM 87110
Contact Nancy Harjo, (505) 837-2290; fax: (505) 837-2053; e-mail: nancy@amerind-corp.org
Internet http://www.amerind-corp.org/grants.shtml
Areas of Interest Community Development; Housing; Native Americans

Santa Fe Community Foundation Grants 805

Santa Fe Community Foundation
PO Box 1827
Santa Fe, NM 87504-1827
Contact Dolores Roybal, Program Officer, (505) 988-9715 ext 2; fax: (505) 988-1829; e-mail: droybal@santafecf.org
Internet http://www.santafecf.org/grantfr.htm
Requirements IRS 501(c)3 tax-exempt organizations serving residents of Santa Fe, Los Alamos, Rio Arriba, Taos, San Miguel, and Moro Counties in New Mexico are eligible.
Restrictions The foundation does not award grants to individuals or for religious purposes, political purposes, capital outlay or capital campaigns, endowment, or governmental agencies experiencing operational budget cuts.
Areas of Interest Arts, General; Children's Museums; Civic Affairs; Day Care; Education; Environmental Programs; Family; Finance; Fund-Raising; Health Care; Homosexuals, Female; Homosexuals, Male; Leadership; Marketing; Poverty and the Poor; Program Evaluation; Public Relations; Rural Areas; Social Services; Training and Development; Volunteers
Sample Awards Santa Fe Children's Museum (Santa Fe, NM)—for a comprehensive three-year summer program for children aged five to seven from low-income Santa Fe families, $130,000. El Bien Estar de Familias Daycare Ctr (Tierra Amarilla, NM)—operating support for this child care center that serves the rural Chama/Tierra Amarilla area of New Mexico, $10,000.

New York

Achelis Foundation Grants 806

Achelis Foundation
767 Third Ave, 4th Fl
New York, NY 10017
Contact Joe Dolan, Executive Director, (212) 644-0322; fax: (212) 759-6510; e-mail: main@achelis-bodman-fnds.org
Internet http://fdncenter.org/grantmaker/achelis-bodman
Requirements Applicants must be New York tax-exempt incorporated agencies or institutions.
Restrictions The foundation does not consider requests for annual appeals, fund-raising events, capital campaigns, international projects, small arts groups, film, or travel.
Areas of Interest Adolescents; Adult and Continuing Education; Alzheimer's Disease; Arts, General; Basic Skills Education; Biomedical Research Training; Career Education and Planning; Child Abuse; Civic Affairs; Cognitive Development/Processes; Conservation, Natural Resources; Disasters; Economic Development; Education; Education Reform; Entrepreneurship; Environmental Programs; Equipment/Instrumentation; Family; Head Injury; Health Care; Hospitals; Housing; Independent Living Programs; Inner Cities; Job Training Programs; Literacy; Nursing Homes; Parent Education; Prison Reform; Public Planning/Policy; Rehabilitation/Therapy; Religion; Science Education; Social Services; Social Work Education; Veterinary Medicine Education; Youth Programs
Sample Awards Save the Children (Westport, CT)—for relief efforts for refugees and other victims of the fighting in Afghanistan, as part of a round of grants responding to the September 11 attacks and their aftermath, $20,000 (2001). Bill of Rights Institute (Washington, DC)—to develop and market Citizenship and Character, an instructional supplement for American government and history classes in US high schools, as part of a round of grants responding to the September 11 attacks and their aftermath, $15,000 (2001). Columbia U, Mailman School of Public Health (New York, NY)—for activities by the Center for Public Health Preparedness designed to improve the ability of medical institutions in New York City to respond to public-health emergenices, especially biological terrorism, as part of a round of grants responding to the September 11 attacks and their aftermath, $100,000 (2001).

Max A. Adler Charitable Foundation Grants 807

Max A. Adler Charitable Foundation
1010 Times Sq Bldg
Rochester, NY 14614
Contact David Gray, President, (585) 232-7290; fax: (585) 232-7260
Requirements New York 501(c)3 nonprofit organizations serving the greater Rochester area are eligible.
Areas of Interest Arts, General; Children and Youth; Health Care; Higher Education; Jewish Services
Sample Awards Nazareth College (Rochester, NY)—for its capital campaign to expand the size of its campus, $50,000 (2003).

Joseph Alexander Foundation Grants   808

Joseph Alexander Foundation
400 Madison Ave, Ste 906
New York, NY 10017
Contact Robert Weintraub, President, (212) 355-3688
Requirements Nonprofit organizations are eligible to apply.
Areas of Interest Alcohol/Alcoholism; Children and Youth; Drugs/Drug Abuse; Family Planning; Higher Education; Hospitals; International Organizations; Israel; Religion; Social Services Delivery; Welfare Reform

ALFJ General Grants Program   809

Astraea Lesbian Foundation for Justice
116 E 16th St, 7th Fl
New York, NY 10003
Contact Program Associate, (212) 529-8021; fax: (212) 982-3321; e-mail: grants@astraeafoundation.org
Internet http://www.astraeafoundation.org
Requirements Organizations that have the least access to traditional funding sources will be given priority.
Areas of Interest Arts, General; Civil/Human Rights; Cultural Activities/Programs; Cultural Diversity; Elderly; Film Production; Homelessness; Homosexuals, Female; Leadership; Minorities; Poverty and the Poor; Publication; Rural Areas; Social Services; Video Production; Violent Behavior; Women's Health; Youth Programs
Sample Awards Ctr for Young Women's Development (San Francisco, CA)—for GAL, a peer-directed program for lesbian young women who are homeless or otherwise on their own, $3000. Women of Color Building Project (Minneapolis, MN)—for general support, $4000.

Altria Arts Grants   810

Altria Corporate Services
120 Park Ave
New York, NY 10017
Contact Grants Administrator, (917) 663-4000
Internet http://www.altria.com/responsibility/04_05_02_05_00_VisArts_Main.asp
Areas of Interest Arts, General; Cultural Outreach; Dance; Theater; Museums; Visual Arts

Altria Group Contributions Program   811

Altria Group, Inc
120 Park Ave
New York, NY 10017
Contact Manager, Corporate Contributions (program areas other than arts), or Manager, Cultural Program (arts), (212) 880-3366 or (800) 883-2422
Internet http://www.altria.com/responsibility/04_05_01_00_whatwefund.asp
Requirements IRS 501(c)3 organizations are eligible.
Restrictions Generally, support will not be provided to/for fund-raising benefits; capital campaigns, endowments, or building fund drives; film, video, or television projects; one-time or annual events; individuals; political or lobbying organizations; religious, fraternal, or veterans groups; research or other activities related to specific diseases or disease-prevention (with the exception of AIDS); athletic or sports-related activities; travel funds; organizations that discriminate on the basis of race, creed, gender, sexual preference, or national origin; or

organizations already supported through United Way contributions.
Areas of Interest AIDS; Adult and Continuing Education; Agriculture Education; Art Education; Arts, General; Children and Youth; Civic Affairs; Conservation, Natural Resources; Disaster Relief; Dramatic/Theater Arts; Education Reform; Elderly; Elementary Education; Environmental Education; Environmental Programs; Food Distribution; Food Service Industry; Human Learning and Memory; Hunger; Internet; Job Training Programs; Literacy; Museums; Music; Nutrition/Dietetics; Secondary Education; Teacher Education; Teacher Education, Inservice; Volunteers
Sample Awards California Farm Water Coalition (Sacramento, CA)—to produce a series of posters about water use in California farming regions, $10,000 (2003). Farms Leadership (Witners, CA)—for a program that provides farm-based experiences to California high school students, $25,000 (2003). Kansas Foundation for Agriculture in the Classroom (Manhattan, KS)—to expand the Connecting Kansas Kids to Crops, Critters, and Conservation education program, $25,000 (2003). National Cattlemen's Foundation (Denver, CO)—for a program designed to help farmers and ranchers become effective spokespeople for the beef and cattle industries on environmental issues, $25,000 (2003).

Altria Theater Grants   812

Altria Group Inc
120 Park Ave
New York, NY 10017
Contact Manager, Cultural Program, (800) 883-2422 or (212) 880-3366
Internet http://www.altria.com/responsibility/04_05_01_01_grantcalendar.asp
Requirements Applicant organization must have received a letter of invitation; be a US 501(c)3 nonprofit, tax-exempt organization; and pay all of its management and artistic staff.
Restrictions Generally, theater departments at universities or colleges are ineligible.
Areas of Interest Arts, General; Performance Art; Performing Arts; Theater/Film Criticism

American Express Foundation Grants   813

American Express Foundation
200 Vessey St, 3 World Financial Center
New York, NY 10285
Contact Linda Hassan, Manager, Philanthropic Program, (212) 640-5662; fax: (212) 693-1033
Internet http://www.americanexpress.com/corp/philanthropy
Requirements The company awards grants to US-based nonprofit organizations with an international focus and organizations outside the United States that can document nonprofit status.
Areas of Interest AIDS Education; African Americans; Art Education; Arts, General; Audience Development; Civic Affairs; Communications; Community Outreach Programs; Community Service Programs; Cultural Diversity; Disabled; Drugs/Drug Abuse; Economic Self-Sufficiency; Education Reform; Environmental Programs; Financial Education; Geography; Health Care; Hispanics; International Programs; Job Training

Programs; Literacy; Minorities; Opera/Musical Theater; Restoration and Preservation; Restoration and Preservation, Structural/Architectural; School-to-Work Transition; Social Services; Women; Youth Programs

Sample Awards Captain Youth and Family Services (Clifton Park, NY)—to establish a mentoring program and a financial-education course for youths and families, $24,364 over 18 months (2004). Family Service of Southern Wisconsin and Northern Illinois (Beloit, WI)—to teach survivors of domestic violence about finances, $15,000 (2004). Northeast Economic Development (Norfolk, NE)—to provide financial education to low-income immigrants, $30,000 over two years (2004). Women at Work (Pasadena, CA)—to help low-income women obtain better paying jobs and manage their money, $30,000 over two years.

Anderson-Rogers Foundation Grants 814

Anderson-Rogers Foundation
327 W 19th St
New York, NY 10011
Contact Grants Administrator
Internet http://fdncenter.org/grantmaker/arfdn/index.
html
Requirements 501(c)3 tax-exempt organizations are eligible.
Restrictions The foundation does not fund scholarships or make grants to individuals or religious organizations.
Areas of Interest Adult and Continuing Education; Child Abuse; Child Welfare; Children and Youth; Environmental Education; Environmental Health; Environmental Programs; Habitat; Land Management; Literacy; Parent Education; Parent Involvement; Social Change; Water Resources, Environmental Impacts

Animal Welfare Trust Grants 815

Animal Welfare Trust
PO Box 737, 141 Halstead Ave, Ste 201
Mamaroneck, NY 10543
Contact Trust Administrator, (914) 381-6177; fax: (914) 381-6176; e-mail: email@animalwelfaretrust.org
Internet http://fdncenter.org/grantmaker/awt/prog.
html
Requirements Grants will be made largely to organizations classified as public charities under section 501(c)3 of the IRS code. Under certain circumstances grants will be considered outside the boundaries of public charities, including organizations outside the United States that can meet appropriate legal standards.
Areas of Interest Animal Care; Animal Rights; Animal Welfare
Sample Awards Remote Area Medical—to support a spay/neuter project on Arizona Indian Reservation, $7000 (2002). HEART- Humane Education Advocates Reaching Teachers—for a program to teach humane education and promote compliance with existing legislation, $15,000 (2002). Delta Society—to publish a manual on standards for companion animals in nursing homes, $7000 (2002).

ANLAF International Fund for Sexual Minorities Grants 816

Astraea National Lesbian Action Foundation
116 E 16th St, 7th Fl
New York, NY 10003
Contact Christine Lipat, Program Officer, (212) 529-8021 ext 12; fax: (212) 982-3321; e-mail: grants@astraeafoundation.org
Internet http://www.astraea.org/grants/int-fund-guide.
html
Requirements Groups must be based in Latin America, the Caribbean, Asia, the Pacific, Eastern Europe, the former Soviet Republics, the Middle East, and Africa.
Restrictions Astraea Foundation generally does not fund organizations with budgets above $500,000.
Areas of Interest Age Discrimination; Children and Youth; Cultural Activities/Programs; Disabled; Economics; Education; Feminism; Homosexuals, Female; Homosexuals, Male; Mental Disorders; Minorities; Political Science; Racism/Race Relations; Rural Areas; Sexism; Social Stratification/Mobility; Women
Sample Awards Audre Lorde Project (Brooklyn, NY)—for the LBTST Women of Color Organizing Initiative, $4000. Triangle Project (Cape Town, Africa)—for expansion of services to the lesbian/gay/bisexual/transsexual communities in rural areas of the Western Cape, $4000.

AT&T Arts and Culture Grants 817

AT&T Foundation
32 Ave of the Americas, 6th Fl
New York, NY 10013
Contact Program Contact, (212) 387-4801; fax: (212) 387-4882
Internet http://www.att.com/foundation/guidelines.
html#arts
Requirements To qualify for consideration, organizations must have been professionally managed for at least five years and must compensate both artistic and managerial personnel.
Restrictions Requests will not be considered for projects that influence legislation, endowments, memorials, brick-and-mortar campaigns, sports event sponsorships, tickets for fund-raising events, or advertising or donated products.
Areas of Interest Arts Administration; Dance; Dramatic/Theater Arts; Exhibitions, Collections, Performances; Films; Museums; Music; Opera/Musical Theater; Orchestras; Performing Arts; Touring Arts Programs
Sample Awards Center Theatre Group (Los Angeles, CA)—to produce a play entitled The Tale of the Allergist's Wife, $35,000 (2002).

AT&T International Programs 818

AT&T Foundation
32 Avenue of the Americas, 24th Fl
New York, NY 10013
Contact Ronald Dabney, Communications Manager, (212) 387-4867; fax: (212) 387-4433; e-mail: rdabney@attmail.com
Internet http://www.att.com/foundation/index.html
Restrictions The foundation does not support projects in the early stages of research and planning; membership

subscriptions; competitions and contests; film and media productions or broadcast underwriting; research studies, unless related to projects the foundation already supports; fellowships, internships, or residencies, unless associated with projects the foundation already supports; endowed or named chairs at educational or research institutions; catalogs and publications, except those associated with projects the foundation already supports; and equipment donations.

Areas of Interest Arts, General; Business; Cultural Activities/Programs; Disaster Relief; Distance Education; Education; Government; Health Care; International Programs; Public Planning/Policy; Social Services; Technology

Sample Awards American Red Cross (Washington, DC)—to support earthquake-relief efforts in El Salvador and in India, $1 million (2001). China Development Foundation for Science and Technology (Beijing, China)—to support the New Experiments in Arts and Technology program, $75,000 (1999). International Council for Distance Education (Oslo, Sweden)—for conferences to help promote global distance learning among universities, governments, and corporations, $554,000.

Bass and Edythe and Sol G. Atlas Fund Grants   819

Bass and Edythe and Sol G. Atlas Fund
185 Great Neck Rd
Great Neck, NY 11021
Contact Sandra Atlas Bass, President, (516) 487-9030
Requirements Nonprofit organizations in New York are eligible.
Restrictions Unsolicited requests for funds are not accepted.
Areas of Interest Child Welfare; Children and Youth; Churches; Community Service Programs; Disabled; Health Care; Hospices; Hospitals; Israel; Jewish Services; Religion; Social Services
Sample Awards United Jewish Appeal Federation (New York, NY)—for operating support, $125,000. Diskin Orphan Home of Israel (Brooklyn, NY)—for operating support, $14,500. St. Jude's Children's Research Hospital (Memphis, TN)—for operating support, $20,500.

Atran Foundation Grants   820

Atran Foundation
23-25 E 21st St, 3rd Fl
New York, NY 10010
Contact Diane Fischer, President, (212) 505-9677
Requirements 501(c)3 tax-exempt Jewish organizations are eligible.
Restrictions Grants are not made to individuals.
Areas of Interest Higher Education; Hospitals; International Programs; Israel; Jewish Services; Jewish Studies; Visual Impairments; Women
Sample Awards Yivo Institute for Jewish Research (New York, NY)—for project support, $90,000. Brandeis University (Waltham, MA)—for operating support, $28,000. Folksbiene Yiddish Theater (New York, NY)—for operating support, $15,000.

Avon Products Foundation Grants   821

Avon Products Foundation
1345 Avenue of the Americas
New York, NY 10105-0196
Contact Kathleen Walas, President, (212) 282-5518; fax: (212) 282-6049
Internet http://www.avoncompany.com/women/avonfoundation
Requirements Applying organizations must be tax-exempt; national and municipal organizations are eligible. Request the guidelines brochure prior to submitting a formal proposal.
Restrictions Grants do not support individuals; memberships; lobbying organizations; political activities and organizations; religious, veteran, or fraternal organizations; fundraising events; and journal advertisements.
Areas of Interest Breast Cancer; Cancer Detection; Children and Youth; Cultural Outreach; Elderly; Humanities; Minorities; Performing Arts; Women; Women's Education; Women's Employment; Women's Health
Sample Awards George Washington U Medical Faculty Assoc (Washington, DC)—for salary support for a bilingual health educator and a social worker for the Mobile Mammography Program, $100,000 (2003). National Domestic Violence Hotline (Austin, TX)—to produce Spanish-language outreach materials for a public-awareness campaign about domestic violence, $25,000 (2003). State U of New York at Albany (NY)—for scholarships that enable nontraditional female students to transfer from community colleges, $72,000 over two years (2003). Women's Housing and Economic Development Corp (New York, NY)—to provide financial-education and financial-counseling services to 100 low-income mothers, through the Self Sufficiency Project, $25,000 (2003).

George F. Baker Trust Grants   822

George F. Baker Trust
477 Madison Ave, Ste 1650
New York, NY 10022
Contact Rocio Suarez, Executive Director, (212) 755-1890; fax: (212) 319-6316; e-mail: rocio@bakernye.com
Restrictions Grants are not made to individuals.
Areas of Interest Civic Affairs; Elementary Education; Environmental Programs; Higher Education; Hospitals; International Relations; Private and Parochial Education; Religion; Secondary Education; Social Services
Sample Awards West Granville Christian Academy (West Granville, MA)—for operating support, $25,000. Saint Paul's Community Development Corp (Patterson, NJ)—for operations and program support, $20,000.

Banfi Vintners Foundation Grants   823

Banfi Vintners Foundation
1111 Cedar Swamp Rd
Glen Head, NY 11545
Contact John Troiano, Executive Director, (516) 626-9200
Areas of Interest Arts, General; Civic Affairs; Health Care; Higher Education; Hospitals; Humanities; International Programs; Preventive Medicine; Public Affairs; Religion; Science; Social Sciences; Wildlife

Sample Awards Colgate U (Hamilton, NY)—for operating support, $75,000. Friends for Long Island's Heritage (Syosset, NY—for operating support, $25,000. Huntington Hospital Assoc (Huntington, NY)—for operating support, $25,000. Cornell U (Ithaca, NY)—for operating support, $465,000.

Bank of Tokyo-Mitsubishi Community Grants Program 824
Bank of Tokyo-Mitsubishi Trust Company
1251 Avenue of the Americas, 15th Fl
New York, NY 10020-1104
Contact Fiona Aitken, (212) 782-4548 or (212) 782-4000; fax: (212) 782-6420; e-mail: bgilroy@btmna.com or nahq@btmna.com
Internet http://www.btmny.com
Requirements New York, NY, nonprofits are eligible.
Restrictions Grants are not awarded to support individuals; religious, sectarian, fraternal,veterans, or labor organizations; political or lobbying groups; organizations outside operating areas; fund-raising activities; or for deficit reduction.
Areas of Interest Business Development; Community Development; Community Service Programs; Day Care; Economic Development; Economically Disadvantaged; Elderly; Families; Housing; Legal Services; Neighborhoods; Small Businesses; Social Services; Vocational/Technical Education; Volunteers; Youth Programs

Barker Welfare Foundation Grants 825
Barker Welfare Foundation
PO Box 2
Glen Head, NY 11545
Contact Sarane Ross, President, (516) 759-5592; fax: (516) 759-5497
Requirements IRS 501(c)3 organizations in Illinois, Indiana, and New York are eligible.
Restrictions Appeals for the following will be declined: organizations outside of Illinois, Indiana, and New York; national health, welfare, or education agencies; scholarships, fellowships, loans, etc.; medical and scientific research; private elementary and secondary schools, colleges, universities, etc.; films, program advertising, conferences, etc.; start-up organizations, emergency funds, and deficit financing; lobbying-related or legislative activities; or endowment funds.
Areas of Interest Arts, General; Civic Affairs; Cultural Activities/Programs; Education; Environmental Education; Family; Health Care; Homelessness; Juvenile Delinquency; Literacy; Reading; Social Services; Youth Programs
Sample Awards Reading Is Fundamental (Chicago, IL)—for the purchase of books, $5000. Travelers and Immigrants Aid of Chicago (Chicago, IL)—for the homeless services program, $10,000. La Porte County Juvenile Service Ctr Task Force (Michigan City, IN)—for general operating support, $3000. Arts Connection (New York, NY)—for the Young Talent program, $15,000 over two years. Central Park Conservancy (New York, NY)—for the Environmental Education program in Central Park, $15,000.

Bay Foundation Grants 826
Bay Foundation
17 W 94th St
New York, NY 10025
Contact Robert Ashton, Executive Director, (212) 663-1115; fax: (212) 932-0316
Requirements Nonprofits in Connecticut, Massachusetts, Maine, New Hampshire, New Jersey, New York, Rhode Island, and Vermont are eligible.
Restrictions Grants do not support requests for endowments, building construction or maintenance, religious projects, scholarships, travel, films, television or video productions, conferences, or annual fund appeals.
Areas of Interest Biodiversity; Botanical Gardens; Children and Youth; Cultural Heritage Preservation; Economic Development; Elementary Education; Libraries; Mathematics Education; Museums; Native American Studies; Natural History; Science Education; Secondary Education; Educational Technology; Writing/Composition Education; Zoos
Sample Awards American Assoc for State and Local History (Nashville, TN)—to update the book Starting Right: A Guide to Museum Planning, $13,100 (2003).

Beldon Fund Grants 827
Beldon Fund
99 Madison Ave, 8th Fl
New York, NY 10016
Contact Holeri Faruolo, (800) 591-9595 or (212) 616-5600; fax: (212) 616-5656; e-mail: info@beldon.org
Internet http://www.beldon.org
Restrictions Grants do not support international efforts, academic or university efforts, school-based environmental education, land acquisition, wildlife or habitat preservation, film or video production, deficit reduction, endowments, capital campaigns, acquisitions of museums, service delivery, scholarshp, publications, or arts/culture.
Areas of Interest Business; Environmental Education; Environmental Health; Environmental Planning/Policy; Environmental Programs; Health Promotion; Toxic Substances; Water Pollution; Water Resources
Sample Awards Clean Water Fund (Washington, DC)—for support of the Colorado office, $15,000. Legal Environmental Assistance Foundation (Tallahassee, FL)—for an underground injection-well program, $10,000. Tides Ctr (San Francisco, CA)—for the Good Neighbor project, $15,000. Resource Councils Education Project (Billings, MT)—to provide challenge grants to six member groups and for a regional corporate analysis project, $100,000.

Arthur and Rochelle Belfer Foundation Grants 828
Arthur and Rochelle Belfer Foundation, Inc
767 Fifth Ave, 46th Fl
New York, NY 10153-0002
Contact Robert Belfer, President
Restrictions Grants are not made to individuals.
Areas of Interest Education; Elderly; Higher Education; Hospitals; Jewish Services; Jewish Studies; Museums; Women

Sample Awards Dana-Farber Cancer Institute (Boston, MA)—for general support, $1 million. Anti-Defamation League of B'nai B'rith (New York, NY)—for operating support, $22,000. American Friends of Israel Museum (New York, NY)—for operating support, $5000.

Frances and Benjamin Benenson Foundation Grants   829

Frances and Benjamin Benenson Foundation
708 Third Ave, 28th Fl
New York, NY 10017
Contact Charles Benenson, President, (212) 867-0990
Requirements Nonprofits of the Jewish and Roman Catholic faiths are eligible.
Restrictions Grants are not made to individuals.
Areas of Interest Community Service Programs; International Programs; Jewish Services; Jewish Studies; Religion
Sample Awards New Israel Fund (Washington, DC)—for operating support, $10,000. Yale U (New Haven, CT)—to support the Hillel House campaign, $5000.

Birds Eye Foods Foundation Grants   830

Birds Eye Foods Foundation
PO Box 20670
Rochester, NY 14602-0670
Contact Susan Riker, Birds Eye Foods Foundation, (585) 264-3155
Internet http://www.birdseyefoods.com/corp/about/foundation.asp
Requirements Nonprofit organizations operating where Birds Eye employees and plants are located (Bergen, Brockport, Fulton, and Oakfield, NY; Montezuma, GA; Berlin, PA; Cincinatti, OH; Algona and Tacoma, WA; Oxnard and Watsonville, CA; Darien, Fairwater, Green Bay, and Fennville, MI; and Waseca, MN) are eligible to apply. Application consists of a letter outlining the project to be supported, the amount requested, an overview of the requesting organization, and a copy of the 501(c)3 letters.
Restrictions Grants are not available to religious or political groups, or to individuals. The foundation does not support land acquisitions, start-up funds, internships, pilot projects, publications, conferences/seminars, matching grants, loans, or multiple year funding.
Areas of Interest Agriculture; Arts, General; Community Service Programs; Cultural Activities/Programs; Education; Health Care; Youth Programs

Bodman Foundation Grants Program   831

Bodman Foundation
767 Third Ave, 4th Fl
New York, NY 10017
Contact Program Contact, (212) 644-0322; fax: (212) 759-6510; e-mail: main@achelis-bodman-fnds.org
Internet http://fdncenter.org/grantmaker/achelis-bodman
Requirements Grants are made primarily to tax-exempt agencies and institutions in New York City and northern New Jersey.
Restrictions The trustees generally do not participate in annual appeals, dinner functions, and fund-raising events; loans and deficits; international projects; small art, dance, music, and theater groups; direct grants to individuals (such as scholarships and financial aid); grants for books, films, and travel; national health and national mental health organizations; nonprofit organizations outside of New York and New Jersey; or government agencies, public schools, and nonprofit programs and services significantly funded or wholly reimbursed by government.
Areas of Interest Alcohol/Alcoholism; Biomedical Research; Child Welfare; Computer Education/Literacy; Consumer Behavior; Cultural Activities/Programs; Dance; Drugs/Drug Abuse; Economic Development; Education Reform; Entrepreneurship; Environmental Programs; Family; Health Care; Homelessness; Hospitals; Intervention Programs; Job Training Programs; Leadership; Literacy; Parent Education; Parent Involvement; Rehabilitation/Therapy; Religion; Science Education; Social Services; Urban Areas; Veterinary Medicine; Volunteers; Youth Programs
Sample Awards Catholic Relief Services (Baltimore, MD)—for relief efforts for refugees and other victims of the fighting in Afghanistan, $20,000 (2001). STRIVE/East Harlem Employment Services (New York, NY)—for its Community Partnership, a citywide job training and placement effort by 15 nonprofit groups to assist workers displaced by the terrorist attacks and the economic recession, $75,000 (2001). Manhattan Institute for Policy Research (New York, NY)—for research, articles, panels, and other events on rebuilding New York, as part of a round of grants responding to the September 11 attacks and their aftermath, $100,000 (2001). New York Historical Society (NY)—for an exhibition and public program series in collaboration with the Skyscraper Museum on the conception, design, engineering, building, and destruction of the World Trade Center, $20,000 (2001).

Booth Ferris Foundation Grants   832

Booth Ferris Foundation
345 Park Ave, 4th Fl
New York, NY 10154
Contact Barbara Maurer, (212) 789-5690; e-mail: maurer_barbara@jpmorgan.com
Internet http://fdncenter.org/grantmaker/boothferris
Requirements Nonprofits, K-12, and higher educational institutions in New York are eligible.
Restrictions The foundation does not support federated campaigns; community chests; individuals; research; or educational institutions for scholarships, fellowships, or unrestricted endowments.
Areas of Interest Adult and Continuing Education; Basic Skills Education; Chemistry; Cultural Activities/Programs; Curriculum Development; Elementary Education; Environmental Programs; Higher Education, Private; Religious Studies; Secondary Education; Social Services; Teacher Education; Theology; Urban Areas
Sample Awards Kenyon College (Gambier, OH)—for the chemistry department, $150,000 (2000). Bennington College (Bennington, VT)—for its BA/MA in Teaching program, $200,000 (2000).

Robert Bowne Foundation Grants   833

Robert Bowne Foundation
345 Hudson St
New York, NY 10014

Contact Anne Lawrence, Program Officer, (212) 229-7227; fax: (212) 886-0400; e-mail: alawrence@ robertbownefoundation.org
Internet http://www.robertbownefoundation.org/ index.php
Requirements Nonprofit organizations in the greater New York City area, with emphasis on the boroughs outside Manhattan, may submit letters of application.
Restrictions Grants are not awarded to religious organizations, primary or secondary schools, colleges or universities, individuals, or to support capital campaigns or endowments.
Areas of Interest Adult and Continuing Education; After-School Programs; Arts, General; Basic Skills Education; Children and Youth; Education; Family; Hispanics; Literacy; Reading Education; Writing/Composition Education; Youth Programs
Sample Awards Coalition for Hispanic Family Services (NY)—to support the Arts and Literacy after-school program, $25,000. Forest Hills Community House (NY)— to support its after-school program, $25,000.

Bristol-Myers Squibb Co Foundation International Grants   834

Bristol-Myers Squibb Co Foundation
345 Park Ave, Ste 4364
New York, NY 10154
Contact Grants Administrator, (212) 546-4000; fax: (212) 546-9574
Internet http://www.bms.com/sr/grants/data/index. html
Restrictions The foundation does not support individuals; conferences, special events, or videos; political, fraternal, social, or veterans organizations; religious or sectarian activities, unless they benefit the entire community; organizations funded through federated campaigns; endowments; or courtesy advertising.
Areas of Interest Biomedical Research; Cancer/ Carcinogenesis; Health Care; International Programs; Nutrition/Dietetics
Sample Awards To work with government agencies and local nonprofit groups to help women and children affected by HIV/AIDS in the sub-Saharan African nations of Botswana, Lesotho, Namibia, South Africa, and Swaziland, $30 million (2003).

Brooklyn Benevolent Society Grants   835

Brooklyn Benevolent Society
488 Atlantic Ave
Brooklyn, NY 11217
Contact Cornelius Heaney, Secretary, (718) 875-2066
Requirements Nonprofit organizations of the Christian and Roman Catholic faiths in New York are eligible.
Areas of Interest Child Welfare; Community Service Programs; Higher Education; Religion; Religious Studies; Secondary Education; Social Services; Women; Youth Programs
Sample Awards Fordham U (New York, NY)—for general support, $10,000. Our Lady of Perpetual Help High School (Brooklyn, NY)—for general support, $7500. Salvation Army Wayside Home and School for Girls (NY)—for general support, $6000.

J. Homer Butler Foundation Grants   836

J. Homer Butler Foundation
30 W 16th St
New York, NY 10011
Contact Dorothy Montalto, Grant Administrator, (212) 242-7340; fax: (718) 442-5088
Areas of Interest Catholic Church; Child Welfare; Churches; Community Service Programs; Hansen's Disease; Health Care; Hospitals; International Programs; Private and Parochial Education; Religious Studies; Women
Sample Awards Xavier Jesuit Community (New York, NY)—for general support, $5000. Gospel Outreach (Hillsboro, MO)—for leprosy programs in India, $2000.

Bydale Foundation Grants   837

Bydale Foundation
11 Martine Ave
White Plains, NY 10606
Contact Milton Solomon, Vice President, (914) 683-3519
Requirements US 501(c)3 nonprofits are eligible.
Areas of Interest Arts, General; Civil/Human Rights; Conservation, Natural Resources; Cultural Activities/ Programs; Environmental Effects; Environmental Programs; Higher Education; International Relations; Public Planning/Policy; Social Services; Water Resources
Sample Awards Clean Water Fund (Washington, DC)—$5000. Greenhouse Crisis Foundation (Washington, DC)—$20,000. Greenpeace USA (Washington, DC)—$2500.

Louis Calder Foundation Grants   838

Louis Calder Foundation
61 E 45th St
New York, NY 10169
Contact Grants Administrator, (212) 687-1680
Requirements Nonprofit organizations serving the New York City area and its residents are eligible. Typical recipients include schools, hospitals and other medical agencies, youth groups, human service agencies, museums, libraries, and arts groups.
Restrictions Awards to performing arts groups or private colleges are by invitation only.
Areas of Interest Academic Achievement; After-School Programs; Arts, General; Children and Youth; Education; Environmental Programs; Family; Health Care; Hospitals; Libraries; Literacy; Museums; Reading; Religion; Scholarship Programs, General; Social Services; Youth Programs
Sample Awards Saint John's U (Jamaica, NY)—to endow a scholarship fund, $333,000 challenge grant. Canisius College (Buffalo, NY)—for scholarships for New York City students who demonstrate academic promise and acute financial need, $250,000 challenge grant. Citizens Advice Bureau (New York, NY)—for support to implement a whole language-based after-school program for South Bronx children, $25,000.

Carnahan-Jackson Foundation Grants   839

Carnahan-Jackson Foundation
1 East Ave, 3rd Fl
Rochester, NY 14604
Contact Janet Schumacher, Vice-President

Requirements IRS 501(c)3 organizations serving western New York, particularly Chautauqua County, are eligible.

Areas of Interest Churches; Community Development; Curriculum Development; Dance; Disabled; Drugs/Drug Abuse; Ecology; Education; Higher Education; Hospitals; Housing; Libraries; Performing Arts; Scholarship Programs, General; Youth Programs

Carnegie Corporation of New York Education Grant Program   840

Carnegie Corporation of New York
437 Madison Ave
New York, NY 10022
Contact Daniel Fallon, Program Chair, (212) 371-3200; fax: (212) 754-4073
Internet http://www.carnegie.org/sub/program/education.html
Requirements Grants are made primarily to academic institutions and national and regional organizations. Grantseekers who would like to approach the foundation with a preliminary request for funding are encouraged to submit a letter of inquiry. If the project described in the letter fits the foundation's guidelines, the sender will be contacted and asked to submit a proposal in the corporation's format.
Restrictions The foundation does not operate scholarship, fellowship, or travel grant programs; it does not make grants for basic operating expenses, endowments, or facilities of educational or human services institutions, nor does it make program-related investments.
Areas of Interest Academic Achievement; Children and Youth; Education Reform; Preschool Education; Higher Education; Urban Education
Sample Awards Dillard U (New Orleans, LA)—and U of Colorado at Boulder (CO)—for the second year of a partnership between the two universities that merges their respective strengths in the humanities, information technology, literature, and mathematics, $350,000 jointly (2003). Boston College (Chestnut Hill, MA), Florida A&M U (Tallahassee, FL), Stanford U (Palo Alto, CA), U of Connecticut (Storrs, CA), U of Texas (El Paso, TX), U of Washington (Seattle, WA), and U of Wisconsin (Milwaukee, WI)—to restructure and enhance their schools of education, approximately $30 million over five years distributed among the schools(2003). District of Columbia College Access Program (Washington, DC)—for operating support of this organization that seeks to increase the number of students from public high schools who enroll in college, in commemoration of the September 11 attacks, $1 million (2003).

Thomas and Agnes Carvel Foundation Grants   841

Thomas and Agnes Carvel Foundation
35 E Grassy Sprain Rd
Yonkers, NY 10710
Contact William Griffin, President, (914) 793-7300
Requirements IRS 501(c)3 organizations in New York, New Jersey, and Connecticut are eligible.
Restrictions Grants are not made to individuals.
Areas of Interest Children and Youth; Nutrition/Dietetics

Sample Awards Seton Hall (South Orange, NJ)—to provide full scholarships to 10 high-school students from Newark, NJ, who commit to a year of volunteer service in Newark upon graduation, $50,000.

Mary Flagler Cary Charitable Trust Grants   842

Mary Flagler Cary Charitable Trust
122 E 42nd St, Rm 3505
New York, NY 10168
Contact Grants Administrator, (212) 953-7700; fax: (212) 953-7720; e-mail: info@carytrust.org
Internet http://www.carytrust.org
Requirements Grants are made to tax-exempt organizations whose programs fall within the trust's interests.
Restrictions Grants are not made to individuals or for scholarships, fellowships, capital funds, annual campaigns, seed grants, emergency funds, deficit financing, or endowment funds.
Areas of Interest Arboretums; Coastal Processes; Conservation, Natural Resources; Ecology; Environmental Programs; Leadership; Music; Music Composition; Music Education; Music Recording; Neighborhoods; Poverty and the Poor; Urban Areas; Wetlands
Sample Awards American Symphony Orchestra (New York, NY)—for general support of its concert season at Avery Fisher Hall, $45,000. Uprose (Brooklyn, NY)—support for the Sunset Park Environmental Justice Community Organizing initiative, $20,000. National Audubon Society (New York, NY)—general support of the society's Florida Everglades program, $40,000.

CBS Foundation Grants   843

CBS Foundation
1515 Broadway, 50th Fl
New York, NY 10036
Contact Karen Zatorski , (212) 258-6000
Internet http://www.cbs.com
Requirements IRS 501(c)3 organizations are eligible.
Restrictions The program does not make loans or grants for advertising, endowments, or for capital costs including construction and renovation. Individuals are not eligible.
Areas of Interest Civic Affairs; Communications; Cultural Activities/Programs; Education; Family; Fine Arts; Higher Education; Journalism Education; Minority Education; Performing Arts; Youth Programs

Central New York Community Foundation Grants   844

Central New York Community Foundation
500 S Salina St, Ste 428
Syracuse, NY 13202-3302
Contact Kim Scott, Program Contact, (315) 422-9538; fax: (315) 471-6031; e-mail: kim@cnycf.org
Internet http://www.cnycf.org/seekers/grants.cfm
Requirements New York 501(c)3 tax-exempt organizations in Onondaga and Madison Counties are eligible.
Restrictions The foundation generally does not make grants for annual operating budgets, except when it is seed or bridge money; endowments; sectarian purposes; loans or assistance to individuals; or medical research.
Areas of Interest Community Development; Computer Grants; Health Care; Inner Cities; Opera/Musical The-

ater; Patient Care and Education; Racism/Race Relations; Volunteers

Sample Awards Urban League of Onondaga County (Syracuse, NY)—for salary support of technicians at its computer centers in inner-city Syracuse, $15,000. Earlville Opera House (Carlville, NY)—to renovate a workshop and studio space for year-round use, $20,000. Syracuse Community Health Ctr (Syracuse, NY)—to construct an education and resource center for patients, $39,500. Interreligious Council of Central New York (Syracuse, NY)—for its Communitywide Dialog on Racism, Race Relations, and Racial Healing program, $20,000.

Chautauqua Region Community Foundation 845 Grants

Chautauqua Region Community Foundation
418 Spring St
Jamestown, NY 14701
Contact Randall Sweeney, Executive Director, (716) 661-3390; fax: (716) 488-0387; e-mail: crcf@crcfonline.org
Internet http://www.crcfonline.org/Grants.htm
Requirements Nonprofit organizations may apply for grants in support of projects serving communities in Chautauqua County, excluding the Fredonia/Dunkirk area, which is served by the Northern Chautauqua Community Foundation.
Areas of Interest Arts, General; Children and Youth; Cultural Activities/Programs; Education; Government; Housing; Infants; Libraries; Nutrition/Dietetics; Philanthropy; Public Administration; Scholarship Programs, General; Shelters; Small Businesses; Social Services
Sample Awards Salvation Army (NY)—to support the purchasing of infant formula and diapers, $500. James Prendergast Library Assoc (NY)—to support acquisition of books on and for small business, $2500. Research and Planning for Human Services (NY)—to support human services coordination activities, $4000.

Citigroup Foundation Grants   846

Citigroup Foundation
850 Third Ave, 13th Fl
New York, NY 10043
Contact Charles Raymond, President, (212) 559-9163; fax: (212) 793-5944; e-mail: citigroupfoundation@citigroup.com
Internet http://www.citigroup.com/citigroup/corporate/foundation/guide.htm
Requirements 501(c)3 nonprofit organizations in communities served by Citibank or a Citigroup company are eligible.
Restrictions Religious, veterans, or fraternal organizations are not eligible unless their project would benefit the entire community.
Areas of Interest Academic Achievement; Arts, General; Business Education; Communications; Community Development; Computer Grants; Consumer Behavior; Consumer Education/Information; Cultural Activities/Programs; Curriculum Development; Disaster Relief; Economic Development; Education; Elementary Education; Environmental Programs; Financial Education; Literacy; Health Care; Health Services Delivery; Housing;

International Economics; International Programs; Mentoring Programs; Minority Education; Neighborhoods; Secondary Education; Service Delivery Programs; Social Services; Teacher Education; Technology Education; Welfare-to-Work Programs; Women's Education

Sample Awards PhD Project (Montvale, NJ)—to increase the number of African American, American Indian, and Hispanic American faculty members at business schools nationwide, $50,000 (2003). American National Red Cross (Washington, DC)—for relief efforts related to the recent widespread wildfires in California, $50,000 (2003). Habitat for Humanity International (Americus, GA)—for its nationwide program through which Citigroup employees build homes in collaboration with deserving families who would not otherwise be able to afford a house, $1 million (2002). Maryland Public Television (Owings Mills, MD)—for the Sense and Dollars Web site, an effort to teach young people to earn, spend, save, and invest money wisely, $25,000 (2002).

Liz Claiborne Foundation Grants   847

Liz Claiborne Foundation
1440 Broadway
New York, NY 10018
Contact Melanie Lyons, Director, (212) 626-5704; fax: (212) 626-5304
Internet http://www.lizclaiborne.com/lizinc/foundation/default.asp
Requirements 501(c)3 nonprofits in Montgomery, AL; New York, NY; Hudson County, NJ; and Mount Pocono, PA are eligible.
Restrictions Religious organizations and individuals are ineligible.
Areas of Interest AIDS; Arts, General; Cultural Programs/Activities; Education; Elementary Education; Environmental Programs; Family; Minority Education; Seconday Education; Social Services Delivery; Women
Sample Awards New York State Public/Private Initiatives, Twin Towers Fund (New York, NY)—to benefit the families of firemen, policemen, emergency medical personnel, and other public-safety and government workers injured or killed in the September 11 terrorist attacks, $1 millio. employee matching gifts to the disaster-relief efforts and donated apparel for rescue workers and victims of the attacks.

Clark Foundation Grants   848

Clark Foundation
1 Rockefeller Plaza, 31st Fl
New York, NY 10020
Contact Charles Hamilton, Executive Director, (212) 977-6900
Requirements Nonprofit organizations in upstate New York and New York, NY, are eligible.
Areas of Interest Children and Youth; Cultural Activities/Programs; Education; Environmental Programs; Food Distribution; Health Care; Hospitals; Philanthropy; Surgery; Youth Programs
Sample Awards Big Brothers Big Sisters of New York (New York, NY)—to provide nonprofit groups with seed grants in order to establish community-based mentor programs throughout New York City, $250,000 (2001).

Community Foundation for Greater Buffalo 849 Grants

Community Foundation for Greater Buffalo
712 Main St
Buffalo, NY 14202
Contact Program Contact, (716) 852-2857; e-mail: mail@cfgb.org
Internet http://www.cfgb.org/hpgrants.html
Requirements IRS 509(a) organizations in or benefiting residents of Allegany, Cattaraugus, Chautauqua, Erie, Genesee, Niagara, Orleans, and Wyoming Counties, NY, are eligible.
Restrictions Grant requests are not considered for endowment funds, religious purposes, projects outside the western New York region, or schools not registered with the state education department.
Areas of Interest Child Welfare; Child/Maternal Health; Children and Youth; Civic Affairs; Community Development; Education; Elementary Education; Family; Health Care; Inner Cities; Opera/Musical Theater; Philanthropy; Poverty and the Poor; Private and Parochial Education; Scholarship Programs, General
Sample Awards Greater Buffalo Opera Comp (Buffalo, NY)—to refurbish and renovate a set for a production of Carmen, $10,000. Bison Fund-Buffalo Inner-City Scholarship Opportunity Network (Buffalo, NY)—for elementary school students, to provide low-income, inner-city parents with the option of choosing a private or parochial school for their children, $10,000.

Community Foundation of Herkimer and 850 Oneida Counties Grants

Community Foundation of Herkimer and Oneida Counties
270 Genessee St
Utica, NY 13502
Contact Susan Smith, Senior Programs Officcer, (315) 735-8212; fax: (315) 735-9363; e-mail: commfdn@borg.com
Requirements The community foundation supports only nonprofit organizations in Oneida and Herkimer Counties in New York.
Restrictions Grants will not normally be made for endowments, ongoing operations, annual budgets or deficit financing, religious purposes, or financial assistance or scholarships to individuals.
Areas of Interest Community Development; Day Care; Emergency Services; Scholarship Programs, General; Senior Citizen Programs and Services
Sample Awards Colgate College—to support scholarships for students from Oneida and Herkimer Counties, $2500. Ilion Central School District—start-up funding for school-based child care center, $47,265. Central Oneida County Volunteer Ambulance Corps—to purchase a cardiac monitor/defibrillator, $8495. West Side Senior Center—to purchase a new copier, $1495.

Aaron Copland Fund for Music Performing 851 Ensembles Program

Aaron Copland Fund for Music
30 W 26th St, Ste 1001
New York, NY 10010-2011
Contact Philip Rothman, Director of Grantmaking Programs, (212) 366-5260 ext 29; fax: (212) 366-5265; e-mail: center@amc.net

Internet http://www.amc.net/resources/grants/performing.html
Requirements Applications may be submitted by nonprofit professional performing ensembles with a history of substantial commitment to contemporary American music and with plans to continue that commitment.
Restrictions In general, support will not be provided to orchestras. Individuals, student ensembles, and presenters without a core ensemble are not eligible. Grants will not be made for the purpose of commissions to composers.
Areas of Interest Music; Music Appreciation; Performing Arts

Aaron Copland Fund for Music Performing 852 Ensembles

American Music Center
30 W 26th St, Ste 1001
New York, NY 10010-2011
Contact Philip Rothman, (212) 366-5260 ext 29
Internet http://www.amc.net/resources/grants/performing.html
Requirements Applicants must meet the following requirements: nonprofit tax-exempt status; performance history of at least two years at the time of application; at least 20 percent of the ensemble's programming (in terms of duration) for the preceding two seasons consists of contemporary American music; and demonstrated commitment to contemporary American music.
Restrictions Individuals, student ensembles, festivals, and presenters without a core ensemble are not eligible. Grants will not be made for the purpose of commissioning composers.
Areas of Interest Music; Music Appreciation; Performing Arts

Aaron Copland Fund Supplemental Program 853 Grants

Aaron Copland Fund for Music
30 W 26th St, Ste 1001
New York, NY 10010-2011
Contact Philip Rothman, American Music Center, (212) 366-5260 ext 29
Internet http://www.amc.net/resources/grants/performing.html
Requirements Nonprofit organizations with a history of substantial commitment to contemporary American music that have been in existence for at least two years at the time of application are eligible.
Restrictions No grants are made to individuals.
Areas of Interest Music

Corning Incorporated Foundation 854 Educational Grants

Corning Incorporated Foundation
MP-LB-02
Corning, NY 14831
Contact Karen Martin, Associate Director, (607) 974-8719; fax: (607) 974-4756; e-mail: swainKa@corning.com
Internet http://www.corning.com/inside_corning/foundation.asp
Requirements All requests to the foundation for support must be made in writing. Grant seekers are advised to

submit a two- to three-page letter of inquiry, signed by the senior administrative officer of the organization.

Restrictions Grants do not support individuals; political parties, campaigns, or causes; labor or veterans' organizations; religious or fraternal groups; volunteer emergency squads; athletic activities; courtesy advertising; or fundraising events.

Areas of Interest Career Education and Planning; Community Service Programs; Computer Grants; Curriculum Development; Education; Educational Technology; Engineering; Higher Education; Libraries; Scholarship Programs, General; Science

Sample Awards Wilson College (Chambersburg, PA)—for the Learning Resources Ctr, $5000. Corning City School District (Painted Post, NY)—to support computerization and curriculum enrichment, $33,000. Junior Achievement of Elmira (Corning, NY)—for general program support, $3000.

Nathan Cummings Foundation Grants   855
Nathan Cummings Foundation
475 10th Ave, 14th Fl
New York, NY 10018
Contact Program Contact, (212) 787-7300; fax: (212) 787-7377; e-mail: info@cummings.ncf.org; arts e-mail: arts@cummings.ncf.org; environment e-mail: enviro@cummings.ncf.org; health e-mail: health@cummings.ncf.org; Jewish life e-mail: jlife@cumming
Internet http://www.ncf.org/guidelines/guidelines.html
Restrictions The foundation does not contribute to endowments, debt reduction, capital campaigns, capital construction, equipment purchases, or museum collections acquisitions.
Areas of Interest Arts, General; Children and Youth; Cultural Diversity; Cultural Outreach; Environmental Programs; Government; Health Care; Jewish Studies; Poverty and the Poor; Refugees; Religion; Religious Studies
Sample Awards Cultural Initiatives-Silicon Valley (San Jose, CA)—for research leading to a community arts program, $50,000 (2002). Better Government Assoc (Chicago, IL)—for campaign finance-reform effors, $32,000 (2002). Hebrew Union College-JIR (New York, NY)—for a flexible master's-degree program for lay Jewish leaders, $67,700 (2002).

Dammann Fund Grants   856
Dammann Fund
521 5th Ave, 31st Fl
New York, NY 10175
Contact Penelope Johnston, c/o Engel and Davis, LLP, (212) 956-4118; fax: (212) 262-9321
Requirements Nonprofits in the greater metropolitan New York, NY, area including southern Connecticut; Boston, MA, and surrounding communities are eligible.
Restrictions Grants are not made to individuals or for scholarships, fellowships, matching gifts, or loans.
Areas of Interest Children and Youth; Disabled; Domestic Violence; Education; Family; Mental Disorders; Mental Health; Rehabilitation/Therapy
Sample Awards Institute for Community Living (New York, NY)—to support residential and rehabilitation services for people with mental and physical disabilities,

$12,000. Boston Medical Ctr Corp (Boston, MA)—for the Domestic Violence Guardian and Litem Program, $30,000. Louise Wise Services (New York, NY)—for the Teen Dad Program, $30,000. Northside Ctr for Child Development (New York, NY)—for therapeutic and educational programs for the Harlem community, $25,000.

Charles A. Dana Neuroscience Research Grants   857
Charles A. Dana Foundation
745 Fifth Ave, Ste 900
New York, NY 10151-0002
Contact Lori Jean Irvine, Program Associate, (212) 223-4040; fax: (212) 317-8721; e-mail: ljirvine@dana.org
Internet http://www.dana.org/grants
Requirements Grants support US organizations whose interests focus on education, health, and neuroscience.
Areas of Interest Addictions; Alzheimer's Disease; Brain; Child Psychology/Development; Depression; Diagnosis, Medical; Drugs/Drug Abuse; Genetics; Hearing Impairments; Human Learning and Memory; Neurological Disorders; Pain; Parkinson's Disease; Psychiatry; Schizophrenia; Spinal Cord Injury; Stroke; Visual Impairments

Dana Foundation Grants   858
Dana Foundation
745 Fifth Ave, Ste 700
New York, NY 10151-0002
Contact Grants Administrator, (212) 223-4040; fax: (212) 317-8721; e-mail: danainfo@dana.org
Internet http://www.dana.org/grants
Areas of Interest Art Eucation; Education; Biomedical Research; Elementary Education; Health Care; Immunology; Brain; Genetics; Neurological Disorders; Neuroscience; Science
Sample Awards Mount Sinai School of Medicine (NY)—for research on neuroimmunology, $300,000 (2002). Clarice Smith Performing Arts Ctr, U of Maryland (College Park, MD)—for a training program for arts specialists who teach public school, $25,500 (2002). U of Texas (Austin, TX)—to support the Dana Center for Educational Innovation, $350,000 (2002).

Dolan Foundations Grants   859
Dolan Foundations
1 Media Crossways
Woodbury, NY 11797
Contact Dr. Robert Vizza, President, (516) 803-9201
Requirements Schools and other nonprofits in New York are eligible. Applicants outside New York should call or write prior to submitting proposals.
Areas of Interest Disabled; Education; Health Care; Higher Education; Hospitals; Mental Health; Rehabilitation/Therapy; Science; Technology
Sample Awards John Carroll U (Cleveland, OH)—to construct a science and technology center, $20,000.

Dreitzer Foundation Grants   860
Dreitzer Foundation
330 Madison Ave, 35th Fl
New York, NY 10017

Contact Grants Administrator, (212) 557-7700; fax: (212) 286-8513
Requirements 501(c)3 tax-exempt organizations in New York are eligible.
Areas of Interest Health Care; Homelessness; Social Services Delivery; Youth Programs
Sample Awards Partnership for the Homeless (New York, NY)—grant recipient, $50,000. Ethical Culture Society of Queens (Bayside, NY)—grant recipient, $25,000.

Freeman Foundation Grants 861
Freeman Foundation
345 Park Ave, 4th Fl
New York, NY 10154
Contact Elizabeth Wong, (212) 464-2482; fax: (212) 464-2305; e-mail: wong_elizabeth@jpmorgan.com
Areas of Interest Asia, East (Far East); Conservation, Agriculture; Conservation, Natural Resources; Economics; Environmental Programs; Forests and Woodlands; Higher Education; International Exchange Programs; International Relations; International Trade and Finance; Land Use Planning/Policy; Medical Education; Nature Centers
Sample Awards U of Hawaii (HI)—to establish the Integrating International Language Study and Service Learning in Asia program at Kapi'olani Community College, through which students will develop second-language skills, increase their understanding of East Asian cultures, and participate in community service, $1.2 million (2003). Johns Hopkins U (Baltimore, MD)—for a professorship and fellowship at the Hopkins-Nanjing Center for Chinese and American Studies, $520,000 (2003). Cleveland Museum of Art (OH)—to develop a curriculum using distance-learning technologies that will make the museum's collection of Asian art available to students, $722,457 over three years (2003).

Samuel Freeman Charitable Trust Grants 862
Samuel Freeman Charitable Trust
114 W 47th St
New York, NY 10036-1532
Contact Linda Franciscovich, c/o US Trust Company, (212) 852-3683; fax: (212) 852-3377
Requirements US nonprofit organizations may apply.
Areas of Interest Cancer/Carcinogenesis; Education; Higher Education; Literature; Philanthropy; Restoration and Preservation; Science; Secondary Education; Transportation

Fund for the City of New York Grants 863
Fund for the City of New York
121 Avenue of the Americas, 6th Fl
New York, NY 10013
Contact Grants Administrator, (212) 925-6675; e-mail: info@fcny.org
Internet http://www.fcny.org
Requirements Grants are awarded to projects with an intended impact on New York City and are limited to qualifying charitable organizations.
Restrictions The fund cannot make grants to individuals, to support endowment and capital campaigns, nor to support academic studies.

Areas of Interest AIDS; Children and Youth; Civic Affairs; Community Development; Governmental Functions; Housing; Nonprofit Organizations; Urban Areas

Gebbie Foundation Grants 864
Gebbie Foundation
110 W Third St, Hotel Jamestown Bldg, Rm 308
Jamestown, NY 14702-1277
Contact Dr. Thomas Cardman, Executive Director, (716) 487-1062; fax: (716) 484-6401; e-mail: gebfnd@netsync.net
Requirements IRS 501(c)3 organizations are eligible. Preference will be given to requests from the Jamestown/Chautauqua County region.
Restrictions Grants are not awarded to support sectarian or religious organizations, higher education institutions (except to institutions that were recipients of lifetime contributions of donor), individuals, or endowments.
Areas of Interest Arts, General; Biomedical Research; Children and Youth; Cultural Activities/Programs; Education; Exercise; Family; Health Care; Higher Education; Hospitals; Water Resources
Sample Awards Fund for the Arts in Chautauqua County—to support an annual campaign, $90,000. Berry College (Mount Berry, GA)—toward renovations of Blackstone Hall, $25,000. WCA Hospital—to purchase exercise equipment, $3055. Chautauqua Watershed Conservancy—for seed money to expand operations, $28,580.

Howard Gilman Foundation Grants 865
Howard Gilman Foundation
111 W 50th St
New York, NY 10020
Contact Harry Brown, Program Associate, (212) 307-1073; fax: (212) 262-4108; e-mail: hbrown@gilman.com
Internet http://www.howardgilman.org
Requirements 501(c)3 nonprofit organizations are eligible.
Restrictions Religious and political agencies are ineligible.
Areas of Interest AIDS; Arts, General; Biomedical Research; Cardiovascular Diseases; Conservation, Natural Resources; Cultural Activities/Programs; Environmental Programs; HIV; Music; Sports Medicine; Wildlife
Sample Awards Brooklyn Academy of Music (Brooklyn, NY)—for endowment and operating support, $5 million.

Herman Goldman Foundation Grants 866
Herman Goldman Foundation
61 Broadway, 18th Fl
New York, NY 10006
Contact Richard Baron, Executive Director, (212) 797-9090
Requirements Applicant organizations must submit a copy of the IRS determination letter.
Restrictions Grants to individuals will not be considered.
Areas of Interest Art Education; Arts, General; Children and Youth; Civil/Human Rights; Critical Care Medicine; Drama; Education; Health Care; Medical Education; Performing Arts

Sample Awards Boca Raton Community Hospital (Boca Raton, FL)—to support construction of an urgent care center, $20,000. New York U School of Medicine—to support Medical Ctr scholarships, $20,000. American Civil Liberties Union Foundation—to continue support of the Children's Rights Project, $10,000. Dramatic Risks—to support the development of exemplary projects in the performing arts, theatrical writing, and the arts in education, $5000.

GreenPoint Foundation Grants 867

GreenPoint Foundation
90 Park Ave, 4th Fl
New York, NY 10016
Contact Gwen Perry, Foundation Manager, (212) 834-1215; fax: (212) 834-1406; e-mail: gperry@ GreenPoint.com
Internet http://www.greenpoint.com/index. cfm?spPathname=static/com-grants5less.htm
Requirements 501(c)(3) nonprofits that serve the needs of the communities in which GreenPoint Bank does business are eligible.
Restrictions Grants do not support capital campaigns, endowments, scholarship funds, special events, other short-term projects, religious organizations, or membership organizations.
Areas of Interest Health Care; Health Care Access; Health Promotion; Housing; Service Delivery Programs
Sample Awards Families of employees of Keefe, Bruyette and Woodf (New York, NY)—for families of employees killed in the September 11 attacks on the World Trade Center, $250,000. American Red Cross, Disaster Relief Fund (Washington, DC)—to provide disaster-relief services to victims of the September 11 terrorist attacks, $25,000.

Stella and Charles Guttman Foundation 868 Grants

Stella and Charles Guttman Foundation
122 E 42nd St. Ste 2010
New York, NY 10168
Contact Elizabeth Olofson, Executive Director, (212) 371-7082; fax: (212) 371-8936; e-mail: info@ guttmanfdn.org
Requirements Charitable 501(c)3 or 170(b)1 organizations are eligible with a strong emphasis on New York City and Israel.
Restrictions The foundation does not make grants directly to individuals or to organizations not qualified as charitable, for foreign travel or study, to initiate or defend public interest litigation, to support anti-vivisectionist causes, or to religious organizations for religious observances.
Areas of Interest Arts, General; At-Risk Youth; Cancer/Carcinogenesis; Children and Youth; Cultural Activities/Programs; Disabled; Drugs/Drug Abuse; Education; Elderly; Employment Opportunity Programs; Family Planning; International Relations; Israel; Mental Health; Science; Social Services Delivery; Women's Health
Sample Awards Educational Alliance (New York, NY)—for general support, $25,000. Creative Ctr for Women with Cancer (New York, NY)—for general support, $25,000. Givat Haviva Educational Foundation (New York, NY)—for the Children Teaching Children program and Ibn Rouchd School in Jat, Israel, $16,000.

Arkell Hall Foundation Grants 869

Arkell Hall Foundation
PO Box 240
Canajoharie, NY 13317-0240
Contact Joseph Santangelo, Vice President & Treasurer, (518) 673-5417; fax: (518) 673-5493
Requirements IRS 501(c)3 organizations directly impacting the Western Montgomery County, NY, community are eligible.
Restrictions Requests that do not include written proof of 501(c)3 status will not be considered. Projects or organizations with large service areas, such as national or regional, will not qualify for funding, nor will projects in which the target community is not the primary area of focus.
Areas of Interest Adult and Continuing Education; Basic Skills Education; Elderly; Health Care; Higher Education; Literacy; Medical Education; Nursing Homes; Religion; Senior Citizen Programs and Services; Single-Parent Families; Women
Sample Awards Cornell University, College of Human Ecology (Ithaca, NY)—for general support, $20,000. College of Saint Rose (Albany, NY)—to support scholarships for single mothers, $3000.

Hartford Aging and Health Program Awards 870

John A. Hartford Foundation
55 E 59th St, 16th Fl
New York, NY 10022-1178
Contact Corinne Rieder, Executive Director, (212) 832-7788; fax: (212) 593-4913; e-mail: mail@ jhartfound.com
Internet http://www.jhartfound.org
Requirements US health, education, and social service organizations may apply.
Restrictions Requests will be denied for general research or for projects lasting more than three years.
Areas of Interest Aging/Gerontology; Career Education and Planning; Geriatrics; Health Care Administration; Health Care Assessment; Health Care Economics; Health Care Financing; Health Services Delivery; Hospitals; Medicine, Internal; Pharmacology; Social Services; Training and Development
Sample Awards American Academy of Nursing (Washington, DC)—to coordinate the foundation's Building Academic Geriatric Nursing Capacity program, and to support doctoral and postdoctoral scholars and nurses pursuing business degrees, $3.05 million (2003). American Federation for Aging Research (New York, NY)—to support nine new scholars, and to extend the Paul B. Beeson Physician Faculty Scholars in Aging Research Program, $4,827,654 over five years (2003). Duke U (Durham, NC)—to support the work of Harvey Cohen, $300,000 over three years (2003). U of Michigan at Ann Arbor (MI)—to support the work of Jeffrey Halter, $300,000 (2003).

Hearst Foundation and William Randolph Hearst Foundation Grants Program   871

Hearst Foundation
888 Seventh Ave, 45th Fl
New York, NY 10106-0057
Contact Mayra Cedeno, Grants Administrator, (212) 586-5404; fax: (212) 586-1917
Internet http://www.hearstfdn.org
Requirements Grants are made only to tax-exempt organizations that are not private foundations. Eligible nonprofits include those working in pediatrics, perinatology, substance abuse, teen pregnancy, homelessness, and infant mortality.
Restrictions Grants are to be used exclusively for charitable purposes within the United States and its possessions. Grants are not made to individuals and may not be used for political purposes. The foundation does not purchase tickets, tables, or advertising for fund-raising events.
Areas of Interest Cultural Activities/Programs; Education; Health Care; Legal Education; Minorities; Orchestras; Poverty and the Poor; Religion; Scholarship Programs, General; Secondary Education; Social Services; Youth Programs
Sample Awards Georgia Institute of Technology (GA)—to endow a scholarship for minorities and women pursuing master's degrees in the College of Engineering, $100,000 (2004). Quincy U (IL)—to endow a scholarship fund for minority students majoring in education, health care, mathematics, or science, $100,000 (2004). Poets and Writers (Los Angeles, CA)—to support literary activities in California, $100,000 (2003). Vanderbilt U Medical Ctr (Nashville, TN)—for the Maternal and Infant Health Outreach Worker Program, $150,000 (2003).

F.B. Heron Foundation Grants   872

F.B. Heron Foundation
100 Broadway, 17th Fl
New York, NY 10005
Contact Mary Jo Mullan, Program Officer, c/o Rockefeller and Company Inc, (212) 404-1800; fax: (212) 404-1805
Internet http://fdncenter.org/grantmaker/fbheron
Requirements US nonprofits may apply.
Areas of Interest Business Development; Career Education and Planning; Child Psychology/Development; Child/Maternal Health; Chronic Illness; Community Service Programs; Day Care; Disabled; Economic Self-Sufficiency; Employment Opportunity Programs; Health Promotion; Homelessness; Homeownership; Independent Living Programs; Parent Education; Preschool Education; Shelters; Training and Development
Sample Awards Rosalie Manor, Inc. (Milwaukee, WI)—to support a First Time Parents program to promote health child development, $75,000. Wheelock College (Boston, MA)—for the Ctr for Career Development in Early Child Care, $50,000. Beyond Shelter (Los Angeles, CA)—for general support, $50,000.

Humanitas Foundation Grants   873

Humanitas Foundation
1114 Ave of the Americas, 28th Fl
New York, NY 10036

Contact Kathleen Mahoney, President, (212) 704-2300
Requirements Applications are accepted from national Roman Catholic organizations, dioceses, diocesan offices, groups of parishes, social agencies, religious orders, and other groups. Roman Catholic organizations with tax-exempt rulings also may apply.
Restrictions Applications will not be accepted from Catholic elementary or secondary schools, colleges, universities, or seminaries. Nor are proposals accepted to fund individuals or individual parishes.
Areas of Interest Adult and Continuing Education; Alcohol/Alcoholism; Catholic Church; Community Outreach Programs; Counseling/Guidance; Day Care; Drugs/Drug Abuse; Emergency Services; Family; Health Care; Homelessness; Hunger; Job Training Programs; Leadership; Minorities; Poverty and the Poor; Refugees; Religious Studies; Shelters
Sample Awards Woodstock Theological Ctr (Washington, DC)—for the Preaching the Just Word program, $25,000. Catholic Charities USA (Alexandria, VA)—for the emergency assistance fund, $40,000. Kidane-Mehret Geez Rite Catholic Church (Washington, DC)—for pastoral work among Ethiopian and Eritrean communities, $30,000.

Carl C. Icahn Foundation Grants   874

Carl C. Icahn Foundation
767 5th Ave, 47th Fl
New York, NY 10153-0023
Contact Gail Golden, Secretary-Treasurer
Requirements New York and New Jersey nonprofits are eligible to apply.
Restrictions No grants are provided to individuals.
Areas of Interest Arts, General; Child Abuse; Child Welfare; Cultural Activities/Programs; Education; Health Care; Jewish Services
Sample Awards Foundation For a Greater Opportunity (New York, NY)—$365,000. Choate Rosemary Hall Foundation, (Wallingford, CT)—$50,000.

Icahn Family Foundation Grants   875

Icahn Family Foundation
767 Fifth Ave, 47th Fl
New York, NY 10153
Contact Gail Golder Icahn, Vice-President
Areas of Interest Arts, General; Children and Youth; Education; Elementary Education; Secondary Education; Education Reform; Higher Education; Equipment/Instrumentation; Genetics
Sample Awards Princeton University (Princeton, NJ)—for Carl C. Icahn Laboratory for Genomics, $3,650,000 (2002). Mount Sinai School of Medicine of New York University (New York, NY)—for medical research, $1,010,000 (2002).

Independence Community Foundation Grants   876

Independence Community Foundation
182 Atlantic Ave
Brooklyn, NY 11201
Contact Marilyn Gelber, Executive Director, (718) 722-2300; fax: (718) 722-5757; e-mail: inquiries@icfny.org

Internet http://www.icfny.org/site2/content/grant_categories.asp

Requirements The foundation supports programs within New York City and Nassau County that are locally or community-based.

Restrictions The foundation does not fund individuals or endowments.

Areas of Interest Arts, General; Community Service Programs; Cultural Activities/Programs; Disabled; Dropouts; Economic Self-Sufficiency; Education; Job Training Programs; Literacy; Neighborhoods; Nonprofit Organizations

Sample Awards Partnership for the Homeless (New York, NY)—for an educational program for children in newly homeless families, $100,000 over two years (2003). Therapy and Learning Ctr (New York, NY)—for furniture and learning materials at this early-childhood-education program, $25,000 (2003). Hicksville Gregory Museum (NY)—for audio equipment for self-guided tours by students, $14,300 (2003). WBGO (Newark, NJ)—for internships at this radio station for high-school and college students, $10,000 (2003).

Christian A. Johnson Endeavor Foundation Grants 877

Christian A. Johnson Endeavor Foundation
1060 Park Ave, Apt 1F
New York, NY 10128
Contact Julie Kidd, President, (212) 534-6620; fax: (212) 410-5909

Restrictions The foundation does not award grants to individuals; neighborhood or community projects; city, county, state, or federal government-affiliated agencies; institutions controlled by religious institutions; or in the areas of health care and medical research.

Areas of Interest Art Education; Curriculum Development; Higher Education, Private; International Studies; Performing Arts; Visual Arts

Sample Awards New England College (Henniker, NH)—to develop the college's curriculum, with an emphasis on its liberal arts courses, $250,000 (2001).

Daisy Marquis Jones Foundation Grants 878

Daisy Marquis Jones Foundation
1600 South Ave, Ste 250
Rochester, NY 14620
Contact Roger Gardner, President, (585) 461-4950; fax (585) 461-9752; e-mail: mail@dmjf.org
Internet http://www.dmjf.org

Requirements Grants are awarded to qualified 501(c)3 nonprofit organizations that are located in Monroe and Yates Counties, NY.

Restrictions Requests will not be considered for support of basic research, the arts, religious purposes, scholarships, private schools, endowments, or to individuals.

Areas of Interest Children and Youth; Criminal Justice; Day Care; Dental Health and Hygiene; Elderly; Health Promotion; Preschool Education; Public Broadcasting; Senior Citizen Programs and Services; Visual Impairments; Volunteers; Women; Youth Programs

Sample Awards Seneca Park Zoo Society (Rochester, NY)—for the Butterfly Beltway program, which will provide educational events for poor children and activities for nursing-home residents, $12,696 (2003). YMCA of Greater Rochester (NY)—to construct Camp Northpoint, $75,000 (2003). Flower City Habitat for Humanity (Rochester, NY)—to construct a single-family home, $40,000 (2003). Advertising Council of Rochester (NY)—for an educational program for nonprofit groups, $10,000 (2003).

Joy Family Foundation Grants 879

Joy Family Foundation
5436 Main St
Williamsville, NY 14221
Contact Marsha Sullivan, Executive Director, (716) 633-6600; fax: (716) 633-0600; e-mail: info@joyfamilyfoundation.org

Requirements New York nonprofit organizations are eligible.

Areas of Interest AIDS; Aging/Gerontology; Alcohol/Alcoholism; Catholic Church; Children and Youth; Drugs/Drug Abuse; Education; Family; Hospitals; Literacy; Social Services; Women

Sample Awards Burchfield-Penny Art Center (Buffalo, NY)—for capital campaign, $25,000. Christ the King Seminary (East Aurora, NY)—grant recipient, $10,000. Computers for Children (Buffalo, NY)—for computer refurbishment, $10,000.

JPMorganChase Regrant Program for Small Ensembles 880

Meet the Composer
75 Ninth Ave, Fl 3R, Ste C
New York, NY 10011
Contact Grants Administrator, (212) 645—6949 ext 101; e-mail: mtrevino@meetthecomposer.org
Internet http://www.meetthecomposer.org/programs/fundforsmall.html

Requirements 501(c)3 tax-exempt organizations in the five boroughs of New York City, with organized music programs for at least three years, and an annual budget of less than $300,000 are eligible. Eligible organizations must have an existing organizational structure and an on-going artistic product.

Areas of Interest Music; Music Composition

Alfred Jurzykowski Foundation Grants 881

Alfred Jurzykowski Foundation
15 E 65th St
New York, NY 10021
Contact Bluma Cohen, Executive Director, (212) 535-8930

Requirements US tax-exempt organizations are eligible for funding for projects in Poland and Brazil.

Restrictions Grants are not awarded to individuals or for endowment funds or loans.

Areas of Interest Brazil; Poland; Social Services

Klingenstein Fund Grants Program 882

Esther A. and Joseph Klingenstein Fund
787 Seventh Ave, 6th Fl
New York, NY 10019
Contact John Klingenstein, President, (212) 492-618; fax: (212) 492-7007

Requirements Applicants should be tax-exempt organizations. A specific form is not required. Applications should include basic information about the organization; a detailed description of the proposed project including a budget; information about other sources of support received or sought for the project; the organization's latest audited financial statement; and a copy of its IRS classification.

Restrictions The fund does not contribute to endowments and rarely contributes to buildings or other kinds of capital projects.

Areas of Interest Animal Research Policy; Communications; Environmental Programs; Epilepsy; Family Planning; Health Care; Journalism; Neuroscience; Population Control; Private and Parochial Education; Public Planning/Policy; Religion; Secondary Education

Sample Awards Teachers College Columbia U (New York, NY)—for program support, $578,595. American Jewish Committee (New York, NY)—for work on issues of separation of church and state, $40,000. Foundation for Biomedical Research (Washington, DC)—for animal biomedical research, $25,000.

Klingenstein Third Generation Foundation   883
Grants in Depression

Klingenstein Third Generation Foundation
787 Seventh Ave, 6th Fl
New York, NY 10019-6016
Contact Sally Klingenstein, Executive Director, (212) 492-6179; fax: (212) 492-7007; e-mail: sally@ktgf.org
Internet http://www.ktgf.org/depress.html
Requirements US tax-exempt organizations are eligible.
Restrictions Grants do not support direct services.
Areas of Interest Adolescent Psychiatry; Adolescent Psychology; Attention Deficit Disorder; Child Psychiatry; Child Psychology/Development; Depression; Family; Intervention Programs; Mental Health; Training and Development
Sample Awards American Academy of Child and Adolescent Psychiatry (Washington, DC)—for general support, $15,000 (2003). Columbia U, Carmel Hill Ctr for Early Diagnosis and Treatment (New York, NY)—to create brochures on mental-health disorders written in different languages and at a low reading level, $15,000 (2003). State U of New York (Buffalo, NY)—fellowship support for James Waxmonsky, for research on child and adolescent depression, $30,000 over two years (2003).

Koessler Family Foundation Grants   884

Kenneth L. and Katherine G. Koessler Family Foundation Inc
124 Brantwood Rd
Snyder, NY 14226
Contact Stephen Juhasz, Grant Manager
Requirements Western New York nonprofits are eligible.
Areas of Interest Child/Maternal Health; Higher Education; Hospices; Hospitals
Sample Awards Canisius College (Buffalo, NY)—for its capital campaign, $1 million matching grant. Childrens Hospital of Buffalo (Buffalo, NY)—for general support, $60,000. Kenmore Mercy Foundation (Kenmore, NY)—to construct a new patient tower, $24,000.

Eugene M. Lang Foundation Grants   885

Eugene M. Lang Foundation
535 5th Ave, Ste 906
New York, NY 10017
Contact Program Contact, (212) 949-4100
Requirements Organizations in New York and Pennsylvania are eligible to apply.
Restrictions Grants are not made to individuals, or for building funds, equipment and materials, capital or endowment funds, deficit financing, publications, or matching gifts.
Areas of Interest Arts, General; Biomedical Research; Education; Health Care; Higher Education; Homelessness; Minorities; Performing Arts; Preschool Education; Single-Parent Families; Social Services
Sample Awards New York-Presbyterian Hospital (New York, NY)—for a six-year health-sciences education program for selected inner-city youths, designed to boost their academic success and facilitate their entry into health careers, $1.25 million (2003).

Lifebridge Foundation Grants   886

Lifebridge Foundation
PO Box 793, Times Square Sta
New York, NY 10108
Contact Larry Auld, Program Director, (212) 757-9711; fax: (212) 757-0246; e-mail: lifebridgenyc@aol.com
Internet http://www.lifebridge.org/policy.htm
Requirements Nonprofit organizations, individuals sponsored by nonprofit organizations, and individuals working independently on specific projects are eligible for funding. The foundation generally preselects its grantees, but also accepts introductory letters. A letter should be no more than three pages and should describe how the organization or project specifically reflects foundation's purposes and aims. Do not include any other supporting materials. Individuals seeking support for a specific project should include a resume or brief biography only.
Restrictions No introductory letters sent via e-mail will be accepted.
Areas of Interest Arts, General; Cultural Diversity; Death/Mortality; Education; Environmental Programs; Land Management; Parapsychology

Albert A. List Foundation Grants   887

Albert A. List Foundation
1328 Broadway, Ste 524, PMB 117
New York, NY 10001-2121
Contact Viki Laura List, President, (212) 631-0065 or (888) 826-1402; fax: (888) 826-1402; e-mail: listfdn@earthlink.net
Internet http://fdncenter.org/grantmaker/listfdn/index.html
Requirements US 501(c)3 nonprofits are eligible.
Restrictions Grants are not made to individuals.
Areas of Interest Abortion; Arts, General; Citizenship; Civil/Human Rights; Education; Family; Government; Grassroots Leadership; Homosexuals, Female; Homosexuals, Male; Human Reproduction/Fertility; Intellec-

tual Freedom; Legal Services; Mass Media; Radio; Social Change; Training and Development
Sample Awards Colorado Legal Initiatives Project (CO)—to support litigation to assure civil rights protection to gays, $76,000. Families USA Foundation—to provide the hands-on training program How to Use Talk Radio, $30,000. National Abortion Rights Action League Foundation—to support grassroots networks to protect and advance reproductive health and rights, $50,000. Art Institute of Chicago (Chicago, IL)—to plan a series of student leadership seminars to help train young artists as citizens and leaders, $8500.

Little River Foundation Grants 888
Little River Foundation
101 Park Ave, Ste 3500
New York, NY 10178-0061
Contact Dale Hogoboom, Assistant Treasurer
Requirements Only residents of Maryland, New Jersey, New York, Pennsylvania, and Virginia may apply.
Areas of Interest AIDS; Adult and Continuing Education; Africa; Alcohol/Alcoholism; Animal Rights; Basic Skills Education; Brain; Cancer/Carcinogenesis; Conservation, Natural Resources; Drugs/Drug Abuse; Environmental Programs; Higher Education; Hospitals; International Studies; Legal Education; Legal Services; Literacy; Preschool Education; Religion; Secondary Education
Sample Awards Grace Episcopal Church (The Plains, VA)—for facilities improvement, $25,000. Piedmont Environmental Council (Warrenton, VA)—for the building program, $87,000. Johns Hopkins U (Baltimore, MD)—for brain tumor research, $25,000. Princeton U (Princeton, NJ)—for annual support, $25,000.

Loews Foundation Grants 889
Loews Foundation
655 Madison Ave
New York, NY 10021
Contact Candace Leeds, (212) 521-2650; fax: (212) 521-2634
Requirements Organizations in Israel are eligible to apply.
Areas of Interest Israel; Jewish Services; Scholarship Programs, General

Lucille Lortel Foundation New York City 890
Theater Grants
Lucille Lortel Foundation
322 Eighth Ave, 21st Fl
New York, NY 10001
Contact Fran Kumin, (212) 924-2817 ext 212; fax: (212) 989-0036; e-mail: fkumin@aol.com
Internet http://www.lortel.org
Requirements An applicant theater must have been in operation as a professional, nonprofit, producing organization in New York, NY, for at least three years and have a current annual operating budget of $200,000 to $2.5 million.
Areas of Interest Performing Arts
Sample Awards 49 small and mid-size nonprofit theaters in New York City that were affected by the attacks on the World Trade Center (NY)—for operating support, $1 million total (2002).

G. Harold and Leila Y. Mathers Charitable 891
Foundation Grants
G. Harold and Leila Y. Mathers Charitable Foundation
103 S Bedford Rd, Ste 101
Mount Kisco, NY 10549-3440
Contact James Handelman, Executive Director, (914) 242-0465
Requirements US research organizations are eligible.
Areas of Interest Biological Sciences; Science
Sample Awards Fox Chase Cancer Ctr (Philadelphia, PA)—for genetic research, $660,000 over three years (2002).

Andrew W. Mellon Foundation Grants 892
Andrew W. Mellon Foundation
140 E 62nd St
New York, NY 10021
Contact Program Contact, (212) 838-8400; fax: (212) 223-2778
Internet http://www.mellon.org/awmpd.html
Requirements Tax-exempt organizations worldwide are eligible.
Restrictions Grants or loans are not made to individuals. Grants are not given to strictly local organizations.
Areas of Interest Classical Studies; Conservation, Natural Resources; Cultural Activities/Programs; Dramatic/Theater Arts; Environmental Programs; Faculty Development; Higher Education; History Education; Libraries, Academic; Library Automation; Literacy; Performing Arts; Political Science Education; Population Studies; Public Affairs; Religion; Technology; Theology; Youth Programs
Sample Awards Buffalo State College (NY)—for a professorship in and equipment for the art-conservation department, $995,000 over six years (2004). Johns Hopkins U, Bloomberg School of Public Health (Baltimore, MD)—for research on refugee health, $600,000 (2004). New York U, Institute of Fine Arts (New York, NY)—for graduate-level instruction in the history of Latin American art, $244,000 (2004). Swarthmore College (PA)—for programs to encourage undergraduate students to consider careers in library science, $500,000 (2004).

Merrill Lynch Philanthropic Program 893
Grants
Merrill Lynch & Company Foundation
2 World Financial Ctr, 5th Fl
New York, NY 10281-6100
Contact Westina Matthews, Vice President, Philanthropic Programs, (212) 236-4319; fax: (212) 236-8007; e-mail: SDimaggio@exchange.ml.com
Internet http://www.ml.com/philanthropy/grants/index.htm
Requirements Tax-exempt 501(c)3 organizations are eligible.
Restrictions Grants will not be made to private foundations; individuals; fundraising activities related to individual sponsorships (e.g., walk-a-thons, marathons); seed money for new organizations; political causes, candidates, and campaigns as well as organizations designed specifically for lobbying; religious, fraternal, social, or other membership organizations providing services mainly to their own constituencies; athletic events and

sports tournaments (Special Olympics is eligible); and fundraising events (dinners, luncheons).

Areas of Interest Children and Youth; Education; Entrepreneurship; Finance

Sample Awards Harlem Educational Activities Fund (New York, NY)—for a five-week program in entrepreneurship and investment education for students entering the eighth grade, $30,000 (2003). For projects through Investing Pays Off, a program that teaches young people about business, entrepreneurship, and finance, $3.2 million divided among 24 groups in Southern California and the San Francisco Bay area (2002).

Mertz Gilmore Foundation Grants 894

Mertz Gilmore Foundation
218 E 18th St
New York, NY 10003-3694

Contact Jay Beckner, Executive Director, (212) 475-1137; fax: (212) 777-5226; e-mail: info@mertzgilmore.org

Internet www.mertzgilmore.org

Restrictions The foundation does not make grants for political purposes such as lobbying or propaganda. In addition, proposals are not accepted for individuals; endowments, annual fund appeals, or fundraising events; conferences, workshops; sectarian religious concerns; scholarships, fellowships, research, loans, or travel; film or media projects; or publications.

Areas of Interest Civic Affairs; Civil/Human Rights; Cultural Activities/Programs; Dance; Defense Studies; Developing/Underdeveloped Nations; Energy Conservation; Environmental Programs; Higher Education; Homosexuals, Female; Homosexuals, Male; Immigrants; Industry; Israel; Law; Palestine; Peace/Disarmament; Renewable Energy Sources; Technology

MetLife Foundation General Grants 895

MetLife Foundation
1 Madison Ave
New York, NY 10010-3690

Contact Sibyl Jacobson, President and CEO, (212) 578-6272; fax: (212) 685-1435

Internet http://www.metlife.com/Companyinfo/Community/Found/index.html

Requirements Tax-exempt organizations are eligible. Giving is made on a national level but preference is given to requests from Connecticut, New Jersey, and New York.

Restrictions Grants do not support religious or sports groups, political activities, hospital capital fund campaigns, United Way-funded groups, local chapters of national nonprofits, disease-specific organizations, patient care, drug treatment, community health clinics, elementary and secondary schools, endowments, courtesy advertising, or festival participation.

Areas of Interest Civic Affairs; Community Development; Cultural Activities/Programs; Education; Health Promotion; Public Broadcasting; Social Services Delivery

Sample Awards Roberto Malinow, Cold Spring Harbor Laboratory (NY)—for research and personal use, as part of the Award for Medical Research in Alzheimer's Disease program, $250,000 (2004). Business Committee for the Arts (Long Island City, NY)—to produce museum

and cultural calendars and distribute them in public elementary schools in select cities, $445,000 (2004). National Urban League (New York, NY)—to help selected cities with employment, health, youth-development, and other projects, $1 million (2004). New York Blood Ctr (New York, NY)—to improve the process of screening and identifying rare blood types, $325,000 over two years (2004).

MONY Foundation Grants 896

MONY Foundation
1740 Broadway, 10-36
New York, NY 10019

Contact Program Contact, (212) 708-2468; fax: (212) 708-2001; e-mail: lynn_stekas@mony.com

Internet http://www.mony.com/Foundation

Restrictions Grants do not support private foundations; fully participating members of the United Way; religious, fraternal, athletic, social, or veterans' organizations; individuals; capital fund drives; endowments; or deficit financing.

Areas of Interest After-School Programs; At-Risk Youth; Children and Youth; Community Service Programs; Minorities; Volunteers; Youth Programs

J.P. Morgan Chase Corporate Contributions 897 Grants

J.P. Morgan Chase
60 Wall St
New York, NY 10260-0060

Contact Corporate Contributions, (212) 552-1112; fax: (212) 648-5082

Internet http://www.jpmorganchase.com/cm/cs?pagename=Chase/Href&urlname=jpmc/community/grants/programs

Requirements Grants are made to tax-exempt organizations that are not classified as private foundations. The charitable trust rarely contributes to projects outside of New York City except in the fields of higher education and international affairs.

Restrictions Grants are not given to individuals, drug abuse programs, programs for specific disease or disability, scholarships, fellowships, United Way recipients, or to churches and other religious organizations unless the programs for which support is sought are entirely nonsecular in nature.

Areas of Interest Arts, General; Business Development; Children and Youth; Community Development; Economic Development; Disadvantaged (Economically); Cultural Programs/Activities; Diversity; Education; Education Reform; Elementary Education; Employment Opportunity Programs; Financial Education; Job Training Programs; Minority Education; Museums; Public Education; Public Planning/Policy; Religion; Secondary Education; Service Delivery Programs; Visual Arts; Youth Programs

Sample Awards Aspen Institute, Initiative for Social Innovation through Business (New York, NY)—to conduct an annual competition designed to boost the leadership and ethical decision-making capacity of business-school students, $1 million (2002). To be distributed among 240 arts and cultural groups in the New York area—for general operating support, $4 million (2002). To be distributed among various nonprofit groups and relief agenices—to assist individuals and organizations affected by the September 11 attacks, $10 million (2002).

Ms. Foundation for Women Reproductive Rights Coalition and Organizing Grants 898

Ms. Foundation for Women
120 Wall St, 33rd Fl
New York, NY 10005
Contact Grants Administrator, (212) 742-2300; fax: (212) 742-1563; e-mail: info@ms.foundation.org
Internet http://www.ms.foundation.org/wmspage. cfm?parm1=5
Requirements Priority will be given to state coalitions and membership organizations mounting proactive strategies and that address reproductive rights in the context of women's health, consumer rights, patient rights, racial justice, economic justice, or other contexts that broaden beyond a single issue. Regional, national, or academically oriented organizations must have strong connections to grassroots groups, and/or their work must be informed by local organizing efforts.
Restrictions The foundation does not support individuals, national organizations, state or regional intermediaries, research institutes or think tanks, or capital and endowment campaigns.
Areas of Interest Abortion; Child/Maternal Health; Contraceptives; Family Planning; Human Reproduction/ Fertility; Sex Education

Ms. Foundation Women and AIDS Fund Grants 899

Ms. Foundation for Women
120 Wall St, 33rd Fl
New York, NY 10005
Contact Grants Administrator, (212) 742-2300; fax: (212) 742-1653; e-mail: info@ms.foundation.org
Internet http://www.ms.foundation.org/wmspage. cfm?parm1=5
Requirements Grants are awarded to nonprofit groups working in the United States and Puerto Rico. The leadership of the specific project must be substantially made up of women with HIV/AIDS. Priority will be given to independent, women-focused organizations and programs.
Restrictions Start-up projects in organizations that have no track record in women and AIDS will not be considered. The fund does not support videos, stand-alone conferences, individuals, scholarships, fundraising events, university-based research, or government agencies.
Areas of Interest AIDS; Women; Women's Health

New-Land Foundation Grants 900

New-Land Foundation
1114 Ave of the Americas, 46th Fl
New York, NY 10036-7798
Contact Program Contact, (212) 479-6162
Restrictions Individuals are ineligible.
Areas of Interest Civil/Human Rights; Criminal Justice; Environmental Programs; Leadership; Peace/Disarmament; Population Control
Sample Awards Ms. Foundation for Women (New York, NY)—$60,000. Institute for Policy Studies (Washington, DC)—$40,000. Land and Water Fund of the Rockies (Boulder, CO)—$25,000.

New World Foundation Grants 901

New World Foundation
666 W End Ave
New York, NY 10025
Contact Grants Administrator, (212) 249-1023; fax: (212) 472-0508; info@newwf.org
Internet http://www.newwf.org/grant_programs/main. html
Areas of Interest Community Development; Education; Equal Educational Opportunity; Equal Employment Opportunity; Grassroots Leadership; Peace/Disarmament; Public Health

New York Community Trust Grants Program 902

New York Community Trust
2 Park Ave, 24th Fl
New York, NY 10016
Contact Joyce Bove, Vice President for Program and Projects, (212) 686-0010 ext 552; fax: (212) 534-8528; e-mail: info@nycommunitytrust.org or grants@ nycommunitytrust.org
Internet http://www.nycommunitytrust.org/newsite/ 02_grantmaking/2.0_grantmakingindex.html
Restrictions The trust does not support endowments, building construction/renovation, deficit financing, films, or religion.
Areas of Interest AIDS; Alcohol Education; Arthritis; Arts, General; Biomedical Research; Children and Youth; Civic Affairs; Civil/Human Rights; Community Development; Conservation, Natural Resources; Cultural Activities/Programs; Disabled; Drug Education; Economic Development; Education; Elderly; Employment Opportunity Programs; Environmental Programs; Family; Health Care; Health Planning/Policy; Health Services Delivery; Homelessness; Housing; Humanities; Hunger; Juvenile Law; Libraries; Mental Health; Mental Retardation; Neighborhoods; Recreation and Leisure; Rehabilitation/Therapy; Restoration and Preservation; Social Services; Technology; Visual Impairments; Women; Writing/Composition Education; Youth Programs
Sample Awards Groundwork (Brooklyn, NY)—for after-school reading classes, homework assistance, and art and music activities, $60,000 (2003). Greater Yellowstone Coalition (Bozeman, MT)—for ecosystem conservation of New York's Island Park area, $50,000 (2003). Hamilton-Madison House (New York, NY)—for its new day-care program for elderly Chinese people with dementia, $40,000 (2003). American Indian Law Alliance (New York, NY)—to strengthen its legal services for American Indians living in New York City, $41,000 over two years (2003).

New York Foundation Grants 903

New York Foundation
350 Fifth Ave, Rm 2901
New York, NY 10118
Contact Maria Mottola, Executive Director, (212) 594-8009
Internet http://www.nyf.org/Guidelines.asp
Requirements A letter outlining proposed project, budget needs, and amount of grant to be requested should precede a formal application. Applicants must reside in New York.

Restrictions The foundation never makes grants to individuals or to capital campaigns. It does not consider support of research studies, films, conferences, or publications; or requests outside New York City except from organizations working on statewide issues of concern to youth, the elderly, or the poor.

Areas of Interest Community Development; Disabled; Disadvantaged (Economically); Education; Elderly; Environmental Programs; Minorities; Public Affairs; Senior Citizen Programs and Services; Welfare Reform; Youth Programs

Sample Awards New York Statewide Senior Action Council(Albany, NY)—for general support of this statewide, membership-based advocacy organization, $45,000 (2002). Afghan Communicator (New York, NY)— to create an information center, assess community needs, and educate the public about Afghanistan, Islam, and the Afghan community, $40,000 (2002). New York AIDS Coalition (New York, NY)—to retain a community organizer to engage grassroots HIV/AIDS leaders in the Coalition's efforts $45,000 (2002). Picture the Homeless (New York, NY)— for an organization led by homeless people to end the criminalization of homelessness and build a movement that demands housing as a human right, $45,000 (2002).

New York Life Foundation Grants 904
New York Life Foundation
51 Madison Ave, Rm 1600
New York, NY 10010-1655
Contact Program Contact, (212) 576-7341; fax: (212) 576-6220; e-mail: NYLFoundation@newyorklife.com
Internet http://www.newyorklife.com/foundation/index.html
Requirements Nonprofit 501(c)3 organizations may submit grant requests. The foundation funds projects in New York City, where New York Life's Home Office is located. The foundation also considers multi-site projects implemented by national organizations. These projects must serve two or more of the following locations: Atlanta, Cleveland, Dallas, Kansas City, Minneapolis, Tampa and San Francisco/San Ramon.
Restrictions The foundation does not support sectarian or religious organizations or activities; fraternal, social, professional, athletic, or veterans groups; seminars or conferences; preschool, primary, or secondary education; endowments; memorials; basic or applied research; capital campaigns; or fund-raising activities.
Areas of Interest AIDS; After-School Programs; Arts, General; At-Risk Youth; Business; Career Education and Planning; Children and Youth; Community Service Programs; Cultural Activities/Programs; Economics; Financial Education; Health Planning/Policy; Insurance/Actuarial Science; Literacy; Medical Education; Middle School Education; Public Affairs; Scholarship Programs, General; Youth Programs
Sample Awards Girls Inc (New York, NY)—for adolescent girls to participate in a mentoring program that engages them in community-service projects, $358,000 over three years (2003). Boys & Girls Clubs of America (Atlanta, GA)—for library materials, technology, and other resources for students at 10 learning centers in Boys & Girls Clubs nationwide, $870,000 over two years (2003). Trust for Public Land (San Francisco, CA)—to create playgrounds at three New York City elementary schools, $750,000 (2003). Harlem Educational Activities Fund (New York, NY)—to provide high-potential youths with academic-enrichment and leadership-development activities, $291,000 over two years (2003).

New York Times Company Foundation 905
Grants
New York Times Company Foundation
229 W 43rd St
New York, NY 10036
Contact Jack Rosenthal, President, (212) 556-1091; fax: (212) 556-4450
Internet http://www.nytco.com/company/foundation/index.html
Requirements A brief letter describing the purpose for which funds are requested, including details of other potential sources of support, is sufficient for an application. Proof of tax-exempt status is also required.
Restrictions Grants are not made to individuals, to sectarian religious institutions and causes, or for drug, alcohol, or health-related purposes.
Areas of Interest Arts, General; Communications; Community Service Programs; Cultural Activities/Programs; Disadvantaged (Economically); Environmental Programs; Ethics; Higher Education; Intellectual Freedom; International Programs; Journalism; Law; Libraries; Mass Communication; Minority Education; Museums; Performing Arts; Professional Associations; Scholarship Programs, General; Urban Affairs; Wildlife
Sample Awards Kids Voting (Boston, MA)—for programs on voting and civic participation, $5000 (2002). Goddard Riverside Community Ctr (New York, NY)—to provide college-related guidance to students in overburdened high schools, $10,000 (2002). Lower East Side Tenement Museum (NY)—for general operating support, $15,000 (2002). Committee to Protect Journalists (NY)—for programs that support journalists who are harassed or imprisoned abroad, $25,000 (2002).

Norman Foundation Grants 906
Norman Foundation
147 E 48th St
New York, NY 10017
Contact June Makela or Wanda Peguero, (212) 230-9830; fax: (212) 230-9849; e-mail: info@normanfdn.org
Internet http://www.normanfdn.org/index.html
Requirements Projects may have local, regional, or national impact. Programs must be tax-exempt and focused on domestic US issues.
Restrictions Grants are not made to individuals, or to support conferences, scholarships, universities, research, films, media and arts projects, direct social service delivery programs, capital funding projects, fundraising drives, or other grantmaking organizations.
Areas of Interest Civil/Human Rights; Conservation, Agriculture; Conservation, Natural Resources; Economic Development; Environmental Law; Grassroots Leadership; Immigrants; Public Planning/Policy; Social Change
Sample Awards Missouri Rural Crisis Center (Columbia, MO)—renewed support for efforts to protect family farms and the environment, $20,000 (2003). Project

HIP-HOP (Boston, MA)—renewal support for youth organizing on education issues, $20,000 (2003). Southeast Regional Economic Justice Network (Durham, NC)—support of the African American/Latino project, $20,000 (2003). Border Action Network (Tucson, AZ)—support of education activities on the impact of growing militarization of the US-Mexico border, $20,000 (2003).

Jessie Smith Noyes Foundation Grants 907
Jessie Smith Noyes Foundation
6 E 39th St, 12th Fl
New York, NY 10016-0112
Contact Victor De Luca, President, (212) 684-6577; fax: (212) 689-6549; e-mail: noyes@noyes.org
Internet http://www.noyes.org
Requirements 501(c)3 tax-exempt organizations are eligible.
Restrictions Normally, the foundation will not consider requests for direct service, endowments, loans or scholarships to individuals, capital construction funds, conferences, media events, production of media and TV programming, or general fund-raising drives. General research projects are not funded per se.
Areas of Interest Conservation, Agriculture; Environmental Law; Environmental Programs; HIV; Hazardous Wastes; Human Reproduction/Fertility; Nonprofit Organizations; Sustainable Development
Sample Awards Idaho Women's Network (Boise, ID)—for operating and program support through the Organizational Strengthening Awards Program, based on its leadership, finances, commitment to diversity, and organizational longevity, $100,000 (2002). National Campaigns for Sustainable Agriculture (Pine Bush, NY)—for operating and program support, $100,000 (2001). New York City Environmental Justice Alliance (New York, NY)—for operating and program support, $100,000 (2001). HIV Law Project (New York, NY)—for operating and program support, $100,000 (2001).

NYFA Artists in the School Community 908
  Planning Grants
New York Foundation for the Arts
355th Ave, Rm 2901
New York, NY 10018
Contact Grants Administrator, (212) 366-6900 ext 321; e-mail: ASC_Plannning@nyfa.org.
Internet http://www.nyfa.org/asc_planning/index.html
Requirements Activities must benefit pre-K through grade 12 students. Schools, school districts, BOCES, teacher centers, colleges and universities or on Indian nation land in New York State are eligible to apply. New York State nonprofit organizations may work collaboratively with schools and artists; however the school must be the lead organization.
Restrictions Nonprofit cultural organizations are not eligible to apply.
Areas of Interest Art Education; Artists in Residence; Elementary Education; Secondary Education

NYSCA Architecture, Planning, and Design 909
  (APD) Grants
New York State Council on the Arts
175 Varick St
New York, NY 10014-4604
Contact Program Director, Architecture, Planning, and Design, (212) 627-4455; TDD: (800) 895-9838
Internet http://www.nysca.org/public/programs_funding.html
Requirements New York State organizations that present documented proof of nonprofit status are eligible to apply.
Areas of Interest Architecture; Architecture History; Design Arts; Graphic Design; Industrial Design; Interior Design; Landscape Architecture/Design; Regional/Urban Design; Restoration and Preservation, Structural/Architectural; Rural Planning/Policy; Urban Planning/Policy

NYSCA Arts in Education Grants 910
New York State Council on the Arts
915 Broadway, 8th Fl
New York, NY 10010-7199
Contact Gary Dayton, Arts in Education, (212) 741-5257; TDD: (212) 387-7049; e-mail: gdayton@nysca.org
Internet http://www.nysca.org/public/programs_guidelines.html
Requirements Nonprofit cultural and environmental organizations based in New York State may submit applications; under state law, public schools and BOCES may not apply directly to the council. Programs for students in grades pre-K-12 are eligible for funding.
Restrictions The program will not fund arts exposure programs or programs that are solely assembly programs or one-time visits or performances, programs that do not take place during the school day, programs that appear to substitute for or replace arts specialists, more than 50 percent of the direct expenses of individual projects, and programs that are exclusively teacher training. Programs for children during nonschool hours are not eligible.
Areas of Interest Art Education; Artists in Residence; Curriculum Development; Elementary Education; Environmental Studies; Preschool Education; Secondary Education; Teacher Education

NYSCA Dance Grants 911
New York State Council on the Arts
175 Varick St
New York, NY 10014-4604
Contact Beverly D'Anne, Program Director, or Debbie Lim, Associate, (212) 741-3232 or (212) 741-3331; TDD: (212) 387-7049; e-mail: bdanne@nysca.org or dlim@nysca.org
Internet http://www.nysca.org/public/programs_guidelines.html
Requirements Eligible to apply are nonprofit New York State performing arts organizations that have been producing and/or presenting under the same artistic and fiscal direction for at least two years (administrative direction for service organizations). Organizations desiring support for mime performances should refer to the Theater program. Eligibility varies for different programs; contact program staff for exact requirements.
Restrictions Support will generally not be provided for projects and programs to which public access is limited by the nature of the presentation including in-school, classroom, workshop, training, social services, therapeutic, and recreational projects and programs. Requests for

support of dance publications, formerly covered under Services to the Field, are no longer funded by the program.

Areas of Interest Audience Development; Choreography; Dance; Performing Arts

NYSCA Electronic Media and Film Grants 912

New York State Council on the Arts
175 Varick St, 3rd Fl
New York, NY 10014
Contact Program Officer, (212) 627-4455
Internet http://www.nysca.org/public/pdf/electronic_media_film.pdf
Requirements New York State nonprofit organizations that can furnish documented proof of their nonprofit status are eligible to apply. To be eligible for multiyear support, an organization must have received two consecutive years of support for the same activity from this program or the former film or media programs.
Areas of Interest Art Criticism; Artists in Residence; Audience Development; Audio Production; Film Production; Information Science/Systems; Media Arts; Planning/Policy Studies; Publication; Radio; Restoration and Preservation; Television; Touring Arts Programs; Video Production

NYSCA Folk Arts Grants 913

New York State Council on the Arts
915 Broadway, 8th Fl
New York, NY 10010-7199
Contact Robert Baron, Program Director, (212) 741-7755; TDD: (212) 387-7049; e-mail: rbaron@nysca.org
Internet http://www.nysca.org/public/programs_guidelines.html
Requirements Eligible to apply are New York State organizations that can document their proof of nonprofit status. Each category also carries its own specific requirements; see the NYSCA guidelines book for details.
Areas of Interest Folk/Ethnic Arts

NYSCA Museum Grants 914

New York State Council on the Arts
175 Varick St
New York, NY 10014-4604
Contact Kristin Herron, Director, (212) 741-7848; e-mail: KHerron@nysca.org
Internet http://www.nysca.org/public/programs_guidelines.html
Requirements Eligible to apply are New York State nonprofit organizations that document proof of nonprofit status.
Restrictions This program does not provide funding for fund-raising, public relations, marketing (except to address audience development for underserved populations), and membership campaigns and activities. No more than one application can be submitted in the exhibition category for any two consecutive years. Support is no longer provided for establishment of a new education or public programs department in a museum.
Areas of Interest Anthropology; Art Conservation; Audience Development; Cultural Diversity; Cultural Heritage Preservation; Exhibitions, Collections, Performances; History; Museum Education; Museums; Science

NYSCA Music Grants 915

New York State Council on the Arts
175 Varick St
New York, NY 10014-4604
Contact James Jordan, Program Director, or John Condon, Associate, (212) 741-6562 or (212) 741-6563; TDD: (212) 387-7049; e-mail: jjordan@nysca.org or jcondon@nysca.org
Internet http://www.nysca.org/public/programs_guidelines.html
Requirements Eligible to apply are New York State nonprofit organizations that can provide proof of nonprofit status. Generally, the program will consider for support only those organizations that have been producing, presenting, and/or serving the music field under the same artistic and administrative direction for at least two years. New applicants are required to have two artistic evaluations (audits) on file prior to the March 1 application deadline.
Restrictions The program will not provide support for projects and programs to which public access is limited by the nature of the presentation, including in-school programs, nursing homes, classroom activities, social services, and therapeutic and recreational programs.
Areas of Interest Band Music; Chamber Music; Folk Music; Jazz; Music; Music Recording; Music, Experimental; Music, Vocal; Musical Instruments; Musicians in Residence; Opera/Musical Theater; Orchestras; Radio; Touring Arts Programs

NYSCA Presenting Organizations Grants 916

New York State Council on the Arts
175 Varick St
New York, NY 10014-4604
Contact Bella Shalom, Program Director, or Kara Yeargans, Associate, (212) 741-2227 or (212) 741-2221; TDD: (800) 895-9838; e-mail: bshalom@nysca.org or kyeargans@nysca.org
Internet http://www.nysca.org/public/programs_guidelines.html
Requirements Eligible to apply are New York State nonprofit organizations that can document proof of their nonprofit status. Generally this program will consider for support only organizations that have been presenting under stable administrative direction for at least two years and are committed to paying artists a guaranteed, specified dollar amount as a fee; the two-year requirement does not apply to new presenter development applicants. The organization must have been funded through the presenting program for the last three years to be eligible for multiyear support. Each category has its own requirements and restrictions; see the NYSCA guidelines book for details.
Restrictions Single-day festivals will not be eligible for support unless they are a part of a larger presenting season.
Areas of Interest Audience Development; Cultural Diversity; Dance; Dramatic/Theater Arts; Mime; Music; Performance Art; Performing Arts

NYSCA Special Arts Services Grants 917

New York State Council on the Arts
175 Varick St
New York, NY 10014-4604
Contact Helen Cash Jackson, Director, (212) 741-7148; TDD: (800) 895-9838; e-mail: hcash@ nysca.org
Internet http://www.nysca.org/public/programs_ guidelines.html
Requirements Organizations eligible for support include performing arts organizations, visual arts organizations, multi-arts centers, and media organizations. Organizations must be nonprofit, located in the state of New York, and able to document proof of nonprofit status. The program requires that an organization be in existence a minimum of two years by the date of application before funding can be considered. All returning applicants to SAS must have two current program audits on file by March 1.
Restrictions Organizations whose projects are directed toward general audiences or organizations whose artists do not represent those communities specified are not eligible for support under this program. Organizations that receive exhibition support from other council programs will not be considered for exhibition support in the SAS.
Areas of Interest African Americans; Asian Americans; Cultural Diversity; Folk/Ethnic Arts; Hispanics; Media Arts; Native Americans; Performing Arts; Touring Arts Programs; Training and Development; Visual Arts

NYSCA Theater Grants 918

New York State Council on the Arts
175 Varick St
New York, NY 10014
Contact Program Contact, (212) 627-4455
Internet http://www.nysca.org/public/pdf/theatre.pdf
Requirements Applicants must be nonprofit New York State theater organizations that are able to document proof of their nonprofit status. In addition to general council criteria, first-time applicants must have documented records of producing and/or presenting theater under the same artistic leadership for at least two years prior to submitting a request for support; exceptions to this policy are the applicants to the new theater advancement, performance art initiative, and special projects categories; see the NYSCA guidelines book for details.
Restrictions This program will not support classes, training, or student productions; popular entertainment and events (carnivals, circuses, sideshows, parades, cabaret activities, and variety shows) are generally excluded from support. The program generally does not fund the subsidy of rehearsal or performance space. Support of commercial productions will not be considered, and theater groups that collect fees from company members for any reason will not receive program support.
Areas of Interest Children's Theater; Dramatic/Theater Arts; Opera/Musical Theater; Performing Arts

NYSCA Visual Arts Grants 919

New York State Council on the Arts
175 Varick St
New York, NY 10014-4604
Contact Elizabeth Merena, Program Director, (212) 741-5222; TDD: (800) 895-9838; e-mail: emerena@ nysca.org
Internet http://www.nysca.org/public/programs_ guidelines.html
Requirements Applicants must be nonprofit New York organizations that can document proof of their nonprofit status. To be eligible, applicants must provide for direct payment of fees to artists in all of their program/project requests that include artists' participation. The program will consider requests only from universities and colleges, whether public or private, in project support categories, and any funds awarded must be matched on a one-to-one cash basis.
Restrictions Funding is not available for educational projects, workshops, and general audience instruction programs; operating costs of starting new organizations; cooperative galleries and other organizations that serve and/or exhibit only the work of their own membership, staff, and/or board; start-up costs for new periodicals; commercial publications; exhibitions and/or projects that primarily include nonprofessional participants; jurors' fees; juried programs/projects that require artists to pay entry fees; nonexhibition related catalogs; fund-raising events and/or projects; reception costs; capital expenditures and/or permanent equipment purchase; surveys; short-term demonstrations; or slide registries. General program support is no longer available for performance art programs.
Areas of Interest Art Criticism; Art, Experimental; Artists in Residence; Disabled; Interdisciplinary Arts; Minorities; Performance Art; Visual Arts; Women

John R. Oishei Foundation Grants 920

John R. Oishei Foundation
1 HSBC Ctr, Ste 3650
Buffalo, NY 14203
Contact Thomas Baker, Executive Director and Secretary, (716) 856-9490; fax: (716) 856-9493; e-mail: info@oisheifdt.org
Internet http://www.oisheifdt.org/applying.htm
Requirements It is the general policy of the foundation to confine its support to activities located in the Buffalo, NY, metropolitan region.
Restrictions Grants do not support endowments; capital requests (buildings or equipment); deficit funding or loans; individual scholarships or fellowships (except within specific foundation programs); travel, conferences, seminars, or workshops; or fundraising events.
Areas of Interest Asian Americans; Biomedical Research; Computer Technology; Criminal Behavior; Cultural Activities/Programs; Education; Finance; Health Care; Higher Education; Hispanic Education; Native American Education; Scholarship Programs, General; Social Services; Technology
Sample Awards State U of New York at Buffalo (NY)— to recruit, pay, and support the research of scientists at the Buffalo Life Sciences Complex, $2 million challenge grant (2003). Canisius College (Buffalo, NY)—for a program that provides faculty members with technology, travel, and other resources designed to enhance undergraduate teaching, $840,000 over five years (2002).

OSI Reproductive Health and Rights Program Grants 921

Open Society Institute
400 W 59th St, 4th Fl
New York, NY 10019
Contact Grants Program Assistant, (212) 548-0600; fax: (212) 548-4679; e-mail: prhr@sorosny.org
Internet http://www.soros.org/repro/grant_guidelines. htm
Requirements 501(c)3 organizations are eligible. Proposals will be accepted for activities in the United States, Central and Eastern Europe, the former Soviet Union, the countries of southern Africa, Guatemala, Haiti, and Mongolia.
Areas of Interest Abortion; Child/Maternal Health; Civil/Human Rights; Communications; Contraceptives; Death/Mortality; Grassroots Leadership; Health Care Access; Human Reproduction/Fertility; International Programs; Legal Services; Medical Ethics; Medical Technology; Political Behavior; Population Control; Public Planning/Policy; Service Delivery Programs; Social Services; Violent Behavior; Women's Health
Sample Awards Planned Parenthood of Maryland (Baltimore, MD)—for the Maryland Emergency Contraception Project, $55,804 (2003). Reproductive Health Technologies Project (Washington, DC)—for general support, $150,000 over two years (2003). U of California at San Francisco (CA)—for a project entitled Early Abortion: Advancing New Standards, $174,741 (2003). U of Rochester (NY)—for the Early Abortion Grand Round Series and Summer Fellowship in Reproductive Health, $92,536 (2003).

Ottinger Foundation Grants 922

Ottinger Foundation
80 Broad St, 17th Fl
New York, NY 10004
Contact Michele Lord, Executive Director, (212) 764-3878; fax: (212) 764-4298; e-mail: info@ ottingerfoundation.org
Internet http://www.ottingerfoundation.org/guidelines. html
Requirements IRS 501(c)3 tax-exempt organizations may apply. Due to the large number of proposals received, initial letters of inquiry are discouraged and will not receive a response. E-mail proposals will also not be accepted.
Restrictions The foundation does not make grants to organizations that traditionally enjoy popular support, such as universities, museums, hospitals, or schools. The foundation does not support individuals, academic research, film or video projects, the construction or restoration of buildings, conferences, books, or local programs that do not have national significance.
Areas of Interest Citizenship; Civil/Human Rights; Economics; Environmental Programs; Grassroots Leadership; Mass Media; Training and Development; Voter Educational Programs
Sample Awards Maine Citizen Leadership Fund (ME)—for voter education and registration activities in Maine, $10,000. Southern California Industrial Areas Foundation (CA)—for the Active Citizenship Campaign, $10,000. Washington Environmental Alliance for Voter Education (WA)—for general support, $10,000.

Land and Water Fund—for constituency building in the Rocky Mountain and desert states, $10,000.

Park Foundation Grants 923

Park Foundation
PO Box 550
Ithaca, NY 14851
Contact Linda Madeo, Executive Director, (607) 272-9124; fax: (607) 272-6057
Requirements 501(c)3 nonprofits serving the US eastern seaboard, including central New York and the Southeast, are eligible.
Restrictions For-profit organizations and individuals are not eligible.
Areas of Interest Animal Rights; Coastal Processes; Education; Environmental Programs; Higher Education; Philanthropy; Scholarship Programs, General; Television
Sample Awards North Carolina State University (Raleigh, NC)—for Park Scholarships, $647,710). Beach Preservation Assoc of Pine Knoll Shores (Atlantic Beach, NC)—for general operating support, $150,000. North Carolina State U (Raleigh, NC)—for the Park Scholarship program, $226,018.

Josephine Bay Paul and C. Michael Paul Foundation Grants 924

Josephine Bay Paul and C. Michael Paul Foundation
PO Box 20218, Park W Finance Station
New York, NY 10025
Contact Frederick Bay, Executive Director, (212) 932-0408; fax: (212) 932-0316
Restrictions Grants are not made to individuals (except Biodiversity Leadership awards), building campaigns, sectarian religious programs, or to other than publicly recognized charities.
Areas of Interest Art Education; Artists in Residence; Biology, Molecular; Chamber Music; Citizenship; Community Service Programs; Conflict/Dispute Resolution; Education Reform; Environmental Programs; Ethics; Evolutionary Biology; Oceanography
Sample Awards Symphony Space (New York, NY)—to expand and endow its education program, the Curriculum Arts Project, $150,000 challenge grant (2002).

Pfizer Foundation Grants 925

Pfizer Inc
235 E 42nd St
New York, NY 10017-5755
Contact Paget Walker, Grants Associate, (800) 733-4717 or (212) 733-4250
Internet http://www.pfizer.com/subsites/philanthropy/ caring/index.html
Requirements Nonprofit 501(c)3 organizations and schools are eligible.
Restrictions The following types of organizations or activities are excluded from support: fundraising events or activities such as telethons, walkathons, and races; specific performances or concerts; sporting events; endowment campaigns; building fund drives and capital campaigns (except science lab renovations in partner schools and universities); film, video, television, or radio projects (except as part of a health literacy program); requests for loans or debt retirement; trips, tours, or cul-

tural exchange programs; conferences, seminars, briefing programs, and similar activities (except in instances where the event evolves from Pfizer programs in health care and science education); organizations already supported through United Way contributions; operating expenses of United Way local agencies (except through annual United Way campaigns); grants to individuals; political causes or candidates; anti-business organizations; or organizations that practice discrimination or limit membership on the basis of race, creed, gender, age, sexual preference, or national origin.

Areas of Interest AIDS; Antibiotics; Community Services Programs; Cultural Programs/Activities; Curriculum Development; Developing/Underdeveloped Nations; Disadvantaged (Economically); Disaster Relief; Education; Elementary Education; Health Care; Health Promotion; HIV; Infectious Diseases/Agents; International Programs; Preventive Medicine; Public Health; Science Education; Secondary Education; Surgery; Visual Impairments

Sample Awards U of the Pacific (Stockton, CA)—to support a research scholar in the doctorate program in pharmaceutical and chemical sciences, $100,000 (2003). CDC Foundation (Atlanta, GA)—for a fellowship program that provides medical students with training in epidemiology and public health at the Ceners for Disease Control and Prevention, $300,000 (2003). Saint Vincent Catholic Medical Ctrs (New York, NY)—to provide mental-health services to New York City firefighters and paramedics, as well as their families, who were affected by the September 11 attacks on the World Trade Center, $400,000 (2002).

Philip Morris Fund Grants 926
Philip Morris Fund
120 Park Avenue, 17th floor
New York, NY 10017-5592
Contact Program Area Manager, (917) 663-5000; fax: (917) 663-2167
Internet http://www.pmusa.com/policies_practices/community_involvement/corporate_contributions.asp
Requirements Nonprofit organizations may submit grant requests.
Restrictions Grants are not awarded to support athletic groups; social clubs, fraternal, veterans, or labor groups; political organizations; educational institutions already supported through fund-raising organizations; sectarian or denominational religious groups; marathons or similar sports events; endowments or revolving funds; courtesy advertising; raffle tickets; conferences, workshops, seminars, or trips; or production or distribution of audio-visual materials.
Areas of Interest Arts, General; Civic Affairs; Cultural Activities/Programs; Education; Elementary Education; Health Care; International Programs; Scholarship Programs, General; Secondary Education; Social Services
Sample Awards Rancho Viejo Elementary School (Yuma, AZ)—for operating support, $39,308. National Merit Scholarship Corp (Evanston, IL)—for scholarships, $404,195.

Pinkerton Foundation Grants 927
Pinkerton Foundation
630 Fifth Ave, Ste 1755
New York, NY 10111
Contact Joan Colello, Executive Director, (212) 332-3385; fax: (212) 332-3399; e-mail: pinkfdn@mindspring.com
Internet http://fdncenter.org/grantmaker/pinkerton
Requirements Grants are awarded primarily to New York City 501(c)3 nonprofit public charitable organizations.
Restrictions The foundation does not grant requests for emergencies, medical research, direct provision of health care, religious education, conferences, publications, or capital projects.
Areas of Interest At-Risk Youth; Children and Youth; Family; Housing; Learning Disabilities; Life Skills Training; Literacy; Mental Retardation; Shelters
Sample Awards Food and Hunger Hotline (New York, NY)—for start-up of a life skills course for at-risk mothers and their children in transition from city shelters to permanent housing, $15,000. Henry Street Settlement (New York, NY)—for pilot family literacy program, $25,000 each of two years.

Prospect Hill Foundation Grants 928
Prospect Hill Foundation
99 Park Ave, Ste 2220
New York, NY 10016-1601
Contact Constance Eiseman, Executive Director, (212) 370-1165; fax: (212) 599-6282
Internet http://fdncenter.org/grantmaker/prospecthill
Requirements Giving is primarily in the northeastern US, including NY and RI. Social service grants are limited to New York groups.
Restrictions The foundation does not support scholarly research or religious activities.
Areas of Interest Conservation, Natural Resources; Environmental Programs; Food Distribution; Human Reproduction/Fertility; Nuclear Weapons; Parent Education; Peace/Disarmament; Population Control; Social Services; Teen Pregnancy
Sample Awards Nuclear Control Institute (Washington, DC)—for general support, $50,000 final grant installment. Saint Luke's-Roosevelt Hospital Ctr (New York, NY)—toward child birth and parenting education for adolescents, $25,000. Friends of Olana (Hudson, NY)—toward completion of an historic landscape report on Olana, $12,000.

Paul Rapoport Foundation Grants 929
Paul Rapoport Foundation
220 E 60th St, Ste 3H
New York, NY 10022
Contact Jane Schwartz, Executive Director, (212) 888-6578; fax: (212) 980-0867
Internet http://fdncenter.org/grantmaker/rapoport
Requirements Nonprofit organizations in the New York, NY, metropolitan area are eligible.
Restrictions The foundation does not support medical research, cultural or artistic activities, or other foundations. Grants are not awarded to individuals or for endowment funds or building campaigns.

Areas of Interest AIDS; AIDS Education; AIDS Prevention; HIV; Homosexuals, Female; Homosexuals, Male; Legal Services; Recreation and Leisure; Rehabilitation/Therapy; Youth Programs

Sample Awards Servicemenbers Legal Defense Network (Washington, DC)—for general operating support of its work to assist members of the US military who have been harmed by official policies on sexual orientation, $20,000 over two years and $10,000 matching grant over two years (2001).

Rochester Area Community Foundation Grants   930

Rochester Area Community Foundation
500 East Ave
Rochester, NY 14607-1912
Contact Deborah Ellwood, Program Contact, (585) 271-4100; fax: (585) 271-4292; e-mail: dellwood@racf.org
Internet http://www.racf.org/page12216.cfm
Requirements Nonprofits in Monroe, Livingston, Ontario, Orleans, Genessee, and Wayne Counties, NY, are eligible.
Restrictions Grants do not support partisan political organizations or religious projects, individuals, annual campaigns, deficit financing, land acquisition, endowments, or emergency funds.
Areas of Interest Arts, General; Child Psychology/Development; Community Development; Cultural Activities/Programs; Education; Elderly; Environmental Programs; Health Services Delivery; Libraries; Philanthropy; Rural Areas; Scholarship Programs, General; Social Services; Transportation
Sample Awards Gilliam-Grant Community Ctr (Bergen, NY)—to provide flexible transportation services to senior citizens living in the rural northeastern corner of Genessee County, $30,000. Richmond Memorial Library (Rochester, NY)—to insure that library services are available to homebound and other elderly people, $50,000 operating support.

Rockefeller Brothers Fund Grants   931

Rockefeller Brothers Fund
437 Madison Ave
New York, NY 10022-7001
Contact Benjamin Shute Jr., Secretary, (212) 812-4200; fax: (212) 812-4299; e-mail: rock@rbf.org
Internet http://www.rbf.org/howapply.html
Requirements A prospective grantee in the United States or foreign counterpart must be either a tax-exempt organization or an organization seeking support for a project that would qualify as educational or charitable.
Restrictions The fund does not make grants to individuals, nor does it as a general rule support research, graduate study, or the writing of books or dissertations by individuals.
Areas of Interest Arts, General; Civic Affairs; Conservation, Natural Resources; Cultural Activities/Programs; Education; Environmental Programs; Health Promotion; Government; Leadership; Marine Resources; Rural Areas; Sustainable Development
Sample Awards To be distributed among 25 students— for fellowships for students of color entering the teaching profession, which provide graduate-school tuition and other assistance to outstanding minority college students who are committed to teaching at public schools, $552,500 over five years (2003). Asian Cultural Council (New York, NY)—for its unrestricted grants program, $200,000 (2002). Via Foundation for Local Initiatives (Prague, Czech Republic)—for general support and for a program that seeks to connect the physical and social environments of participating communities, $130,000 over years (2002). United Way of New York City (NY)—for its Child Care and Early Education Fund, $100,000 over two years (2002). U of South Africa (Pretoria, South Africa)—to refine, develop, and evaluate the effect of its family-based literacy model, $98,000 over two years (2002).

Samuel Rubin Foundation Grants   932

Samuel Rubin Foundation
777 United Nations Plaza
New York, NY 10017-3521
Contact Cora Weiss, President, (212) 697-8945; fax: (212) 682-0886; e-mail: info@samuelrubinfoundation.org
Internet http://www.samuelrubinfoundation.org
Restrictions Funds are not granted to individuals or for buildings, endowments, or scholarships.
Areas of Interest Civil/Human Rights; Economics; International Planning/Policy; Peace/Disarmament; Political Science; Social Change

Helena Rubinstein Foundation Grants   933

Helena Rubinstein Foundation
477 Madison Ave, 7th Flr.
New York, NY 10022-5802
Contact Diane Moss, President, (212) 750-7310; fax: (212) 750-9798
Internet http://fdncenter.org/grantmaker/rubinstein/index.html
Requirements Only New York residents may apply.
Areas of Interest Academic Achievement; Arts, General; Children and Youth; Community Service Programs; Education; Health Care; Vocational Counseling; Youth Programs
Sample Awards New York City Outward Bound Ctr (NY)—for programs to help high school students develop self-esteem, self-reliance, social responsibility, and improved academic performance, $10,000. Goodwill Industries of Greater New York (NY)—to support the capital campaign, $10,000. Winston Preparatory School (NY)—salary support for a vocational guidance counselor, $5000.

Fan Fox and Leslie R. Samuels Foundation Grants Program   934

Fan Fox and Leslie R. Samuels Foundation
350 Fifth Ave, Ste 4301
New York, NY 10118
Contact Julio Urbina, (212) 239-3030; fax: (212) 239-3039; e-mail: jurbina@samuels.org or info@samuels.org
Internet http://www.samuels.org
Requirements The foundation funds organizations in the New York City area only. Only 501(c)3 tax-exempt organizations are invited to apply.

Restrictions The foundation does not give grants to individuals or for scholarships, and does not support research, film, or video, nor does it fund education or social services. The foundation no longer actively solicits applications for support of arts-in-education programs at the primary and secondary level.

Areas of Interest Elderly; Health Care; Performing Arts

Sample Awards Cornell U, Weill Medical College (New York, NY)—for Partnership for Caring awards for projects that help make the use of proxies ad other healthcare agents more effective for elderly people who must rely on others to make healthcare decisions for them, $200,000 over 18 months (2002).

Sandy Hill Foundation Grants 935

Sandy Hill Foundation
PO Box 30
Hudson Falls, NY 12839-0030
Contact Floyd Rourke, Trustee, (518) 747-5805
Requirements Nonprofit organizations in the tri-county upstate New York area are eligible.
Areas of Interest Education; Health Care; Shelters; Social Services; Visual Impairments
Sample Awards Eva's Shelter (Paterson, NJ)—to purchase a building, $161,318. Seton Hall U (South Orange, NJ)—for an endowed scholarship fund, $100,000. Seeing Eye (Morristown, NJ)—for general operating support, $20,000.

Santa Maria Foundation Grants 936

Santa Maria Foundation
PO Box 604138
Bayside, NY 11360-4138
Contact Margaret Devine, Administrative Assistant
Areas of Interest Catholic Church; Homeless Shelters; Housing; Religious Welfare Programs; Single-Parent Families
Sample Awards Roman Catholic Communities of Mount Desert Island, (ME)—for general operating support, $50,000. Greenwood Foundation (New York, NY)—for general operating support. Saint Vincent Ministry—for general operating support, $35,000.

Scherman Foundation Grants 937

Scherman Foundation
16 E 52nd St, Ste 601
New York, NY 10022-5306
Contact Sandra Silverman, Executive Director, (212) 832-3086; fax: (212) 838-0154; e-mail: info@scherman.org
Internet http://www.scherman.org/html/policy.html
Requirements Tax exempt 501(c)3 organizations are eligible.
Restrictions The foundation does not accept applications via the internet or fax. Funding is not given to: individuals; colleges, universities, or professional schools; medical, science, or engineering research; capital campaigns; conferences; or specific media or arts productions.
Areas of Interest AIDS; Arts; Community Services; Domestic Violence; Environment; Family Planning; HIV; Housing; Human Rights; Human Services; Liberty; Minorities; Natural Resources; Peace; Reproduction; Security; Social Services

Sample Awards Tolentine Zeiser Community Life Ctr (Bronx, NY)—for a domestic violence prevention program, $25,000. Search for Common Ground (Washington, DC)—for operating support, $25,000. Fund for the City of New York (New York, NY)—for a public schools HIV/AIDS technical assistance project, $15,000.

Schlumberger Foundation Grants 938

Schlumberger Foundation
277 Park Ave
New York, NY 10172
Contact Arthur Alexander, Executive Secretary, (212) 350-9400; fax: (212) 350-9457
Requirements Applying organizations must be 501(c)3 tax-exempt. Grants to educational institutions are made to colleges and universities located in the United States and Canada.
Restrictions Grants are not awarded directly to individuals or to organizations outside the United States and Canada.
Areas of Interest Dramatic/Theater Arts; Earth Sciences; Electronics/Electrical Engineering; Engineering; Engineering Education; Environmental Programs; Fine Arts; Higher Education; Museums; Music; Professional Associations; Science Education; Special Education; Technology Education

Shubert Foundation Grants 939

Shubert Foundation
234 W 44th St
New York, NY 10036
Contact Vicki Reiss, Executive Director, (212) 944-3777; fax: (212) 944-3767
Internet http://www.shubertfoundation.org/grantprograms/default.asp
Requirements Tax-exempt 501(c)3 organizations may apply for grant support.
Restrictions Grants are not awarded to individuals or for capital or endowment funds, seed money, research, conduit organizations, renovation projects, audience development, productions for specialized audiences, scholarships, fellowships, or matching gifts.
Areas of Interest Arts Administration; Dance; Dramatic/Theater Arts; Opera/Musical Theater; Performing Arts
Sample Awards Vivian Beaumont Theater (New York, NY)—for general operating support, $275,000. Crossroads Theatre Comp (New Brunswick, NJ)—for operating support, $25,000. Alvin Ailey American Dance Theater (New York, NY)—for operating support, $85,000.

Sister Fund Grants for Women's Organizations 940

Sister Fund
116 E 16th St, 7th Fl
New York, NY 10003
Contact Sunita Mehta, Director of Grants and Programs, (212) 260-4446; fax: (212) 260-4633; e-mail: info@sisterfund.org
Internet http://www.sisterfund.org/about_mission.php
Requirements Nonprofit organizations are eligible to apply.

Restrictions Funding will not be given to: groups which do not have their own 501(c)3 or a fiscal sponsor with 501(c)3 IRS tax determination; individuals; state, county or municipal agencies; capital/building acquisition or improvements; scholarship funds or student aid; or deficit financing.

Areas of Interest Civil/Human Rights; Economic Development; Economically Disadvantaged; Education; HIV; Homosexuals, Female; Human Reproduction/Fertility; Minorities; Political Behavior; Public Planning/Policy; Refugees; Religion; Social Change; Theology; Violent Behavior; Women; Women's Education; Women's Employment; Women's Health; Women's Rights; Women's Studies

Sample Awards Catholics for Free Choice (Washington, DC)—for the Women, Religion, and Public Policy Project, $10,000. Assistance to Iranian Refugees (New York, NY)—to aid female Iranian asylum seekers through case management, advocacy, education, and organizing services, $10,000. Iris House (New York, NY)—to renovate a new facility to provide services to HIV-positive women, $25,000.

Alfred P. Sloan Foundation Grants   941
Alfred P. Sloan Foundation
630 Fifth Ave, Ste 2550
New York, NY 10111
Contact Program Contact, (212) 649-1649; fax: (212) 757-5117
Internet http://www.sloan.org
Restrictions Grants are not extended to religion, the creative or performing arts, medical research, or health care. Grants are not made for endowments or for buildings or equipment and are made only occasionally for general support or for activities outside the United States.
Areas of Interest Civic Affairs; Distance Education; Drugs/Drug Abuse; Economics; Environmental Programs; Higher Education; Nonprofit Organizations; Philanthropy; Science; Science Education; Technology; Technology Education
Sample Awards Massachusetts Institute of Technology (MA)—to study the future use of nuclear power in the United States, $450,000 (2002). U of Maryland Foundation (MD)—to develop an institutional framework to help prevent the dangerous use of biological pathogens, $500,000 (2002). City U of New York system (NY) and George Mason U (NY)—for the September 11 Digital Archives, $700,000 jointly (2002).

Sony Electronics Charitable Contributions   942
  Program Grants
Sony Electronics Inc
550 Madison Ave, 33rd Fl
New York, NY 10022-3211
Contact Ann Morfogen, (212) 833-6873; fax: (212) 833-6862; e-mail: Ann_Morfogen@sonyusa.com
Internet http://www.sony.com/SCA/philanthropy/guidelines.shtml
Requirements US nonprofits, including schools and school districts, are eligible.
Restrictions Sony does not award grants to organizations that practice discrimination, partisan political organizations, religious organizations, labor unions, endowment or capital campaigns of national organizations, or-

ganizations whose primary purpose is to influence legislation, testimonial dinners in general, for-profit publications seeking advertisements, individuals seeking self-advancement, or foreign or non-US organizations.
Areas of Interest Arts, General; Basic Skills Education; Civic Affairs; Cultural Activities/Programs; Elementary Education; Health Services Delivery; Higher Education; Literacy; Minorities; Secondary Education; Social Services Delivery; Technology Education

Sprague Foundation Grants Program   943
Seth Sprague Educational and Charitable Foundation
114 W 47th St
New York, NY 10036-1532
Contact Carolyn Larke, c/o US Trust Company of New York, fax: (212) 852-3377; Linda Franciscovich, c/o US Trust Company of New York, fax: (212) 852-3377
Requirements Only residents of New York and Massachusetts may apply.
Restrictions No grants are provided to individuals, for building funds, or for loans.
Areas of Interest Arts and Culture; Children and Youth; Civic Affairs; Community Development; Cultural Activities/Programs; Education; Government; Health Care; Hospitals; Human Services; Performing Arts; Public Administration; Secondary Education; Social Services

Morgan Stanley Foundation Grants   944
Morgan Stanley Foundation
1601 Broadway, 12th Fl
New York, NY 10019
Contact Joan Steinberg, Director of Community Affairs, (212) 259-1235; fax: (212) 259-1253; e-mail: whatadifference@msdw.com
Internet http://www.morganstanley.com/about/inside/community.html?page=about
Requirements New York 501(c)3 organizations in company-operating areas are eligible.
Restrictions Grants do not support United Way member agencies, individuals, endowment or building funds, capital campaigns, deficit financing, equipment acquisition, scholarships, fellowships, special projects, journal advertisements, research, publications, conferences, fund-raising dinners, or benefit events.
Areas of Interest Adult and Continuing Education; Arts, General; Child/Maternal Health; Civic Affairs; Community Development; Cultural Activities/Programs; Economic Development; Education; Elderly; Health Care; Homeownership; Housing; Job Training Programs; Law Enforcement; Literacy; Neighborhoods; Performing Arts; Preventive Medicine; Social Services; Teacher Education; Women
Sample Awards Victims Relief Fund (NY)—to support the fund, which was established to support emergency-assistance and other nonprofit rescue and relief organizations, and to match all employee gifts to aid victims of the September 11 terrorist attacks, $10 million minimum.

Starr Foundation Grants   945
Starr Foundation
70 Pine St, 14th Fl
New York, NY 10270

Contact Florence Davis, President, (212) 770-688; e-mail: florence.davis@starrfdn.org or grants@ starrfoundation.org
Internet http://fdncenter.org/grantmaker/starr
Areas of Interest Biomedical Research; Cultural Activities/Programs; Disabled; Disadvantaged(Economically); Employment Opportunity Programs; Environmental Studies; Food Distribution; Genetics; Health Care; Health Services Delivery; Higher Education; Hospitals; Housing; Insurance/Actuarial Science; International Relations; International Trade and Finance; Job Training Programs; Libraries, Academic; Literacy; Medical Education; Poverty and the Poor; Public Affairs; Scholarship Programs, General; Social Services; Visual Impairments
Sample Awards New York Blood Ctr (New York, NY)—to augment the cord-blood inventory that benefits ptients needing bone-marrow transplants, $5 million (2003). Temple U, Beasley School of Law (Philadelphia, PA)—to endow its master's-of-law program in China, which educates Chinese judges, legal officials, law professors, and lawyers in US and international law, $2.5 million (2002). Massachusetts Institute of Technology, School of Humanities, Arts, and Social Sciences (Cambridge, MA)—to endow the MIT Center for International Studies, $10 million (2002). Johns Hopkins U (Baltimore, MD)—for the Southeast Asia Studies program at the Nitze School of Advanced International Studies, $600,000 (2002).

Steele-Reese Foundation Grants 946
Steele-Reese Foundation
32 Washington Square W
New York, NY 10011
Contact William Buice, (212) 505-2696
Internet http://www.Steele-Reese.org
Requirements Applicant should submit a letter requesting guidelines. Only residents of Georgia, Idaho, Kentucky, Montana, North Carolina, Texas, and Wyoming are eligible to apply. Personal and telephone inquiries are not encouraged.
Restrictions The foundation does not make grants to individuals, to community chest or similar drives, for conferences or workshops, for efforts to influence elections or legislation, for planning purposes or experimental projects, for emergencies, or for permanent support except for occasional endowment grants to organizations where stability is critically important.
Areas of Interest Education; Health Care; Higher Education; Humanities; Rural Areas; Social Services
Sample Awards Warren Wilson College (Asheville, NC)—for an endowment for faculty salaries, $200,000 over four years.

Sulzberger Foundation Grants 947
Sulzberger Foundation
229 W 43rd St, Ste 1031
New York, NY 10036
Contact Grants Administrator, (212) 556-1755
Requirements Nonprofit organizations in New York and Tennessee are eligible. Preference is given to requests from New York City and Chatanooga.
Restrictions Individuals are not eligible. Loans and matching grants are not awarded.

Areas of Interest Arts, General; Conservation, Natural Resources; Education; Environmental Programs; Health Care; Health Services Delivery; Hospitals; Social Services Delivery
Sample Awards New York Times Company Foundation (New York, NY)—for the Neediest Cases Fund, $100,000 (2003).

Surdna Foundation Arts Teachers Fellowships 948
Surdna Foundation
330 Madison Ave, 30th Fl
New York, NY 10017
Contact Grants Administrator, (212) 557-0010; fax: (212) 557-0003; e-mail: request@surdna.org
Internet http://www.surdna.org/programs/artsteachersfellowships.html
Requirements Permanently assigned full- and part-time arts teachers in specialized, public arts high schools who have been teaching for at least five years are eligible. Dance, music, theater-arts, and visual-arts teachers are eligible.
Restrictions
Areas of Interest Art Education; Dance; Dance Education; Music; Music Education; Performing Arts; Teacher Education; Theater Arts; Theater/Film Criticism; Visual Arts

Surdna Foundation Grants 949
Surdna Foundation
330 Madison Ave, 30th Fl
New York, NY 10017-5001
Contact Edward Skloot, Executive Director, (212) 557-0010; fax: (212) 557-0003; e-mail: request@ surdna.org
Internet http://www.surdna.org
Requirements 501(c)3 organizations may apply. The foundation urges applicants to send two- to three-page letters of intent before sending proposals. IRS nonprofit status certification, recent audited financial statements, and project budget should also be included.
Restrictions Grants are not made to individuals or given to organizations outside the United States. The foundation generally does not fund capital campaigns or building construction. Unsolicited proposals are not accepted in the arts program.
Areas of Interest Art Education; Biodiversity; Citizenship; Civic Affairs; Community Development; Conflict/Dispute Resolution; Economic Self-Sufficiency; Energy; Environmental Programs; Family; Housing; Land Use Planning/Policy; Leadership; Nonprofit Organizations; Performing Arts; Poverty and the Poor; Preschool Education; Problem Solving; Transportation; Urban Areas; Youth Programs
Sample Awards CompuMentor (San Francisco, CA)—to promote technology use by nonprofit groups by increasing the availability of donated and discounted technology products and by providing technology-related education and assistance, $750,000 over three years (2003). Ballet Hispanico (New York, NY)—to strengthen its School of Dance's advanced-level training program in the areas of curriculum, scholarships, performance, and career preparation, faculty support, and recruitment, as part of the joint Doris Duke Charitable

Foundation-Surdna Foundation Talented Students in the Arts Initiative, $450,000 (2002). Julliard School (New York, NY)—for the newly inaugurated Institute for Jazz Studies, in partnership with Jazz at Lincoln Center, including support for faculty salaries and marketing and performance-related expenses, $240,000 (2002). CyberSkills for Vermont Nonprofits (Burlington, VT)—to develop and improve the technological capacity of Vermont nonprofit groups, as part of this collaborative program involving CCTV/CyberSkills Vermont, the Vermont Alliance of Nonprofit Organizations, and the Vermont Public Interest Research Group, $450,000 over three years (2002).

Third Wave Foundation Grants 950

Third Wave Foundation
511 W 25th St, Ste 301
New York, NY 10001
Contact Program/Development Associate, (212) 675-0700; fax: (212) 255-6653; email: info@ thirdwavefoundation.org
Internet http://www.thirdwavefoundation.org/ programs/default.htm
Requirements Though US citizenship is not required, scholarship applicants must be studying at an American university, community college, or vocational school. Applicant organizations and/or programs must be based in the United States.
Areas of Interest Civil/Human Rights; Disabled; Economics; Homosexuals, Female; Homosexuals, Male; Human Reproduction/Fertility; Microenterprises; Minorities; Poverty and the Poor; Racism/Race Relations; Scholarship Programs, General; Sexism; Women

Tides Foundation Drug Policy Reform 951 Grants

Tides Foundation
40 Exchange Pl, Ste 1111
New York, NY 10005
Contact Grants Administrator, (212) 509-1049; fax: (212) 509-1059; e-mail: fdp@tides.org
Internet http://www.tidesfoundation.org/drug_policy. cfm
Requirements 501(c)3 tax-exempt organizations and organizations with 501(c)3 fiscal sponsors are eligible.
Restrictions The fund does not support the production of videos or films; writing and publication of books and other publications, but may consider strategic distribution of publications; capital expenditures; dissertations, postgraduate work, or research; individuals; journalistic and academic projects; direct service projects outside of the United States (exception, organizations responding to the Latin America Target Area RFP); or traditional abstinence-only treatment programs.
Areas of Interest AIDS; Drugs/Drug Abuse; HIV; Minorities; Public Education; Public Policy/Planning

U.S. Trust Corporation Foundation Grants 952

U.S. Trust Corporation Foundation
114 W 47th St
New York, NY 10036

Contact Carol Strickland, Chairman of the Corporate Contributions Committee, (212) 852-1330; fax: (212) 852-1341; e-mail: cstrickland@ustrust.com or foundation@ustrust.com
Internet http://www.ustrust.com/ustrust/html/aboutUs/ community/corpcon.html
Requirements Grant giving is concentrated in the communities in which US Trust does business, and is directed to 501(c)3 nonprofit organizations.
Restrictions Grants are not made to individuals for education or other purposes; educational, religious, veterans, fraternal, or labor organizations unless engaged in a significant project benefiting the entire community; organizations, projects, or programs outside the United States; political organizations or candidates; organizations requesting support for advertising; organizations supported by umbrella organizations; or organizations with operating budgets of $150,000 or less.
Areas of Interest Community Service Programs; Cultural Activities/Programs; Dramatic/Theater Arts; Economic Self-Sufficiency; Housing; Inner Cities; Problem Solving; General; Service Delivery Programs; Urban Affairs; Youth Programs

Unilever US Grants 953

Unilever United States Foundation
390 Park Ave
New York, NY 10022
Contact John Gould Jr., (212) 888-1260; fax: (212) 318-3600
Internet http://www.unilever.com/ environmentsociety/communitynew
Requirements 501(c)3 nonprofit organizations in company-operating areas including California, Georgia, Indiana, Maryland, Missouri, New Jersey, and New York are eligible to apply.
Areas of Interest Civic Affairs; Education; Environmental Programs; Health Care; Service Delivery Programs

Laura B. Vogler Foundation Grants 954

Laura B. Vogler Foundation
PO Box 610508
Bayside, NY 11361-0508
Contact Lawrence D'Amato, President, (718) 423-3000; fax: (718) 631-4808
Internet http://fdncenter.org/grantmaker/vogler
Requirements Nonprofit organizations in New York City and Long Island, NY, may submit proposals.
Restrictions Grants are not awarded to support building or endowment funds, annual fund-raising campaigns, or matching gifts.
Areas of Interest Adolescents; Children and Youth; Education; Elderly; Health Care; Homelessness; Preschool Education; Shelters; Social Services; Women
Sample Awards Shield Institute (NY)—for a joint activities program for preschoolers and the elderly, $2500. Mercy Ctr Ministries Inc (NY)—to support three shelters for homeless young women and parenting teens, $3500.

Weeden Foundation Grants 955

Weeden Foundation
747 3rd Ave, 34th Fl
New York, NY 10017

Contact Program Contact, (212) 888-1672; fax: (212) 888-1354; e-mail: weedenfdn@weedenfdn.org
Internet http://www.weedenfdn.org
Requirements 501(c)3 nonprofit organizations are eligible.
Areas of Interest Biodiversity; Conservation, Natural Resources; Ecology; Family Planning; Land Use Planning/Policy; Population Control; Wildlife; Women
Sample Awards Alaska Conservation Foundation (AK)—$15,000. Alternatives to Growth Oregon (OR)—$50,000. Population Coalition—$25,000.

Marie C. and Joseph C. Wilson Foundation Grants   956
Marie C. and Joseph C. Wilson Foundation
160 Allens Creek Rd
Rochester, NY 14618-3309
Contact Ruth Fleischmann, Executive Director, (585) 461-4699 or 461-4696; fax: (585) 473-5206; e-mail: mcjcwilsonfdn@frontiernet.net
Internet http://www.mcjcwilsonfoundation.org/funding.cfm
Requirements 501(c)3 nonprofit organizations serving the Rochester, NY, area are eligible.
Restrictions Grants will not be made to individuals, partisan political organizations, or to support lobbying efforts. Requests for capital projects also will not be considered.
Areas of Interest Academic Achievement; Adolescent Health; Adult and Continuing Education; Community Development; Disabled; Elderly; Environmental Programs; Family; Health Care; Health Services Delivery; Immigrants; Inner Cities; Legal Services; Literacy; Poverty and the Poor; Preschool Education; Social Services Delivery; Technology Education; Youth Programs
Sample Awards Garth Fagan Dance (Rochester, NY)—for dance scholarships and partial salary support for apprentice instructors, $12,500 (2003). Andrews Ctr (Rochester, NY)—for foster care for children with special needs, $10,000 (2003). Rochester Museum and Science Ctr, Water Education Collaborative (NY)—for the Community Water Watch and Great Lawns/Great Lakes projects, $20,000 (2003). Victim Resource Ctr of the Finger Lakes (Newark, NY)—for crisis-intervention services for victims of domestic violence and sexual assault, $13,500 (2003).

North Carolina

Arts and Science Council Grants   957
Arts and Science Council—Charlotte/Mecklenburg
227 W Trade St, Ste 250
Charlotte, NC 28202
Contact Grants Program, (704) 372-9667; fax: (704) 372-8210; e-mail: asc@artsandscience.org
Internet http://www.artsandscience.org/index.asp?fuseaction=GrantsServices.GrantPrograms
Requirements Artists and organizations in North Carolina's Anson, Cabarrus, Cleveland, Gaston, Iredell, Lincoln, Mecklenburg, Rutherford, Rowan, Stanly, or Union Counties or South Carolina's York County are eligible.

Areas of Interest Art Education; Artists' Fellowships; Arts Administration; Cultural Heritage Preservation; History; Science

Belk Foundation Grants   958
Belk Foundation
2801 W Tyvola Rd
Charlotte, NC 28217-4500
Contact Paul Wyche Jr., Trustee, (704) 357-1000
Requirements 501(c)3 nonprofits may apply, preference is given to organizations in North Carolina.
Restrictions Grants are not made to individuals.
Areas of Interest Arts, General; Cultural Activities/Programs; Higher Education; Hospitals; Religion; Wildlife; Youth Programs

Blumenthal Foundation Grants   959
Blumenthal Foundation
PO Box 34689
Charlotte, NC 28234
Contact Philip Blumenthal, Trustee, (704) 377-9237 or (704) 377-6555 ext 2305
Requirements North Carolina Christian, interdenominational, Jewish, nondenominational, and Presbyterian nonprofits, as well as the Salvation Army, are eligible.
Areas of Interest Civil/Human Rights; Community Service Programs; Environmental Education; Family; Higher Education; Hospitals; Jewish Services; Jewish Studies; Refugees; Religion; Religious Studies; Social Services; Youth Programs
Sample Awards Carolina Agency for Jewish Education (Charlotte, NC)—$35,000. Lubavitch of North Carolina (Charlotte, NC)—$12,000. Presbyterian Hospital Foundation (Charlotte, NC)—$10,000.

Burlington Industries Foundation Grants   960
Burlington Industries Foundation
PO Box 21207, 3330 W Friendly Ave
Greensboro, NC 27420
Contact Delores Sides, Executive Director, (336) 379-2303
Requirements 501(c)3 organizations in Burlington communities (South Carolina, North Carolina, and Virginia), are eligible for grant support.
Restrictions The foundation does not provide funding for: individuals; conferences; seminars; workshops; endowment funds; outdoor dramas; films or documentaries; medical research operating expenses; or loans. The foundation generally does not support sectarian or denominational religious organizations, national organizations, private secondary schools, or historic preservation projects.
Areas of Interest Arts & Culture; Children and Youth; Civic Affairs; Crime Prevention; Community Development; Disabled; Elderly; Elementary Education; Emergency Services; Family; Health Care; Health Services Delivery; Higher Education; Hospices; Hospitals; Law Enforcement; Libraries; Medical Education; Minorities; Minority Education; Museums; Nursing Education; Professional Associations; Recreation and Leisure; Secondary Education; Vocational/Technical Education; Youth Programs
Sample Awards U of North Carolina School of Nursing (NC)—for operating support, $4000.

Community Foundation of Greater   **961**
Greensboro Grants
Community Foundation of Greater Greensboro
100 S Elm, Ste 307
Greensboro, NC 27401-2638
Contact Program Contact, (336) 379-9100; fax: (336)
378-0725; e-mail: grants@cfgg.org
Internet http://www.cfgg.org/guidelines.htm
Requirements Nonprofit organizations in Greensboro,
NC, are eligible.
Areas of Interest Arts, General; At-Risk Youth; Civic
Affairs; Civil/Human Rights; Community Develop-
ment; Cultural Activities/Programs; Cultural Diversity;
Environmental Programs; Films; Health Care; Scholar-
ship Programs, General; Social Services
Sample Awards Eastern Music Festival (Greensboro,
NC)—for the 2003 Piedmont Jazz Festival, $10,000
(2003). Guilford County Council of PTAs (Greensboro,
NC)—to promote greater parental involvement in
schools, $40,000 (2003). Piedmont Authority of Re-
gional Transportation (Greensboro, NC)—to coordinate
a regional medical-transportation program, $10,000 over
two years (2003). North Carolina Ctr for Nonprofits (Raleigh, NC)—for scholarships to enable local nonprofit
groups to attend a statewide conference, $10,000 (2003).

Moses Cone-Wesley Long Community   **962**
Health Foundation Grants
Moses Cone-Wesley Long Community Health Founda-
tion
PO Box 4426
Greensboro, NC 27404-4426
Contact Program Director, (336) 832-9555; fax: (336)
832-9559; e-mail:
Internet http://www.mcwlhealthfoundation.org
Requirements North Carolina nonprofit organizations,
government agencies, schools, academic and research
institutions, and collaborative consortia serving Greens-
boro, Winston-Salem, and High Point are eligible.
Areas of Interest AIDS Prevention; Alcohol/Alcohol
Abuse; Drugs/Drug Abuse; Fitness; Health Care; Health
Care Access; Health Education; Health Promotion;
Health Services Delivery; Injury; Mental Health; Nutri-
tion; Obesity; Sexual Behavior; Sexually Transmitted
Diseases; Smoking Behavior; Teacher Education; Teen
Pregnancy
Sample Awards Guilford County Schools (Greensboro,
NC)—for tobacco-education and smoking-cessation
programs, and to provide outdoor physical-fitness equip-
ment, a curriculum, and teacher training at 11 additional
elementary schools, $150,000 and $146,300, respec-
tively (2003). Healthserve Medical Clinic (Greensboro,
NC)—for operating support, $600,000 (2003). Moses
Cone Health System (Greensboro, NC)—to expand the
Congregational Nurse Program to 23 additional congre-
gations and to maintain programs at 23 local churches,
$497,248 (2003). U of North Carolina (Greensboro,
NC)—to train health advisers to help immigrants gain
access to health services, $125,000 (2003).

Cumberland Community Foundation Grants 963
Cumberland Community Foundation
PO Box 2345, 308 Green St
Fayetteville, NC 28302-2171

Contact Donna Keen, (910) 483-4449; fax: (910)
483-2905; e-mail: info@cumberlandcf.org
Internet http://www.cumberlandcf.org/grant.html
Requirements The foundation will normally make
grants only to 501(c)3 organizations in Cumberland
County and surrounding counties in North Carolina.
However, under some circumstances, grants will be
made to other tax-exempt organizations, provided that
the funds are used for charitable purposes.
Restrictions Grants are not made to or for individual
needs, sectarian purposes, operating deficits, annual
campaigns or special events, endowments, operating
budgets of organizations fully supported by other
funders, political and partisan groups, low-risk groups,
or research.
Areas of Interest Arts, General; Child Welfare; Civic
Affairs; Community Development; Conservation, Natural Resources; Cultural Activities/Programs; Education;
Environmental Programs; Health Care; Social Services

Dickson Foundation Grants   **964**
Dickson Foundation
301 S Tryon St, Ste 1800
Charlotte, NC 28202
Contact Grants Administrator, (704) 372-5404
Requirements Giving is primarily in North Carolina.
Areas of Interest Children and Youth; Education;
Health Care; Health Promotion; Higher Education; Sec-
ondary Education; Youth Programs
Sample Awards Lenoir-Rhyne College (Hickory,
NC)—to construct a building that will house classrooms
and laboratories for the nursing, occupational-therapy,
and sports medicine programs, $100,000 (2002).

Dover Foundation Grants   **965**
Dover Foundation
PO Box 208
Shelby, NC 28151
Contact Hoyt Bailey, President, (704) 487-8888; fax:
(704) 482-6818; e-mail: doverfnd@shelby.net
Requirements Applicants must reside in North
Carolina.
Restrictions The foundation ordinarily does not make
grants to organizations whose principal activities are out-
side the United States; political activities or entities; indi-
viduals or their projects; advertising; newsletters, maga-
zines, or books; or trips or tours.
Areas of Interest Biomedical Research; Business Edu-
cation; Community Development; Education; Mental
Health
Sample Awards Gardner-Webb U, School of Business
(Boiling Springs, NC)—to endow a faculty position at
the School of Business, $500,000. Heineman Medical
Research Center of Charlotte (Charlotte, NC)—for support, $50,000.

Duke Endowment Grants   **966**
Duke Endowment
100 N Tryon St, Ste 3500
Charlotte, NC 28202-4012
Contact Dr. Elizabeth Locke, President, (704)
376-0291; fax: (704) 376-9336; e-mail: elocke@tde.
org

Internet http://www.dukeendowment.org/programs.cfm
Requirements Nonprofit organizations and United Methodist churches in North or South Carolina, or any group collaborating with these organizations, are eligible.
Areas of Interest Child/Maternal Health; Education; Health Care; Higher Education; Minorities; Religion
Sample Awards Prevent Child Abuse and Neglect Initiative (Raleigh, NC)—for efforts to reduce cases of child abuse and neglect, $2,459,399 (2003). Duke U Health System (Durham, NC)—for a medical-research fund, $100,000 (2003). Shady Grove United Methodist Church (Saint George, SC)—for economic development, as part of the Program for the Rural Carolinas, $150,000 (2003). Johnson C. Smith U (Charlotte, NC)—for merit-based, full-tuition scholarship. study-abroad program. and capital and staff support, $3.975 million (2003).

Golden LEAF Foundation Grants 967
Golden LEAF (Long-term Economic Advancement Foundation) Foundation
800 Tiffany Blvd, Ste 200
Rocky Mount, NC 27804
Contact Grants Administrator, (888) 684-8404 or (252) 442-7474; fax: (252) 442-7404; e-mail: info@goldenleaf.org
Internet http://www.goldenleaf.org
Requirements North Carolina 501(c)3 tax-exempt organizations are eligible.
Areas of Interest Agricultural Management; Agriculture; Economic Development; Education; Employment Opportunity Programs; Job Training Programs; Rural Areas; Rural Education; Teacher Education
Sample Awards Beaufort County Community College (NC)—to provide students with job skills related to heavy equipment and transport technology, $182,800 (2003). North Carolina Community College System (NC)—for job-training scholarships for community-college students in North Carolina regions that have traditionally depended on tobacco farming and production, $300,000 (2003). North Carolina State U (NC)—for various projects on agricultural alternatives to tobacco farming, $1.2 million (2003). School of Education at East Carolina (NC)—to begin and evaluate a program to recruit and retain teachers in eight rural counties of eastern North Carolina, $350,000 (2003).

Goodrich Corporation Foundation Grants 968
Goodrich Foundation
Four Coliseum Centre, 2730 W Tyvola Rd
Charlotte, NC 28217-4578
Contact Contributions Administrator, (704) 423-7000; fax: (704) 423-7069
Internet http://www.goodrich.com/CDA/GeneralContent/0,1136,59,00.html
Requirements 501(c)3 tax-exempt organizations are eligible.
Restrictions The foundation generally will not support: multiyear grants in excess of five years; individuals, private foundations, endowments, churches or religious programs, fraternal/social/ labor/veterans organizations; groups with unusually high fundraising or administrative expenses; political parties, candidates, or lobbying activities; travel funds for tours, exhibitions, or trips by individuals or special interest groups; organizations that discriminate because of race, color, religion, national origin, or areas covered by applicable federal, state, or local laws; local athletic/sports programs or equipment, courtesy advertising benefits, raffle tickets and other fundraising events; organizations that receive sizable portions of their support through municipal, county, state, or federal dollars; individual United Way agencies that already benefit from Goodrich contributions to the United Way; or international organizations.
Areas of Interest Adult and Continuing Education; Arts, General; Civic Affairs; Community Service Programs; Cultural Activities/Programs; Education; Elementary Education; Engineering Education; Health Care; Higher Education; Hospitals; Mathematics Education; Science Education; Secondary Education; Service Delivery Programs

MRBF Small Grants for Grassroots Organizations 969
Mary Reynolds Babcock Foundation
2920 Reynolda Rd
Winston-Salem, NC 27106
Contact Cynthia Stivender, (336) 748-9222; fax: (336) 777-0095; e-mail: info@mrbbf.org
Internet http://www.mrbf.org/fund/gld.aspx
Requirements Southeastern organizations must be rooted in their local community, have a governing board that represents and is accountable to their constituency, have a track record of effectiveness in addressing racism or poverty in low-income communities, and have operating budgets of no more than $100,000 to be eligible.
Areas of Interest Civil/Human Rights; Cultural Diversity; Government; Grassroots Leadership; Philanthropy; Poverty and the Poor; Racism/Race Relations

North Carolina Arts Council Folklife Projects Grants 970
North Carolina Arts Council
Department of Cultural Resources
Raleigh, NC 27601-2807
Contact Wayne Martin, (919) 733-7877; e-mail: wayne.martin@ncmail.net
Internet http://www.ncarts.org/guidelines/grant_program.cfm?ID=6
Requirements North Carolina nonprofit organizations are eligible.
Areas of Interest Folk Medicine; Folk Music; Folk/Ethnic Arts; Arts Festivals; Workshops; Audio Production; Film Production; Video Production; Radio; Publication; Arts Administration

North Carolina Arts Council General Support Grants 971
North Carolina Arts Council
Department of Cultural Resources
Raleigh, NC 27601-2807
Contact Linda Bamford, (919) 733-9044; e-mail: linda.bamford@ncmail.net
Internet http://www.ncarts.org/guidelines/grant_program.cfm?ID=7

Requirements North Carolina dance, literary, music, theater, and visual arts organizations may apply. This category is designed to support groups that, over time, have consistently produced strong artistic programs and demonstrated responsible administrative practices. Organizations not previously funded in this category must contact the council staff to discuss eligibility before submitting applications.

Restrictions University museums or galleries are not eligible to apply in this category.

Areas of Interest Arts Administration; Dance; Dramatic/Theater Arts; Literature; Music; Visual Arts

North Carolina Arts Council Literary, 972 Performing, and Visual Arts Program Support Grants

North Carolina Arts Council
Department of Cultural Resources
Raleigh, NC 27601-2807
Contact Jeff Pettus, Visual Arts Director, (919) 715-0836; e-mail: jeff.pettus@ncmail.net
Internet http://www.ncarts.org/guidelines/grant_category.cfm?ID=11
Requirements North Carolina nonprofit organizations that produce literary, performing, or visual arts programs may apply. Statewide service organizations also may apply. Grants must be matched dollar-for-dollar by the organization.
Areas of Interest Dance; Dramatic/Theater Arts; Educational/Public Television; Literature; Music; Performing Arts; Radio; Visual Arts

North Carolina Arts Council Local Arts 973 Council Salary Assistance Grants

North Carolina Arts Council Local Arts Council
Department of Cultural Resources
Raleigh, NC 27601-2807
Contact Janie Wilson, Arts and Communities Director, (919) 715-8269; e-mail: janie.wilson@ncmail.net
Internet http://www.ncarts.org/guidelines/grant_category.cfm?ID=13
Requirements A local arts agency that is a North Carolina nonprofit organization or local government agency involved in activities in two or more art forms and that exists to provide programs, financial support, or services for arts organizations, individual artists, and the community as a whole is eligible.
Areas of Interest Arts Administration

North Carolina Arts Council Management/ 974 Technical Assistance Grants

North Carolina Arts Council
Department of Cultural Resources
Raleigh, NC 27699-4632
Contact Linda McGloin, Outreach Coordinator, (919) 715-8273; e-mail: linda.mcgloin@ncmail.net
Internet http://www.ncarts.org/guidelines/grant_category.cfm?ID=17
Requirements Any North Carolina nonprofit arts organization or organization that provides arts programs, such as schools or community organizations, may apply.
Areas of Interest Arts Administration; Audience Development; Cultural Activities/Programs

North Carolina Arts Council Outreach 975 Program Grants

North Carolina Arts Council
Department of Cultural Resources
Raleigh, NC 27601-2807
Contact http://www.ncarts.org/guidelines/grant_program.cfm?ID=31
Internet http://www.ncarts.org/services.cfm
Requirements North Carolina nonprofit, tax-exempt arts organizations, primarily based in and focused on the African American, Asian American, Hispanic, or Native American communities, may apply. Single-discipline organizations that are not the primary constituents of other council sections are eligible for support, as well as multidisciplinary organizations that serve a wide range of art forms including the performing, visual, and literary arts in their cultures.
Areas of Interest Arts Administration; Cultural Diversity; Disabled; Health Care; African Americans; Asian Americans; Hispanics; Native Americans; Performing Arts; Visual Arts; Literature

North Carolina Community Development 976 Grants

Cannon Foundation
PO Box 548
Concord, NC 28026-0548
Contact Frank Davis, Executive Director, (704) 786-8216; fax: (704) 785-2051
Internet http://www.thecannonfoundationinc.org
Requirements IRS 501(c)3 organizations serving North Carolina communities are eligible. Churches and governmental agencies also may apply.
Restrictions Grants are not awarded for endowments, loans, scholarships, or fellowships.
Areas of Interest Arts & Culture; Children and Youth; Community Service Programs; Environmental Programs; Health Care; Higher Education; Hospitals; Preservation and Restoration; Religion; Social Services
Sample Awards Lenoir-Rhyne College (Hickory, NC)—for equipment and technology upgrades, $156,000 (2003). Mars Hill College (Mars Hill, NC)—to purchase two boilers and a fire-alarm system, $150,000 (2002).

North Carolina GlaxoSmithKline 977 Foundation Grants

North Carolina GlaxoSmithKline Foundation
5 Moore Dr
Research Triangle Park, NC 27709
Contact Marilyn Foote-Hudson, Executive Director, (919) 483-2140; fax: (919) 315-3015
Internet http://www.gsk.com/community/ncfound.htm
Requirements The foundation makes grants only to North Carolina 501(c)3 tax-exempt organizations and institutions or to governmental agencies.
Restrictions Grants are not made to individuals for construction or restoration projects, or for international programs unless specifically exempted by the board. Funds are not ordinarily provided to programs that benefit a limited geographic region.
Areas of Interest Art Education; Biology; Chemistry; Chemistry Education; Computer Science; Developmentally Disabled; Education; Health Care; Health Sci-

ences; Mathematics; Pharmacy Education; Physical Sciences; Science; Undergraduate Education; Volunteers

Sample Awards U of North Carolina (Chapel Hill, NC)—to strengthen the fundraising ability of small U of North Carolina campuses and affiliated organizations, including the North Carolina School of the Arts and the UNC Ctr for Public Television, $400,000 (2001). North Carolina School of the Arts (Winston-Salem, NC)—to provide arts-education scholarships for students from North Carolina, $100,000 challenge grant (2001). Shaw U (Raleigh, NC)—to provide scholarships to students majoring in chemistry and who will go on to pursue graduate study in pharmacy, $200,000 (2001). Meredith College (Raleigh, NC)—to support an undergraduate research opportunities program, in which upperclass students join with faculty members to conduct research in biology, chemistry, computer science, mathematics, and the health and physical sciences, $600,000 (2000).

Progress Energy Grants 978

Progress Energy
PO Box 1551
Raleigh, NC 27602-1551
Contact Merrilee Jacobson, Contributions Specialist, (919) 546-6441; fax: (919) 546-4338
Internet http://www.progress-energy.com/community
Requirements Tax-exempt organizations in North and South Carolina may apply.
Restrictions Grants will not be made to support individuals; political candidates; fraternal, veterans, or labor organizations; religious activities; courtesy advertising; memberships; athletic teams or programs; or individual K-12 schools or school districts.
Areas of Interest Community Development; Community Service Programs; Economic Development; Education; Environmental Programs; Preschool Education; Social Services
Sample Awards Smart Start Preschool (Wake County, NC)—for program support. North Carolina Zoological Society (NC)—for operating support, $10,000.

Kate B. Reynolds Charitable Trust Grants 979

Kate B. Reynolds Charitable Trust
128 Reynolds Village
Winston-Salem, NC 27106
Contact E. Ray Cope, President, (336) 723-1456; fax: (336) 723-7765
Internet http://www.kbr.org/html/applications/app.html
Requirements Nonprofit 501(c)3 organizations in North Carolina are eligible.
Restrictions Grants are not awarded to individuals.
Areas of Interest Elderly; Health Care; Hispanics; Sexually Transmitted Diseases; Women's Health
Sample Awards Hospice and Palliative Care Ctr (Winston-Salem, NC)—to provide 10 additional beds at the Reynolds Hospice Home, $400,000 (2003).

Z. Smith Reynolds Foundation Grants 980

Z. Smith Reynolds Foundation
147 S Cherry St, Ste 200
Winston-Salem, NC 27101-5287

Contact Thomas Ross, Executive Director, (800) 443-8319 or (336) 725-7541; fax: (336) 725-6069; e-mail: tomr@zsr.org or info@zsr.org
Internet http://www.zsr.org/grantmaking.htm
Requirements The foundation makes grants only to nonprofit, tax-exempt, charitable organizations and institutions in North Carolina.
Restrictions Reynolds gives low priority to requests for endowments, brick-and-mortar projects, equipment, and for indirect or overhead costs at higher education or established institutions.
Areas of Interest Academic Achievement; At-Risk Youth; Children and Youth; Civic Affairs; Civil/Human Rights; Counseling/Guidance; Cultural Activities/Programs; Economic Development; Education; Environmental Programs; Minorities; Nonprofit Organizations; Public Affairs; Public Policy/Planning; Scholarship Programs, General; Secondary Education; Social Services; Women
Sample Awards North Carolina Museum of Natural Sciences (Raleigh, NC)—to start up a comprehensive environmental-education program in five eastern North Carolina counties that are rich in natural resources and have high percentages of low-income or Latino residents, $300,000 (2002).

Sisters of Mercy of North Carolina 981
Foundation Grants

Sisters of Mercy of North Carolina Foundation
2115 Rexford Rd, Ste 401
Charlotte, NC 28211
Contact Grants Administrator, (704) 366-0087; fax: (704) 366-8850; e-mail: contact@somncfdn.org
Internet http://www.somncfdn.org/grantseekers.html
Requirements Tax-exempt health care, education, and social service organizations in North and South Carolina are eligible to apply.
Restrictions The foundation does not ordinarily support projects, programs, or organizations that serve a limited audience; biomedical or clinical research; units of the federal government; political activities; publication of newsletters, magazines, books and the production of videos; conferences and travel; endowment funds; capital fundraising campaigns; annual giving campaigns; or social events or similar fundraising activities.
Areas of Interest Children and Youth; Diversity; Economically Disadvantaged; Education; Elderly; Health Care; Social Services; Social Services Delivery; Volunteers; Women

Wachovia Foundation Grants 982

Wachovia Foundation
301 S College St, NC0143
Charlotte, NC 28288-0143
Contact Connie Smith, Program Contact, (904) 489-3268; e-mail: connie.e.smith@wachovia.com
Internet http://www.wachovia.com/inside/page/0,,139_414_430,00.html
Requirements Applicant organizations must have a 501(c)3 nonprofit tax-exempt classification, be located or provide service in Wachovia's markets, have broad community support and address specific community needs; and demonstrate fiscal and administrative stability.

Restrictions Grants are not made to support individuals; travel or conferences; political causes or candidates; organizations whose primary purpose is to influence legislation; religious, veteran, or fraternal organizations for programs limited to specific groups; retirement homes or communities; precollege-level private schools; or organizations already receiving support through United Way or a United Arts drive, except for approved capital campaigns.

Areas of Interest Arts, General; Children and Youth; Civic Affairs; Community Development; Cultural Activities/Programs; Dropouts; Economic Self-Sufficiency; Education; Health Care; Health Promotion; Health Services Delivery; Literacy; Private and Parochial Education; Quality of Life; Social Services

Sample Awards U of North Carolina at Chapel Hill (NC)—for the Kenan-Flagler Business School's new Center for Corporate Finance, and for a professorship in banking and finance at the School of Law, $1.1 million and $300,000 respectively (2003). North Carolina State U Foundation (Raleigh, NC)—for undergraduate scholarships, graduate fellowships, enrichment activities for the graduate business program, diversity programs, and support for minority students at the College of Management, $1 million (2003). Lutheran Family Services in the Carolinas (Raleigh, NC)—to upgrade technology, $25,000 (2003).

Warner Foundation Grants   983
Warner Foundation
501 Washington St, Ste D
Durham, NC 27701
Contact Grants Administrator, (919) 530-8842; fax: (919) 530-8852; e-mail: info@thewarnerfoundation.org
Internet http://www.thewarnerfoundation.org
Requirements North Carolina nonprofit organizations are eligible.
Restrictions Grants do not support operating a private school, repayment of outstanding debt, sectarian or missionary purposes, or endowments.
Areas of Interest Economic Development; Economic Self-Sufficiency; Racism/Race Relations

North Dakota

Fargo-Moorhead Area Foundation Grants   984
Fargo-Moorhead Area Foundation
609 1 First Ave N, Ste 205
Fargo, ND 58102
Contact Jan Ulferts Stewart, Executive Director, (701) 234-0756; fax: (701) 234-9724; e-mail: office@areafoundation.org
Internet http://www.areafoundation.org
Requirements The foundation welcomes grant requests from 501(c)3 organizations in Cass and Clay Counties in North Dakota and Minnesota or those serving residents of these counties.
Restrictions Grants are generally not made for ongoing operation expenses (except limited experimental or start-up periods), annual membership drives, religious organizations for religious purposes, or to individuals.

Areas of Interest Arts, General; Civic Affairs; Cultural Activities/Programs; Education; Health Care; Recreation and Leisure; Social Services; Youth Programs

North Dakota Community Foundation   985
  (NDCF) Grants
North Dakota Community Foundation
PO Box 387, 1025 N Third St
Bismarck, ND 58502
Contact Kevin Dvorak, President, (701) 222-8349; fax: (701) 222-8257; e-mail: kdvorak@ndcf.net
Internet http://www.ndcf.net/Grants/grantsindex.html
Requirements North Dakota nonprofit organizations are eligible.
Restrictions Grants are not made to individuals.
Areas of Interest Arts, General; Cultural Activities/Programs; Elderly; Health Care; Mental Health; Parks; Recreation and Leisure; Youth Programs

North Dakota Council on the Arts Access   986
  Program Grants
North Dakota Council on the Arts
1600 E Century Ave, Ste 6
Bismarck, ND 58503
Contact Community Services Coordinator, (701) 328-7590; fax: (701) 328-7595; e-mail: comserv@state.nd.us
Internet http://www.state.nd.us/arts/grants/community_arts_access.htm
Requirements Applicant organization must be a nonprofit corporation with articles on file with the state of North Dakota; comply with applicable state and federal laws; be located in and serve a community of less than 6000 people according to the most recent census, or serve a special constituency or underserved audience; and provide a one-to-one match for grant funds requested. However, up to 50 percent of the total match may be in-kind goods or services, with documentation.
Restrictions Organizations supported through the Institutional Support and Mini-Grant programs, requests for Artists in Residence or LEAP activities, reduction of a deficit, and projects completed at the time of the application are ineligible.
Areas of Interest Arts Administration; Arts, General; Audience Development; Minorities; Rural Areas

North Dakota Council on the Arts   987
  Institutional Support Program Grants
North Dakota Council on the Arts
1600 E Century Ave, Ste 6
Bismarck, ND 58503
Contact Jan Webb, Executive Director, (701) 328-7590; fax: (701) 328-7595; TDD: (800) 366-6888; e-mail: comserv@state.nd.us
Internet http://www.state.nd.us/arts/grants/inst_supp.htm
Requirements Applicant North Dakota-based organizations must comply with all NDCA general policy guidelines; comply with applicable state and federal laws; submit complete and accurate applications and provide at least 50 percent of the total cash cost of the project; and submit current long-range plans that include goals and measurable objectives for the organization. Applicants whose operating budgets exceed $100,000 must be

tax-exempt and submit independent audits for the most recently completed fiscal year. Presentation, production, or service of the arts must be the primary activity of the applicant organization.

Restrictions The following are ineligible: organizations supported through Access; capital architectural improvements or purchase or long-term rental of equipment or property; benefits or hospitality costs; fellowships, scholarships, or tuition fees; activities restricted to an organization's membership; and proposals which match federal funds with federal funds.

Areas of Interest Arts Administration; Cultural Activities/Programs; Exhibitions, Collections, Performances; Publication; Finance; Audience Development

North Dakota Council on the Arts Special Project Grants   988

North Dakota Council on the Arts
1600 E Century Ave, Ste 6
Bismarck, ND 58503
Contact Jan Webb, Executive Director, (701) 328-7590; fax: (701) 328-7595; TDD: (800) 366-6888; e-mail: jwebb@state.nd.us
Internet http://www.state.nd.us/arts/grants/spec_proj.htm
Requirements Applicant organizations must comply with all NDCA general policy guidelines and be based in North Dakota.
Restrictions The following are ineligible: organizations supported through Access or Institutional Support; capital architectural improvements or purchase or long-term rental of equipment or property; benefits or hospitality costs; fellowships, scholarships, or tuition fees; activities restricted to an organization's membership; and proposals which match federal funds with federal funds.
Areas of Interest Touring Arts Programs

Alex Stern Family Foundation Grants   989

Alex Stern Family Foundation
609 1/2 1st Ave N
Fargo, ND 58102
Contact Donald Scott, Executive Director, (701) 237-0170
Requirements Moorhead, MN, and Fargo, ND, nonprofit organizations are eligible.
Restrictions Grants are not awarded to individuals or for endowments.
Areas of Interest Alcohol/Alcoholism; Arts, General; Cancer/Carcinogenesis; Child Welfare; Community Development; Cultural Activities/Programs; Education; Elderly; Family; Hospices; Minorities; Social Services

Ohio

Akron Community Foundation Grants   990

Akron Community Foundation
345 W Cedar St
Akron, OH 44307-2407
Contact Carolyn Christian, Vice President of Programs, (330) 376-8522; fax: (330) 376-0202; e-mail: acf_fund@ix.netcom.com
Internet http://www.akroncommunityfdn.org/grants

Requirements IRS 501(c)3 nonprofit Summit County, OH, organizations are eligible.
Restrictions The foundation generally does not consider requests for general operating support, computers, office equipment, or travel expenses. Grants may not be used for endowments, scholarships, religious purposes, capital campaigns, or deficit expenses. Organizations that do not operate programs in Summit County are not eligible for grants. Grants are not made to individuals.
Areas of Interest Adult and Continuing Education; Alcohol/Alcoholism; Civic Affairs; Civil/Human Rights; Consumer Behavior; Criminal Behavior; Cultural Programs; Drugs/Drug Abuse; Education; Elementary Education; Energy; Environmental Programs; Higher Education; Humanities; Job Training Programs; Law Enforcement; Leadership; Literacy; Performing Arts; Preschool Education; Public Health; Mental Health; Recreation and Leisure; Secondary Education; Social Services; Vocational/Technical Education;
Sample Awards 26 organizations (Akron, OH)—for arts, civic-involvement, education, health, and human-services projects, through the Millennium Fund for Children, $37,074 distributed (2003). Good Samaritan Hunger Ctr (Akron, OH)—for general support, $20,000 (2003). Battered Women's Shelter (Akron, OH)—for general support, $13,000 (2003). Neighborhood Development Corp of Akron (OH)—for prostate-cancer education and screening services, $15,000 (2003).

Molly Bee Fund Grants   991

Molly Bee Fund
20325 Center Ridge Rd, Ste 629
Rocky River, OH 44116
Contact Thomas Allen, (440) 331-8220
Restrictions Grants are not made to individuals.
Areas of Interest Arts, General; Cultural Activities/Programs; Education; Hospitals

Beerman Foundation Grants   992

Beerman Foundation
11 W Monument Bldg, 8th Fl
Dayton, OH 45402
Contact William Weprin, Vice President, (937) 222-1285
Requirements Nonprofit organizations in Ohio are eligible.
Areas of Interest Archives; Baptist Church; Churches; Community Service Programs; English Education; Health Care; Higher Education; Hospitals; International Programs; Jewish Services; Minority Education; Presbyterian Church; Religion; Religious Studies; Theology
Sample Awards Temple Beth (Dayton, OH)—for operating support, $975. Hebrew Union College (Cincinnati, OH)—for operating support, $3800. Jewish Community Complex (Dayton, OH)—for operating support, $50,000.

Bethesda Foundation Grants   993

Bethesda Foundation
10506 Montgomery Rd, Ste 304
Cincinnati, OH 45242

Contact Tim McDowell, Program Contact, (513) 745-1615; fax: (513) 745-1623; e-mail: bethesdafoundation@trihealth.com or Tim_McDowell@trihealth.com
Internet http://www.bethesdafoundation.com
Requirements Nonprofit organizations in Hornell, NY, are eligible.
Areas of Interest AIDS; Alcohol/Alcoholism; Drugs/Drug Abuse; Education; Health Care; Hospitals; Nutrition/Dietetics; Scholarship Programs, General; Social Services

Bicknell Fund Grants   994
Bicknell Fund
1422 Euclid Ave, Ste 1010
Cleveland, OH 44115-2078
Contact Robert Acklin, Secretary/Treasurer, (216) 363-6482
Internet http://fdncenter.org/grantmaker/bicknellfund
Requirements Ohio 501(c)3 organizations in the greater Cleveland area are eligible.
Restrictions Grants are not awarded to individuals; organizations located outside the Cleveland, OH, area to fund endowments; or for political advocacy. Multiyear grants are not awarded.
Areas of Interest Arts; Civic Affairs; Disadvantaged (Economically); Education; Homeless; Humanities; Public Affairs; Social Services Delivery

William Bingham Foundation Grants   995
William Bingham Foundation
20325 Center Ridge Rd, Ste 629
Rocky River, OH 44116
Contact Program Contact, (440) 331-6350; fax: (440) 331-6810; e-mail: info@WBinghamFoundation.org
Internet http://fdncenter.org/grantmaker/bingham/guide.html
Restrictions Grants are not made to individuals or to organizations located outside the United States.
Areas of Interest Arts, General; Distance Education; Elementary Education; Environmental Programs; Fellowship Programs, General; Health Care; Poetry; Prisoners; Secondary Education; Social Services; Women
Sample Awards Yale University (New Haven, CT)—for a five-year grant to expand Fox International Fellowships, $250,000. Women in Transition (Warwick, RI)—to fund a case manager for female ex-offenders, $31,000. Academy of American Poets (NY)—to develop an online poetry classroom, $10,000.

Blade Foundation Grants   996
Blade Foundation
541 N Superior St
Toledo, OH 43660
Contact William Block Jr., President, (419) 245-6210
Requirements Ohio nonprofits and individuals are eligible.
Areas of Interest Cultural Activities/Programs; Education; Scholarship Programs, General; Social Services

Cincinnati Bell Foundation Grants   997
Cincinnati Bell Foundation
201 E Fourth St, Rm 102-560
Cincinnati, OH 45202
Contact Robert Horine, Public Affairs Director, (513) 397-7545
Internet http://home.cincinnatibell.com/corporate/community
Requirements 501(c)3 nonprofit organizations in the Cincinnati Bell service area are eligible. Giving primarily in northern KY, the greater Cincinnati, OH, area, and in other cities in which the company has a significant corporate presence.
Areas of Interest Arts, General; Audiovisual Materials; Civic Affairs; Compensatory Education; Cultural Activities/Programs; Elementary Education; Higher Education; Mentoring Programs; Secondary Education; Social Services; Videos; Youth Programs
Sample Awards Cincinnati Zoo (Cincinnati, OH)—for general support, $100,000. College of Mount Saint Joseph (Cincinnati, OH)—to equip a media and video center in the college's new student center, $75,000.

Cleveland-Cliffs Foundation Grants   998
Cleveland-Cliffs Foundation
1100 Superior Ave, Ste 1800
Cleveland, OH 44114-2589
Contact Vice President-Assistant Treasurer, (216) 694-5700; fax: (216) 694-4880; e-mail: publicrelations@cleveland-cliffs.com
Internet http://www.cleveland-cliffs.com/GeneralInformation
Requirements Nonprofit organizations in the mining communities in which Cleveland-Cliffs Inc operates, including Michigan, Minnesota, and the greater Cleveland area, are eligible.
Areas of Interest Animal Rights; Child Abuse; Civic Affairs; Cultural Activities/Programs; Education; Environmental Programs; Health Care; Higher Education; Literature; Museums; Philanthropy; Religion; Science; Social Services; Technology
Sample Awards Case Western Reserve U (Cleveland, OH)—for operating support, $25,000. Great Lakes Museum of Science, Environment, and Technology (Cleveland, OH)—for capital support, $15,000. Cleveland Bicentennial Commission (Cleveland, OH)—for operating support, $20,000.

Cleveland Foundation Grants Program   999
Cleveland Foundation
1422 Euclid Ave, Ste 1400
Cleveland, OH 44115
Contact Steven A. Minter, President, (216) 861-3810; tty: (216) 861-3806; fax: (216) 589-9039; e-mail: Idunford@clevefdn.org
Internet http://www.clevelandfoundation.org/page1550.cfm
Requirements Grants are made available primarily to Ohio tax-exempt private agencies and sometimes to governmental agencies in which case the limits of eligibility are more strictly defined. Only programs in greater Cleveland and Lake and Geauga Counties are considered for support.

Restrictions Grants are not made to individuals or for ongoing operating expenses, annual appeals or membership drives, fundraising, religious groups, travel, community services such as police and fire protection, publications, or video productions.

Sample Awards Cleveland State U (OH)—for the Ruth Ratner Miller Center for Greater Cleveland's Future, $180,000 (2003). Independent Pictures (Cleveland, OH)—for operating support, $15,000 (2002). Neighborhood Progress (Cleveland, OH)—to develop a sustainability and neighborhood-development plan, $38,500 (2002). Shaker Lakes Regional Nature Ctr (Cleveland, OH)—for renovation and a new construction project, $100,000 (2002).

CMA Foundation Grants 1000

Columbus Medical Association Foundation
431 E Broad St
Columbus, OH 43215
Contact Jewell Garrison, Director of Programs, (614) 240-7420; fax: (614) 240-7415; email: garrison@cmaf-ohio.org
Internet http://www.cmaf-ohio.org/cmaf
Requirements Nonprofit organizations in central Ohio, including Franklin, Delaware, Fairfield, Licking, Madison, Pickaway, and Union Counties, are eligible.
Areas of Interest African Americans; At-Risk Youth; Biomedical Research; Breast Cancer; Cancer Detection; Health Promotion; Health Services Delivery; Hospitals; Mentoring Programs; Preventive Medicine
Sample Awards Children's Hunger Alliance (Columbus, OH)—to promote school-breakfast programs, $30,000 (2003). Educational Council Foundation (Columbus, OH)—to train middle- and high-school educators to provide information about positive health behaviors, $50,000 maximum (2003). Franklin County Health Dept (Columbus, OH)—to expand its anti-tobacco activities, $30,000 maximum (2003). Mount Carmel Health Systems Foundation (Columbus, OH)—to provide education, information, and self-care skills training to people who have experienced heart failure, $90,000 (2003).

Columbus Foundation Grants 1001

Columbus Foundation
1234 E Broad St
Columbus, OH 43205
Contact Grants Administrator, (614) 251-4000; fax: (614) 251-4009; e-mail: nonprofitinfo@columbusfoundation.org
Internet http://www.columbusfoundation.org/gd5/_gd_templates/pages/gdPageSecondary.aspx?page=30
Requirements 501(c)3 tax-exempt organizations in the central Ohio region are eligible.
Restrictions Individuals are ineligible. Requests for religious purposes, budget deficits, endowments, conferences, scholarly research, or projects that are normally the responsibility of a public agency are generally not funded. Funding is not available for projects when funds are available elsewhere.
Areas of Interest Arts; Biomedical Research; Eye Diseases; Conservation; Education; Glaucoma; Health; Hearing Impairments; Humanities; Neighborhoods; Philanthropy; Social Services; Urban Affairs

Sample Awards Children's Hospital Foundation (Columbus, OH)—to provide outpatient diagnosis and treatment services to poor people, $60,000 (2003). Elder Choices of Central Ohio (Columbus, OH)—for a professional-development program designed to encourage staff retention, $25,000 (2003). LifeCare Alliance (Columbus, OH)—to provide meals for 500 chronically ill and disabled people who are homebound, $50,000 (2003). Northwest Counseling Services (Columbus, OH)—for a program to help prevent substance abuse and violence among youths, $27,000 (2003).

Dana Corporation Foundation Grants 1002

Dana Corporation Foundation
PO Box 1000
Toledo, OH 43697
Contact Ed McNeal, (419) 535-4500
Internet http://www.dana.com
Requirements 501(c)3 organizations in communities where Dana Corporation facilities are located are eligible.
Restrictions The foundation does not make grants to individuals or to organizations that practice discrimination, religious groups for denominational purposes, political activities, or United Way-supported organizations for operating expenses. The foundation does not purchase tickets to charitable or fund-raising events or support goodwill advertising.
Areas of Interest Arts, General; Civic Affairs; Cultural Activities/Programs; Education; Environmental Programs; Health Care; Social Services; Youth Programs

Dayton Power and Light Foundation Grants 1003

Dayton Power and Light Company Foundation
1065 Woodman Dr
Dayton, OH 45432
Contact Ginny Strausburg, Executive Director, (937) 259-7924; fax: (937) 259-7923
Internet http://www.waytogo.com/support_community.html
Requirements 501(c)3 organizations in the greater Dayton, OH, area are eligible.
Restrictions The foundation prefers not to support capital campaigns; college fund-raising associations; conduit organizations; endowment or development funds; fraternal, labor, or veterans organizations; hospital operating budgets; individual members of federated campaigns; individuals; national organizations outside the DP&L service territory; religious organizations; sports leagues; or telephone or mass-mail solicitations. Grants are rarely made to tax-supported institutions.
Areas of Interest Adult and Continuing Education; Basic Skills Education; Civic Affairs; Cultural Activities/Programs; Engineering Education; Health Care; Literacy; Social Services
Sample Awards Dayton Art Institute (OH)—to support the capital campaign, $25,000. United Way of the Greater Dayton Area (OH)—to support the annual campaign, $200,000.

Eaton Charitable Fund Grants 1004

Eaton Charitable Fund
1111 Superior Ave, 24th Fl
Cleveland, OH 44114-2584

Contact James Mason, Community Affairs, (216) 523-4944 or (216) 523-5000; fax: (216) 479-7013; e-mail: jamesmason@eaton.com
Internet http://web.eaton.com/NASApp/cs/ContentServer?pagename=EatonCom%2FPage%2FEC_T_ArticleFull&c=Page&cid=1007421140590
Requirements Proposals should be submitted to the local Eaton manager. Applicant organizations must be 501(c)3 tax exempt charities and be located in communities where the company has operations.
Restrictions Eaton does not contribute to annual operating budgets of hospitals; debt retirement of any organization; endowment; religious, fraternal, or labor organizations; or individuals or individual endeavors.
Areas of Interest Community Development; Education
Sample Awards 81,640 Eaton Multicultural Scholars Program, Cleveland, O. $15,000 Habitat for Humanity, Sumter, S. $7,500 United Performing Arts Fund, Milwaukee, W. and $5,000 YMCA of North Oakland County, Rochester Hills, MI.

Ellie Fund Grants   1005
Ellie Fund
1422 Euclid Ave, Ste 627
Cleveland, OH 44115-1952
Contact c/o Foundation Management Serices, (216) 621-2901; e-mail: ellie@fmscleveland.com
Internet http://www.fmscleveland.com/ellie/guidelines.cfm
Requirements Grants are awarded only to tax-exempt, nonprofit organizations, and never to individuals.
Restrictions Requests for annual appeals, fundraisers, symposia, and seminars will not be considered.
Areas of Interest Children and Youth; Intervention, Types of (Health/Safety/Medical); Literacy; Mental Health; Safety; Service Delivery Programs

FAF Community Arts Fund Operating   1006
    Support Program Grants
Fine Arts Fund
2649 Erie Ave
Cincinnati, OH 45208-2087
Contact Grants Administrator, (613) 871-2787; fax: (513) 871-2706; e-mail: faf@artsincincinnati.org
Internet http://www.artserv.org/grant.html
Requirements Organizations must have 501(c)3 tax-exempt status; three or more years of incorporated operation; an active board of volunteers that advises the organization in areas such as audience development, publicity, community relations, fund-raising, and finance; proof of fiscal accountability and management; policies and programming that demonstrate attendance by, as well as accessibility to, a broad public audience; and demonstrated focus on the greater Cincinnati area.
Restrictions Individuals and units or support groups of state agencies, community centers, government, college or university departments, school systems, ar churches and synagogues are not eligible for operating support.
Areas of Interest Arts Administration; Audience Development; Cultural Activities/Programs; Fine Arts; Fund-Raising; Volunteers

FirstEnergy Foundation Community Grants 1007
FirstEnergy Foundation
76 S Main St
Akron, OH 44308-1812
Contact Donna Valentine, Director, (330) 761-4246
Internet http://www.firstenergycorp.com/community/engine;jsessionid=INAZT05FBFMZFUVWYRIZONY?s=com.firstenergycorp.community.www.Home&o=1268297&q=1&p=%2FFirstEnergy+Foundation
Requirements 501(c)3 organizations in northern Ohio, with emphasis on the Cleveland and Toledo areas, are eligible.
Restrictions Support is not given to individuals or to national or international organizations or for political organizations, endowment funds, equipment purchase, deficit financing, research, scholarships, fellowships, or loans.
Areas of Interest Civic Affairs; Community Development; Cultural Activities/Programs; Education; Environmental Programs; Health Care; Higher Education; Hospitals; Junior and Community Colleges; Museums; Music; Performing Arts; Public Affairs; Religious Studies; Restoration and Preservation; Secondary Education; Social Services; Theology; Vocational/Technical Education; Youth Programs; Zoos
Sample Awards United Way Services (Cleveland, OH)—for operating support, $493,000. Musical Arts Assoc (Cleveland, OH)—for operating support, $43,394. Cleveland Initiative for Education (Cleveland, OH)—for operating support, $40,000.

FirstEnergy Foundation Grants   1008
FirstEnergy Foundation
76 S Main St
Akron, OH 44308
Contact Community Initiatives, (330) 761-4246
Internet http://www.firstenergycorp.com/community
Requirements New Jersey, Ohio, and Pennsylvania nonprofit organizations are eligible.
Areas of Interest Arts, General; Community Development; Cultural Activities/Programs; Education; Environmental Programs; Health Care; Hospitals; Minorities; Social Services; Urban Affairs

Ginn Foundation Grants   1009
Ginn Foundation
13938 A Cedar Rd #239
Cleveland Heights, OH 44118
Contact Grants Administrator, e-mail: info@ginnfoundation.org
Internet http://www.ginnfoundation.org/index.html
Requirements Nonprofit organizations in Cuyahoga County, OH, may apply.
Restrictions The foundation will not fund requests for support of advocacy activities. Nor will it make grants to endowment, capital, or annual fund campaigns. The foundation will not fund special events or attendance at conferences or symposia.
Areas of Interest At-Risk Youth; Children and Youth; Community Service Programs; Education; Health Care; Jewish Services; Nonprofit Organizations
Sample Awards Intergenerational School (Cleveland, OH)—to fund a portion of the salary and benefits for a

communications/development coordinator, $15,000 (2003). Covenant (Cleveland, OH)—to fund expansion of a program to treat and counsel chemically dependent and/or dual-diagnosed indigent, at-risk youth, $40,000 (2003). Bellefaire Jewish Children's Bureau (Cleveland, OH)—$37,800 to fund the salary and benefits of an after-school treatment program coordinator, $37,800 (2003). Cleveland Music School Settlement (OH)—to conduct a community needs assessment and for general operating expenses, $20,000 (2003).

Greater Cincinnati Foundation Grants 1010

Greater Cincinnati Foundation
200 W Fourth St
Cincinnati, OH 45202-2602
Contact Miles Wilson, Vice President for Grants and Programs, (513) 241-2880; fax: (513) 852-6886; e-mail: wilsonm@greatercincinnatifdn.org
Internet http://www.greatercincinnatifdn.org/page241.cfm
Requirements Nonprofit, charitable 501(c)3 organizations located in greater Cincinnati, northern Kentucky, and southeast Indiana are eligible.
Restrictions The foundation does not make grants for ongoing operating expenses of existing institutions; individuals; religious organizations for religious purposes; endowments; scholarship and scholarly or medical research; annual fund-raising drives; community services that are primarily supported by tax dollars; travel grants; nor schools, hospitals, nursing homes, or retirement centers.
Areas of Interest Arts, General; Audience Development; Cultural Programs; Community Development; Education; Environmental Programs; Health Care; Health Services Delivery; Higher Education; Social Services; Social Services Delivery
Sample Awards Otto Armleder Memorial Education Ctr (Cincinnati, OH)—for scholarships for disadvantaged children, through the Richard T. Farmer Fund, $5 million challenge grant (2003). Cincinnati Fire Museum (OH)—for audience development and collections management, $30,000 (2002). Greater Cincinnati Community Shares (OH)—for organizational development, $38,760 (2002). College of Mount Saint Joseph (Cincinnati, OH)—for the Teacher Apprentice program, $50,000 (2002).

Greater Columbus Arts Council Operating 1011 Grants

Greater Columbus Arts Council
100 E Broad St, Ste 2250
Columbus, OH 43215
Contact Program Officer, Community Funding, (614) 224-2606; fax: (614) 224-7461; e-mail: info@gcac.org
Internet http://www.gcac.org/funding/orgsOppSupport.asp
Requirements Applicant organizations must have had 501(c)3 status for at least three consecutive years prior to the date of application, demonstrate that the organization's primary focus and actual operation are artistic in nature, provide cultural programming of the highest caliber, employ professional management staff, demonstrate a wide-ranging impact on the city of Columbus, operate with a community-based board of trustees, operate with a clearly articulated artistic plan, and demonstrate fiscal accountability.
Areas of Interest Arts Administration; Dramatic/Theater Arts; Economic Development; Orchestras; Tourism
Sample Awards Actors' Theater Company (Columbus, OH)—for general operating support, $15,544. Columbus Symphony Orchestra (Columbus, OH)—for general operating support, $208,083. The Thurber House (Columbus, OH)—for general operating support, $44,103.

Walter L. Gross Jr. Family Foundation 1012 Grants

Walter L. Gross Jr. Family Foundation
9435 Waterstone Blvd, Ste 390
Cincinnati, OH 45249
Contact Jeffrey Gross, Trustee, (513) 785-6060
Requirements Ohio nonprofit organizations are eligible.
Areas of Interest Animal Care; Animal Rights; Arts, General; Churches; Community Development; Community Outreach Programs; Education; Environmental Programs; Health Care; Higher Educaton; Human Services; Medical Programs; Religion; Social Services; Social Services Delivery
Sample Awards Habitat for Humanity (Cincinnati, OH)—for general support, $10,000. Miami U Foundation (Oxford, OH)—for general support, $300,000. Our Daily Bread (Cincinnati, OH)—for general support, $2000.

Agnes Gund Foundation Grants 1013

Agnes Gund Foundation
517 Broadway, 3rd Fl
East Liverpool, OH 43920
Contact Agnes Gund, (330) 385-3400
Requirements Although there are no funding restrictions there is a focus on New York City.
Areas of Interest Arts, General; Cultural Activities/Programs; Cultural Outreach; Dance; Education; Health Care; Higher Education; Museums; Music; Performing Arts
Sample Awards Museum of Modern Art (New York, NY)—for general operating support, $1 million. Cleveland Museum of Art (OH)—for general operating support, $200,000. Virginia Museum of Fine Arts (Richmond, VA)—for general operating support, $100,000. Creative Capital Foundation (New York, NY)—for general operating support, $75,000.

George Gund Foundation Grants 1014

George Gund Foundation
45 Prospect Ave W, 1845 Guildhall Bldg
Cleveland, OH 44115
Contact David Bergholz, Executive Director, (216) 241-3114; fax: (216) 241-6560; e-mail: info@gundfdn.org
Internet http://www.gundfdn.org/guidelines_f.html
Requirements The foundation makes grants only to nonprofit, tax-exempt organizations or to qualified governmental units or agencies.
Restrictions Grants are not made outside of the United States. Grants are not awarded to support capital needs, endowments, debt reduction, benefit events, conferences, publications, the disabled, or the elderly. With the

exception of retinal disease research, reproductive health, community health, and AIDS, the funder is not active in the health field.

Areas of Interest AIDS; Arts, General; Civic Affairs; Community Development; Economic Development; Education; Environmental Programs; Eye Diseases; Family; Great Lakes; Health Care; Housing; Human Reproduction/Fertility; Neighborhoods; Poverty and the Poor; Public Health; Public Planning/Policy; Social Services

Sample Awards Urban League of Greater Cleveland (OH)—for organizational development, $50,000 (2003). Heartwood Inc (Bloomington, IN)—for operating support of this forest-preservation group, $20,000 (2003). Berea Children's Home (OH)—for its government-affairs and public-policy program, $35,800 (2003). U of Michigan at Ann Arobr (MI)—for the Great Lakes Radio Consortium training program for environmental journalists, $25,000 (2003).

Huffy Foundation Grants   1015

Huffy Foundation
225 Byers Rd
Miamisburg, OH 45342
Contact Pam Booher, Secretary, (937) 866-6251
Requirements Nonprofit organizations in company locations may apply. Requests should include a description of the organization and its history and purpose, a description of the people it serves, summary of total budget and funding for the past and present years, and names of Huffy employees who serve on the organization's governing board.
Restrictions Grants are not made to individuals, in support of political activities or of religious organizations for religious purposes, or non tax-exempt organizations. Grants are seldom made for medical research; to organizations receiving support from United Way; to endowments; or for operating funds for organizations located outside the corporation communities.
Areas of Interest Alcohol/Alcoholism; Arts, General; Child Welfare; Cultural Activities/Programs; Dramatic/Theater Arts; Drugs/Drug Abuse; Education; Health Care; Higher Education; Hospitals; Museums; Philanthropy; Public Administration; Social Services; Women; Youth Programs

Iddings Foundation   1016

Iddings Benevolent Trust
Ketting Tower, Suite 1620
Dayton, OH 45423
Contact Maribeth Graham, Administrator, (937) 224-1773; fax: (937) 224-1871
Requirements Applicants must be Ohio-based, tax-exempt organizations whose purpose is to improve the community environment and lives of the citizens, and whose primary focus is on the greater Dayton area.
Restrictions Grants are not made to individuals or to organizations outside Ohio. Additionally, there will be no endowment support.
Areas of Interest AIDS; Community Development; Cultural Activities/Programs; Curriculum Development; Education; Environmental Programs; Health Care; Literacy; Mental Health; Scholarship Programs, General; Social Services

Sample Awards AIDS Foundation of Miami Valley (OH)—for staff support over two years, $19,125. Miami Valley Literacy Council (OH)—for salary support of a curriculum director, $5000.

Kroger Company Foundation Grants   1017

Kroger Company Foundation
1014 Vine St
Cincinnati, OH 45202-1100
Contact Lynn Marmer, President, (513) 762-4999 ext 3; fax: (513) 762-1295
Internet http://www.kroger.com/corpnewsinfo_charitablegiving.htm
Requirements Nonprofit organizations in Kroger communities may submit grant proposals. National and regional organizations that provide services to areas of company operations also may be considered.
Restrictions Support is not given to individuals or for religious purposes, endowment campaigns (unless the endowment is an important part of a broader campaign that meets the foundation's objectives), medical research, conferences, dinners, or sporting events.
Areas of Interest Arts, General; Children and Youth; Civic Affairs; Education; Hunger; Minorities; Social Services; Women; Women's Health; Youth Programs

Lubrizol Foundation Grants Program   1018

Lubrizol Corporation
29400 Lakeland Blvd, 053A
Wickliffe, OH 44092
Contact Kenneth Iwashita, President, (440) 347-5080; fax: (440) 347-1858; e-mail: kmi@lubrizol.com
Internet http://www.lubrizol.com/foundation
Requirements Tax-exempt Ohio and Texas organizations are eligible to apply.
Restrictions Funds are not awarded directly to individuals or to endowments.
Areas of Interest Adult and Continuing Education; Art Education; Arts, General; Basic Skills Education; Chemical Engineering; Chemistry; Citizenship; Civic Affairs; Environmental Programs; Health Care; Higher Education; Hospices; Hospitals; Leadership; Literacy; Mechanical Engineering; Museums; Nature Centers; Parks; Performing Arts; Private and Parochial Education; Public Broadcasting; Recreation and Leisure; Rehabilitation/Therapy; Scholarship Programs, General; Secondary Education; Social Services; Youth Programs
Sample Awards Purdue U—to expand the Lubrizol HP Process Systems Engineering Laboratory, $15,000. Cleveland Institute of Art—for a scholarship, $4000.

S. Livingston Mather Charitable Trust Grants   1019

S. Livingston Mather Charitable Trust
25825 Science Park Dr, Ste 110
Beachwood, OH 44122
Contact Janet Havener, Vice President, c/o Glenmede Trust Company, (216) 514-7862; fax: (216) 378-2917
Requirements Only residents of Ohio may apply.
Restrictions Ordinarily, grants will not be made for scientific and medical research in areas appropriately supported by government and the United Way or any medical or hospital activities.

Areas of Interest Child Welfare; Cultural Activities/Programs; Education; Environmental Programs; Mental Health; Social Services; Youth Programs

Mathile Family Foundation Grants   1020
Mathile Family Foundation
PO Box 13615
Dayton, OH 45413-0615
Contact Brenda Carnal, Program Contact, (937) 264-4600; fax: (937) 264-4805; e-mail: brenda. carnal@cymi.com
Requirements Ohio nonprofit organizations are eligible. Giving primarily is limited to the Dayton area.
Restrictions Grants are not made to individuals or for endowment funds.
Areas of Interest Business Education; Children and Youth; Education; Food Distribution; Homelessness

McGregor Foundation Grants   1021
McGregor Foundation
1422 Euclid Ave, Ste 627
Cleveland, OH 44115-1952
Contact Susan Althans, c/o Foundation Management Services, e-mail: salthans@fmscleveland.com
Internet http://mcgregorfoundation.org/guidelines.html
Requirements Tax-exempt nonprofit organizations located within Cuyahoga County, OH, with preference given to communities traditionally served by The A.M. McGregor Home, are eligible. Currently no unsolicited grant applications from organizations outside Cuyahoga County will be accepted.
Restrictions The foundation discourages capital requests from long-term residential care facilities or requests for debt reduction, annual funds, research, symposia, or endowments. No grants are awarded to individuals.
Areas of Interest Geriatrics; Health Education; Health Promotion
Sample Awards Alzheimer's Disease and Related Disorders Assoc, Cleveland Area Chapter (OH)—to develop a centralized information system for programs and services at multiple sites, $74,983 (2004). Concordia Care (Cleveland Heights, OH)—for salary support of a full-time chaplain, $28,000 (2004). Fairhill Ctr (Cleveland, OH)—for a telephone hotline operated by the Intergenerational Resource Ctr, $35,255 (2004). Ideastream (Cleveland, OH)—to produce a national series on issues related to care giving, $25,000 (2004).

Milacron Foundation Grants   1022
Milacron Foundation
2090 Florence Ave
Cincinnati, OH 45206
Contact John Francy, Assistant Secetary, (513) 487-5912; fax: (513) 487-5586
Requirements Michigan and Ohio 501(c)3 nonprofit organizations are eligible.
Restrictions Grants are not made to individuals.
Areas of Interest Arts, General; Community Development; Higher Education; Religion; Youth Programs

Burton D. Morgan Foundation Grants   1023
Burton D. Morgan Foundation
PO Box 1500
Akron, OH 44309-1500
Contact Marie Erb, Program Contact, (330) 643-0219; fax: (330) 258-6559; e-mail: admin@bdmorganfdn.org
Internet http://www.bdmorganfdn.org
Requirements IRS 501(c)3 organizations in northeastern Ohio are eligible.
Restrictions The foundation does not make grants to/for individuals, multiyear commitments, annual fund drives, units of government, organizations and institutions that are primarily tax supported, or social service organizations or programs.
Areas of Interest Arts, General; Business; Career Education and Planning; Cultural Activities/Programs; Economics; Education; Higher Education; Mental Health; Religion
Sample Awards Ashland U (OH)—to establish a center for entrepreneurial studies, $3.25 million (2002). Denison U (Granville, OH)—to build a center that will house alumni offices and offices related to career counseling and off-campus internships, $8 million. College of Wooster (Wooster, OH)—$8 million. Old Trail School (Akron, OH)—$960,000.

John P. Murphy Foundation Grants   1024
John P. Murphy Foundation
50 Public Sq, Ste 924
Cleveland, OH 44113-2203
Contact Allan Zambie, Executive Vice President, (216) 623-4770; fax: (216) 623-4773
Internet http://www.fdncenter.org/grantmaker/jpmurphy
Requirements Ohio nonprofits may request grant support. Primary concern of the foundation is Cuyahoga County, OH, and its surrounding counties.
Restrictions Grants are not awarded to support endowments or scholarships.
Areas of Interest Arts, General; Community Service Programs; Cultural Activities/Programs; Dance; Health Care; Higher Education; Museums; Music; Religion; Social Services
Sample Awards Cleveland Ballet (Cleveland, OH)—$202,000. Ursuline College (Pepper Pike, OH)—$74,000. Rock and Roll Hall of Fame and Museum (Cleveland, OH)—$60,000.

Nationwide Foundation Grants   1025
Nationwide Foundation
1 Nationwide Plaza, MD 1-22-05
Columbus, OH 43215-2220
Contact Stephen Rish, President, (614) 249-5095; fax: (614) 249-3147
Internet http://www.nationwide.com/about_us/involve/fndatn.htm
Requirements Seventy percent of grants are awarded to nonprofit organizations in the greater Columbus, OH, area, with the rest going to organizations in which Nationwide has a large number of employees and agents.
Restrictions Individuals, organizations that support political candidates or political philosophies, public elementary and secondary schools, lobbying groups, and

fraternal or veterans organizations are not eligible for these grants. Research is not funded.

Areas of Interest Alcohol/Alcoholism; Business; Children and Youth; Dance; Disabled; Dramatic/Theater Arts; Drugs/Drug Abuse; Economics; Elderly; Fine Arts; Health Care; Higher Education; Legal Education; Mental Health; Minority Education; Museums; Music; Religious Welfare Programs; Social Services; Urban Affairs

Sample Awards American Red Cross, National Disaster Relief Fund (Washington, DC)—to assist victims of disasters worldwide, and to provide disaster-relief services to victims of the September 11 terrorist attacks, $500,000 over five years and $500,000, respectively (2001). Otterbein College (Westerville, OH)—for its campaign to construct a new recreation and fitness center, $500,000 (2001).

NMF Federated Department Stores Grants 1026
Federated Department Stores Inc
7 W Seventh St
Cincinnati, OH 45202
Contact Dixie Barker, Corporate Contributions Manager, (513) 579-7569; fax: (513) 579-7185
Internet http://www.federated-fds.com/community/report/chapter2/index_1_4.asp
Restrictions Grants are not given to individuals or to groups whose primary purpose is religious or political or that operate primarily outside the company's retail markets.
Areas of Interest AIDS; Arts, General; Breast Cancer; Cultural Activities/Programs; Domestic Violence; Education; Health Care; Higher Education; Literacy; Minority Education; Social Services; Women
Sample Awards Florida State U, College of Human Sciences (Tallahassee, FL)—to endow programs for students pursuing merchandising careers, $605,000 (2002).

Nord Family Foundation Grants 1027
Nord Family Foundation
747 Milan Ave
Amherst, OH 44001
Contact John Mullaney, Executive Director, (800) 745-8946 or (440) 984-3939; fax: (440) 984-3934; e-mail: execdir@nordff.org or info@nordff.org
Internet http://www.nordff.org
Requirements Most of the foundation's grants are made in Lorrain County, OH. Grants are also made in certain other geographic areas, including Cuyahoga County, OH; Denver, CO; and Columbia, SC.
Restrictions The foundation does not support debt reduction, research projects, and tickets or advertising for fundraising activities.
Areas of Interest Arts, General; Business; Children and Youth; Civic Affairs; Computer Education/Literacy; Cultural Outreach; Education; Family; Health Care; Health Promotion; Neighborhoods; Social Services
Sample Awards Firelands Assoc for the Visual Arts (Oberlin, OH)—for general operating support, $30,000 (2003). Colorado Homeless Families (Westminster, CO)—to provide transitional housing and support services to homeless families, $10,000 (2003). Communities in Schools (Columbia, SC)—for programs in the Richland One schools, focusing on children in grades four through 12 and their families, $22,500 (2003). Com-

munity Health Partners Foundation (Lorain, OH)—for the Health Ministry/Parish Nursing Program's work in Latino communities, $25,000 (2003).

Nordson Corporation Foundation Grants 1028
Nordson Corporation Foundation
28601 Clemens Rd
Westlake, OH 44145
Contact Kathy Ladiner, (440) 892-1580; e-mail: klandier@nordson.com
Internet http://www.nordson.com/corporate/grants.html
Requirements Private, nonprofit organizations in California, Georgia, Ohio, Rhode Island, and southeastern Massachusetts may apply.
Restrictions Funding is not provided for organizations whose services are not provided within the foundation's geographic areas of interest; direct grants or scholarships to individuals; organizations not eligible for tax-deductible support; organizations not exempt under Section 501(c)3 of the Internal Revenue Code; political causes, candidates, organizations or campaigns; organizations that discriminate on the basis of race, sex, or religion; or special occasion, goodwill advertising, i.e., journals or dinner programs.
Areas of Interest Arts, General; Children and Youth; Civic Affairs; Cultural Activities/Programs; Education; Elementary Education; Health Care; Higher Education; Higher Education, Private; Leadership; Literacy; Neighborhoods; Public Planning/Policy; Secondary Education; Social Services; Urban Affairs; Volunteers
Sample Awards Ctr for Leadership in Education (Lorain, OH)—for general operating support, $250,000. Salvation Army of Lorain (Lorain, OH)—for the capital campaign, $50,000. Neighborhood House Assoc of Lorain County (Lorain, OH)—for rejuvenation of the Cityview Ctr, $39,625.

Ohio Arts Council Operating Support I Grants 1029
Ohio Arts Council
727 E Main St
Columbus, OH 43205-1796
Contact Patricia Henahan, Grants Office Director, (614) 466-2613; TDD: (614) 466-4541; e-mail: pat.henahan@oac.state.oh.us
Internet http://www.oac.state.oh.us/grantsprogs/guidelines/guide_orgsupport.asp
Requirements Applicants must be incorporated as a nonprofit 501(c)3 organization in the state of Ohio.
Restrictions Primarily educational organizations that award academic credits, organizations receiving operating funds from other state agencies, organizations whose main purpose is not the arts, divisions or departments of larger institutions, or national service organizations are ineligible for funding through this program.
Areas of Interest Arts Administration; Craft Arts; Dance; Design Arts; Dramatic/Theater Arts; Folk/Ethnic Arts; Literature; Media Arts; Music; Visual Arts

Ohio Arts Council Performing Arts on Tour 1030
Ohio Arts Council
727 E Main St
Columbus, OH 43205-1796

Contact Kathy VanHorn Cain, Presenting/Touring Program, Division of Arts for Communities, (614) 466-2613; TDD: (614) 466-2613; e-mail: kathy.cain@ oac.state.oh.us

Internet http://www.oac.state.oh.us/grantsprogs/ guidelines/guide_communities.asp

Requirements This program supports Ohio organizations presenting the performing arts, music, dance, and theater. OAC will fund producing organizations acting as presenters in special situations only. Top priority will be given to organizations that apply for residencies of an Ohio artist. Lower priority is given to organizations applying for residencies of non-Ohio residents. A major institution is able to apply for Fee Support and for money for Presenting New Works.

Restrictions It is not the intent of this program to provide orchestras, opera companies, or theaters with soloists. If funding is received through Fee Support or Presenting New Works, additional funding cannot be received for those artists' fees through Operating Support.

Areas of Interest Dance; Dramatic/Theater Arts; Music; Performing Arts; Touring Arts Programs

Ohio Arts Council Statewide Service Organizations Grants   1031

Ohio Arts Council
727 E Main St
Columbus, OH 43205-1796
Contact Dia Huekler Foley, Grants Office Assistant Director, (614) 466-2613; TDD: (614) 466-4541; e-mail: dia.foley@oac.state.oh.us

Internet http://www.oac.state.oh.us/grantsprogs/ guidelines/guide_intro.asp

Requirements Only Ohio residents may apply.

Restrictions Organizations that receive direct funding from the state of Ohio may not apply for funding through this program.

Areas of Interest Arts Administration; Arts, General; Craft Arts; Dance; Design Arts; Dramatic/Theater Arts; Folk/Ethnic Arts; Literature; Media Arts; Music; Visual Arts

F.J. O'Neill Charitable Corporation Grants 1032

F.J. O'Neill Charitable Corporation
3550 Lander Rd
Cleveland, OH 44124
Contact Grants Administrator, (216) 464-2121

Requirements Ohio nonprofit organizations serving the Cleveland area are eligible.

Areas of Interest Biomedical Research; Churches; Education; Higher Education; Religion; Secondary Education

William J. and Dorothy K. O'Neill Foundation Grants   1033

William J. and Dorothy K. O'Neill Foundation
30195 Chagrin Blvd, Ste 250
Cleveland, OH 44124
Contact Program Contact, (216) 831-9667; fax: (216) 831-3779; e-mail: oneillfdn@aol.com

Internet http://www.oneillfdn.org/application.htm

Requirements 501(c)3 organizations in metropolitan areas where O'Neill family members currently live are eligible, including Washington, DC; Orlando/Upper Keys, FL; Big Island, HI; Baltimore/Annapolis, MD; New York/Long Island, NY; Cincinnati/Cleveland, OH; Columbus and Licking County, OH; Richmond/Virginia Beach, VA; and Houston, TX.

Restrictions The foundation does not make grants to individuals, to organizations that are wholly outside the United States, or in response to form letters for annual appeals.

Areas of Interest Animal Care; Arts, General; Children and Youth; Criminal Behavior; Cultural Activities/Programs; Community Development; Disabled; Education; Employment Opportunity Programs; Environmental Programs; Family; Health Care; Housing; Law Enforcement; Poverty and the Poor; Social Services Delivery

Sample Awards Cleveland Zoological Society (Cleveland, OH)—for an educational exhibit, $100,000 (2003). Cleveland Metro Parks (Cleveland, OH)—for a regional park conference, $7500 (2003). Big Brothers Big Sisters of Cleveland (Cleveland, OH)—for strategic plan, $10,000 (2003).

Owens Corning Foundation Grants   1034

Owens Corning Foundation
1 Owens Corning Pkwy
Toledo, OH 43659
Contact George Kiemle, Chair, (419) 248-6719; fax: (419) 248-5689

Internet http://www.owenscorning.com/acquainted/ support

Requirements Nonprofits in company-operating areas worldwide may apply.

Restrictions The foundation does not support debt retirement, endowment campaigns, individuals, religious organizations for religious activities, political organizations, groups promoting ideological points of view, travel, or for-profit organizations.

Areas of Interest Civic Affairs; Cultural Activities/Programs; Elementary Education; Environmental Programs; Fine Arts; Higher Education; Housing; Performing Arts; Secondary Education

Elisabeth Severance Prentiss Foundation Grants Program   1035

Elisabeth Severance Prentiss Foundation
1900 E Ninth St. Loc. 2066
Cleveland, OH 44114
Contact Frank Rizzo, c/o National City Bank, (216)222-2760

Requirements Grants are awarded to promote and improve medical services in the greater Cleveland, OH, area.

Restrictions Grants are not awarded to individuals for scholarships, fellowships, or grants in aid; or to organizations for fund-raising campaigns, surveys, assessments, studies, or planning activities.

Areas of Interest AIDS; Biomedical Research; Elderly; Health Care; Hospitals; Medical Education; Science; Women

Sample Awards Case Western Reserve U (Cleveland, OH)—to renovate the Health Center Library, $1 million (2003).

Procter and Gamble Fund Grants 1036

Procter and Gamble Fund
PO Box 599
Cincinnati, OH 45201
Contact Carol Talbot, (513) 983-1100; fax: (513)
945-8979; e-mail: talbot.cg@pg.com
Internet http://www.pg.com
Requirements 501(c)3 organizations in communities
where Procter and Gamble Company manufacturing
plants are located are eligible.
Areas of Interest Arts Administration; Business; Civic
Affairs; Cultural Activities/Programs; Curriculum De-
velopment; Dance; Disaster Relief; Dramatic/Theater
Arts; Economic Development; Economics Education;
Elementary Education; Environmental Programs; Food
Banks; Health Care; Hospitals; International Programs;
Job Training Programs; Libraries; Minority Schools;
Music; Public Planning/Policy; Secondary Education;
Social Services; Teacher Education; Technology Educa-
tion; Visual Arts; Volunteers; Youth Programs; Zoos
Sample Awards Hispanic Assoc of Colleges and Uni-
versities (San Antonio, TX)—to promote Hispanics'
success in higher education and careers, $12,000 (2003).
Disaster Relief Fund (Washington, DC) and American
Red Cross (Washington, DC)—for relief efforts following a series of deadly tornadoes in the Midwest,
$100,000 and $25,000 respectively (2003). Tuskegee U
(AL)—to construct a new facility for the College of Business and Information Science, as part of the university's
Legacy Campaign, $2 million (2003). TechnoServe
(Norwalk, CT)—for its work with small-scale coffee
growers in Latin America, including help with improving the quality of their product and exploring alternatives
to coffee production, $1.5 million (2002).

Reinberger Foundation Grants 1037

Reinberger Foundation
27600 Chagrin Blvd
Cleveland, OH 44122
Contact Robert Reinberger, President, (216)
292-2790; fax: (216) 292-4466
Requirements Most organizations receiving assistance
are in the Cleveland and Columbus, OH, areas.
Areas of Interest Biomedical Research; Cultural Activ-
ities/Programs; Environmental Programs; Higher Education; Natural Sciences; Social Services
Sample Awards Otterbein College (Westerville, OH)—
for the planning phase of a new natural sciences facility,
$200,000 over two years.

Helen Steiner Rice Foundation Grants 1038

Helen Steiner Rice Foundation
PO Box 0236, 221 E Fourth St, Ste 2100
Cincinnati, OH 45201-0236
Contact Andrea Cornett, Grant Coordinator, (513)
451-9241; e-mail: hsrice@fuse.net
Internet http://www.helensteinerrice.com/grants.html
Requirements Nonprofit organizations in the greater
Cincinnati area and Lorain, OH, may submit grant appli-
cations.
Restrictions Grants are not awarded to individuals or for
support of capital campaigns or building funds.
Areas of Interest Adult and Continuing Education;
Aging/Gerontology; Basic Skills Education; Churches;
Disabled; Elderly; Family; Health Care; Health Services
Delivery; Homelessness; Literacy; Minorities; Pre-
school Education; Transportation; Volunteers; Women
Sample Awards Wesley Hall (Cincinnati, OH)—for a
program for disadvantaged elderly, $35,000. Interfaith
Hospitality Network (Cincinnati, OH)—for its transpor-
tation program, $12,500. YWCA of Cincinnati
(Cincinnati, OH)—to support a school-readiness pro-
gram for disadvantaged families, $10,000.

Richland County Foundation Grants 1039

Richland County Foundation
24 W 3rd St, Ste 100
Mansfield, OH 44902-1209
Contact Pamela Siegenthaler, President, (419)
525-3020; fax: (419) 525-1590; e-mail:
psiegenthaler@rcfoundation.org
Internet http://www.rcfoundation.org
Requirements Only Ohio residents may apply.
Restrictions Grants are not awarded for sectarian reli-
gious purposes, annual campaigns, fellowships, special-
ized research, ongoing support, or travel.
Areas of Interest Civic Affairs; Clinics; Cultural Activ-
ities/Programs; Economic Development; Education;
Health Services Delivery; Higher Education; Social Ser-
vices
Sample Awards Ohio State U (Mansfield, OH)—for an
endowment fund, $97,500 matching grant. Mansfield
City Schools (Mansfield, OH)—for Project Success,
$28,125. Third Street Community Clinic (Mansfield,
OH)—for general support, $20,000.

Saint Ann Foundation Grants 1040

Saint Ann Foundation
1422 Euclid Ave
Cleveland, OH 44115-1901
Contact Cynthia Drennan, (216) 241-9300; fax: (216)
241-9345; e-mail mail@socstannfdn.org
Internet http://www.socstannfdn.org/SoC/
SoCMission.html
Requirements The mission, programs, and services of
the grant applicant should be consistent with the mission
and values of the foundation. The applicant organization
must be tax-exempt and nonprofit as defined by the IRS.
Proposals will be considered from organizations located
in the following counties in Ohio: Ashland, Cuyahoga,
Geauga, Lake, Lorain, Medine, Summit and Wayne.
Projects of religious communities will be considered
from LCWR Region VI (Ohio, Kentucky, Tennessee)
and South Carolina.
Restrictions The foundation does not fund: annual appeals or membership drives; capital construction; endowment funds; debt retirement; grants to individuals; or
fund-raising campaigns.
Areas of Interest Community Development; Disadvantaged (Economically); Religious Welfare Programs;
Service Delivery Programs; Social Services; Social Services Delivery
Sample Awards Cuyahoga County Department of Senior and Adult Services (Cleveland, OH)—for operating
support of the Cuyahoga County Grandparent and Other
Kinship Caregiver Initiative, $236,000 over two years
(2003). Crown Point Ecology Ctr (Bath, OH)—to examine the land-use issues of religious congregations in

northeastern Ohio, $20,000 (2003). Intercommunity Justice and Peace Ctr (Cincinnati, OH)—to build capacity and strengthen community outreach efforts, $20,000 (2003). Project AIMM (Nerinx, KY)—for operating support, $20,000 (2003).

Sisters of Charity Foundation of Canton Grants 1041

Sisters of Charity Foundation of Canton
220 Market Ave S, Ste 310
Canton, OH 44702
Contact Lou Capaldi, Grants Manager, (330) 454-5800; fax: (330) 454-5909; e-mail: lcapaldi@ scfcanton.org
Internet http://www.scfcanton.org/grant.html
Requirements Ohio tax-exempt, nonprofit organizations in the Stark County area are eligible. Proposals from surrounding counties including Carroll, Holmes, Tuscarawas, and Wayne may be considered.
Restrictions Grants normally are not awarded to fund requests for capital campaigns, or operating expenses/debt reduction of established organizations, unless it can be demonstrated that the program services will have significant impact on addressing the root causes of poverty. Grants do not support annual appeals or membership drives, endowment funds, or individuals.
Areas of Interest Child/Maternal Health; Children and Youth; Disadvantaged (Economically); Education; Elementary Education; Family; Health Care; Health Promotion; Health Services Delivery; Poverty and the Poor; Religion; Religious Welfare Programs; Secondary Education; Service Delivery Programs; Social Services; Social Services Delivery
Sample Awards United Methodist Church (Canton, OH)—for an outreach program for middle-school students, $15,000 (2003). YWCA of Canton (OH)—for operating support and security at the New Beginnings Shelter, $42,500 (2003). Domestic Violence Project (Canton, OH)—to centralize services and develop a new site, $200,000 (2003). Massillon City Schools (OH)—to continue an after-school program, $125,000 (2003).

Kelvin and Eleanor Smith Foundation Grants 1042

Kelvin and Eleanor Smith Foundation
26380 Curtiss Wright Pkwy, Ste 105
Cleveland, OH 44143
Contact Carol Zett, Grants Manager, (216) 289-5789; fax: (216) 289-5948
Requirements Nonprofit organizations in the greater Cleveland, OH, area are eligible.
Restrictions Grants are not made in support of individuals or for endowment funds, scholarships, fellowships, matching gifts, or loans.
Areas of Interest Botanical Gardens; Education; Environmental Programs; Health Care; Libraries, Academic; Performing Arts; Visual Arts
Sample Awards Case Western Reserve University, Kelvin Smith Library (Cleveland, OH)—for capital campaign, $200,000. Cleveland Museum of Art (Cleveland, OH)—for annual fund, $125,000.

Stark Community Foundation Grants 1043

Stark Community Foundation
220 Market Ave S, Unizan Plz, Ste 750
Canton, OH 44702-2107
Contact Jackie Gilin, Grants Coordinator, (330) 454-3426; fax: (330) 454-5855; e-mail: jgilin@starkcf.org
Internet http://www.starkcommunityfoundation.org/grant.htm
Requirements Grants are made to 501(c)3 tax-exempt organizations that are public charities and government bodies in or directly benefiting Stark County, OH.
Restrictions Ineligible activities and organizations include operating expenses of well-established organizations, deficit financing for programs or capital expenditures, endowment funds, religious organizations for religious purposes, annual appeals and membership contributions, and conferences and recognition events.
Areas of Interest After-School Programs; Arts and Culture; Building Grants; Buildings, Residential; Civic Affairs; Community and Civic; Community Development; Community Service Programs; Economic Development; Education; Health and Health Services; Health Personnel/Professions; Higher Education; Housing; Humanities; Leadership; Neighborhoods; Scholarships, General
Sample Awards United Way of Central Stark County (Canton, OH)—for operating support, $140,117. Canton County Day School (Canton, OH)—for operating support, $73,500. Walsh U (North Canton, OH)—for program support, $182,000.

Stocker Foundation Grants 1044

Stocker Foundation
559 Broadway Ave, 2nd Fl
Lorain, OH 44052-1744
Contact Patricia O'Brien, Executive Director, (440) 246-5719; fax: (440) 246-5720; e-mail: pobrien@ stockerfoundation.org
Internet http://www.stockerfoundation.org/grants.shtml
Requirements Funds are made to organizations in Lorain County, Ohio; Cochise, Pima, and Santa Cruz counties in Arizona; and Dona Ana County, New Mexico.
Restrictions Grants do not support annual campaigns, conferences, deficit financing, government services, public school services required by law, or research projects.
Areas of Interest Art Education; Children and Youth; Community Service Programs; Curriculum Development; Disabled; Education; Elementary Education; Health Care; Health Care Access; Leadership; Secondary Education; Social Services; Social Services Delivery; Women
Sample Awards Douglas Ctr for Performing Arts (Douglas, AZ)—to support the youth theater program, $3500.

Stranahan Foundation Grants 1045

Stranahan Foundation
4159 Holland-Sylvania Rd, Ste 206
Toledo, OH 43623-2590

Contact Pam Roberts, (419) 882-5575; fax: (419) 882-2072; e-mail: proberts@stranahanfoundation.org
Internet http://www.stranahanfoundation.org
Requirements Nonprofit organizations in Ohio are eligible to apply.
Restrictions Grants are not made to individuals.
Areas of Interest Arts; Community Development; Education; Higher Education; Museums

Wolfe Associates Grants Program 1046
Wolfe Associates Inc
34 S Third St
Columbus, OH 43215
Contact Rita Wolfe Hoag, (614) 460-3782
Requirements Organizations must be nonprofit with 501(c)3 status. Funding is kept almost exclusively to the Columbus and central Ohio area.
Restrictions No grants are awarded to individuals, or for research, demonstration projects, publications, or conferences.
Areas of Interest Arts and Culture; Cancer/Carcinogenesis; Children and Youth; Community Development; Education; Elementary Education; Environmental Programs; Higher Education; Hospitals; Human Services; Jewish Services; Medical Programs; Scholarship Programs, General; Secondary Education; Social Services; Youth Programs
Sample Awards YMCA of Central Ohio (Columbus, OH)—for operating support, $30,000. Columbus Jewish Foundation (Columbus, OH)—for operating support, $8000.

Youngstown Foundation Grants 1047
Youngstown Foundation
PO Box 1162
Youngstown, OH 44501
Contact G.M. Walsh, Executive Director, (216) 744-0320; fax: (330) 758-4663
Requirements Nonprofits in Mahoning County, OH, may submit applications for grant support.
Restrictions Grants are not made to individuals.
Areas of Interest Nonprofit Organizations

Oklahoma

Mervin Bovaird Foundation Grants 1048
Mervin Bovaird Foundation
401 S Boston Ave, Ste 3300
Tulsa, OK 74103-4070
Contact R. Casey Cooper, President and Trustee, c/o Boesche, McDermott, and Eskridge, (918) 592-3300
Requirements Nonprofits of the Christian, Methodist, Roman Catholic, and United Methodist faiths in Tulsa, OK, are eligible.
Areas of Interest Churches; Family; Homelessness; Hospitals; Nursing Homes; Private and Parochial Education; Religion; Shelters; Social Services; Youth Programs
Sample Awards Salvation Army (Tulsa, OK)—for facilities and program expansion, $50,000. John 3:16 Mission (Tulsa, OK)—for the family/youth center, $25,000.

Kirkpatrick Foundation Grants 1049
Kirkpatrick Foundation
PO Box 268822
Oklahoma City, OK 73126-8822
Contact Susan McCalmont, Secretary, (405) 840-2882; fax: (405) 840-2946; e-mail: kirkpatrickfoundation@msn.com
Requirements Only residents of Oklahoma may apply.
Restrictions Grants are not awarded to individuals or in support of hospitals, religious organizations, or mental health agencies.
Areas of Interest Adult and Continuing Education; Arts, General; Basic Skills Education; Children and Youth; Cultural Activities/Programs; Literacy; Museums; Orchestras; Performing Arts; Restoration and Preservation; Visual Arts
Sample Awards Oklahoma City Art Museum (Oklahoma City, OK)—for general operating support, $20,000. Oklahoma Philharmonic Society (Oklahoma City, OK)—for general operating support, $20,000.

Oklahoma City Community Programs and 1050 Grants
Oklahoma City Community Foundation
PO Box 1146
Oklahoma City, OK 73103-1146
Contact Program Contact, (405) 235-5603; fax: (405) 235-5612; e-mail: info@occf.org or n.anthony@occf.org
Internet http://www.occf.org/occf/programs-grants/index.html
Requirements 501(c)3 nonprofit organizations serving the greater Oklahoma City area, and programs that benefit persons living in the greater Oklahoma City metropolitan area, are eligible.
Restrictions Grants are not awarded to individuals or to benefit specific individuals.
Areas of Interest After-School Programs; Arts, General; Computer Grants; Cultural Activities/Programs; Education; Emergency Programs; Health Care; Neighborhoods; Recreation and Leisure; Scholarship Programs, General; Social Services; Transportation; Volunteers
Sample Awards Arts Council of Oklahoma City (OK)—to support a collaborative summer program of the Oklahoma City Parks and Recreation Department, After School Options, and four local school districts, $20,000. Mesta Park Neighborhood Assoc (OK)—to create a new median strip to reduce the volume of traffic around NW 18th St and N Shartel Blvd, $10,000. Neighborhood Alliance (OK)—for a computer-resource center, $22,788.

C.W. Titus Foundation Grants 1051
C.W. Titus Foundation
1801 Philtower Bldg
Tulsa, OK 74103-4123
Contact Grants Administrator
Requirements Missouri and Oklahoma nonprofit organizations are eligible.
Areas of Interest Arts, General; Community Development; Cultural Activities/Programs; Hospices; Hospitals; Social Services; Social Services Delivery

Sample Awards Southwest Missouri State U Foundation (Springfield, MO)—to construct and equip a new master-control facility for the university's Ozarks Public Television station, $1 million.

William K. Warren Foundation Grants　　**1052**
William K. Warren Foundation
PO Box 470372
Tulsa, OK 74147-0372
Contact Grants Administrator, (918) 492-8100
Areas of Interest Biomedical Research; Education; Health Care; Religion; Religious Welfare Programs; Social Services Delivery
Sample Awards Salvation Army of Tulsa (OK)—for general operating support, $135,000. Saint Anthony Hospital Foundation (Oklahoma City, OK)—for general support, $100,000.

Oregon

Carpenter Foundation Grants　　**1053**
Carpenter Foundation
711 E Main St, Ste 10
Medford, OR 97504
Contact Polly Williams, Programs Officer, (541) 772-5851; fax: (541) 773-3970; e-mail: carpfdn@internetcds.com
Internet http://www.carpenter-foundation.org
Requirements Nonprofit organizations in the Jackson and Josephine Counties of Oregon may submit proposals.
Areas of Interest Alcohol/Alcoholism; Arts, General; Children and Youth; Conservation, Natural Resources; Drugs/Drug Abuse; Education; Emergency Services; Faculty Development; Family; Health Care; Housing; Public Administration; Public Affairs; Regional Planning/Policy; Scholarship Programs, General; Social Services
Sample Awards Community Emergency Resources and Vital Services (OR)—for operating support. Three Rivers and Josephine County Joint Unit School District (Murphy, OR)—for child and family agency services, $10,000. Southern Oregon State College (Ashland, OR)—for faculty development and scholarship fund, $20,000.

Collins Foundation Grants　　**1054**
Collins Foundation
1618 SW First Ave, Ste 505
Portland, OR 97201
Contact Cynthia Adams, Director of Programs, (503) 227-7171; fax: (503) 295-3794; email: caddams@collinsfoundation.org
Internet http://www.collinsfoundation.org
Requirements Grants are made to 501(c)3 nonprofit agencies domiciled in Oregon. The proposed project must directly benefit the citizens of Oregon.
Restrictions Grants are not made to individuals or to organizations sponsoring requests intended to be used by or for the benefit of an individual. Grants normally are not made to elementary, secondary, or public higher education institutions; or to individual religious congregations. Grants normally are not made for development of-

fice personnel, annual fundraising activities, endowments, operational deficits, financial emergencies, or debt retirement.
Areas of Interest Arts, General; Biology; Conservation, Natural Resources; Cultural Activities/Programs; Disabled; Environmental Studies; Equipment/Instrumentation; Health Care; Higher Education; Mental Disorders; Religion; Social Services; Wildlife; Youth Programs
Sample Awards Pacific U (PO)—to build a library, $275,000 (2003). Portland Ctr Stage (OR)—for general operating support, $75,000 (2003). Contemporary Crafts Gallery (Portland, OR)—for its 2002-03 exhibition season, $25,000 (2003). George Fox U (Newberg, OR)—to offer a new bachelor's degree in engineering, $200,000 (2003).

Ford Family Foundation Grants　　**1055**
Ford Family Foundation
1600 NW Stewart Pkwy
Roseburg, OR 97470
Contact Norman Smith, President, (541) 957-5574; fax: (541) 957-5720
Internet http://www.tfff.org/main/guidelines.html
Requirements Nonprofit organizations in Oregon, with emphasis given to requests from Douglas and Coos Counties, and small and midsize communities in rural Oregon and in Siskiyou County, CA, are eligible.
Restrictions Grants are not made to individuals or to support endowment funds.
Areas of Interest Civic Affairs; Community Development; Education; Health Care; Rural Areas; Rural Education; Rural Health Care; Social Services; Youth Programs
Sample Awards Doernbecher Children's Hospital (Portland, OR)—to expand the Children's Cancer Center, $2 million challenge grant (2003).

Jackson Foundation Grants Program　　**1056**
Jackson Foundation
PO Box 3168
Portland, OR 97208
Contact Robert Depew, US National Bank of Oregon, (503) 275-4414
Requirements Grants are awarded to nonprofit 501(c)3 tax-exempt agencies located within the state of Oregon.
Restrictions No support for churches or temples. No grants to individuals; or for matching gifts, scholarships, fellowships, or building or equipment funds for religious organizations; no loans to individuals.
Areas of Interest Alcohol/Alcoholism; Arts, General; Children and Youth; Disabled; Drugs/Drug Abuse; Economic Development; Education; Environmental Programs; Health Care; Housing; Junior and Community Colleges; Minorities; Philanthropy; Women
Sample Awards Emanuel Medical Center Foundation (Portland, OR)—for general support, $10,000. Portland Community College Foundation (OR)—for program support, $5000.

Jeld-Wen Foundation Grants　　**1057**
Jeld-Wen Foundation
PO Box 1329
Klamath Falls, OR 97601

Contact Carol Chestnut , Grants Administrator, (541) 882-3451

Requirements Giving is primarily in company-operating areas in Arizona, Florida, Iowa, Kentucky, North Carolina, Ohio, Oregon, South Dakota, and Washington.

Restrictions The fund will not award grants for proposals providing service to a very narrow segment of the community.

Areas of Interest Education; Youth Programs

Sample Awards Tower Theater Foundation (Bend, Oregon)—grant recipient, $500,000.

Samuel S. Johnson Foundation Grants 1058

Samuel S. Johnson Foundation
PO Box 356
Redmond, OR 97756

Contact Elizabeth Hill Johnson, President, (541) 548-8104; fax: (541) 548-2014; e-mail: ssjohnson@ empnet.com

Requirements Grants are awarded to organizations in Oregon.

Restrictions Grants do not support annual campaigns, deficit financing, construction, endowments, or sole underwriting of major proposals or projects.

Areas of Interest Adult and Continuing Education; After-School Programs; Alcohol/Alcoholism; Animal Care; Crime Prevention; Domestic Violence; Drugs/ Drug Abuse; Family; Health Care; History; Hospices; Literacy; Museums; Religion; Rural Health Care; Safety; Scholarship Programs, General; Shelters; Youth Programs

Sample Awards Northeast Community School (Portland, OR)—for after-school and summer-enrichment programs, $15,000. Oregon Historical Society (Portland, OR)—for a school program, $5000. Jesuit High School, Clark Library (Portland, OR)—for books and computer equipment, $10,000.

McKenzie River Gathering Foundation 1059 Grants

McKenzie River Gathering Foundation
454 Willamette
Eugene, OR 97401

Contact Anita Rodgers, Program Director, (541) 485-2790; e-mail: anita@mrgfoundation.org

Internet http://www.mrgfoundation.org

Requirements Applicant organizations must be located in Oregon, organizing for progressive social change, committed to developing diversity, and have limited access to other funding.

Restrictions Grants are not awarded to/for social service agencies, schools, health centers, scholarships, cooperatives, individuals, or organizations based outside of Oregon, even if they have an Oregon project.

Areas of Interest AIDS; Civil/Human Rights; Domestic Violence; Environmental Programs; Forestry Management; HIV; Hispanics; Homelessness; Human Reproduction/Fertility; Labor Relations; Peace/Disarmament; Racism/Race Relations; Water Resources

Sample Awards Central Oregon Environmental Ctr (Bend, OR)—for general support, $3000. Latino Coalition (Eugene, OR)—for general support, $3000.

Fred Meyer Foundation Grants 1060

Fred Meyer Foundation
3800 SE 22nd Ave
Portland, OR 97242

Contact Mary Loftin, Community Affairs, (800) 858-9202 ext 5605 or (503) 797-7155; e-mail: foundation@fredmeyer.com

Internet http://www.fredmeyer.com/corpnewsinfo_ charitablegiving_art4_foundation.htm

Requirements Grants will be awarded to nonprofits in communities served by Fred Meyer Stores located in Alaska, Idaho, Oregon, Utah, and Washington.

Restrictions Grants do not support athletic programs, religious activities, travel expenses, or groups that discriminate.

Areas of Interest Adolescents; Alternative Modes of Education; Arts, General; Children and Youth; Children's Theater; Cultural Activities/Programs; Education; Elementary Education; Family; Food Preparation; Health Promotion; Homelessness; Literacy; Nutrition/Dietetics; Parent Education; Poverty and the Poor; Preschool Education; Safety; Transportation; Volunteers

Sample Awards Perseverance Theater (Juneau, AK)— for a series of arts and cultural presentations for school-age children, $10,500. Community Transitional School (Portland, OR)—to purchase a school bus for this private alternative school serving homeless preschool through eighth-grade students in the Portland area, $25,000. Share Our Strength's Portland Operation Frontline (Portland, OR)—for a six-week class in which volunteer chefs teach basic cooking, food budgeting, and nutritional skills to low-income teenage parents, $15,000.

Meyer Memorial Trust Grants Program 1061

Meyer Memorial Trust
425 NW 10th Ave, Ste 400
Portland, OR 97209

Contact Grants Administrator, (503) 228-5512; e-mail: mmt@mmt.org

Internet http://www.mmt.org

Requirements General purpose and small grants are awarded to 501(c)3 nonprofit organizations in Oregon and Clark County, WA. Teachers and other staff members from public and private elementary and secondary schools in Oregon and Clark County, WA, are eligible for teacher initiatives grants.

Restrictions Meyer does not fund general administrative overhead or indirect rate allocations. Requests for special projects will receive priority over requests for ongoing operations.

Areas of Interest Arts, General; Audience Development; Children and Youth; Classroom Instruction; Community Development; Dramatic/Theater Arts; Education; Health Care; Higher Education; Humanities; Music, Vocal; Social Services; Technology; Youth Programs

Sample Awards Albany Library (OR)—for equipment that will enable patrons to check out their own library materials, $11,460 (2003). Three Rivers Land Conservancy (Lake Oswego, OR)—for a project to spur individual donations for regional land-conservation activities, $95,000 (2003). Assoc for Human Advancement and Development (Portland, OR)—for an after-school program for Hmong-American children, $50,000 (2003). All Women's Health Services (Portland, OR)—for staff and marketing costs, $10,000 (2003).

Nike Corporate Contributions Program Grants 1062

Nike Inc
PO Box 4027
Beaverton, OR 97076
Contact Public Affairs, (503) 671-6453; fax: (503) 532-0418
Internet http://www.nike.com/nikebiz/nikebiz. jhtml?page=26
Requirements Nonprofits, including schools, school districts, colleges and universities, and community-based organizations, may request grant support.
Restrictions Requests are denied for support of capital campaigns; fraternal, religious, or political groups; research programs or studies; sponsorship advertising; endowments; or coverage of operating deficits.
Areas of Interest Biotechnology; Children and Youth; Cultural Outreach; Dance; Education; Environmental Programs; Literacy; Minorities; Parks; Recreation and Leisure; Social Services; Sports; Women
Sample Awards National Congress of American Indians (Washington, DC)—for its intern and fellowship program for American Indian and Alaska Native students enrolled at higher education institutions, $25,000 (2003). Challenged Athlete Foundation (Del Mar, CA)—for award money designated by Rudy Garcia-Tolson, the winner of the 2002 Casey Martin Award, $25,000 (2003). 30 Boys and Girls Clubs in 14 cities—for programs that involve physical activities for youths, $1.5 million in cash and equipment (2003). Portland Parks and Recreation (OR)—to refurbish nearly 90 existing outdoor basketball courts in more than 30 Portland parks, $2 million (2002).

Oregon Community Foundation Grants 1063

Oregon Community Foundation
1221 Southwest Yamhill, No 100
Portland, OR 97205
Contact Program Contact, (503) 227-6846 ext 414; fax: (503) 274-7771; e-mail: info@ocfl.org
Internet http://www.ocf1.org
Requirements Oregon nonprofit organizations may apply.
Restrictions Grants are not awarded to individuals or religious organizations for religious purposes or for endowments, annual campaigns, deficit financing, research, publications, films, or conferences.
Areas of Interest Adult and Continuing Education; Basic Skills Education; Career Education and Planning; Civic Affairs; Community Development; Cultural Activities/Programs; Education; Health Care; Literacy; Minorities; Minority Health; Nursing; Public Administration; Reading Education; Social Services; Youth Programs; Youth Violence
Sample Awards Boys and Girls Club of Portland Metropolitan Area (Portland, OR)—for its gang-prevention program, $12,500 (2003).

Oregon Soccer Foundation for Youth Grants 1064

Oregon Soccer Foundation for Youth
4840 SW Western Ave, Ste 800
Beaverton, OR 97005
Contact Oregon Youth Soccer Association, (800) 275-7353 or (503) 626-4625; fax: (503) 520-0302
Internet http://www.oregonyouthsoccer.org/test/foundation
Areas of Interest Children and Youth; Sports

Portland General Electric Foundation Grants 1065

Portland General Electric Foundation
121 SW Salmon St, One World Trade Center, 3rd Fl
Portland, OR 97204
Contact Julie Franz, Contributions Coordinator, (503) 464-8779; fax: (503) 464-2223; e-mail: Julie_Franz@pgn.com
Internet http://www.pgefoundation.org/eligibility.html
Requirements 501(c)3 nonprofits in Oregon are eligible.
Restrictions The foundation does not fund: bridge grants, debt retirement or operational deficits; endowment funds; general fund drives or annual appeals; political entities, ballot measure campaigns or candidates for political office; organizations that discriminate against individuals on the basis of creed, color, gender, sexual orientation, age, religion or national origin; fraternal, sectarian and religious organizations; individuals; travel expenses; conferences, symposiums, festivals, events, team sponsorships or user fees; salaries of employees, with the exception of costs relating directly to the funded project; or capital requests that include building improvements, equipment purchases or anything considered an asset of the organization.
Areas of Interest Arts & Culture; Community Development; Cultural Diversity; Education; Education Reform; Elementary Education; Environmental Programs; Family; Health Promotion; Higher Education; Homeless; Job Training Programs; Leadership; Libraries; Minorities; Minority Health; Music Education; Preschool Education; Secondary Education; Volunteers

Regional Arts and Cultural Council General Support Grants 1066

Regional Arts and Cultural Council
620 SW Main St, Ste 420
Portland, OR 97205
Contact Lorin Schmit Dunlop, Grant Specialist, (503) 823-5408; fax: (503) 823-5432; e-mail: lsdunlop@racc.org
Internet http://www.racc.org
Requirements Organizations must have 501(c)3 status, have been in existence for a minimum of three years, have paid professional staff and continuous administration throughout the year, and meet RACC guidelines for eligible expenses. Organizations must be based in Multnomah, Washington, or Clackamas Counties in Oregon.
Areas of Interest Arts Administration

Pennsylvania

Air Products and Chemicals Grants 1067

Air Products and Chemicals Corporation
7201 Hamilton Blvd
Allentown, PA 18195-1501
Contact Marta Boulos Gabriel, Program Contact;
e-mail: bilheir@airproducts.com
Internet http://www.airproducts.com/Responsibility/
SocialResponsibility
Requirements 501(c)3 nonprofit organizations in company-operating areas are eligible.
Restrictions Grants are not made to/for individuals, sectarian or denominational organizations, political candidates or activities, veterans organizations, organizations receiving United Way support, labor groups, elementary or secondary schools, capital campaigns of national organizations, hospital operating expenses, national health organizations, or goodwill advertising.
Areas of Interest Arts, General; Audience Development; Community Development; Cultural Activities/Programs; Economic Development; Economics Education; Education; Educational/Public Television; Environmental Programs; Equal Educational Opportunity; Equal Employment Opportunity; Exercise; Health Care; Health Promotion; Higher Education; Libraries; Minority Education; Museums; Public Broadcasting; Safety; Social Services; Special Education; Urban Planning/Policy

Alcoa Foundation Grants 1068

Alcoa Foundation
201 Isabella St
Pittsburgh, PA 15212-5858
Contact Program Contact, (412) 553-2348; fax: (412) 553-4498
Internet http://www.alcoa.com/global/en/community/foundation.asp
Requirements The foundation awards grants to nonprofit public charities in communities where Alcoa has a presence. Local Alcoans work within their communities to evaluate organizations and make recommendations for funding to Alcoa Foundation. Nonprofit organizations that serve localized communities should find the Alcoa facility nearest to them and write a one-page letter describing their mission, nature of request, connection to the areas of excellence and offering contact information. If interested, the Alcoa location contact will notify the requesting organization and invite them to submit more information. Areas of operation include western Pennsylvania; Davenport, IA; Evansville, IN; Massena, NY; New Jersey; Cleveland, OH; Knoxville, TN; and Rockdale, TX.
Restrictions The foundation does not make gifts to local projects other than those near Alcoa plant or office locations; endowment funds, deficit reduction, or operating reserves; hospital capital campaign programs unless the hospital presents a comprehensive area analysis that justifies, on a regional rather than an individual institutional basis, the need for the capital improvement; individuals, except for the scholarship program for children of Alcoa employees; tickets and other promotional activities; trips, tours, or student exchange programs; or documentaries and videos.

Areas of Interest Arts, General; Biomedical Research; Business Education; Civic Affairs; Cultural Activities/Programs; Cultural Diversity; Economics Education; Education; Engineering Education; Environmental Programs; Health Care; Hospitals; International Programs; Mathematics Education; Minority Education; Minority Schools; Religion; Science; Science Education; Secondary Education; Social Services
Sample Awards Clarkson U (Potsdam, NY)—for diversity-related student activities, a global-perspectives exchange program, and scholarships for minority students, $55,000 (2003).

Allegheny Foundation Grants 1069

Allegheny Foundation
1 Oxford Ctr, 301 Grant St, Ste 3900
Pittsburgh, PA 15219-6401
Contact Matthew Groll, Executive Director, (412) 392-2900
Internet http://www.scaife.com/alleghen.html
Requirements Initial inquiries should be in letter form signed by the organization's president, or authorized representative, and have the approval of the board of directors. The letter should include a concise description of the specific program for which funds are requested. Additional information must include a budget for the program and for the organization, the latest audited financial statement, an annual report, and a board of director's list. A copy of the organization's 501(c)3 letter is required. Only Pennsylvania residents may apply.
Restrictions Grants are not made to individuals.
Areas of Interest Civic Affairs; Education; Nonprofit Organizations; Public Affairs; Public Planning/Policy; Restoration and Preservation
Sample Awards Allegheny Institute for Public Policy—$50,000. Fineview Citizens Council Inc—$10,000. Pennsylvania Assoc of Nonprofit Organizations—$35,000.

Allegheny Technologies Charitable Trust 1070

Allegheny Technologies
1000 Six PPG Pl
Pittsburgh, PA 15222
Contact Jon Walton, Trustee, (412) 394-2800; fax: (412) 394-3034
Internet http://www.alleghenytechnologies.com
Requirements 501(c)3 tax-exempt organizations in company-operating areas are eligible.
Areas of Interest Arts, General; Civic Affairs; Cultural Activities/Programs; Education; Health Care; Public Affairs; Social Services
Sample Awards Pittsburgh Symphony Society (Pittsburgh, PA)—grant recipient, $55,000.

American Eagle Outfitters Foundation Grants 1071

American Eagle Outfitters Foundation
150 Thorn Hill Dr
Warrendale, PA 15086
Contact Foundation Administrator
Internet http://www.ae.com/corp/foundation2.htm
Requirements 501(c)3 public charities are eligible.
Restrictions The foundation will not contribute to: fashion shows or other requests for clothing donations except

for occasions where the company may provide disaster-related support to communities resulting from acts of nature (i.e., floods, tornadoes, hurricanes, fires, etc.); organizations that discriminate based on race, creed, color, sex, age, national origin, veteran status, or physical or mental disabilities; individual religious organizations; political organizations, campaigns, or candidates for political office; lobbying groups; medical or health-related causes; veteran or fraternal organizations; individuals; goodwill advertising in journals or program books; capital campaigns such as building grants; organizations that spend more than 30 percent of their total budget on fundraising efforts; or programs in communities without AE stores.

Areas of Interest Civil Service; College Students; Disaster Relief; Diversity; Early Childhood Education; Education; Literacy; Quality of Life; Youth and Education; Youth Programs

Sample Awards KaBOOM (Chicago, IL)—to construct three parks for skateboarding, in-line skating, and biking, $250,000 (2003). Jumpstart (Boston, MA)—to recruit AmeriCorps members to help preschoolers develop language, literacy, and social skills, and for stipends and operating support for AmeriCorps members, $600,000 over four years (2003).

Ametek Foundation Grants   1072
Ametek Foundation
PO Box 1764, 37 N Valley Rd, Bldg 4
Paoli, PA 19301-0801
Contact Kathryn Londra, (610) 647-2121; fax: (610) 296-3412
Requirements IRS 501(c)3 organizations are eligible.
Restrictions Grants are not made to individuals or to political, fraternal, or veterans organizations.
Areas of Interest Arts, General; Biomedical Research; Civic Affairs; Education; Environment; Health Care; Higher Education; Hospitals; Museums; Philanthropy; Scholarship Programs, General; Social Services; Vocational/Technical Education
Sample Awards Rochester City School District (Rochester, NY)—grant recipient, $116, 231. Gnaden Huetten Memorial Hospital (Lehighton, PA)—grant recipient, $1000. Abilities, Inc of Florida (Clearwater, FL)—grant recipient, $15,000.

Arcadia Foundation Grants   1073
Arcadia Foundation
105 E Logan St
Norristown, PA 19401
Contact Marilyn Lee Steinbright, President, (610) 275-8460; fax: (610) 275-8460
Requirements Eastern Pennsylvania organizations whose addresses have zip codes of 18000-19000 are eligible.
Restrictions Grants are not awarded to support individuals, deficit financing, land acquisition, fellowships, demonstration projects, publications, or conferences.
Areas of Interest Children and Youth; Education; Health Care

Arronson Foundation Grants   1074
Arronson Foundation
1 S Broad St, Ste 2100
Philadelphia, PA 19107
Contact Joseph Kohn, President & Secretary, (215) 238-1700 or (215) 238-1968
Requirements Nonprofit organizations in Pennsylvania, with emphasis on the Philadelphia area, are eligible to apply.
Areas of Interest Churches; Health Care; Higher Education; Hospices; International Programs; Jewish Services; Religion; Religious Studies; Youth Programs
Sample Awards Federation of Allied Jewish Appeal (Philadelphia, PA)—for operating support, $100,000.

Bailey-Fischer and Porter Grants   1075
Bailey-Fischer and Porter
125 E County Line Rd
Warminster, PA 18974
Contact Maria Novak, (215) 674-6000; fax: (215) 674-7183
Requirements Philadelphia nonprofits are eligible.
Areas of Interest Arts, General; Civic Affairs; Education; Public Affairs

Bayer Foundation Grants   1076
Bayer Foundation
100 Bayer Rd, Bldg 4
Pittsburgh, PA 15205-9741
Contact Rebecca Lucore, Executive Director, (412) 777-2000
Internet http://www.bayerus.com/about/community/i_foundation.html
Requirements 501(c)3 nonprofit organizations in Bayer operating communities are eligible. Submit proposals to regional offices in Ohio, California, North Carolina, Indiana, Missouri, Massachusetts, Rhode Island, New Jersey, Pennsylvania, and Connecticut.
Restrictions Grants do not support charitable dinners and events, programs to influence legislation, endowments, deficit reduction or operating reserves, religious groups, student trips, athletic sponsorships, community advertising, telephone solicitations, or operating support for United Way agencies.
Areas of Interest Art Education; Arts, General; Business Administration; Civic Affairs; Cultural Outreach; Curriculum Development; Economic Development; Education; Job Training Programs; Literacy; Neighborhoods; Nonprofit Organizations; Science Education; Social Services; Social Services Delivery
Sample Awards Robert Morris College (Moon Township, PA)—for the Bayer Ctr for Nonprofit Management, which awards master's degrees in business administration with a focus on nonprofit management and that offers technical and consulting services, educational programs, and research and referral services to nonprofit organizations in Pennsylvania, $500,000.

Will R. Beitel Childrens Community   1077
Foundation Grants
Will R. Beitel Childrens Community Foundation
PO Box 292
Nazareth, PA 18064-0292
Contact Thomas Kelchner, (610) 861-8929

Requirements Pennsylvania nonprofit organizations serving Northampton County are eligible.
Areas of Interest Child Psychology/Development; Community Development; Education; Family; Social Services

Claude Worthington Benedum Foundation 1078
Grants
Claude Worthington Benedum Foundation
233 Fourth Ave
Pittsburgh, PA 15222
Contact William Getty, President, or Beverly Walter, Grants Program Director, (800) 223-5948 or (412) 288-0360; fax: (412) 288-0366
Internet http://fdncenter.org/grantmaker/benedum
Requirements Southwestern Pennsylvania and West Virginia nonprofit organizations may apply.
Restrictions Support is not given for national health and welfare campaigns, medical research, religious activities, fellowships, scholarships, annual campaigns, or travel.
Areas of Interest Arts, General; Community Development; Computer Engineering; Economic Development; Education; Environmental Programs; Families; Health Care; Health Care Access; Health Services Delivery; Higher Education; Housing; Orchestras; Personnel Training and Development; Rural Health Care; Social Services; Teacher Education
Sample Awards Carnegie Hall West Virginia (Lewisburg, WV)—for a professional-development series for art educators, $35,000 (2003). Foundation for California U of Pennsylvania (California, PA)—to initiate computer-training programs in Pennsylvania's Allegheny and Washington Counties, $68,000 over two years (2003). Literacy Volunteers of West Virginia (Charleston, WV)—to provide literacy services to adults in West Virginia, $60,000 (2003). Stop Abusive Family Environments (Welch, WV)—for operating support and for its low-cost-housing program, $100,000 (2003).

Beneficia Foundation Grants 1079
Beneficia Foundation
1 Pitcairn Pl, Ste 3000
Jenkintown, PA 19046
Contact Feodor Pitcairn, Executive Director, (215) 887-6700
Requirements Nonprofit tax-exempt organizations are eligible.
Restrictions Individuals are not eligible.
Areas of Interest Arts, General; Conservation, Natural Resources; Ecology; Environmental Programs; Marine Resources; Opera/Musical Theater; Tropical Zones
Sample Awards Opera Co of Philadelphia (PA)—for general support, $45,000. Ctr for Marine Conservation (Washington, DC)—for general support, $30,000. The Nature Conservancy, New Jersey Field Office (Chester, NJ)—for the Johnson Swamp Preserve, $5000.

Berks County Community Foundation 1080
Grants
Berks County Community Foundation
PO Box 212, 501 Washington St
Reading, PA 19603-0212
Contact Richard Mappin, Vice President for Grantmaking, (610) 685-2223; e-mail: richardm@bccf.org or info@bccf.org
Internet http://www.bccf.org/scholarships/index.html
Requirements Individuals, nonprofit organizations, and other public and private organizations in Pennsylvania may apply.
Areas of Interest Alcohol/Alcoholism; Arts, General; Cultural Activities/Programs; Drugs/Drug Abuse; Economic Development; Education; Environmental Programs; Fine Arts; Health Care; Music; Social Services; Youth Programs
Sample Awards To be distribute among nine nonprofit organizations in Berk County (PA)—for programs for children and youths, as recommended by the Youth Advisory Committee, $16,752 (2003). to be distributed among 118 students in Berks County (PA)—for scholarships for postsecondary education, $142,000 (2003).

CIGNA Foundation Grants 1081
CIGNA Foundation
1601 Chestnut St, TL06B
Philadelphia, PA 19192-1540
Contact Program Contact, e-mail: communityrelations@cigna.com
Internet http://www.cigna.com/general/about/community/grant_information.html
Requirements Organizations with 501(c)3 tax-exempt status are eligible.
Restrictions The foundation will not consider applications for grants to individuals, organizations operating to influence legislation or litigation, political organizations, or religious activities. In general, the foundation will not consider applications from organizations receiving substantial support through the United Way or other CIGNA-supported federated funding agencies; hospitals' capital improvements; or research, prevention, and treatment of specific diseases.
Areas of Interest Adult and Continuing Education; Arts, General; Basic Skills Education; Civic Affairs; Cultural Activities/Programs; Death/Mortality; Health Care; Higher Education; Infants; International Programs; Literacy; Minority Education; Public Planning/Policy; Secondary Education; Social Services
Sample Awards Hartford Action Plan in Infant Health (Hartford, CT)—to prevent infant mortality, $750,000.

Connelly Foundation Grants 1082
Connelly Foundation
1 Tower Bridge, Ste 1450
West Conshohocken, PA 19428
Contact Victoria Flaville, Vice President, (215) 834-3222; fax: (610) 834-0866; e-mail: info@connellyfdn.org
Internet http://www.connellyfdn.org/guidelines.html
Requirements Grants are usually restricted to organizations located within the area of its geographic concentration, which includes the city of Philadelphia and the greater Delaware Valley region.
Areas of Interest Adult and Continuing Education; Arts, General; Churches; Cultural Activities/Programs; Elementary Education; Higher Education; Hospitals; Poverty and the Poor; Religion; Secondary Education; Social Services

William B. Dietrich Foundation Grants   1083
William B. Dietrich Foundation
PO Box 58177
Philadelphia, PA 19102-8177
Contact William Dietrich, President, (215) 979-1919
Requirements Pennsylvania nonprofits are eligible to apply.
Restrictions No grants are provided for individuals.
Areas of Interest AIDS; Aging/Gerontology; Arts and Culture; Cancer/Carcinogenesis; Children and Youth; Conservation, Elderly; Natural Resources; Higher Education; History; Human Services; Museums; Restoration and Preservation, Structural/Architectural; Secondary Education; Social Services; Youth Programs
Sample Awards Woodmere Art Museum (Philadelphia, PA)—to expand its administrative offices, $200,000. Wellness Community of Philadelphia (PA)—to restore and renovate an 18th-century barn that will serve as a new facility for this group that offers programs and services for people with cancer and their families, $350,000.

Dominion Foundation Grants   1084
Dominion Foundation
625 Liberty Ave, 21st Fl
Pittsburgh, PA 15222-3199
Contact James Mesloh, Executive Director, (412) 690-1430; fax: (412) 690-7608
Internet http://www.dom.com/about/community/foundation/index.jsp
Requirements IRS 501(c)3 nonprofit organizations in company-operating areas (Connecticut, Louisiana, Ohio, New York, North Carolina, Pennsylvania, Virginia, and West Virginia) are eligible.
Restrictions Grants are not made to individuals; organizations for strictly sectarian purposes; fraternal, political, advocacy, or labor organizations; operating funds of United Way-supported agencies; or courtesy advertising in programs, parties, or benefit performances.
Areas of Interest Arts, General; Community Development; Cultural Activities/Programs; Education; Elementary Education; Environmental Education; Health Care; Mathematics Education; Museums; Nonprofit Organizations; Photography; Science Education; Secondary Education; Social Services
Sample Awards National Museum of American Art (Washington, DC)—to support a major exhibition and other programs related to its photography collection, including new acquisitions, research, publications, and media projects. Oberlin College (OH)—to teach students how to apply environmental education to real-world problems.

Samuel S. Fels Fund Grants   1085
Samuel S. Fels Fund
1616 Walnut St, Ste 800
Philadelphia, PA 19103-5313
Contact Helen Cunningham, Executive Director, (215) 731-9455; fax: (215) 731-9457
Internet http://www.samfels.org/apps.html
Requirements Philadelphia nonprofits may apply for grants.
Restrictions Grants are not awarded to support multiyear projects, umbrella-funding groups, scholarships, travel, research, capital funds, major equipment, endowments, deficit financing, ticket purchases, ads, fund-raising events, or emergency aid.
Areas of Interest After-School Programs; Arts, General; Community Service Programs; Curriculum Development; Education; Women's Education
Sample Awards Philadelphia Citizens for Children and Youth (PA)—for after-school programs. Community Women's Education project (PA)—for general operating support.

FMC Foundation Grants   1086
FMC Foundation
1735 Market St
Philadelphia, PA 19103
Contact Program Contact, (215) 299-6000; fax: (215) 299-5998
Internet http://www.fmc.com
Requirements Grants are awarded to 501(c)3 organizations in FMC-plant communities. US-based organizations with an international focus are eligible.
Restrictions Grants are not made to individuals.
Areas of Interest Business Education; Chemistry Education; Community Development; Economics Education; Education; Engineering Education; Health Care; Higher Education; Hospitals; Medical Education; Minority Education; Public Affairs; Scholarship Programs, General; Social Services; Urban Planning/Policy

Grundy Foundation Grants   1087
Grundy Foundation
PO Box 701, 680 Radcliffe St
Bristol, PA 19007
Contact Roland Johnson, Executive Director, (215) 788-5460; fax: (215) 788-0915; e-mail: grundyf@voicenet.com
Requirements Pennsylvania 501(c)3 organizations in Bucks County are eligible.
Restrictions Grants are not made to support operating expenses, political or religious organizations, or individuals.
Areas of Interest Children and Youth; Cultural Activities/Programs; Disabled; Dramatic/Theater Arts; Elderly; Health Care; Hospitals; Restoration and Preservation
Sample Awards Bristol Riverside Theater (Bristol, PA)—for the performance season. Behanna (Southampton, PA)—for renovations to Swigart House.

Heinz Endowments Grants   1088
Heinz Endowments
30 Dominion Tower, 625 Liberty Ave
Pittsburgh, PA 15222
Contact Maxwell King, President, (412) 281-5777; fax: (412) 281-5788; e-mail: info@heinz.org
Internet http://www.heinz.org
Requirements Grants are limited to 501(c)3 nonprofit organizations and 509(a) public charities in Pennsylvania and generally to the southwestern Pennsylvania region.
Restrictions Individuals and for-profit organizations are not eligible.
Areas of Interest Arts, General; At-Risk Youth; Audience Development; Child Psychology/Development; Child/Maternal Health; Children and Youth; Commu-

nity and School Relations; Cultural Activities/Programs; Disaster Relief; Ecology, Aquatic; Economic Development; Education; Entrepreneurship; Environmental Programs; Family; Higher Education; International Studies; Neighborhoods; Nonprofit Organizations; Solid Waste Disposal; Technology; Urban Areas

Sample Awards Pennsylvania Child Care Assoc (Harrisburg, PA)—for scholarships to help home-based child-care providers receive additional training in early-childhood education, $300,000 (2003). Pittsburgh Theological Seminary (PA)—for the development of a faith-based intervention model for families with young children, $100,000 (2002). Allegheny Conference on Community Development (PA)—to support a regional land-use initiative, $100,000 (2002). Black Contractors Assoc (PA)—for a construction employees training project, $75,000 (2002).

H.J. Heinz Company Foundation Grants   1089
H.J. Heinz Company Foundation
PO Box 57
Pittsburgh, PA 15230
Contact Tammy Aupperle, Program Director, (412) 456-5773; fax: (412) 456-7859; e-mail: heinz. foundation@hjheinz.com
Internet http://www.heinz.com/jsp/foundation.jsp
Requirements Nonprofits in company-operating areas are eligible. Contact program staff for company locations.
Restrictions Requests are denied for general scholarships, fellowships, travel, political causes, individuals, or religious groups.
Areas of Interest Children and Youth; Cultural Activities/Programs; Health Care; Disadvantaged (Economically); Education; Families; Nutrition/Dietetics; Social Services; Youth Programs; Minorities; Women
Sample Awards North Side Leadership Conference (Pittsburgh, PA)—to provide employment and education programs for local residents, $2 million. Civic Light Opera (Pittsburgh, PA)—for the Millenium Creche, $10,000. Mon Valley Initiative (Pittsburgh, PA)-for operating support, $25,000.

Allen Hilles Fund Grants   1090
Allen Hilles Fund
PO Box 540
Philadelphia, PA 19462
Contact Judith Bardes, Manager, e-mail: Judy1@aol. com
Internet http://www.dvg.org/Hilles/index.html
Requirements Philadelphia-area and Wilmington, DE, nonprofit organizations are eligible.
Restrictions Funding requests for endowments, scholarships, capital expenditures, political purposes, or agency promotion (i.e., marketing, development, publication of annual reports, or fundraising events) are denied.
Areas of Interest Disadvantaged (Economically); Economic Development; Education; Health Care Access; Religion; Violence in Schools; Women; Women's Health
Sample Awards Elizabeth Blackwell Health Ctr for Women (Philadelphia, PA)—for the Access to Underserved Initiative, $4000. American Friends Service Committee (Philadelphia, PA)—for nonviolence

workshops in area schools, $5000. Eastern Philadelphia Organizing Project (PA)—for operating support, $10,000.

Hillman Foundation Grants   1091
Hillman Foundation
2000 Grant Bldg
Pittsburgh, PA 15219
Contact Ronald Wertz, President, (412) 338-3466; fax: (412) 338-3463; email: foundation@hillmanfo. com
Requirements Nonprofit, charitable organizations serving Pittsburgh and southwestern Pennsylvania are eligible.
Restrictions Grants are not awarded to support group travel or meetings, such as conferences or seminars.
Areas of Interest Arts, General; Cancer/Carcinogenesis; Civic Affairs; Cultural Activities/Programs; Education; Health Care; Orchestras; Social Services; Youth Programs
Sample Awards Chatham College (Pittsburgh, PA)—to endow and operate the Pennsylvania Center for Women, Politics, and Public Policy, $2.95 million (2003).

Hirtzel Memorial Foundation Grants   1092
Orris C. Hirtzel and Beatrice Dewey Hirtzel Memorial Foundation
PO Box 185
Pittsburgh, PA 15230
Contact Laurie Moritz, Grants Administrator, c/o Mellon Financial Corporation, (412) 234-0023
Requirements New York nonprofit organizations in Ripley, Chautauqua County, and Pennsylvania nonprofit organizations in North East, Erie County, are eligible.
Areas of Interest Community Development; Education; Health Care; Health Promotion; Health Services Delivery; Higher Education; Human Services; Medical Research; Neighborhoods; Scholarships, General; Social Services Delivery
Sample Awards Mercyhurst College (Erie, PA)—to establish the Institute on Aging and Geriatric Health, $1 million.

Roy A. Hunt Foundation Grants   1093
Roy A. Hunt Foundation
1 Bigelow Sq, Ste 630
Pittsburgh, PA 15219-3030
Contact Grants Administrator, (412) 281-8734; fax: (412) 255-0522; e-mail: info@rahuntfdn.org
Internet http://www.rahuntfdn.org/programs.shtml
Requirements Tax-exempt organizations are eligible.
Areas of Interest Arts, General; Community Development; Conservation, Natural Resources; Cultural Programs/Activities; Environmental Programs; Health Care; Health Services Delivery; International Affairs; Libraries; Peace/Disarmament; Public Affairs; Religion; Violent Behavior; Youth Violence
Sample Awards Peace Development Fund (Amherst, MA)—general operating support, $4000 (2003). Shadyside Hospital Foundation (Pittsburgh, PA)—for the Hillman Cancer Ctr capital campaign, $10,000 (2003). Buddhist Ray (New York, NY)—for the Tricycle magazine, $5000 (2003). Ligonier Valley Library (PA)—for general operating support, $4000 (2003).

Stewart Huston Charitable Trust Grants   1094
Stewart Huston Charitable Trust
50 S First Ave, 2nd Fl
Coatesville, PA 19320
Contact Scott Huston, Program Director, (610)
384-2666; fax: (610) 384-3396; e-mail: admin@
stewarthuston.org
Internet http://www.stewarthuston.org
Requirements 501(c)3 nonprofit organizations are eligible.
Restrictions Grants are not awarded for scholarship support to individuals, endowment purposes, purchases of tickets or advertising for benefit purposes, coverage of continuing operating deficits, or document publication costs. Support is not provided to intermediate or pass-through organizations (other than United Way) that in turn allocate funds to beneficiaries or to fraternal organizations, political parties or candidates, veterans, labor or local civic groups, volunteer fire companies, or groups engaged in influencing legislation.
Areas of Interest Alcohol/Alcohol Abuse; Archaeology; Arts and Culture; At-Risk Youth; Child/Maternal Health; Civic Affairs; Critical Care Medicine; Cultural Activities/Programs; Diversity; Drugs/Drug Abuse; Economically Disadvantaged; Education; Elderly; Food Banks; Health and Health Services; Health Care; Homeless Shelters; Hospices; Human Services; Preservation and Restoration; Philanthropy; Poverty and the Poor; Protestant Church; Public Education; Religion; Social Services; Special Education
Sample Awards Maternal and Child Health Consortium—for operating support. Coatesville Cultural Society (Coatesville, PA)—for its capital campaign, $10,000. Chester County Medical Ctr (West Grove, PA)—for its capital campaign to renovate the center's emergency room, $10,000.

Independence Foundation Grants Program 1095
Independence Foundation
200 S Broad St, Ste 1101
Philadelphia, PA 19102
Contact Susan Sherman, President, (215) 985-4009; fax: (215) 985-3989
Requirements 501(c)3 tax-exempt organizations serving Philadelphia and the surrounding counties including Bucks, Chester, Delaware, and Montgomery are eligible.
Restrictions Grants will not be made to individuals or for building and development funds or to support travel, research, or publications.
Areas of Interest Alzheimer's Disease; Arts, General; Cultural Activities/Programs; Disadvantaged (Economically); Family Planning; Health Care; Health Care Access; Health Care Assessment; Health Care Economics; Health Promotion; Legal Services; Managed Care; Nursing; Urban Affairs
Sample Awards La Salle U, Neighborhood Nursing Center (Philadelphia, PA)—to provide healthcare and educational services to uninsured residents of northwest Philadelphia, $125,000 (2001).

T. James Kavanagh Foundation Grants   1096
T. James Kavanagh Foundation
234 E State St
Sharon, PA 16146
Contact Thomas Kavanagh, Trustee, (610) 356-0743
Requirements Giving is strictly limited to the US, with emphasis on southern NJ and PA. Any Roman Catholic affiliate, church, school, college, or hospital will be considered.
Restrictions Grants will not be awarded outside of the United States, not even to US missions or to help their agencies abroad. No funding will be given for individuals; endowment funds; seed money; deficit financing; land acquisition; publications; conferences; scholarships or fellowships; matching gifts; or loans.
Areas of Interest Catholic Church; Education; Elementary Education; Music; Opera; Private and Parochial Education; Religion; Religious Program; Secondary Education; Scholarship Programs, General
Sample Awards Saint Joseph's R.C. School (Sharon, PA)—for the learning assistance program, $10,000. Opera Company of Philadelphia (Philadelphia, PA)—$10,000. Merion Mercy Academy (Merion Station, PA)—$5000.

Laurel Foundation Grants   1097
Laurel Foundation
2 Gateway Ctr, Ste 1800
Pittsburgh, PA 15222
Contact Donna Panazzi, Executive Director, (412) 765-2400; fax: (412) 765-2407
Requirements Nonprofit organizations in western Pennsylvania may submit applications.
Restrictions Grants are not made to individuals.
Areas of Interest Conservation, Natural Resources; Cultural Activities/Programs; Curriculum Development; Environmental Programs; Family Planning; Health Care; Museums; Performing Arts; Population Control; Visual Impairments; Vocational/Technical Education
Sample Awards Pennsylvania Assoc for the Blind (Pittsburgh, PA)—for facility improvements and program expansion, $10,000.

**Katherine Mabis McKenna Foundation   1098
Grants**
Katherine Mabis McKenna Foundation
PO Box 186
Latrobe, PA 15650
Contact Linda McKenna Boxx, (724) 537-6900
Requirements Philadelphia nonprofit organizations are eligible. Preference is given to requests from Westmoreland County.
Areas of Interest Arts, General; Conservation, Natural Resources; Education; Environmental Programs; Higher Education
Sample Awards Seton Hill U (Greensburg, PA)—to construct a recreational facility that will include fitness rooms, a gymnasium, and a running trace, $2 million (2003).

**Mellon Financial Corporation Foundation   1099
Grants**
Mellon Financial Corporation Foundation
One Mellon Ctr, 500 Grant St, 18th Fl
Pittsburgh, PA 15258
Contact James McDonald, President, (412) 234-2732

Internet http://www.mellon.com/communityaffairs/
charitablegiving.html
Requirements IRS 501(c)3 charitable organizations in
Delaware, Maryland, Massachusetts, New Jersey, and
Philadelphia are eligible.
Restrictions Support is not available for loans or assistance to individuals; ecclesiastical programs of churches
or other sectarian organizations; political parties, campaigns, or candidates; or fraternal fraternal organizations. Grants do not support scholarships and fellowships; travel grants, conferences, specialized health campaigns; or endowment funds.
Areas of Interest Business Development; Economic
Development; Employment Opportunity Programs;
Homeownership; Housing; Literacy; Nonprofit Organizations; Poverty and the Poor

Richard King Mellon Foundation Grants   1100
Richard King Mellon Foundation
500 Grant St, Ste 4106
Pittsburgh, PA 15219-2502
Contact Michael Watson, Vice President and Director,
(412) 392-2800; fax: (412) 392-2837
Internet http://fdncenter.org/grantmaker/rkmellon
Requirements Projects originating in Pittsburgh and
southwestern Pennsylvania are given special priority.
Restrictions Grants are not made to individuals. The
foundation does not consider requests for individuals or
organizations that pass funds to other agencies or pro-
jects outside of the United States.
Areas of Interest Biological Sciences; Children and
Youth; Citizenship; Civic Affairs; Civics Education;
Cultural Activities/Programs; Economic Development;
Education; Employment Opportunity Programs; Environmental Programs; ; FamiliesHealth Care; Higher Ed-
ucation; Job Training Programs; Land Management; Libraries, Academic; Management; Private and Parochial
Education; Nonprofit Organizations; Social Services;
Urban Areas; Vocational Education; Wildlife; Youth
Programs
Sample Awards Chatham College (Pittsburgh, PA)—to
construct an athletic and fitness center, $4 million
(2003). Pennsylvania State U (University Park, PA)—to
help construct a new facility for the Smeal College of
Business Administration, $3 million (2002). Duquesne
U (Pittsburgh, PA)—for unrestricted use, in honor of the
university's president, $1 million (2001). U of Pittsburgh
at Johnstown (PA)—to integrate technology into the academic curriculum, $500,000 (2001).

1957 Charity Trust Grants   1101
1957 Charity Trust
PO Box 7236
Philadelphia, PA 19101-7236
Contact Judith Bardes, Manager, (610) 828-8145
Requirements Nonprofit organizations in the
five-county region in southeastern Pennsylvania may
submit grant applications.
Restrictions The foundation does not make grants to individuals.
Areas of Interest Adult and Continuing Education; Basic Skills Education; Community Development; Conservation, Natural Resources; Cultural Activities/Pro-
grams; Environmental Programs; Housing; Leadership;

Literacy; Preschool Education; Social Services; Youth
Programs
Sample Awards YWCA of Coatesville (Coatesville,
PA)—for the capital campaign, $7200. Immaculate
Heart of Mary Ctr for Literacy and GED Programs (Phil-
adelphia, PA)—program support, $1000. Resources for
Human Development (Philadelphia, PA)—for the En-
dow-A-Home project, $4500.

William Penn Foundation Grants   1102
William Penn Foundation
2 Logan Sq, 11th Fl
Philadelphia, PA 19103-2707
Contact Janet Haas, President, (215) 988-1830; fax:
(215) 988-1823; e-mail: moreinfo@williampennfdn.
org
Internet http://www.williampennfoundation.org/
info-url3564/info-url.htm
Requirements Grants are awarded to IRS 501(c)3
tax-exempt organizations in the Pennsylvania counties
of Montgomery, Chester, Bucks, and Delaware; and
Camden County, NJ. Environmental grants are made in a
larger region, approximately a 100-mile radius from
Philadelphia. In some instances, government agencies
may be eligible if no nonprofit organization can conduct
the equivalent activity.
Restrictions Grants are not made to individuals.
Areas of Interest Adolescents; Architecture; Art Education; Arts, General; Child Psychology/Development;
Child/Maternal Health; Children and Youth; Citizenship; Community Development; Corporate/Strategic
Planning; Cultural Activities/Programs; Education; Elementary Education; Environmental Education; Environmental Programs; Family; Higher Education; Horticulture; Human Learning and Memory; Leadership; Literature; Museums; Orchestras; Performing Arts; Preschool
Education; School-to-Work Transition; Secondary Education; Urban Areas; Visual Arts
Sample Awards Philadelphia Sketch Club (PA)—to
make structural repairs to its historic building, and to establish the position of full-time executive director,
$137,700 over three years (2003). Preschool Project, An
Early Childhood Resource Ctr (Philadelphia, PA)—to
provide services to Latino preschoolers and their families, and to help renovate a facility, $418,364 over three
years (2003). Lancaster Farmland Trust (PA)—to ac-
quire and protect agricultural land in Lancaster County,
PA, $216,000 over two years (2003). Pennsylvania Land
Trust Assoc (Harrisburg, PA)—to strengthen its capacity
to provide technical-assistance and policy programs,
$150,000 over two years (2003).

Pew Charitable Trusts Grants   1103
Pew Charitable Trusts
2005 Market St, Ste 1700
Philadelphia, PA 19103-7077
Contact Grants Information Manager, (215) 575-9050;
fax: (215) 575-4939; e-mail: info@pewtrusts.com
Internet http://www.pewtrusts.com/grants/index.cfm
Requirements Grants are made only to 501(c)3
tax-exempt organizations that are not private founda-
tions.
Restrictions Grants are not made to individuals or for
endowments, capital campaigns, unsolicited construc-

tion requests, debt reduction, or scholarships or fellow-ships that are not part of a program initiated by the trusts.

Areas of Interest Adult and Continuing Education; Allied Health Education; Area Studies; Basic Skills Education; Campaign Finance Reform; Child Psychology/Development; Children and Youth; Civics Education; Cultural Activities/Programs; Curriculum Development; Economics; Education; Education Reform; Environmental Education; Environmental Programs; Faculty Development; Fish and Fisheries; Health Care; Higher Education; Hospitals; Humanities; Language; Libraries; Literacy; Medical Education; Nursing; Nursing Education; Nutrition/Dietetics; Performing Arts; Problem Solving; Public Planning/Policy; Religion; Science Education; Social Services; Touring Arts Programs

Sample Awards Pace U (New York, NY)—for a campaign to reduce harmful air emissions from US power plants, $3.5 million (2003). Council of Chief State School Officers (Washington, DC)—to promote support for high-quality preschool education and activities among educators working with older children, $240,000 (2003). Hedwig House (Norristown, PA)—to provide employment education and counseling to people with mental illness, $170,000 over two years (2003). Church Memorial Park (Chester, Canada)—for general operating support, $143,000 (2003).

**Pew Charitable Trusts Programs to Serve   1104
    Vulnerable Adults**
University of Pennsylvania Institute on Aging /Pew
Charitable Trusts
3615 Chestnut St
Phildadelphia, PA 19104-6006
Contact Dr. Kathryn Jedrziewski, Pew Fund:
Programs to Serve Elderly People, (215) 573-9746;
e-mail: elderorg@mail.med.upenn.edu
Internet http://www.uphs.upenn.edu/aging/elderorg
Requirements 501(c)3 and 509(a) organizations in the Philadelphia area in the county of Bucks, Chester, Delaware, Montgomery, or Philadelphia are eligible to apply.
Restrictions The following will not be considered for support: nursing homes, personal care and boarding homes, assisted living facilities, and retirement communities; capital support; individuals; scholarships; endowments; annual appeals and membership contributions; debt reduction; medical and disease-specific research; or expenditures that are reimbursable.
Areas of Interest Adults; Aging/Gerontology; Elderly; Health Care; Health Services Delivery; Jewish Services
Sample Awards Aid for Friends (Philadelphia, PA)—service-delivery grant, for continued operating support to provide home visits and meals to isolated, homebound, elderly people, $120,000 (2004). Eldernet of Lower Merion and Narberth (Bryn Mawr, PA)—service-delivery grant, for continued operating support to provide a range of support services to needy elderly people, and capacity-building grant, for development of outcome assessment tools and installation of a financial and fundraising software system, 30,000 and $15,000 respectively (2004). Health Promotion Council of Southeastern Pennsylvania (Philadelphia, PA)—service-delivery grant, to support the Healthy Living for Asian Elders project, providing health promotion and disease management services for Asian elders, $120,000 (2004). Jewish Community Ctrs of Greater Philadelphia (Philadelphia, PA)—service-delivery grant, for continued support of home-delivered meals, social services, and health care services to older adults $112,000 (2004).

**Pew Philadelphia Cultural Leadership   1105
    Program Grants**
Pew Charitable Trusts
2005 Market St, Ste 1700
Philadelphia, PA 19103-7077
Contact Marian Godfrey, Director, Culture Program, (215) 575-4870; fax: (215) 575-4939; e-mail: culturemail@pewtrusts.org
Internet http://www.pewtrusts.com/grants/index.cfm
Requirements 501(c)3 nonprofits operating in Bucks, Chester, Delaware, Montgomery, or Philadelphia Counties; have a minimum of $150,000 of annual operating revenue as evidenced by the organization's most recent audit; possess a board-approved strategic plan that extends through the proposed three-year grant period that is in active use by board, staff, and volunteers; be professionally managed with at least one full-time, paid professional staff member; provide programming that is available to the general public; attract a substantial local constituency; and show no working capital deficit in the most recent audited fiscal year.
Restrictions Requests will not be considered for endowments; debt reduction; support for general operations or core programs of organizations outside the Philadelphia five-county area; museum, collection or library acquisitions; computer or multimedia hardware or software, except as part of trusts-initiated programs; grants made directly to individual artists, except as part of trusts-initiated programs; individual commissions, exhibitions, performing arts productions, or television or radio broadcasts, except as part of trusts-initiated programs; cultural exchange activities, except as part of trusts-initiated programs; arts education projects, except as part of the Philadelphia Cultural Leadership Program or other artistic initiatives; conferences or symposia, except as part of trusts-initiated programs; media and technology projects, except those that forward specific culture program interests and priorities; and programs originating outside the United States of America.
Areas of Interest Cultural Programs; Leadership

Philadelphia Foundation Grants   1106
Philadelphia Foundation
1234 Market St, Ste 1800
Philadelphia, PA 19107
Contact Program Contact, (215) 563-6417; fax: (215) 563-6882; e-mail: sspivey@philafound.org
Internet http://www.philafound.org/grants/grants.htm
Requirements IRS 501(c)3 tax-exempt organizations located in Bucks, Chester, Delaware, Montgomery, and Philadelphia Counties of Pennsylvania are eligible. Organizations with budgets of less than $500,000 may apply for general operating support or for support of specific projects. Organizations with budgets between $500,000 and $1.5 million may apply for project support only.
Restrictions Grants are rarely made to affiliates of national or international organizations, government agencies, organizations not located in Southeastern Pennsylvania, organizations with budgets of more than $1.5 mil-

lion, private schools, or umbrella-funding organizations. Requests usually are denied for capital campaigns, conferences, deficit financing, endowments, publications, research projects, tours, and trips. Individuals are ineligible.

Areas of Interest African Americans; Asian Americans; Children and Youth; Civil/Human Rights; Community Development; Cultural Activities/Programs; Cultural Diversity; Economic Development; Education; Environmental Programs; Family; Health Care; Hispanics; Housing; Leadership; Parent Education; Social Services; Teen Pregnancy; Visual Impairments

Sample Awards HomeCare Assoc (Philadelphia, PA)—to expand educational activities and support for home health aides, $14,000 (2003). Metropolitan Career Ctr (Philadelphia, PA)—to provide low-income adults with job-training and employment opportunities, $25,000 (2003). Bryn Mawr Rehab Hospital (Malvern, PA)—for the Patient Therapy Scholarship Fund, $10,000 (2003).

Phoenixville Community Health Foundation Grants 1107

Phoenixville Community Health Foundation
1260 Valley Forge Rd, Ste 102
Phoenixville, PA 19460
Contact Carol Poinier, Grants, Operations Manager, (610) 917-9890; fax: (610) 917-9861; e-mail: pchf1@juno.com
Internet http://www.pchf1.org/gmakeover.html
Requirements Pennsylvania 501(c)3 tax-exempt organizations serving Chester and Montgomery Counties are eligible.
Restrictions Grants are not awarded for direct scholarship support to individuals; purchases of tickets or advertising for benefit purposes; coverage of continuing operating deficits; document publication; pass-through grant support through a third party (except United Way); and fraternal organizations, political parties or candidates, veterans, labor or local civic groups, or groups engaged in influencing legislation.
Areas of Interest Adolescent Health; Allied Health Education; Behavioral Sciences; Child Abuse; Child/Maternal Health; Civic Affairs; Dental Health and Hygiene; Elder Abuse; Elderly; Environmental Health; Homelessness; Housing; Medical Education; Nursing Education; Public Health; Violent Behavior; Volunteers
Sample Awards Phoenixville Area Children's Learning Ctr (PA)—to provide financial assistance to low-income families whose children attend the center, $12,000 partial challenge grant (2003). Phoenixville Area Police Athletic League (PA)—for this youth-development recreation program, $10,000 partial challenge grant (2003). Phoenixville Public Library (PA)—to develop a fundraising plan and for salary support of a part-time fundraiser, $50,000 over two years (2003). Spring-Ford Counseling Services (Royersford, PA)—to provide family counseling, $15,000 (2003).

PPG Industries Foundation Grants 1108

PPG Industries Foundation
1 PPG Pl
Pittsburgh, PA 15272
Contact Sue Sloan, Senior Program Officer, (412) 434-2453; fax: (412) 434-4666

Internet http://www.ppg.com/fin_divinvest/indus_found.htm
Requirements Grants are not available to individuals or for use outside the United States. The foundation does not support advertising, sponsorships, endowments, political or religious purposes, or special events. Loans are not made. Operating grants are not made to United Way agencies. Write preliminary inquiry prior to submitting proposal.
Areas of Interest Arts, General; Chemistry; Civic Affairs; Civil/Human Rights; Cultural Activities/Programs; Education; Employment Opportunity Programs; Health Care; Higher Education; Music, Vocal; Neighborhoods; Safety; Social Services; Volunteers
Sample Awards Robert Morris U (Moon Township, PA)—to renovate the Career and Leadership Development Ctr, $350,000 (2003).

Gilroy and Lillian P. Roberts Charitable Foundation Grants 1109

Gilroy and Lillian P. Roberts Charitable Foundation
10 Presidential Blvd, Ste 250
Bala Cynwyd, PA 19004
Contact Stanley Merves, Treasurer, (610) 668-1998
Restrictions Individuals are not eligible.
Areas of Interest Arts, General; Education; Fine Arts; Health Care; Higher Education; Hospitals; Jewish Services; Religion; Social Services Delivery
Sample Awards Temple University (Philadelphia, PA)—for Merves Professorship in Accounting, $155,000 (2003).

Rohm & Haas Corporate Contributions Program 1110

Rohm & Haas
LaSalle University, 1900 W Olney Avenue
Philadelphia, PA 19141-1199
Contact Jason Rash, Consulting and Board Services Coordinator, (215) 951-1709; fax: (215) 951-1925; e-mail: rash@lasalle.edu
Internet http://www.rohmhaas.com/community/giving/programs.htm
Requirements Only requests in writing from nonprofit 501(c)3 organizations that are soundly managed and have constructive objectives will be recognized.
Areas of Interest Arts, General; Business Development; Chemistry Education; Community Development; Higher Education; Hospitals; Humanities; Museums; Music; Technology Education

Sarah Scaife Foundation Grants Program 1111

Sarah Scaife Foundation
1 Oxford Ctr, 301 Grant St, Ste 3900
Pittsburgh, PA 15219
Contact Michael Gleba, Vice President of Programs, (412) 392-2900
Internet http://www.scaife.com/sarah.html
Restrictions Grants are not made to individuals or to national organizations for general fund-raising purposes.
Areas of Interest Biomedical Research; Cultural Activities/Programs; Education; Ethics; Health Care; Information Science/Systems; Public Affairs; Public Planning/Policy; Recreation and Leisure; Science

Sample Awards U of Pittsburgh (Pittsburgh, PA)—to construct facilities for the planned Pittsburgh Institute for Neurodegenerative Diseases, $5.4 million.

W.W. Smith Charitable Trust Grants   **1112**
W.W. Smith Charitable Trust
200 Four Falls Corporate Ctr, Ste 300
West Conshohocken, PA 19428
Contact Frances Pemberton, Trust Administrator, (610) 397-1844; fax: (610) 397-1680
Requirements Grant recipients are limited to organizations within the five-county area of Pennsylvania including Buck, Chester, Delaware, Montgomery, and Philadelphia Counties. Organizations must be tax-exempt and not classified as private foundations or private operating foundations.
Restrictions After three consecutive years of funding, at least two years must elapse before further applications from the organization may be considered.
Areas of Interest AIDS; Cancer/Carcinogenesis; Cardiovascular Diseases; Children and Youth; Elderly; Food Distribution; Higher Education; Scholarship Programs, General; Shelters; Undergraduate Education
Sample Awards La Salle U (Philadelphia, PA)—for financial aid for students, $98,000. Philadelphia College of Bible (Langhorne, PA)—for financial aid for students, $58,000.

Staunton Farm Foundation Grants   **1113**
Staunton Farm Foundation
650 Smithfield St, Centre City Tower, Ste 210
Pittsburgh, PA 15222
Contact Joni Schwager, Executive Director, (412) 281-8020; fax: (412) 232-3115; e-mail: jschwager@stauntonfarm.org
Internet http://www.stauntonfarm.org
Requirements Nonprofit organizations in the 10-county area in southwestern Pennsylvania including Washington, Greene, Fayette, Westmoreland, Armstrong, Butler, Lawrence, Beaver, Indiana, and Allegheny are eligible.
Areas of Interest Mental Health
Sample Awards Comprehensive Substance Abuse Services of Southwestern Pennsylvania (PA)—to fund two counselor positions in Latrobe for two years, $ 87,200 (2002). Early Learning Institute (PA)—to fund a mobile therapy social worker, $23,500 (2002). Pittsburgh Psychoanalytic Foundation (PA)—for the Pittsburgh Coalition for Psychotherapy 2 yrs) $60,000 for two years (2002). Pittsburgh Mercy Foundation (PA)—to support A Child's Place at Mercy, $120,000 for three years (2002).

Harry C. Trexler Trust Grants   **1114**
Harry C. Trexler Trust
33 S Seventh St, Ste 205
Allentown, PA 18101
Contact Thomas Christman, (610) 434-9645; fax: (610) 437-5721
Requirements Potential grantees are nonprofit organizations located in Allentown or Lehigh County, PA, and rendering exclusive or substantial services to the people residing therein.

Restrictions Grants are not made to individuals or for endowment funds, research, scholarships, or fellowships.
Areas of Interest Children and Youth; Community Development; Disabled; Disadvantaged (Economically); Education; Elderly; Higher Education; Libraries, Public; Performing Arts; Service Delivery Programs; Recreation and Leisure
Sample Awards Muhlenberg College (Allentown, PA)—for arts center expansion, $150,000 (2002). Allentown Art Museum (Allentown, PA)—for operating support, $75,000 (2002). Good Shepherd Home and Rehabilitation (Allentown, PA)—for renovation of building, $50,000 (2002).

Tyco Electronics Foundation Grants   **1115**
Tyco Electronics Foundation
PO Box 3608, MS 140-10
Harrisburg, PA 17105-3608
Contact Mary Rakoczy, (717) 592-4869; fax: (717) 592-4022; e-mail: mjrakocz@tycoelectronics.com
Internet http://www.tycoelectronics.com/about/foundation/vision.stm
Requirements Organizations receiving funding must have IRS tax-exempt status and be located in company-operating areas (Roanoke, VA; the Triangle area of North Carolina; Rock Hill, SC; and central Pennsylvania).
Restrictions The foundation generally will not support organizations in geographic areas where Tyco Electronics has few or no employees; individuals, private foundations, national organizations, or service clubs; fraternal, social, labor, or veterans organizations; organizations that discriminate on the basis of race, religion, color, national origin, physical or mental conditions, veteran or marital status, age, or sex; churches or religious organizations in general; political campaigns; general operating needs of United Way agencies; loans or investments; or programs that pose a potential conflict of interest.
Areas of Interest Arts, General; Career Education and Planning; Civic Affairs; Community Development; Counseling/Guidance; Cultural Activities/Programs; Economic Self-Sufficiency; Education; Educational/Public Television; Environmental Education; Health Services Delivery; Higher Education; Mathematics Education; Radio; Science Education; Secondary Education

Union Benevolent Association Grants   **1116**
Union Benevolent Association
117 S 17th St, Ste 2300
Philadelphia, PA 19103-5022
Contact Joanne Denworth, President; (215) 568-2225; fax: (215) 563-2204
Requirements Nonprofit organizations in Philadelphia, PA, may submit letters of application.
Restrictions Grants do not support national organizations, religious organizations for religious purposes, government agencies, or individuals.
Areas of Interest Community Development; Education; Environmental Programs; Family Planning; Health Care; Housing; Social Services
Sample Awards Germantown Settlement (PA)—$2500 (2001). Adoption Ctr of Delaware Valley (PA)—$2000 (2001). Atwater Kent Museum (PA)—$1500 (2001).

Recording for the Blind and Dyslexic (PA)—$1000 (2001).

Rhode Island

Dunn Foundation K-12 Grants   1117
Dunn Foundation
320 Thames St, Rm 274
Newport, RI 02840
Contact Program Contact, (401) 367-0026
Internet http://www.dunnfoundation.org/grants1.htm
Requirements Nonprofit national, regional, or state-wide organizations conducting programs that are suitable for replication, rather than being tied to a specific community, are eligible. Programs must have measurable outcomes and demonstrate the ability to attract support from other donors and the broader educational community.
Restrictions Grants do not support real property acquisition, endowments, individuals, religious groups, or political organizations. Unsolicited applications are not accepted.
Areas of Interest Architecture; Arts, General; Citizenship; Conservation, Natural Resources; Curriculum Development; Economics; Elementary Education; Environmental Education; Instructional Materials and Practices; Public Planning/Policy; Restoration and Preservation; Secondary Education

Rhode Island Foundation Grants   1118
Rhode Island Foundation
1 Union Station
Providence, RI 02903
Contact Karen Voci, Senior Vice President for Program, (401) 274-4564; fax: (401) 331-8085
Internet http://www.rifoundation.org/grants.html
Requirements Rhode Island nonprofits organizations may apply.
Restrictions The foundation does not make grants for endowments, research, religious groups, hospital equipment, capital needs of health organizations, or to educational institutions for general operating expenses.
Areas of Interest After-School Programs; Aging/Gerontology; Arts, General; Children and Youth; Community Development; Cultural Activities/Programs; Dramatic/Theater Arts; Economic Development; Education; Elderly; Family; Fund-Raising; Health Care; Health Services Delivery; Homelessness; Immigrants; Libraries; Libraries, Public; Literacy; Performing Arts; Public Administration; Restoration and Preservation; School Dental Programs; Social Services Delivery
Sample Awards Festival Ballet Providence (RI)—for audience-development activities, #23,000 (2003). Martin Luther King Community Ctr (Newport, RI)—to strengthen its after-school academic-support program, $20,000 (2003). Landmark Medical Ctr (Woonsocket, RI)—for a community-outreach program that provides holistic health-care services and health management to local senior citizens, $25,000 (2003). Thirty-one nonprofit organizations (RI)—to provide clothing, food, housing, medical care, and utility assistance to needy Rhode Island residents, $108,500 (2003).

Rhode Island State Council on the Arts   1119
Grants to Individuals/Organizations
Rhode Island State Council on the Arts
95 Cedar St, Ste 103
Providence, RI 02903-1034
Contact Estelle Verte, Grants Coordinator, (401) 222-3882; fax: (401) 521-1351; e-mail: estelle@risca.state.ri.us or info@risca.state.ri.us
Internet http://www.arts.ri.gov/grants.htm
Requirements Nonprofit Rhode Island organizations are eligible. All grants to organizations require a dollar-for-dollar cash match. Grants to individual artists do not require a dollar-for-dollar match.
Areas of Interest Art Education; Arts Administration; Audience Development; Community Development; Cultural Diversity; Volunteers

Textron Corporate Contributions Grants   1120
Textron Charitable Trust
40 Westminster Street
Providence, RI 02903
Contact Cate Roberts, Director of Community Affairs, (401) 457-3172; fax: (401) 457-2225
Internet http://www.textron.com/profile/community.html
Requirements Textron targets its giving to nonprofit agencies located in its headquarters state of Rhode Island and those locations where the company has divisional operations. Organizations outside of Rhode Island should contact the local Textron company.
Restrictions Grants do not support organizations without 501(c)(3) tax-exempt status; individuals, including political candidates; churches, seminaries, or other religious organizations for religious activities; political causes and organizations representing fraternal or self-segregated populations; or organizations that discriminate by race, color, creed, gender, sexual preference, or national origin.
Areas of Interest Children and Youth; Counseling/Guidance; Employment Opportunity Programs; Fine Arts; Health Care; Higher Education; Job Training Programs; Literacy; Minorities; Minority Employment; Museums; Performing Arts; Public Broadcasting; Restoration and Preservation, Structural/Architectural; Shelters; Social Services; Visual Arts; Women; Women's Employment
Sample Awards U of Rhode Island (RI)—for its campaign to rebuild the College of Business Administration, $300,000.

Women's Fund of Rhode Island Grants   1121
Rhode Island Foundation
1 Union Station
Providence, RI 02903
Contact Karen Voci, Senior Vice President for Program, (401) 274-4564; fax: (401) 331-8085
Internet http://www.rifoundation.org/womens_apply_intro.htm
Requirements 501(c)3 nonprofits that serve women and girls who reside in Rhode Island and organizations applying through 501(c)3 fiscal agents that serve the target populations and area are eligible. The fund prefers to support organizations that have limited access to other donors.

Restrictions The fund will not support projects that discriminate on the basis of ethnicity, race, color, creed, religion, gender, national origin, age, disability, marital status, sexual orientation, gender identity, or any veteran's status; or projects that present or incorporate religion in any manner. Grants do not support individuals or scholarships, capital or endowment, biomedical research or debt reduction, fundraising events or campaigns to elect candidates to public office.

Areas of Interest Civil/Human Rights; Economic Development; Health Education; Leadership; Literacy; Service Delivery Programs; Women; Women's Education; Women's Health; Women's Employment

South Carolina

Bailey Foundation Grants   **1122**
Bailey Foundation
PO Box 494
Clinton, SC 29325
Contact Thomas Sebrell, Administrator, (864) 938-2632; fax: (864) 938-2669
Requirements Nonprofit organizations in South Carolina are eligible.
Areas of Interest Community Service Programs; Health Care; Higher Education; Private and Parochial Education; Religion; Religious Studies; Scholarship Programs, General; Youth Programs
Sample Awards First Presbyterian Church (Clinton, SC)—for the Into Tomorrow and Beyond program, $100,000. Broad Street United Methodist Church (Statesville, NC)—for building construction, $25,000. Presbyterian College (Clinton, SC)—to construct new classrooms, $40,000. First Assembly of God (Clinton, SC)—for roof repairs and to purchase a sound system, $4000.

Mary Black Foundation Grants   **1123**
Mary Black Foundation
945 E Main St
Spartanburg, SC 29302
Contact Program Contact, (864) 573-9500; fax: (864) 573-5805; e-mail: info@maryblackfoundation.org
Internet http://www.maryblackfoundation.org/application.html
Requirements Nonprofit organizations in Spartanburg County, SC are eligible.
Restrictions The foundation does not award grants for direct support to individuals for projects or scholarships, budget deficits, religious organizations for religious purposes that are not related to the foundation's mission, directly influencing legislation or supporting candidates for office, general fund-raising drives or events, or capital campaigns.
Areas of Interest Elderly; Health Promotion; Health and Safety Education; Parent Education; Preventive Medicine; Restoration and Preservation; Youth Violence
Sample Awards Health Resource Ctr (Spartanburg, SC)—to publish and distribute Parent Talk, a newsletter on child rearing, $15,000 (2001). Senior Ctrs of Spartanburg County (SC)—for a home-repair program for elderly people, $28,000. Healthy Spartanburg (SC)—for general operating support, $25,000. Stop the Vio-

lence Collaboration of Spartanburg (SC)—to hold a series of violence-prevention institutes for seventh and eighth graders, $25,000.

Close Foundation Grants   **1124**
Close Foundation
1826 Second Baxter Crossing
Fort Mill, SC 29708
Contact Angela McCrae, Executive Director, (803) 548-2002; fax: (803) 548-1797
Requirements IRS 501(c)3 organizations serving designated communities in South Carolina are eligible.
Areas of Interest Community Service Programs; Education; Health Care; Recreation and Leisure; Religion

Community Foundation Serving Coastal   **1125**
    South Carolina Grants
Community Foundation Serving Coastal South Carolina
90 Mary St
Charleston, SC 29403
Contact Madeleine McGee, President, (843) 723-3635; fax: (843) 577-3671; e-mail: mmcgee@tcfgives.org
Internet http://www.communityfoundationsc.org
Requirements 501(c)3 South Carolina nonprofits in Berkeley, Charleston, and Dorchester Counties and from Georgetown to Beaufort, SC, are eligible.
Restrictions Grants do not support individuals (except for designated scholarship funds), endowments, deficit financing, dinners, and rarely building funds.
Areas of Interest Arts, General; Civil/Human Rights; Criminal Justice; Cultural Activities/Programs; Ecology; Education; Environmental Programs; Health Care; Marine Resources; Religion; Rural Education; Social Services
Sample Awards City of Charleston, Department of Recreation (SC)—to bring marine ecology and recycling programs to students in the Enterprise Community Zone, as well as to rural schools, $4600.

John I. Smith Charities Grants   **1126**
John I. Smith Charities Inc
PO Box 608
Greenville, SC 29608
Contact Bill Bridges, (864) 271-5930
Requirements Nonprofit organizations in South Carolina are eligible to apply.
Areas of Interest Basic Skills Education; Child Welfare; Churches; Disabled; Higher Education; Literacy; Medical Education; Performing Arts; Religious Studies; Theology; Visual Arts
Sample Awards Peace Ctr for the Performing Arts (Greenville, SC)—program support, $50,000. Columbia Theological Seminary (Decatur, GA)—program support, $100,000. Child's Haven (Greenville, SC)—program support, $2000.

South Carolina Arts Commission General   **1127**
    Support for Organizations Grants
South Carolina Arts Commission
101 Business Park Blvd, Ste 2100
Columbia, SC 29203-9498

Contact Stephanie Cook, Grants Manager, (803) 734-8769; e-mail: scook@arts.state.sc.us
Internet http://www.state.sc.us/arts/grants/organizations/index.html
Requirements An organization must meet basic eligibility requirements as a professional single-discipline organization in South Carolina in the performing, literary, visual, or media arts. Applicant must provide a two-to-one or three-to-one cash match to the requested amount.
Areas of Interest Arts Administration; Cultural Activities/Programs; Literature; Media Arts; Performing Arts; Visual Arts

South Dakota

Kind World Foundation Grants   1128
Kind World Foundation
PO Box 980
Dakota Dunes, SD 57049
Contact Arlene Curry, Executive Director, (605) 232-9139; fax: (605) 232-3098; e-mail: acurry@kindworld.org
Areas of Interest Animal Rights; Arts, General; Education; Environmental Programs; Higher Education; Social Services
Sample Awards Morningside College (Sioux City, IA)—for marketing and financial aid programs, $125,000.

Tennessee

AFG Industries Grants   1129
AFG Industries Inc
PO Box 929
Kingsport, TN 37662
Contact Human Resources, (800) 251-0441or (423) 229-7200; fax: (423) 229-7459
Internet http://www.afgglass.com
Requirements Tennessee nonprofits are eligible.
Areas of Interest Arts, General; Civic Affairs; Education; Health Care; Humanities; Public Affairs; Social Services

Aladdin Industries Foundation Grants   1130
Aladdin Industries Foundation Inc
703 Murfreesboro Rd
Nashville, TN 37210-4521
Contact L.B. Jenkins, Secretary & Treasurer, (615) 748-3360
Internet http://gbgm-umc.org/units/cim/nmi/grantinfo/3501-2.htm
Requirements Most grants are awarded in Tennessee. Proposals are reviewed quarterly.
Areas of Interest Arts, General; Business; Cultural Activities/Programs; Drugs/Drug Abuse; Education; Elderly; Health Care; Performing Arts; Scholarship Programs, General; Social Services; Youth Programs

Aristech Foundation Grants   1131
Aristech Foundation
703 Murfreesboro Rd
Nashville, TN 37210-4521

Contact L.B. Jenkins, (615) 748-3360
Requirements 501(c)3 nonprofits in Tennessee are eligible.
Areas of Interest Children and Youth; Education; Elderly; Performing Arts; Service Delivery Programs; Social Services Delivery; Youth Programs

Bridgestone/Firestone Grants   1132
Bridgestone/Firestone Trust Fund
535 Marriott Dr
Nashville, TN 37214
Contact Bernice Csaszar, Administrator, (615) 937-1415; fax: (615) 937-1414; e-mail: bfstrustfund@bfusa.com
Requirements IRS 501(c)3 nonprofit tax-exempt organizations in Arkansas, Colorado, Connecticut, Florida, Kentucky, Illinois, Indiana, Iowa, Louisianna, Michigan, North Carolina, Ohio, Oklahoma, Pennsylvania, South Carolina, Tennessee, Texas, Utah, and Wisconsin are eligible.
Restrictions Grants are not awarded to individuals or groups that discriminate, political groups or members of a single religious organization, or elementary/secondary schools.
Areas of Interest Arts, General; Civic Affairs; Education; Health Care; Social Services

Thomas W. Briggs Foundation Grants   1133
Thomas W. Briggs Foundation
845 Crossover Ln, Ste 138
Memphis, TN 38117
Contact Joanne Tilley, Director, (901) 680-0276; fax: (901) 767-1135
Requirements Tennessee nonprofit organizations are eligible.
Areas of Interest After-School Programs; Crime Prevention; Education; Higher Education; Social Services; Youth Programs
Sample Awards Childrens Museum of Memphis (Memphis, TN)—for program support, $40,000 (2001). Rhodes College (Memphis, TN)—for program support, $25,000 (2001).

Commission on Religion in Appalachia   1134
   Grants
Commission on Religion in Appalachia
PO Box 52910
Knoxville, TN 37950-2910
Contact Gaye Evans, (865) 584-6133; e-mail: corainappa@aol.com
Internet http://www.geocities.com/appalcora/About.html
Requirements Nonprofits in the Appalachian regions of Mississippi, Alabama, Georgia, South Carolina, North Carolina, Tennessee, Kentucky, Virginia, West Virginia, Ohio, Pennsylvania, Maryland, and New York are eligible.
Areas of Interest Appalachia; Churches; Civil/Human Rights; Domestic Violence; Food Distribution; Health Care; Housing; Private and Parochial Education; Religion; Social Services; Women

Frist Foundation Grants   1135

Frist Foundation
3319 W End Ave, Ste 900
Nashville, TN 37203-1076
Contact Peter Bird, (615) 292-3868; fax: (615)
292-5843; email: info@fristfoundation.org
Internet http://www.fristfoundation.org/html/fund.
html
Requirements 501(c)3 nonprofits in Davidson County,
TN, area may apply.
Restrictions The foundation does not support: individuals or their projects, private foundations, political activities, or advertising or sponsorships. The foundation does not ordinarily support: projects, programs, or organizations that serve a limited audience or a relatively small number of people; organizations during their first three years of operation; disease-specific organizations seeking support for national projects and programs; biomedical or clinical research; hospitals; organizations whose principal impact is outside of Middle Tennessee; endowments; social events or similar fund-raising activities; or religious organizations for religious purposes.
Areas of Interest Community Service Programs; Economic Development; Health Care; Housing; Leadership; Music; Nonprofit Organizations; Religion; Social Services; Technology; Youth Programs
Sample Awards Domestic Violence Intervention Ctr (TN)—to translate domestic violence educational materials into Spanish, $3000 (2002). Mockingbird Theatre (TN)—for general support, $5000 (2002). Metropolitan Nashville Public Schools (TN)—to establish a pilot reading program at Haywood Elementary School, $65,000 (2002). Faith Family Medical Clinic of Nashville (TN)—to help establish a medical clinic for low-income working people, $105,000 (2002).

Hyde Family Foundations Grants   1136

Hyde Family Foundations
6075 Poplar Ave, Ste 335
Memphis, TN 38119
Contact Teresa Sloyan, Executive Director, (901) 685-3400; fax: (901) 683-3147
Requirements Giving is limited to Tennessee with strong emphasis on Memphis, TN.
Restrictions Grants are not made to individuals.
Areas of Interest Arts, General; Cultural Activities/Programs; Dance; Education; Music; Public Planning/Policy; Radio; Service Delivery Programs; Social Services
Sample Awards Ballet Memphis, (TN)—for general support, $626,081. Blues Foundation (Memphis, TN)—for radio show and general operating and other support, $100,616.

Lyndhurst Foundation Grants   1137

Lyndhurst Foundation
517 E Fifth St
Chattanooga, TN 37403-1826
Contact Jack Murrah, President, (423) 756-0767; fax: (423) 756-0770; e-mail: jmurrah@
lyndhurstfoundation.org
Internet http://www.lyndhurstfoundation.org
Requirements Organizations in southern Appalachia area may apply (including Tennessee, Georgia, South Carolina, North Carolina, and Alabama). Arts organizations in Chattanooga, TN, are eligible for arts grants.
Areas of Interest Arts, General; Community Service Programs; Cultural Activities/Programs; Environmental Programs; Leadership; Parks; Urban Areas.
Sample Awards Riverfront/Downtown Planning and Design Ctr (TN)—for operating support. National Parks and Conservation Assoc (TN)—for operating support.

Louie M. and Betty M. Phillips Foundation   1138
Grants

Louie M. and Betty M. Phillips Foundation
200 42nd Ave N
Nashville, TN 37209
Contact Louie Buntin, (615) 385-5949; fax: (615) 385-2507; e-mail: louie@phillipsfoundation.org
Internet http://www.phillipsfoundation.org
Requirements Nonprofit organizations are eligible. With rare exceptions, grants are limited to organizations in the greater Nashville, TN, area.
Restrictions The foundation does not support individuals or their projects, private foundations, political activities, advertising, or sponsorships. In general, the foundation does not support projects, programs, or organizations that serve a limited audience or a relatively small number of people; disease-specific organizations; biomedical or clinical research; organizations whose principal impact is outside the Nashville area; or tax-supported institutions.
Areas of Interest Arts, General; Civic Affairs; Community Development; Community Service Programs; Education; Health Care; Health Care Access; Health Promotion; Social Services; Social Services Delivery

William B. Stokely Jr. Foundation Grants   1139

William B. Stokely Jr. Foundation
620 Campbell Station Rd, Ste 27
Knoxville, TN 37922-1636
Contact William Stokely III, President, (865) 966-4878
Requirements Tennessee organizations with 501(c)3 tax-exempt status are eligible.
Restrictions The foundation does not donate funds to individuals.
Areas of Interest Arts and Culture; Children and Youth; Cultural Activities/Programs; Health Care; Health Services Delivery; Higher Education; Hospitals; Museums; Public Affairs; Religion; Scholarship Programs, General; Youth Programs

Tennessee Arts Commission Arts Projects   1140
Grants

Tennessee Arts Commission
401 Charlotte Ave
Nashville, TN 37243-0780
Contact Kim Leavitt, (615) 532-5934; fax: (615) 741-8559; TDD: (615) 741-1701; e-mail: kim.leavitt@
state.tn.us
Internet http://www.arts.state.tn.us/grantprograms.htm
Requirements Applicants must be nonprofit organizations chartered in Tennessee that have proof of federal tax-exempt status. In addition, organizations must be service or single-discipline arts organizations that have a statewide mission. An organization may receive funds

for no more than two projects in the same fiscal year. Multiple events, such as a performance series, should be submitted as one application. Prior to submitting an application, qualifying organizations must discuss their project proposal with staff members.
Areas of Interest Artists in Residence; Arts Administration; Arts Festivals; Audience Development; Exhibitions, Collections, Performances; Literature; Periodicals; Touring Arts Programs

Tennessee Arts Commission General Operating Support Grants   1141
Tennessee Arts Commission
401 Charlotte Ave, Citizens Plz Bldg
Nashville, TN 37243-0780
Contact Bob Kucher, Deputy Director, Arts Program Division, (615) 741-2093; fax: (615) 741-8559; e-mail: bob.kucher@state.tn.us
Internet http://www.arts.state.tn.us/grantprograms.htm
Requirements Applicants in this category must be established Tennessee arts-committed organizations responsible for their own programming. Most applicants are single-entity groups dedicated to one arts discipline, but cross-disciplinary supporting or sponsoring agencies, such as arts councils, arts festivals, or arts centers, also are eligible.
Restrictions Applications may not be sent by fax or electronic mail. Funds may not be used for capital improvements (buildings or construction); for equipment purchases; for the elimination of an accumulated deficit; seed money for starting new organizations; in-school, curriculum-based projects; or endowment funds.
Areas of Interest Arts Administration; Arts and Culture

Tennessee Arts Commission Major Cultural 1142 Institutions Grants
Tennessee Arts Commission
401 Charlotte Ave
Nashville, TN 37243-0780
Contact Bob Kucher, Deputy Director, Arts Programs, (615) 741-2093; fax: (615) 741-8559; e-mail: bob.kucher@state.tn.us
Internet http://www.arts.state.tn.us/grantprograms.htm
Requirements Applicants must have a history of commission funding in arts projects and/or Arts Build Communities or general operating support for at least three of the past five years. Organizations must be governed by a board of directors or trustees drawn from, when possible, and reflective of the community at large. Applicants must be single-entity agencies, e.g. museums, symphonies, theater companies, etc., responsible for their own programming. The applicants must be dedicated primarily to one art discipline. Organizations must be located in Tennessee.
Restrictions No funds may be used for capital improvements (buildings or construction); for equipment purchases; for the elimination of an accumulated deficit; in-school, curriculum-based projects; endowment campaigns or programs; or out-of-state travel expenses.
Areas of Interest Arts Administration; Arts and Culture; Dramatic/Theater Arts; Museums; Orchestras

Tennessee Arts Commission Rural Arts   1143 Project Support
Tennessee Arts Commission
401 Charlotte Ave
Nashville, TN 37243-0780
Contact Lisa Hester, Director of Arts Access, (615) 532-9797; e-mail: lisa.hester@state.tn.us
Internet http://www.arts.state.tn.us/grantprograms.htm
Requirements An application to the TAC may be made by any 501(c)3 nonprofit organization or government agency chartered in Tennessee and located in a non-MSA (Non-Metropolitan Statistical Area) county. Grants must be matched dollar-for-dollar. Prior to submitting an application, qualifying organizations must discuss their project proposal with staff members.
Areas of Interest Artists in Residence; Arts Administration; Arts Festivals; Audience Development; Exhibitions, Collections, Performances; Performing Arts; Touring Arts Programs; Computer Software; Computer Education/Literacy; Technology; Rural Areas

Texas

Abell-Hanger Foundation Grants   1144
Abell-Hanger Foundation
PO Box 430
Midland, TX 79702-0430
Contact David Smith, Executive Director, (915) 684-6655; fax: (915) 684-4474; e-mail: ahf@abell-hanger.org
Internet http://www.abell-hanger.org
Requirements Applicant organizations must be located in Texas and be 501(c)3 tax-exempt. National organizations with significant operations in, or providing material benefits to the citizens of, Texas will be considered based on the degree of operations/benefits within the state.
Restrictions The foundation does not fund grants, scholarships, or fellowships for individuals.
Areas of Interest Adoption; Art Education; Business Education; Communications; Cultural Activities/Programs; Disabled; Environmental Programs; Fine Arts; Health Services Delivery; Higher Education; Higher Education, Private; Nursing Education; Religion; Scholarship Programs, General; Science Education; Teacher Education; Youth Programs
Sample Awards Abilene Habitat for Humanity in Abilene (TX)—to construct 21 homes, $10,500 matching grant (2002). Institute for the Study of Earth and Man (Dallas, TX)—for graduate student research funds, $35,000 (2002). Abused Children's Shelter in (Odessa, TX)—for unrestricted operating support, $30,000 (2002). Roaring Springs Community Volunteers (TX)—for improvements to the community center, $8000 (2002).

Alcon Foundation Grants Program   1145
Alcon Foundation
6201 S Freeway
Fort Worth, TX 76134
Contact Mary Dulle, Chair, (817) 293-0450; e-mail: Mary.Dulle@Alconlabs.com
Requirements Grants are not made for building programs.
Areas of Interest Education; Ophthalmology; Vision

Sample Awards National Sjogrens Syndrome Assoc (Phoenix, AZ)—for general operating support, $2500.

AMR/American Airlines Foundation Grants 1146
AMR/American Airlines Foundation
PO Box 619616, MD 5575
Dallas/Fort Worth Airport, TX 75261-9616
Contact Grants Administrator, (817) 967-3545; fax: (817) 967-9784
Internet http://www.amrcorp.com/corpinfo.htm
Requirements IRS 501(c)3 nonprofit, tax-exempt organizations located in cities where the airline operates a hub or has a major facility and/or an employee base are eligible.
Restrictions Grants do not support endowments; annual operating support fund drives; organizations that discriminate on the basis of race, religion, sex, or national origin; religious, fraternal, social, or veterans' organizations; political or partisan organizations or candidates; organizations established to influence legislation or specific elections; individuals; organizations receiving support from United Way fund drives; basic academic or scientific research; athletic events or sponsorships; or social functions or advertising in commemorative journals, yearbooks, or special event publications (these requests are forwarded to the appropriate local sales office for consideration).
Areas of Interest Arts, General; Child/Maternal Health; Community Development; Cultural Activities/Programs; Education; Emergency Programs; Health Care; Social Services
Sample Awards Southern Methodist U (Dallas, TX)—for MBA students participating in a global-leadership program at the Cox School of Business, $1 million value in air travel. Roundabout Theatre Co (New York, NY)—for general operations at the American Airlines Theatre (formerly the Selwyn Theatre), $8.5 million.

M.D. Anderson Foundation Grants　1147
M.D. Anderson Foundation
PO Box 2558
Houston, TX 77252-8037
Contact Charlene Slack, Secretary-Treasurer, (713) 216-4513
Requirements Texas nonprofit organizations are eligible.
Areas of Interest Education Reform; Higher Education; Hospitals; Humanities Education; Private and Parochial Education; Religion; Scholarship Programs, General; Teacher Education
Sample Awards U of Texas (Austin, TX)—for the law school, $800,000 (2002). U of Saint Thomas (Houston, TX)—to construct a humanities and education building, $250,000 (2000).

Assisi Foundation Grants　1148
Assisi Foundation
6077 Primacy Pkwy, Ste 253
Memphis, TX 38119
Contact Barry Flynn, Executive Director, (901) 684-1564; fax: (901) 684-1997
Internet http://www.assisifoundation.org/proposal.html

Requirements Memphis-area and Shelby County, TN, nonprofit organizations are eligible.
Areas of Interest Animal Care; Animal Rights; Art Education; Civic Affairs; Computer Education/Literacy; Education; Ethics; Health Care; Higher Education; Literacy; Racism/Race Relations; Religion; Social Services; Training and Development
Sample Awards Catholic Diocese of Memphis, Dept of Education (TN)—for campus improvements at the Immaculate Conception Schools, $75,000 (2003). Personal and Career Development (Memphis, TN)—to produce and print YouthXpress, a monthly publication produced by young people, $25,000 challenge grant (2003). alt. Consulting (Memphis, TN)—to provide technical assistance to local nonprofit organizations, $10,000 (2003). Catholic Diocese of Memphis (TN)—for technology equipment needed to connect parishes, schools, and charitable groups electronically, $65,700 (2003).

Marilyn Augur Family Foundation Grants　1149
Marilyn Augur Family Foundation
3131 Turtle Creek Blvd, Ste 1000
Dallas, TX 75219
Contact Nancy Roberts, (214) 522-5586; fax: (214) 522-0245; e-mail: maf@waymark.net
Internet http://fdncenter.org/grantmaker/augur/app.html
Requirements Texas nonprofit organizations are eligible.
Restrictions Generally, the foundation does not give grants in the area of arts and culture.
Areas of Interest Religion; Social Services Delivery

Harry Bass Foundation Grants　1150
Harry Bass Foundation
4809 Cole Ave, Ste 252
Dallas, TX 75205
Contact Grants Administrator, (214) 599-0300; fax: (214) 599-0405
Internet http://www.harrybassfoundation.org/about.asp
Requirements Texas 501(c)3 tax-exempt organizations are eligible.
Restrictions In general, grants are not made for purposes of church or seminary construction; annual fundraising events or general sustentation drives; professional conferences and symposia; out-of-state performances or competition expenses; or to other private foundations.
Areas of Interest Arts; Children and Youth; Cultural Activities/Programs; Education; Religion; Social Services Delivery
Sample Awards Dallas Ctr for the Performing Arts (Dallas, TX)—to design and construct the Dallas Center for the Performing Arts, $1 million over five years (2003).

Lee and Ramona Bass Foundation Grants　1151
Lee and Ramona Bass Foundation
309 Main St
Fort Worth, TX 76102
Contact Valleau Wilkie Jr., Executive Director; (817) 336-0494; fax: (817) 332-2176; e-mail: cjohns@sidrichardson.org
Internet http://www.sidrichardson.org

Requirements Eligible organizations must have 501(c)3 status. Grant requests must be limited to programs and projects within the state of Texas.
Restrictions No grants can be made to individuals.
Areas of Interest Arts, General; Cultural Activities/Programs; Education; Health Care; Social Services

Belo Foundation Grants 1152
Belo Foundation
PO Box 655237
Dallas, TX 75625-5237
Contact Judith Garrett Segura, President, (214) 977-6661; fax: (214) 977-6620
Internet http://www.belo.com/about/foundation.xml
Requirements The foundation supports charitable organizations focusing on its areas of interest in the cities where Belo has companies.
Areas of Interest Art in Public Places; Children and Youth; Citizenship; Education; Higher Education; Journalism Education; Land Use Planning/Policy; Parks; Urban Areas
Sample Awards YMCA of Metropolitan Dallas (Dallas, TX)—for capital support of its campaign to build eight new facilities and to expand and improve 15 existing branches, $75,000. Bacone College (Muskogee, OK)—for its capital campaign, $10,000.

Mary E. Bivins Foundation Grants 1153
Mary E. Bivins Foundation
PO Box 1727
Amarillo, TX 79105
Contact Judy Mosely, (806) 379-9400
Internet http://www.bivinsfoundation.org
Requirements Christian nonprofits in Texas are eligible.
Areas of Interest Religion; Religious Studies; Religious Welfare Programs; Scholarship Programs, General; Higher Education
Sample Awards Ozark Christian College (Joplin, MO)—for scholarships, $23,805. Abilene Christian U (Abilene, TX)—for scholarships, $3300.

Brown Foundation of Houston Grants 1154
Brown Foundation of Houston
PO Box 130646
Houston, TX 77219-0646
Contact Nancy Pittman, Executive Director, (713) 523-6867; fax: (713) 523-2917; e-mail: bfi@ brownfoundation.org
Internet http://www.brownfoundation.org/Guidelines. asp
Restrictions The foundation does not expect to award grants to individuals in the form of scholarships or any other assistance; grants to religious organizations for religious purposes; testimonial dinners, fundraising events, or marketing events; directly or indirectly to support candidates for political office or to influence legislation; grants to other private foundations; or grants to cover past operating deficits or debt retirements.
Areas of Interest Archives; Arts, General; Cancer/ Carcinogenesis; Children and Youth; Churches; Community Service Programs; Conservation, Natural Resources; Education; Elementary Education; Higher Education; Patient Care and Education; Performing Arts;

Private and Parochial Education; Religion; Secondary Education; Visual Arts
Sample Awards U of Arkansas (Fayetteville, AR)—to endow a chair in English literacy designed to increase the reading and writing competency of Arkansas high-school graduates through summer workshops and graduate-assistant tutoring, $1.5 million (2003). Infernal Bridegroom Productions (Houston, TX)—to implement its new strategic plan, $25,000 (2002). Johns Hopkins U (Baltimore, MD)—for the Mattin Center, the new student arts and activities facility at the university's Homewood campus, $1 million (2002). U of Texas Health Science Ctr at Houston (TX)—to construct a building dedicated to research on molecular medicine, $20,000 over five years (2002).

Burlington Resources Foundation Grants 1155
Burlington Resources Foundation
5050 Westheimer St, Ste 1400
Houston, TX 77056
Contact Dee McBride, Grants Administrator, (713) 624-9366; fax: (713) 624-9955; e-mail: dmcbride@ br-inc.com
Internet http://www.br-inc.com/community/ community_policies.asp
Requirements Contributions are limited to nonprofit, tax exempt US organizations which have obtained IRS status under Section 501(c)3 of the IRS Code, and, where appropriate, under Section 170(c). Proof of the exemption must be submitted with grant applications.
Restrictions Grants do not support religious organizations for religious purposes; war veterans and fraternal service organizations; endowment funds; national health organizations and programs; grants or loans to individuals; fund-raising events; corporate memberships or contributions to chambers of commerce, taxpayer associations and other bodies whose activities are expected to directly benefit the company; or political organizations, campaigns and candidates.
Areas of Interest Art, General; Child Abuse; Community Development; Community Service Programs; Conservation; Crime Prevention; Drugs/Drug Abuse; Public Education; Educational/Public Television; Governmental Functions; Higher Education; Historic Preservation; Hospitals; Human Services; Medical Programs; Minorities; Parks; Performing Arts; Private Education; Public Broadcasting; Public Education; Runaway Youth; Senior Citizen Programs and Services; Social Services; Visual Arts; Women; Youth Programs
Sample Awards Christian Community Service (Houston, TX)—$25,000. Jewish Day School of Metropolitan Seattle (Seattle, WA)—$25,000. YMCA of Greater Seattle (Seattle, WA)—$15,000.

CACHH General Assistance Program 1156
Expansion Arts Support Grants
Cultural Arts Council of Houston/Harris County
3201 Allen Pkwy, Ste 250
Houston, TX 77019
Contact Liz Alexander, Grants Department, (713) 527-9330; fax: (713) 630-5210; e-mail: liz@cachh.org or info@cachh.org
Internet http://www.cachh.org

Requirements Houston 501(c)3 nonprofit multicultural arts organizations are eligible. The organization must be governed by a board of directors that meets regularly and have been in operation at least one year before the deadline.
Areas of Interest Arts Administration; Disabled; Inner Cities; Minorities; Native Americans

CACHH General Assistance Program Organizational Support Grants 1157
Cultural Arts Council of Houston/Harris County
3201 Allen Pkwy, Ste 250
Houston, TX 77019
Contact Liz Alexander, Grants Department, (713) 527-9330; fax: (713) 630-5210; e-mail: liz@cachh.org
Internet http://www.cachh.org/GAP.organizational. support.grants.html
Requirements Houston 501(c)3 nonprofit cultural arts or university arts organizations are eligible. The organization must be governed by a board of directors that meets regularly, and have been in operation at least three years before the deadline.
Areas of Interest Arts Administration; Cultural Activities/Programs

Effie and Wofford Cain Foundation Grants 1158
Effie and Wofford Cain Foundation
4131 Spicewood Springs Rd, Ste A-1
Austin, TX 78759
Contact Mrs. Lynn Fowler, Executive Director, (512) 346-7490; fax: (512) 346-7491
Requirements The foundation only makes grants to 501(c)3 tax-exempt organizations in Texas.
Restrictions Individuals are ineligible.
Areas of Interest African Americans; Aging/Gerontology; Baptist Church; Biomedical Research; Child Psychology/Development; Community Service Programs; Disabled; Elementary Education; Episcopal Church; Government; Health Care; Hispanics; Homelessness; Hospitals; Medical Education; Methodist Church; Nursing Education; Presbyterian Church; Preschool Education; Public Administration; Religion; Secondary Education
Sample Awards Texas College (Tyler, TX)—for its concert choir, $14,000 (2003). Seton Fund (Austin, TX)—for the Seton Medical Center Expansion and Renovation Project, $500,000 (2002).

Amon G. Carter Foundation Grants 1159
Amon G. Carter Foundation
PO Box 1036
Fort Worth, TX 76101-1036
Contact Terry Woodfin, Program Contact, (817) 332-2783; fax: (817) 332-2787; e-mail: terry@agcf.org
Internet http://www.agcf.org
Restrictions Grants, loans, or scholarships are not made to individuals.
Areas of Interest Arts, General; Civic Affairs; Education; Elderly; Food Distribution; Health Services Delivery; Humanities; Museums; Performing Arts; Religion; Social Services; Visual Arts; Youth Programs
Sample Awards Amon Carter Museum (TX)—program support, $5.57 million. Meals on Wheels (TX)—program support, $35,000. J.L. West Presbyterian Special Care—capital campaign support, $50,000.

CH Foundation Grants 1160
CH Foundation
PO Box 94038
Lubbock, TX 79493-4038
Contact Kay Sanford, President, (806) 792-0448; fax: (806) 792-7824
Requirements Texas nonprofits are eligible.
Areas of Interest Arts, General; Cultural Activities/Programs; Elementary Education; Higher Education; Hospitals; Medical Education; Museums; Nursing Education; Orchestras; Private and Parochial Education; Religion; Secondary Education; Social Services
Sample Awards Texas Tech U (Lubbock, TX)—for general support for museums, $175,000. All Saints Episcopal School (Lubbock, TX)—for the building fund, $100,000. Lubbock Symphony Orchestra (Lubbock, TX)—for general support, $25,000.

Coastal Bend Community Foundation Grants 1161
Coastal Bend Community Foundation
600 Building, Ste 1716
Corpus Christi, TX 78473
Contact Jim Moloney, Executive Vice President, (361) 882-9745; fax: (361) 882-2865; e-mail: jmoloney@ cbcfoundation.org
Internet http://www.cbcfoundation.org/grant.html
Requirements Nonprofit organizations in Texas in Aransas, Bee, Jim Wells, Kleberg, Nueces, Refugio, and San Patricio counties, may submit grant proposals.
Areas of Interest Community Development; Education
Sample Awards Texas A&M U (Corpus Christi, TX)—for program support, $10,000. HIV/AIDS Housing Ctr (Corpus Christi, TX)—for operating support, $12,500.

Cockrell Foundation Grants 1162
Cockrell Foundation
1000 Main St, Ste 3250
Houston, TX 77002
Contact M. Nancy Williams, Executive Vice President, (713) 209-7500; fax: (713) 209-7599; e-mail: foundation@cockrell.com
Internet http://www.cockrell.com/foundation/contact_ information.asp
Requirements Texas 501(c)3 nonprofit organizations in Houston are eligible.
Areas of Interest Cultural Activities/Programs; Higher Education; Hospitals; Museums; Natural Sciences; Religious Studies; Social Services; Youth Programs
Sample Awards U of Texas at Austin (TX)—for the College of Engineering, $550,000.

ConocoPhillips Grants Program 1163
ConocoPhillips
600 N Dairy Ashford, 3130 Marland Bldg
Houston, TX 77079
Contact Program Contact, (281) 293-1000
Internet http://www.conocophillips.com/about/ contributions.asp

Requirements Applications are accepted from areas where ConocoPhillips has a strong business presence, e. g., Texas and Oklahoma. All contributions are to be used within the United States.

Restrictions ConocoPhillips does not award funds to individuals, church groups, fund raisers, specific disease-oriented groups, political candidates, or for travel, endowment, or bricks and mortar.

Areas of Interest Alcohol/Alcoholism; Arts, General; At-Risk Youth; Business; Child Welfare; Civic Affairs; Community and School Relations; Computer Science; Cultural Activities/Programs; Drugs/Drug Abuse; Elderly; Elementary Education; Engineering; Environmental Programs; Ethics; Fire Prevention; Geology; Geophysics; Health Care; Higher Education; Humanities; International Economics; International Programs; International Relations; Leadership; Legal Services; Marketing; Mathematics Education; Minorities; Public Planning/Policy; Science Education; Secondary Education; Social Services; Training and Development; Values/Moral Education; Volunteers; Women; Youth Programs

Sample Awards U of Texas (Austin, TX)—for scholarships, fellowships, and special programs in business, engineering, law, and the natural sciences, $1 million (2003).

Cooper Industries Foundation Grants 1164

Cooper Industries Foundation
PO Box 4446
Houston, TX 77210
Contact Leonor Carrosquilla, Secretary, (713) 209-8607; fax: (713) 209-8982; e-mail: evans@ cooperindustries.com
Internet http://www.cooperindustries.com/about/ index.htm
Requirements Organizations must be in the United States. Nonprofit organizations with 501(c)3 tax-exempt status in the communities where Cooper Industries has plant facilities and concentrations of employees are eligible to apply. Initial contact should be by letter including operating budget, evidence of tax-exempt status, purpose of request, and annual report if published.
Restrictions Grants are not made to religious, political, labor, lobbying, fraternal, or veterans organizations; national or state health and welfare organizations; or primary and secondary schools. Grants also are not made to support endowment funds; individuals; trips or tours; tickets, tables, or advertising for benefit purposes; intermediary funding agencies; nor to any organizations whose policies are inconsistent with national equal opportunity policies.
Areas of Interest Art Education; Arts, General; AIDS; Cancer/Carcinogenesis; Civic Affairs; Cultural Activities/Programs; Disabled; Disadvantaged (Economically); Education; Emergency Programs; Environmental Programs; Health Care; Higher Education; Libraries; Literacy; Mentoring Programs; Museums; Neighborhoods; Public Broadcasting; Safety; Scholarship Programs, General; Social Services; Vocational/ Technical Education; Volunteers; Youth Programs
Sample Awards Literacy Volunteers of Greater Syracuse (Syracuse, NY)—for operating support, $33,000. AIDS Foundation of Houston (Houston, TX)—for pro-

gram support, $1500. Dana-Farber Cancer Institute (Boston, MA)—for program support, $1000.

Dave Coy Foundation Grants 1165

Dave Coy Foundation
PO Box 121
San Antonio, TX 78291-0121
Contact Gregg Muenster, c/o Bank of America, (210) 270-5371
Requirements Nonprofits in Bexar County, TX, are eligible.
Restrictions Grants are not made to individuals.
Areas of Interest Alcohol/Alcoholism; Children and Youth; Drugs/Drug Abuse; Housing; Jewish Services; Religion; Religious Studies; Senior Citizen Programs and Services; Social Services; Transportation
Sample Awards Salvation Army (San Antonio, TX)—for operating support for a program for male substance abusers, $125,000. Jewish Community Center of San Antonio (San Antonio, TX)—for senior transportation, $40,000. San Antonio Metropolitan Ministry (San Antonio, TX)—to upgrade housing beds and mattresses, $35,000. Amarillo Senior Citizens Assoc (Amarillo, TX)—for operating support, $15,000.

Cullen Foundation Grants 1166

Cullen Foundation
601 Jefferson, 40th Fl
Houston, TX 77002
Contact Alan Stewart, Executive Director, (713) 651-8837; e-mail: salexander@cullenfdn.org
Internet http://www.cullenfdn.org
Requirements Texas 501(c)3 and 170(c) nonprofit organizations are eligible.
Areas of Interest Community Service Programs; Cultural Activities/Programs; Cultural Outreach; Education; Elementary Education; Health Care; Higher Education; Performing Arts; Public Affairs; Secondary Education
Sample Awards U of Texas Health Science Ctr (Houston, TX)—for the capital campaign, $10 million (2002). Charter School Resource Ctr of Texas (San Antonio, TX)—for operational support, $100,00. Baylor College of Medicine (Houston, TX)—for emergency flood relief for labs destroyed by tropical storm Allison, $125,000. Houston Museum of Natural Science (TX)—to support the annual campaign, $125,000.

Dallas Women's Foundation Grants 1167

Dallas Women's Foundation
4300 MacArthur Ave, Ste 255
Dallas, TX 75209-6524
Contact Sarah Nelson, Director, Grants and Research, (214) 965-9977 ext. 108; fax: (214) 526-3633; e-mail: snelson@dallaswomensfoundation.org
Internet http://www.dallaswomensfoundation.org/ grants/highlights.html
Requirements The foundation awards grants to Texas nonprofit agencies that have received a 501(c)3 designation from the IRS. At least 50 percent of the population served must be residents of Dallas, Denton, or Collin County, with priority given to organizations serving residents of Dallas County. Also, 75 percent of the clients

benefiting from the grant funding must be women and/or girls.

Restrictions The foundation does not fund individuals, campaigns to elect public officials or for political or lobbying efforts, programs that promote religious activities, projects that take place before the completion of the grant making process, projects inconsistent with federal, state and local nondiscrimination ordinances regarding equal employment opportunity, grants that ultimately will go wholly to another agency, other than the applicant, or organizations which have the ability to levy taxes.

Areas of Interest AIDS; Alcohol/Alcoholism; At-Risk Youth; Child/Maternal Health; Domestic Violence; Gender Equity; Girls; HIV; Immigrants; Job Training Programs; Refugees; Shelters; Women; Youth Programs;

Sample Awards Brighter Tomorrows (Dallas, TX)—to expand shelter and other services of this domestic-violence group to outlying areas of Dallas, $20,000. Charities Home Ctr (Dallas, TX)—to implement a new retail-skills training program for refugee and immigrant women, $20,000. Magdalen House (Dallas, TX)—for general operating support of this detoxification facility for women with alcohol abuse problems, $20,000. AIDS Arms (Dallas, TX)—to provide case-management services to HIV-positive women and children, $20,000.

Michael and Susan Dell Foundation Grants 1168
Michael and Susan Dell Foundation
PO Box 163867
Austin, TX 78716-3867
Contact Grants Administrator
Internet http://www.msdf.org
Requirements Texas nonprofit organizations are eligible.
Areas of Interest After-School Programs; Child Abuse; Child Sexual Abuse; Child Welfare; Children and Youth; Child/Maternal Health; College-Preparatory Education; Day Care; Domestic Violence; Early Childhood Education; Education; Foster Care; Health Care Access; Health Insurance; Health Promotion; Jewish Services; Safety; Youth Programs
Sample Awards Jewish Community of Austin (TX)—to enhance the quality of Jewish life in Austin and around the world through charitable, educational, social service, cultural, religious, and recreational endeavors, $50,000 (2003). Texas High School Project (TX)—to increase high-school-graduation and college-enrollment rates by redesigning existing high schools and creating new ones, including charter schools and schools through which students can earn college credits, $20 million (2003). Austin Musical Theatre (TX)—to support the general operating fund of the Austin Musical Theatre, $100,000 (2003). Caritas (Austin, TX)—to provide rent, utilities, food, and support to people in need, $3000 (2003).

ExxonMobil Education Foundation Grants 1169
ExxonMobil Education Foundation
5959 Las Colinas Blvd
Irving, TX 75039-2298
Contact Program Contact, (972) 444-1106; fax: (972) 444-1405; e-mail: contributions@exxonmobil.com

Internet http://www.exxon.mobil.com/corporate/About/CommunityPartnerships/Corp_A_Partnership.asp
Requirements The foundation makes grants only to tax-exempt organizations. A two-page letter of inquiry is required.
Restrictions The foundation rarely contributes to endowments or make grants for construction or remodeling of facilities. Funds are not provided for equipment acquisition. Scholarships and grants to individuals are not awarded.
Areas of Interest At-Risk Youth; Demography; Education Reform; Educational Planning/Policy; Elementary Education; Engineering Education; Higher Education; Mathematics Education; Minority Education; Science Education; Secondary Education; Teacher Education; Technology Education; Undergraduate Education; Women's Education
Sample Awards U of Texas at Austin, Ctr for American History (TX)—to catalog and preserve a collection of ExxonMobil's historical archives, $300,000 (2004). Society of Women Engineers (Chicago, IL)—to develop curricula to prepare girls in elementary and high school for careers in scientific fields, $600,000 (2003). Texas State History Museum Foundation (Austin, TX)—to produce a large-screen film about Texas, and to create accompanying education materials for use by schools and the museum, $1.5 million and $63,000 respectiviely Tom Joyner Foundation (Dallas, TX)—for scholarships for students at engineering, mathematics, and science 11 historically black colleges and universities, $200,000 (2003).(2003).

Leland Fikes Foundation Grants Program 1170
Leland Fikes Foundation
3050 Lincoln Plaza, 500 N Akard
Dallas, TX 75201
Contact Nancy Solana, (214) 754-0144
Requirements Only Texas organizations are eligible to apply.
Restrictions Grants are not awarded to individuals.
Areas of Interest Arts, General; Biomedical Research; Cultural Activities/Programs; Education; Family Planning; Health Care; Mental Health; Obstetrics-Gynecology; Social Services; Women's Health
Sample Awards Planned Parenthood (TX)—for operating support.

George Foundation Grants 1171
George Foundation
310 Morton St, Ste C
Richmond, TX 77469
Contact Dee Koch, Grant Officer, (281) 342-6109; fax: (281) 341-7635; e-mail: dkoch@ thegeorgefoundation.org
Internet http://www.thegeorgefoundation.org/Guide.htm
Requirements Nonprofit organizations in Fort Bend County, TX, may submit grant proposals.
Restrictions The foundation will not consider grant applications for fundraising events; loans; individuals; organizations without tax-exempt status; organizations that practice discrimination by race, color, creed, religion, gender, age or national origin; proposals that in-

clude a commitment of continued support by the foundation; or political interests of any kind.

Areas of Interest Adult and Continuing Education; Basic Skills Education; Biomedical Research; Children and Youth; Elderly; Elementary Education; Family; Health Care; Language; Linguistics/Philology; Literature; Mental Retardation; Museums; Philanthropy; Preschool Education; Religion; Restoration and Preservation; Science; Secondary Education; Social Services Delivery

Sample Awards Associated Catholic Charities of the Diocese of Galveston-Houston (TX)—to assist in providing two full-time bilingual counselors to serve Fort Bend families in crisis, 140,000 three-year grant (2003). Montrose Clinic (TX)—to assist in funding operating expenses of the HIV Primary Care Clinic to serve Fort Bend residents living with HIV/AIDS, $25,000 (2003). Stehlin Foundation for Cancer Research (TX)—to support research projects involving the Camptothecin family of drugs, $50,000 matching grant (2003). Wharton County Junior College (TX)—to provide scholarships for 60 Fort Bend County students during the 2003-04 academic school year, $50,000 (2003).

Paul and Mary Haas Foundation Contributions and Student Scholarships 1172
Paul and Mary Haas Foundation
PO Box 2928
Corpus Christi, TX 78403
Contact Karen Wesson, Director, (361) 887-6955; fax: (361) 883-5992; email: haasfdn@aol.com
Requirements Grants are made to Texas organizations with 501(c)3 status. Initial inquiries should be made in the form of a one- to two-page written proposal.
Areas of Interest Adult and Continuing Education; Arts, General; Basic Skills Education; Civic Affairs; Curriculum Development; Education; Elderly; Family; Finance; Health Care; Literacy; Neighborhoods; Philanthropy; Religion; Scholarship Programs, General; Vocational/Technical Education
Sample Awards Corpus Christi Neighborhood Ctrs (TX)—for general operating support, $5000.

Halliburton Foundation Grants 1173
Halliburton Foundation
10200 Bellaire Blvd
Houston, TX 77072-5206
Contact Chief Executive Officer, (281) 575-3000; e-mail: fhoufoundation@halliburton.com
Internet http://www.halliburton.com/about/community.jsp
Areas of Interest Arts & Culture; Civic Affairs; Education; Elementary Education; Health; Higher Education; Junior and Community Colleges; Secondary Education; Social Services

Hillcrest Foundation Grants 1174
Hillcrest Foundation
PO Box 830241
Dallas, TX 75283-0241
Contact Daniel Kelly, Vice President, Bank of America, (214) 209-1965
Requirements 501(c)3 organizations in Texas may apply.

Restrictions The following types of requests will not be considered: political organizations, individuals, loans, scholarships for individuals, tuition, or seminars.
Areas of Interest Education; Health Promotion; Higher Education; Poverty and the Poor; Transportation
Sample Awards MediSend International (Dallas, TX)—to purchase a recycling and warehouse center for this organization that recycles medical equipment and redistributes it to needy countries, $50,000 (2003). Camp Fire USA Lone Star Council (Dallas, TX)—for salary support, capital improvements, and a program-awareness campaign associated with its after-school telephone service for youths who are without adult supervision, $10,000 (2003). Southern Methodist U (Dallas, TX)—to construct the James M. Collins Executive Education Center as part of the university's business school, $1 million (2002).

Hoglund Foundation Grants 1175
Hoglund Foundation
3729 Normandy
Dallas, TX 75205
Contact Kelly Compton, Executive Director, (214) 526-6522; fax: (214) 526-6465; e-mail: khc@hoglundfdtn.org
Internet http://www.hoglundfdtn.org/hoglguid.html
Requirements Texas nonprofit organizations are eligible.
Restrictions Grants are not made to individuals.
Areas of Interest Child Psychology/Development; Child/Maternal Health; Education; Health Sciences; Health Services Delivery; Social Services

Inland Foundation Inc Grants 1176
Inland Foundation Inc
303 S Temple Dr
Diboll, TX 75941
Contact Evonne Nerren, Secretary Treasurer, (936) 829-1721
Internet http://www.templeinland.com/index.asp
Requirements Grants are awarded to nonprofits in plant locations, including Fort Smith, AR; Buena Park, El Centro, Los Angeles, Neward, Santa Fe Springs, and Tracy, CA; Denver, CO; Orlando, FL; Rome, GA; Chicago, IL; Crawfordsville, Evansville, Indianapolis, and Newport, IN; Garden City and Kansas City, KS; Louisville and Maysville, KY; Minden, LA; Minneapolis, MN; Hattiesburg, MS; Saint Louis, MO; Edison and Spotswood, NJ; Middletown, OH; Biglerville, and Hazleton, PA; Vega Alta, Puerto Rico; Lexington and Rock Hill, SC; Elizabethton and New Johnsonville, TN; Dallas, Edinburg, and Orange, TX; and Petersburg, VA.
Restrictions The foundation does not make grants to individuals, religious organizations for sectarian purposes, or individual professors or departments within universities.
Areas of Interest Arts, General; Community Service Programs; Cultural Activities/Programs; Education; Health Care

Harris and Eliza Kempner Fund Grants 1177
Harris and Eliza Kempner Fund
2201 Market St, Ste 601
Galveston, TX 77550-1529

Contact Elaine Perachio, Executive Director, (409) 762-1603; fax: (409) 762-5435; e-mail: information@ kempnerfund.org
Internet http://www.kempnerfund.org/app/guidelines.html
Requirements Grants are made primarily to Texas residents.
Areas of Interest Arts, General; Cognitive Development/Processes; Community Development; Economic Development; Education; Environmental Programs; Health Care; International Relations; Population Control; Science Education; Social Services; Third World Nations; Youth Programs
Sample Awards U of Texas Medical Branch (Galveston, TX)—for its fundraising campaign to support programs to improve access to car. healtcare educatio. and research on infectious diseases, vaccines, and chronic diseases, $1 million (2003).

Kimberly-Clark Foundation Grants   1178
Kimberly-Clark Foundation
PO Box 619100
Dallas, TX 75261-9100
Contact Carolyn Mentesana, Vice President, (972) 281-1200; fax: (972) 281-1490
Internet http://www.kimberly-clark.com/aboutus/kc_ foundation.asp
Requirements Nonprofit organizations in Kimberly-Clark locations are eligible.
Areas of Interest AIDS; AIDS Counseling; African Americans; Civic Affairs; Cultural Activities/Programs; Education; Environmental Programs; Health Care; Higher Education; International Programs; Museums; Nursing; Performing Arts; Poverty and the Poor; Public Broadcasting; Scholarship Programs, General; Social Services; Youth Programs
Sample Awards Marquette U (Milwaukee, WI)—for the Raynor Library's Information Commons and the Thompson Center for Excellence in Education, $1.1 million over five years. US Fund for Unicef (New York, NY)—to provide education, health, legal, and mental-health services to African children orphaned because of AIDS, $2.6 million over four years. UNICEF—to provide services to the more than 13 million chldren worldwide orphaned as a result of AIDS, including health and nutritional services, community care, group homes, access to education, grief counseling, and legal advice on how to keep siblings together, $2.6 million.

Marcia and Otto Koehler Foundation   1179
     Grants
Marcia and Otto Koehler Foundation
PO Box 121
San Antonio, TX 78291-0121
Contact Gregg Muenster, Senior Vice President, Bank of America, (210) 270-5371; fax: (210) 270-5552
Requirements Grants are awarded only to organizations in Bexar County, Texas.
Restrictions Grants will not be made to individuals or to support other foundations or endowments; salaries; operating deficits; political organizations; or churches, synagogues, or parishes.
Areas of Interest Arts, General; Cultural Activities/Programs; Education; Medical Programs; Museums; Social Services

Sample Awards Centro Alameda (San Antonio, TX)— to restore a marquee, canopy, and facade, $30,000. McNay Art Museum (San Antonio, TX)—to sponsor an art exhibit, $50,000.

Albert and Bessie Mae Kronkosky   1180
     Charitable Foundation Grants
Albert and Bessie Mae Kronkosky Charitable Foundation
112 E Pecan, Ste 830
San Antonio, TX 78205
Contact Grants Administrator, (888) 309-9001 or (210) 475-9000; fax: (210) 354-2204; e-mail: kronfndn@kronkosky.org
Internet http://www.kronkosky.org
Requirements Nonprofits in Texas counties, including Bandera, Bexar, Comal, and Kendall, are eligible to receive grant support.
Restrictions Grants do not support economic development, annual fund and fundraising event sponsorships, political or lobbying activities, or religious organizations for sectarian purposes.
Areas of Interest Animal Rights; Child Abuse; Child Welfare; Child/Maternal Health; Computer Grants; Cultural Activities/Programs; Disabled; Disaster Relief; Elderly; Leadership; Libraries; Museums; Nonprofit Organizations; Parks; Values/Moral Education; Veterinary Medicine; Wildlife; Youth Programs; Zoos
Sample Awards Alamo Area Resource Ctr (San Antonio, TX)—for case-management, counseling, nutritional, and other services for people with HIV/AIDS, $130,000 (2003). Horses Helping the Handicapped (Boerne, TX)—to provide services to youths with emotional, mental, or physical impairments, $23,000 (2003). Boys and Girls Club of Bandera County (TX)—for leadership training and after-school activities, $60,000 (2003). American Academy of Arts and Sciences (Cambridge, MA)—to create an exhibit tailored to the developmental needs of young children, $3 million (2003).

Lightner Sams Foundation of Wyoming   1181
     Grants
Lightner Sams Foundation of Wyoming
5400 LBJ Fwy, Ste 515
Dallas, TX 75240
Contact Larry Lightner, (972) 458-8811; fax: (972) 458-8812; e-mail: foundation@lightnersams.org
Requirements Giving is primarily made to Texas nonprofit organizations.
Areas of Interest Animal Care; Arts, General; Cultural Activities/Programs; Education; Social Services; Wildlife
Sample Awards Goodwill Industries of Dallas (Dallas, TX)—for capital campaign, $12,500. American Foundation for the Blind (Dallas, TX)—for operating support, $1000.

Lowe Foundation Grants   1182
Lowe Foundation
5151 San Felipe, Ste 400
Houston, TX 77056
Contact Barbara Hendry, Secretary, (713) 622-5420 ext 320; fax: (713) 960-1672; e-mail: info@ thelowefoundation.org

Internet http://www.thelowefoundation.org/
guidelines.htm
Requirements 501(c)3 organizations in Texas may apply for grant support.
Areas of Interest Arts, General; Child/Maternal Health; Critical Care Medicine; Health Care; Higher Education; Pediatrics; Women's Health
Sample Awards U of Texas Southwestern Medical Ctr at Dallas (Dallas, TX)—to endow a professorship in pediatric critical care, $100,000.

Lubbock Area Foundation Grants   1183
Lubbock Area Foundation
1655 Main, Ste 209
Lubbock, TX 79401
Contact Kathleen Stocco, Executive Director, (806) 762-8061; fax: (806) 762-8551; e-mail: contact@ lubbockareafoundation.org
Internet http://www.lubbockareafoundation.org/grant. htm
Requirements Nonprofit organizations in Lubbock, TX, and its surrounding counties are eligible for grant support.
Restrictions Grants are not awarded to individuals or for retirement of debts or loans.
Areas of Interest Adult and Continuing Education; Alcohol/Alcoholism; Arts, General; Basic Skills Education; Civic Affairs; Community Development; Cultural Activities/Programs; Drugs/Drug Abuse; Education; Environmental Programs; Health Care; Job Training Programs; Literacy; Public Administration; Restoration and Preservation; Social Services
Sample Awards Junior League of Lubbock (Lubbock, TX)—for construction of a new headquarters, $1500. Salvation Army of Lubbock (Lubbock, TX)—for kitchen equipment, $2400. South Plains Food Bank (Lubbock, TX)—for a job training program, $2500.

Eugene McDermott Foundation Grants   1184
Eugene McDermott Foundation
3808 Euclid Ave
Dallas, TX 75205
Contact Grants Administrator, (214) 521-2924
Requirements Texas nonprofit organizations are eligible.
Areas of Interest Biomedical Research; Children and Youth; Civil/Human Rights; Community Development; Education; Elementary Education; Health Care; Higher Education; History; Hospitals; International Relations; Minorities; Museums; Public Affairs; Secondary Education; Service Delivery Programs
Sample Awards U of Texas Southwestern Medical Ctr (Dallas, TX)—to establish a chair in cardiothoracic anesthesiology, $1 million (2003).

Meadows Foundation Grants   1185
Meadows Foundation of Texas
3003 Swiss Ave
Dallas, TX 75204-6090
Contact Program Contact, (800) 826-9431 or (214) 826-9431; fax: (214) 827-7042; email: grants@mfi.org
Internet http://www.mfi.org
Requirements Grants are made to qualified organizations in Texas or programs benefiting Texas residents.

Restrictions Grants are not made to individuals or for church or seminary construction, annual fund-raising events or drives, biomedical research, out-of-state performances or competition expenses, or professional conferences and symposia.
Areas of Interest Arts, General; Civic Affairs; Cultural Activities/Programs; Curriculum Development; Education; Educational Administration; Elementary Education; Engineering; Health Care; Hospitals; Jewish Studies; Public Affairs; Racism/Race Relations; Scholarship Programs, General; Science; Social Services; Teacher Education; Technology; Violent Behavior
Sample Awards Salvation Army of Dallas (TX)—for a public-awareness campaign to encourage people to support local charities that might face economic trouble because so many donors contributed to the September 11 recovery, $150,000 (2002). U of Texas at Austin, McDonald Observatory (TX)—for professional-development workshops for teachers and presentations and hands-on activities for students at the new McDonald Observatory Visitors Center, $105,000 over three years (2002). Texas International Theatrical Arts Society (Dallas, TX)—for emergency operating support needed to counter revenue losses, $179,000 (2002).

J. P. Morgan Chase Texas Foundation, Inc   1186 Grants
J. P. Morgan Chase Texas Foundation, Inc
PO Box 2558
Houston, TX 77252
Contact Jana Gunter, Trustee, (713) 216-4004
Requirements Organizations and projects must be based in Houston and have a broad impact on the Houston community.
Restrictions The foundation does not fund individuals, scholarships, churches/religious organizations, or elementary or secondary schools.
Areas of Interest Adult and Continuing Education; Basic Skills Education; Biomedical Research; Business; Business Education; Civic Affairs; Crime Control; Disabled; Economics; Educational/Public Television; Elementary Education; Health Care; Hospitals; Hunger; Literacy; Minorities; Museums; Neighborhoods; Performing Arts; Secondary Education; Social Services; Urban Affairs; Youth Programs; Zoos

J.C. Penney Company Grants   1187
J.C. Penney Company Inc
PO Box 10001
Dallas, TX 75301-8101
Contact Community Relations and Corporate Communications, (972) 431-1349; fax: (972) 431-1355; e-mail: info@jcpenney.com
Internet http://www.jcpenney.net/company/commrel/ guidelin.htm
Requirements K-12, higher education, 501(c)3 nonprofits, and 170(c)1 state agencies may request grant support.
Areas of Interest Arts, General; Business Education; Children and Youth; Civic Affairs; Cultural Activities/ Programs; Education Reform; Elementary Education; Family; Health Care; Higher Education; Preschool Education; Secondary Education; Social Services; Volunteers

Sample Awards YMCA of the USA (Chicago, IL)—for scholarships to training programs designed to better prepare YMCA employees and volunteers nationwide to work at after-school program, $150,000 (2004).

Pollock Foundation Grants   **1188**
Pollock Foundation
2626 Howell St, Ste 895
Dallas, TX 75204
Contact Robert Pollock, Trustee, (214) 871-7155; fax: (214) 871-8158
Requirements Texas nonprofit organizations are eligible. Preference is given to requests from Dallas.
Areas of Interest Children and Youth; Cultural Activities/Programs; Dental Education; Health Care; Jewish Services; Libraries; Library Science; Nursing; Public Health; Social Services; Social Services Delivery; Youth Programs
Sample Awards Southwestern Medical Foundation (Dallas, TX)—to establish a center for research on intestinal cancer at the U of Texas Southwestern Medical Center, $1 million (2002).

Powell Foundation Grants   **1189**
Powell Foundation
2121 San Felipe, Ste 110
Houston, TX 77019-5600
Contact Caroline Sabin, Executive Director, (713) 523-7557; fax: (713) 523-7553; e-mail: info@ powellfoundation.org
Internet http://www.powellfoundation.org/ powellguide.htm
Requirements Texas tax-exempt organizations serving Harris, Walker, and Travis counties are eligible.
Restrictions Normally, the foundation will not consider requests for building funds or grant commitments extending into successive calendar years. The foundation does not support grants to religious organizations for religious purposes; testimonial dinners, fundraising events, or advertising; other private foundations; past operating deficits or debt retirement; or individuals. Normally, the foundation will not consider requests for building funds or grant commitments extending into successive calendar years.
Areas of Interest Aging/Gerontology; Arts, General; Community Service Programs; Disadvantaged (Economically); Education; Elderly; Elementary Education; Environmental Health; Environmental Programs; Health Care; Higher Education; Minorities; Performing Arts; Social Services; Social Services Delivery; Visual Arts
Sample Awards U of Texas at Austin (TX)—to establish an endowment for the UTeach program, which trains students to become mathematics and science teachers, $1 million (2002).

RadioShack Neighborhood Answers Grant 1190
RadioShack Corporation
100 Throckmorton, Ste 700B
Fort Worth, TX 76102
Contact Community Relations, (817) 415-3700; fax: (817) 415-0939; e-mail: corporate.citizenship@ radioshack.com
Internet http://www.radioshackcorporation.com/cr/ contrib_program.shtml

Requirements An applicant organization must have 501(c)3 tax-exempt status; offer solutions to help prevent family violence/abuse and/or child abduction; and directly impact or benefit, through programs and/or services, a RadioShack community.
Restrictions Grants cannot be considered for individuals; endowments or private foundations that are themselves grant-making organizations; construction or major renovation projects; to fund advertising or marketing programs; fundraising events and sponsorships (i.e., golf tournaments, dinners, auctions); multiyear grants; religious, political, and fraternal organizations; or trips, sporting events, tours, and transportation.
Areas of Interest Child Abuse; Child Welfare; Children and Youth; Domestic Violence; Familial Abuse

Sid W. Richardson Foundation Grants   **1191**
Sid W. Richardson Foundation
309 Main St
Fort Worth, TX 76102
Contact Valleau Wilkie Jr., Executive Director, (817) 336-0494; fax: (817) 332-2176
Internet http://www.sidrichardson.org
Requirements Proposals must cover programs and projects within Texas.
Restrictions Grants are not made to individuals.
Areas of Interest Alcohol/Alcoholism; Art Education; Arts Administration; Business Education; Children and Youth; Crime Prevention; Dance; Disabled; Drugs/Drug Abuse; Economics Education; Elderly; Elementary Education; Food Distribution; Higher Education; History; Hospitals; Housing; Museums; Nursing; Orchestras; Organ Transplants; Performing Arts; Preschool Education; Preventive Medicine; Science; Secondary Education; Social Services; Visual Arts; Youth Programs
Sample Awards U of Texas at Austin (TX)—for the Port Aransas Marine Science Institute, $165,000 (2003). U of Saint Thomas (Houston, TX)—to create a master's degree program in bilingual education, $100,000 (2002). U of Texas at Austin (TX)—for the Dana Center for Math and Science Education, $100,000 (2002).

Dora Roberts Foundation Grants   **1192**
Dora Roberts Foundation Grants
PO Box 2050
Fort Worth, TX 76113
Contact Konnie Darrow, c/o Bank One Texas, (817) 884-4772
Requirements Texas nonprofit organizations are eligible.
Areas of Interest Children and Youth; Education; Health Care; Higher Education; Hospitals; Protestant Church; Religion; Social Services Delivery

David Robinson Foundation Grants   **1193**
David Robinson Foundation
11550 IH-10 W, Ste 155
San Antonio, TX 78230
Contact Grants Administrator, (210) 696-8061; fax: (210) 696-7754
Requirements Texas nonprofit organizations are eligible.
Areas of Interest Agriculture; Family Planning; Single-Parent Families; Religion; Social Services Delivery

Rockwell Fund Inc Grants 1194

Rockwell Fund Inc
1330 Post Oak Blvd, Ste 1825
Houston, TX 77056
Contact Carolyn Watson, Program Officer, (713) 629-9022; fax: (713) 629-7702; e-mail: cwatson@rockfund.org
Internet http://www.rockfund.org
Requirements Grants are made only to nonprofit, tax-exempt organizations in Texas with priority given to those in the Houston area.
Restrictions Grants are not awarded for the following: grants to individuals; underwriting for benefits, dinners, galas; fundraising special events; mass appeal solicitations; or medical or scientific research projects.
Areas of Interest Child/Maternal Health; Civic Affairs; Curriculum Development; Education; Environmental Programs; Health Care; Health Services Delivery; Higher Education; Hospitals; Humanities; Instructional Materials and Practices; Performing Arts; Pregnancy; Preservation and Restoration; Rehabilitation/Therapy; Religion; Service Delivery Programs; Social Services; Youth Programs
Sample Awards Gladney Fund (Fort Worth, TX)—to support the adoption and maternity services organization's Houston regional office, $10,000.

San Antonio Area Foundation Grants 1195

San Antonio Area Foundation
110 Broadway, Ste 230
San Antonio, TX 78205
Contact Program Contact, (210) 225-2243; fax: (210) 225-1980; e-mail: gift@saafdn.org
Internet http://www.saafdn.org/Pages/grantsframes.html
Requirements Grants are made to organizations in the San Antonio, TX, area.
Areas of Interest Adult and Continuing Education; Animal Care; Arts, General; Basic Skills Education; Biomedical Research; Community Service Programs; Cultural Activities/Programs; Health Care; Higher Education; Literacy; Medical Education; Nursing Education; Orchestras; Preschool Education; Social Services
Sample Awards San Antonio Symphony (TX)—for the Young People's Concert series, $25,000. Southwest Foundation for Biomedical Research (San Antonio, TX)—to purchase equipment, $15,000.

Harold Simmons Foundation Grants 1196

Harold Simmons Foundation
5430 LBJ Fwy, Ste 1700
Dallas, TX 75240-2697
Contact Lisa Simmons Epstein, President, (972) 233-2134
Requirements Dallas, TX, nonprofits are eligible.
Restrictions Grants are not awarded to support individuals or for endowment funds or loans.
Areas of Interest Adult and Continuing Education; Arts, General; Basic Skills Education; Child Psychology/Development; Civil/Human Rights; Community Service Programs; Developing/Underdeveloped Nations; Health Care; Higher Education; International Programs; Literacy; Religion; Scholarship Programs, General; Social Services; Youth Programs

Sample Awards Southern Methodist U (TX)—for scholarship programs, $1.2 million. YMCA of Metropolitan Dallas (Dallas, TX)—for its capital campaign to build eight new facilities and expand and improve 14 existing branches, $100,000.

Dr. Bob and Jean Smith Foundation Grants 1197

Dr. Bob and Jean Smith Foundation
3811 Turtle Creek Ctr, No 2150 LB 53
Dallas, TX 75219
Contact Sally Smith, Grants Administrator, (214) 521-3461 or Patty Smith, CFO
Requirements Texas nonprofit organizations are eligible. Preference is given to Dallas-based organizations.
Restrictions Individuals are ineligible.
Areas of Interest Health Care; Higher Education; Medical Education
Sample Awards Southern Methodist U (TX)—for an auditorium in the new museum, $1 million (2001).

Victor E. Speas Foundation Grants 1198

Victor E. Speas Foundation
PO Box 831041
Dallas, TX 75283-1041
Contact David Ross, Senior Vice President, Bank of America, (800) 357-7094
Requirements Nonprofit organizations in Missouri counties, including Jackson, Clay, Platte, and Cass, are eligible.
Areas of Interest AIDS; Alcohol/Alcoholism; Children and Youth; Disabled; Drugs/Drug Abuse; Elderly; Health Care; Higher Education; Medical Education; Women; Youth Programs

Sterling-Turner Charitable Foundation Grants 1199

Sterling-Turner Charitable Foundation
815 Walker St, Ste 1543
Houston, TX 77002-5724
Contact Eyvonne Moser, Executive Director, (713) 237-1117; fax: (713) 223-4638; e-mail: patricia@sterlingturnerfoundation.org
Internet http://sterlingturnerfoundation.org
Requirements Nonprofit Texas organizations may submit written requests for grants.
Restrictions Individuals are ineligible.
Areas of Interest Adult and Continuing Education; Basic Skills Education; Catholic Church; Churches; Civic Affairs; Conservation, Natural Resources; Cultural Activities/Programs; Elderly; Fine Arts; Health Care; Higher Education; Hospices; Hospitals; Jewish Services; Literacy; Museums; Performing Arts; Protestant Church; Religion; Secondary Education; Social Services; Urban Affairs; Youth Programs
Sample Awards Kinkaid School (Houston, TX)—for program support, $10,000. Houston Baptist U (Houston, TX)—for program support, $25,000. Museum of Fine Arts of Houston (Houston, TX)—for operating support, $166,667.

Strake Foundation Grants 1200

Strake Foundation
712 Main St, Ste 3300
Houston, TX 77002
Contact George Strake Jr., President, (713) 216-2400; fax: (713) 216-2401; e-mail: foundation@strake.org
Requirements Awards are made to organizations located only in the United States, primarily in Texas.
Restrictions Awards are not made to support elementary schools or individuals, nor for deficit financing, consulting services, technical assistance, publications, or loans.
Areas of Interest Adult and Continuing Education; Arts, General; Basic Skills Education; Catholic Church; Cultural Activities/Programs; Higher Education, Private; Hospitals; Literacy; Museums; Private and Parochial Education; Secondary Education
Sample Awards College of Saint Thomas More (Fort Worth, TX)—to support courses and materials related to the college's new bachelor of arts degree, $10,000.

Sturgis Charitable and Educational Trust Grants 1201

Roy and Christine Sturgis Charitable and Educational Trust
PO Box 830241
Dallas, TX 75283-0241
Contact Daniel Kelly, Vice President, Bank of America, (214) 209-1965
Requirements 501(c)3 nonprofit organizations in Texas and Arkansas are eligible.
Restrictions Grants will not be awarded to support political organizations, loans, scholarships or tuition for individuals, or seminars.
Areas of Interest Arts, General; Cultural Activities/Programs; Education; Health Care; Restoration and Preservation; Social Services; Youth Programs
Sample Awards Governor's Mansion Assoc (Little Rock, AR)—for major renovations at the Arkansas Governor's Mansion, including the construction of a grand hall that will be used for official functions, $500,000 (2000).

Swalm Foundation Grants 1202

Swalm Foundation
14800 St. Mary's Ln, Ste 107
Houston, TX 77079
Contact Kathleen Carroll, Office Manager, (281) 497-5280; fax: (281) 497-7340; e-mail: kcarroll@swalm.org
Internet http://www.swalm.org/guide.htm
Requirements Texas nonprofit organizations are eligible.
Restrictions The foundation does not support: capital projects; social service programs which require or include formal instruction in or adherence to the tenets of a particular religion; construction or operations of individual churches, synagogues, or mosques; capital campaigns and operations of institutions of higher learning, medical facilities, or medical research institutions; private schools, charter schools, or experimental programs in public education; giving campaigns of large national or international organizations; galas or other social fundraisers; programs with limited support from the community and other available funding sources, including government support; endowments; scholarships or fellowships to individuals; or an organization that has more than six months' operating reserves, true administrative costs exceeding 20 percent of its budget, disproportionate salaries, or an endowment spending policy of less than four to five percent of net assets for endowments greater than $1 million.
Areas of Interest Adult and Continuing Education; After-School Programs; Arts and Culture; Basic Skills Education; Child Abuse; Child Welfare; Community Development; Community Services; Conservation; Disabled; Domestic Violence; Early Childhood Education; Economically Disadvantaged; Elementary Education; Environment; Health Education; Health Services Delivery; Higher Education; Homeless; Housing; Human Services; Libraries; Literacy; Mental Health; Mental Retardation; Parenting Education; Preschool Education; Scholarship Programs, General; Senior Citizen Programs and Services; Social Services; Volunteerism; Youth Programs

T.L.L. Temple Foundation Grants 1203

T.L.L. Temple Foundation
109 Temple Blvd, Ste 300
Lufkin, TX 75901
Contact A. Wayne Corely, Executive Director, (936) 639-5197
Requirements Nonprofit organizations in Texas counties constituting the East Texas Pine Timber Belt are eligible.
Restrictions Grants do not support private foundations or individuals, nor are grants made in support of deficit financing.
Areas of Interest Adult and Continuing Education; Animal Welfare; Arts and Culture; Civic Affairs; Community Development; Community Service Programs; Cultural Activities/Programs; Economically Disadvantaged; Education; Elementary Education; Governmental Functions; Health Care; Higher Education; Hospices; Hospitals; Human Services; Mental Health; Scholarship Programs, General; Social Services; Substance Abuse
Sample Awards Alzheimer's Disease and Related Disorders Assoc (Chicago, IL)—for the Temple Foundation Discovery Awards for Alzheimer's Disease Research, $2.5 million (2001).

Temple-Inland Foundation Grants 1204

Temple-Inland Foundation
PO Drawer 338, 303 S Temple Dr
Diboll, TX 75941
Contact Evonne Nerren, (936) 829-1721; fax: (936) 829-7727
Internet http://www.templeinland.com
Restrictions Ineligible applicants include fraternal, veterans, political, local social, and service organizations.
Areas of Interest Churches; Community Development; Elementary Education; Health Care; Health Services Delivery; Higher Education; Hospitals; Museums; Performing Arts; Scholarship Programs, General; Secondary Education

Trull Foundation Grants   **1205**
Trull Foundation
404 Fourth St
Palacios, TX 77465
Contact Grants Administrator, (361) 972-5241; fax: (361) 972-1109; e-mail: info@trullfoundation.org
Internet http://www.trullfoundation.org
Requirements 501(c)3 tax-exempt organizations and departments, agencies, and other services operated within federal, state, or local government agencies and institutions and agencies affiliated with organized religions and religious bodies are eligible.
Restrictions The foundation usually will not make long term commitments; make grants for buildings, endowments, or research; repeat grants to the same project longer than three years; or fund operational expenses except during initial years.
Areas of Interest Children and Youth; Education; Elementary Education; Religion; Scholarship Programs, General; Secondary Education; Social Services Delivery
Sample Awards Children's Discovery Museum (Victoria, TX)—for the Children's Discovery Museum Building Renovation, $2500 (2003). Hawk Watch International (Salt Lake City, UT)—for the South Texas Raptor Migration Project and Education Project, $2500 (2003).

Verizon Foundation Grants   **1206**
Verizon Foundation
1255 Corporate Dr, MC SVC05BC62
Irving, TX 75038
Contact Patrick Gaston, President, (800) 360-7955; fax: (212) 840-6988; e-mail: Patrick.G.Gaston@Verizon.com
Internet http://foundation.verizon.com/index.shtml
Requirements Eligible applicants are 501(c)3 nonprofit organizations and accredited higher education institutions.
Restrictions The foundation does not provide direct support to elementary and secondary schools for basic operations, teacher salaries, or other expenses generally supported by federal, state, and local taxes; building funds for educational institutions; government-funded organizations; athletic programs; student trips or cultural exchanges; fraternal, athletic, social, or veterans' groups; organizations that discriminate; single disease organizations; or operating support for colleges, universities, or United Way-funded agencies.
Areas of Interest Academic Achievement; Adult and Continuing Education; Alcohol Education; At-Risk Youth; Cultural Activities/Programs; Dramatic/Theater Arts; Drug Education; Economic Development; Educational Technology; Educational/Public Television; Hospitals; Job Training Programs; Literacy; Mathematics Education; Minority Education; Minority Schools; Museums; Performing Arts; Safety; Science Education; Social Services; Technology; Telecommunications
Sample Awards Illinois Wesleyan U (Bloomington, IL)—to upgrade equipment in the Internet computer laboratory at Sheean Library, $25,000. Classroom Inc (New York, NY)—to design a nationwide curriculum in information technology for ninth- and 10th-grade students, $200,000. United Negro College Fund (Fairfax, VA)—to expand a summer program that brings together UNCF-institution students and GTE scientists for technology research, $420,000.

Wortham Foundation Grants   **1207**
Wortham Foundation
2727 Allen Pkwy, Ste 1570
Houston, TX 77019
Contact Barbara Snyder, Grants Administrator, (713) 526-8849; fax: (713) 526-7222; e-mail: bsnyder@wortham.org
Requirements Houston nonprofit organizations in Harris County, TX, are eligible.
Restrictions Grants are generally not awarded to colleges, universities, hospitals, or individuals.
Areas of Interest Arts, General; Civic Affairs; Community Development; Environmental Programs; Museums; Opera/Musical Theater; Performing Arts
Sample Awards Houston Grand Opera (Houston, TX)—for a multiple-year program to record, preserve, and disseminate the company's opera productions, $300,000. Museum of Fine Arts (Houston, TX)—for capital support, $1.5 million.

M.B. and Edna Zale Foundation Grants   **1208**
M.B. and Edna Zale Foundation
3102 Maple Ave, Ste 225
Dallas, TX 75201
Contact Leonard Krasnow, President, (214) 855-0627; fax: (214) 220-0633
Requirements Only residents of Florida, New York, and Texas may apply.
Areas of Interest Drugs/Drug Abuse; Economic Self-Sufficiency; Education; Family; Gun Control; Jewish Studies; Job Training Programs; Middle East; Minorities; Parent Education; Poverty and the Poor; Preventive Medicine; Violent Behavior

Utah

Ruth Eleanor Bamberger and John Ernest   **1209**
    Bamberger Memorial Foundation Grants
Ruth Eleanor Bamberger and John Ernest Bamberger Memorial Foundation
136 S Main, Ste 418
Salt Lake City, UT 84101
Contact Eleanor Roser, (801) 364-2045
Requirements Only residents of Utah may apply.
Restrictions Grants are not awarded to individuals (except for scholarships to local students) or for endowment or building funds, research, or matching gifts.
Areas of Interest Child Welfare; Elementary Education; Environmental Programs; Health Care; Health Services Delivery; Hospitals; Medical Education; Nursing Education; Scholarship Programs, General; Secondary Education; Wildlife; Youth Programs
Sample Awards Community Health Ctrs (Salt Lake City, UT)—to strengthen health care services at four Salt Lake-area clinics, $10,000.

M. Bastian Family Foundation Grants   **1210**
M. Bastian Family Foundation
51 W Center St, Ste 305
Orem, UT 84057
Contact McKay Matthews, Program Contact, (801) 225-2455

Requirements Utah and Virginia nonprofit organizations are eligible.

Areas of Interest AIDS; Arts, General; Diabetes; Health Care; Higher Education; Music; Pediatrics; Religion; Scholarship Programs, General; Social Services; Wildlife

Sample Awards Brigham Young U (Provo, UT)—for scholarship endowment, $200,000. Pediatric AIDS Foundation (Los Angeles, CA)—for general support, $20,000. American Diabetes Assoc (Alexandra, VA)—for research, $100,000.

George S. and Dolores Dore Eccles Foundation Grants 1211
George S. and Dolores Dore Eccles Foundation
79 S Main St, 12th Fl
Salt Lake City, UT 84111
Contact Lisa Eccles, Executive Director, (801) 246-5331
Requirements Giving primarily in Utah.
Areas of Interest Arts, General; Children and Youth; Economics; Higher Education; Hospitals; Medical Programs; Performance Art; Visual Arts
Sample Awards Westminster College of Salt Lake City (UT)—for undergraduate scholarships, $1.2 million over three years (2002).

Utah Arts Council General Support Grants 1212
Utah Arts Council
617 E South Temple
Salt Lake City, UT 84102-1177
Contact Sherry Waddingham, Grants Officer, (801) 236-7550; fax: (801) 236-7556; TDD: (800) 346-4128; e-mail: swaddingham@utah.gov
Internet http://www.arts.utah.org/grants
Requirements Established Utah arts organizations are eligible. Grants must be matched with at least an equal amount of cash. Applicants must submit a copy of an audit by an independent accounting firm for the preceding fiscal year.
Areas of Interest Arts; Arts Administration; Arts and Culture; Creative Writing; Literature; Performing Arts; Visual Arts

Vermont

Kelsey Trust Grants 1213
Kelsey Trust
PO Box 30
Middlebury, VT 05753
Contact Paula Johnson, Grants Manager, c/o Vermont Community Foundation, (802) 388-3355
Internet http://www.vermontcf.org/grants-kelsey.html
Requirements Nonprofit organizations in the Lake Champlain Valley drainage basin; eastern Adirondacks, in New York; and western Vermont, north of Rutland, may submit applications for grant support.
Areas of Interest Adult and Continuing Education; Basic Skills Education; Child Psychology/Development; Children and Youth; Conservation, Natural Resources; Environmental Programs; Family; Family Planning;

Health Care; Literacy; Preschool Education; Vocational/Technical Education
Sample Awards Planned Parenthood of Northern Adirondack (Plattsburgh, NY)—for program support, $10,000. Fletcher Allen Health Care (Burlington, VT)—for program support, $3000. Bristol Family Center (Bristol, VT)—for program support, $1000.

New England Grassroots Environment Fund Grants 1214
New England Grassroots Environment Fund
PO Box 1057
Montpelier, VT 05601
Contact Cheryl King Fischer, Executive Director, (802) 223-4622; fax: (802) 229-1734; e-mail: fischer@grassrootsfund.org
Internet http://www.grassrootsfund.org/guide_1.html
Requirements 501(c)3 nonprofit, grassroots organizations in Maine, Massachusetts, New Hampshire, Rhode Island, and Vermont are eligible. Grassroots groups are defined as being largely volunteer driven, having no more than two paid full-time staff members, and an annual budget (including projects) of less than $100,000. Proposals may be considered from larger community-based groups for projects at the grassroots level.
Restrictions Grants do not support lobbying or partisan political purposes.
Areas of Interest Churches; Computer Grants; Environmental Programs; Grassroots Leadership; Networking (Computers); Sustainable Development; Training and Development; Volunteers; Water Resources; Wildlife
Sample Awards Maine Wolf Coalition (South China, ME)—to purchase a computer, other office equipment, and furniture, $2250. Toxics Action Ctr (Boston, MA)—to finance scholarships to allow local activists to attend an annual training conference, $175. New Hampshire Council of Churches (Concord, NH)—to hire an intern to set up a network of faith-based environmental groups and congregations, $2500. Saugatucket River Heritage Corridor (Wakefield, RI)—for general operating support, $2500.

Virginia

Arlington Community Foundation Grants 1215
Arlington Community Foundation
2525 Wilson Blvd
Arlington, VA 22201
Contact Executive Director, (703) 243-4785; fax: (703) 243-4796
Internet http://www.arlcf.org/grants.html
Requirements Virginia residents and nonprofit organizations are eligible.
Restrictions The foundation does not make grants for endowments, capital campaigns, religious purposes, individual debts, or political lobbying.
Areas of Interest Adult and Continuing Education; Aging/Gerontology; Arts, General; Children and Youth; Community Development; Government; Health Care; Literacy; Minorities; Performing Arts; Public Administration; Reading Education; Scholarship Programs, General; Social Services Delivery

Bedford Community Health Foundation Grants   1216

Bedford Community Health Foundation
PO Box 1104
Bedford, VA 24523
Contact Program Contact, (540) 586-5292; fax: (540) 587-5819; e-mail: bchf@library.bedford.va.us
Internet http://www.bchf.org
Requirements Nonprofits serving Bedford and Bedford County are eligible.
Restrictions Individuals are not eligible.
Areas of Interest Health Care; Scholarship Programs, General

Beirne Carter Foundation Grants   1217

Beirne Carter Foundation
1802 Bayberry Ct, Ste 301
Richmond, VA 23226
Contact Grants Administrator, (804) 521-0272; fax: (804) 521-0274; e-mail: bcarterfn@aol.com
Internet http://www.bcarterfdn.org
Requirements Virginia 501(c)3 nonprofits are eligible.
Restrictions Grants will not normally be made to endowment funds, to organizations supported primarily by government funds (such as public schools), for ongoing operating expenses or existing deficits, or debt reduction.

Areas of Interest Audiovisual Materials; Ecology; Education; Health Care; Local History; Natural Resources; Religion; Scholarship Programs, General; Youth Programs
Sample Awards Saint Timothy's School (Stevenson, MD)—to endow merit scholarships, $50,000. Foundation for Historic Christ Church (Irvington, VA)—for production of an audiovisual program, $18,500. YMCA (Richmond, VA)—to support the capital development program, $10,000.

Chesapeake Corporation Foundation Grants 1218

Chesapeake Corporation Foundation
PO Box 2350
Richmond, VA 23218-2350
Contact J.P. Causey Jr., (804) 697-1000; fax: (804) 697-1199
Internet http://www.cskcorp.com
Requirements Nonprofits internationally are eligible.
Restrictions Grants do not support athletic purposes or individuals, except for employee-related scholarships.
Areas of Interest Civic Affairs; Community Development; Cultural Programs/Activities; Education; Elementary Education; Health Care; Higher Education; International Programs; Secondary Education

Eastman Kodak American Greenways Awards   1219

Conservation Fund
1800 N Kent St, Ste 1120
Arlington, VA 22209-2156
Contact Eastman Kodak American Greenways Grants, (703) 525-6300; fax: (703) 525-4610; e-mail: greenways@conservationfund.org
Internet http://www.conservationfund.org/?article=2372

Requirements Local, regional, and statewide nonprofit organizations are eligible. Public agencies also may apply, but community organizations will receive preference.
Areas of Interest Environmental Programs

Ethyl Corporation Grants   1220

Ethyl Corporation
PO Box 2189
Richmond, VA 23218
Contact Human Resources and External Affairs, (804) 788-5720; fax: (804) 788-5636; e-mail: contributions@ethyl.com
Internet http://www.ethyl.com/nav/default.asp?sec=contact&page=cont
Requirements Organizations in company-operating locations worldwide are eligible, including the United States, Australia, Belgium, Brazil, Canada, England, France, Germany, Japan, Russia, Saudi Arabia, and Singapore.
Restrictions Grants are not awarded to religious organizations for religious purposes, individuals for personal gain, or fraternal groups.
Areas of Interest Arts, General; Civic Affairs; Cultural Activities/Programs; Economics Education; Education; Exercise; Health Care; Higher Education; Private and Parochial Education; Recreation and Leisure; Scholarship Programs, General; Secondary Education; Social Services; Undergraduate Education

Gannett Foundation Grants   1221

Gannett Foundation
7950 Jones Branch Dr
McLean, VA 22107
Contact Irma Simpson, Manager, (703) 854-6069; fax: (703) 854-2002; e-mail: isimpson@gcil.gannett.com
Internet http://www.gannettfoundation.org/GUIDELINES.htm
Requirements 501(c)3 nonprofit organizations in Gannett-operating areas are eligible.
Restrictions The foundation does not fund individuals; national or regional organizations unless their programs address specific community needs; elementary or secondary schools (except to provide special initiatives or programs not provided by regular school budgets); programs where the primary purpose is promotion of a specific religious doctrine or tenet; political action or legislative advocacy groups; medical or other research organizations; or multiyear pledges or campaigns.
Areas of Interest Adult and Continuing Education; African Americans (Student Support); Arts, General; At-Risk Youth; Basic Skills Education; Cultural Activities/Programs; Disadvantaged (Economically); Economic Development; Education; Families; Health Care; HIV; Literacy; Mental Health; Neighborhoods; Nutrition/Dietetics; Problem Solving; Vocational/Technical Education; Youth Programs
Sample Awards 100 Black Men of Middle Tennessee (Nashville, TN)—for a scholarship endowment, $150,000. Building Our Pride in Chambersburg (PA)—funding for teachers and supplies for a summer enrichment and nutrition program, $3800.

General Dynamics Corporation Grants 1222
General Dynamics Corporation
3190 Fairview Park Dr
Falls Church, VA 22042-4523
Contact Diane Mossler, (703) 876-3305; fax: (703) 876-3600
Internet http://www.generaldynamics.com
Areas of Interest Arts, General; Civic Affairs; Community Service Programs; Cultural Activities/Programs; Health Services Delivery; Public Affairs; Social Services Delivery

Harvest Foundation Grants 1223
Harvest Foundation
PO Box 5183, 1 Ellsworth St
Martinsville, VA 24115
Contact Grants Administrator, (276) 632-3329; fax: (276) 632-1878
Internet http://www.theharvestfoundation.org
Requirements 501(c)3 tax-exempt organizations located in, or for programs focused in, Virginia's Martinsville and/or Henry Counties are eligible.
Restrictions The foundation does not fund organizations that discriminate based upon race, creed, gender, or sexual orientation; scholarships, fellowships, or grants to individuals; sectarian religious activities, political lobbying, or legislative activities; profit-making businesses; emergency needs or extremely time sensitive requests; or direct replacement of discontinued government support.
Areas of Interest Academic Achievement; Citizenship; Community Services; Education; Health Care; Health Care Access; Health Promotion; Literacy; Safety; Social Services Delivery
Sample Awards Family Life Services, Free Medical Clinic (VA)—for general operations and to help with financial reporting and board development, $22,000 (2003). Martinsville City Schools (VA)—to enable the district's six schools to begin addressing the performance of students in the areas of literacy and math, $75,000 (2003). Partners for Livable Communities (VA)—to initiate a project to identify needs and develop specific solutions to make the community more livable for its older residents, $35,000 (2003). Gateway Streetscape Foundation (VA)—for a greenhouse and equipment to expand the capabilities and effectiveness of the urban greening program, $10,067 (2003).

Jenkins Foundation Grants 1224
Community Foundation Serving Richmond and Central Virginia
7325 Beaufont Springs Dr, Ste 210
Richmond, VA 23225
Contact Jill McCormick, Senior Program Officer, (804) 330-7400; fax: (804) 330-5992; email: jmccormick@tcfrichmond.org
Internet http://www.tcfrichmond.org/Page2954.cfm#Jenkins
Requirements IRS 501(c)3 organizations undertaking health-related programs serving the indigent population in Richmond, VA, and the surrounding counties of Henrico, Chesterfield, Goochland, Powhatan, and Hanover are eligible.
Areas of Interest Assisted-Living Programs; Dental Health and Hygiene; Geriatrics; Health Care; Nursing; Poverty and the Poor; Rural Health Care; Service Delivery Programs
Sample Awards Virginia Home (Richmond, VA)—to renovate, expand, and improve its facilities, $50,000 (2002). Brother's Keepers Ministries (Richmond, VA)—for salary support of counselors and a secretary, and for an organizational evaluation, $28,000. YWCA of Richmond County (VA)—to renovate facilities that house services for survivors of domestic violence and sexual assault, $100,000. Legal Information Network for Cancer (Richmond, VA)—to provide cancer patients with legal representation and technical assistance, $10,000.

Freddie Mac Foundation Grants 1225
Freddie Mac Foundation
8250 Jones Branch Dr, MS A40
McLean, VA 22102
Contact Carliss Hill, Grants Manager, (703) 918-2222; fax: (703) 918-8895
Internet http://www.freddiemacfoundation.org
Requirements Eligible organizations must be tax exempt under IRS code 501(c)3 and located primarily in the metropolitan District of Columbia area; Montgomery, Prince Georges, and Howard Counties in Maryland; Fairfax, Arlington, and Prince William Counties in Virginia.
Restrictions Grants do not support individuals, religious groups for religious purposes, debt liabilities, or endowment campaigns.
Areas of Interest At-Risk Youth; Career Education and Planning; Charter Schools; Child Abuse; Child Welfare; Computer Education/Literacy; Day Care; Disaster Relief; Education Reform; Family; Intervention Programs; Literacy; Mentoring Programs; Parent Involvement; Preschool Education; Teacher Education, Inservice; Training and Development; Transportation
Sample Awards Advocates for Homeless Families (Frederick, MD)—for the Families Forward program, through the Helping Hand Emergency Fund, $12,500 (2003). Community Bridges (Silver Spring, MD)—for the Jump Start Girls program, through the Helping Hand Emergency Fund, $25,000 (2003). Hannah House (Washington, DC)—for a supportive-housing program, through the Helping Hand Emergency Fund, $15,000 (2003). Metropolitan Ctr for Assault Prevention (Wheaton, MD)—for efforts to prevent child abuse, through the Helping Hand Emergency Fund, $50,000 (2003).

Mark and Catherine Winkler Foundation Grants 1226
Mark and Catherine Winkler Foundation
4900 Seminary Rd, Ste 900
Alexandria, VA 22311
Contact Lynne Ball, Assistant Treasurer, (703) 998-0400
Requirements Northern Virginia nonprofit organizations are eligible.
Areas of Interest Behavioral/Social Sciences; Biomedical Research; Children and Youth; Community Development; Conservation, Natural Resources; Education; Environmental Programs; Health Care; Higher Education; Social Services; Social Services Delivery; Surgery

Sample Awards Colorado College (Colorado Springs, CO)—to create a professorship and to add a new junior faculty position in the psychology department, $1.5 million (2002).

Mars Foundation Grants 1227

Mars Foundation
6885 Elm St
McLean, VA 22101
Contact Grants Administrator, (703) 821-4900; fax: (703) 448-9678
Internet http://www.mars.com
Requirements US 501(c)3 nonprofit organizations are eligible.
Areas of Interest Arts, General; Civic Affairs; Costume; Cultural Activities/Programs; Education; Environmental Programs; Health Care; Restoration and Preservation; Social Services; Wildlife
Sample Awards Colonial Williamsburg (Williamsburg, VA)—for new 17th- and 18th-century costumes for the casts of the Cry Witch! program, $25,000 (2001).

Mitsubishi Electric America Foundation Grants 1228

Mitsubishi Electric America Foundation
1560 Wilson Blvd, Ste 1150
Arlington, VA 22209
Contact Program Officer, (703) 276-8240; fax: (703) 276-8260; TDD: (202) 857-0036
Internet http://www.meaf.org/grants.html
Requirements Grants are made only to 501(c)3 tax-exempt nonprofit organizations.
Restrictions The foundation does not support individuals; intermediary organizations; ethnic, fraternal, labor, or political organizations; religious organizations for religious purposes; endowments; the purchase of tickets for fundraising; or advertising, mass mailing, or conference expenses.
Areas of Interest After-School Programs; Disabled; Disabled Student Support; Disabled, Accessibility for; Educational Technology; Visual Impairments
Sample Awards Children's Hospital Medical Ctr (Cincinnati, OH)—to develop and disseminate a training program that uses handheld computers to increase the independence and employability of youths with cognitive disabilities, $120,000 over three years (2003). Computer Technologies Program (Berkeley, CA)—for a mentor program that matches disabled youths with information-technology professionals with disabilities, $100,000 over two years (2003). Girls Scouts of the Nation's Capital (Washington, DC)—to disseminate the Starfish Troops program, which provides scouting opportunities to girls in hospitals, rehabilitation centers, and long-term care facilities, $25,000 (2003).

Norfolk Southern Foundation Grants 1229

Norfolk Southern Foundation
PO Box 3040
Norfolk, VA 23514-3040
Contact Deborah Wyld, Executive Director, (757) 629-2881; fax: (757) 629-2361; e-mail: dhwyld@ nscorp.com
Internet http://www.nscorp.com/nscorp/html/ foundation.html

Requirements 501(c)3 organizations east of the Mississippi River are eligible.
Areas of Interest Arts, General; Cultural Activities/Programs; Higher Education
Sample Awards Colonial Williamsburg Foundation (Williamsburg, VA)—for a new program that will incorporate the military experiences of 18th-century blacks into Colonial Williamsburg's overall programs, $18,086 (2002).

NSF Biological Field Stations and Marine Laboratories (FSML) Grants 1230

National Science Foundation
4201 Wilson Blvd
Arlington, VA 22230
Contact Dr. Gerald Selzer, Program Director, (703) 292-8470; e-mail: gselzer@nsf.gov
Internet http://www.nsf.gov/pubs/2001/nsf0159/ nsf0159.htm
Requirements US colleges and universities, free-standing research and education institutions, and US chartered corporations with formally constituted research and education programs at field stations or marine laboratories are eligible to apply.
Areas of Interest Biological Sciences; Databases; Equipment/Instrumentation; Instrumentation, Scientific; Marine Sciences

NSF Education and Human Resources Project Grants 1231

National Science Foundation
4201 Wilson Blvd, Rm 805
Arlington, VA 22230
Contact Program Contact, (703) 292-8600; e-mail: jramaley@nsf.gov
Internet http://www.ehr.nsf.gov
Requirements Public and private colleges (two-year and four-year) and universities, state and local educational agencies, nonprofit and private organizations, professional societies, science academies and centers, science museums and zoological parks, research laboratories, and other institutions with an educational mission may apply.
Areas of Interest Education; Higher Education; Leadership; Mathematics Education; Museums; Science Education; Technology Education; Zoos

Richmond and Central Virginia Strengthening Families—Strengthening Communities Grants 1232

Community Foundation Serving Richmond and Central Virginia
7325 Beaufont Springs Dr, Ste 210
Richmond, VA 23225
Contact Susan Brown Davis, Program Officer, (804) 330-7400; fax: (804) 330-5992; e-mail: sdavis@ tcfrichmond.org
Internet http://www.tcfrichmond.org/Page2954.cfm
Requirements Proposals will be accepted from charitable organizations that serve the residents of metropolitan Richmond and Central Virginia.
Areas of Interest Children and Youth; Community Development; Day Care; Economic Self-Sufficiency; Fam-

ily; Housing; Neighborhoods; Parent Education; Poverty and the Poor; Scholarship Programs, General

Sample Awards U of Virginia (VA)—to construct a performing arts cente. and to endow a student marching-and-concert band, $10 million and $1.5 million, respectively (2003). Congregations Around Richmond Involved to Assure Shelter (VA)—for the case-management componenet of its Family Focus program, $10,000 (2002). Coal Pit Learning Ctr (Glen Allen, VA)—for its free preschool and after-school daycare services and to support board and resource development, $15,000 (2002). Sacred Heart Ctr (Richmond, VA)—to implement Bridges of Hope, a new after-school and summer program that offers academic, cultural, and recreational activities to middle school-aged youths, $125,000 (2002).

Robins Foundation Grants   1233
Robins Foundation
PO Box 1124
Richmond, VA 23218-1124
Contact William Roberts Jr., (804) 697-6917; fax: (804) 697-7233
Internet http://www.robins-foundation.org
Requirements 501(c)3 organizations based in Virginia are eligible. Organizations based in Virginia that have or support programs outside Virginia or the United States also are eligible.
Restrictions In general, the foundation does not make grants to support annual operating funds or budgets, special events or fundraising benefits, or religious purposes unless they are otherwise compatible with the objectives of the foundation.
Areas of Interest At-Risk Youth; Children and Youth; Cultural Activities/Programs; Disabled, Accessibility for; Economic Self-Sufficiency; Education; Environmental Programs; Family; Higher Education; Hospitals; Religion; Science; Social Services
Sample Awards Virginia Foundation for Independent Colleges (Richmond, VA)—to increase accessibility for mobility-impaired students and faculty members at its 15 member colleges, $152,000 (2000).

Catherine Filene Shouse Foundation Grants 1234
Catherine Filene Shouse Foundation
127 S Fairfax St, No 400
Alexandria, VA 22314
Contact Camille Warren, Secretary, (703) 549-1055
Restrictions Individuals are ineligible.
Areas of Interest Arts Administration; Arts, General; Career Education and Planning; Cultural Activities/Programs; Education; Health Care; Higher Education; Leadership; Performing Arts
Sample Awards MGH Institute of Health Professions (Boston, MA)—to renovate a building in the Charlestown Navy Yard that will serve as its future home, $2 million (2001). U of Rochester, Eastman School of Music (Rochester, NY)—for the Arts Leadership Program, which prepares students for administrative and executive roles at arts groups, $3.26 million (2000).

Virginia Commission for the Arts General   1235
Operating Support Program
Virginia Commission for the Arts
223 Governor St
Richmond, VA 23219
Contact Donna Champ Banks, Program Coordinator, (804) 225-3132; fax: (804) 225-4327; e-mail: donna. banks@arts.virginia.gov
Internet http://www.arts.state.va.us/genoper.htm
Requirements Nonprofit, tax-exempt Virginia organizations are eligible to apply.
Areas of Interest Arts Administration

Virginia Environmental Endowment   1236
Kanawha and Ohio River Valleys
Program
Virginia Environmental Endowment
PO Box 790, 1051 E Cary St, 3 James Ctr, Ste 1400
Richmond, VA 23218-0790
Contact Gerald McCarthy, Executive Director, (804) 644-5000; e-mail: info@vee.org
Internet http://www.vee.org/programs.cfm
Requirements Constructive, result-oriented projects that are conducted by existing nonprofit organizations are funded. Activities that unite business, government, and civic interests for environmental improvement are encouraged, as are projects that serve as models for other communities. Organizations must be in Kentucky or West Virginia.
Areas of Interest Business; Citizenship; Civic Affairs; Ecology, Aquatic; Education; Environmental Education; Environmental Health; Environmental Programs; Fish and Fisheries; Public Health; Regional Planning/ Policy; Water Pollution; Water Resources
Sample Awards U of Charleston (WV)—for the metals analysis component of the Kanawha River Project, $25,000.

Virginia Environmental Endowment   1237
Virginia Program Grants
Virginia Environmental Endowment
PO Box 790, 1051 E Cary St
Richmond, VA 23206-0790
Contact Gerald McCarthy, Executive Director, (804) 644-5000; e-mail: info@vee.org
Internet http://www.cvco.org/vee/programs.htm
Requirements Eligible for funding are constructive, result-oriented projects that are conducted by existing Virginia nonprofit organizations. Activities that unite business, government, and civic interests for environmental improvement are encouraged, as are projects that serve as models for other communities.
Areas of Interest Botanical Gardens; Business; Citizenship; Civic Affairs; Conservation, Natural Resources; Economic Development; Environmental Education; Environmental Law; Environmental Planning/Policy; Environmental Programs; Forestry Management; Government; Land Use Planning/Policy; Marine Sciences; Pollution Control; Poverty and the Poor; Sustainable Development
Sample Awards Commonwealth of Virginia (Richmond, VA)—for the Governor's Natural Resources Leadership Summit, $10,000 (2003). Nature Conservancy Action Fund of Virginia (Charlottesville, VA)— for a campaign to increase support for natural-resources

programs in Virginia, $74,445 (2003). Valley Conservation Council (Staunton, VA)—to expand its Community Partnership conservation initiatives in Botetourt County, $16,000 (2003). U of Virginia (VA)—for an environmental-education project that uses Internet technology to serve secondary-school students in Virginia's Eastern Shore region, $105,399 (2003).

webMethods Foundation Grants   1238
webMethods Foundation
3930 Pender Dr
Fairfax, VA 22030
Contact Grants Administrator, (703) 460-6080; fax: (703) 460-2599; e-mail: foundation@webMethods.org
Internet http://www.webMethods.org
Requirements 501(c)3 charitable organizations within a 100-mile radius of Washington, DC, are eligible.
Areas of Interest Children and Youth; Disadvantaged (Economically); Family; Homelessness; Housing

Washington

ATR Foundation One-Year Basic Grants   1240
A Territory Resource Foundation
603 Stewart St, Ste 1007
Seattle, WA 98101
Contact Program Contact, (206) 624-4081; fax: (206) 382-2640; e-mail: grants@atrfoundation.org
Internet http://www.atrfoundation.org/grants/index.htm
Requirements Only residents of Idaho, Montana, Oregon, Washington, and Wyoming may apply.
Areas of Interest Agricultural Economics; Civil/Human Rights; Environmental Programs; Public Affairs; Public Planning/Policy; Rural Areas; Social Change
Sample Awards Idaho Rural Council (Boise, ID)—for general support to preserve Idaho's rural way of life by protecting the environment and promoting a more just agricultural economy through organizing, education, and policy development, $12,000.

ATR Foundation Three-Year Support Grants   1241
A Territory Resource Foundation
603 Stewart St, Ste 1007
Seattle, WA 98101
Contact Grants Manager, (206) 624-4081; fax: (206) 382-2640; e-mail: grants@atrfoundation.org
Internet http://www.atrfoundation.org/grants/index.htm
Requirements Only organizations in Idaho, Montana, Oregon, Washington, and Wyoming may apply. To be eligible for these grants, organizations must have received a spring, fall, major, or one-year basic grant from ATR within the last five years.
Areas of Interest Civil/Human Rights; Public Affairs; Social Change
Sample Awards Chaya (Seattle, WA)—for grassroots organizing and leadership-development activities dealing with violence among immigrants and refugees from South Asia, $45,000 over three years (2003). Environmental Justice Action Group (Portland, OR)—for community-based organizing activities that address air pollu-

tion and its effects on the health of Portland residents, $45,000 over three years (2003). Powder River Basin Resource Council (Douglas, WY)—for community-based efforts to conserve Wyoming's land, mineral, and water resources and to protect air quality in the state, $45,000 over three years (2003). VOZ: Worker's Rights Education Project (Portland, OR)—to promote the rights of immigrant workers, particularly day laborers, through organizing, leadership development, and community education, $45,000 over three years (2003).

Brainerd Foundation Grants   1242
Brainerd Foundation
1601 Second Ave, Ste 610
Seattle, WA 98101-1541
Contact Paul Brainerd, President, or Ann Krumboltz, Executive Director, (206) 448-0676; fax: (206) 448-7222; e-mail: info@brainerd.org
Internet http://www.brainerd.org
Requirements Nonprofit organizations in the Pacific Northwest are eligible.
Restrictions The foundation does not favor proposals for school education programs, land acquisition, endowments, capital campaigns, projects sponsored by government agencies, basic research, fellowships, or books or videos that are not part of a broader strategy.
Areas of Interest Civic Affairs; Communications; Deserts and Arid Zones; Ecology; Environmental Economics; Environmental Effects; Environmental Law; Environmental Programs; Environmental Studies; Grassroots Leadership; Mass Media; Mining; Organizational Theory and Behavior
Sample Awards Alaska Wilderness League (Washington, DC)—to protect the wildlands, fisheries, and wildlife resources of Alaska, $40,000 (2003). Ctr for Environmental Citizenship (Washington, DC)—to help environmental groups in the US Northwest promote participation and leadership among youths, $35,000 (2003). Mineral Policy Ctr (Washington, DC)—for a campaign to revamp state and federal mining laws and regulations, $30,000 (2003). Wilderness Society (Washington, DC)—for public education on the conservation of federally protected wildlands in the US West, $100,000 (2003).

Bullitt Foundation Grants   1243
Bullitt Foundation
1212 Minor Ave
Seattle, WA 98101
Contact Amy Solomon, Program Officer , (206) 343-0807; fax: (206) 343-0822; e-mail: asolomon@bullitt.org
Internet http://www.bullitt.org
Requirements Nonprofit organizations in the Pacific Northwest, including Washington, Oregon, Idaho, western Montana, coastal rainforests in Alaska, and British Columbia, Canada are eligible.
Restrictions The foundation does not consider requests for university overhead costs.
Areas of Interest Air Pollution; Climatology; Conservation, Agriculture; Conservation, Natural Resources; Energy Conservation; Environmental Education; Environmental Law; Environmental Programs; Health Promo-

tion; Leadership; Toxic Substances; Transportation; Water Resources; Wildlife; Youth Programs

Sample Awards North Seattle Community College Foundation (WA)—to support a model project for watershed educational activities, $10,000. Washington's National Park Fund (WA)—to support a program for youth from local school districts, $5000.

Community Foundation of South Puget Sound Grants 1244

Community Foundation of South Puget
111 Market St NE, Ste 375
Olympia, WA 98501
Contact Grants Administrator, (360) 705-3340; e-mail: legacy@thecommunityfoundation.com
Internet http://www.thecommunityfoundation.com/grantguidelines.html
Requirements The foundation awards grants to Washington tax-exempt organizations primarily for use in Thurston, Mason, and Lewis Counties, except on instructions of the donor at the time of the gift or bequest.
Restrictions Grants do not support religious organizations for religious purposes; individuals; annual campaigns of organizations (direct mail or special events); political or lobbying activities; organizations that discriminate based on race, creed, or ethnic group; capital campaigns for bricks and mortar or endowment funds; or for multiple year commitments.
Areas of Interest Cultural Activities/Programs; Education; Health; Social Services Delivery

Comprehensive Health Education Foundation Grants 1245

Comprehensive Health Education Foundation
22419 Pacific Hwy S
Seattle, WA 98198
Contact Sue Haughton, (206) 824-2907 ; fax: (206) 824-3072; e-mail: foundation.grants@chef.org
Internet http://www.chef.org/about/grants.php?var=x&PHPSESSID=9cfa37001872ca0e2169466a2a7e0a67
Requirements Washington State 501(c)3 tax-exempt organizations and units of government that are nondiscriminatory in policy and practice regarding disabilities, age, sex, sexual orientation, race, ethnic origin, or creed are eligible.
Restrictions Support will not be provided for building or land acquisitions; equipment or furniture purchases; endowment funds; emergency funds; grants to individuals; fellowships/scholarships; research; debt retirement; fundraising activities; general fund drives; indirect overhead; or CHEF programs or products.
Areas of Interest Children and Youth; Elderly; Health Care; Health Education; Health Promotion; Mental Health; Parent Education
Sample Awards Vanessa Behan Crisis Nursery (WA)—for parent education classes and support groups, $5000 (2002). Spokane School District #81 (WA)—for a blended curriculum for the fifth grade that includes classroom teachers and fitness and health specialists, $8500 (2002). Market Foundation (WA)—for the Senior Wellness program, which gives impoverished urban seniors the opportunity to learn how to improve their health, $5000 (2002).

Forest Foundation Grants 1246

Forest Foundation
820 A St, Ste 345
Tacoma, WA 98402
Contact Frank Underwood, Executive Director, (253) 627-1634
Requirements Washington nonprofit organizations in Pierce County are eligible. Capital requests outside of Pierce County will be considered.
Restrictions Grants do not support individuals, endowment funds, debt retirement, annual appeals, research, fellowships, films, publications, or scholarships.
Areas of Interest Arts, General; Environmental Programs; Social Services; Social Services Delivery
Sample Awards Seattle Ctr Foundation (WA)—for its capital campaign for the Marion Oliver McCaw Hall performing arts center, $250,000 (2003).

Foundation Northwest Grants 1247

Foundation Northwest
221 N Wall St, Ste 624
Spokane, WA 99201-0826
Contact C. Hanford, Vice President, (509) 624-2606; fax: (509) 624-2608; email: info@foundationnw.org
Internet http://www.foundationnw.org
Requirements Grant applications are accepted for projects that will enrich the quality of life in the communities of eastern Washington and northern Idaho. Eligible Washington counties include Adams, Asotin, Columbia, Ferry, Garfield, Lincoln, Pend Oreille, Spokane, Steven, and Whitman. Eligible Idaho counties include Benewah, Bonner, Boundary, Clearwater, Idaho, Kootenai, Latah, Lewis, Nez Perce, and Shoshone.
Restrictions Grants do not support endowments, debt retirement, lobbying, sectarian religious purposes, individuals, travel, sports teams and classes, projects that taxpayers or commercial interests normally support, fundraising campaigns, publications or films (unless an integral part of a foundation-supported program), or nondonor-supported research.
Areas of Interest Civic Affairs; Community Development; Cultural Activities/Programs; Dramatic/Theater Arts; Education; Music; Philanthropy; Social Services

Bill and Melinda Gates Foundation Grants 1248

Bill and Melinda Gates Foundation
PO Box 23350
Seattle, WA 98122
Contact Program Contact, (206) 709-3140; e-mail: info@gatesfoundation.org
Internet http://www.gatesfoundation.org/grants/eligibilityandguidelines/default.htm
Requirements 501(c)3 tax-exempt organizations are eligible. Priority is given to requests in the Pacific Northwest, including Idaho, Oregon, and Washington.
Areas of Interest Cancer Prevention; Child/Maternal Health; Computer Grants; Developing/Underdeveloped Nations; Disaster Relief; Education; Educational Technology; Emergency Programs; Health Care; Health Promotion; International Programs; Internet; Libraries; Middle School Education; Neighborhoods; Poverty and the Poor; Pregnancy; Preventive Medicine; Regional Planning/Policy; Secondary Education; Teacher Education, Inservice; Technology; Women's Health

Sample Awards International Partnership for Microbicides (Silver Spring, MD)—to accelerate the discovery, development, and accessibility of topical microbicides that can prevent HIV transmission, $60 million (2003). Foundation for California Community Colleges (Sacramento, CA)—to create 15 early-college high-schools at which students can earn either college credits or an associate's degree, $9 million (2003). Portland Community College (OR)—to create eight alternative high schools, $4.9 million (2003). Big Picture Co (Providence, RI)—to provide technical assistance to a network of groups working to duplicate high-quality alternative high schools, to expand and improve existing schools, to convert programs that offer GEDs into schools that offer high-school diplomas, and to initiate policy and other efforts, $1.9 million (2003).

Glaser Progress Foundation Grants 1249

Glaser Progress Foundation
PO Box 91123
Seattle, WA 98111
Contact Leslie McDonald, Operations Director, (206) 728-1050; fax: (206) 728-1123; e-mail: leslie@ glaserprogress.org or grants@glaserprogress.org
Internet http://www.glaserprogress.org
Requirements US 501(c)3 tax-exempt organizations are eligible.
Areas of Interest Animal Care; Internet; Media; Social Change; Technology
Sample Awards Yale U (New Haven, CT)—for the G-ECON Project, to explore the relationship between economics and geography, $100,000 (2002). Doris Day Animal Foundation (Washington, DC)—for general support of the Chimpanzee Collaboratory, $14,000 (2003). Independent Media Institute (San Francisco, CA)—to support AlterNet's online magazine and digest, $20,000 (2002). Columbia University (New York, NY)—to support the Access Project for the Global Fund to Fight AIDS, Tuberculosis, and Malaria, $450,000 (2002).

Greater Tacoma Community Foundation 1250 Grants

Greater Tacoma Community Foundation
PO Box 1995, 1019 Pacific Ave
Tacoma, WA 98401-1995
Contact Lynn Rumball, Program Officer, (253) 383-5622; fax: (253) 272-8099; e-mail: lrumball@gtcf. org
Internet http://www.tacomafoundation.org
Requirements IRS 501(c)3 tax-exempt organizations serving the greater Tacoma-Pierce County area are eligible.
Restrictions Grants will not be made for/to annual campaign appeals, individuals, political or lobbying activities, religious organizations for religious purposes, deficit reduction, or publications except those that grow out of research and experiments underwritten by the foundation.
Areas of Interest Arts, General; Civic Affairs; Cultural Activities/Programs; Economic Development; Education; Health Care; Minority Education; Social Services; Youth Programs

Sample Awards Kids in Distressed Situations (New York, NY)—to provide donated products to low-income children and families in Tacoma and Pierce County, WA, through the Emergency Food Network, $25,000 (2002).

Handsel Foundation Grants 1251

Handsel Foundation
PO Box 1322
Freeland, WA 98249
Contact Diane Johnson, President, (360) 331-7282; fax: (360) 331-5793; e-mail: handselfdn@aol.com
Requirements US nonprofit organizations are eligible. Grants typically support projects in the western United States.
Areas of Interest Animal Care; Computer Grants; Computer Software; Economic Development; Hearing Impairments; Native American Education; Native Americans
Sample Awards Humane Society of Del Norte (Crescent City, CA)—to purchase computer and office equipment, $5500. Turtle Mountain Community College (Belcourt, ND)—to purchase computer equipment, software, and furniture, $22,270. American Indian Higher Education Consortium (Alexandria, VA)—for publication of the American Indian Higher Education Journal, $4000. Hearing Impaired Press (Berkeley, CA)—to assist with operating expenses for the OWL Program, $20,712.

Harder Foundation Grants 1252

Harder Foundation
401 Broadway
Tacoma, WA 98402
Contact Mary Martin, Office Manager, (253) 593-2121; fax: (253) 593-2122; e-mail: harder1@ wolfenet.com
Requirements Nonprofit environmental groups or projects in Alaska, Colorado, Florida, Idaho, Montana, Nevada, Oregon, Utah, Washington, and Wyoming are eligible.
Restrictions Local projects with limited scope, environmental education programs, and public policy development are not funded.
Areas of Interest Ecology; Environmental Programs; Fish and Fisheries; Forests and Woodlands; Water Resources; Wildlife
Sample Awards Greater Yellowstone Coalition—to support a project for grizzly bear protection, $12,000. Save Our Wild Salmon Coalition—for general support, $14,500.

Kitsap Community Foundation Grants 1253

Kitsap Community Foundation
PO Box 3670
Silverdale, WA 98383
Contact Executive Director, (360) 698-3622; e-mail: kcf@kitsapfoundation.org
Internet http://www.kitsapfoundation.org/grantgd. html
Requirements Washington 501(c)3 nonprofit organizations in Kitsap County and its neighboring communities are eligible.
Restrictions Generally, the foundation does not make grants to annual campaign appeals; endowments; indi-

viduals; political or lobbying activities; religious organizations for sacramental or theological purposes; publications except those that grow out of research and experiments underwritten by the foundation; or deficit reduction.

Areas of Interest Arts; Cultural Activities/Programs; Civic Affairs; Community Development; Education; Environmental Programs; Health; Recreation; Social Services Delivery; Youth Programs

Kongsgaard-Goldman Foundation Grants 1254

Kongsgaard-Goldman Foundation
1932 First Ave, Ste 602
Seattle, WA 98101
Contact Martha Kongsgaard, Vice President, (206) 448-1874; fax: (206) 448-1973; e-mail: kgf@ kongsgaard-goldman.org
Internet http://www.kongsgaard-goldman.org/ program.html
Requirements Organizations classified as 501(c)3 or 149(1)f (Canada) may apply. Grants are limited to organizations in the Pacific Northwest (Washington, Oregon, Idaho, Alaska, Montana) and British Columbia, Canada.
Restrictions Grants are not awarded to support direct services, clinical and health services, medical research grants to individuals, wildlife rehabilitation programs, land acquisition, or funding of individual scholarships or fellowships.
Areas of Interest Arts, General; Churches; Civic Affairs; Civil/Human Rights; Environmental Programs; Hearing Impairments; Humanities; Jewish Services; Leadership; Special Education; Training and Development
Sample Awards Chamber Music In Napa Valley (Napa, CA)—for general support, $5000 (2002). Pacific Crest Biodiversity Project (Seattle, WA)—to support the NW Old Growth Campaign and the Wildlands Restoration Program, $8000 (2002). Jewish Family Service (Seattle, WA)—to promote the growth and development of Jews of all ages in greater King County to lead productive and meaningful lives, $20,000 (2002).

Byron W. and Alice L. Lockwood 1255 Foundation Grants

Byron W. and Alice L. Lockwood Foundation
11033 NE 24th St, Ste 200
Bellevue, WA 98004
Contact Grants Administrator, (206) 232-1881
Requirements Washington nonprofit organizations are eligible. Grants are awarded primarily in Washington's Seattle and Puget Sound areas.
Areas of Interest Arts, General; Biomedical Research; Education; Health Care; Health Care Administration; Higher Education; Hospitals; Housing; Museums; Religion; Religious Welfare Programs; Social Services Delivery
Sample Awards Seattle's Union Gospel Mission (Seattle, WA)—for capital improvements at the men's shelter, $50,000 (2003).

Medina Foundation Grants 1256

Medina Foundation
801 2nd Ave, Ste 1300
Seattle, WA 98104
Contact Gregory Barlow, Executive Director, (206) 464-5231; fax: (206) 652-8791; e-mail: medina@ medinafoundation.org
Internet http://www.medinafoundation.org/guidelin. htm
Requirements Organizations operating within the greater Puget Sound region or to projects significantly affecting its residents are eligible. The greater Puget Sound region is defined as the following counties: Clallum, Grays Harbor, Island, Jefferson, King, Kitsap, Mason, Pacific, Pierce, San Juan, Skagit, Snohomish, Thurston, and Whatcom.
Restrictions Requests will not be accepted from public schools or cultural programs.
Areas of Interest Alcohol Education; Alternative Modes of Education; Career Education and Planning; Compensatory Education; Disabled; Drug Education; Family; Food Distribution; Housing; Leadership; Mentoring Programs; Middle School Education; Personnel Training and Development; Private and Parochial Education; Religious Welfare Programs; Service Delivery Programs; Social Services; Vocational/Technical Education
Sample Awards Seattle's Union Gospel Mission (Seattle, WA)—for capital improvements at the men's shelter, $50,000 (2003).

Microsoft Community Affairs Washington 1257 State Contributions

Microsoft Corporation
1 Microsoft Way
Redmond, WA 98052-6399
Contact Bruce Brooks, (425) 936-8185; fax: (425) 936-7329; e-mail: giving@microsoft.com
Internet http://www.microsoft.com/giving
Requirements The corporation contributes cash and software to 501(c)3 nonprofits in the Puget Sound, WA, area.
Restrictions Charitable grants are not made to individuals; political, labor, religious, or fraternal organizations; amateur sports groups, teams, or events; conferences or symposia; hospitals or medical clinics; or programs serving people and communities outside the United States (some exceptions are made for pilot programs initiated by Microsoft subsidiaries).
Areas of Interest Arts Administration; Arts, General; Civic Affairs; Computer Grants; Computer Software; Cultural Activities/Programs; Curriculum Development; Economic Development; Education; Environmental Programs; Family; Food Distribution; Government; Higher Education; Information Science/Systems; Job Training Programs; Libraries, Public; Social Services; Technology; Training and Development; Youth Programs
Sample Awards Elderhealth Northwest (Seattle, WA)—to construct low-cost housing units for elderly people, $50,000 (2002). Urban Enterprise Ctr (Seattle, WA)—to foster effective dialogues on race and to expand job creation and economic development in the Central and Rainier Valley neighborhoods of Seattle, $25,000 (2002). Washington Early Learning Foundation (Seattle, WA)—for a statewide public-awareness campaign on early childhood development, $15,000 (2001). Boys and Girls Clubs of King County (Seattle, WA)—for its capital campaign, $175,000 (2000).

Norcliffe Foundation Grants 1258
Norcliffe Foundation
999 Third Ave, First Interstate Ctr, Ste 1006
Seattle, WA 98104
Contact Dana Pigott, President, (206) 682-4820
Requirements Washington 501(c)3 organizations may apply.
Restrictions Grants are not awarded to individuals or for deficit financing.
Areas of Interest Adult and Continuing Education; Basic Skills Education; Biomedical Research; Conservation, Natural Resources; Cultural Activities/Programs; Dramatic/Theater Arts; Elderly; Higher Education; Hospitals; Literacy; Religion; Restoration and Preservation; Secondary Education; Vocational/Technical Education; Youth Programs
Sample Awards Seattle Center Foundation (Seattle, WA)—to construct Marion Oliver McCaw Hall, $1 million.

RealNetworks Foundation Grants 1259
RealNetworks Foundation
PO Box 91123
Seattle, WA 98111-9223
Contact Grants Administrator, (206) 892-6644; fax: (206) 956-8249; e-mail: info@realfoundation.org
Internet http://www.realfoundation.org/grants/index.html
Areas of Interest Internet; Quality of Life; Technology
Sample Awards Reporters Without Borders (Paris, France)—for operating support, $31,000 (2003). Family Services (Seattle, WA)—for services for homeless children, $10,000 (2003). American Anti-Slavery Group (Boston, MA)—for the iAbolish Anti-Slavery Web site, $20,000 (2003).

Seattle Foundation Grants 1260
Seattle Foundation
425 Pike St, Ste 510
Seattle, WA 98101
Contact Ceil Erickson, Director of Community Grantmaking Program, (206) 622-2294 ext 141; e-mail: erickson@seattlefoundation.org
Internet http://www.seafound.org/grantseekers/index.html
Requirements IRS 501(c)3 tax-exempt organizations located in King County, WA, are eligible.
Restrictions Grants are not made to individuals or to religious organizations for religious purposes. Grants will not be awarded for endowment; general purposes; funding of conferences or seminars; discriminatory purposes on the basis of race or creed; or the production of books, films, or videos.
Areas of Interest Children and Youth; Citizenship; Conservation, Natural Resources; Cultural Activities/Programs; Dental Health; Education; Elderly; Health Promotion; Jewish Services; Neighborhoods; Physical Medicine and Rehabilitation; Public Affairs; Rehabilitation/Therapy; Social Services Delivery
Sample Awards Civic Light Opera (Seattle, WA)—to purchase a sound system, and for operating support, $10,000 (2003). Jewish Family Service (Seattle, WA)—for its capital-renovation campaign, $25,000 (2003). Ctr for Environmental Law and Policy (Seattle, WA)—for

operating costs and computer equipment, $10,000 (2003). Northwest Medical Teams International-Western Washington (Bellevue, WA)—to support the Mobile Dental Unit Program in western Washington State, $15,000 (2003).

Simpson Fund Grants 1261
Simpson Fund
1301 Fifth Ave, Ste 2800
Seattle, WA 98101-2613
Contact Grants Administrator, (206) 224-5198; e-mail: cmusgra@simpson.com
Internet http://www.simpson.com/fundinfo.cfm
Requirements Contributions are limited to Simpson communities: Washington—downtown Seattle, Tacoma, Mason County, Grays Harbor County, and Thurston County; Oregon—Lincoln and Tillamook Counties; and California—Del Norte and Humboldt Counties.
Areas of Interest Arts, General; Community Service Programs; Conservation, Natural Resources; Economic Development; Education; Environmental Programs; Forest Products Industry; Forestry and Woodlands; Health Care; Health Services Delivery

SVP Early Childhood Development and 1262 Parenting Grants
Social Venture Partners
1601 Second Ave, Ste 605
Seattle, WA 98101-1541
Contact Paul Shoemaker, Executive Director, (206) 374-8757; fax: (206) 728-0552; e-mail: paulshoe@svpseattle.org or info@svpseattle.org
Internet http://www.svpseattle.org/grant_guidelines/early_childhood.htm
Requirements Programs must serve King County in Washington. Applicants must be classified as nonprofit 501(c)3 public charities or public schools or school districts qualifying under section 170(c) of the IRS code.
Restrictions The foundation does not consider requests from individuals, organizations that discriminate, religious organizations for sectarian purposes, sports teams, and political or lobbying organizations. The foundation does not consider requests for auctions or fund-raising events, debt reduction, endowment funds or capital campaigns, litigation or legal expenses, land acquisition, productions, or performances.
Areas of Interest Children and Youth; Counseling/Guidance; Curriculum Development; Education; Equipment/Instrumentation; Instructional Materials and Practices; Parent Involvement; Program Evaluation; Service Delivery Programs; Teacher Education, Inservice; Volunteers
Sample Awards Kimball Elementary School (WA)—to continue funding for the counselor and coordinator positions as well as start-up funds for an extended learning program, $45,000. Youth Eastside Services (WA)—to hire program evaluation and research staff, a parenting volunteer coordinator, and to network the YES agency, $60,000.

Washington Mutual Foundation Grants   1263
Washington Mutual Foundation
999 3rd Ave, FIS2913
Seattle, WA 98104
Contact Marc Frazer, (800) 258-0543 or (206) 461-4663
Internet http://www.wamu.com
Requirements Nonprofits serving low-to-moderate income areas in California, Florida, Idaho, Illinois, Massachusetts, Montana, Nevada, New York, Oregon, Texas, Utah, and the state of Washington are eligible.
Restrictions Recipients of United Way funds are ineligible.
Areas of Interest Children and Youth; Disaster Relief; Elementary Education; Housing; Secondary Education
Sample Awards American National Red Cross (Washington, DC)—for relief efforts related to the recent widespread wildfires in California, $250,000 (2003). New Teacher Project (New York, NY)—for Teaching for Results, a series of seminars designed to support midcareer professionals in Atlanta, Los Angeles, and New York as they make the transition to teaching careers, $1.25 million (2003). Local Initiatives Support Corp (New York, NY)—to support urban and rural neighborhood-revitalization efforts at various sites nationwide, and to support the organization's national operations, Center for Home Ownership, and rural-development programs, $1.15 million (2002). Neighborhood Reinvestment Corp (Washington, DC)—for the National NeighborWorks Week 2002 and to provide scholarship support to people attending Neighborhood Reinvestment Training Institutes, $1.6 million (2002).

Weyerhaeuser Company Foundation Contributions Program   1264
Weyerhaeuser Company Foundation
PO Box 9777
Federal Way, WA 98063-9777
Contact Elizabeth Crossman, President, (253) 924-3159; fax: (253) 924-3658; e-mail: foundation@weyerhaeuser.com
Internet http://www.weyerhaeuser.com/citizenship/philanthropy/default.asp
Requirements Applying organizations must have nonprofit, tax-exempt status. The foundation concentrates on direct services in the communities where Weyerhaeuser has significant land holdings and operating facilities, including Alabama, Arkansas, Mississippi, North Carolina, Oklahoma, Oregon, and Washington. A limited number of smaller awards are also made to other locales where fewer employees are based.
Restrictions Grants are not awarded to individuals or for political campaigns, activities that influence legislation, religious organizations seeking funds for theological purposes, or funds to purchase tickets or tables at fundraising benefits.
Areas of Interest Arts, General; Community Development; Cultural Activities/Programs; Curriculum Development; Education; Environmental Programs; Forest Products Industry; Forests and Woodlands; Health Care; Land Management; Public Affairs; Public Planning/Policy; Social Services; Youth Programs
Sample Awards World Forestry Ctr (Portland, OR)—for its capital campaign, including exhibit renovation and a marketing study, $1 million (2002).

Whatcom Community Foundation Grants   1265
Whatcom Community Foundation
119 Grand Ave, Ste A
Bellingham, WA 98225
Contact Grants Administrator, (360) 671-6463; fax: (360) 671-6437; e-mail: wcf@whatcomcf.org
Internet http://www.nas.com/~wcf
Requirements Washington tax-exempt nonprofit organizations serving Whatcom County are eligible.
Restrictions Grants do not support capital requests (bricks and mortar); endowment funds; debt retirement; political campaigns; religious activities; memberships in civic organizations or trade associations; courtesy advertising; tickets for benefits; fundraising events, individuals; for-profit organizations; or organizations that discriminate on the basis of gender, religion, sexual orientation, ethnicity, national origin, or physical ability.
Areas of Interest Children and Youth; Community Services; Education; Environmental Programs; Family; Quality of Life
Sample Awards Safe Start Consortium (WA)—for a staff position to coordinate multi-agency strategic planning and fund development for reducing the exposure of young children to violence, $10,000. National Information Center for Ecology (WA)—for a project involving children in wildlife habitat enhancement along Fever Creek in Bellingham, $5000. Cornwall Park Church of God (WA)—for a summer program for children in first through fifth grades who have endured high-stress experiences, $4000. Lynden Pioneer Museum (WA)—for the museums' elementary educational workshops, $400.

Women's Funding Alliance Grants   1266
Women's Funding Alliance
603 Stewart St, Ste 207
Seattle, WA 98101
Contact LeAnne Moss, Executive Director, (206) 467-6733; fax: (206) 467-7537; e-mail: leanne@wfalliance.org or wfa@wfalliance.org
Internet http://www.wfalliance.org/grants.htm
Requirements Washington nonprofits are eligible.
Areas of Interest Children and Youth; Civil/Human Rights; Cultural Diversity; Domestic Violence; Education; Employment Opportunity Programs; Human Reproduction/Fertility; Leadership; Poverty and the Poor; Sexual Abuse; Women
Sample Awards Casa Latina (Seattle, WA)—to help low-income Latinas develop leadership skills and find jobs, $10,000 (2003). Safeplace (Olympia, WA)—to provide services for women affected by domestic violence and sexual assault, $10,000 (2003). Seattle Girls' School (WA)—to hire a development director, $10,000 (2003). Southern Sudanese Women's Assoc (Seattle, WA)—to set up an office and begin a program for Sudanese girls, $10,000 (2003).

West Virginia

Daywood Foundation Grants   1267
Daywood Foundation
1600 Bank One Ctr
Charleston, WV 25301
Contact William Booker, Secretary-Treasurer, (304) 345-8900

Requirements West Virginia nonprofits in Barbour, Charleston, Greenbrier, Kanawha, and Lewisburg Counties are eligible.

Restrictions Grants do not support endowment funds, research, individuals, or individual scholarships or fellowships.

Areas of Interest Arts, General; Community Development; Higher Education; Social Services; Youth Programs

West Virginia Commission on the Arts 1268 Major Institutions Support Grants

West Virginia Commission on the Arts
1900 Kanawha Blvd E
Charleston, WV 25305-0300
Contact Barbara Anderson, Grants Coordinator, (304) 558-0220; fax: (304) 558-2779; TDD: (304) 558-0220; e-mail: barbie.anderson@wvculture.org
Internet http://www.wvculture.org/arts/grantsbk.html# programs
Requirements Applicant organizations must have a minimum operating base of at least $500,000; be in existence for five years as a West Virginia nonprofit organization, during which time a permanent, paid, professional staff has administered the organization's programming on an annual basis; serve a large audience that represents a broad cross section of citizens, including people who are disabled or institutionalized, senior citizens, lower income groups, and culturally diverse audiences; demonstrate compliance with Section 504 of the Rehabilitation Act; and contribute to the development of West Virginia's culture.
Restrictions Organizations whose primary thrust is education and that award academic credits; organizations whose main purpose is not the arts; divisions or departments of larger institutions; national service organizations; and organizations receiving funds from other state agencies are ineligible.
Areas of Interest Arts Administration; Arts, General; Community Development; Community Outreach Programs; Cultural Diversity; Disabled; Economically Disadvantaged; Elderly; Museums; Orchestras

West Virginia Commission on the Arts 1269 Planning and Organizational Development Grants

West Virginia Commission on the Arts
1900 Kanawha Blvd E
Charleston, WV 25305
Contact Barbara Anderson, Grants Coordinator, (304) 558-0220; fax: (304) 558-2779; e-mail: barbie. anderson@wvculture.org
Internet http://www.wvculture.org/arts/grantsbk.html# programs
Requirements Only residents of West Virginia may apply.
Areas of Interest Arts Administration

Wisconsin

Helen Bader Foundation Grants 1270

Helen Bader Foundation
233 N Water St, 4th Fl
Milwaukee, WI 53202
Contact Program Contact, (414) 224-6464; fax: (414) 224-1441; e-mail: info@hbf.org
Internet http://www.hbf.org/index.html
Requirements 501(c)3 tax-exempt organizations are eligible. Grants will only be approved for foreign entities that meet specific charitable status requirements.
Restrictions The foundation does not provide financial support for ongoing operating expenses, deficits, fundraising, loans, or as direct support for individuals.
Areas of Interest Alzheimer's Disease; Business Development; Child Psychology/Development; Economic Development; Education; Family; Human Learning and Memory; International Programs; Israel; Jewish Studies; Neighborhoods; Nonprofit Organizations; Religion; Senile Dementia; Sports
Sample Awards Saint Ann Ctr for Intergenerational Care (Milwaukee, WI)—to enhance its therapeutic recreational activities for older adults, $141,042 over three years (2002). America's Black Holocaust Museum (Milwaukee, WI)—for general operating support, $10,000 (2002). Assoc for the Absorption of Immigrants in Haifa (Israel)—for its prekindergarten programs for new immigrant children, $20,000 (2002). Esperanza Unida (Milwaukee, WI)—for its construction-training program for low-income young adults, $40,000 (2002).

Lynde and Harry Bradley Foundation 1271 Grants Program

Lynde and Harry Bradley Foundation
PO Box 510860
Milwaukee, WI 53203-0153
Contact Michael Joyce, President, (414) 291-9915; fax: (414) 291-9991
Internet http://www.bradleyfdn.org/app.html
Requirements Tax-exempt and nonprofit organizations should prepare a letter of inquiry presenting a concise description of the project, its objectives and significance, and the qualifications of the organizations and individuals involved. If the project appears to fall within the foundation's mandate, a brochure with detailed proposal requirements will be sent to the applicant.
Restrictions The foundation favors projects that are normally not financed by public funds and will consider requests from religious organizations that are not denominational in character. Grants without significant importance to the foundation's areas of interest will only under special conditions be considered for endowment or deficit financing proposals. Grants will not be made to individuals, for overhead costs, or for fund-raising counsel.
Areas of Interest Academic Achievement; Civic Affairs; Cultural Activities/Programs; Curriculum Development; Economic Development; Education; Fellowship Programs, General; Gifted/Talented Education; Health Services Delivery; Higher Education; International Planning/Policy; Local Government; Neighborhoods; Poverty and the Poor; Private and Parochial Education; Public Affairs; Public Planning/Policy; Publication; Scholarship Programs, General; Social Services; State Government; Urban Areas

Sample Awards Princeton U (NJ)—for research on US national-security strategy in Asia, $20,000 (2003). Bel Canto Chorus (Milwaukee, WI)—for general support, $30,000 (2003). Northwest Side Community Development Corp (Milwaukee, WI)—for program support, $15,000 (2003). La Casa de Esperanza (Waukesa, WI)— for capital support, $25,000 (2003).

Brico Fund Grants   1272
Brico Fund
205 E Wisconsin Ave, Ste 200
Milwaukee, WI 53202
Contact Program Contact, (414) 272-2747; fax: (414) 272-2036; e-mail: bricofund@bricofund.org
Internet http://www.bricofund.org
Requirements The fund supports organizations with projects and programs within the Greater Milwaukee community. Some funding is done statewide or nationally for programs of broader scope.
Restrictions Grants do not support conferences and meetings, disease-specific programs, educational institutions, individuals, media projects, medical institutions, religions, or organizations with a focus on animals.
Areas of Interest Civil/Human Rights; Conservation, Natural Resources; Economic Development; Environmental Programs; Women
Sample Awards 1000 Friends (WI)—for the opening of a Milwaukee office to explore transportation and smart growth issues, $30,000 (2003. Fondy Market—to support building of the market, $50,000 (2003). Growing Power—for operating support, $115,000 (2003). Midtown Neighborhood Assoc—to support an urban tree house and education program, $35,000 (2003). Urban Ecology $ 20,000

Frank G. and Freida K. Brotz Family   1273
  Foundation Grants
Frank G. and Freida K. Brotz Family Foundation
PO Box 551, 3518 Lakeshore Rd
Sheboygan, WI 53082-0551
Contact Grants Commissioner, (920) 458-2121
Requirements Wisconsin nonprofits are eligible.
Areas of Interest Community Service Programs; Higher Education; Hospitals; Private and Parochial Education; Religion; Religious Studies; Youth Programs
Sample Awards YMCA (Sheboygan, WI)—for capital development, $50,000. Christ Child Academy (Sheboygan, WI)—for general support, $15,000. Tyme Out Youth Ministry (Pewaukee, WI)—for general support, $2500.

Greater Green Bay Community Foundation 1274
  Grants
Greater Green Bay Community Foundation
302 N Adams St, Ste 100
Green Bay, WI 54301
Contact Steve Schumeisser, Treasurer, (920) 432-0800; fax: (920) 432-5577; email: bret@ggbcf.org
Internet http://www.ggbcf.org/grants.html
Requirements Nonprofits with operations in Brown, Door, Kewaunee, Oconto, and Shawano Counties, WI, are eligible.
Areas of Interest Arts, General; Community Development; Cultural Activities/Programs; Education; Envi-

ronmental Programs; Health Care; Museums; Nonprofit Organizations; Restoration and Preservation; Social Services
Sample Awards Children's Museum of Green Bay (Green Bay, WI)—for the "Pets are People Too" Exhibit, $7,000. Greater Green Bay YMCA (Green Bay, WI)— for Swim Smart & Family Nights, $3,367.

Johnson Controls Foundation Grants   1275
  Program
Johnson Controls Foundation
PO Box 591, 5757 N Green Bay Ave
Milwaukee, WI 53201-0591
Contact Program Contact, (414) 524-2296
Internet http://www.johnsoncontrols.com/CorpValues/foundation.htm
Requirements Nonprofits and colleges and universities are eligible.
Restrictions In general, no grants will be made to public or private preschools, elementary schools, or secondary institutions. Grants are not usually made for specific medical or scientific research projects.
Areas of Interest Arts, General; Basic Skills Education; Children and Youth; Civic Affairs; Cultural Activities/Programs; Disabled; Elderly; Equipment/Instrumentation; Health Care; Higher Education; Hospitals; Private Education; Public Education; Science; Social Services; Engineering; Computer Software
Sample Awards Milwaukee School of Engineering (Milwaukee, WI)—to develop a specialized software-engineering laboratory, $1 million.

Johnson Foundation Wingspread   1276
  Conference Support Program
Johnson Foundation
33 E Four Mile Rd
Racine, WI 53402
Contact Barbara Schmidt, Program Secretary, (262) 639-3211; fax: (262) 681-3327; e-mail: bschmidt@johnsonfdn.org
Internet http://www.johnsonfdn.org/progint/index.html
Requirements To be invited to submit a full proposal, applicants first must submit a brief concept letter, consisting of: a clear statement of purpose; a draft agenda; the identification of key participants; and an estimated budget and schedule. The letter should describe how the conference will: enhance collaboration and community; include diverse opinions and perspectives; identify solutions; and result in action.
Restrictions Proposals are limited to 501(c)3 organizations, educational institutions, or agencies of government. The foundation does not make grants, sponsor retreats, fundraisers, meetings of single organizations, or for-profit events. The facilities are not available for rent.
Areas of Interest Arts & Culture, Civic Affairs; Community Development; Disabled; Economic Development; Education; Elementary Education; Environmental Programs; Families; Secondary Education; Youth Programs

Madison Community Foundation Grants   1277

Madison Community Foundation
PO Box 5010, 2 Science Ct
Madison, WI 53705
Contact Amy Overby, Vice President of Grantmaking,
(608) 232-1763; fax: (608) 232-1772; e-mail:
frontdesk@madisoncommunityfoundation.org or
aoverby@madisoncommunityfoundation.org
Internet http://www.madisoncommunityfoundation.
org
Requirements Nonprofit organizations serving Dane
County, WI, are eligible.
Restrictions Grants are not awarded to individuals or for
religious purposes, annual campaigns, endowments, def-
icit financing, political activities, or equipment.
Areas of Interest Adolescents; Children and Youth;
Community Development; Computer Grants; Cultural
Outreach; Dramatic/Theater Arts; Economic Develop-
ment; Education; Elderly; Environmental Programs;
Health Care; Hospices; Parent Education; Recreation
and Leisure; Social Services
Sample Awards Briarpatch (Madison, WI)—to support
a program that assists parents with the specific chal-
lenges of raising adolescents, $15,000. American
Players Theatre (Madison, WI)—for construction of
on-site restrooms, $10,000. Hospicecare (Madison,
WI)—for a new computer system, $10,000. YWCA
(Madison, WI)—for facility renovations, $30,000.

Faye McBeath Foundation Grants   1278

Faye McBeath Foundation
1020 N Broadway
Milwaukee, WI 53202
Contact Sarah Dean, Executive Director, (414)
272-2626; fax: (414) 272-6235; e-mail: info@
fayemcbeath.org
Internet http://www.fayemcbeath.org/grant_process.
asp
Requirements Organizations in Wisconsin are eligible.
Restrictions The foundation does not fund annual
drives, endowments, scholarships, emergencies, or research.
Areas of Interest Allied Health Education; Child Welfare; Civic Affairs; Community Service Programs; Education; Elderly; Employment Opportunity Programs;
English Education; Food Distribution; Government
Studies; Health Care; Job Training Programs; Local
Government; Medical Education; Nonprofit Organizations; Nursing Education; Public Health; Teacher Education; Transportation; Writing/Composition Education
Sample Awards Journey House (Milwaukee, WI)—for
after-school education and recreation programs for girls,
$15,000 (2003). Hunger Task Force of Milwaukee
(WI)—to distribute food to poor elderly people, $30,000
(2003). Salvation Army (Milwaukee, WI)—for the
Christmas Tree of Lights campaign, $10,000 (2003).
Prevent Blindness-Wisconsin (Milwaukee, WI)—to
provide vision screenings to children at 10 daycare centers throughout Milwaukee, $10,000 (2003).

Mead Witter Foundation Grants   1279

Mead Witter Foundation, Inc.
PO Box 39
Wisconsin Rapids, WI 54495-0039
Contact Susan Feith, Vice President and Executive
Director, (715) 424-3004; fax: (715) 424-1314
Requirements Wisconsin 501(c)3 organizations may
apply.
Restrictions The foundation does not support religious,
athletic, or fraternal groups, except when these groups
provide needed special services to the community at
large; direct grants or scholarships to individuals; community foundations; or flow-through organizations that
redispense funds to other charitable causes.
Areas of Interest Arts, General; Education; Environmental Programs; Health Care; Higher Education;
Scholarship Programs, General; Secondary Education;
Social Services; Youth Programs
Sample Awards Family Ctr (Wisconsin Rapids, WI)—
to construct a facility that will house a residential shelter
for victims of domestic violence and the organization's
administrative offices, $1 million challenge grant
(2003).

Miller Brewing Corporate Contributions   1280
Program Grants

Miller Brewing Corporation
3939 W Highland Blvd
Milwaukee, WI 53201-0482
Contact Gil Llanas, (414) 931-3110; fax: (414)
931-6352
Internet http://www.millerbrewing.com/
inthecommunity/default.asp
Requirements Nonprofits must be near Miller operating
locations, in Irwindale, CA; Albany, GA; Trenton, OH;
Eden, NC; Fort Worth, TX; and Milwaukee, WI.
Areas of Interest African Americans (Student Support);
Education; Family; Hispanic Education; Junior and
Community Colleges; Job Training Programs; Legal Ed-
ucation; Minority Education; Vocational/Technical Ed-
ucation

Rockwell International Corporate Trust   1239
Grants Program

Rockwell International Corporate Trust
1201 S Second St
Milwaukee, WI 53204
Contact Trust Administrator, (562) 797-3311
Internet http://www.rockwellautomation.com/about_
us/citizenship.html
Restrictions Organizations are not eligible if they have
not received a permanent, tax-exempt ruling determination from the federal government; if they cannot provide
current full, certified, audited financial statements; or if
they are private foundations. Funding will not be considered for the following purposes: general endowments,
deficit reduction, grants to individuals, federated campaigns, organizations or projects outside the United
States, religious organizations for religious purposes, or
fraternal or social organizations.
Areas of Interest Art Education; Arts, General; Community Development; Computer Science; Cultural Ac-
tivities/Programs; Disabled; Education; Engineering;
Health Care; Health Services Delivery; Higher Education; Hospitals; Social Services; Technology; Youth Programs
Sample Awards U of California at Irvine (Irvine, CA)—
to create a multimedia learning and research center

where students in the arts, computer science, engineering, and other fields can collaborate on art and design projects using state-of-the-art digital technology.

Sensient Technologies Foundation Grants 1281

Sensient Technologies Foundation Inc
777 E. Wisconsin Ave
Milwaukee, WI 53202-5304
Contact Doug Arnold, (414) 347-3727; fax: (414) 347-4783
Requirements California, Indiana, Missouri, and Wisconsin nonprofits, including school districts, are eligible.
Areas of Interest Arts, General; Community Development; Education; Family; Food Distribution; Higher Education; Homelessness; Social Services; Hospitals; Biomedical Research; Mental Health; Crisis Counseling; Minorities; Nutrition/Dietetics; Performing Arts; Public Planning/Policy; Long-Term Care; Hospices; Urban Planning/Policy; Volunteers

Stackner Family Foundation Grants 1282

Stackner Family Foundation
PO Box 597
Hartland, WI 53209
Contact John Treiber, Executive Director, (414) 646-7040; fax: (414) 646-5409; email: Stackner@execpc.com
Requirements Nonprofit organizations in the greater Milwaukee, WI, area may request grant support.
Sample Awards Horizon House (Milwaukee, WI)—for an outpatient program, $4000. Penfield Childrens Ctr (Milwaukee, WI)—for the capital campaign, $10,000.

Wisconsin Arts Board Arts Challenge Initiative Grants 1283

Wisconsin Arts Board
101 E Wilson St, 1st Fl
Madison, WI 53702
Contact Mark Fraire, Grant Programs and Services Specialist, (608) 264-8191; fax: (608) 267-0380; TDD: (608) 267-9629; e-mail: mark.fraire@arts.state.wi.us
Internet http://arts.state.wi.us/static/aci.htm
Requirements Only nonprofit arts organizations in Wisconsin are eligible to apply.
Areas of Interest Arts Administration; Arts and Culture; Fund-Raising; Minorities

Wyoming

Homer A. Scott and Mildred S. Scott Foundation Grants 1284

Homer A. Scott and Mildred S. Scott Foundation
PO Box 2007
Sheridan, WY 82801-2007
Contact Lynn Mavrakis, Executive Director, (307) 672-1448; fax: (307) 672-1443
Requirements Sheridan, WY, nonprofit organizations are eligible.
Restrictions No grants to individuals.
Areas of Interest Children and Youth; Communications; Higher Education; Leadership; Mental Health; Social Services
Sample Awards Senior Citizens Coordinating Council (Sheridan, WY)—$75,780 (2002). Sheridan College Foundation (Sheridan, WY)—$73,639 (2002). YMCA of Sheridan County (Sheridan, WY)—$61,933 (2002).

Wyoming Arts Council Community Services Grants 1285

Wyoming Arts Council
2320 Capitol Ave
Cheyenne, WY 82002
Contact Rita Basom, Community Services Program Manager, (307) 777-7109; fax: (307) 777-5499; TDD: (307) 777-5964; e-mail: rbasom@state.wy.us
Internet http://wyoarts.state.wy.us/gto.html
Requirements Wyoming nonprofit tax-exempt organizations are eligible to apply.
Areas of Interest Performing Arts; Visual Arts; Literature; Media Arts; Folk/Ethnic Arts; Multidisciplinary Arts

Subject Index

Note: Numbers refer to entry numbers.

Art, Experimental

Art in Public Places

Artists' Fellowships

Artists in Residence

Arts Administration

Asia, East (Far East)

Asian Americans

At-Risk Youth

John Edward Fowler Memorial Foundation Grants, 291
Fuller Foundation Grants, 764
Gannett Foundation Grants, 1221
GATX Corporation Grants Program, 414
Ginn Foundation Grants, 1009
Stella and Charles Guttman Foundation Grants, 868
Heinz Endowments Grants, 1088
Stewart Huston Charitable Trust Grants, 1094
Jacobs Family Foundation Grants, 128
JoMiJo Foundation Grants, 132
Freddie Mac Foundation Grants, 1225
McKesson Foundation Grants, 146
MONY Foundation Grants, 896
New York Life Foundation Grants, 904
Pinkerton Foundation Grants, 927
Luther I. Replogle Foundation Grants, 306
Z. Smith Reynolds Foundation Grants, 980
Robins Foundation Grants, 1233
Skillman Foundation Grants Program, 632
Staples Foundation for Learning Grants, 596
Target Foundation Grants, 695
US Bank Foundation Grants, 697
Verizon Foundation Grants, 1206
Whiting Foundation Grants, 639

Athletics *see* **Sports**

Audience Development
Air Products and Chemicals Grants, 1067
American Express Foundation Grants, 813
Colorado Council on the Arts Grants for Artists and Organizations, 213
FAF Community Arts Fund Operating Support Program Grants, 1006
FleetBoston Financial Foundation Grants, 575
Georgia Power Foundation Grants, 353
Greater Cincinnati Foundation Grants, 1010
Walter and Elise Haas Fund Grants, 107
Heinz Endowments Grants, 1088
McKesson Foundation Grants, 146
Meyer Memorial Trust Grants Program, 1061
Mississippi Arts Commission Arts-Based Community Development Program Grants, 703
Nevada State Council on the Arts Community Arts Development Grants, 753
New Hampshire State Council on the Arts Professional Advancement Grants, 767
North Carolina Arts Council Management/Technical Assistance Grants, 974
North Dakota Council on the Arts Access Program Grants, 986
North Dakota Council on the Arts Institutional Support Program Grants, 987
NYSCA Dance Grants, 911
NYSCA Electronic Media and Film Grants, 912
NYSCA Museum Grants, 914
NYSCA Presenting Organizations Grants, 916
Rhode Island State Council on the Arts Grants to Individuals/Organizations, 1119

Tennessee Arts Commission Arts Projects Grants, 1140
Tennessee Arts Commission Rural Arts Project Support, 1143
Alvin and Fanny Blaustein Thalheimer Foundation Grants, 552

Audio Production
North Carolina Arts Council Folklife Projects Grants, 970
NYSCA Electronic Media and Film Grants, 912

Audiovisual Materials
Beirne Carter Foundation Grants, 1217
Cincinnati Bell Foundation Grants, 997

Aviation
America West Airlines Foundation Grants, 12
Ray Foundation Mental Health and Substance Abuse Prevention Grants, 759

Band Music *see also* **Orchestras**
Illinois Arts Council Music Program Grants, 421
NYSCA Music Grants, 915

Baptist Church
Beerman Foundation Grants, 992
Effie and Wofford Cain Foundation Grants, 1158
V.V. Cooke Foundation Grants, 503

Basic Skills Education
Achelis Foundation Grants, 806
Atkinson Foundation Community Grants, 46
Atlanta Foundation Grants, 341
Azadoutioun Foundation Grants, 555
Ball Brothers Foundation Grants, 460
James Ford Bell Foundation Grants, 645
Berrien Community Foundation Grants, 607
F.R. Bigelow Foundation Grants, 648
Guido A. and Elizabeth H. Binda Foundation Grants, 609
Boettcher Foundation Grants, 206
Booth Ferris Foundation Grants, 832
Boston Foundation Grants Program, 558
Robert Bowne Foundation Grants, 833
Albert W. Cherne Foundation Grants, 658
Chicago Board of Trade Foundation Grants, 392
CIGNA Foundation Grants, 1081
Community Foundation of Central Illinois Grants, 401
Cowles Charitable Trust Grants, 777
Crail-Johnson Foundation Grants, 73
Dade Community Foundation Grants, 316
Fred Harris Daniels Foundation Grants, 570
Dayton Power and Light Foundation Grants, 1003
Fairfield County Community Foundation Grants, 250
Field Foundation of Illinois Grants, 412
Gannett Foundation Grants, 1221
Catherine Manley Gaylord Foundation Grants, 715
George Foundation Grants, 1171
Richard and Rhoda Goldman Fund Grants, 102
Paul and Mary Haas Foundation Contributions and Student Scholarships, 1172
Arkell Hall Foundation Grants, 869
Hallmark Corporate Foundation Grants, 717

John H. and Wilhelmina D. Harland Charitable Foundation Grants, 354
Household International Corporate Giving Program Grants, 418
Johnson Controls Foundation Grants Program, 1275
Kelsey Trust Grants, 1213
Kirkpatrick Foundation Grants, 1049
Little River Foundation Grants, 888
Lubbock Area Foundation Grants, 1183
Lubrizol Foundation Grants Program, 1018
Miranda Lux Foundation Grants, 139
Mardag Foundation Grants, 680
McCune Charitable Foundation Grants, 803
J. P. Morgan Chase Texas Foundation, Inc Grants, 1186
Nevada Community Foundation Grants, 752
1957 Charity Trust Grants, 1101
Norcliffe Foundation Grants, 1258
Norton Foundation Grants, 509
Oppenstein Brothers Foundation Grants, 726
Oregon Community Foundation Grants, 1063
Pew Charitable Trusts Grants, 1103
Principal Financial Group Foundation Grants, 488
Helen Steiner Rice Foundation Grants, 1038
Joseph H. and Florence A. Roblee Foundation Grants, 729
Saint Paul Foundation Grants, 692
San Antonio Area Foundation Grants, 1195
Sara Lee Foundation Grants, 446
Harold Simmons Foundation Grants, 1196
John I. Smith Charities Grants, 1126
Sony Electronics Charitable Contributions Program Grants, 942
Sprint Foundation Grants, 497
Sterling-Turner Charitable Foundation Grants, 1199
Strake Foundation Grants, 1200
Hattie M. Strong Foundation Grants, 307
Swalm Foundation Grants, 1202
Whirlpool Foundation Grants, 638
G.N. Wilcox Trust Grants, 369
Wilson-Wood Foundation Grants, 339
Woodward Governor Company Charitable Trust Grants, 458

Behavioral Sciences
Phoenixville Community Health Foundation Grants, 1107
Whitehall Foundation Neurobiology Research Grants, 338

Biochemistry
Millipore Foundation Grants, 583

Biodiversity
Bay Foundation Grants, 826
Columbia Foundation Grants Program, 68
Foundation for Deep Ecology Grants, 90
Max and Anna Levinson Foundation Grants, 801
New England Biolabs Foundation Grants, 585
Orchard Foundation Grants, 523
Surdna Foundation Grants, 949
Weeden Foundation Grants, 955

Biological Sciences *see also* **Agriculture; Biomedical Research**
Flinn Foundation Grants Programs, 26

Pentair Education and Community Programs, 687
Piper Jaffray Companies Community Support Grants, 688
Prince Charitable Trusts District of Columbia Grants, 304
Saint Paul Foundation Grants, 692
Catherine Filene Shouse Foundation Grants, 1234
Star Tribune Foundation Grants, 693
Tyco Electronics Foundation Grants, 1115
United Airlines Foundation Education Grants, 451

Catholic Church
Anthony R. Abraham Foundation Grants, 310
William Blair and Company Foundation Grants, 383
Helen V. Brach Foundation Grants, 386
Otto Bremer Foundation Grants, 650
James Graham Brown Foundation Grants, 500
J. Homer Butler Foundation Grants, 836
Morris and Gwendolyn Cafritz Foundation Grants, 282
Campaign for Human Development Grants, 283
Eugene B. Casey Foundation Grants, 531
Charity Inc Grants, 657
Coleman Foundation Grants, 399
Collins C. Diboll Private Foundation Grants, 513
Carrie Estelle Doheny Foundation Grants, 79
Stella B. Gross Charitable Trust Grants, 103
Crescent Porter Hale Foundation Grants, 108
Huisking Foundation Grants, 254
Humanitas Foundation Grants, 873
J.W. and Ida M. Jameson Foundation Grants, 129
Joy Family Foundation Grants, 879
T. James Kavanagh Foundation Grants, 1096
Marion I. and Henry J. Knott Foundation Grants Program, 542
Thomas and Dorothy Leavey Foundation Grants, 136
I.A. O'Shaughnessy Foundation Grants, 686
Raskob Foundation for Catholic Activities Grants, 278
Sage Foundation Grants, 631
Santa Maria Foundation Grants, 936
Sterling-Turner Charitable Foundation Grants, 1199
Strake Foundation Grants, 1200

Central America
Arca Foundation Grants, 280
New Prospect Foundation Grants, 433

Chamber Music
Clarence E. Heller Charitable Foundation Grants, 110
Illinois Arts Council Music Program Grants, 421
James Irvine Foundation Grants, 126
NYSCA Music Grants, 915
Josephine Bay Paul and C. Michael Paul Foundation Grants, 924

Chemical Engineering
Lubrizol Foundation Grants Program, 1018

Chemistry *see also* **Biochemistry**
Booth Ferris Foundation Grants, 832

Herbert H. and Grace A. Dow Foundation Grants, 615
Marion I. and Henry J. Knott Foundation Grants Program, 542
Loctite Corporate Contributions Program, 258
Lubrizol Foundation Grants Program, 1018
Millipore Foundation Grants, 583
North Carolina GlaxoSmithKline Foundation Grants, 977
PPG Industries Foundation Grants, 1108

Chemistry Education
FMC Foundation Grants, 1086
North Carolina GlaxoSmithKline Foundation Grants, 977
Rohm & Haas Corporate Contributions Program, 1110
Thomas B. and Elizabeth M. Sheridan Foundation Grants, 551

Chicanos *see* **Hispanics**

Child Abuse
Achelis Foundation Grants, 806
Anderson-Rogers Foundation Grants, 814
Arizona Republic Foundation Grants, 21
Arizona Republic Newspaper Corporate Contributions Grants, 22
Burton G. Bettingen Grants, 54
Burlington Resources Foundation Grants, 1155
Cleveland-Cliffs Foundation Grants, 998
Crail-Johnson Foundation Grants, 73
Dade Community Foundation Grants, 316
Doris and Victor Day Foundation Grants, 407
Michael and Susan Dell Foundation Grants, 1168
Gaylord and Dorothy Donnelley Foundation Grants, 409
FHL Foundation Grants, 800
Huie-Dellmon Trust Grants, 514
Carl C. Icahn Foundation Grants, 874
Albert and Bessie Mae Kronkosky Charitable Foundation Grants, 1180
Herbert and Gertrude Latkin Charitable Foundation Grants, 135
Freddie Mac Foundation Grants, 1225
McGregor Fund Grants, 624
Pacific Life Foundation Grants, 156
PacifiCare Health Systems Foundation Grants, 157
Phoenixville Community Health Foundation Grants, 1107
Pinellas County Grants, 330
RadioShack Neighborhood Answers Grant, 1190
Swalm Foundation Grants, 1202

Child/Maternal Health *see also* **Obstetrics-Gynecology; Pediatrics**
Aetna Foundation Grants, 244
AMR/American Airlines Foundation Grants, 1146
Baxter International Foundation Grants, 381
Blowitz-Ridgeway Foundation Grants, 385
California Wellness Foundation Work and Health Program Grants, 64
Community Foundation for Greater Buffalo Grants, 849
Crail-Johnson Foundation Grants, 73
Dallas Women's Foundation Grants, 1167
Deaconess Foundation Grants, 709

Michael and Susan Dell Foundation Grants, 1168
Walt Disney Company Foundation Grants, 75
Duke Endowment Grants, 966
DuPont Corporate Contributions Program Grants, 276
Edwards Memorial Trust Grants, 668
Flinn Foundation Grants Programs, 26
Bill and Melinda Gates Foundation Grants, 1248
Health Foundation of Greater Indianapolis Grants, 466
Heinz Endowments Grants, 1088
F.B. Heron Foundation Grants, 872
Hoglund Foundation Grants, 1175
HRK Foundation Grants, 675
Stewart Huston Charitable Trust Grants, 1094
Jewish Fund Grants, 621
Johnson & Johnson Grants Program, 785
Kansas Health Foundation Grants, 493
F.M. Kirby Foundation Grants, 787
Koessler Family Foundation Grants, 884
Albert and Bessie Mae Kronkosky Charitable Foundation Grants, 1180
Lowe Foundation Grants, 1182
Lucent Technologies Foundation Grants, 788
J.M. McDonald Foundation Grants Program, 230
Mid-Iowa Health Foundation Grants, 486
Ms. Foundation for Women Reproductive Rights Coalition and Organizing Grants, 898
OSI Reproductive Health and Rights Program Grants, 921
Pajaro Valley Community Health Grants, 162
William Penn Foundation Grants, 1102
Phoenixville Community Health Foundation Grants, 1107
Prince Charitable Trusts Chicago Grants, 439
Rockwell Fund Inc Grants, 1194
Sisters of Charity Foundation of Canton Grants, 1041
Morgan Stanley Foundation Grants, 944

Child Psychology/Development
Helen Bader Foundation Grants, 1270
Will R. Beitel Childrens Community Foundation Grants, 1077
Temple Hoyne Buell Foundation Grants, 209
Effie and Wofford Cain Foundation Grants, 1158
Chestnut Hill Charitable Foundation, Inc Grants, 568
Chicago Board of Trade Foundation Grants, 392
Colorado Interstate Gas Grants, 214
Constellation Energy Group and Baltimore Gas and Electric Corporate Contributions, 534
Charles A. Dana Neuroscience Research Grants, 857
Robert and Polly Dunn Foundation Grants, 349
Francis Families Foundation Grants, 713
Stella B. Gross Charitable Trust Grants, 103
Miriam and Peter Haas Fund Grants, 106
Heinz Endowments Grants, 1088
F.B. Heron Foundation Grants, 872
Hoglund Foundation Grants, 1175

Children's Museums

Children's Theater

Choral Music see Music, Vocal

Choreography

Christianity see Religion

Chronic Illness

Churches see also Catholic Church; Jewish Studies; Protestant Church; Religion; Religious Studies

Cigarettes see Tobacco

Cinema see Films

Citizenship

Civil/Human Rights

Education of Minorities see Hispanic Education; Native American Education

Education of Women see Women's Education

Education Reform

Educational Administration

Educational Evaluation/Assessment

Educational Planning/Policy

Educational Psychology

Educational/Public Television

Educational Technology

Health Care Access

Hearing Impairments

Heart Disease see Cardiovascular Diseases

Hepatitis

Heredity see Genetics

High School Education see Secondary Education

Higher Education see also Faculty Development; Junior and Community Colleges; Libraries, Academic; Undergraduate Education

Housing *see also* **Homelessness; Homeownership; Supportive Housing Programs**

Learning Disabilities

Legal Education

Legal Services

Leisure *see* **Parks; Recreation and Leisure; Tourism**

Lesbians *see* **Homosexuals, Female**

Liberal Arts *see* **Humanities Education**

Libraries *see also* **Libraries, Academic; Libraries, Public**

Music *see also* **Band Music; Chamber Music; Dance; Folk Music; Jazz; Music, Vocal; Opera/Musical Theater; Orchestras**

Music Appreciation

Oceanography *see also* **Marine Sciences**
Richard and Rhoda Goldman Fund Grants, 102
Josephine Bay Paul and C. Michael Paul Foundation Grants, 924

Old Age *see* **Elderly; Geriatrics**

Oncology
Genentech Corporate Contributions Grants, 98
International Paper Grants, 256
NCI Cancer Biology Research Grants, 546

Opera/Musical Theater
American Express Foundation Grants, 813
ArvinMeritor Foundation Grants, 606
AT&T Arts and Culture Grants, 817
Paul and Edith Babson Foundation Grants, 556
Beneficia Foundation Grants, 1079
Boston Foundation Grants Program, 558
Central New York Community Foundation Grants, 844
Community Foundation for Greater Buffalo Grants, 849
Fuller Foundation Grants, 764
Greenburg-May Foundation Grants, 328
Hartford Foundation for Public Giving Grants, 252
William and Flora Hewlett Foundation Performing Arts Grants, 115
Illinois Arts Council Music Program Grants, 421
George Frederick Jewett Foundation Grants Program, 130
Edward S. Moore Foundation Grants, 262
NYSCA Music Grants, 915
NYSCA Theater Grants, 918
Saint Paul Foundation Grants, 692
Shubert Foundation Grants, 939
Union Pacific Foundation Grants Program, 748
Wortham Foundation Grants, 1207

Ophthalmology
Alcon Foundation Grants Program, 1145

Oral Hygienists *see* **Dental Health and Hygiene**

Orchestras
Alabama State Council on the Arts Operating Support, 2
AT&T Arts and Culture Grants, 817
Barr Fund Grants, 380
Claude Worthington Benedum Foundation Grants, 1078
CH Foundation Grants, 1160
Walt Disney Company Foundation Grants, 75
Dorrance Family Foundation Grants, 25
Fremont Area Community Foundation Grants, 617
Fuller Foundation Grants, 764
Greater Columbus Arts Council Operating Grants, 1011
Hearst Foundation and William Randolph Hearst Foundation Grants Program, 871
Clarence E. Heller Charitable Foundation Grants, 110
Hillman Foundation Grants, 1091
Illinois Arts Council Music Program Grants, 421
Illinois Tool Works Foundation Grants, 423

Kirkpatrick Foundation Grants, 1049
Lucent Technologies Foundation Grants, 788
Montana Community Foundation Grants, 737
NJSCA General Operating Support Grants, 791
Kenneth T. and Eileen L. Norris Foundation Grants, 153
NYSCA Music Grants, 915
William Penn Foundation Grants, 1102
Sid W. Richardson Foundation Grants, 1191
San Antonio Area Foundation Grants, 1195
Taubman Endowment for the Arts, 634
Tennessee Arts Commission Major Cultural Institutions Grants, 1142
Union Pacific Foundation Grants Program, 748
George R. Wallace Foundation Grants, 603
West Virginia Commission on the Arts Major Institutions Support Grants, 1268

Organ Transplants
Sid W. Richardson Foundation Grants, 1191

Organizational Theory and Behavior
General Mills Foundation Grants, 670
Charles G. Koch Charitable Foundation Grants, 294
David and Lucile Packard Foundation Grants, 158
Peace Development Fund Grants, 586
San Francisco Foundation Grants, 174

Parapsychology
Lifebridge Foundation Grants, 886

Parent Education
Achelis Foundation Grants, 806
Anderson-Rogers Foundation Grants, 814
Bender Foundation Grants, 281
Mary Black Foundation Grants, 1123
Bodman Foundation Grants Program, 831
Helen V. Brach Foundation Grants, 386
Community Foundation for Southern Arizona Grants, 24
Comprehensive Health Education Foundation Grants, 1245
Do Right Foundation Grants, 77
Alexander Eastman Foundation Grants, 763
Stella B. Gross Charitable Trust Grants, 103
F.B. Heron Foundation Grants, 872
Horizons Community Issues Grants, 121
Walter S. Johnson Foundation Grants, 131
Madison Community Foundation Grants, 1277
Robert R. McCormick Tribune Foundation Grants Programs, 430
Fred Meyer Foundation Grants, 1060
Midsouth Foundation Grants, 702
Pacific Life Foundation Grants, 156
Philadelphia Foundation Grants, 1106
Piper Jaffray Companies Community Support Grants, 688
Prospect Hill Foundation Grants, 928
Richmond and Central Virginia Strengthening Families—Strengthening Communities Grants, 1232
Skillman Foundation Grants Program, 632

Star Tribune Foundation Grants, 693
Union Bank of California Foundation Grants, 194
Whirlpool Foundation Grants, 638
M.B. and Edna Zale Foundation Grants, 1208

Parent Involvement
America West Airlines Foundation Grants, 12
Anderson-Rogers Foundation Grants, 814
Bodman Foundation Grants Program, 831
Crail-Johnson Foundation Grants, 73
GenCorp Foundation Grants, 97
Freddie Mac Foundation Grants, 1225
Milken Family Foundation Grants, 148
Northern Trust Company Charitable Trust and Corporate Giving Program, 434
Prince Charitable Trusts Chicago Grants, 439
SVP Early Childhood Development and Parenting Grants, 1262

Parks *see also* **Recreation and Leisure**
Bacon Family Foundation Grants, 205
Belo Foundation Grants, 1152
Bersted Foundation Grants, 382
Brunswick Foundation Grants, 387
Burlington Resources Foundation Grants, 1155
Community Foundation of Muncie and Delaware County Grants, 463
Cooper Foundation Grants, 743
Mary D. and Walter F. Frear Eleemosynary Trust Grants, 366
Gateway Foundation Grants, 714
Georgia-Pacific Grants, 352
Walter and Elise Haas Fund Grants, 107
Fred C. and Mary R. Koch Foundation Grants Program, 494
Albert and Bessie Mae Kronkosky Charitable Foundation Grants, 1180
Lubrizol Foundation Grants Program, 1018
Lyndhurst Foundation Grants, 1137
Nike Corporate Contributions Program Grants, 1062
North Dakota Community Foundation (NDCF) Grants, 985
Harold Whitworth Pierce Charitable Trust Grants, 587
Prince Charitable Trusts Chicago Grants, 439
Prince Charitable Trusts Rhode Island Grants, 441
Schumann Fund for New Jersey Grants, 797

Parochial Education *see* **Private and Parochial Education**

Patient Care and Education *see also* **Health Care; Health Promotion; Nursing**
Brown Foundation of Houston Grants, 1154
Central New York Community Foundation Grants, 844
Rathmann Family Foundation Grants, 549

Peace/Disarmament *see also* **Diplomacy**
AED New Voices Fellowship Program, 279
CarEth World Peace and Justice Grants, 566

Sponsoring Organizations Index

Note: Numbers refer to entry numbers.

Geographic Index

Note: This index lists grants for which applicants must be residents of or located in a specific geographic area. Numbers refer to entry numbers.

North Carolina

North Dakota

Northeast

Ohio

Oklahoma